University Neighborhood Centers

A BIBLIOGRAPHY OF SOCIAL SURVEYS

REPORTS OF FACT-FINDING STUDIES MADE AS A BASIS FOR SOCIAL ACTION; ARRANGED BY SUBJECTS AND LOCALITIES

Reports to January 1, 1928

By ALLEN EATON, Department of Surveys and Exhibits, in Collaboration with SHELBY M. HARRISON, Director, Department of Surveys and Exhibits, Russell Sage Foundation

NEW YORK
RUSSELL SAGE FOUNDATION
1930

COPYRIGHT, 1930, BY
RUSSELL SAGE FOUNDATION

WM. F. FELL CO·PRINTERS
PHILADELPHIA

TABLE OF CONTENTS

INTRODUCTION
DEVELOPMENT AND SPREAD OF SOCIAL SURVEYS . xi
By Shelby M. Harrison

PART I
GENERAL SOCIAL SURVEYS
Urban 1
Rural 10

PART II
SURVEYS IN SPECIALIZED FIELDS
Accidents and Accident Prevention 16
Adolescence 18
Aged 19
Agriculture 19
Almshouses 19
Americanization 20

Blindness, Sight Conservation, and Disease of the Eye . . . 20
Boy Life 22
Burial 23

Cancer 23
Cardiacs 24
Charities 24
Child Health and Hygiene 27
Child Labor 29
Child Marriages 37
Child Welfare 37
Chinese 47
Churches 47
City and Regional Planning 47
City, County, and State Administration 61

A BIBLIOGRAPHY OF SOCIAL SURVEYS

	PAGE
Clinics and Dispensaries	70
Community Studies	71
Continuation and Part-Time Schools	71
Convalescence	73
Correction	73
Cost of Living	73
Crime and Criminals	79
Crippled, Disabled, and Handicapped	81
Czechs	83
Dance Halls	84
Deaf	84
Defective (Mental)	84
Delinquency and Correction	84
Dependency	88
Deportation	89
Desertion	90
Detention	90
Disabled	90
Disaster	91
Disease of the Eye	91
Dispensaries	91
Domestic Workers	91
Education	91
Eight-Hour Day	126
Elections	126
Epileptics	126
Exceptional Children	127
Family Welfare	127
Feebleminded	128
Finns	130
Fire	130
Food	131
Gangs	132
Garbage, Refuse, and Sewage	132
German	133
Girls	133
Government	134
Greeks	134

CONTENTS

	PAGE
Handicapped	134
Health Administration	134
Health and Sanitation	139
Health in Industry	154
Health Insurance	159
Homeless	159
Hospitals and Sanatoria	160
Housing	161
Illegitimacy	173
Immigration and Americanization	176
Indians	180
Industrial Conditions and Relations	181
Industrial Education	202
Industrial Hygiene	204
Infant Mortality	204
Infantile Paralysis	207
Insane	209
Insurance	209
Italians	209
Jails	211
Japanese	211
Jugo-Slavs	211
Juvenile Court	212
Juvenile Delinquency	212
Kindergartens	215
Labor	215
Libraries	216
Lithuanians	217
Loans	217
Magyars	218
Markets	218
Marriage Laws	218
Maternal Deaths	219
Maternity Homes	219
Mental Hygiene	219
Mexicans	226
Midwife	226

v

A BIBLIOGRAPHY OF SOCIAL SURVEYS

	PAGE
Migration	227
Military Camps	227
Milk	227
Minimum Wage	228
Mortality	230
Motion Pictures	230
Music	230
Negro Education	230
Negroes	232
Neighborhood Houses and Settlements	237
Nurseries and Nursing	238
Old Age	239
Parish	239
Parks	239
Part-Time Schools	239
Pauper	239
Penal Institutions	240
Penitentiary	240
Pensions	240
Playgrounds	242
Poles	242
Police	242
Poliomyelitis	243
Pool Room	243
Population	243
Posture	244
Pre-Natal Care	244
Pre-School	244
Prisons	245
Probation and Parole	250
Prohibition	251
Prostitution	251
Psychiatric	252
Race Relations	253
Recreation	253
Reformatories	258
Regional Planning	259
Relief	259

CONTENTS

	PAGE
Religion	260
Religious Education	267
Rural	267
Rural Education	270
Rural Health and Sanitation	276
Russians	279
Sanatoria	279
Sanitation	279
School Buildings and Plants	280
School Health and Sanitation	285
School Organization and Administration	288
Settlements	296
Sex Delinquency	296
Sight Conservation	297
Slavs	297
Slovaks	298
Slums	298
Social Agencies	298
Social Evil	302
Social Insurance	303
Spanish	304
Streets	304
Sub-Normal, Retarded, and Exceptional Children	304
Taxation	306
Teachers	309
Tenements	309
Theatres	309
Trachoma	309
Truancy and Non-Attendance	311
Tuberculosis	312
Unemployment	320
Unmarried Mothers	324
Vagrants	324
Venereal Disease	324
Vice	325
Violent Deaths	327
Vocational Guidance and Training	328

	PAGE
Wages	333
Ward	333
White Slave Traffic	333
Widows	333
Workhouses	333
Zoning	333

PART III
PUBLICATIONS ON PURPOSE, METHOD, AND STANDARDS IN SURVEYS

GENERAL SOCIAL SURVEYS—URBAN	334
GENERAL SOCIAL SURVEYS—RURAL	338
PUBLICATIONS IN SPECIALIZED FIELDS	339
Boy Life	339
Charities	340
Child Health and Hygiene	340
Child Labor	340
Child Welfare	340
Chinese	341
Churches	341
City and Regional Planning	341
City, County, and State Administration	342
Community Studies	343
Cost of Living	343
Crime and Criminals	344
Crippled, Disabled, and Handicapped	344
Defective (Mental)	344
Delinquency and Correction	344
Dependency	344
Education	344
Fire	347
Government	347
Health and Sanitation	347
Health in Industry	349
Hospitals and Sanatoria	349
Housing	350

CONTENTS

	PAGE
Immigration and Americanization	350
Industrial Conditions and Relations	351
Japanese	351
Libraries	351
Mental Hygiene	351
Nurseries and Nursing	352
Parish	352
Playgrounds	352
Police	352
Population	352
Prisons	352
Race Relations	352
Recreation	352
Religion	353
Religious Education	354
Rural	355
Rural Education	355
Rural Health and Sanitation	355
Sanitation	356
School Buildings and Plants	356
School Health and Sanitation	356
School Organization and Administration	356
Social Agencies	356
Tuberculosis	357
Unemployment	357
Vocational Guidance and Training	357
Zoning	358

PART IV
GEOGRAPHICAL INDEX
Surveys Classified by Localities   359

INTRODUCTION
DEVELOPMENT AND SPREAD OF SOCIAL SURVEYS
By Shelby M. Harrison

TO POINT to great and rapid change as one of the outstanding features of American community life is now almost a commonplace. The quick and potent ebb and flow of forces which affect physical aspects and influence social action are not unexpected in the younger settlements of a new country. Change is inherent in growth, and most of them have grown. But the moving forces in this country have not been confined to these newer parts, neither to frontier sections nor those rural and urban districts which have but recently passed out of their pioneer stage. The last thirty to fifty years have transformed the aspect and realities of our older communities also, in ways ranging from the size and kinds of houses in which people live to the size, form, and functioning of their social and political organizations. Mere growth in numbers of people, residences, and enterprises has been one influence at work; but there have been others—among them tremendous developments in the control and use of natural forces. The increase in the use of machinery in farming, the building of good roads, the widespread distribution of electric power, among other things, have wrought remarkable changes in the rural sections of the country; but the use of machinery and new physical energy have brought an even greater change in the urban centers, where commerce and industry have become most highly organized and developed.

The constant rearrangement of elements that make up community life, resulting from new ideas, new opportunities, new interests and energies at work, has taken many forms, among them the transfer of individuals and families to new and different physical environments or the springing up of new environments around their old homes and neighborhoods; the movement of racial, industrial, and agricultural groups away from old associations into new and often difficult ones; a different distribution of people in the various age groupings in many of our largest population centers, and in our rural districts as well, from that obtaining heretofore; the transfer of many of the home industries and functions of a decade or two ago to bakeries, clothing factories, and other shops and agencies outside the home; new forms of transportation and greater general mobility of population; increased leisure time for many people and new forms of recreation facilities, public and private; and a clear tendency, on the one hand, through the great increase in huge multiple dwellings and office buildings, toward the concentration of larger and larger numbers of people on smaller pieces of land, and on the other hand, the apparent tendency toward decentralization in urban regions—toward the removal both of factories and workers' homes from congested central districts to neighboring belts of satellite communities.

Such far-reaching changes in the manner of life and in the social relationships of people have created new community needs and problems, illustrations of which are on every hand. Fifty-odd years ago, for example, one of our leading cities regarded it as comparatively safe to pump its drinking water out of the rivers flowing through it, and thence, unfiltered, to the homes of its citizens; but the building of industrial plants and homes for workers above the intakes in the rivers, and the location of other cities up the streams which dumped their sewage into the water, so polluted the supply that the typhoid death rate in that city became among the highest of any in the country—over fifty times as high as that now found in some of our largest cities. Other things besides the bad water supply contributed to the high mortality rate, but it is significant that almost immediately following the completion of facilities for the filtration of the water supply the typhoid death rate dropped over half.

Similarly, people faced new problems of housing and health when the atmosphere became so laden with smoke and dust as to shut out much of the available sunlight; of safe food when the road from producer to consumer became longer and more complex; of play and recreation when all of the vacant space near peoples' homes was built upon and motor cars crowded streets, which were the only playgrounds left to city children; of mental well-being because of the speed and tension of modern urban life;

INTRODUCTION

of family welfare when technological and other developments in industrial processes reduced the employment of wage-earners, and in turn family incomes.

The community not touched by these forces of change, both to its profit and its loss, as values are commonly reckoned, is exceptional indeed; and many have attempted new adjustments to meet their newly emerging needs. Organized education, for example, not so long ago began to see its field of endeavor taking on different aspects, many of them unfamiliar, little understood and otherwise perplexing; and experiments aimed to develop educational methods more realistically related to the life into which children were soon to work and live have been undertaken. Numerous religious organizations also have seen that certain types of their work demanded better adaptation to modern requirements, whether these have been created by new attitudes toward religion, new racial groupings, or new physical conditions of city and rural life. And, though slower to act, many of our governmental bodies have read the signs of the times and set about modifying their work, reorganizing, dropping old functions, and adding new.

But adjustments and new adaptations of the importance called for could not be intelligently undertaken without more information than was ordinarily available. Facts were seen to be a primary requirement: first, in securing a better understanding of the new needs; second, in the formulation of plans for action; and third, as a means of interesting citizens both in the needs revealed and in their duty to do something. Even where facts regarding local conditions were in hand—and the cases were rare—the statistics during these periods of rapid change quickly became out of date. If action in the community was to be taken to promote desirable tendencies and to thwart the undesirable; if evils were to be corrected and burdens lifted, and forces working for advance were to be strengthened; and if such action was to be based upon reliable information, it was obvious that some special effort was needed to secure such information in every modern community from time to time, if not continuously.

In other words, changing community conditions, the increasing demand for united action by citizens in order to control tendencies in the public interest, and the growing conviction that control and improvement can be more intelligent and effective if based on knowledge, have combined to make the social study or survey almost one of the indispensable activities of the modern community, whether it be neighborhood, parish, village, city, region, or state.

FORERUNNERS OF SURVEYING AND EARLY BEGINNINGS

But these developments did not come all at once. They were part of a gradual evolution in which many forces had a part. As far back as the eighties, and in greater degrees in later years, as pointed out in a recent paper by Paul U. Kellogg and Neva R. Deardorff,[1] the charity organization movement in this country had begun to expand its conception of the aid that might be rendered to sick or hungry families. While direct material relief was seen to be a necessary part of the assistance given, it was also realized that a larger service could be rendered if the causes of the family's breakdown were discovered and removed. The first essential in carrying out such a purpose was the ascertaining of the facts in each particular case—the "all-round diagnosis of the causes and the all-round application of the resources of the community to relief and rehabilitation."

Further, among the four or five major features of the charity organization program stress was being laid upon effort not only to remove disabilities already experienced by the family, but to take social action to prevent future disabilities; to prevent the deaths of fathers of families, for example, insofar as they were caused by industrial accidents, polluted water, and the like; or to remedy bad housing, which was often a factor in family discord and breakdowns. Thus when the same form of family distress was seen to recur in a particular locality social workers began to suspect something wrong with living conditions, and stimulated by these recurring clues they here and there set investigations on foot which disclosed the facts necessary for better understanding of causes and for planning community action. The anti-tuberculosis movement and the movement for tenement house reform in New York had their origins and gathered much of their support

[1] "Social Research as Applied to Community Progress." In Proceedings of the First International Conference of Social Work, Paris, 1928.

INTRODUCTION

from the sequence of diagnosis and treatment of disabled families, observation of recurring disabilities, and investigation of living conditions.

During the nineties leaders in the study of economic and social problems in some of our universities were also beginning to urge the application of the inductive method to social questions. They were turning from the methods of logic to the methods of science, as the latter were then being applied in the natural and physical world; and meanwhile our state legislatures were occasionally instituting fact-finding investigations into problems faced by their state governments, more particularly on their financial and administrative sides.

Moreover, as we made the turn into the new century, new aids were being developed which enabled research to be more reliable and fruitful. The beginnings of a technique in social investigation were discernible; and extension and improvement in the public record-keeping in vital statistics and other matters of social welfare, backward as we still are in some of these respects, were getting under way; attention was being given by scholars and others to the refinement of statistical methods; social problems were being increasingly recognized as complex and ramifying far in many directions; and the conviction was growing that environment plays an important role in the lives of individuals and that improvement in it has great value both as a corrective and a constructive force.

Thus new tools for use in social investigation were being fashioned while the need of them and their value was being more and more recognized—at a time when social and civic leaders began to see that the strands of community life were being thrown into new and unfamiliar patterns, that these undirected interweavings meant the aggravation of many old hardships to persons and families and the introduction of new and oppressive ones, that the welfare and destinies of many were less in their own keeping then ever before because of social conditions outside their own control, and that the community should feel an increasing responsibility for doing something of practical value to retrieve lost ground and to gain new footholds. And the more practical the efforts to these ends and the more intelligent the planning, as already suggested, the more necessary it became to study existing situations as an indispensable part of the work to be undertaken.

While this closer coordination of civic action and social investigation had begun to show itself in the last two decades of the last century, it has risen more clearly above the horizon since 1900; and although antecedent tendencies were prophetic of an epoch in which something of the discrepancy between the use of scientific methods in the physical and in the social sciences might be corrected, so far as local studies were concerned it was not until the Pittsburgh Survey in 1907 that these tendencies took definite form. In it a new type of endeavor was born which not only articulated developing needs and developing scientific tools, but also gave illustration and impetus to an idea that was destined to spread widely.

There were, however, a number of individual pieces of work immediately preceding the Pittsburgh Survey which shared with it in the effort to secure a more realistic understanding of conditions under which multitudes of people were living, and in the endeavor to enlist the interest of citizens in improving these conditions. The most outstanding among these were the books by Jacob Riis on "slum" conditions[1] which pictured out of first-hand experience unhealthful, insanitary, and oppressive surroundings, menacing and thwarting the lives of thousands of people in the most crowded sections of New York; the series of articles by Lincoln Steffens on The Shame of the Cities[2] in which, after weeks spent in seven of our larger metropolitan centers, he portrayed conditions which he hoped might bring into action the civic pride he believed to be latent, and which, when aroused, would prove a power for improvement; the Hull House Maps and Papers describing conditions in a crowded section of Chicago; the investigations made in connection with the work of the New York State Tenement House Commission of 1900,[3] appointed by Theodore Roosevelt, then governor of the state, which resulted

---

[1] Riis, Jacob A., How the Other Half Lives. Chas. Scribner's Sons, New York, 1890.

[2] Steffens, Lincoln, The Shame of the Cities. McClure, Phillips and Company, New York, 1904.

[3] DeForest, Robert W., and Veiller, Lawrence, editors, The Tenement House Problem. Macmillan Company, New York, 1903.

INTRODUCTION

in the establishment of the first Tenement House Department for New York City; a few investigations into the cost of living of wage-earners; the important series of studies of Life and Labour of the People in London by Charles Booth;[1] and the investigation of the problem of poverty in York, England, by B. Seebohm Rowntree.[2] Nevertheless the Pittsburgh undertaking stood out as something different from these—on a footing of its own; purposeful, as these were; using some of the skill of the journalist, as indeed the earlier ones had—yet having characteristics which made it individual and distinctive.

The First Survey: Pittsburgh

While, as far as one could ascertain, on one or two prior occasions the term "survey" had been applied to inquiries having certain social aspects,[3] the word in the sense in which it has become so familiar in this country was first applied to the series of community-wide, coordinated social inquiries in Pittsburgh. This pioneer effort in the great western Pennsylvania steel district was directed by Paul U. Kellogg and carried out by Charities and the Commons,[4] then under the editorship of Edward T. Devine, the cost being met by a grant from the Russell Sage Foundation, which also published the findings. It has been described by Mr. Kellogg as: "an appraisal . . . of how human engineering had kept pace with mechanical in the American steel district . . . an attempt to throw light on these and kindred economic forces not by theoretical discussion of them, but by spreading forth the objective facts of life and labor which

[1] Booth, Charles, Life and Labour of the People in London. Macmillan and Company, Ltd., London, 1902.

[2] Rowntree, B. Seebohm, Poverty, a Study of Town Life. Macmillan and Company, Ltd., London, 1901.

[3] See reference on page 146 to Report on the Croton Water Shed: a Sanitary Survey of the Croton Water Shed, in the Health Department Report, New York City, 1891. While this investigation had certain public health aspects, it, however, was almost entirely an engineering study. Similarly, Patrick Geddes in 1904, in the Introduction to his book on City Development: A Study of Parks, Gardens, and Culture Institutes, refers to a Photographic Survey as part of his town-planning study. This material, however, had largely to do with the physical aspects or appearance of parts of a city; and in Chapter II, when he speaks of a Social Survey of Dunfermline, he had in mind studies like those of London by Booth and of York by Rowntree.

[4] Now The Survey (magazine).

should help in forming judgment as to their results . . . [an attempt] to get at certain underlying factors in this [Pittsburgh's] growth as they affected the wage-earning population, . . . an inventory of such an American community."[1]

Some of the elements which made the Pittsburgh Survey distinctive may be gleaned from other descriptions by Mr. Kellogg. These, in abbreviated quotations, are as follows: "First of all, the survey takes its unit of work from the surveyor. It has to do with a subject matter, to be sure, but that subject matter is subordinated to the idea of a definite geographical area. Just as a geological survey is not geology in general, but the geology of a given mountain range or watershed, so, even when a special subject matter is under study, the sociological survey adds an element of locality, of neighborhood or city, state or region, to what would otherwise pass under the general term of an investigation. In the second place, the survey takes from the physician his art of applying to the problems at hand standards and experience worked out elsewhere, just as the medical profession has been studying hearts and lungs until they know the signals which tell whether a man's organs are working or not, and what to look for in making a diagnosis. In the third place, the survey takes from the engineer his working conception of the structural relation of things. There is a building element in surveys. When we look at a house, we know that carpenters have had a good deal to do with it; also bricklayers, steamfitters, and the rest of the building trades. But your engineer, like your general contractor and architect, has to do with the work of each of these crafts in its relation to the work of every other. So it is with a survey, whether it deals with the major elements entering a given community which has structural parts or a given master problem.[2] In the fourth place, the survey takes from the charity organization movement its case-work method of bringing problems down to

[1] Kellogg, Paul U., The Pittsburgh District: Civic Frontage. Russell Sage Foundation, New York, 1914, p. 493–495.

[2] In a more recent elaboration of this feature Mr. Kellogg and Dr. Deardorff put the point as follows: "The procedure brought the resources of cognate professions to bear on common problems that interested them all. The staff included social workers, engineers, lawyers, city planners, sanitarians, physicians, statisticians, economists, labor investigators, and the like. It was on the borderlands between the ordinary divisions of inquiry that some of the most

human terms; by figures, for example, of the household cost of sickness—not in sweeping generalizations but in what Mr. Woods called 'piled-up actualities.' In the fifth place, the survey takes from the journalist the idea of graphic portrayal, which begins with such familiar tools of the surveyor as maps and charts and diagrams, and reaches far through a scale in which photographs and enlargements, drawings, casts, and three-dimension exhibits exploit all that the psychologists have to tell us of the advantages which the eye holds over the ear as a means for communication. The survey's method is one of publicity."[1]

Thus, while employing the methods of social research as developed at the time, and also contributing something to their further development, the greatest claim of the Pittsburgh project for distinction lay perhaps in its success in combining the methods and skills of the social investigator with those of specialists in other fields.

The subject matter of the Pittsburgh Survey included the study of wages, hours of work, work accidents, and other questions of industrial relations and conditions for both men and women workers; of family budgets and home conditions among steel workers; typhoid fever and other problems related to health and sanitation; housing of the working population; the local system of taxation; the public schools; city planning and civic improvement possibilities; the hospital and other institutional needs of

---

valuable results were obtained. Thus the long neglected hazard of work accidents was found at the first staff conferences ramifying in so many directions that practically every member was faced with one phase or another of it. It bore upon the relief funds of the labor unions, the multitudinous benefit societies of the immigrant races, and the relief plans of corporations; it had led to the organization of employer's liability associations and employees' liability associations; it was bringing pensioners to the charitable societies and inmates to the children's institutions; it was a dominating factor in the local system of state subsidies to charitable institutions; it was the concern of the coroner's office, the office of foreign consuls and the health bureau, where it was one of the two causes which gave Pittsburgh its high general death rate; it had to do in a minute degree with the discipline, intelligence, grit, and moral backbone of the working force in the mills; in the courts it harked back to the fundamental issues of public policy and freedom of contract; and in its effect on income on the standard of living of workingmen's families it set its stamp on the next generation." Kellogg, Paul U., and Deardorff, Neva R., "Social Research as Applied to Community Progress." In Proceedings of the First International Conference of Social Work, Paris, 1928, Vol. I, p. 791.

[1] Kellogg, Paul U., "The Spread of the Survey Idea." In Proceedings of the Academy of Political Science, July, 1912, Vol. II, No. 4.

the city; certain phases of the crime situation and the administration of justice; playgrounds and recreation; dependent children in institutions; and a number of other related questions.

The investigations were made by a special staff who had the cooperation of a large number of leaders and organizations in national social and public health movements, together with organizations and leaders in social and civic work in Pittsburgh, the latter including three outstanding citizens who sponsored the undertaking throughout.

The chief findings were presented graphically in a public exhibition in Pittsburgh, summaries of the various reports were also published as articles in Charities and the Commons, and the full reports were issued in six volumes under the titles: The Pittsburgh District—Civic Frontage; Wage-Earning Pittsburgh; Women and the Trades; Homestead, the Households of a Mill Town; Work-Accidents and the Law; and the Steel Workers. Much of the Survey's data also reached the public through addresses at national conventions, newspaper articles and editorials, discussions at luncheon meetings, and articles in a wide range of magazines.

BETWEEN PITTSBURGH AND SPRINGFIELD

Except for the survey of the Polish district in Buffalo in 1910 which was aimed not only to show important needs of that colony but to arouse interest and enlist support for a comprehensive survey of the whole city, during the two years that followed the publication of the findings of the Pittsburgh Survey very little evidence was observable in other cities of a demand to be surveyed. This may have been due in part to the fact that it took time for the significance of the Pittsburgh undertaking for other cities to be understood. However, by 1911 interest in community surveys began to show itself elsewhere.

Following a quick journalistic survey of Birmingham, chosen as a type of the new and growing industrial centers of the South, which was made by The Survey magazine, four city-wide organizations, the Chamber of Commerce, Associated Charities, Ministerial Association, and the Central Trades Assembly, joined in sponsoring a survey of Syracuse, N. Y.; and by 1912 enough

INTRODUCTION

cities desiring surveys had sought advice and cooperation from The Survey magazine and the Russell Sage Foundation to make the latter feel warranted in establishing a Department of Surveys and Exhibits,[1] appointing as director Shelby M. Harrison, a former member of the Pittsburgh Survey staff. The two main objectives which the Department set for itself were the spreading of the survey idea and the further development of survey methods. In the furthering of both of these objects advice and assistance were made available to outside organizations on their specific undertakings. As demonstration projects the Department has conducted a number of preliminary and general surveys, among these being its surveys in Scranton, Pa., Newburgh, N. Y., and Topeka, Kans.; but its most important undertaking aside from its participation in the recent surveys of the New York Regional Plan was the survey in 1914 of Springfield, Ill. At that time the city contained roughly 60,000 people and because of wide diversity in its economic and social activities had much in common not only with the other 47 state capitals, but also with a large group of other cities of the country.

The Springfield Survey

The Springfield Survey included nine main lines of inquiry: the work of the public schools; the care of mental defectives, the insane, and alcoholics; recreation needs and facilities; housing legislation and trends; public health and sanitation; public and private charities; industrial conditions and relations; delinquency and the correctional system; and the administration of city and county offices, other than those included in the previous divisions. Building upon the experience of Pittsburgh and other surveys, four main steps, in addition to the organizing of staff and local forces in Springfield, were stressed: first, the investigation of the facts of local problems; second, the analysis and interpretation of the data gathered; third, the formulation of suggestions and recommendations for action growing out of the analyses; and fourth, the educational use of the facts and recommendations.

[1] There was at the same time considerable interest throughout the country, particularly among social work organizations, in the graphic presentation of information of social value to wider and wider audiences; and because of its important relation to the educational use of survey findings the two types of work were united in this new Department.

In general terms the method of investigation comprised study of the records, published and unpublished, compiled and uncompiled, of organizations and institutions in the community and of outside agencies which had data on Springfield; personal visits to and observation of Springfield organizations and institutions in operation; the gathering of facts through intensive studies or tests planned for certain sections of the city, or of the population; special studies of the activities of particular agencies or groups of agencies and interviews with officers in charge; first-hand observation of conditions throughout the city; written inquiries and personal interviews with individuals in possession of experience or information pertaining to the problem in hand; and studies of legislation relating to local conditions and procedures.

The Springfield Survey added a number of new features, although some of them may claim distinction only in the degree of emphasis which they were given. The inquiry was initiated locally and sponsored throughout by a very representative group of citizens, including a former lieutenant governor, a state senator, a state commissioner, the city superintendent of schools, other public officials, business men, labor leaders, clergymen, doctors, women's club leaders, editors, teachers, and social workers. Seventeen agencies, national and state, public and private, collaborated in the enterprise; a large proportion of the cost was borne by the locality; over 900 citizens participated as volunteer workers, taking part in the field investigations or in the preparation of the Survey Exhibition; and a highly intensive and diversified educational campaign was carried out to help the public to understand and reckon with the Survey's findings.

While many citizens had a part in the Survey from its beginning, the people of Springfield took over the Survey, so to speak, to a much greater degree during the preparation and course of the Survey Exhibition, held in the large and imposing First Regiment Armory. It was attended by thousands of visitors, including many from distant parts of the state. The Exhibition at one stroke placed them in possession of the leading facts, ideas, and recommendations of the surveyors; and in addition afforded an opportunity to participate personally in the venture. In this way they not only felt a sense of proprietary interest but became

INTRODUCTION

in fact part owners. Here was a broad new channel through which many citizens might help to put the Survey's information and suggestions to work; and through 40 and more exhibit committees they took up the task.

These groups of workers included an advisory committee, a general executive committee, committees on automobiles, decoration, drayage, lettering, lighting, photographs, printed matter, speakers, special days, ushers, and many others. As the campaign grew, more and more people lent their help, not only because their committee leaders were energetic and enthusiastic and the spirit of the campaign contagious, but because the things they had to do were interesting. They made models and mechanical devices, tried their hands at art work, wrote special stories for the newspapers, handled office matter, snapped photographs, and made public addresses before churches, lodges, labor unions, school clubs, and other organizations and societies. They helped stage and take part in the short plays written to bring out some of the important lessons of the Survey.

The Exhibition became an event in the community which gave further "news" value to the Survey's facts and conclusions, and for two months preceding its opening a special campaign of publicity and promotion was carried on which kept the subject before the people. Those familiar with publicity work will recognize the value of such things as the invitations sent out by a hospitality committee to mayors throughout the state; exhibit models and devices displayed from time to time in public places; unexplained cartoons posted in the windows at exhibition headquarters; the street railway company's offer to transport school children free to the Exhibition; prizes offered for the five best grammar school essays on "What I Saw at the Springfield Survey Exhibition"; special days assigned to societies and organizations; a daily department in one of the newspapers under "The Survey Question Box"; proclamation by the mayor making the last day of the exhibit Springfield Exhibition Day, and urging "all citizens of Springfield to take this last opportunity to inspect and study the many interesting and instructive things there to be found."

In addition to the Exhibition other channels to public attention were used in spreading the Survey's data. As each division of the inquiry completed its work the findings were fully summarized for the local press, the newspapers of the city printing from 12 to 30 articles on each. Material was also used by local, state and national trade papers, magazines, and other periodicals. Complete reports for each of the nine survey divisions and a volume summarizing all these reports were printed and circulated both locally and among those interested outside the city. The material also gained some currency through numerous public meetings where it was under discussion.

The Survey Idea Further Defined

As it has worked out in practice, then, the social or community survey is seen to embody a number of distinct characteristics. It is an enterprise which draws upon and utilizes in a single endeavor the experience and skills of:

1. The civic and social workers in discovering in their everyday service to the community clues to current social situations needing better understanding;
2. The engineer in seeing the structural relations of different types of community conditions to each other;
3. The surveyor in relating his work and study to a definite geographical area;
4. The social research worker, in formulating specific questions for study, investigating and analyzing the pertinent facts, and drawing warranted generalizations;
5. The physician, city planner, and social worker, in bringing problems down to human terms and in prescribing or planning treatment; and
6. The journalist and publicity worker in interpreting facts and new knowledge in terms of human experience and presenting them in ways which will engage the attention and stimulate democratic action.

In short, the social survey is a cooperative undertaking which applies scientific method to the study and treatment of current related social problems and conditions having definite geographical limits and bearings, plus such a spreading of its facts, conclusions, and recommendations as will make them, as far as possible, the common knowledge of the community and a force for intelligent coordinated action.

INTRODUCTION

In the Introduction to Lincoln Steffens' Shame of the Cities, published in 1904, he makes this interesting comment upon his own method of work and purpose:

> This is all very unscientific, but then, I am not a scientist. I am a journalist. I did not gather with indifference all the facts and arrange them patiently for permanent preservation and laboratory analysis. I did not want to preserve, I wanted to destroy the facts. My purpose was no more scientific than the spirit of my investigation and my reports; it was, as I said above, to see if the shameful facts, spread out in all their shame, would not burn through our civic shamelessness and set fire to American pride. That was the journalism of it. I wanted to move and to convince.

Twenty-five years later, in his presidential address before the annual meeting of the American Sociological Society, December, 1929, Professor William F. Ogburn, in forecasting trends and requirements in the development of a more scientific sociology, said:

> One of these new habits will be the writing of wholly colorless articles, and the abandonment of the present habit of trying to make the results of science into literature. . . . Articles will always be accompanied by the supporting data, hence the text will be shorter and the records longer. . . . The articles in the new social science journals will be in some ways greatly expanded social science abstracts, that is, an abstract in the sense that the scientific essentials will be abstracted from the irrelevant interpretation, popularization and emotionalism. . . . The sociologist will of course work on the problems that tend to make sociology an organized systematic body of knowledge, but also he will choose for his researches the study of those problems the solution of which will benefit the human race and its culture, particularly those problems that present the greatest acuteness. But the scientific sociologist will attack these problems once chosen with the sole idea of discovering new knowledge.

While neither of these points of view would necessarily exclude or minimize the importance of the other nor the value of the other's resulting product, they nevertheless clearly differentiate between two types of activities—one the work of the scientist in adding to the sum of human knowledge and the other the work of the journalist in so presenting the new knowledge that it may affect life and events. And such a differentiation helps us to see the nature of the social survey. It is not scientific research alone, nor journalism alone, nor social planning alone, nor any other one type of social or civic endeavor; it is a combination of a number of these. In its best form the survey unites the contributions of the research worker who brings to light new information bearing upon related problems and needs in a definite locality, of the experienced social planner in offering suggestions for improvement based upon the new knowledge, and the expert in educational publicity in spreading widely both information and suggestions, and in interpreting their significance.

General and Specialized Surveys

The first surveys covered a broad range of subjects; they were general studies of entire communities, these communities ranging in size and form all the way from the local neighborhood or parish, city ward, town, and city up to counties and states. A tendency set in, however, after a few years, toward employing the survey to appraise one major phase of community life, such as health and sanitation, public education, housing, recreation, employment and industrial relations, child welfare, dependency and charitable effort to reduce or relieve it, and delinquency and correction. Outstanding examples of these are the series of investigations in Cleveland, the first one of which, that on education, made under the direction of Leonard P. Ayres, has been of influence in the spread of the survey of special fields. This was the most complete inquiry into a city school system up to that time—perhaps up to the present. In organizing the undertaking Dr. Ayres broke up the major questions of school equipment, organization and administration into 23 separate divisions, and each was made the subject of intensive investigation. These divisions are indicated by their titles: child accounting in the public schools (which dealt with problems of the school census, retardation, elimination, size of classes, truancy, and compulsory attendance); educational extension; schools and classes for exceptional children; the school and the immigrant; school buildings and equipment; school organization and administration; overcrowded schools and the platoon plan; the teaching staff; education through recreation; health work in the public schools; household arts and school lunches; the public library and the public schools; what the schools teach and might teach; measur-

INTRODUCTION

ing the work of the public schools; financing the public schools; and eight topics in the field of vocational training. Each of these studies was reported upon in a separate monograph of pocket size, and on the date of issue was made the subject of a public discussion at a luncheon conference, always well attended, held in the assembly hall of one of the large downtown Cleveland hotels. The verbal summaries and conference discussions were later fully reported in the local newspapers. The series of monographs was also summarized in two volumes, one entitled The Cleveland School Survey, by Dr. Ayres, and the other, Wage-Earning and Education, by R. R. Lutz.

Other phases of the Cleveland series included surveys of recreation, criminal justice, and hospitals and health. Additional illustrations of these studies in special fields are to be seen in the surveys of municipal administration by the National Institute of Public Administration and the New York and other Bureaus of Municipal Research; the church surveys in Springfield, Mass., and St. Louis by the Institute of Social and Religious Research; surveys of state school systems by the General Education Board and the Carnegie Foundation for the Advancement of Teaching; and the numerous studies of unemployment and crime under way during 1929 in different parts of the United States.

Both types of survey, the general and that specializing in a single field, have their peculiar uses. The general survey is of value not only where definite measures for social improvement need to be outlined along a broad front, but where interest and a sense of responsibility for conditions still lie relatively dormant and need arousing. Doubtless one of the chief reasons for the shift toward the more specialized inquiry is the fact that in this country many communities have now passed beyond the "awakening" stage and are ready to deal in a more intensive way with special problems or groups of them, taking them up one by one. Moreover, as the technical equipment of surveyors has improved, surveys in single fields have become so intensive and comprehensive that the accumulated findings in a single field often promise to be as much as a community can well assimilate before being diverted to new topics—and in some cases doubtless as much as it can be responsible for or finance at a given time.

Perhaps the most conspicuous exception to this trend is the present practice of surveying communities comprehensively as a basis for city and regional plans—a procedure which seems not only warranted but inevitable because of the intimate relation between the numerous physical, industrial, public health, recreational, housing, legal, financial, and engineering phases of the city's or region's future development. Another group of exceptions of almost equal importance is the series of investigations being conducted in rural districts. These range from the securing of a fact-basis for community organization in the township or county all the way to the study of future programs for rural states. The comprehensive general survey has been used with apparent advantage also as a basis for the Better Cities Contests which have been conducted for a number of years by the Wisconsin State Conference of Social Work; also with conspicuously good effect in studying conditions and problems of racial or otherwise homogeneous groups populating fairly sharply defined areas, as, for instance, the recent survey of conditions among American Indians, made by the Brookings Institution and directed by Lewis Meriam.[1]

Spread of Both Types

That the survey idea has gained wide acceptance and adoption in practice since the completion of the first ventures is to be seen in the story told by this Bibliography. The basis used in selecting the survey reports here included was the definition of the idea as worked out in practice. That is to say, in listing survey projects only those were included which embodied the elements or features regarded as essential to the idea and as differentiating them from strictly research, planning, or journalistic undertakings. This does not mean that every feature included in the definition is to be found in every survey here recorded, nor are they present in the same proportions in all cases; but it does mean that in making the selections only those were taken which, from the information available to the compilers, appeared to include at least the following: the social question or questions under study were related

---

[1] Meriam, Lewis, and Associates, The Problem of Indian Administration. Institute for Government Research (Brookings Institution), Washington, 1928.

INTRODUCTION

to a definite geographical area; they either grew out of current efforts to improve social and civic conditions or were sufficiently related to current problems to raise the presumption that the data collected could be of use, if not immediately, at least in the not distant future; the studies represented a collection of facts bearing upon these problems rather than essays or the statement of reasoned opinions; the findings of the studies were published and circulated. A few reports published in mimeographed form, where the circulation was not limited to a comparatively small number, were included, but the vast majority of the material was in the form of printed reports.

With these points in mind as much information as possible beyond what was indicated by the title of the survey or its report was sought, and in a very large proportion of cases this search included an examination of the published report itself. The result was the selection of a total of 2,775 titles of projects which had been completed up to January 1, 1928.[1]

With longer use and increasing experience in surveys it was to be expected that some differentiation as to their functions and some specialization as to their uses would develop, and this is exactly what has happened. Thus they divide themselves first into two major groupings, general social surveys and surveys in specialized fields, the former numbering 154 and the latter 2,621. Of the general social surveys, 82 deal with urban conditions and 72 with those of rural areas.

The surveys in specialized fields represent upwards of 125 separate groupings made up on the basis of questions or problems investigated. Those relating to the general grouping of schools and education head the list with 625; health and sanitation come next with 469; industrial conditions, next with 296; city and regional planning, and delinquency and correction each runs

---

[1] This total includes a certain amount of duplication, since the main divisions of certain general and a few specialized surveys, where they were reported on separately, were counted as individual projects. In attempting, however, to get some indication of the spread of surveys in terms of separate projects, it is probably not far from the numerical facts to take the figure 2,775, certainly 2,700, since these duplications are doubtless roughly offset by the number of reports, though relatively small, it is believed, which were not discovered in this search. At the time this Introduction was written it is safe to say that the total number of survey projects in this country has gone beyond 2,800.

over 150; and housing runs over 100. The sub-groupings under these general heads are as follows:

Schools and Education	Number of Surveys
Continuation and Part Time Schools	16
Education (General surveys of the field)	334
Industrial Education	19
Libraries	12
Negro Education	14
Pre-School	2
Religious Education	5
Rural Education	54
School Buildings and Plants	44
School Organization and Administration	69
Sub-Normal, Retarded, and Exceptional Children	13
Truancy and Non-Attendance	10
Vocational Guidance	33
Total	625

Health and Sanitation	
Blindness, Sight Conservation, and Disease of the Eye	16
Cancer	5
Cardiacs	2
Child Health	13
Clinics and Dispensaries	9
Convalescence	4
Food	4
Garbage, Refuse, and Sewage	11
Health Administration	43
Health and Sanitation (General surveys of the field)	124
Health in Industry	40
Health Insurance	2
Hospitals and Sanatoria	13
Infant Mortality	23
Infantile Paralysis	11
Maternal Deaths	2
Midwife	2
Milk Problem	10
Nurseries and Nursing	12
Posture	2
Pre-Natal Care	2
Rural Health and Sanitation	18

INTRODUCTION

	Number of Surveys	
School Health and Sanitation	22	
Trachoma	9	
Tuberculosis	65	
Venereal Disease	5	
Total		469

Industrial and Work Conditions and Relations

Accidents (Practically all industrial)	19	
Child Labor	61	
Domestic Workers	1	
Eight-Hour Day	2	
Industrial Conditions and Relations (General)	169	
Minimum Wage	18	
Unemployment	26	
Total		296

City and Regional Planning — 155

Delinquency and Correction

Crime and Criminals	20	
Delinquency and Correction (General)	27	
Detention	5	
Juvenile Delinquency	30	
Police	7	
Prisons	46	
Probation and Parole	7	
Reformatories	2	
Sex Delinquency	6	
Workhouses	2	
Total		152

Housing — 112

Other major fields in which the number of surveys have run fairly large are city, county, and state administration, with 88; child welfare, with 68; recreation, with 53; mental hygiene, with 52; cost of living, with 46; religion, 48; conditions among Negroes, 39; taxation, 35; immigration and Americanization, 36; social agencies, 28; and vice, with 26.

These figures indicate something of the spread in number of survey types, and in the range of subjects investigated. The longitudinal spread, so to speak, throughout the country is equally striking. Every state in the Union is represented, those states for which the largest number of surveys were found being New York, with 392; Ohio, with 206; Pennsylvania, 196; Illinois, 191; Massachusetts, 188; California, 109; New Jersey, 96; Missouri and Georgia, each 78; Minnesota, 75; Wisconsin, 75; Indiana, 72; Connecticut, 71; and with 40 or more in each of the following states: Michigan, Texas, Colorado, Maryland, South Carolina, and Virginia. As would be expected, the greatest local concentration of surveys is to be found in the large cities; thus we find in New York City, 184[1]; Chicago, 109; Cleveland, 95; Philadelphia, 49; Boston and Pittsburgh, each with 46; Milwaukee, 33; Cincinnati, 32; St. Louis, 30; Minneapolis, 28; Baltimore, 26; San Francisco, 21; and Detroit, 18.

Social Surveys in Foreign Countries

For the most part this search for surveys was limited to the United States and Canada, although some notable examples are to be found in other countries, among them the surveys of York, already referred to, Edinburgh and other cities of England and Scotland;[2] Constantinople, Prague, Peking, and Africa. Some of these are included in the present volume; also a number of others

[1] In 1926 the Welfare Council of New York City published a list of some 527 reports of social studies dealing with welfare questions in New York City and carried to completion in the period 1915 through 1925. The number is larger than those here listed for New York City chiefly because the list was not limited to surveys as defined here and because it included studies reported on in typewritten form.

[2] Outstanding among these, in addition to Rowntree's York, are the following:

Bowley, A. L., and Burnett-Hurst, A. R., Livelihood and Poverty: A Study of the Economic Conditions of Working Class Households in Northampton, Warrington, Stanley, Reading (and subsequently Bolton). G. Bell and Sons, Ltd., London, 1915.

Bowley, A. L., and Hogg, M. H., Has Poverty Diminished? A Sequel to Livelihood and Poverty. (An investigation after ten years of the same cities—Northampton, Warrington, Stanley, Reading, and Bolton.) P. S. King and Son, Ltd., London, 1925.

Crawford, A. F. Sharman, Cork: A Civic Survey. Cork Town Planning Association, Hodder and Stoughton, Ltd., London, 1926.

Gilchrist, E. J., Ipswich: A Survey of the Town. Ipswich Local Committee of the Conference on Christian Politics, Economics and Citizenship, 1924.

Hawkins, C. B., Norwich: A Social Study. Philip Lee Warner, London, 1910.

Mess, Henry A., Industrial Tyneside: A Social Survey made for the Bureau of Social Research for Tyneside. Ernest Benn, Ltd., London, 1928.

INTRODUCTION

made in Mexico, South America, and elsewhere. The basis upon which some surveys were chosen and others not was that those were included which seemed to be traceable in a measure to the development and spread of surveys in America, the evidence of this relationship being found chiefly in the fact that the surveys chosen in other countries were under the direction of, or included on their staffs, workers from this country.

The Demand for Survey Aids: Publications on Purpose and Methods

Another evidence of the vitality of the survey idea is to be found in the apparent demand for information on the experience had by social surveyors in outlining the purposes and aims of their surveys and in developing survey methods. In Part III of the present volume references will be found to some 187 published documents treating of such experience. They deal with these aspects of general social surveys in urban centers to the extent of 43 books, pamphlets or articles; in rural areas, to the extent of 10 documents; and publications of this character relating to specialized fields of inquiry number 133. The list includes a number of books written chiefly as college texts; and the subject has also made its way into numerous college courses.[1]

O'Rourke, Horace T., The Dublin Civic Survey. Dublin Civic Survey Committee for the Civics Institute of Ireland, Hodder and Stoughton, Ltd., London, 1925.

Rackstraw, Marjorie, editor, A Social Survey of the City of Edinburgh. Joint Committee, Committee of the Social Union and the Edinburgh Council of Social Agencies, Edinburgh, Oliver and Boyd, 1926.

[1] Among publications dealing with survey purposes and methods which have been issued in the United States since the date when the listings here were closed are the following:

American Public Health Association, Appraisal Form for City Health Work. Standards for measuring city health department work. By the Committee on Administrative Practice of the American Public Health Association. 3d edition, 1929. American Public Health Association, 370 Seventh Ave., New York.

Bartlett, Harriet M., "The Social Survey and The Charity Organization Movement." In American Journal of Sociology, September, 1928.

Caswell, Hollis Leland, City School Survey: An Interpretation and Appraisal. Columbia University Press, New York, 1929.

Continuing Committee of the Annual Conference on Research, Young Men's Christian Association of the United States and Canada, Association Survey Methods and Results, Section B of Research and Studies II. General Board of the Young Men's Christian Associations, New York, 1930.

A BIBLIOGRAPHY OF SOCIAL SURVEYS

The subject has also gained a place in numerous conferences on social and civic work, the most recent being the 1930 meeting of the National Conference of Social Work in Boston, where the Division on Social Forces devoted two of its main sessions to a symposium on survey objectives, practice, and procedures.

Douglass, H. Paul, How to Study the City Church. Doubleday, Doran and Company, Garden City, N. Y., 1928.

Good, Carter Victor, How to Do Research in Education. Warwick and York, Baltimore, 1928.

Hogg, Margaret H., "Sources of Incomparability and Error in Employment-Unemployment Surveys." In Journal of the American Statistical Association, September, 1930.

Lundberg, George A., "Field Work: The Interview and Social Survey." In A Study in Methods of Gathering Data, Longmans, Green and Company, New York, 1929.

Manny, Theodore B., "Method and Scope of the Survey of Local Rural Government." In Rural Municipalities, Century Company, New York, 1930.

Metropolitan Life Insurance Company, The Community Health Study Campaign-Schedule. New York.

Morse and Burnham, Every Community Survey of New Hampshire. Home Missions Council, 105 East 22d Street, New York, 1928.

Odum and Jocher, "Types of Method: The Survey." Chapter XVI in An Introduction to Social Research, Holt and Company, New York, 1929.

Palmer, Vivien M., Field Studies in Sociology: A Student's Manual. University of Chicago Press, Chicago, 1928.

Rice, Stuart A., editor, Statistics in Social Studies. Papers prepared for annual meeting of American Statistical Association, 1929. University of Pennsylvania Press, Philadelphia, 1930.

Smith, T. V., and White, L. D., editors, Chicago, an Experiment in Social Research. University of Chicago Press, Chicago, 1929.

West Virginia Country Life Council, Country Community Score Card. Extension Division, College of Agriculture, West Virginia University Circular 255, July, 1928.

Woodhouse, Mr. and Mrs. Chase Going, "The Field of Research on the Economic and Social Problems of the Home." In Journal of Home Economics, Vol. XX, Nos. 3, 4, 5, 1928.

(Numerous publications issued by the Social Science Research Council, New York, are also in the nature of aids in the conduct of social studies and research.)

Among valuable publications in other countries which discuss various phases of survey methods, purposes, and standards, the following British material will be of special interest:

Branford, Sybella, and Farquharson, Alexander, An Introduction to Regional Surveys. Prepared at the instance of the Cities Committee, Leplay House. Leplay House Press, 1924, Westminster, 65 Belgrave Road, S. W. 1.

Butler, C. V., and Simpson, C. A., Village Survey-Making, an Oxfordshire Experiment. H. M. Stationery Office, London, 1928.

Geddes, Patrick, "The Survey of Cities, and City Survey for Town Planning Purposes, of Municipalities and Government." Chapters XV and XVI in Cities in Evolution. Williams and Norgate, London, 1915.

INTRODUCTION

INSTITUTIONS INTERESTED, SPONSORING, AND PARTICIPATING

The spread of interest is strikingly shown in another way—in the very wide range of organizations which have initiated, sponsored, conducted, or in other ways participated in surveys. A glance through the Bibliography will show these to include: special national, state, and local survey committees; various university and college organizations such as sociology departments, extension divisions, college agricultural experiment stations and departments of rural sociology and economics; national, state, and local public health and medical associations, antituberculosis societies, associations of clinics, visiting nurse associations, family welfare and charity organization societies, councils of social agencies, child labor committees, consumers' leagues, civic clubs and federations, committees on conservation, bureaus of municipal research, commissions on efficiency and economy, housing associations and committees, immigration commissions, playground and recreation committees and associations, committees on industrial relations, commissions on interracial relations, child study and child welfare organizations, juvenile protective associations, park commissions, city and regional planning committees, city improvement associations, chambers of commerce and other business men's organizations, taxpayers' leagues, societies for the control of cancer, national life insurance companies, young men's and young women's Christian associations, social hygiene bureaus and associations, citizens' committees on finance, crime commissions, committees on the feeble-minded and on mental hygiene, committees on aged and dependent persons, public education and educational research associations, prison inquiry commissions, probation associations, hospital organizations, committees on unemployment, vice commissions; national governmental bodies, like the United States Public Health Service, United States Children's Bureau, Women's Bureau, United States Office of Education, United States Bureau of Agricultural Economics; state governmental bodies, like state industrial commissions, state boards of health, charities, corrections, finance, immigration and housing, public welfare, labor, industry, and agriculture; local governmental bodies in many of these fields, particularly in health and education, and a few city councils.

A BIBLIOGRAPHY OF SOCIAL SURVEYS

The range of participating organizations also includes national, state, and local departments, federations and branches of national religious bodies, national and local foundations and community trusts, local research organizations, rotary clubs, women's civic organizations, city and civic clubs, federations of women's clubs, social settlements and neighborhood associations, health demonstrations, state and local councils of churches, local chapters of the American Red Cross, community chests, councils of social agencies, and a few library organizations.

Wider Acceptance of Fact-Basis for Public Opinion and Program Making

Indeed, practically every type of private organization interested in improving the conditions under which people live and work, and a large number of municipal, state, and federal bodies have made the study of social conditions an important feature of their regular work. They have done this for the purpose not only of giving citizens the raw fact material necessary to form intelligent opinion upon matters of public concern, but also to provide the information necessary to develop plans for the current work of their various organizations. This is a development of great significance. It means that in planning public undertakings leaders in these very numerous types of work are less and less willing to base decisions, or to ask others to act, upon assumptions or best guesses. On the contrary they are resting their cases more and more upon ascertained knowledge, even though it may not be exact and they must therefore often be content with approximate accuracy. Thus, whether these efforts during the last twenty-five years to get at the truth go under the title of surveys, investigations, inquiries, reconnoitres, researches, or some other name, their spread marks an important period in the social history of this country—a period of transition from a great absence of basic information for social and community planning to a more factual basis.

The movement has further significance. It shows that national organizations no longer are content to work out, away from the local scene, standardized programs for their local branches to be clamped down upon community situations regardless of how well

INTRODUCTION

they fit. Rather they prefer, with what guidance and help they can give from their broader range of vision and experience, to see programs fostered by local effort grow out of ascertained knowledge of the peculiar elements in each situation. This trend would seem to acknowledge the need of greater local autonomy in some types of public service.

Continuing Survey and Research Agencies

Another tendency which appears to be evident from this compilation of social inquiries is the institution of more or less permanent survey or research bureaus in different localities. Sometimes the bureau is an independent organization, in other cases it is attached to one of a variety of community institutions. Bureaus of municipal research, and local community trusts and foundations are examples of the former, while the latter vary among private agencies from research bureaus in welfare councils, councils of social agencies, church federations, housing associations, city planning committees, educational associations, census study committees and university departments of sociology, political science, economics, education, medicine, and law, to bureaus in public departments of health and public welfare, and to city and county governmental commissions on city planning.

The tendency, moreover, is perhaps even more marked where the scope is national. In this field, as already indicated, many privately supported organizations and not a few publicly supported agencies carry more or less permanent staffs of workers equipped to make or to cooperate in making at least a limited number of local surveys in different parts of the country. Examples of the former are to be found in the Bureau of Jewish Social Research, National Institute of Public Administration, Young Men's Christian Association, Young Women's Christian Association, National Catholic Welfare Conference, National Child Labor Committee, Federal Council of Churches of Christ in America, National Industrial Conference Board, National Tuberculosis Association, National Recreation Association, American Social Hygiene Association, Foreign Policy Association, the Brookings Institution, the National Bureau of Economic Research, the Commonwealth Fund, the Milbank Memorial Fund, and the Russell Sage Foundation. Examples of public agencies are to be found in the United States Public Health Service, the Children's Bureau, the Women's Bureau, Office of Education, and some of the bureaus in the United States Department of Agriculture.[1]

The setting-up of these local and continuing survey bureaus has made it possible to combine certain features of the general community survey with those of the specialized survey in a particular field. In some cities, for example, successive studies of special fields have been undertaken with the result that after a few years the major divisions of social and civic concern in the locality have been covered. Such inquiries have the advantage usually of making it possible to center public attention upon one set of related problems at a time, presumably to consider them more fully, and possibly to develop a plan of action before passing on to another group of questions. In practice it affords opportunity for more thorough work both on the investigational and the educational sides. An outstanding illustration of this method is to be found in the series of surveys carried out in Cleveland, already referred to, most of them by the Survey Committee of the Cleveland Foundation, which included the Cleveland Education Survey with its more than 20 separate reports; the Cleveland Recreation Survey, reported in 7 volumes; the Cleveland Hospital and Health Survey, in 10 volumes, and a preliminary study of Cleveland's Relief Agencies, reported in one volume.

Local child health and general health demonstrations, notably those conducted by several of the national foundations, by pursuing their work through a period of years, and by utilizing the survey both to draw their base lines for recording conditions from which later measurements of trends could be made, and also to outline plans of work to suit the peculiar needs of the community, exhibit certain features of the continuing study and survey method.

[1] Other departments and bureaus of the national government, such as the Census Bureau and the Bureau of Labor Statistics, regularly collect and report valuable data on social questions, but these are more in the nature of basic statistical compilations than surveys, as here defined.

INTRODUCTION

More Funds for Surveys

The Pittsburgh Survey, as has been seen, was paid for in very large part with funds supplied by a national foundation located not in Pittsburgh but in New York City. In the early years of the Survey funds to meet the necessary expenses were in large part supplied by national rather than local organizations. Indeed it has been pointed out that the wide development in social investigation has been due not alone to the growth of the scientific spirit and of a widespread social consciousness, paralleling advances in methods of social research and in the technical equipment of investigators, but also to the rise of the great foundations with their deepening appreciation of research. Before 1900 there were only three foundations in this country, in the more or less generally accepted meaning of that term. By 1907, when the Russell Sage Foundation was established, there were only eight. By 1922 the number had reached 33; 77 in 1924; and over 150 by 1930. The community trust, an endowed institution in many instances also making contributions to social research, has also developed largely in the last decade or two. The first one, the Cleveland Foundation, was established in 1914; by 1924 there were 50, and by 1930 more than 60. The total endowment of the ten largest foundations runs upwards of $600,000,000 and that of the community trusts in 1929 was estimated at upwards of $32,000,000.[1]

Moreover, local funds from other sources, while seldom easy to secure for research purposes, have been put into surveys in larger measure as time has gone on. A major proportion of the Springfield Survey was paid for locally, the largest single sums coming from the local Board of Education and several private organizations and individuals; much of it in small contributions. While the value of survey work is not yet fully recognized nor has the community reached the point where it will pay for its surveys on an expert basis, as it does when it calls in an engineer to pass upon the safety of a public bridge or a chemist to pass judgment upon the water supply, nevertheless increasing numbers of cities see that the saving of lives, the safeguarding of health, and

[1] "Foundations in Social Work." In Social Work Year Book, Russell Sage Foundation, New York, 1930, p. 168–171.

promotion of the common welfare through organized, intelligently planned attacks upon disease, ignorance, crime, and other evils have legitimate claims upon the public and private purse.

Educational Use of Survey Findings

The importance of putting real effort into interpreting the findings of a survey has been recognized from the beginning. As already pointed out, educational use of the data is essential to the idea. The Pittsburgh Survey was undertaken by a group interested in spreading information through journalism; and it and later surveys have used not only the printed page, be it newspaper, magazine, pamphlet, or book, but also the spoken word, and graphic devices of many kinds. Nevertheless, a glance over the many projects employed and reflection upon a considerable acquaintance with the procedure followed leads to the conviction that as a rule nothing like the attention and skill has gone into the educational use of the material that has been expended upon its collection.[1] One of the interesting and more significant developments, however, has been a considerable increase in knowledge of the educational processes themselves and a growing skill in their use. In certain undertakings a desire to take advantage of the method of "learning by doing" governed the use of large numbers of volunteers in presenting data to the public; and the so-called "project" method familiar to study classes and conference groups has been employed to spread knowledge of the

---

[1] Some minor defects in this connection may be indicated here. A large number of the reports examined for this Bibliography lacked essential descriptive information regarding the enterprise itself. Titles, too often even with the aid of sub-titles, gave no clear idea of the field covered; the names of organizations and individuals responsible for the survey and the names of the author or authors of the report were not always clearly stated; even the name of the place surveyed in some cases was difficult to find; the date was sometimes omitted or buried deep in the text; and many of the reports gave no publisher's name nor indication where copies might be secured. While these omissions would occasion little or no difficulty in the locality where the survey was made, particularly if it had been widely participated in; nevertheless in large cities these would constitute important deficiencies, certainly if the report was to be used outside the vicinity studied. It would be helpful locally, and undoubtedly among students of social events, if each report could carry the following information where it can be easily found: descriptive name of report; place studied; names of persons and organizations conducting the survey; the author of the report; date of publication; name and address of publisher; the price or whether copies may be had free; if not to be had from publisher where else it can be obtained or consulted.

INTRODUCTION

data. The trend would then seem to be, though seemingly slow, toward a recognition of the importance of putting survey findings before people in ways which will gain them attention and thought, and will bridge the gap between information and action.

THE SURVEYING PROCESS GOES ON

Although in outlining the scope of this Bibliography it was necessary to set a definite date when the listing would have to be finished, as far as it has been possible to judge no sharp change in current trend has taken place since the time of its conclusion. The date set was January 1, 1928. During the intervening period, while the reports collected were being examined, supplementary data secured, and the various subject and locality classifications being worked out, numerous surveys have been under way. Since no thorough search has been made, it is not possible to record them all, perhaps not even all of the outstanding ones; but among those that have come to our attention are the following:

Child Welfare

- Boys and Girls in Salt Lake City, by Rotary Club and Business and Professional Women's Club in Salt Lake City.
- Child Labor in Agriculture and Farm Life in the Arkansas Valley, Colorado, by Bertram H. Mautner and W. Lewis Abbott. National Child Labor Committee.
- Child Labor in New Jersey. Part I, Employment of School Children. Part II, Children Engaged in Industrial Home Work, by Nettie P. McGill and Mary Skinner. Children's Bureau, United States Department of Labor.
- Child Workers on City Streets, by Nettie P. McGill. Children's Bureau, United States Department of Labor.
- Children in Agriculture, by Nettie P. McGill. Children's Bureau, United States Department of Labor.
- Children in Fruit and Vegetable Canneries, A Survey in Several States, by Ellen Nathalie Matthews. Children's Bureau, United States Department of Labor.
- Children in Street Work, by Nettie P. McGill. Children's Bureau, United States Department of Labor.
- National Study of Catholic Children's Homes, by National Conference of Catholic Charities.
- State Survey of Crippled Children (Massachusetts), by State Department of Public Welfare.
- Study of Children Employed in Enid, Oklahoma City, Lawton, and Tulsa (Oklahoma), by National Child Labor Committee.

A BIBLIOGRAPHY OF SOCIAL SURVEYS

City and Regional Planning

    Regional planning surveys of the Committee on Regional Plan of New York and Its Environs, of the National Capital Park and Planning Commission in Washington, of the Regional Planning Federation of the Philadelphia Tri-State District, and of the Regional Planning Association of Chicago; together with a series of social studies in Chicago by the Local Community Research Committee at the University of Chicago.

    Study of city planning problems in New York, by the Mayor's Committee on Plan and Survey.

Community Studies

    Community Welfare in San Diego, California, by George B. Mangold for the Welfare Council of San Diego and the San Diego County Welfare Commission.

    Jewish Communal Survey of Greater New York, by Bureau of Jewish Social Research (First Section: Studies in the New York Jewish Population).

    Middletown, a Study in Contemporary Culture; and a series of village surveys, by the Institute of Social and Religious Research.

Delinquency, Correction, Administration of Justice

    Administration of Justice in Boston, The, by a group from the Harvard Law School.

    Administration of Justice in New Jersey, The, by the National Institute of Public Administration.

    Central Registration Bureau of the Municipal Court of Philadelphia, by Philadelphia Bureau of Municipal Research.

    Health Survey of American Prisons, by National Society of Penal Information.

    Illinois Crime Survey, The, by the Illinois Association for Criminal Justice.

    Juvenile Courts in Utah, The, by the National Probation Association.

    Juvenile Delinquency in Maine, by the Social Service Division of the Children's Bureau, United States Department of Labor.

    Parole and the Indeterminate Sentence, a report to the Chairman of the Parole Board of Illinois. Committee on the Study of the Workings of the Indeterminate-Sentence Law and of Parole in the State of Illinois (Bruce, Burgess, Harno, and Landesco).

    Police Department, The, by Buffalo Municipal Research Bureau. Survey of Causes and Effects of Crime in New York, by the Baumes Crime Commission.

    Survey of Chicago Police Department, by Citizens Police Committee.

    Study of the Prevalence and Treatment of Delinquency among Boys, A, by Dorothy Williams Burke. Children's Bureau, United States Department of Labor.

    Survey of Police Department of Minneapolis, Minnesota, by August Vollmer, City Council.

INTRODUCTION

Survey of the Los Angeles County Juvenile Court, by the National Probation Association.

Treatment of Adult Offenders and Children in Luzerne County, The, by Leon Stern. Wyoming Valley Welfare Council (Pennsylvania), Wilkes-Barre.

Government Administration and Public Finance

Administration of Indian Affairs, The, by the Institute for Government Research, Brookings Institution.

Capital Expenditure Program, A, by Buffalo Municipal Research Bureau, Inc.

Comparative Assessed Valuation for 1927 and 1928 in Iowa, by Des Moines Bureau of Municipal Research.

Cost of Government, The, Wayne County, Michigan, 1928–1929, by Detroit Bureau of Governmental Research

Government and Administration of the District of Columbia, The, by L. F. Schmeckebier and W. F. Willoughby. Institute for Government Research, Brookings Institution.

Report on the Audit and Analysis of the Accounts of the Town of Milford for the year 1927, by the Taxpayers' Research League of Delaware.

San Francisco-San Mateo Survey, The, by the San Francisco Bureau of Governmental Research.

Health and Sanitation

Appraisal of Public Health Activities of Portland, Oregon, An, by James Wallace. Committee on Administrative Practice, American Public Health Association.

Health Inventory of New York City, by M. M. Davis and M. C. Jarrett. Welfare Council of New York City.

Health Survey of Cambridge, Massachusetts, in Relation to Tuberculosis, by M. P. Horwood for the Anti-Tuberculosis Association.

Health Survey of Holyoke, Massachusetts, by Murray P. Horwood.

Health Survey of New Haven, Connecticut, by New Haven Community Chest.

Hospital and Health Survey of Philadelphia, by Haven Emerson for Chamber of Commerce.

Hospital and Health Survey of Washington, D. C., by Survey Committee of the American Public Health Association.

Investigations by the United States Public Health Service, Office of Education, Women's Bureau, and Children's Bureau.

Noise Abatement in New York City, by the Noise Abatement Commission.

Providence (R. I.) Health Survey, by James Wallace, for Committee on Administrative Practice, American Public Health Association.

Recheck of Survey of the Organization and Activities of the Board of Health of the City of Augusta, Ga., by Haven Emerson.

A BIBLIOGRAPHY OF SOCIAL SURVEYS

Report of a Survey of the Department of Health and Relief, Hartford, Connecticut, by the Mayor and Court of Common Council.

Report on a Survey of the Organization and Activities of the Board of Health of the City of Augusta, Ga., by Waller and Fuchs for Special Health Committee, City Council of Augusta.

Review of Health Conditions and Needs in Pitt County, North Carolina, A, by A. F. Walker and Anne Whitney. Metropolitan Life Insurance Company. (Similar studies of health conditions and needs, conducted as a part of the work of the Department of Public Welfare of the General Federation of Women's Clubs and printed by the Metropolitan Life Insurance Company, have been made in Knoxville, Tenn., Middletown and Syracuse, N. Y., and Winston-Salem, N. Car.)

Sanitary and Health Surveys of Mentor and Madison Villages, Ohio, by the Lake County Department of Health.

Sanitary Survey of Greece, by Health Organization of the League of Nations.

School Health Study (70 Cities), by American Child Health Association.

Studies undertaken in connection with the health demonstrations of the Milbank Memorial Fund and with the child health demonstrations of the Commonwealth Fund.

Study of Clinics in Cincinnati, by American Public Health Association and Cincinnati Public Health Federation.

Study of Costs of Medical Care, by Committee on the Costs of Medical Care.

Survey of Health and Other Conditions in Palestine, by the Joint Palestine Survey Commission.

Survey of Health Department and Hospital Facilities of St. Louis, by Committee on Administrative Practice, American Public Health Association.

Survey of Public Health Activities in Los Angeles, California, by I. V. Hiscock and H. F. Scoville for the Bureau of Efficiency of Los Angeles County and the Committee on Administrative Practice, American Public Health Association.

Survey of Public Health Activities, by Montreal Health Survey Committee.

Survey of the Medical Facilities of Shelby County, Indiana, A, 1929, by Allon Peebles for the Committee on the Costs of Medical Care, 910 Seventeenth St., N. W., Washington, D. C.

Mental Hygiene

Mental Hygiene Survey of Boston, by Massachusetts Society for Mental Hygiene, and other local collaborating agencies.

Problem of the Feeble-Minded in New Jersey, The, by Research Department, Training School at Vineland, New Jersey.

Survey of Mental Health Services in Chicago and Illinois, by Illinois Society for Mental Health.

INTRODUCTION

Survey of Mental Hygiene Facilities and Resources in New York City, A, by a group of experts for the National Committee for Mental Hygiene and the State Charities Aid Association.

Negroes

Comprehensive Study of the Condition of Negro Children in North Carolina, A, by N. Car. State Board of Charities and Public Welfare.

Negro Health Survey of Chicago, by City Department of Health.

Study of Conditions among Negroes in Richmond, Virginia, by Council of Social Agencies.

Schools and Education

Public Education in Virginia, by Professor M. V. O'Shea for Virginia Legislature.

Report of a Commission to Survey Public Education, by Charles H. Elliott for the State of New Jersey.

Report of the Survey of Elmore County, Alabama, Schools for the State Department of Education.

Report of the Survey of the Schools of Maple Heights, Ohio, by George D. Strayer. Teachers College Institute of Educational Research.

Report of the Survey of the Schools of Newburgh, New York, by George D. Strayer. Teachers College Institute of Educational Research.

School Building Program for the City of Paducah, Kentucky, A, by George D. Strayer and N. L. Engelhardt.

Survey of Education in West Virginia, by L. V. Cavins. West Virginia Department of Education.

Survey of Land-Grant Colleges, by United States Office of Education.

"Survey of Retarded Children in Public Schools of Massachusetts," by Neil A. Dayton. In American Journal of Psychiatry, Vol. VII, No. 5, p. 22.

Miscellaneous

Behind the Scenes in Candy Factories: New York City, by Consumers' League of New York.

British Columbia Library Survey, by British Columbia Library Commission.

Economic and Social Study of Charles County, Virginia, An, by J. J. Carson. University of Virginia.

Employment of Women at Night, The, by Mary D. Hopkins. Women's Bureau, United States Department of Labor.

Industrial Village Churches, by Edmund deS. Brunner. Institute of Social and Religious Research.

Minneapolis Churches and Their Comity Problems, by Wilbur C. Hallenbeck for the Institute of Social and Religious Research.

Near East and American Philanthropy, The, by F. A. Ross and others. General Committee of the Near East Survey.

Public and Private Social Work in Vancouver, by Vancouver Community Chest and Survey Committee.

A BIBLIOGRAPHY OF SOCIAL SURVEYS

Public Welfare Administration in Louisiana, by Elizabeth Wisner. Social Service Monographs No. 11, University of Chicago.

Small Loan Situation in New Jersey in 1929, The, by Willford Isbell King. New Jersey Industrial Lenders' Association, Trenton.

Some Southern Cotton Mill Workers and Their Villages, by J. J. Rhyne. University of North Carolina.

Study of Rural Vermont, by the Vermont Commission on Country Life.

Survey of Interracial Relations, The, by the National Conference on Interracial Relations.

Survey of Milwaukee's Playground and Playfield Needs, by D. C. Enderis and Gilbert Clegg. Milwaukee (Wis.) Common Council.

Survey of Recreational Facilities in Rochester, New York, A, by Charles B. Raitt for the Rochester Bureau of Municipal Research, Inc.

United States Looks at Its Churches, The, by C. L. Fry. Institute of Social and Religious Research.

Welfare of Prisoners' Families in Kentucky, by Ruth S. Bloodgood. Children's Bureau, United States Department of Labor.

SURVEY TENDENCIES SUMMARIZED

Starting with the Pittsburgh Survey in 1907–1909, which combined in a new form the social investigation within a given area of related current problems and the analysis and interpretation of its findings in ways to make them educational forces in the community, certain developments and tendencies in the use of surveys have emerged. Important among these are: (1) a wider participation of local people and organizations in the various features of the surveys, some of these much more marked than others; (2) a development of survey types and a differentiation between them according to the functions which each is best suited to perform—in other words, the making of a distinction between a general survey and the comprehensive and intensive investigation of a special field, the latter being accomplished through the breaking up of the whole unit of social concern into subdivisions and the application of more extended study to each; (3) when an inquiry is proposed, an increasing care in the type of survey to be selected; (4) an increasing use of the survey method in foreign countries; (5) the growth of a considerable body of material dealing with survey policies, methods, and standards; (6) the wide range of organizations initiating, sponsoring, and conducting surveys; (7) the consequent and apparent

INTRODUCTION

acceptance in practically all types of social and civic work of the survey as important in informing the public on social questions, and as a basis for planning community programs; (8) the shifting of interest from readymade programs evolved in distant central headquarters to the development of plans made through surveys to fit the peculiar needs of the communities concerned; (9) an important increase in funds being devoted to local research and surveys; (10) the setting up of more or less permanent local councils and other agencies equipped to make consecutive studies in their own cities over a period of years; (11) growing attention to social surveys in textbooks and other writings on social subjects and in college courses; and (12) relatively few instances in which the educational use of findings would seem to have been given sufficient emphasis.

It may be added, with some considerable assurance, that the great growth in the use of the survey, partly resulting from a tendency to apply inductive methods to social questions and the increased effort to improve methods of measuring social phenomena, has in turn added vitality and new impetus to these trends themselves, and has also greatly increased the demand on both public and private agencies for better social statistics.

* * * * *

How to Use the Bibliography

A word should be added about the arrangement of the material in this Bibliography. It is classified in two ways: according to the subject matter of the reports, and according to the locality studied. Part I lists reports of general social surveys, Part II reports of surveys of special phases of the local community life, and Part III material discussing the purpose of both types of surveys, methods employed in making them, and standards of measurement used. Part IV lists reports grouped by locality.

In the arrangement according to subject the following data are given: (1) title of study; (2) name of author or authors; (3) name of publisher; (4) date of publication; (5) number of pages the report contains; and (6) price at which it can be obtained; if it is out of print that fact is noted. The arrangement according to place, the Geographical Index, gives the information in briefer form, but reference is always made to the page on which fuller information appears.

In the Table of Contents will be found a complete list of the subject headings under which reports and publications have been listed and the page reference on which each subject heading begins.

If the reader wishes to learn what reports have been made in the field of general social surveys, that is, surveys covering several subjects in one community, he will turn to Part I, where the General Social Surveys are listed. Here he will find them divided into (1) General Social Surveys—Urban and (2) General Social Surveys—Rural; each division is arranged alphabetically according to locality.

If he wishes to learn what has been done in some specialized field, say in that of Education, he will turn to Part II and look under the head of Education. There he will find listed all the surveys dealing with the general subject of Education. If he is interested in specific phases of this subject he will be instructed in the note at the beginning of the section under what other headings to search for information; for instance, Industrial Education, Negro Education, School Buildings and Plants, and so forth. These titles are listed in their alphabetical place in the same Part.

The publications setting forth the purpose of the social survey, methods employed in making it, and the standards of measurement used will be found in Part III, where this material is arranged also under subjects.

If the reader wishes to know what surveys have been made in a certain community he will turn to Part IV, the Geographical Index, where he will find all the reports that have been listed in Parts I and II classified as to locality. He will look first for the country or state in which the particular town or county is located. Under the name of the locality will then be found the surveys made there and the page references to Parts I and II where the fuller information concerning the reports appears.

Copies of most of the reports and publications listed in this Bibliography may be consulted in the Library of the Russell Sage Foundation.

PART I
GENERAL SOCIAL SURVEYS

A DISTINCTION is here made between surveys which cover several major fields of social interest and those which take up a single field or problem. Examples of the former are the Pittsburgh Survey and the Springfield (Ill.) Survey; of the latter, the Cleveland Education Survey, the Health Survey of New Haven, and the Providence (R. I.) Housing Survey. The former type is listed here under the broad title of General Social Surveys. A number of other reports which also take up topics in several related fields will be found under the sub-heading RELIGION in PART II.

URBAN

ALABAMA, BIRMINGHAM. **Birmingham: Smelting Iron Ore and Civics.** In The Survey. Vol. xxvii, No. 14.
> By—Ethel Armes, John A. Fitch, Morris Knowles, W. M. McGrath, A. J. Kelway, Graham Romeyn Taylor, and Shelby M. Harrison. PUBLISHER—The Survey, New York City. 1912. 104 p. Out of print.

ARKANSAS, LITTLE ROCK. **Community Study of Little Rock.**
> By—Southwestern Division, American Red Cross. PUBLISHER—The same, Little Rock. 1921. 164 p. Free.

ASIA MINOR, SMYRNA. **A Survey of Some Social Conditions in Smyrna.**
> By—Social Survey Committee. MIMEOGRAPHED—The same, Smyrna. 1921. 24 p. Out of print.

CALIFORNIA, LOS ANGELES. **The Better City. A sociological study of a modern city.**
> By—Dana W. Bartlett. PUBLISHER—The Neuner Company Press, Los Angeles. 1907. 248 p. Out of print.

CALIFORNIA, LOS ANGELES. **A Community Survey Made in Los Angeles City.**
> By—Commission of Immigration and Housing. PUBLISHER—The same, San Francisco. 1918. 74 p. Free.

CALIFORNIA, LOS ANGELES. **Study of the Housing and Social Conditions in the Ann Street District of Los Angeles.** Under the Direction of the Department of Sociology of the University of Southern California.
 BY—Gladys Patrie. PUBLISHER—Society for the Study and Prevention of Tuberculosis, Los Angeles. 1918. 28 p. Free.

CALIFORNIA, SAN DIEGO. **Pathfinder Social Survey of San Diego.** Report of a limited investigation of social conditions.
 BY—Edith Shatto King and Frederick A. King. PUBLISHER—College Woman's Club, San Diego. 1914. 48 p. 15 cents.

CANADA. REPORTS OF PRELIMINARY AND GENERAL SOCIAL SURVEYS IN CANADA. **Fort William,** 36 p.; **Hamilton,** 49 p.; **London,** 99 p.; **Port Arthur,** 27 p.; **Regina,** 48 p.; **Sydney,** 29 p.; **Vancouver,** 32 p.
 BY—B. M. Stewart. PUBLISHER—Board of Social Service and Evangelism, Presbyterian Church, Toronto. 1913. 30 cents each.

CANADA, MONTREAL. **The City below the Hill.** A sociological study of a portion of the city of Montreal.
 BY—Herbert Brown Ames. PUBLISHER—Bishop Engraving and Printing Company, Montreal. 1897. 87 p. Out of print.

CANADA, TORONTO. **What Is the Ward Going to Do with Toronto?** A report on undesirable living conditions in one section of the city of Toronto.
 BY—Bureau of Municipal Research. PUBLISHER—The same, Toronto. 1918. 75 p. Out of print.

CHINA, PEKING. **Peking: A Social Survey.**
 BY—S. A. Gamble and J. S. Burgess. PUBLISHER—George H. Doran Company, New York City. 1921. 538 p. $5.00.

CHINA, SUNG-KA-HONG. **A Social Survey.** Brown in China, Monograph No. 1.
 BY—Harold S. Bucklin, Director. PUBLISHER—Shanghai College. 1924. 1060. 60 cents.

COLORADO, BOULDER COUNTY. **Boulder County Studies.** 1919–1921. University of Colorado Bulletin. Vol. XXI, No. 9. General Series No. 174.
 BY—Extension Division, University of Colorado. PUBLISHER—The same, Boulder. 1921. 167 p. Free.

CZECHOSLOVAKIA. **Czechoslovakia.** A survey of economic and social conditions.
 BY—Joseph Gruber. PUBLISHER—Macmillan Company, New York City. 1924. 256 p. $2.00.

GENERAL SOCIAL SURVEYS

CZECHOSLOVAKIA, PRAGUE. **Prague: The American Spirit in the Heart of Europe.** The Survey. Vol. XLVI, No. 11.
> BY—Ruth Crawford, Bedrich Shepanek, Herbert Adolphus Miller, and William L. Chenery. PUBLISHER—The Survey, New York City. 1921. 34 p. 25 cents.

DISTRICT OF COLUMBIA, WASHINGTON. **Neglected Neighbors.**
> BY—Charles F. Weller. PUBLISHER—John C. Winston Company, Philadelphia, Pennsylvania. 1909. 342 p. Out of print.

GEORGIA, ATHENS AND CLARKE COUNTY. **Report of a Survey of Athens and Clarke County.**
> BY—A. S. Edwards. PUBLISHER—American Red Cross, Athens. 1921. 12 p. Free.

GEORGIA, AUGUSTA AND RICHMOND COUNTY. **The Augusta Survey.** A community improvement study of Augusta and Richmond County.
> BY—Carter Taylor, Director. PUBLISHER—Augusta Civic Organizations and Georgia Council of Social Agencies, Augusta. 1924. 274 p. Free.

ILLINOIS, CHICAGO. **The American Girl in the Stockyards District.** An investigation carried on under the direction of the Board of the University of Chicago Settlement and the Chicago Alumnæ Club of the University of Chicago.
> BY—Louis Montgomery. PUBLISHER—University of Chicago Press. 1913. 70 p. 29 cents.

ILLINOIS, CHICAGO. **A Community Survey in the Twenty-First Ward.** In the City Club Bulletin. Vol. 6, No. 5.
> BY—G. B. St. John. PUBLISHER—City Club, Chicago. 1913. 19 p. 10 cents per copy.

ILLINOIS, GALESBURG. **An Analysis of the Social Structure of a Western Town.** Reprinted from The Charities Review.
> BY—Arthur W. Dunn. PUBLISHER—University of Chicago Press. 1896. 53 p. Out of print.

ILLINOIS, JACKSONVILLE AND MORGAN COUNTY. **Community Study in Jacksonville and Morgan County.**
> BY—Evelina Belden, Director. MIMEOGRAPHED—Morgan County Chapter, American Red Cross, Jacksonville. 1920. 108 p. 50 cents.

A BIBLIOGRAPHY OF SOCIAL SURVEYS

ILLINOIS, SPRINGFIELD. **The Springfield Survey.** A study of social conditions in an American city. In 3 volumes.
>By—Shelby M. Harrison, Director. PUBLISHER—Russell Sage Foundation, New York City.
>Vol. I. 1918. 540 p.; Vol. II. 1918. 675 p.; Vol. III. 1920. 422 p. Out of print.

>The nine sections of the Springfield Survey have been issued separately and will be found under the following sub-headings in Part II: Charities; City, County, and State Administration; Delinquency and Correction; Education; Health and Sanitation; Housing; Industrial Conditions and Relations; Mental Hygiene; and Recreation.

ILLINOIS, SPRINGFIELD. **Social Conditions in an American City.** Summary of the findings of the Springfield Survey.
>By—Shelby M. Harrison. PUBLISHER—Russell Sage Foundation, New York City. 1920. 439 p. Out of print.

>A brief summary of the main findings and conclusions of the Springfield Survey by Shelby M. Harrison, under the title, In Lincoln's Home Town, will be found in The Survey, Vol. xxxvii, No. 3.

INDIANA. **A Social and Economic Survey.**
>By—F. D. and F. H. Streightoff. PUBLISHER—W. K. Stewart Company, Indianapolis. 1916. 261 p. $1.25.

INDIANA, SUGAR CREEK TOWNSHIP AND THORNTOWN. **Know Your Community Better Study.**
>By—American Red Cross of Thorntown. PUBLISHER—The same. 1920. 38 p. Free.

KANSAS. SOCIAL SURVEYS OF KANSAS CITIES.
Armourdale. The report of a social survey of Armourdale, a community of 12,000 people living in the industrial district of Kansas City. 1919. 91 p. Free.
Clay Center. 1918. 34 p. Free.
Council Grove. 1917. 15 p. Out of print.
Lawrence. 1917. 122 p. Out of print.
Minneapolis. 1918. 39 p. Free.
>By—Manuel C. Elmer, Director. PUBLISHER—University of Kansas, Lawrence.

KANSAS, BELLEVILLE. **Belleville Social Survey.**
>By—E. W. Burgess and J. J. Sippy. PUBLISHER—Social Survey Committee of the Belleville Welfare Society. 1915. 70 p. 25 cents.

GENERAL SOCIAL SURVEYS

KANSAS, TOPEKA. THE TOPEKA IMPROVEMENT SURVEY.
  I. **A Public Health Survey of Topeka.** By Franz Schneider, Jr. 97 p. Out of print.
  II. **Delinquency and Correction.** By Zenas L. Potter. 64 p. 15 cents.
  III. **Municipal Administration in Topeka.** By D. O. Decker. 43 p. 15 cents.
  IV. **Industrial Conditions in Topeka.** By Zenas L. Potter. 56 p. Out of print.
  By—Shelby M. Harrison, Director. PUBLISHER—Russell Sage Foundation, New York City. 1914.

KENTUCKY, LOUISVILLE. **Jewish Neighborhood Survey.** In Jewish Charities. Vol. 7, No. 8.
  By—Charles Strull and Bess Glassman. PUBLISHER—National Conference of Jewish Social Service, New York City. 1916. 4 p. Out of print.

MAINE, AUGUSTA. **The Augusta Survey.** A community study and population census of the city of Augusta.
  By—L. Eva Summers, Director. PUBLISHER—Augusta Branch, National Civic Federation. 1921. 155 p. Free.

MARYLAND, BALTIMORE. **Study of Social Statistics in the City of Baltimore for the Year 1916–1917.** Report No. 16.
  By—Bureau of State and Municipal Research. PUBLISHER—City Council, Baltimore. 1919. 60 p. Free.

MASSACHUSETTS, BOSTON. **The City Wilderness, South End.** 1898. 319 p.
Americans in Process, North and West Ends. 1902. 389 p.
  By—Robert A. Woods. PUBLISHER—Houghton, Mifflin and Company, New York City. Out of print.

MASSACHUSETTS, BOSTON. **The Trend of Jewish Population in Boston.** A study to determine the location of a Jewish communal building. Monograph Vol. 1, No. 1.
  By—Ben Rosen. PUBLISHER—Federated Jewish Charities, Boston. 1921. 28 p. 75 cents.

MASSACHUSETTS, LOWELL. **The Record of a City.** A social survey of Lowell.
  By—George F. Kenngott. PUBLISHER—Macmillan Company, New York City. 1912. 257 p. $3.00.

MICHIGAN, HAMTRAMCK. **A Survey of Social, Educational, and Civic Conditions with Some Recommendations.**
   By—W. E. Kreusi. PUBLISHER—Citizens of Detroit. 1915. 15 p. Out of print.

MINNESOTA, HENNEPIN COUNTY. **The Mound District: A Suburban Home Community.** A study of living conditions and activities in a suburban community of Hennepin County as a basis for community development.
   By—Manuel C. Elmer. PUBLISHER—Hennepin County Tuberculosis Association, Minneapolis. 1922. 31 p. Free.

MINNESOTA, SOUTH MINNEAPOLIS. **A Neighborhood in South Minneapolis.**
   By—Manuel C. Elmer, Director. PUBLISHER—University of Minnesota, Minneapolis. 1922. 45 p. Postage.

MINNESOTA, STILLWATER. **Report of a Social Survey.** A study of social conditions and activities in Stillwater as a basis for a constructive program of community well-being.
   By—Manuel C. Elmer, Director. PUBLISHER—University of Minnesota, Minneapolis. 1920. 14 p. 25 cents.

MISSOURI, COLUMBIA. **What You Should Know about Your City.** Some results of a social survey of Columbia.
   By—C. A. Ellwood and others. PUBLISHER—Charity Organization Society, Columbia. 1913. 15 p. Free.

MISSOURI, SPRINGFIELD. **Springfield Social Survey.**
   By—W. T. Cross and R. H. Leavell. PUBLISHER—Social Survey Council, Springfield. 1911. 33 p. Out of print.

NEW JERSEY, JERSEY CITY. **Study of the First Ward, Jersey City.**
   By—M. A. Fruh. PUBLISHER—Whittier House, Jersey City. 1912. 33 p. Out of print.

NEW JERSEY, NEWARK. **The Ironbound District.** A study of a district in New Jersey.
   By—W. D. Price. PUBLISHER—Neighborhood House, Newark. 1912. 27 p. Out of print.

NEW JERSEY, PRINCETON. **Some Unsolved Problems of a University Town.**
   By—Arthur Evans Wood. PUBLISHER—University of Pennsylvania, Philadelphia. 1920. 76 p. $1.25.

NEW YORK, MOUNT VERNON. **Community Survey.**
   By—Bureau of Jewish Social Research. MIMEOGRAPHED—The same, New York City. 1925. 96 p. Free.

GENERAL SOCIAL SURVEYS

NEW YORK, NEWBURGH. **The Newburgh Survey.** Reports of limited investigations of social conditions in Newburgh.
    BY—Zenas L. Potter and others. PUBLISHER—Russell Sage Foundation, New York City. 1913. 104 p. Out of print.

NEW YORK CITY. WEST SIDE STUDIES.
  Vol. 1. **The Middle West Side.** By O. H. Cartwright; **Mothers Who Must Earn.** By Katharine Anthony. 223 p. $2.00.
  Vol. 2. **Boyhood and Lawlessness; The Neglected Girl.** By Ruth S. True. 143 p. Out of print.
    BY—Pauline Goldmark, Director. PUBLISHER—Russell Sage Foundation, New York City. 1914.

NEW YORK CITY. **A Social Survey of the Washington Street District of New York City.**
    BY—P. B. Myers, Jr. PUBLISHER—Trinity Church Men's Committee, New York City. 1914. 70 p. Out of print.

NEW YORK CITY [BROOKLYN]. **A Neighborhood Survey of Brownsville.**
    BY—Alter F. Landesman. PUBLISHER—Hebrew Educational Society, Brooklyn. 1927. 16 p. Free.

NEW YORK, ROCHESTER. **Fourth Ward Survey: Know Your City.**
    BY—E. A. Rumball. PUBLISHER—Common Good Publishing Company, Rochester. 1911. 32 p. 10 cents.

NEW YORK, SAG HARBOR. **The Sag Harbor Survey.**
    BY—Board of Home Missions of the Presbyterian Church. PUBLISHER—The same, New York City. 1911. 15 p. Out of print.

NORTH CAROLINA, MECKLENBURG COUNTY AND CHARLOTTE. **Agricultural Mecklenburg and Industrial Charlotte.** Social and economic. Department of Rural Social-Economics. University of North Carolina.
    BY—Edgar T. Thompson. PUBLISHER—Charlotte Chamber of Commerce. 1926. 317 p. Free.

NORTH DAKOTA, FARGO. **Social Survey of Fargo.**
    BY—Manuel C. Elmer. PUBLISHER—Associated Charities of Fargo. 1915. 46 p. 25 cents.

OHIO, CLEVELAND. **A Review of the Surveys of the Cleveland Foundation.**
    BY—Raymond Moley. PUBLISHER—Cleveland Foundation. 1923. 106 p. Free.

OHIO, COLUMBUS. **The Neighborhood.** A study of local life in the city of Columbus. In the American Journal of Sociology. Vol. XXVII, Nos. 4, 5, and 6.
> By—E. D. McKenzie. PUBLISHER—University of Chicago Press. 1922. 65 p. 75 cents per copy.

OREGON, LANE COUNTY. **Community Life in Lane County.** Commonwealth Review of the University of Oregon. Vol. II, Nos. 1 and 2.
> By—Joseph D. Boyd. PUBLISHER—University of Oregon, Eugene. 1920. 33 p. Free.

PENNSYLVANIA, COOPERSBURG. **Coopersburg Survey, Being a Study of the Community around Coopersburg, Lehigh County.**
> By—T. Maxwell Morrison. PUBLISHER—Moravian Country Church Association, Easton. 1915. 34 p. 25 cents.

PENNSYLVANIA, PHILADELPHIA. **Study of Housing and Social Conditions in Selected Districts in Philadelphia.**
> By—F. A. Craig. PUBLISHER—Henry Phipps Institute, Philadelphia. 1915. 89 p. Out of print.

PENNSYLVANIA, PHILADELPHIA. **Preliminary Study for Philadelphia Young Men's Hebrew Association Building Campaign.**
> By—Jewish Welfare Board. PUBLISHER—The same, New York City. 1921. 53 p. Free.

PENNSYLVANIA, PITTSBURGH. THE PITTSBURGH SURVEY. In Charities and the Commons. Vol. XXI, Nos. 14, 19, and 23.
I. The People. 123 p.
II. The Place and Its Social Forces. 165 p.
III. The Work. 144 p.
> By—Paul U. Kellogg, Editor. PUBLISHER—Charity Organization Society of the City of New York. 1909. Out of print.

PENNSYLVANIA, PITTSBURGH. **Report of the Economic Survey of Pittsburgh.**
> By—J. T. Holdsworth. PUBLISHER—City Council of Pittsburgh. 1912. 229 p. Out of print.

PENNSYLVANIA, PITTSBURGH. **Pittsburgh District: Civic Frontage.** The Pittsburgh Survey.
> By—Edward T. Devine and others. PUBLISHER—Russell Sage Foundation, New York City. 1914. 554 p. $2.50.

PENNSYLVANIA, PITTSBURGH. **Social Survey of the 22d and 23d Wards North Side.**
> By—First United Presbyterian Church. PUBLISHER—The same, Pittsburgh. 1915. 56 p. Out of print.

GENERAL SOCIAL SURVEYS

PENNSYLVANIA, PITTSBURGH. THE PITTSBURGH SURVEY. Findings in six volumes, listed separately in their special subject classification in Part II.
>**Women and the Trades;** under Industrial Conditions and Relations.
>**The Steel Workers;** under Industrial Conditions and Relations.
>**Wage-Earning Pittsburgh;** under Industrial Conditions and Relations.
>**Work-Accidents and the Law;** under Accidents and Accident Prevention.
>**Homestead: The Households of a Mill Town;** under Family Welfare.
>>By—Paul U. Kellogg, Editor. PUBLISHER—Russell Sage Foundation, New York City.

PENNSYLVANIA, SCRANTON. **Scranton in Quick Review.** Report of a Pathfinder Survey of living conditions which point to the need of a more intensive local survey.
>By—Shelby M. Harrison and others. PUBLISHER—Century Club, Scranton. 1913. 31 p. 10 cents.

RHODE ISLAND, NEWPORT. **Newport Survey of Social Problems.**
>By—Carol Aronovici. PUBLISHER—Newport Survey Committee. 1911. 59 p. Out of print.

RHODE ISLAND, PROVIDENCE. **A Modern City.**
>By—William Kirk. PUBLISHER—University of Chicago Press. 1909. 363 p. Out of print.

TENNESSEE, JACKSON AND MADISON COUNTY. **Social Survey of the City of Jackson and Madison County.**
>By—A. F. Kuhlman, Director. PUBLISHER—Jackson-McClaran Chapter, American Red Cross, Jackson. 1920. 139 p. $1.00.

TURKEY, CONSTANTINOPLE. **Constantinople Today, or the Pathfinder Survey of Constantinople.** A study of oriental social life.
>By—Clarence Richard Johnson, Director. PUBLISHER—Macmillan Company, New York City. 1922. 418 p. $5.00.

WISCONSIN, ASHLAND. **A Citizens' Survey of Ashland.** A comprehensive fact-finding study by the citizens of Ashland of their education, industry, municipal government, recreation, city planning, social work, library, town and country relations, and religion.
>By—Citizens of Ashland. PUBLISHER—Wisconsin Conference of Social Work, Madison. 1927. 207 p. $2.00.

In addition to reports **presenting findings** of General Social Surveys in urban communities, as listed above, publications dealing with **methods of conducting** such studies will be found in Part III, PURPOSE, METHOD, AND STANDARDS, page 334.

A BIBLIOGRAPHY OF SOCIAL SURVEYS

RURAL

ARIZONA. **A Social Survey of Arizona.**
    By—Mary Kidder Rak. PUBLISHER—University Extension Division, University Station, Tucson. 1921. 86 p. Free.

ARKANSAS. **Rural Survey in Arkansas.**
    By—Warren H. Wilson and J. O. Ashenhurst. PUBLISHER—Department of Church and Country Life, Presbyterian Church, New York City. 1913. 31 p. Out of print.

CALIFORNIA, MARIN AND SONOMA COUNTIES. **Rural Survey of Marin and Sonoma Counties.**
    By—Hermann N. Morse. PUBLISHER—Board of Home Missions, Presbyterian Church in the U. S. A., New York City. 1916. 39 p. 10 cents.

CALIFORNIA, TULARE COUNTY. **Rural Survey of Tulare County.**
    By—O. F. Wisner and Hermann N. Morse. PUBLISHER—Board of Home Missions, Presbyterian Church in the U. S. A., New York City. 1915. 116 p. 10 cents.

CANADA. RURAL SURVEYS.
  Report of a Rural Survey of the Agricultural, Educational, Social, and Religious Life, Turtle Mountain District, Including the Municipalities of Whitewater, Morton and Winchester. 1914. 78 p. 30 cents.
  Rural Survey of Swan River Valley. 1913. 73 p. 30 cents.
    By—W. A. Riddell. PUBLISHER—Board of Social Service and Evangelism, Presbyterian Church, Toronto.

CANADA. **Rural Planning and Development.** A study of rural conditions and problems in Canada.
    By—Thomas Adams. PUBLISHER—Commission of Conservation of Canada, Ottawa. 1917. 281 p. Out of print.

CHINA, PHENIX VILLAGE [KWANTUNG]. **Country Life in South China.** The sociology of familism.
    By—Daniel Harrison Kulp. PUBLISHER—Bureau of Publications, Teachers College, Columbia University, New York City. 1925. 367 p. $3.50.

CHINA, YENSHAN COUNTY, CHIHLI PROVINCE. **An Economic and Social Survey of 150 Farms.** University Publication Bulletin No. 13.
    By—J. Lossing Buck. PUBLISHER—College of Agriculture and Forestry, University of Nanking. 1926. 110 p. 30 cents.

GENERAL SOCIAL SURVEYS

GEORGIA. SOCIAL AND ECONOMIC SURVEYS OF GEORGIA COUNTIES.
Floyd County. By Estelle Hughes. 1917. 15 p.
Fulton and Bibb Counties. 1913. 8 p.
Muscogee County. By Ella Jones. 1917. 14 p.
Putnam County. 1912. 5 p.
Webster County. By Ella Kidd and E. C. Bronson. 1912. 10 p.
BY—Georgia Club, State Normal School. PUBLISHER—The same, Athens. Out of print.

ILLINOIS. **A Rural Survey in Illinois.**
BY—W. H. Wilson and C. S. Adams. PUBLISHER—Board of Home Missions, Presbyterian Church in the U. S. A., New York City. 1912. 32 p. Out of print.

INDIANA. **A Rural Survey in Indiana.** A sociological study of 32 rural communities.
BY—Ralph A. Felton and Clarence A. Neff. PUBLISHER—Board of Home Missions, Presbyterian Church in the U. S. A., New York City. 1911. 91 p. Out of print.

IOWA. **Social Surveys of Three Rural Townships in Iowa.** University of Iowa Monographs. Studies in the Social Sciences. Vol. V, No. 2.
BY—Paul S. Pierce. PUBLISHER—University of Iowa, Iowa City. 1917. 88 p. 50 cents.

IOWA. RURAL SOCIAL SURVEYS.
Rural Social Survey of Orange Township, Blackhawk County. Bulletin No. 184. 1918. 54 p.
A Rural Social Survey of Lone Tree Township, Clay County. Bulletin No. 193. 1920. 34 p.
A Rural Social Survey of Hudson, Orange, and Jesup Consolidated School Districts, Blackhawk and Buchanan Counties. Bulletin No. 224. 1924. 45 p.
BY—George H. VanTungeln. PUBLISHER—Agricultural Experiment Station, Iowa State College of Agriculture and Mechanic Arts, Ames. Free.

KENTUCKY. **Rural Survey in Kentucky.**
BY—E. Fred Eastman. PUBLISHER—Department of Church and Country Life, Presbyterian Church, New York City. 1912. 48 p. Out of print.

MARYLAND. **A Rural Survey in Maryland.**
BY—Warren H. Wilson and Anna B. Taft. PUBLISHER—Board of Home Missions, Presbyterian Church in the U. S. A., New York City. 1912. 113 p. Out of print.

MINNESOTA. SOCIAL AND ECONOMIC SURVEYS OF COMMUNITIES IN MINNESOTA.
  Social and Economic Survey of a Community in Red River Valley. Current Problems No. 5. By Louis D. H. Weld. 1915. 86 p. 25 cents.
  Social and Economic Survey of a Community in Northeastern Minnesota. Current Problems No. 45. By Gustav P. Warber. 1915. 115 p. 25 cents.
  Social and Economic Survey of a Rural Township in Southern Minnesota. Studies in Economics No. 1. By Carl W. Thompson and G. P. Warber. 1913. 75 p. 50 cents.
    PUBLISHER—University of Minnesota, Minneapolis.
MISSOURI. **Rural Survey in Missouri.**
    By—Warren H. Wilson. PUBLISHER—Department of Church and Country Life, Presbyterian Church, New York City. 1912. 42 p. Out of print.
MISSOURI, ASHLAND. **Ashland Community Survey.** An economic, social, and sanitary survey in Howard County.
    By—Carl C. Taylor and E. W. Lehmann. PUBLISHER—College of Agriculture, University of Missouri, Columbia. 1920. 16 p. Free.
MISSOURI, MORGAN COUNTY. **A Rural Survey of Morgan County.** Monthly Bulletin Vol. XVI, No. 2.
    By—W. L. Nelson. PUBLISHER—Missouri State Board of Agriculture, Columbia. 1916. 51 p. Free.
MONTANA, RAVALLI COUNTY. **Social Study of Ravalli County.** Bulletin No. 160. University of Montana.
    By—Walter H. Baumgartel. PUBLISHER—Agricultural Experiment Station, Bozeman. 1923. 32 p. Free.
NEW JERSEY. **Social Aspects of the Jewish Colonies of South Jersey.**
    By—Philip Reuben Goldstein. PUBLISHER—University of Pennsylvania, Philadelphia. 1921. 74 p. Free.
NORTH CAROLINA. ECONOMIC AND SOCIAL STUDIES OF NORTH CAROLINA COUNTIES.
  Forsyth County. By Charles N. Siewers. 1924. 92 p.
  Gaston County. By S. H. Hobbs, Jr. 1920. 96 p.
  Halifax County. By Sidney B. Allen and B. Stanford Travis, Jr. 1920. 75 p.
  Pitt County. By Pitt County Club. 1920. 77 p.
  Rockingham County. By Rockingham County Club. 1918. 72 p.

GENERAL SOCIAL SURVEYS

Rutherford County. By R. E. Price. 1918. 61 p.
Sampson County. By S. H. Hobbs, Jr. 1917. 55 p.
Wake County. By G. B. Lay. 1918. 67 p.
 PUBLISHER—Department of Rural Social Science, University of North Carolina, Chapel Hill. Free.

OHIO. RURAL LIFE SURVEYS.
Southeastern Ohio. By R. A. Felton. 1913. 64 p.
Southwestern Ohio. By Paul L. Vogt. 1913. 93 p.
Greene and Clermont Counties. By Paul L. Vogt. 1914. 82 p.
Northwestern Ohio. By R. A. Felton. 1914. 70 p.
 BY—W. H. Wilson, Director. PUBLISHER—Board of Home Missions, Presbyterian Church in the U. S. A., New York City. 10 cents each.

OREGON, LANE COUNTY. **Rural Survey of Lane County.** Bulletin, Vol. 13, No. 14.
 BY—F. C. Ayer and H. N. Morse. PUBLISHER—University of Oregon, Eugene. 1916. 109 p. Free.

PENNSYLVANIA. **Rural Survey in Pennsylvania.**
 BY—Warren H. Wilson and T. Maxwell Morrison. PUBLISHER—Department of Church and Country Life, Presbyterian Church, New York City. 1914. 40 p. Out of print.

PENNSYLVANIA, BUCKS COUNTY. **A Social Survey of Bucks County: Three Rural Townships.**
 BY—Joseph Marchant Hayman. PUBLISHER—Protestant Episcopal Church, Philadelphia. 1915. 79 p. 50 cents.

SOUTH CAROLINA. ECONOMIC AND SOCIAL STUDIES OF SOUTH CAROLINA COUNTIES
Anderson County. Bulletin No. 126. By Olin D. Johnson, Frank T. Meeks, L. B. Cox, and A. M. Bowen. 1923. 127 p.
Chesterfield County. Bulletin No. 111. By Isom Teal, A. L. Campbell, and Claude A. Sherrill. 1922. 88 p.
Dillon County. Bulletin No. 110. By Edgar T. Thompson and Dewey Stephens. 1922. 85 p.
Fairfield County. Bulletin No. 142. By S. W. Nicholson, A. M. Faucette, and R. W. Baxter. 1924. 83 p.
Florence County. Bulletin No. 103. By J. P. McNeill, Jr., and John A. Chase, Jr. 1921. 67 p.
Greenville County. Bulletin No. 102. By Guy A. Gulick. 1921. 89 p.

A BIBLIOGRAPHY OF SOCIAL SURVEYS

Kershaw County. Bulletin No. 120. By George H. Whittkowsky and J. L. Moseley, Jr. 1923. 89 p.

Lancaster County. Bulletin No. 132. By Ernest E. Beaty and Carl W. McMurray. 1923. 115 p.

Lexington County. Bulletin No. 122. By J. E. Stockman and D. S. Shull. 1923. 93 p.

Marion County. Bulletin No. 130. By Sarah E. Godbold and G. A. Williamson, Jr. 1923. 113 p.

Orangeburg County. Bulletin No. 124. By J. M. Green, Jr., and W. F. Fairey, Jr. 1923. 110 p.

Richland County. Bulletin No. 136. By Elizabeth D. English and B. M. Clark. 1924. 94 p.

Sumter County. Bulletin No. 112. By Ralph H. Ramsey, Jr., and A. H. Green. 1922. 111 p.

Union County. Bulletin No. 128. By Robert M. Hope, Fant Kelly, Charles M. Gee, and Douglas Jeter. 1923. 108 p.

PUBLISHER—Department of Rural Science, University of South Carolina, Columbia. Free.

TENNESSEE. **Rural Survey in Tennessee.**

By—Warren H. Wilson and Anton T. Boisen. PUBLISHER—Department of Church and Country Life, Presbyterian Church, New York City. 1912. 48 p. 10 cents.

TENNESSEE. SURVEYS OF TENNESSEE COUNTIES.

Survey of Union County. University Record. Division of Extension Series. Vol. I, No. 2. By B. O. Duggan. 1924. 48 p.

Survey of Crockett County. University Record. Division of Extension Series. Vol. I, No. 3. By W. W. Armentrout. 1924. 31 p.

Educational, Economic, and Community Survey of Bledsoe County. University Record. Division of Extension Series. Vol. IV, No. 2. By D. M. Brown. 1927. 39 p.

PUBLISHER—University of Tennessee Press, Knoxville. Out of print.

TEXAS, TRAVIS COUNTY. **A Social and Economic Survey of Southern Travis County.** Bulletin, 1916, No. 65.

By—Lewis H. Haney and George S. Wehrwein. PUBLISHER—University of Texas, Austin. 1916. 149 p. 35 cents.

UNITED STATES. **Rural Primary Groups.** A study of agricultural neighborhoods. Agricultural Experiment Station of the University of Wisconsin and the U. S. Department of Agriculture cooperating. Research Bulletin 51.

By—J. H. Kolb. PUBLISHER—University of Wisconsin, Madison. 1921. 81 p. Free.

GENERAL SOCIAL SURVEYS

UTAH, ESCALANTE. **A Social Survey of Escalante.** Brigham Young University Studies No. 1.
    BY—Lowry Nelson. PUBLISHER—Brigham Young University, Provo. 1925. 44 p. Free.

VIRGINIA. ECONOMIC AND SOCIAL SURVEYS OF VIRGINIA COUNTIES.
  Albemarle County. University Record. Vol. VII, No. 2. By Elizabeth Fahrney. 1922. 111 p. 20 cents.
  Clarke County. University Record. Vol. IX, No. 12. By Paul L. Warner. 1925. 127 p. 25 cents.
  Fairfax County. University Record. Vol. VIII, No. 12. By Lehman Nickell and Cary J. Randolph. 1924. 127 p. 20 cents.
  King and Queen County. University Record. Vol. IX, No. 10. By Joseph Ryland Mundie. 1925. 98 p. 25 cents.
  Princess Anne County. University Record. Vol. VIII, No. 9. By E. E. Ferrebee and J. Pendleton Wilson, Jr. 1924. 96 p. 25 cents.
  Rockingham County. University Record. Vol. IX, No. 1. By J. S. Peters and W. F. Stinespring. 1924. 131 p. 20 cents.
    PUBLISHER—University of Virginia, Charlottesville.

In addition to reports **presenting findings** in Rural Surveys, as listed above, publications dealing with **methods of conducting** such studies will be found in PART III, PURPOSE, METHOD, AND STANDARDS, page 338.

PART II

SURVEYS IN SPECIALIZED FIELDS

ACCIDENTS AND ACCIDENT PREVENTION

See also INDUSTRIAL CONDITIONS AND RELATIONS; and VIOLENT DEATHS.

CALIFORNIA. Report to the Industrial Accident Commission of the State of California on Special Investigations of Serious Permanent Injuries from January, 1914, to June, 1918.
> BY—L. O. Adams. PUBLISHER—Industrial Accident Commission, San Francisco. 1919. 15 p. Free.

CALIFORNIA, LOS ANGELES COUNTY. Causes of Fatal Accidents on Highways. Sociological Monographs No. 2.
> BY—William Smith. PUBLISHER—Southern California Sociological Society, Los Angeles. 1916. 16 p. Out of print.

MASSACHUSETTS. One Thousand Industrial Accidents Suffered by Massachusetts Children.
> BY—Lucile Eaves. PUBLISHER—Women's Educational and Industrial Union, Boston. 1922. 9 p. 10 cents.

MASSACHUSETTS. See also WISCONSIN in this section.

MISSOURI, KANSAS CITY. Report of the Investigation of 100 Industrial Accidents in Kansas City. In fourth Annual Report of the Board of Public Welfare of Kansas City.
> BY—L. A. Halbert. PUBLISHER—Board of Public Welfare, Kansas City. 1912. 25 p. Out of print.

NEW JERSEY. Industrial Accidents to Women in New Jersey, Ohio, and Wisconsin. U. S. Department of Labor. Bulletin of the Women's Bureau No. 60.
> BY—Kathleen Jennison and Elizabeth Benham. PUBLISHER—Superintendent of Documents, Government Printing Office, Washington, D. C. 1927. 316 p. 45 cents.

NEW JERSEY. See also WISCONSIN in this section.

SURVEYS IN SPECIALIZED FIELDS

ACCIDENTS AND ACCIDENT PREVENTION—Continued

NEW YORK. **Causes and Prevention of Industrial Accidents.** Report to the Legislature of the State of New York by the Commission Appointed to Inquire into the Question of Employers' Liability and Other Matters.
> BY—The Commission. PUBLISHER—State of New York, Albany. 1911. 116 p. Free.

NEW YORK. STUDIES OF INDUSTRIAL ACCIDENTS.
Asphyxiation in Garages and Other Automobile Accidents. Bulletin No. 1. 1920. 23 p.
An Analysis of One Hundred Accidents on Power Punch Presses with Suggestions as to the Installation of Suitable Guards on Such Machines. Bulletin No. 131. 1924. 8 p.
An Analysis of Three Hundred Accidents in Woodworking Factories with Suggestions as to Safe Practice and Suitable Machine Guards. Bulletin No. 139. 1925. 63 p.
> BY—Division of Industrial Hygiene, State Department of Labor. PUBLISHER—The same, Albany. Free.

NEW YORK. STUDIES OF INDUSTRIAL ACCIDENTS.
Children's Work Accidents. Special Bulletin No. 116. By Edith Hilles. 1923. 42 p.
Some Social and Economic Effects of Work Accidents to Women. A study of five hundred women compensated for permanent partial injuries. Special Bulletin No. 127. By Charlotte E. Carr. 1924. 67 p.
Some Recent Figures on Accidents to Women and Minors. Special Bulletin No. 144. By Martha Luginbuhl. 1926. 69 p.
> PUBLISHER—Bureau of Women in Industry, State Department of Labor, Albany. Free.

OHIO. **Accidents to Working Children of Ohio.**
> BY—Consumers' League of Ohio, National Child Labor Committee, Consumers' League of Cincinnati, Toledo Consumers' League, and Young Women's Christian Associations of Ohio. PUBLISHER—Consumers' League of Ohio, Cleveland. 1927. 87 p. 50 cents.

OHIO. *See also* NEW JERSEY in this section.

PENNSYLVANIA. **Accidents to Working Children in Pennsylvania.**
> BY—Estelle Lauder, Eileen F. Evans, and Beatrice McConnell. PUBLISHER—Consumers' League of Eastern Pennsylvania, Philadelphia. 1925. 67 p. Free.

ACCIDENTS AND ACCIDENT PREVENTION—Continued

PENNSYLVANIA, PITTSBURGH. **Work-Accidents and the Law.** The Pittsburgh Survey.
> BY—Crystal Eastman. PUBLISHER—Russell Sage Foundation, New York City. 1910. 335 p. Out of print.

UNITED STATES. **Accidents and Accident Prevention.** Vol. IV. Report on Conditions of Employment in the Iron and Steel Industry in the United States.
> BY—Charles P. Neill, Director. PUBLISHER—Superintendent of Documents, Government Printing Office, Washington, D. C. 1913. 350 p. 40 cents.

UNITED STATES. INDUSTRIAL ACCIDENT AND HYGIENE SERIES. U. S. Department of Labor.

Accidents and Accident Prevention in Machine Building. Bulletin No. 256. 1917. 119 p. 15 cents.

Causes and Prevention of Accidents in the Iron and Steel Industry. 1910–1919. Bulletin No. 298. 1922. 398 p. 35 cents.
> BY—Lucian W. Chaney. PUBLISHER—Superintendent of Documents, Government Printing Office, Washington, D. C.

WISCONSIN. **Industrial Accidents to Employed Minors in Wisconsin, Massachusetts, and New Jersey.** U. S. Department of Labor. Children's Bureau Publication No. 152.
> BY—Edith S. Gray. PUBLISHER—Superintendent of Documents, Government Printing Office, Washington, D. C. 1926. 119 p. 15 cents.

WISCONSIN. *See also* NEW JERSEY in this section.

ADOLESCENCE

MASSACHUSETTS. **Influence of Occupation on Health during Adolescence.** Report of a physical examination of 679 male minors under 18 in the cotton industries of Massachusetts. U. S. Public Health Service Bulletin No. 78.
> BY—M. Victor Safford. PUBLISHER—Superintendent of Documents, Government Printing Office, Washington, D. C. 1916. 51 p. 10 cents.

NEW YORK CITY. **The Adolescent Offender.** A study of the age-limit of the Children's Court.
> BY—Lawrence Veiller. PUBLISHER—Committee on Criminal Courts, Charity Organization Society, New York City. 1923. 85 p. Free.

SURVEYS IN SPECIALIZED FIELDS

ADOLESCENCE—Continued

NEW YORK CITY. **Determinants of Sex Delinquency in Adolescent Girls.** Based on Intensive Studies of 500 Cases. No. 38.
> By—Anne T. Bingham. PUBLISHER—Probation and Protection Association, New York City. 1923. 93 p. 50 cents.

AGED

> See DEPENDENCY; PENSIONS; and SOCIAL AGENCIES.

AGRICULTURE

> See PART I, GENERAL SOCIAL SURVEYS—URBAN and RURAL, and PART II, in CHILD LABOR; CHILD WELFARE; COST OF LIVING; EDUCATION; INDUSTRIAL CONDITIONS AND RELATIONS; INDUSTRIAL EDUCATION; JAPANESE; MILK; RURAL; TUBERCULOSIS; UNEMPLOYMENT; and VOCATIONAL GUIDANCE AND TRAINING.

ALMSHOUSES

> See also DEPENDENCY; and RELIEF.

CONNECTICUT. **Some American Almshouses.** A study of a group of almshouses in Connecticut, New Jersey, New York, and Pennsylvania.
> By—Estelle Stewart, Director. PUBLISHER—Women's Department, National Civic Federation, New York City. 1927. 95 p. Free.

MISSOURI. **Condition of the County Almshouses of Missouri.**
> By—Charles A. Ellwood. PUBLISHER—University of Missouri, Columbia. 1904. 31 p. Out of print.

NEW JERSEY. See CONNECTICUT in this section.

NEW JERSEY, NEWARK. **The Poor and Alms Department and the Almshouse of Newark.** A survey made by the Department of Surveys and Exhibits of the Russell Sage Foundation.
> By—Francis H. McLean. PUBLISHER—Board of City Commissioners, Newark. 1919. 71 p. Out of print.

NEW YORK. See CONNECTICUT in this section.

OHIO, CINCINNATI. **The Hamilton County Home.** A social survey of the almshouse in Cincinnati.
> By—Eugenia Lea Remelin and Ellery Francis Reed. MIMEOGRAPHED—Helen S. Trounstine Foundation and Women's City Club, Cincinnati. 1927. 57 p. $1.00.

ALMSHOUSES—Continued

PENNSYLVANIA. *See* CONNECTICUT in this section.

SOUTH CAROLINA. **Handbook of Jail, Chaingang, and Almshouse Management.** Quarterly Bulletin. Vol. IV, No. 3.
> BY—Frank E. Broyles. PUBLISHER—State Board of Charities and Corrections, Columbia. 1918. 59 p. Free.

TENNESSEE, HAMILTON COUNTY. **Report of a Study of the Hamilton County Workhouse and Almshouse.**
> BY—C. Spencer Richardson. PUBLISHER—Appraisal Committee, Hamilton County Court, Chattanooga. 1917. 42 p. Out of print.

VIRGINIA. **Southwest Virginia County Almshouse Survey.** In The Disappearance of the County Almshouse in Virginia.
> BY—Arthur W. James. PUBLISHER—State Board of Public Welfare, Richmond. 1926. 10 p. Free.

AMERICANIZATION

> *See* IMMIGRATION AND AMERICANIZATION.

BLINDNESS, SIGHT CONSERVATION, AND DISEASE OF THE EYE

> *See also* MIDWIFE; and TRACHOMA.

MARYLAND. **Report of the Commission to Investigate the Conditions of the Adult Blind in Maryland.**
> BY—The Commission. PUBLISHER—Commonwealth of Maryland, Annapolis. 1907. 20 p. Free.

MASSACHUSETTS. **Report of the Massachusetts Commission on the Adult Blind.**
> BY—The Commission. PUBLISHER—Commonwealth of Massachusetts, Boston. 1904. 32 p. Out of print.

MASSACHUSETTS. **Ophthalmia Neonatorum in Ten Massachusetts Cities.** A study by the Research Department of the Boston School of Social Work.
> BY—Henry Copley Greene. PUBLISHER—American Association for the Conservation of Vision, New York City. 1911. 41 p. Out of print.

MASSACHUSETTS. **Report of Ten-Year Survey Committee on the Work of the Massachusetts Commission for the Blind.** 1906–1916.
> BY—C. F. Fraser. PUBLISHER—Massachusetts Association for Promoting the Interests of the Blind, Boston. 1917. 42 p. Free.

SURVEYS IN SPECIALIZED FIELDS

BLINDNESS, SIGHT CONSERVATION, AND DISEASE OF THE EYE—Continued

MASSACHUSETTS. **Report of the Special Commission Relative to the Registration, Care, and Relief of Blind Persons.** House No. 755.
> By—The Commission. PUBLISHER—Commonwealth of Massachusetts, Boston. 1920. 13 p. Free.

MASSACHUSETTS. **Final Report of the Special Commission on the Blind to Investigate Relative to the Employment, Training, and Placement of the Blind.** House No. 1170.
> By—The Commission. PUBLISHER—Commonwealth of Massachusetts, Boston. 1925. 53 p. Free.

MINNESOTA. **Report of the Minnesota Commission for the Blind.**
> By—The Commission. PUBLISHER—State Board of Control, St. Paul. 1923. 119 p. Free.

NEW YORK. **Report of the Commission to Investigate the Condition of the Blind in the State of New York.**
> By—The Commission. PUBLISHER—General Assembly, Albany. 1906. 586 p. Out of print.

NEW YORK, JAMESTOWN. **The Jamestown Eye Survey.** A study of 8,000 school children.
> By—Medical Inspection Bureau in co-operation with the National Committee for the Prevention of Blindness, New York State Commission for the Blind, and the Jamestown Board of Education. PUBLISHER—University of the State of New York Press, Albany. 1926. 26 p. Free.

NEW YORK CITY. **Care and Treatment of the Jewish Blind in the City of New York.**
> By—Florina Lasker, Ella Lasker, and Loula Lasker. PUBLISHER—Bureau of Social Research, New York City. 1918. 109 p. Out of print.

OHIO. **A Mental Survey of the Ohio State School for the Blind.** Ohio Board of Administration Publication No. 9.
> By—Thomas H. Haines. PUBLISHER—State Department of Public Welfare, Columbus. 1916. 24 p. Out of print.

OHIO, CLEVELAND. **The Blind in Cleveland.**
> By—Cleveland Society for the Blind. PUBLISHER—The same. 1918. 72 p. $1.00.

A BIBLIOGRAPHY OF SOCIAL SURVEYS

BLINDNESS, SIGHT CONSERVATION, AND DISEASE OF THE EYE—Continued

OHIO, HAMILTON COUNTY. **Blindness in Hamilton County.** A summary of the activities, laws, and statistics relating to blindness with special reference to the administration of the law regulating "The Relief of the Needy Blind." Studies from the Helen S. Trounstine Foundation. Vol, I, No. 3.

By—Louis Stricker. PUBLISHER—Helen S. Trounstine Foundation, Cincinnati. 1918. 47 p. 50 cents.

PENNSYLVANIA. **Report of the Commission to Study Conditions Relating to Blind Persons in Pennsylvania.**

By—The Commission. PUBLISHER—Commonwealth of Pennsylvania, Harrisburg. 1925. 84 p. Free.

UNITED STATES. **Eye Hazards in Industrial Occupations: A Report of Typical Cases and Conditions with Recommendations for Safe Practice.** Publication No. 12.

By—Gordon L. Berry. PUBLISHER—National Committee for the Prevention of Blindness, New York City. 1917. 145 p. 50 cents.

UNITED STATES. **Eye Sight Conservation Survey.** Bulletin 7.

By—Joshua Eyre Hannum and Guy A. Henry. PUBLISHER—Eye Sight Conservation Council of America, New York City. 1925. 219 p. $1.00.

BOY LIFE

See also PART I, GENERAL SOCIAL SURVEYS—URBAN, and PART II, in CHILD HEALTH AND HYGIENE; CHILD LABOR; CHINESE; INDUSTRIAL CONDITIONS AND RELATIONS; JUVENILE DELINQUENCY; MENTAL HYGIENE; TRUANCY AND NON-ATTENDANCE; and VOCATIONAL GUIDANCE AND TRAINING.

CALIFORNIA, LOS ANGELES. **The City Boy and His Problems.** A survey of boy life in Los Angeles.

By—Emory S. Bogardus. PUBLISHER—Rotary Club of Los Angeles. 1926. 148 p. Free.

CALIFORNIA, SAN FRANCISCO. **A Study of the San Francisco District Council of the Boy Scouts of America.**

By—E. P. Von Allmen. MIMEOGRAPHED—Council of Social and Health Agencies, San Francisco. 1924. 88 p. Free.

ILLINOIS, CHICAGO. **Preliminary Inquiry into Boys' Work in Chicago.**

By—Chicago Council of Social Agencies. PUBLISHER—The same. 1921. 28 p. Free.

SURVEYS IN SPECIALIZED FIELDS

BOY LIFE—Continued

NEW JERSEY, TRENTON. **Some Salient Facts Gathered from Trenton's Boy Life Survey.**
    BY—Boys' Work Committee of the Y. M. C. A. PUBLISHER—Rotary Club, Trenton. 1922. 33 p. Free.

NEW YORK CITY. **A Survey of New York City Boys.**
    BY—F. F. C. Rippon. PUBLISHER—Kiwanis Club, New York City. 1926. 51 p. Free.

TEXAS, AMARILLO. **Boy Life Survey of Amarillo.**
    BY—H. C. Pipkin. MIMEOGRAPHED—Rotary Club of Amarillo. 1922. 10 p. Free.

TEXAS, SAN ANTONIO. **The Wheel of Fortune.** Salient significant facts gleaned from the San Antonio Boy Life Survey.
    BY—Rotary Club Boys' Work Committee and Young Men's Christian Association of San Antonio. PUBLISHER—Rotary Club of San Antonio. 1921. 39 p. Free.

In addition to reports **presenting findings** in Boy Life Surveys, as listed above, publications dealing with **methods of conducting** such studies will be found in PART III, PURPOSE, METHOD, AND STANDARDS, page 339.

BURIAL

UNITED STATES. **Reasons for Present-Day Funeral Costs.** A summary of facts developed by the Advisory Committee on Burial Survey in the course of an impartial study of the burial industry.
    BY—John C. Gebhart. PUBLISHER—Advisory Committee on Burial Survey, New York City. 1927. 39 p. Free.

CANCER
    See also MEXICANS.

CALIFORNIA, SAN FRANCISCO. SAN FRANCISCO CANCER SURVEY. [Studies also made in Albany, Buffalo, and Madison Co., N. Y.; Battle Creek, Mich.; Boston, Mass.; Chicago, Ill.; East Orange and Newark, N. J.; New Orleans, La.; Oakland, Calif.; Rochester, Minn.]
  First Preliminary Report (First and Second Quarterly Reports with Appendices). 1922. 45 p.
  Second Preliminary Report (Third and Fourth Quarterly Reports). 1924. 192 p.
  Third Preliminary Report (Fifth and Sixth Quarterly Reports). 1925. 246 p.

CANCER—Continued

Fourth Preliminary Report (Seventh and Eighth Quarterly Reports). 1926. 228 p.
    By—Frederick L. Hoffman. PUBLISHER—Prudential Insurance Company of America, New York City. Free.

UNITED STATES. **Free Tumor Diagnosis as a Function of State Public Health Laboratories.** Report of a Special Committee of the American Society for the Control of Cancer. Publication Bulletin 11.
    By—Leverett Dale Bristol, Director. PUBLISHER—American Society for the Control of Cancer, New York City. 1916. 12 p. Free.

CARDIACS

    See also CONVALESCENCE; and HOSPITALS AND SANATORIA.

INDIANA, BLOOMINGTON. **The Social Aspect of the Cardiac Case.** A study based upon 154 cardiac cases referred to the Social Service Department of Indiana University. Studies No. 42, Vol. VI.
    By—Lela Frances Thompson. PUBLISHER—University of Indiana, Bloomington. 1919. 44 p. 35 cents.

NEW YORK CITY. **Special Report on Cardiac Classes in the Schools of New York City.**
    By—Committee on Schools, Association for the Prevention and Relief of Heart Disease. PUBLISHER—Board of Education, New York City. 1923. 41 p. Free.

CHARITIES

    See also ALMSHOUSES; CHILD WELFARE; DELINQUENCY AND CORRECTION; DEPENDENCY; IMMIGRATION AND AMERICANIZATION; RELIEF; and SUB-NORMAL, RETARDED, AND EXCEPTIONAL CHILDREN.

CANADA, TORONTO. **Report of the Charities Commission to Make Examination into the Working of the Different Charitable Institutions.**
    By—The Commission. PUBLISHER—The same, Toronto. 1912. 52 p. Out of print.

COLORADO, DENVER. **Summary Report of Field Survey of the Denver Federation for Charity and Philanthropy.**
    By—Institute for Public Service, New York City. PUBLISHER—Colorado Taxpayers' Protective League, Denver. 1916. 32 p. 10 cents.

SURVEYS IN SPECIALIZED FIELDS

CHARITIES—Continued

CONNECTICUT, BRIDGEPORT. **Report on the Department of Public Charities of Bridgeport.** An investigation made by the Russell Sage Foundation.
  By—Margaret F. Byington. PUBLISHER—Board of Public Charities, Bridgeport. 1912. 16 p. Out of print.

CONNECTICUT, NEW LONDON. **Suggestions Concerning Closer Unity of Charity Work in New London.** An investigation.
  By—Maurice Willows. PUBLISHER—Business Men's Association, New London. 1913. 22 p. Out of print.

ILLINOIS. **A Report on Charitable and Correctional Institutions of the State of Illinois.**
  By—James W. Garner. PUBLISHER—Efficiency and Economy Committee of Illinois, Springfield. 1914. 62 p. Out of print.

ILLINOIS, SPRINGFIELD. **The Charities of Springfield.** Charities Section of the Springfield Survey.
  By—Francis H. McLean. PUBLISHER—Russell Sage Foundation, New York City. 1915. 185 p. 25 cents.

INDIANA, INDIANAPOLIS. **Indianapolis Survey.**
  By—Maurice B. Hexter. PUBLISHER—United Jewish Charities, Cincinnati. Ohio. 1919. 27 p. Out of print.

KENTUCKY, LEXINGTON. **Report on the Charities of Lexington.**
  By—Margaret F. Byington. PUBLISHER—City of Lexington. 1918. 51 p. Free.

MICHIGAN. **Report on the Penal, Reformatory, and Charitable Institutions.**
  By—Special Commissioners to Examine Penal, Reformatory, and Charitable Institutions. PUBLISHER—State of Michigan, Lansing. 1871. 133 p. Out of print.

MICHIGAN, GRAND RAPIDS. **Survey of the Charities and Philanthropies of Grand Rapids.**
  By—Edwin W. Booth. PUBLISHER—Charity Organization Society, Grand Rapids. 1911. 16 p. Out of print.

MISSOURI, ST. JOSEPH. **Survey of the Work of the Associated Charities Work Room, Baby Welfare, Humane Society, Riverside Home, Sheltering Arms, Tuberculosis Society, Visiting Nurses, Wesley House, and Negro Orphans.**
  By—St. Joseph Federation for Charity and Philanthropy. PUBLISHER—The same. 1920. 17 p. Free.

A BIBLIOGRAPHY OF SOCIAL SURVEYS

CHARITIES—Continued

NEW JERSEY, ENGLEWOOD. **Report of the Committee of Investigation of Englewood Charities.**
By—Margaret F. Byington. PUBLISHER—The Committee, Englewood. 1911. 15 p. Out of print.

NEW YORK. **Report of the State Commissioner to Examine into the Management and Affairs of the State Board of Charities, the Fiscal Supervisor, and Certain Related Boards and Commissions.**
By—Charles H. Strong. PUBLISHER—State of New York, Albany. 1916. 168 p. Out of print.

NEW YORK CITY. **Report of the Committee on Inquiry into the Departments of Health, Charities, and Bellevue and Allied Hospitals.**
By—Henry C. Wright, Director. PUBLISHER—City of New York. 1913. 788 p. Free.

NEW YORK CITY. **Brief Summary of the Final Report of the Catholic Charities Diocesan Survey.**
By—Catholic Charities Archdiocese. PUBLISHER—The same, New York City. 1920. 15 p. Free.

NEW YORK, ROCHESTER. **Abstract of a Report on the Department of Charities of the City of Rochester.**
By—Francis H. McLean. PUBLISHER—Bureau of Municipal Research, Rochester. 1918. 38 p. Free.

NEW YORK, SYRACUSE. **Report of Investigations for the Associated Charities of Syracuse.** Part I. Report on Finance, Budget and Accounting Methods of the City of Syracuse. Part II. Report on the Syracuse Department of Charities.
By—Fred W. Linders and Helen Drake. PUBLISHER—Bureau of Municipal Research, New York City. 1912. 8 p. 10 cents.

PENNSYLVANIA. **Report of the Citizens' Committee on the Finances of Pennsylvania.** Part III. Survey of the Fiscal Policies of the State of Pennsylvania as Related to Charitable Institutions, Hospitals, State Penal and Correctional Institutions, and State Subsidies of Private Charitable Institutions.
By—The Committee. PUBLISHER—Department of State and Finance, Harrisburg. 1922. 130 p. Out of print.

RHODE ISLAND, PROVIDENCE. **A Community Fund for Charitable Organizations of Providence.** A report of a study.
By—Pierce Williams. PUBLISHER—Providence Community Fund. 1925. 40 p. Free.

SURVEYS IN SPECIALIZED FIELDS

CHARITIES—Continued

TENNESSEE, CHATTANOOGA. **Report on Charitable Organizations of Chattanooga.** In Chattanooga Municipal Record. Vol. 3, No. 3.
> By—Bureau of Municipal Research. PUBLISHER—City of Chattanooga. 1913. 2 p. Out of print.

UNITED STATES. **Study of Nine Hundred and Eighty-five Widows Known to Certain Charity Organization Societies in 1910.**
> By—Mary E. Richmond and Fred S. Hall. PUBLISHER—Russell Sage Foundation, New York City. 1913. 83 p. 25 cents.

VERMONT, BURLINGTON. **Survey of the City of Burlington: Its Charities and Housing Conditions.**
> By—F. H. McLean and U. D. Brown. PUBLISHER—Committee on Social Survey, Burlington. 1915. 85 p. Out of print.

In addition to reports **presenting findings,** as listed above, a publication dealing with **methods of conducting** such studies will be found in Part III, PURPOSE, METHOD, AND STANDARDS, under **Crime and Criminals.**

CHILD HEALTH AND HYGIENE

See also ADOLESCENCE; CHILD LABOR; CHILD WELFARE; CLINICS AND DISPENSARIES; HEALTH AND SANITATION; INFANT MORTALITY; INFANTILE PARALYSIS; ITALIANS; NEGROES; PRENATAL CARE; PRE-SCHOOL; RURAL HEALTH AND SANITATION; TRUANCY AND NON-ATTENDANCE; and TUBERCULOSIS.

ARKANSAS, WARREN AND BRADLEY COUNTY. **A Survey of Conditions Affecting Children in Warren and Bradley County.**
> By—Frances Sage Bradley. PUBLISHER—Bradley County Public Health Association, Warren. 1923. 15 p. Free.

CANADA, MONTREAL AND THE PROVINCE OF QUEBEC. **Child Health Studies in Montreal and the Province of Quebec.**
> By—Child Welfare Association of Montreal. PUBLISHER—The same. 1921. 53 p. Free.

KENTUCKY. **The Nutrition and Care of Children in a Mountain County of Kentucky.** U. S. Department of Labor. Children's Bureau Publication No. 110.
> By—Lydia Roberts. PUBLISHER—Superintendent of Documents, Government Printing Office, Washington, D. C. 1922. 41 p. 10 cents.

CHILD HEALTH AND HYGIENE—Continued

MASSACHUSETTS, BOSTON. **Physical Defects in Children: Report of 602 Cases.** Pamphlet No. 8.
> BY—William R. P. Emerson. PUBLISHER—Nutrition Clinic for Delicate Children, Boston. 1920. 16 p. 10 cents.

MISSOURI. **Progress Report on Field Investigations in Child Hygiene in the State of Missouri.** Public Health Reports. Vol. 35, No. 53.
> BY—C. P. Knight. PUBLISHER—Superintendent of Documents, Government Printing Office, Washington, D. C. 1920. 19 p. 5 cents.

NEW YORK. **A Child Health Survey of New York State.** An inquiry into the measures being taken in the different counties for conserving the health of children.
> BY—Josephine Baker and Dorothy C. Kempf. PUBLISHER—New York League of Women Voters, New York City. 1922. 140 p. 15 cents.

NEW YORK. **The Health of the Working Child.** Special Bulletin, No. 134.
> BY—Bureau of Women in Industry. PUBLISHER—State Department of Labor, Albany. 1924. 91 p. Free.

NEW YORK CITY. **The Health of a Thousand Newsboys in New York City.** A study made in cooperation with the Board of Education.
> BY—Heart Committee, New York Tuberculosis and Health Association. MIMEOGRAPHED—The same, New York City. 1926. 73 p. Free.

NEW YORK CITY. **A Study of 106 Malnourished Children.** Reprinted from the Public Health Nurse, June, 1926.
> BY—East Harlem Nursing and Health Demonstration. PUBLISHER—The same, New York City. 1927. 7 p. Free.

OHIO, CLEVELAND. **A Program for Child Health.** Part III. Cleveland Hospital and Health Survey.
> BY—Josephine Baker. PUBLISHER—Cleveland Hospital Council. 1920. 50 p. 50 cents.

TEXAS, AUSTIN. **Social Survey of the City of Austin.** Delineator Seventh Baby Campaign.
> BY—C. E. Terry and Franz Schneider, Jr. PUBLISHER—The Delineator, New York City. 1917. 40 p. Out of print.

SURVEYS IN SPECIALIZED FIELDS

CHILD HEALTH AND HYGIENE—Continued

UNITED STATES. **A Survey of Evidence Regarding Food Allowances for Healthy Children.**
> By—Lucy H. Gillett. PUBLISHER—New York Association for Improving the Condition of the Poor, New York City. 1917. 24 p. 10 cents.

UNITED STATES. **Infectious Diseases of Children.** A study of 6,078 cases among immigrants with special reference to cross infection and hospital management. U. S. Public Health Service Bulletin, No. 95.
> By—J. G. Wilson. PUBLISHER—Superintendent of Documents, Government Printing Office, Washington, D. C. 1918. 101 p. Free.

In addition to reports **presenting findings** in Child Health and Hygiene Surveys, as listed above, publications dealing with **methods of conducting** such studies will be found in Part III, PURPOSE, METHOD, AND STANDARDS, page 340.

CHILD LABOR
> *See also* ACCIDENTS AND ACCIDENT PREVENTION; CHILD HEALTH AND HYGIENE; CHILD WELFARE; CHINESE; CONTINUATION AND PART-TIME SCHOOLS; EIGHT-HOUR DAY; HEALTH IN INDUSTRY; INDUSTRIAL CONDITIONS AND RELATIONS; JUVENILE DELINQUENCY; TRUANCY AND NON-ATTENDANCE; and VOCATIONAL GUIDANCE AND TRAINING.

ALABAMA. **The Cry of the Children.** A study of child labor in the cotton and woolen mills of Alabama, Georgia, Maine, New Hampshire, and Massachusetts.
> By—Bessie VanVorst. PUBLISHER—Moffat, Yard, and Company, New York City. 1908. 246 p. $1.25.

ALABAMA, BIRMINGHAM. **Newsboys in Birmingham.** In The American Child. Vol. III, No. 4.
> By—Esther Lee Rider. PUBLISHER—National Child Labor Committee, New York City. 1922. 10 p. 25 cents per copy.

CALIFORNIA, SAN FRANCISCO. **Child Labor on the Stage in San Francisco.**
> By—Juvenile Protective Association. PUBLISHER—The same, San Francisco. 1924. 30 p. Free.

COLORADO. **Child Labor in the Sugar-Beet Fields of Colorado.** In Child Labor Bulletin, No. 4.
> By—E. N. Clopper. PUBLISHER—National Child Labor Committee, New York City. 1916. 30 p. 50 cents.

CHILD LABOR—Continued

COLORADO. **Children Working on Farms in Certain Sections of the Western Slope of Colorado.** Publication No. 327.
 By—Charles E. Gibbons and Howard M. Bell. PUBLISHER—National Child Labor Committee, New York City. 1925. 112 p. 50 cents.

CONNECTICUT. **Administration of Child Labor Laws.** Part I. Employment Certificate System in Connecticut. U. S. Department of Labor Children's Bureau Publication No. 12.
 By—Helen L. Sumner and Ethel E. Hanks. PUBLISHER—Superintendent of Documents, Government Printing Office, Washington, D. C. 1915. 69 p. 10 cents.

CONNECTICUT. **Child Laborers in the Shade Grown Tobacco Industry in Connecticut.** Pamphlet No. 11.
 By—Mary Crowell Welles. PUBLISHER—Consumers' League of Connecticut, Hartford. 1916. 6 p. Free.

CONNECTICUT. **Industrial Instability of Child Workers.** A study of employment certificate records in Connecticut. U. S. Department of Labor. Children's Bureau Publication No. 74. Industrial Series No. 5.
 By—Robert Morse Woodbury. PUBLISHER—Superintendent of Documents, Government Printing Office, Washington, D. C. 1920. 86 p. 10 cents.

DISTRICT OF COLUMBIA, WASHINGTON. **Child Labor at the National Capital.** Publication No. 213.
 By—A. J. McKelway. PUBLISHER—National Child Labor Committee, New York City. 1912. 15 p. 10 cents.

GEORGIA. **Child Labor in Georgia.** Publication No. 138.
 By—A. J. McKelway. PUBLISHER—National Child Labor Committee, New York City. 1910. 20 p. 10 cents.

GEORGIA. *See also* ALABAMA in this section.

ILLINOIS. **Work of Children on Illinois Farms.** U. S. Department of Labor. Children's Bureau Publication No. 168.
 By—Dorothy Williams and Mary E. Skinner. PUBLISHER—Superintendent of Documents, Government Printing Office, Washington, D. C. 1926. 48 p. 15 cents.

ILLINOIS, CHICAGO. **Chicago Children in the Street Trades.**
 By—Elsa Wertheim. PUBLISHER—Juvenile Protective Association, Chicago. 1917. 11 p. Out of print.

SURVEYS IN SPECIALIZED FIELDS

CHILD LABOR—Continued

INDIANA. **Child Labor in Indiana.** Pamphlet No. 91.
    By—E. N. Clopper. PUBLISHER—National Child Labor Committee, New York City. 1908. 16 p. Free.

INDIANA. **School or Work in Indiana?** Publication No. 341.
    By—Charles E. Gibbons and Harvey N. Tuttle. PUBLISHER—National Child Labor Committee, New York City. 1927. 30 p. 15 cents.

KENTUCKY. **Enforcement of the Child Labor Law in Kentucky.** Publication No. 331.
    By—Charles E. Gibbons. PUBLISHER—National Child Labor Committee, New York City. 1925. 8 p. 10 cents.

MAINE. *See* ALABAMA in this section.

MARYLAND. **Administration of Child Labor Laws.** Part III. Employment Certificate System in Maryland. U. S. Department of Labor. Children's Bureau Publication No. 41. Industrial Series No. 2.
    By—Francis Henry Bird and Ella Arvilla Merritt. PUBLISHER—Superintendent of Documents, Government Printing Office, Washington, D. C. 1919. 125 p. 15 cents.

MARYLAND. **Child Labor on Maryland Truck Farms.** U. S. Department of Labor. Children's Bureau Publication No. 123.
    By—Alice Channing. PUBLISHER—Superintendent of Documents, Government Printing Office, Washington, D. C. 1923. 52 p. 10 cents.

MASSACHUSETTS. **Report of the Effect of the Child Labor Law of 1913.** House No. 2552.
    By—Robert A. Woods, Director. PUBLISHER—State Board of Labor and Industries, Boston. 1914. 94 p. Free.

MASSACHUSETTS. **Child Labor in Massachusetts.** An inquiry under the auspices of the Massachusetts Child Labor Committee.
    By—Raymond G. Fuller and Mabel A. Strong. PUBLISHER—Massachusetts Child Labor Committee, Boston. 1926. 176 p. $2.00.

MASSACHUSETTS. *See also* ALABAMA in this section.

MASSACHUSETTS, BOSTON. **The Working Children of Boston.** A study of child labor under a modern system of legal regulation. U. S. Department. Children's Bureau Publication No. 89.
    By—Helen Sumner Woodbury. PUBLISHER—Superintendent of Documents, Government Printing Office, Washington, D. C. 1922. 374 p. 25 cents.

A BIBLIOGRAPHY OF SOCIAL SURVEYS

CHILD LABOR—Continued

MASSACHUSETTS, SPRINGFIELD. **Newsboys in Springfield.** In National Vocational Guidance Association Bulletin No. 2.
    BY—Amy Hewes. PUBLISHER—Bureau of Vocational Guidance, Harvard University, Cambridge. 1923. 11 p. 15 cents.

MASSACHUSETTS, WALTHAM. **From School to Work.** A study of children leaving school under 16 years of age to go to work in Waltham. U. S. Department of Labor. Children's Bureau Miscellaneous Publication.
    BY—Margaret Hutton Abels. PUBLISHER—Superintendent of Documents, Government Printing Office, Washington, D. C. 1917. 59 p. Out of print.

MICHIGAN. **People Who Go to Beets.** Pamphlet No. 299.
    BY—Theresa Wolfson. PUBLISHER—National Child Labor Committee, New York City. 1919. 23 p. 15 cents.

MICHIGAN. **Child Labor in the Sugar Beet Fields of Michigan.**
    BY—Walter W. Armentrout, Sara A. Brown, and Charles E. Gibbons. PUBLISHER—National Child Labor Committee, New York City. 1923. 78 p. 20 cents.

MICHIGAN. **Minors in Automobiling and Metal Manufacturing Industries in Michigan.** U. S. Department of Labor. Children's Bureau Publication No. 126.
    BY—Helen M. Dart and Ella Arvilla Merritt. PUBLISHER—Superintendent of Documents, Government Printing Office, Washington, D. C. 1923. 131 p. 25 cents.

MICHIGAN, DETROIT AND GRAND RAPIDS. **Wage-Earning School Children in Detroit and Grand Rapids.** In Child Labor Bulletin. Vol. 7, No. 2.
    BY—C. Edith Kirby. PUBLISHER—National Child Labor Committee, New York City. 1918. 9 p. 50 cents per copy.

MISSOURI. **Children Working in Missouri.** Publication No. 339.
    BY—Charles E. Gibbons and Harvey N. Tuttle. PUBLISHER—National Child Labor Committee, New York City. 1927. 31 p. 10 cents.

MISSOURI, ST. LOUIS. **The Newsboys of St. Louis.** A study by the Missouri School of Social Economy.
    BY—Ina Taylor. PUBLISHER—School of Social Economy, St. Louis. 1910. 15 p. 10 cents.

SURVEYS IN SPECIALIZED FIELDS

CHILD LABOR—Continued

NEW HAMPSHIRE. *See* ALABAMA in this section.

NEW JERSEY. **Pennsylvania Children on New Jersey Cranberry Farms.** Report of an investigation. Publication No. 102.
> BY—Janet S. McKay. PUBLISHER—Public Education and Child Labor Association of Pennsylvania, Philadelphia. 1923. 16 p. 10 cents.

NEW JERSEY. **Work of Children on Truck and Small Fruit Farms in Southern New Jersey.** U. S. Department of Labor. Children's Bureau Publication No. 132.
> BY—Ellen Nathalie Matthews. PUBLISHER—Superintendent of Documents, Government Printing Office, Washington, D. C. 1924. 57 p. 10 cents.

NEW YORK. **Unrestricted Forms of Child Labor in New York State.** Pamphlet No. 168.
> BY—George A. Hall. PUBLISHER—National Child Labor Committee, New York City. 1911. 13 p. Out of print.

NEW YORK. **Administration of Child Labor Laws.** Part 2. Employment Certificate System in New York. U. S. Department of Labor. Children's Bureau Publication No. 17. Industrial Series No. 2.
> BY—Helen L. Sumner and Ethel E. Hanks. PUBLISHER— Superintendent of Documents, Government Printing Office, Washington, D. C. 1917. 134 p. 20 cents.

NEW YORK. **Children in Industry:** A Survey.
> BY—Joseph P. Murphy. PUBLISHER—Associated Industries of New York State, Buffalo. 1919. 87 p. Free.

NEW YORK. **The Trend of Child Labor in New York State.** 1910–1922. Special Bulletin No. 122.
> BY—Edna Shepard. PUBLISHER—Bureau of Women in Industry, State Department of Labor, Albany. 1923. 18 p. Free.

NEW YORK CITY. **Heights and Weights of New York City Children 14 to 16 Years of Age.** A study of measurements of boys and girls granted employment certificates.
> BY—L. K. Frankel and L. I. Dublin. PUBLISHER—Metropolitan Life Insurance Company, New York City. 1916. 53 p. Free.

NEW YORK CITY. **Child Labor and Juvenile Delinquency in Manhattan.** Reprint from Child Labor Bulletin. Vol. 6, No. 3.
> BY—Mabel Brown Ellis. PUBLISHER—National Child Labor Committee, New York City. 1918. 43 p. 10 cents.

A BIBLIOGRAPHY OF SOCIAL SURVEYS

CHILD LABOR—Continued

NEW YORK, WHITE PLAINS. **The Administration of Child Labor and Compulsory Education Laws.** Pamphlet No. 1.
 BY—Lillian A. Quinn. PUBLISHER—Westchester County Children's Association, White Plains. 1920. 31 p. Out of print.

NORTH CAROLINA. **Child Labor in the Carolinas.** Account of investigations made in the cotton mills of North and South Carolina. Pamphlet No. 92.
 BY—A. E. Sedden, A. H. Ulm, and Lewis W. Hine. PUBLISHER—National Child Labor Committee, New York City. 1910. 15 p. Out of print.

NORTH DAKOTA. **Child Labor in North Dakota.** U. S. Department of Labor. Children's Bureau Publication No. 129.
 BY—Ellen Nathalie Matthews. PUBLISHER—Superintendent of Documents, Government Printing Office, Washington, D. C. 1923. 65 p. 15 cents.

OHIO, CINCINNATI. **An Experimental Study of Children at Work and in School between the Ages of Fourteen and Eighteen Years.**
 BY—Helen Thompson Woolley. PUBLISHER—Macmillan Company, New York City. 1926. 762 p. $4.00.

OHIO, CINCINNATI. **A Study of Industrial Injuries to Working Children in Cincinnati during 1926.**
 BY—Frances R. Whitney and Nellie J. Rechenbach. PUBLISHER—Consumers' League of Cincinnati. 1927. 40 p. 50 cents.

OHIO, TOLEDO. STUDIES OF TOLEDO CHILDREN.
 Toledo Children Who Leave School for Work. A study of 329 boys and girls. Pamphlet 31. 1918. 31 p.
 Toledo School Children in Street Trades. Findings of a study of children who sell papers and other articles on the streets of Toledo. 1922. 32 p.
  BY—Consumers' League of Toledo. PUBLISHER—The same. 35 cents each.

OREGON. **Child Labor in Fruit and Hop Growing Districts of the Northern Pacific Coast [Oregon and Washington].** U. S. Department of Labor. Children's Bureau Publication No. 151.
 BY—Alice Channing. PUBLISHER—Superintendent of Documents, Government Printing Office, Washington, D. C. 1926. 52 p. 15 cents.

SURVEYS IN SPECIALIZED FIELDS

CHILD LABOR—Continued

PENNSYLVANIA. **Child Labor and the Welfare of Children in an Anthracite Coal Mining District.** U. S. Department of Labor. Children's Bureau Publication No. 106.
>By—Grace Abbott. PUBLISHER—Superintendent of Documents, Government Printing Office, Washington, D. C. 1922. 94 p. 10 cents.

PENNSYLVANIA, PHILADELPHIA. **Report of a Study of Out-of-School Work among Pupils of Philadelphia Public Schools.** Publication No. 101.
>By—Janet S. McKay. PUBLISHER—Public Education and Child Labor Association of Pennsylvania, Philadelphia. 1923. 16 p. Free.

PENNSYLVANIA, WILKES-BARRE. **Survey of Wage-Earning Girls below Sixteen Years of Age in Wilkes-Barre.** Women in Industry Series No. 11.
>By—Sarah H. Atherton. PUBLISHER—National Consumers' League, New York City. 1915. 65 p. 25 cents.

RHODE ISLAND; PROVIDENCE, PAWTUCKET, AND CENTRAL FALLS. **Industrial Home Work of Children.** U. S. Department of Labor. Children's Bureau Publication No. 100.
>By—Emma Duke, Harry Viteles, and Eloise Shellabarger. PUBLISHER—Superintendent of Documents, Government Printing Office, Washington, D. C. 1922. 80 p. 10 cents.

SOUTH CAROLINA. *See* NORTH CAROLINA in this section.

TEXAS; BRAZOS, BURLESON, HILL, NACOGDOCHES, TAYLOR, AND WASHINGTON COUNTIES. **Child Labor among Cotton Growers of Texas.** A study of children living in rural communities in six counties in Texas. Publication No. 324.
>By—Charles E. Gibbons and Clara B. Armentrout. PUBLISHER—National Child Labor Committee, New York City. 1925. 124 p. 25 cents.

TEXAS, DALLAS. **The Newsboys of Dallas.** A friendly study of the boys, their work and thrift, home life and schooling, and of their general character, association, ambitions, and promise of fitness as future responsible citizens of Dallas.
>By—Civic Federation of Dallas. PUBLISHER—The same. 1921. 32 p. 10 cents.

A BIBLIOGRAPHY OF SOCIAL SURVEYS

CHILD LABOR—Continued

UNITED STATES. **Child Labor and the Night Messenger Service.** Publication No. 141.
 By—Owen R. Lovejoy. PUBLISHER—National Child Labor Committee, New York City. 1910. 15 p. 10 cents.

UNITED STATES. **Child Labor in Canneries.** Publication No. 128.
 By—Pauline Goldmark. PUBLISHER—National Child Labor Committee, New York City. 1910. 8 p. 10 cents.

UNITED STATES. **Child Labor in the Street Trades.** Pamphlet No. 126.
 By—Edward N. Clopper. PUBLISHER—National Child Labor Committee, New York City. 1910. 12 p. Out of print.

UNITED STATES. **Conditions under Which Children Leave School to Go to Work.** Vol. VII. Report on Condition of Woman and Child Wage-Earners in the United States. Senate Document No. 645.
 By—Charles P. Neill, Director. PUBLISHER—Superintendent of Documents, Government Printing Office, Washington, D. C. 1910. 310 p. Out of print.

UNITED STATES. **The Glass Industry and Child Labor Legislation.** Pamphlet No. 157.
 By—Charles L. Chute. PUBLISHER—National Child Labor Committee, New York City. 1911. 11 p. 5 cents.

UNITED STATES. **Work of School Children during Out-of-School Hours.** U. S. Department of Interior. Bureau of Education Bulletin, 1917. No. 20.
 By—C. D. Jarvis. PUBLISHER—Superintendent of Documents, Government Printing Office, Washington, D. C. 1917. 28 p. 5 cents.

UNITED STATES. **Administration of the First Federal Child Labor Law.** U. S. Department of Labor. Children's Bureau Publication No. 78. Legal and Industrial Series No. 6.
 By—Children's Bureau. PUBLISHER—Superintendent of Documents, Government Printing Office, Washington, D. C. 1921. 191 p. 25 cents.

UNITED STATES. **Child Labor in Representative Tobacco-Growing Areas.** U. S. Department of Labor. Children's Bureau Publication No. 155.
 By—Harriet A. Byrne. PUBLISHER—Superintendent of Documents, Government Printing Office, Washington, D. C. 1926. 42 p. 10 cents.

SURVEYS IN SPECIALIZED FIELDS

CHILD LABOR—Continued

VIRGINIA. **Child Labor in Virginia.** Pamphlet No. 171.
> BY—A. J. McKelway. PUBLISHER—National Child Labor Committee, New York City. 1912. 12 p. Out of print.

WASHINGTON. *See* OREGON in this section.

WISCONSIN. **Administration of Child Labor Laws.** Part 4. Employment Certificate System in Wisconsin. U. S. Department of Labor. Children's Bureau Publication No. 85.
> BY—Ethel E. Hanks. PUBLISHER—Superintendent of Documents, Government Printing Office, Washington, D. C. 1921. 152 p. 15 cents.

WISCONSIN, MILWAUKEE. **The Newsboys of Milwaukee.** Bulletin No. 8.
> BY—Alexander Fleisher. PUBLISHER—Milwaukee Bureau of Economy and Efficiency. 1911. 96 p. Out of print.

In addition to reports **presenting findings** in Child Labor Surveys, as listed above, publications dealing with **methods of conducting** such studies will be found in Part III, PURPOSE, METHOD, AND STANDARDS, page 340.

CHILD MARRIAGES

> *See also* MARRIAGE LAWS.

UNITED STATES. **Child Marriages.**
> BY—Mary E. Richmond and Fred S. Hall. PUBLISHER—Russell Sage Foundation, New York City. 1925. 159 p. $1.50.

CHILD WELFARE

> Reports dealing with the general question of child welfare and with two or more phases of the subject are listed here. For reports dealing with a single phase of child welfare *see* ACCIDENTS AND ACCIDENT PREVENTION; BLINDNESS, SIGHT CONSERVATION, AND DISEASE OF THE EYE; BOY LIFE; CHARITIES; CHILD HEALTH AND HYGIENE; CHILD LABOR; CHINESE; CLINICS AND DISPENSARIES; CRIPPLED, DISABLED, AND HANDICAPPED; DEPENDENCY; EDUCATION; FAMILY WELFARE; FEEBLEMINDED; ILLEGITIMACY; IMMIGRATION AND AMERICANIZATION; INDUSTRIAL CONDITIONS AND RELATIONS; INFANT MORTALITY; INFANTILE PARALYSIS; JAPANESE; JUVENILE DELINQUENCY; MARRIAGE LAWS; MATERNAL DEATHS; MENTAL HYGIENE;

CHILD WELFARE—Continued

NEGRO EDUCATION; NURSERIES AND NURSING; PRE-NATAL CARE; PRE-SCHOOL; RECREATION; RURAL EDUCATION; RURAL HEALTH AND SANITATION; SCHOOL HEALTH AND SANITATION; SOCIAL AGENCIES; SUB-NORMAL, RETARDED, AND EXCEPTIONAL CHILDREN; TRUANCY AND NON-ATTENDANCE; and UNMARRIED MOTHERS.

ALABAMA. **Child Welfare in Alabama.** An inquiry by the National Child Labor Committee under the auspices and with the co-operation of the University of Alabama.
BY—E. N. Clopper. PUBLISHER—National Child Labor Committee, New York City. 1918. 249 p. $1.00.

ALABAMA. **A Study of Alabama Laws Affecting Children and Suggestions for Legislation.** In Alabama Childhood. Vol. I, No. 4.
BY—National Child Labor Committee. PUBLISHER—Alabama Child Welfare Commission, Montgomery. 1922. 100 p. Free.

CALIFORNIA. **Child Welfare Work in California.** A study of agencies and institutions.
BY—William H. Slingerland. PUBLISHER—Russell Sage Foundation, New York City. 1916. 247 p. 75 cents.

CALIFORNIA. **Experimental Study of Abnormal Children with Special Reference to the Problem of Dependency and Delinquency.** Publication Vol. 3, No. 1.
BY—Olga Bridgman. PUBLISHER—University of California, Berkeley. 1918. 49 p. 75 cents.

CANADA, BRITISH COLUMBIA. **Report of the British Columbia Child Welfare Survey.**
BY—Robert E. Mills, Director. PUBLISHER—British Columbia Child Welfare Survey Committee, Vancouver. [Available through Canadian Council on Child Welfare, Ottawa, Canada.] 1927. 92 p. Free.

COLORADO. **Child Welfare Work in Colorado.** Bulletin Vol. XX, No. 10.
BY—W. H. Slingerland. PUBLISHER—University of Colorado, Boulder. 1920. 174 p. 25 cents.

CONNECTICUT. **Report of the Connecticut Commission on the Number and Condition of Dependent and Neglected Children in the State.**
BY—The Commission. PUBLISHER—General Assembly of Connecticut, Hartford. 1883. 16 p. Out of print.

SURVEYS IN SPECIALIZED FIELDS

CHILD WELFARE—Continued

CONNECTICUT. **The Problem of the County Home Child.** A study made under the auspices of the Connecticut Board of Charities.
> By—Elizabeth H. Dexter and Grace F. Marcus. PUBLISHER—State Board of Charities, Hartford. 1921. 32 p. Free.

DELAWARE. **People Who Go to Tomatoes [Delaware and Maryland].** A study of 400 families. Pamphlet No. 215.
> By—Harry M. Bremer. PUBLISHER—National Child Labor Committee, New York City. 1914. 17 p. 5 cents.

DELAWARE. **The Chance of a Delaware Child: Assurance of Life and Opportunity through the Good Faith of the State.**
> By—Ina J. Perkins, Director. PUBLISHER—Reconstruction Commission of Delaware, Dover. 1920. 86 p. Out of print.

DELAWARE. **Children Deprived of Parental Care.** A study of children taken under care by Delaware agencies and institutions. U. S. Department of Labor. Children's Bureau Publication No. 81.
> By—Ethel M. Springer. PUBLISHER—Superintendent of Documents, Government Printing Office, Washington, D. C. 1921. 95 p. 10 cents.

DELAWARE, HARE'S CORNER. **Special Investigation of the Delaware Orphan Home and Industrial School at Hare's Corner.** In Report of the Delaware State Board of Charities.
> By—Charles R. Miller. PUBLISHER—State Board of Charities, Wilmington. 1920. 6 p. Free.

DISTRICT OF COLUMBIA. **Report of the Committee Appointed by the Attorney General to Study the Need for Legislation Affecting Children in the District of Columbia Including Drafts of New Juvenile Court Laws.** In Report of Attorney General.
> By—Julia Lathrop, Bernard Flexner, William J. Kerby, Walter C. Clephane, and William H. Baldwin. PUBLISHER—Superintendent of Documents, Government Printing Office, Washington, D. C. 1915. 35 p. Free.

DISTRICT OF COLUMBIA. **Child Welfare in the District of Columbia.** A study of agencies and institutions for the care of dependent and delinquent children.
> By—Hastings H. Hart. PUBLISHER—Russell Sage Foundation, New York City. 1924. 150 p. $2.00.

CHILD WELFARE—Continued

DISTRICT OF COLUMBIA. **Law and Public Welfare in the District of Columbia.** Report of the Commission on Public Welfare Legislation for the District of Columbia to the commissioners of the District.
   BY—The Commission. PUBLISHER—The same, Washington, D. C. 1925. 70 p. Free.

GEORGIA. **Dependent and Delinquent Children in Georgia.** U. S. Department of Labor. Children's Bureau Publication No. 161.
   BY—Emma O. Lundberg, Director. PUBLISHER—Superintendent of Documents, Government Printing Office, Washington, D. C. 1926. 97 p. 15 cents.

IDAHO. **Child Welfare Work in Idaho.** A study of public and private agencies and institutions and methods employed in the care of dependent, delinquent, and defective children.
   BY—W. H. Slingerland. PUBLISHER—Children's Homefinding and Aid Society of Idaho, Boise. 1920. 112 p. 50 cents.

ILLINOIS, CHICAGO. **Opportunities in School and Industry for Children of the Stockyard District.** An investigation carried on under the direction of the board of the University Settlement.
   BY—Ernest L. Talbert. PUBLISHER—University of Chicago Press. 1912. 64 p. 25 cents.

ILLINOIS, CHICAGO. **Baby Farms in Chicago.**
   BY—A. A. Guild. PUBLISHER—Juvenile Protective Association, Chicago. 1917. 31 p. Free.

ILLINOIS, CHICAGO. **Children of Wage-Earning Mothers.** A study of a selected group in Chicago. U. S. Department of Labor. Children's Bureau Publication No. 102.
   BY—Helen Russell Wright. PUBLISHER—Superintendent of Documents, Government Printing Office, Washington, D. C. 1922. 92 p. 10 cents.

INDIANA. **Report of Committee on Delinquent and Dependent Children, Including Truancy, Juvenile Courts, and Poor Relief.**
   BY—The Committee. PUBLISHER—State Association of Town and City Superintendents, Indianapolis. 1908. 40 p. Out of print.

IOWA. **Juvenile Delinquency, Child Labor, Compulsory School Attendance, Child Welfare, Corrections and Charities.** Report of the Iowa State Teachers Association to the Educational Council.
   BY—F. A. Welch, H. E. Blackmar, and Bessie A. McClenahan. PUBLISHER—Iowa Teachers Association, Des Moines. 1918. 19 p. 25 cents.

SURVEYS IN SPECIALIZED FIELDS

CHILD WELFARE—Continued

IOWA. **Analytical Study of a Group of Five and Six Year Old Children.** Studies in Child Welfare. Vol. 1, No. 4.
> By—Clara H. Town. PUBLISHER—Iowa Child Welfare Research Station, University of Iowa, Iowa City. 1921. 87 p. 50 cents.

IOWA. *See also* UNITED STATES in this section.

KENTUCKY, **Child Welfare in Kentucky.** An inquiry for the Kentucky Child Labor Association and the State Board of Health.
> By—Edward N. Clopper, Director. PUBLISHER—National Child Labor Committee, New York City. 1919. 322 p. $1.25.

KENTUCKY, LOUISVILLE. **Child Welfare Work in Louisville.** A study of conditions, agencies, and institutions.
> By—W. H. Slingerland. PUBLISHER—Russell Sage Foundation, New York City. 1919. 152 p. 20 cents.

MARYLAND. *See* DELAWARE in this section.

MASSACHUSETTS. **A Survey of the Rural Children of Western Massachusetts.** Reprinted from The Commonwealth. Vol. 7, No. 6.
> By—Mary Putnam. PUBLISHER—Massachusetts Department of Health, Boston. 1921. 15 p. Free.

MASSACHUSETTS. **Children in Need of Special Care.** Studies based on two thousand case records of social agencies.
> By—Lucile Eaves. PUBLISHER—Women's Educational and Industrial Union, Boston. 1923. 125 p. $1.25.

MASSACHUSETTS. **Fit and Proper.** A study of legal adoption in Massachusetts.
> By—Ida R. Parker. PUBLISHER—Church Home Society, Boston. 1927. 310 p. $1.20.

MASSACHUSETTS; LAWRENCE, METHUEN, ANDOVER, AND NORTH ANDOVER. **Child Welfare Needs in Lawrence, Methuen, Andover, and North Andover.**
> By—Harrison G. Wagner. MIMEOGRAPHED—New England Division, American Red Cross, Boston. 1922. 24 p. Free.

MASSACHUSETTS, NEW BEDFORD. **A Study of the Children's Agencies in the Council of Social Agencies of New Bedford.**
> By—Child Welfare League of America. MIMEOGRAPHED—Council of Social Agencies, New Bedford. 1923. 72 p. Free.

A BIBLIOGRAPHY OF SOCIAL SURVEYS

CHILD WELFARE—Continued

MASSACHUSETTS, SPRINGFIELD. **Unemployment and Child Welfare.** A study made in a middle western and an eastern city during the industrial depression of 1921–1922 [Springfield, Mass., and Racine, Wis.]. U. S. Department of Labor. Children's Bureau Publication No. 125.
> BY—Emma Octavia Lundberg. PUBLISHER—Superintendent of Documents, Government Printing Office, Washington, D. C. 1923. 173 p. 20 cents.

MINNESOTA. **Public Child-Caring Work in Certain Counties of Minnesota, North Carolina, and New York.** U. S. Department of Labor. Children's Bureau Publication No. 173.
> BY—H. Ida Curry. PUBLISHER—Superintendent of Documents, Government Printing Office, Washington, D. C. 1927. 96 p. 15 cents.

MINNESOTA, MINNEAPOLIS. **Survey of Child Caring Institutions of Minneapolis.**
> BY—Committee on Children's Institutions, Minneapolis Council of Social Agencies. PUBLISHER—Council of Social Agencies, Minneapolis. 1922. 19 p. Free.

MISSOURI, ST. LOUIS. **Report of the Municipal Commission on Delinquent, Dependent, and Defective Children.**
> BY—The Commission. PUBLISHER—City Council, St. Louis. 1911. 90 p. Free.

NEBRASKA. **Report of the Nebraska Children's Code Commission.**
> BY—The Commission. PUBLISHER—Department of Public Welfare, Lincoln. 1920. 240 p. Free.

NEW HAMPSHIRE. **Report of the Children's Commission to the Governor and Legislature.**
> BY—The Commission. PUBLISHER—Department of Charities and Corrections, Concord. 1915. 136 p. Free.

NEW HAMPSHIRE, COOS COUNTY. **Child Welfare Needs in Coos County.**
> BY—Anna Russell. MIMEOGRAPHED—New England Division, American Red Cross, Boston, Massachusetts. 1922. 19 p. Free.

NEW JERSEY. **Report of New Jersey Commission on Defective, Delinquent, and Dependent Children and Their Care.**
> BY—The Commission. PUBLISHER—General Assembly of New Jersey, Trenton. 1898. 28 p. Out of print.

SURVEYS IN SPECIALIZED FIELDS

CHILD WELFARE—Continued

NEW JERSEY. CHILD WELFARE IN NEW JERSEY. U. S. Department of Labor. Children's Bureau.
  Part 1. **State Supervision and Personnel Administration.** Publication No. 174. By William J. Blackburn. 77 p. 15 cents.
  Part 2. **State Provision for Dependent Children.** Publication No. 175. By Ruth Berolzheimer and Florence Nesbit. 148 p. 25 cents.
  Part 4. **Local Provision for Dependent and Delinquent Children in Relation to the State's Program.** Publication No. 180. By William J. Blackburn, Ruth Bloodgood, and Mary E. Milburn. 76 p. 15 cents.
    PUBLISHER—Superintendent of Documents, Government Printing Office, Washington, D. C. 1927.

NEW YORK. **How Foster Children Turn Out.** A study and critical analysis of 910 children who were placed in foster homes by the State Charities Aid Association and who are now 18 years of age or over.
    By—Sophie van Senden Theis. PUBLISHER—State Charities Aid Association, New York City. 1924. 239 p. $1.00.

NEW YORK. **Report on Manufacturing in Tenements Submitted to the Commission to Examine the Laws Relating to Child Welfare.**
    By—Bernard L. Shientag. PUBLISHER—State Department of Labor, Albany. 1924. 8 p. Free.

NEW YORK. *See also* MINNESOTA in this section.

NEW YORK, ERIE COUNTY. **Study of the Activities of the Erie County Board of Child Welfare.**
    By—Frances M. Hollingshead, Director. MIMEOGRAPHED—Buffalo Foundation. 1921. 30 p. Free.

NEW YORK CITY. **The Child in the Foster Home.** Studies in Social Work. Child Welfare Series. Monograph No. 2.
    By—Sophie van Senden Theis and Constance Goodrich. PUBLISHER—New York School of Social Work, New York City. 1921. 150 p. 75 cents.

NEW YORK, SYRACUSE. **Child Welfare in Syracuse.**
    By—Lydia Allen De Vilbiss. PUBLISHER—Child Welfare Committee, Syracuse. 1919. 90 p. 25 cents.

NORTH CAROLINA. **Child Welfare in North Carolina.** An inquiry for the North Carolina Conference for Social Service.
    By—W. H. Swift. PUBLISHER—National Child Labor Committee, New York City. 1918. 314 p. $1.00.

CHILD WELFARE—Continued

NORTH CAROLINA. **Rural Children in Selected Counties of North Carolina.** U. S. Department of Labor. Children's Bureau Publication No. 33. Rural Child Welfare Series No. 2.
> By—Frances S. Bradley and Margaretta A. Williamson. PUBLISHER—Superintendent of Documents, Government Printing Office, Washington, D. C. 1918. 118 p. 25 cents.

NORTH CAROLINA. *See also* MINNESOTA in this section.

NORTH DAKOTA. **Report of Children's Code Commission of the State of North Dakota to the Legislative Assembly.**
> By—C. L. Young, Director. PUBLISHER—State of North Dakota, Bismarck. 1922. 56 p. Free.

NORTH DAKOTA. **Dependent and Delinquent Children in North Dakota and South Dakota.** U. S. Department of Labor. Children's Bureau Publication No. 160.
> By—Emma O. Lundberg, Director. PUBLISHER—Superintendent of Documents, Government Printing Office, Washington, D. C. 1926. 124 p. 20 cents.

OKLAHOMA. **Child Welfare in Oklahoma.** An inquiry by the Committee for the University of Oklahoma.
> By—E. N. Clopper, Director. PUBLISHER—National Child Labor Committee, New York City. 1917. 285 p. 75 cents.

OREGON. **Child Welfare Work in Oregon.** A study of public and private agencies and institutions for the care of dependent, delinquent, and defective children for the Oregon Child Welfare Commission. Extension Division Bulletin.
> By—W. H. Slingerland. PUBLISHER—University of Oregon, Eugene. 1918. 131 p. Free.

PENNSYLVANIA. **Child Welfare Work in Pennsylvania.** An investigation.
> By—William H. Slingerland. PUBLISHER—Russell Sage Foundation, New York City. 1915. 352 p. Out of print.

PENNSYLVANIA. **Report on Subsidized Institutions for the Care of Dependent, Delinquent, and Crippled Children.** Pamphlet No. 1.
> By—Abraham Oseroff. PUBLISHER—Public Charities Association of Pennsylvania, Philadelphia. 1915. 80 p. Free.

SURVEYS IN SPECIALIZED FIELDS

CHILD WELFARE—Continued

PENNSYLVANIA. **Summary of Child Welfare Work in Pennsylvania.** A reprint of the introduction to a study of Pennsylvania child helping agencies and institutions.
> BY—Hastings H. Hart. PUBLISHER—Russell Sage Foundation, New York City. 1915. 34 p. 25 cents.

PENNSYLVANIA. **Report to the General Assembly Meeting in 1925 of the Commission Appointed to Study and Revise the Statutes of Pennsylvania Relating to Children.**
> BY—The Commission. PUBLISHER—Commonwealth of Pennsylvania, Harrisburg. 1925. 184 p. Free.

PENNSYLVANIA. **Child Welfare Conditions and Resources in Seven Pennsylvania Counties.** U. S. Department of Labor. Children's Bureau Publication No. 176.
> BY—Neva R. Deardorff. PUBLISHER—Superintendent of Documents, Government Printing Office, Washington, D. C. 1927. 305 p. 25 cents.

PENNSYLVANIA, PITTSBURGH. **Pittsburgh as a Foster Mother.** A concrete community study of child-caring methods.
> BY—Florence L. Lattimore. PUBLISHER—Russell Sage Foundation, New York City. 1914. 113 p. 10 cents.

PORTO RICO. **Child Welfare in the Insular Possessions of the United States.** Part I. Porto Rico. U. S. Department of Labor. Children's Bureau Publication No. 127.
> BY—Helen V. Bary. PUBLISHER—Superintendent of Documents, Government Printing Office, Washington, D. C. 1923. 73 p. 15 cents.

RHODE ISLAND. **Is Rhode Island a Thoughtful Father to Its Children?** A tentative survey.
> BY—M. B. Stillwell and Harold A. Andrews. PUBLISHER—Child Welfare Division, State Board of Health, Providence. 1920. 59 p. Free.

SOUTH DAKOTA. *See* NORTH DAKOTA in this section.

TENNESSEE. **Child Welfare in Tennessee.** An inquiry by the National Child Labor Committee for the Tennessee Child Welfare Commission.
> BY—Edward N. Clopper. PUBLISHER—Department of Public Instruction, Nashville. 1920. 616 p. $1.50.

CHILD WELFARE—Continued

TEXAS. **The Child-Caring Institutions of Texas.** A survey.
> By—Mrs. W. B. Sharp. PUBLISHER—Social Service Committee, Texas Federation of Women's Clubs, Houston. 1916. 20 p. Free.

TEXAS. **The Welfare of Children in the Cotton-Growing Areas of Texas.** U. S. Department of Labor. Children's Bureau Publication No. 134.
> By—Ellen Nathalie Matthews. PUBLISHER—Superintendent of Documents, Government Printing Office, Washington, D. C. 1924. 83 p. 15 cents.

UNITED STATES. **Selective Migration as a Factor in Child Welfare in the United States with Special Reference to Iowa.** Studies in Child Welfare. Vol. 1, No. 7.
> By—Hornell N. Hart. PUBLISHER—Child Welfare Research Station, University of Iowa, Iowa City. 1921. 137 p. $1.00.

UNITED STATES. **The Work of Child-Placing Agencies.** U. S. Department of Labor. Children's Bureau Publication No. 171.
> By—Katharine P. Hewes, L. Josephine Webster, and Mary L. Evans. PUBLISHER—Superintendent of Documents, Government Printing Office, Washington, D. C. 1927. 223 p. 35 cents.

WASHINGTON, TACOMA. **Child Life in Tacoma.** A child welfare survey embracing the fields of health, delinquency, dependency, and club work.
> By—George A. Lundberg. PUBLISHER—Rotary Club of Tacoma. 1926. 57 p. $1.00.

WEST VIRGINIA. **Rural Child Welfare.** An inquiry based upon conditions in West Virginia.
> By—Edward N. Clopper. PUBLISHER—National Child Labor Committee, New York City. 1922. 355 p. $3.00.

WEST VIRGINIA, RALEIGH COUNTY. **The Welfare of Children in Bituminous Coal Mining Communities in West Virginia.** U. S. Department of Labor. Children's Bureau Publication No. 117.
> By—Nettie P. McGill. PUBLISHER—Superintendent of Documents, Government Printing Office, Washington, D. C. 1923. 77 p. 15 cents.

WISCONSIN, RACINE. *See* MASSACHUSETTS, SPRINGFIELD, in this section.

In addition to reports **presenting findings** in Child Welfare Surveys, as listed above, publications dealing with **methods of conducting** such studies will be found in PART III, PURPOSE, METHOD, AND STANDARDS, page 340.

SURVEYS IN SPECIALIZED FIELDS

CHINESE

See also IMMIGRATION AND AMERICANIZATION; and RACE RELATIONS.

CHINA. **An Enquiry into the Scientific Efficiency of Mission Hospitals in China.**
By—Harold Balme and Milton T. Stauffer. PUBLISHER—Missionary Association of Peking. 1920. 39 p. 6 pence.

CHINA. **Christian Education in China.** A study made by an educational commission representing the mission boards and societies conducting work in China.
By—China Educational Commission. PUBLISHER—Foreign Mission Conference of North America, New York City. 1922. 430 p. $2.00.

CHINA, PEKING. **Peking Rugs and Peking Boys.** A study of the rug industry in Peking.
By—C. C. Chu and Thomas C. Blaisdell, Jr. PUBLISHER—Chinese Social and Political Science Association, Peking. 1925. 47 p. 25 cents.

UNITED STATES. **Chinese Migration with Special Reference to Labor Conditions.** U. S. Bureau of Labor Statistics No. 340.
By—Ta Chen. PUBLISHER—Superintendent of Documents. Government Printing Office, Washington, D. C. 1923. 231 p. 25 cents.

In addition to reports **presenting findings,** as listed above, a publication dealing with **methods of conducting** such studies will be found in PART III, PURPOSE, METHOD, AND STANDARDS, under **Race Relations.**

CHURCHES

See PART I, GENERAL SOCIAL SURVEYS—URBAN and RURAL, and PART II, in RECREATION; and RELIGION.

For publications dealing with **methods of conducting** Church Surveys see PART III, PURPOSE, METHOD, AND STANDARDS, under **General Social Surveys,** both **Urban** and **Rural;** and **Religion.**

CITY AND REGIONAL PLANNING

NOTE: The following list of city plan reports is selective rather than inclusive. It presents those found in a search in which the interest centered not so much in the architectural and engineering

CITY AND REGIONAL PLANNING—Continued

aspects of the subject as in those having more immediate social welfare implications. Students of the subject and others who are interested in a more comprehensive list of reports on city and regional planning are referred to the Manual on City Planning and Zoning by Theodore Kimball Hubbard, published by the Harvard University Press, Cambridge, Massachusetts.

See also CITY, COUNTY, AND STATE ADMINISTRATION.

ALABAMA, BIRMINGHAM. **City Plan for Birmingham.**
   By—Warren H. Manning. PUBLISHER—Committee on City Plan, Birmingham. 1919. 47 p. Free.

ARKANSAS, LITTLE ROCK. **Report on the Park System for Little Rock.**
   By—John Nolen. PUBLISHER—Little Rock Parkway Association. 1913. 30 p. Out of print.

CALIFORNIA, LOS ANGELES. **Report of the Municipal Art Commission of Los Angeles.**
   By—Charles M. Robinson. PUBLISHER—Municipal Art Commission, Los Angeles. 1909. 38 p. Free.

CALIFORNIA, OAKLAND. **Plan of Civic Improvement for the City of Oakland.**
   By—Charles M. Robinson. PUBLISHER—City of Oakland. 1913. 20 p. Free.

CALIFORNIA, OAKLAND AND BERKELEY. **Report on a City Plan for the Municipalities of Oakland and Berkeley.**
   By—Warner Hegemann. PUBLISHER—Chamber of Commerce, Berkeley. 1915. 165 p. Free.

CALIFORNIA, PASADENA. **Progress Report of the City Planning Commission.**
   By—The Commission. PUBLISHER—Pasadena Civic Federation. 1917. 32 p. Free.

CALIFORNIA, SACRAMENTO. **Report of the Commission on Its Investigation of the Planning of the Capital of California.**
   By—The Commission. PUBLISHER—The same, Sacramento. 1916. 29 p. Free.

CALIFORNIA, SAN DIEGO. **A Comprehensive Plan for the Improvement of San Diego.**
   By—John Nolen. PUBLISHER—George B. Ellis Company, Boston, Massachusetts. 1908. 109 p. $2.00.

SURVEYS IN SPECIALIZED FIELDS

CITY AND REGIONAL PLANNING—Continued

CALIFORNIA, SAN FRANCISCO. **Report on the Improvement and Adornment of San Francisco.**
    BY—D. H. Burnham. PUBLISHER—City of San Francisco. 1904. 209 p. Out of print.

CALIFORNIA, SAN JOSE. **Beautifying of San Jose.** Report to the Outdoor Art League of San Jose.
    BY—Charles M. Robinson. PUBLISHER—Outdoor Art League, San Jose. 1909. 39 p. Free.

CALIFORNIA, SANTA BARBARA. **Report Regarding the Civic Affairs of Santa Barbara;** also the **Report of the Committee of Eleven on the Improvement of the City Streets.**
    BY—C. M. Robinson. PUBLISHER—Civic League, Santa Barbara. 1909. 36 p. Out of print.

CANADA, OTTAWA AND HULL. **Report of the Federal Plan Commission on a General Plan for the Cities of Ottawa and Hull.**
    BY—The Commission. PUBLISHER—Department of Finance, Ottawa. 1915. 158 p. Out of print.

CANADA, TORONTO. **Report of Civic Improvement Committee for the City of Toronto.**
    BY—W. R. Meredith. PUBLISHER—City Council of Toronto. 1911. 32 p. Out of print.

COLORADO, BOULDER. **The Improvement of Boulder.** Report to the City Improvement Association.
    BY—Frederick Law Olmsted, Jr. and Charles Eliot. PUBLISHER—City Improvement Association, Boulder. 1910. 106 p. Free.

COLORADO, COLORADO SPRINGS. **Colorado Springs: A City Beautiful and a General Plan for Its Improvement.**
    BY—Charles M. Robinson. PUBLISHER—Department of Public Works and Property, Colorado Springs. 1912. 71 p. Out of print.

COLORADO, DENVER. **Proposed Plan for the City of Denver.**
    BY—Charles M. Robinson. PUBLISHER—Art Commission of the City and County of Denver. 1906. 24 p. Out of print.

CONNECTICUT, BRIDGEPORT. REPORTS OF THE CITY PLANNING COMMISSION.
Preliminary Report to the City Plan Commission with Supplementary Material. 1915. 79 p.
Better City Planning for Bridgeport. 1916. 159 p.
    BY—John Nolen. PUBLISHER—Bridgeport Planning Commission. Out of print.

CITY AND REGIONAL PLANNING—Continued

CONNECTICUT, BRISTOL. **Local Survey and City Planning Proposals for Bristol.**
>BY—John Nolen. PUBLISHER—Chamber of Commerce, Bristol. 1920. 35 p. Free.

CONNECTICUT, HARTFORD. **A Plan of the City of Hartford.**
>BY—Carrere and Hastings, Architects. PUBLISHER—Commission on City Plan, Hartford. 1912. 117 p. Out of print.

CONNECTICUT, NEW HAVEN. **Report of the Civic Improvement Commission of New Haven.**
>BY—Cass Gilbert and Frederick L. Olmsted. PUBLISHER—New Haven Civic Improvement Commission. 1910. 138 p. Out of print.

DISTRICT OF COLUMBIA, WASHINGTON. **Preliminary Report to the American Civic Association by the Committee of 100 on the Federal City.**
>BY—The Committee. PUBLISHER—American Civic Association, Washington, D. C. 1924. 95 p. Free.

GEORGIA, COLUMBUS. **City Plan, Columbus.**
>BY—John Nolen. PUBLISHER—Planning Board, Columbus. 1926. 34 p. $1.75.

HAWAII, HONOLULU. **Beautifying Honolulu.**
>BY—Charles M. Robinson. PUBLISHER—Civic Federation of Honolulu. 1907. 39 p. Free.

ILLINOIS, ALTON. **The Advancement of Alton.** A general city plan study for the Board of Trade.
>BY—Charles Mulford Robinson. PUBLISHER—Alton Board of Trade. 1914. 42 p. Free.

ILLINOIS, CHICAGO. **Zoning Chicago.** A report by the Chicago Zoning Commission on plans for a zoning ordinance to be submitted to the city.
>BY—Chicago Zoning Commission. PUBLISHER—The same. 1922. 11 p. Out of print.

ILLINOIS, DECATUR. **The Decatur Plan.**
>BY—Myron Howard West. PUBLISHER—Association of Commerce, Decatur. 1920. 171 p. Free.

ILLINOIS, EAST ST. LOUIS. **City Plan for East St. Louis.**
>BY—Harland Bartholomew. PUBLISHER—War Civics Committee, East St. Louis. 1920. 65 p. Free.

SURVEYS IN SPECIALIZED FIELDS

CITY AND REGIONAL PLANNING—Continued

ILLINOIS, ELGIN. **Plan of Elgin.**
> BY—City Plan Commission. PUBLISHER—Elgin Association of Commerce. 1917. 46 p. Free.

ILLINOIS, JOLIET. **Joliet City Plan.**
> BY—Edward H. Bennett, William E. Parsons, and H. T. Frost. PUBLISHER—Joliet City Plan Commission. 1921. 45 p. Free.

ILLINOIS, ROCKFORD. **Plan for the Improvement and Extension of Rockford.**
> BY—Myron Howard West. PUBLISHER—Rockford City Plan Commission. 1918. 121 p. Free.

INDIANA, ELKHART. **Planning Prospects for Elkhart.** Report on plan proposals based on planning survey, with supplement on zoning.
> BY—John Nolen and Philip W. Foster. PUBLISHER—City Planning Commission, Elkhart. 1923. 24 p. Free.

INDIANA, FORT WAYNE. **Report to the Civic Improvement Association of Fort Wayne.**
> BY—Charles M. Robinson. PUBLISHER—Civic Improvement Association, Fort Wayne. 1909. 123 p. Free.

IOWA, CEDAR RAPIDS. **Report with Regard to Civic Affairs on the City of Cedar Rapids with Recommendations for City Improvement and Beautification.**
> BY—Charles M. Robinson. PUBLISHER—Chamber of Commerce, Cedar Rapids. 1908. 19 p. Free.

IOWA, DAVENPORT. **City Planning for Davenport.**
> BY—Roscoe E. Sawistowsky. PUBLISHER—City Council of Davenport. 1918. 81 p. Free.

IOWA, DUBUQUE. **Report on the Improvement of the City of Dubuque.**
> BY—Charles M. Robinson. PUBLISHER—Commercial Club, Dubuque. 1907. 32 p. Free.

IOWA, MASON CITY. **A Civic Survey of an Iowa Municipality.** A preliminary report on a city plan for Mason City. Publication Vol. XXIV, No. 36.
> BY—Rolland S. Wallis. PUBLISHER—Engineering Extension Department, Iowa State College, Ames. 1926. Part 1. 126 p. Part 2. 31 p. Free.

IOWA, WATERLOO. **The Well-Being of Waterloo.**
> BY—Charles M. Robinson. PUBLISHER—Civic Society of Waterloo. 1910. 35 p. Free.

A BIBLIOGRAPHY OF SOCIAL SURVEYS

CITY AND REGIONAL PLANNING—Continued

KANSAS, WICHITA. **A Comprehensive City Plan for Wichita.**
>By—Harland Bartholomew. PUBLISHER—City Plan Commission, Wichita. 1923. 128 p. Free.

MAINE, BANGOR. **Bangor City Plan.** The burned district.
>By—Warren H. Manning. PUBLISHER—Committee on Civic Improvement, Bangor. 1911. 16 p. Free.

MARYLAND, BALTIMORE. **Partial Report on the City Plan.**
>By—Municipal Art Society of Baltimore. PUBLISHER—The same. 1910. 47 p. Free.

MARYLAND, BALTIMORE. **The Port Development Plan.**
>By—Port Development Plan Commission. PUBLISHER—The same, Baltimore. 1922. 38 p. Free.

MASSACHUSETTS, BOSTON. **The Port of Boston.** A study and a solution of traffic and operating problems and its place in the competition of North Atlantic seaports.
>By—E. J. Clapp. PUBLISHER—Yale University Press, New Haven. 1916. 402 p. $3.00.

MASSACHUSETTS, BOSTON. REPORTS OF THE CITY PLANNING BOARD.
A Survey and a Comprehensive Plan for East Boston. 1916. 128 p.
The North End; A Survey and a Comprehensive Plan. 1919. 97 p.
>By—The Board. PUBLISHER—The same, Boston. Free.

MASSACHUSETTS, BOSTON. **Metropolitan Planning and Development in Boston and Its Environs.**
>By—Committee on Municipal and Metropolitan Affairs. PUBLISHER—Chamber of Commerce, Boston. 1922. 32 p. Free.

MASSACHUSETTS, FALL RIVER. **Report of the City Planning Board.**
>By—Arthur Shurtleff. PUBLISHER—City Planning Board, Fall River. 1922. 43 p. Free.

MASSACHUSETTS, GARDNER. **Recommendations for the Development of the Town of Gardner.**
>By—Gardner Planning Board. PUBLISHER—The same. 1921. 72 p. Free.

MASSACHUSETTS, NORWOOD. **Report of the Planning Board of Norwood.**
>By—Arthur Shurtleff. PUBLISHER—Town Planning Board, Norwood. 1923. 40 p. Free.

MASSACHUSETTS, SPRINGFIELD. **A City Plan for Springfield.**
>By—F. L. Olmsted. PUBLISHER—City Planning Board, Springfield. 1922. 59 p. Free.

SURVEYS IN SPECIALIZED FIELDS

CITY AND REGIONAL PLANNING—Continued

MASSACHUSETTS, SPRINGFIELD. **A City Plan for Springfield.**
> BY—City Planning Board. PUBLISHER—The same, Springfield. 1923. 212 p. Free.

MASSACHUSETTS, WORCESTER. **A City Plan for Worcester.**
> BY—Technical Advisory Corporation. PUBLISHER—City Planning Board, Worcester. 1924. 173 p. Out of print.

MICHIGAN, DETROIT. **Conditions in Detroit.**
> BY—Frederick L. Olmsted. PUBLISHER—City Plan and Improvement Commission, Detroit. 1915. 36 p. Free.

MICHIGAN, DETROIT. **Detroit Suburban Planning.** Report to the City Plan and Improvement Commission.
> BY—Arthur Coleman Comey. PUBLISHER—City Plan Commission of Detroit. 1921. 30 p. Free.

MICHIGAN, DETROIT. **Zoning and Its Application to Detroit.**
> BY—T. Glenn Phillips. PUBLISHER—City Plan Commission, Detroit. 1922. 17 p. $1.00.

MICHIGAN, FLINT. **The City Plan of Flint, Including the Reports of John Nolen and Bion J. Arnold.**
> BY—City Planning Board. PUBLISHER—The same, Flint. 1920. 95 p. Free.

MICHIGAN, GRAND RAPIDS. **Preliminary Report for a City Plan of Grand Rapids.**
> BY—A. W. Brunner and J. M. Carrere. PUBLISHER—City Plan Commission, Grand Rapids. 1909. 48 p. Out of print.

MICHIGAN, KALAMAZOO. **City Planning for Kalamazoo.** A preliminary report on city plan and the sewage problem.
> BY—Harland Bartholomew and W. W. Horner. PUBLISHER—City Commissioners of Kalamazoo. 1921. 13 p. Free.

MICHIGAN, LANSING. **The Lansing Plan: A Comprehensive City Plan Report.**
> BY—Harland Bartholomew. PUBLISHER—City Plan Commission, Lansing. 1922. 62 p. $1.00.

MINNESOTA, MINNEAPOLIS. **Plan of Minneapolis.**
> BY—Edward H. Bennett and Andrew Wright Crawford. PUBLISHER—Civic Commission, Minneapolis. 1917. 227 p. $10.00.

MINNESOTA, ST. PAUL. **Plan for St. Paul.**
> BY—Edward H. Bennett, William E. Parsons, and George H. Herrold. PUBLISHER—Commissioner of Public Works, St. Paul. 1922. 64 p. Free.

A BIBLIOGRAPHY OF SOCIAL SURVEYS

CITY AND REGIONAL PLANNING—Continued

MINNESOTA, STILLWATER. **Plan of Stillwater.**
 BY—A. V. Morell and A. R. Nichols. PUBLISHER—Civic Organization of Stillwater. 1918. 43 p. Free.

MISSOURI, KANSAS CITY. **The Kansas City Zone Plan.**
 BY—City Planning Commission. PUBLISHER—The same, Kansas City. 1922. 8 p. Free.

MISSOURI, ST. LOUIS. **A City Plan for St. Louis.** Reports of the several committees appointed by the Executive Board of the Civic League.
 BY—William Trelease, Director. PUBLISHER—Civic League of St. Louis. 1907. 113 p. Out of print.

MISSOURI, ST. LOUIS. REPORTS ON CITY PLANNING.
River des Peres Plan. 1916. 38 p. Out of print.
A Major Street Plan for St. Louis. 1917. 86 p. Free.
Problems of St. Louis. Being a description from the city planning standpoint of past and present tendencies of growth with general suggestions for impending issues and necessary future improvements. 1917. 140 p. Out of print.
The Zone Plan. 1919. 82 p. Out of print.
A Public Building Group Plan for St. Louis. 1919. 15 p. Free.
The St. Louis Transit System, Present and Future. 1920. 36 p. Out of print.
Plan of St. Louis. 1927. 68 p. Out of print.
 BY—Harland Bartholomew. PUBLISHER—City Plan Commission, St. Louis.

NEBRASKA, OMAHA. **City Planning Needs of Omaha: Street Widening and Extensions, Inner Belt Traffic Way, and River Drive.**
 BY—City Planning Commission. PUBLISHER—The same, Omaha. 1919. 41 p. Free.

NEW JERSEY. *See* NEW YORK CITY in this section.

NEW JERSEY, DOVER. **Town Planning for Dover.**
 BY—Arthur Coleman Comey. PUBLISHER—Common Council of Dover. 1913. 34 p. Out of print.

NEW JERSEY, EAST ORANGE. **City Plan of East Orange.**
 BY—City Planning Commission. PUBLISHER—Technical Advisory Corporation, New York City. 1922. 80 p. Free.

NEW JERSEY, GLEN RIDGE. **Glen Ridge.** The preservation of its natural beauty and its improvement as a place of residence.
 BY—John Nolen. PUBLISHER—Citizens Committee of Glen Ridge. 1909. 45 p. Free.

SURVEYS IN SPECIALIZED FIELDS

CITY AND REGIONAL PLANNING—Continued

NEW JERSEY, JERSEY CITY. **Report of Suggested Plan of Procedure for City Plan Commission.**
    BY—E. P. Goodrich and George B. Ford. PUBLISHER—Department of Parks and Public Property, Jersey City. 1913. 64 p. Free.

NEW JERSEY, MONTCLAIR. **Montclair.** The preservation of its natural beauty and its improvement as a residence town.
    BY—John Nolen. PUBLISHER—Civic Association of Montclair. 1908. 102 p. Out of print.

NEW JERSEY, NEWARK. REPORTS ON CITY PLANNING.
Preliminary Report to the City Plan Commission. By George B. Ford and E. P. Goodrich. 1912. 24 p.
City Planning for Newark. 1913. 163 p.
Comprehensive Plan for Newark. 1915. 180 p.
    BY—City Plan Commission. PUBLISHER—The same, Newark. Out of print.

NEW JERSEY, PATERSON. REPORTS OF THE CITY PLAN COMMISSION.
Zoning: The First Step in Planning. Final report of the Commission on Building Districts and Restrictions. 1921. 54 p. Free.
The Thoroughfares and Traffic of Paterson. 1922. 82 p. Free.
    BY—Herbert S. Swan. PUBLISHER—City Plan Commission, Paterson.

NEW JERSEY, RIDGEWOOD. **Improvement of Ridgewood.**
    BY—Charles M. Robinson. PUBLISHER—Board of Trade, Ridgewood. 1908. 32 p. Free.

NEW YORK, BINGHAMTON. **Better Binghamton.**
    BY—Charles M. Robinson. PUBLISHER—Mercantile Press Club, Binghamton. 1911. 105 p. Out of print.

NEW YORK, JAMESTOWN. **First Annual Report of the Board of Park Commissioners Embracing a Comprehensive Plan for the Establishment of a City Park System.**
    BY—Charles Mulford Robinson. PUBLISHER—Board of Park Commissioners, Jamestown. 1908. 36 p. Free.

NEW YORK CITY. REPORTS ON CITY PLANNING FOR NEW YORK CITY.
Report of the Committee on the Height, Size, and Arrangement of Buildings. 1912. 295 p. Out of print.

CITY AND REGIONAL PLANNING—Continued

Development and Present Status of City Planning in New York City. 1914. 76 p. Free.

Final Report of the Commission on Building Districts and Restrictions. 1916. 299 p. Out of print.

Establishment of Setbacks or Courtyards in the City of New York. 1917. 15 p. Out of print.

>By—Committee on City Plan. PUBLISHER—Board of Estimate and Apportionment, New York City.

NEW YORK CITY. **A Street Tree System for New York City.** Bulletin of the New York State College of Forestry, Syracuse University. Vol. XVI, No. 8.

>By—Laurie Davidson Cox and Hugh P. Baker. PUBLISHER—Syracuse University. 1916. 89 p. Out of print.

NEW YORK CITY. **Joint Report of the New York and New Jersey Port and Development Commission with Comprehensive Plan and Recommendations.**

>By—Port Development Commission. PUBLISHER—State of New York, Albany. 1920. 495 p. Free.

NEW YORK CITY. **The Port of New York Authority Report with Plan for the Comprehensive Development of the Port of New York.**

>By—Commissioners of the Port of New York Authority. PUBLISHER—State of New York, Albany. 1921. 56 p. Free.

NEW YORK CITY. REPORTS OF REGIONAL PLAN OF NEW YORK AND ITS ENVIRONS.

Plan of New York and Its Environs: Report of Progress. By The Plan. 1923. 67 p. Free.

Predicted Growth of New York and Its Environs Based on a Study of Population. By Raymond Pearl and Lowell J. Reed. 1924. 42 p. 25 cents.

Highway Traffic in New York and Its Environs. Engineering Series, Monograph No 1. By Harold M. Lewis and Ernest P. Goodrich. 1925. 127 p. $2.00.

The Transit and Transportation Problem. Engineering Series, Monograph No. 2. By Harold M. Lewis. 1926. 129 p. $2.00.

Land Values: Distribution within New York Region and Relation to Various Factors in Urban Growth. Engineering Series, Monograph No. 3. By Harold M. Lewis, Wayne D. Heydecker, and Raymond A. O'Hara. 1927. 72 p. $2.00.

SURVEYS IN SPECIALIZED FIELDS

CITY AND REGIONAL PLANNING—Continued
The Chemical Industry. Economic Series, Monograph No. 1. By Mabel Newcomer. 1924. 49 p. $1.00.
The Metal Industry. Economic Series, Monograph No. 2. By Vincent W. Lanfear. 1924. 49 p. 75 cents.
The Food Manufacturing Industries. Economic Series, Monograph No. 3. By Faith M. Williams. 1924. 62 p. 75 cents.
The Wood Industries. Economic Series, Monograph No. 4. By Mark C. Mills. 1924. 53 p. 75 cents.
The Tobacco Products Industry. Economic Series, Monograph No. 5. By Lucy Winsor Killough. 1924. 58 p. 75 cents.
The Printing Industry. Economic Series, Monograph No. 6. By A. F. Hinrichs. 1924. 54 p. 75 cents.
The Clothing and Textile Industries. Economic Series, Monographs Nos. 7, 8, and 9. By B. M. Selekman, Henriette R. Walter, and W. J. Couper. 1925. 104 p. $1.00.
The Retail Shopping and Financial Districts. Economic Series, Monographs Nos. 10 and 12. By Donald H. Davenport, Lawrence M. Orton, and Ralph W. Roby. 1927. 54 p. $1.00.
The Wholesale Markets. Economic Series, Monograph No. 11. By George Filipetti. 1925. 69 p. 75 cents.
Other reports in this series to be issued.
PUBLISHER—Regional Plan of New York and Its Environs, New York City.

NEW YORK, OGDENSBURG. **Report of the Improvement Commission of the City of Ogdensburg.**
By—Charles M. Robinson. PUBLISHER—Common Council of Ogdensburg. 1907. 12 p. Free.

NEW YORK, ROCHESTER. **City Plan for Rochester.**
By—A. W. Brunner and Frederick L. Olmsted. PUBLISHER—Civic Improvement Committee, Rochester. 1911. 39 p. Out of print.

NEW YORK, SYRACUSE. **City Planning for Syracuse.**
By—City Planning Commission. PUBLISHER—The same, Syracuse. 1919. 48 p. Free.

NEW YORK, UTICA. **Report of the Committee on Improving and Beautifying Utica.**
By—Smith M. Lindsley and Merwin K. Hart. PUBLISHER—Chamber of Commerce, Utica. 1908. 60 p. Free.

CITY AND REGIONAL PLANNING—Continued

NEW YORK, UTICA. **A Plan for the Development of a System of Major Streets.**
> By—Harland Bartholomew. PUBLISHER—City Planning Commission, Utica. 1922. 37 p. Free.

NORTH CAROLINA, RALEIGH. **A City Plan for Raleigh, Being a Report to the Civic Department of the Women's Club of Raleigh.**
> By—Charles M. Robinson. PUBLISHER—Women's Club of Raleigh. 1913. 99 p. 50 cents.

OHIO, AKRON. **City Plan for Akron.**
> By—John Nolen. PUBLISHER—Akron Chamber of Commerce. 1919. 91 p. $1.00.

OHIO, AKRON. **The Tentative Zoning Plan for Akron.**
> By—Charles F. Fisher. PUBLISHER—City Planning Commission, Akron. 1921. 20 p. Free.

OHIO, CINCINNATI. **Official Plan of the City of Cincinnati.**
> By—City Planning Commission. PUBLISHER—The same, Cincinnati. 1925. 275 p. $2.17.

OHIO, CLEVELAND. REPORTS ON CITY PLANNING.
Report of the Committee on Grouping Plan for Public Buildings to the Cleveland Chamber of Commerce. 1899. 8 p.
Billboards. Report of the City Plan Committee approved by the Board of Directors of the Cleveland Chamber of Commerce. 1921. 9 p.
The Cleveland Thorofare Plan. 1921. 15 p.
The Cleveland Zone Plan. By Morris A. Black. 1922. 16 p.
The Plan for Greater Cleveland. 1923. 23 p.
> By—City Plan Commission. PUBLISHER—Cleveland Chamber of Commerce. Free.

OHIO, COLUMBUS. **The Columbus Zone Plan.**
> By—Robert Whitten and A. H. C. Shaw. PUBLISHER—City Planning Commission, Columbus. 1923. 26 p. Free.

OHIO, HAMILTON. **The City Plan of Hamilton.**
> By—Harland Bartholomew. PUBLISHER—Chamber of Commerce, Hamilton. 1921. 66 p. Free.

OHIO, TOLEDO. CITY PLANNING REPORTS.
Industrial Survey. 24 p. 50 cents.
Major Street Plan. 72 p. 50 cents.

SURVEYS IN SPECIALIZED FIELDS

CITY AND REGIONAL PLANNING—Continued
Port Study. 71 p. 50 cents.
Progress Report. 71 p. Out of print.
Railroad Transportation. 47 p. 50 cents.
Transit Problem. 46 p. Out of print.
> By—Harland Bartholomew. PUBLISHER—City Planning Commission, Toledo. 1924.

OKLAHOMA, OKLAHOMA CITY. **A Report on a Plan for an Outer Parkway and a Plan for an Interior System of Parks and Boulevards.**
> By—W. H. Dunn. PUBLISHER—Board of Park Commissioners, Oklahoma City. 1910. 31 p. Out of print.

OREGON, PORTLAND. REPORTS ON CITY PLANNING.
Zoning and City Planning for Portland. Bulletin No. 1. 1919. 55 p.
Proposed Building Zones. Bulletin No. 4. 1919. 32 p.
Major Traffic Street Plan, Boulevard, and Park System for Portland. 1921. 97 p.
> By—Charles H. Cheney. PUBLISHER—City Planning Commission of Portland. Free.

OREGON, PORTLAND. **A Survey of the Port of Portland.**
> By—Earl Kilpatrick, Director. MIMEOGRAPHED—Portland School of Social Work. 1921. 19 p. Free.

PENNSYLVANIA, ERIE. **Greater Erie.** Plans and reports for the extension and improvement of the city.
> By—John Nolen. PUBLISHER—Chamber of Commerce, Erie. 1913. 254 p. $1.25.

PENNSYLVANIA, PHILADELPHIA. **A Regional Plan for the Philadelphia Metropolitan District, Being the Report of a Preliminary Survey.**
> By—Citizens Committee. PUBLISHER—City Club, Philadelphia. 1924. 36 p. Free.

PENNSYLVANIA, PITTSBURGH. **Main Thoroughfares and the Downtown District.**
> By—Frederick L. Olmsted. PUBLISHER—Pittsburgh Civic Commission. 1910. 169 p. Out of print.

PENNSYLVANIA, PITTSBURGH. **Civic Improvement Possibilities in Pittsburgh.** In The Pittsburgh District Civic Frontage, The Pittsburgh Survey.
> By—Charles Mulford Robinson. PUBLISHER—Russell Sage Foundation, New York City. 1914. p. 49–63. Out of print.

CITY AND REGIONAL PLANNING—Continued

PENNSYLVANIA, PITTSBURGH. REPORTS ON CITY PLANNING.
  A Major Street Plan for Pittsburgh. Report No. 2. 1921. 65 p. 50 cents.
  Transit: A Part of the Pittsburgh Plan. Report No. 3. 1923. 58 p. 50 cents.
  Parks. Report No. 4. 1923. 76 p. 50 cents.
  Railroads of the Pittsburgh District. Report No. 5. 1923. 76 p. 50 cents.
  Waterways: A Part of the Pittsburgh Plan. Report No. 6. 1923. 60 p. 50 cents.
    BY—Citizens' Committee on City Planning. PUBLISHER—The same, Pittsburgh.

PENNSYLVANIA, READING. **Replanning Reading, an Industrial City of a Hundred Thousand.**
    BY—John Nolen. PUBLISHER—George H. Ellis Company, Boston, Massachusetts. 1910. 107 p. Out of print.

RHODE ISLAND, PROVIDENCE. **The Providence Zone Plan.** Report outlining a tentative zone plan for Providence.
    BY—Robert Whitten. PUBLISHER—Joint Standing Committee on Ordinances, Providence. 1923. 31 p. Free.

SOUTH CAROLINA, GREENVILLE. **Beautifying and Improving Greenville.**
    BY—Kelsey and Guild, Architects. PUBLISHER—Municipal League, Greenville. 1907. 48 p. Out of print.

TENNESSEE, MEMPHIS. **A Comprehensive City Plan, Memphis.**
    BY—Harland Bartholomew and others. PUBLISHER—City Plan Commission, Memphis. 1924. 176 p. Free.

TEXAS, DALLAS. **City Plan for Dallas.**
    BY—G. E. Kessler. PUBLISHER—Park Board, Dallas. 1911. 58 p. Out of print.

TEXAS, EL PASO. **The City Plan of El Paso.**
    BY—City Plan Commission. PUBLISHER—The same, El Paso. 1925. 69 p. $1.00.

TEXAS, HOUSTON. **Houston.** Tentative plans for its development.
    BY—Arthur Coleman Comey. PUBLISHER—Houston Park Commission. 1913. 83 p. $2.00.

TEXAS, PARIS. **General City Plan for Paris.**
    BY—W. H. Dunn. PUBLISHER—City Council, Paris. 1915. 25 p. Free.

SURVEYS IN SPECIALIZED FIELDS

CITY AND REGIONAL PLANNING—Continued

VIRGINIA, ROANOKE. **Remodeling Roanoke.** Report to the Committee on Civic Improvement.
> BY—John Nolen. PUBLISHER—Committee on Civic Improvement of Roanoke. 1907. 56 p. Out of print.

WASHINGTON, SEATTLE. **Plan of Seattle.**
> BY—Virgil G. Bogue. PUBLISHER—Municipal Plan Commission, Seattle. 1911. 191 p. Out of print.

WEST VIRGINIA, WHEELING. **Abstracts of Reports upon Several Phases of a City Plan for Greater Wheeling.**
> BY—Morris Knowles. PUBLISHER—Wheeling Improvement Association. 1920. 37 p. Free.

WISCONSIN, MADISON. **Madison a Model City.**
> BY—John Nolen. PUBLISHER—Madison Park and Pleasure Drive Association. 1911. 168 p. Free.

WISCONSIN, MILWAUKEE. **Preliminary Reports of the City Planning Commission of the City of Milwaukee.**
> BY—The Commission. PUBLISHER—The same, Milwaukee. 1911. 46 p. Free.

In addition to reports **presenting findings** in City and Regional Planning Surveys, as listed above, publications dealing with **methods of conducting** such studies will be found in Part III, PURPOSE, METHOD, AND STANDARDS, page 341.

CITY, COUNTY, AND STATE ADMINISTRATION

> NOTE: The following list of studies of city, county, and state administration is selective rather than inclusive; it presents only those reports found in a search in which the interest centered in aspects of the question more or less immediately related to matters of social welfare.
> See also CHILD LABOR; ELECTIONS; FAMILY WELFARE; FIRE; HEALTH ADMINISTRATION; HOUSING; JAPANESE; LOANS; MARKETS; MUSIC; PAUPER; PENSIONS; POLICE; RECREATION; RELIEF; SCHOOL ORGANIZATION AND ADMINISTRATION; and TAXATION.

CALIFORNIA, LOS ANGELES. **Administrative Methods of the City Government of Los Angeles.** Report of a preliminary survey of certain city departments.
> BY—New York Bureau of Municipal Research. PUBLISHER—Municipal League of Los Angeles. 1913. 27 p. Free.

CITY, COUNTY, AND STATE ADMINISTRATION—Continued

CALIFORNIA, SAN FRANCISCO. **Survey Report of the Government of the City and County of San Francisco.**
> By—New York Bureau of Municipal Research. PUBLISHER—Real Estate Board, San Francisco. 1916. 681 p. Free.

COLORADO. REPORTS ON STATE AFFAIRS.
Report on a Survey of the Office of Governor. 30 p.
Report on a Survey of the Office of Secretary of State and on Public Control of Corporations. 45 p.
Report on a Survey of the Office of Auditor of State and of the Office of Public Examiner. 55 p.
Report on a Survey of the Office of State Treasurer. 46 p.
Report on a Survey of State Finances and Budget Procedure. 57 p.
Report on a Survey of the Administration of Public Service Functions Relating to Regulation and Supervision. 46 p.
Report on the Revenue System of the State. 24 p.
Summary of the Findings and Recommendations Relating to the Executive Branch of the State Government. 55 p.
> By—Survey Committee of State Affairs. PUBLISHER—The same, Denver. 1916. Out of print.

COLORADO, DENVER. **Report on a Survey of Certain Departments, City and County of Denver.**
> By—New York Bureau of Municipal Research. PUBLISHER—Colorado Tax Payers Protective League, Denver. 1914. 583 p. $1.50.

CONNECTICUT, BRIDGEPORT. **Report of the Study of the Financial Condition of the City of Bridgeport.**
> By—Bureau of Municipal Research. MIMEOGRAPHED—Bridgeport Chamber of Commerce. 1921. 60 p. Free.

DELAWARE. **County Administration.** A study based upon a survey of county government in the State of Delaware.
> By—Chester Collins Maxey. PUBLISHER—Macmillan Company, New York City. 1919. 203 p. $2.50.

GEORGIA, ATLANTA. **Organization and Administration of the City Government of Atlanta.** Report of a general survey made for the Chamber of Commerce Committee on Municipal Research (exclusive of health and education departments).
> By—Herbert R. Sands. PUBLISHER—Chamber of Commerce, Atlanta. 1912. 64 p. 10 cents.

SURVEYS IN SPECIALIZED FIELDS

CITY, COUNTY, AND STATE ADMINISTRATION—Continued

ILLINOIS. REPORTS OF THE EFFICIENCY AND ECONOMY COMMITTEE OF ILLINOIS.
  Report of the Committee Created under the Authority of the 48th Assembly of Illinois. 1914. 80 p.
  Report of the Committee Created under the Authority of the 49th Assembly of Illinois. 1915. 1051 p.
  By—John Fairlie, Director. PUBLISHER—State of Illinois. Springfield. Postage.

ILLINOIS, CHICAGO. Conditions of Municipal Employment in Chicago. A study in morale.
  By—Leonard D. White. PUBLISHER—City Council, Chicago. 1925. 114 p. Free.

ILLINOIS, CHICAGO AND COOK COUNTY. STUDIES OF CITY AND COUNTY DEPARTMENTS.
  Administration of the Office of Recorder of Cook County. 1911. 63 p. Out of print.
  Administration of the Office of Sheriff of Cook County. 1911. 26 p. Free.
  The Judges and the County Fee Offices. 1911. 15 p. Out of print.
  Methods of Preparing and Administering the Budget of Cook County. 1911. 53 p. Out of print.
  Bureau of Streets; Civil Service Commission; and Special Accounting System of the City of Chicago. 1911. 112 p. Out of print.
  The Park Governments of Chicago. An Inquiry into Their Organization and Methods of Administration. 1911. 182 p. Free.
  Administration of the Office of Clerk of the County Court of Cook County. 1912. 43 p. Free.
  Offices of the Clerks of the Circuit and Superior Courts: A Supplemental Inquiry into Their Organization and Methods of Administration. 1912. 27 p. Free.
  The Office of Sheriff of Cook County: A Supplementary Inquiry Into its Organization and Methods of Administration. 1912. 26 p. Free.
  The Office of County Treasurer of Cook County. An inquiry into the administration of its finances with special reference to the question of interest on public funds. 1913. 67 p. Free.
  The Nineteen Local Governments in Chicago. A multiplicity of overtaxing bodies with many elective offices. 1915. 32 p. Out of print.
  The City Manager Plan for Chicago. Draft of a bill for the reorganization of the municipal government with explanatory statement. 1917. 60 p. Free.

A BIBLIOGRAPHY OF SOCIAL SURVEYS

CITY, COUNTY, AND STATE ADMINISTRATION—Continued

Primary Days and Election Days as Holidays. An instance of governmental absurdity and waste. 1917. 11 p. Free.

Unification of Local Governments in Chicago. 1917. 98 p. Free.

The Water Works System of the City of Chicago. 1917. 207 p. Out of print.

By—Chicago Bureau of Public Efficiency. PUBLISHER—The same.

ILLINOIS, SPRINGFIELD. **City and County Administration in Springfield.** Government Efficiency Section of the Springfield Survey.

By—D. O. Decker and Shelby M. Harrison. PUBLISHER—Russell Sage Foundation, New York City. 1917. 180 p. 25 cents.

INDIANA. **Report of Committee Appointed by Governor Ed Jackson to Make a Survey of Boards and Commissions of Indiana.**

By—The Committee. PUBLISHER—State of Indiana, Indianapolis. 1925. 33 p. Free.

INDIANA. *See also* NEW YORK in this section.

INDIANA, INDIANAPOLIS and MARION COUNTY. **Summary of Recommendations for the Improvement of the Government of the City of Indianapolis and Marion County.** Activities of the Chamber of Commerce. Vol. I.

By—New York Bureau of Municipal Research. PUBLISHER—Chamber of Commerce, Indianapolis. 1918. 15 p. Free.

IOWA. *See* NEW YORK in this section.

KANSAS, TOPEKA. **Municipal Administration in Topeka.** Part III. Topeka Improvement Survey.

By—D. O. Decker. PUBLISHER—Russell Sage Foundation, New York City. 1914. 43 p. 15 cents.

LOUISIANA, NEW ORLEANS. **Administrative Survey of the Government of the City of New Orleans.**

By—Frank Dameron. PUBLISHER—Municipal Survey Commission, New Orleans. 1922. 283 p. $1.00.

MASSACHUSETTS. **Report on Reorganization of Boards and Commissions Having Supervision and Control of State Institutions.**

By—Massachusetts Commission on Economy and Efficiency. PUBLISHER—Commonwealth of Massachusetts, Boston. 1914. 65 p. Out of print.

SURVEYS IN SPECIALIZED FIELDS

CITY, COUNTY, AND STATE ADMINISTRATION—Continued

MASSACHUSETTS. **Report of a Committee to Investigate the Subject of County Government in the Commonwealth and the Relation of the Counties and Their Institutions to the Commonwealth.** Senate Document No. 280.
> By—The Committee. PUBLISHER—Commonwealth of Massachusetts, Boston. 1922. 130 p. Free.

MASSACHUSETTS, NEWTON. **Efficiency Survey of the Departments of Streets, Forestry, and Water and Their Allied Functions.**
> By—Edwin A. Cottrell. PUBLISHER—City of Newton. 1916. 164 p. Free.

MASSACHUSETTS, SPRINGFIELD. **Organization and Administration of the City Government of Springfield.** Report of a general survey.
> By—New York Bureau of Municipal Research. PUBLISHER—City of Springfield. 1913. 93 p. Out of print.

MINNESOTA, MINNEAPOLIS. REPORTS OF THE MINNEAPOLIS CIVIC AND COMMERCE ASSOCIATION.

Report on a Survey of the Business Administration of the Minneapolis Board of Park Commissioners. By Bureau of Municipal Research. 1915. 52 p. Free.

A Survey of the Bonded Debt and the Operation of the Sinking Fund of Minneapolis. By F. L. Olsen. 1922. 48 p. Out of print.
> PUBLISHER—The Association.

MISSOURI, ST. LOUIS. **Organization and Administration of the City Government of St. Louis.**
> By—New York Bureau of Municipal Research. PUBLISHER—The same. 1910. 416 p. Out of print.

NEW HAMPSHIRE, DOVER. **Civic Survey of the City of Dover.**
> By—New Hampshire Committee, Women's Department, National Civic Federation. PUBLISHER—The same, Peterboro. 1918. 40 p. 25 cents.

NEW JERSEY. REPORTS OF THE COMMISSION FOR THE SURVEY OF MUNICIPAL FINANCING.

First Report of the Commission. 1916. 22 p.

Analysis of the Laws Affecting Municipal and County Finances and Taxation. Second edition, revised. 1920. 129 p.
> By—The Commission. PUBLISHER—State Department, Trenton. Free.

CITY, COUNTY, AND STATE ADMINISTRATION—Continued

NEW JERSEY, NEWARK. **Introduction and Explanatory Excerpts from a Survey of the Government, Finances, and Administration of the City of Newark.**
>By—Bureau of Municipal Research. PUBLISHER—The same, New York City. 1919. 71 p. Free.

>Complete report covering 888 pages is on file at the Newark Board of Trade where it may be consulted.

NEW YORK. **Report of an Investigation of the Methods of Fiscal Control of State Institutions.** Part I. New York. Part II. Comparison of the States of New York, Indiana, and Iowa. Publication No. 122.
>By—Henry C. Wright. PUBLISHER—State Charities Aid Association, New York City. 1911. 353 p. Out of print.

NEW YORK. **Report of New York State Legislature Joint Committee to Inquire into Methods of Financial Administration of the State Institutions and Departments.**
>By—The Committee. PUBLISHER—General Assembly of New York State, Albany. 1911. 226 p. Free.

NEW YORK, JAMESTOWN. **Government of the City of Jamestown.** General municipal survey and constructive recommendations.
>By—New York Bureau of Municipal Research. PUBLISHER—Jamestown Board of Commerce. 1917. 413 p. Free.

NEW YORK CITY. **Administrative Reorganization and Constructive Work in the Government of the City of New York.**
>By—Henry Bruere. PUBLISHER—Department of Finance, City of New York. 1915. 50 p. Out of print.

NEW YORK CITY. **Government of the City of New York.** A survey of its organization and functions.
>By—New York City Commissioners of Accounts and New York Bureau of Municipal Research. PUBLISHER—City of New York. 1915. 1343 p. Out of print.

NEW YORK CITY. **Study of County Government within the City of New York and a Plan for Its Reorganization, Prepared for the Constitutional Convention.**
>By—Henry Bruere and Leonard M. Wallstein. PUBLISHER—City of New York. 1915. 47 p. Out of print.

NEW YORK CITY. **New York City's Administrative Progress. 1914-1916.** A survey of various departments under the jurisdiction of the Mayor.
>By—Henry Bruere, Director. PUBLISHER—City Council, New York City. 1916. 351 p. Out of print.

SURVEYS IN SPECIALIZED FIELDS

CITY, COUNTY, AND STATE ADMINISTRATION—Continued

NEW YORK, ROCHESTER. REPORTS ON THE GOVERNMENT OF THE CITY OF ROCHESTER.
Critical Appraisal and Constructive Suggestions. By New York Bureau of Municipal Research. 1915. 546 p.
Report on the Problem of Street Cleaning. By Jake W. Routh and John T. Child. 1918. 133 p.
Report on the Administration of the Bureau of Buildings in the Department of Public Safety. By Frank P. Cartwright. 1921. 57 p.
PUBLISHER—Rochester Bureau of Municipal Research. Free.

OHIO. Report of the Committee for an Investigation of Finances of Municipalities.
BY—The Committee. PUBLISHER—Ohio Legislative Reference Department, Columbus. 1915. 41 p. Out of print.

OHIO. Report of the Joint Committee on Administrative Reorganization with Surveys of State Administration Agencies.
BY—The Committee. PUBLISHER—Bureau of Municipal Research, Akron. 1921. 66 p. Free.

OHIO. Report on State Institutions. Publication No. 20.
BY—Ohio Board of Administration. PUBLISHER—State of Ohio, Columbus. 1921. 50 p. Free.

OHIO, CINCINNATI AND HAMILTON COUNTY. The Government of Cincinnati and Hamilton County.
BY—Lent D. Upson, Director. PUBLISHER—City Survey Committee, Cincinnati. 1924. 535 p. Free.

OHIO, COLUMBUS. Report on a Survey of the City Government.
BY—New York Bureau of Municipal Research. PUBLISHER—City Council, Columbus. 1916. 257 p. 50 cents.

OHIO, CUYAHOGA COUNTY. The Jury System of Cuyahoga County. Report of investigations into jury system and merit system. Bulletin of the Municipal League of Cleveland.
BY—Municipal League of Cleveland. PUBLISHER—The same. 1916. 24 p. 5 cents.

OREGON, PORTLAND. Organization and Business Methods of the City Government of Portland.
BY—New York Bureau of Municipal Research. PUBLISHER—Committee on Municipal Research, Portland. 1913. 118 p. Free.

CITY, COUNTY, AND STATE ADMINISTRATION—Continued

PENNSYLVANIA. **State Budget Systems.** Pennsylvania's appropriation methods and budget system in the state.

By—Committee on State Budget. PUBLISHER—Pennsylvania State Chamber of Commerce, Harrisburg. 1922. 120 p. Free.

PENNSYLVANIA. **Survey of the Fiscal Policies of the State Highway Department, the State Department of Public Printing and Binding, the Department of Workmen's Compensation, and the Policies of the Commonwealth as to Rentals and Buildings.** Part I. Report of the Citizens' Committee on the Finances of Pennsylvania.

By—The Committee. PUBLISHER—Department of State Finance, Harrisburg. 1922. 190 p. Out of print.

PENNSYLVANIA, PHILADELPHIA. **The Water Supply Problem of Philadelphia with a Historical Review of the Water Works Development.**

By—Bureau of Municipal Research of Philadelphia. PUBLISHER —The same. 1922. 53 p. Free.

PENNSYLVANIA, READING. REPORT ON A SURVEY OF THE MUNICIPAL DEPARTMENTS AND SCHOOL DISTRICT.
Department of Parks. 7 p.
Department of Water. 25 p.

By—New York Bureau of Municipal Research. PUBLISHER— Reading Chamber of Commerce. 1913. 10 cents each.

RHODE ISLAND, PROVIDENCE. **Municipal Street Cleaning.** A survey of the problem of street cleaning in the City of Providence. In 25th Annual Report of the Bureau of Industrial Statistics of Rhode Island.

By—George H. Webb and Carol Aronovici. PUBLISHER— Bureau of Industrial Statistics, Providence. 1911. 34 p. Free.

SOUTH CAROLINA, CHARLESTON. **Report on Survey of the Government and Audit of Finances of the City of Charleston.**

By—Bureau of Municipal Research, New York. PUBLISHER— City Council, Charleston. 1924. 284 p. Free.

SOUTH DAKOTA. **Report on the Administrative Organization of the Government of the State of South Dakota.**

By—New York Bureau of Municipal Research. PUBLISHER— State of South Dakota, Pierre. 1922. 74 p. Free.

TEXAS. **County Government in Texas.** Bulletin No. 1732. Municipal Research Series No. 15.

By—Herman G. James. PUBLISHER—University of Texas, Austin. 1917. 118 p. Out of print.

SURVEYS IN SPECIALIZED FIELDS

CITY, COUNTY, AND STATE ADMINISTRATION—Continued

UNITED STATES. **Administration of the "Full Crew" Laws in the United States.** Supplement to Vol. IV, No. 4.
    By—Bureau of State Research of New Jersey. PUBLISHER—The same, Newark. 1917. 131 p. Free.

VIRGINIA, NORFOLK. **Survey of the City Government of Norfolk.**
    By—New York Bureau of Municipal Research. PUBLISHER—Chamber of Commerce, Norfolk. 1915. 529 p. Free.

VIRGINIA, RICHMOND. **Report on a Survey of the City Government of Richmond.**
    By—Bureau of Municipal Research of New York City. PUBLISHER—Civic Association of Richmond. 1917. 949 p. $3.00.

WASHINGTON. **Conditions in State Institutions of Washington with Recommendations for Needed Changes in Administration and Legislation.**
    By—Anna Y. Reed and May B. Goldsmith. PUBLISHER—State of Washington, Olympia. 1912. 92 p. Out of print.

WISCONSIN, MILWAUKEE. SURVEYS OF CITY DEPARTMENTS.
The Citizens' Free Employment Bureau. Bulletin No. 6. By Fred A. King. 1911. 16 p.
Free Legal Aid. Bulletin No. 7. By Fred A. King. 1911. 16 p.
Review of the Bureau's Work. Bulletin No. 9. By B. M. Rastall. 1911. 23 p.
Water Works Efficiency: Water Wastes Survey. Bulletin No. 11. By Roy Palmer and W. R. Brown. 1911. 39 p.
Water Works Efficiency: Present Capacity and Future Requirements. Bulletin No. 14. By F. E. Turneaure. 1912. 23 p.
Water Works Efficiency: Operating Efficiency. Bulletin No. 16. By Roy Palmer. 1912. 31 p.
Eighteen Months' Work, Containing Suggestions for a Municipal Survey. Bulletin No. 19. By John R. Commons. 1912. 44 p.
    PUBLISHER—Milwaukee Bureau of Economy and Efficiency. Out of print.

WISCONSIN, MILWAUKEE. **Report on a Preliminary Survey of Certain Departments of the City of Milwaukee.**
    By—Bureau of Municipal Research of New York. PUBLISHER—City of Milwaukee. 1913. 135 p. Out of print.

WISCONSIN, MILWAUKEE. **A Report to the Public.** A comparative financial study.
    By—Citizens' Bureau of Municipal Efficiency. PUBLISHER—The same, Milwaukee. 1915. 18 p. Out of print.

CITY, COUNTY, AND STATE ADMINISTRATION—Continued

WISCONSIN, MILWAUKEE COUNTY. **Milwaukee County Government, Being a Joint Report by the Committee on Civil Service, County Administration, and County Institutions and Buildings.**
BY—The Committee. PUBLISHER—City Club of Milwaukee. 1916. 18 p. Out of print.

In addition to reports **presenting findings** in City, County, and State Administration Surveys, as listed above, publications dealing with **methods of conducting** such studies will be found in Part III, PURPOSE, METHOD, AND STANDARDS, page 342.

CLINICS AND DISPENSARIES

See also HEALTH AND SANITATION; and HOSPITALS AND SANATORIA.

CANADA, MONTREAL. **A Social Study along Health Lines of the First Thousand Children Examined in the Health Clinic of the Canadian Patriotic Fund.**
BY—Helen R. Y. Reid. PUBLISHER—Canadian Patriotic Fund, Montreal. 1920. 39 p. Out of print.

NEW YORK CITY. **Work of New York's Tuberculosis Clinics.** A critical study of its work.
BY—New York Tuberculosis Clinics. PUBLISHER—Association of Tuberculosis Clinics, New York City. 1910. 87 p. Out of print.

NEW YORK CITY. **The Dispensary Situation in New York City.** Summary and recommendations.
BY—Public Health Committee, New York Academy of Medicine. PUBLISHER—The same, New York City. 1920. 16 p. Free.

NEW YORK CITY. **Tuberculosis Clinics.** Section of Report of New York Dispensaries. Reprinted from the American Review of Tuberculosis. Vol. IV, No. 1.
BY—Public Health Committee, New York Academy of Medicine. PUBLISHER—The same, New York City. 1920. 25 p. Free.

NEW YORK CITY. **Venereal Disease Clinics.**
BY—E. H. Lewinski-Corwin. PUBLISHER—American Social Hygiene Association, New York City. 1920. 14 p. Out of print.

NEW YORK CITY. **Community Dental Service in New York City.** A survey of dental clinics and other organized facilities.
BY—Michael M. Davis, Jr., and Clare Terwilliger. PUBLISHER—Committee on Dispensary Development, United Hospital Fund, New York City. 1924. 48 p. Free.

SURVEYS IN SPECIALIZED FIELDS

CLINICS AND DISPENSARIES—Continued

NEW YORK CITY. **Medical Care for a Million People.** A report on clinics in New York City and of the six years' work of the Committee on Dispensary Development of the United Hospital Fund. 1920–1926.
 BY—The Committee. PUBLISHER—The same, New York City. 1927. 90 p. Free.

PENNSYLVANIA. **A Survey of the Fiscal Policies of the Tuberculosis Hospitals and Dispensaries of Pennsylvania.** Reprint from Part III of the Report of the Citizens' Committee on the Finances of Pennsylvania.
 BY—H. A. Pattison. PUBLISHER—Department of State and Finance, Harrisburg. 1922. 175 p. Free.

UNITED STATES. **Present Status of Venereal Disease Clinics.** Public Health Reports. Vol. 35, No. 47.
 BY—John W. Hart. PUBLISHER—Superintendent of Documents, Government Printing Office, Washington, D. C. 1920. 7 p. 5 cents.

COMMUNITY STUDIES

 See PART I, GENERAL SOCIAL SURVEYS—URBAN and RURAL, and PART II, in JUVENILE DELINQUENCY; RELIGION; and RURAL.

For publications dealing with **methods of conducting** Community Studies see Part III, PURPOSE, METHOD, AND STANDARDS, under **General Social Surveys,** both **Urban** and **Rural; City and Regional Planning; Education; Hospitals and Sanatoria; Recreation; Religion;** and **Rural Education.**

CONTINUATION AND PART-TIME SCHOOLS

 See also CRIPPLED, DISABLED, AND HANDICAPPED; EDUCATION; INDUSTRIAL EDUCATION; SCHOOL ORGANIZATION AND ADMINISTRATION; and VOCATIONAL GUIDANCE AND TRAINING.

CALIFORNIA. **The Administration of the Part-Time School in the Small Community.** Part-Time Education Series No. 13. Division Bulletin No. 14.
 BY—Ralph Edward Berry. PUBLISHER—Vocational Education Division, University of California, Berkeley. 1924. Part I. 46 p. Part II. 59 p. Free.

CONTINUATION AND PART-TIME SCHOOLS—Continued

FOREIGN COUNTRIES. *See* UNITED STATES.

IOWA. **Special Investigation of Children in Industry Attending Part-Time School.** Bulletin No. 17.
    BY—Ellen M. Rourke. PUBLISHER—State Bureau of Labor, Des Moines. 1926. 77 p. Free.

MASSACHUSETTS. **The Needs and Possibilities of Part-Time Education.** Results of an investigation by the Board of Education.
    BY—David Snedden, Director. PUBLISHER—State Board of Education, Boston. 1913. 164 p. Free.

MASSACHUSETTS. **The Continuation Schools of Massachusetts.**
    BY—Massachusetts Child Labor Committee. PUBLISHER—The same, Boston. 1924. 30 p. Free.

MASSACHUSETTS. **The Intelligence of Continuation-School Children in Massachusetts.**
    BY—L. Thomas Hopkins. PUBLISHER—Harvard University Press, Cambridge. 1924. 132 p. $1.00.

OHIO, CLEVELAND. **Continuation Schools.**
    BY—Cleveland Chamber of Commerce. PUBLISHER—The same. 1913. 14 p. Free.

UNITED STATES AND FOREIGN COUNTRIES. **Part-Time Schools.** A survey of experience in the United States and foreign countries with recommendations [Belgium, Canada, Denmark, England, France, Germany, Holland, Italy, Norway, Scotland, Sweden, Switzerland]. Federal Board for Vocational Education Bulletin No. 73.
    BY—H. B. Smith. PUBLISHER—Superintendent of Documents, Government Printing Office, Washington, D. C. 1922. 461 p. 35 cents.

WISCONSIN. THE CONTINUATION SCHOOLS OF WISCONSIN: VOCATIONAL SCHOOL SURVEY.

Adult Education. 1921. 39 p.

"Dual" Control in Wisconsin. 1921. 27 p.

Fundamentals of the Curriculum and of the Course of Study. 1921. 74 p.

Genesis and Purpose of the Vocational School Survey; Beginnings of Continuation Schools in Wisconsin; and History of Continuation Schools in Wisconsin. 1921. 23 p.

Scholarships in the Continuation School. 1921. 15 p.

Technical Trade Training. 1921. 23 p.

Human Engineering in the Continuation School. 1922. 16 p.

SURVEYS IN SPECIALIZED FIELDS

CONTINUATION AND PART-TIME SCHOOLS—Continued
An Inventory Description of Wisconsin's Continuation Schools. 1922. 257 p.
The Teacher Problem. 1922. 16 p.
By—Edward A. Fitzpatrick, Director. PUBLISHER—State Board of Education, Madison. Free.

CONVALESCENCE
See also HOSPITALS AND SANATORIA.
NEW YORK CITY. The Convalescent Treatment of Heart Disease by Graduated Exercise Applied through Natural Work and Play Methods. Reprinted from Medical Record, February 12, 1921.
By—Frederic Brush. PUBLISHER—Sturgis Research Fund, Burke Foundation, White Plains. 1921. 28 p. 10 cents.
NEW YORK CITY. Provision for the Care of Convalescents in New York City. Reprinted from Medical Record, December 19, 1923.
By—Public Health Committee, New York Academy of Medicine. PUBLISHER—Sturgis Research Fund, Burke Foundation, White Plains. 1923. 19 p. 10 cents.
NEW YORK CITY. Study of Country Convalescent Treatment of One Hundred Neuro-Psychiatric Patients.
By—N. F. Cummings. PUBLISHER—Sturgis Research Fund, Burke Foundation, White Plains. 1923. 20 p. 10 cents.
NEW YORK CITY. Convalescence for Neuro-Psychiatric Patients. Report of a study of results in two convalescent homes.
By—Advisory Committee on Convalescence, Hospital Information Bureau, United Hospital Fund of New York. PUBLISHER—Sturgis Research Fund, Burke Foundation, White Plains. 1926. 29 p. Free.

CORRECTION
See DELINQUENCY AND CORRECTION.

COST OF LIVING
See also EDUCATION; INDUSTRIAL CONDITIONS AND RELATIONS; JAPANESE; and RURAL.
CALIFORNIA. Cost of Living Survey. Report relative to the cost of living in California for selected family groups.
By—J. C. Whitman, Director. PUBLISHER—California State Civil Service Commission, Sacramento. 1923. 81 p. Free.

A BIBLIOGRAPHY OF SOCIAL SURVEYS

COST OF LIVING—Continued

CALIFORNIA, LOS ANGELES. **The Relation of Wages to the Cost of Living in Los Angeles.** 1915–1920. Studies in Sociology No. 19.
> BY—Hazel M. Liggett. PUBLISHER—Southern California Sociological Society, Los Angeles. 1921. 11 p. 15 cents.

CONNECTICUT, WATERBURY. **Survey of Cost of Living in Waterbury.**
> BY—R. S. Sperry, Director. PUBLISHER—Chamber of Commerce, Waterbury. 1920. 24 p. Free.

DISTRICT OF COLUMBIA. **High Cost of Living in the District of Columbia.** Senate Report No. 327.
> BY—Committee on the District of Columbia. PUBLISHER—Superintendent of Documents, Government Printing Office, Washington, D. C. 1919. 32 p. Free.

ILLINOIS, AURORA. **Cost of Living Survey.**
> BY—Aurora Chamber of Commerce. PUBLISHER—The same. 1921. 3 p. Free.

ILLINOIS, CHICAGO. **Wages and Family Budget in the Chicago Stockyards District with Wage Statistics from Other Industries Employing Unskilled Labor.** An investigation carried on under the direction of the Board of the University of Chicago Settlement.
> BY—J. C. Kennedy, Director. PUBLISHER—University of Chicago. 1914. 80 p. 25 cents.

IOWA. COST OF LIVING ON IOWA FARMS. Agricultural Experiment Station Bulletin No. 237.

> Part I. **An Economic and Sociological Study of 472 Farm Families and Farm Homes in Boone, Story, and Sac Counties, Iowa.** By George H. Von Tungeln, J. E. Thaden and E. L. Kirkpatrick. 56 p.

> Part II. **Household Expenditures.** By Hazel Kyrk. 79 p.
>> PUBLISHER—Iowa State College of Agriculture and Mechanic Arts, Ames. 1926. Free.

KANSAS. **Cost of Living Survey of Wage Earning Women of the State of Kansas.**
> BY—Linna E. Bresette, Director. PUBLISHER—Women's Division of the Court of Industrial Relations, Topeka. 1921. 42 p. Free.

SURVEYS IN SPECIALIZED FIELDS

COST OF LIVING—Continued

KENTUCKY. **The Cost of Living among Colored Farm Families of Selected Localities of Kentucky, Tennessee, and Texas.**
    BY—U. S. Bureau of Agricultural Economics. PUBLISHER—Superintendent of Documents, Government Printing Office, Washington, D. C. 1925. 13 p. 5 cents.

MARYLAND, BALTIMORE. **Wage-Earning Women and Girls in Baltimore.** A study of the cost of living in 1918. Women in Industry Series No. 15.
    BY—Josephine A. Roche. PUBLISHER—National Consumers' League, New York City. 1921. 36 p. Free.

MASSACHUSETTS. **Report of a Commission on the Cost of Living in Massachusetts.** House Document 1750.
    BY—The Commission. PUBLISHER—State of Massachusetts, Boston. 1910. 752 p. Out of print.

MASSACHUSETTS. REPORTS OF THE COMMISSION ON THE NECESSARIES OF LIFE.
Report of the Commission on the Necessaries of Life. House Document No. 1500. 1920. 182 p.
Report of the Commission on the Necessaries of Life. House Document No. 1260. 1921. 125 p.
Report of the Special Commission on the Necessaries of Life. House Document No. 1400. 1922. 177 p.
Report of the Special Commission on the Necessaries of Life. House Document No. 1250. 1923. 288 p.
    BY—The Commission. PUBLISHER—The same, Boston. Free.

MASSACHUSETTS, FALL RIVER. **The Cost of Living among Wage-Earners, Fall River.** Research Report No. 22.
    BY—National Industrial Conference Board. PUBLISHER—The same, New York City. 1919. 18 p. 50 cents.

MASSACHUSETTS, LAWRENCE. **The Cost of Living among Wage-Earners, Lawrence.** Research Report No. 24.
    BY—National Industrial Conference Board. PUBLISHER—The same, New York City. 1919. 21 p. 50 cents.

MASSACHUSETTS, NEW BEDFORD. **Cost of Living, New Bedford.**
    BY—Special Committee. PUBLISHER—Chamber of Commerce, New Bedford. 1921. 11 p. Free.

MASSACHUSETTS, WORCESTER. **The Cost of Living among Wage-Earners, Worcester.** Special Report No. 16.
    BY—National Industrial Conference Board. PUBLISHER—The same, New York City. 1920. 20 p. 50 cents.

COST OF LIVING—Continued

MICHIGAN, DETROIT. **The Cost of Living among Wage-Earners, Detroit.** Special Report No. 19.
 By—National Industrial Conference Board. PUBLISHER—The same, New York City. 1921. 22 p. 50 cents.

MINNESOTA. **Cost of Living on Minnesota Farms.** 1905–1914. Agricultural Experiment Station Bulletin 162.
 By—F. W. Peck. PUBLISHER—University of Minnesota, Minneapolis. 1916. 31 p. Out of print.

MINNESOTA, MINNEAPOLIS. **The Salary Situation and the Cost of Living.** Report of the Survey Commission. Bulletin of the University of Minnesota. Vol. XXIII, No. 45.
 By—Albert J. Lobb. PUBLISHER—University of Minnesota, Minneapolis. 1920. 55 p. Out of print.

NEW JERSEY, HUDSON COUNTY. **The Cost of Living among Wage-Earners, North Hudson County.** Special Report No. 7.
 By—National Industrial Conference Board. PUBLISHER—The same, New York City. 1920. 21 p. 50 cents.

NEW YORK. **Investigations into Living Costs.** Department of Farms and Markets Bulletin. Vol. II, No. 12.
 By—Martin H. Glynn and John H. Finley. PUBLISHER—Department of Farms and Markets, Albany. 1919. 5 p. Free.

NEW YORK CITY. **Wage-Earners' Budgets.** A study of standards and cost of living in New York City. Greenwich House Series of Social Studies No. 1.
 By—Louise Bolard More. PUBLISHER—Henry Holt and Company, New York City. 1907. 280 p. Out of print.

NEW YORK CITY. **The Standard of Living among Workingmen's Families in New York City.**
 By—Robert Coit Chapin. PUBLISHER—Russell Sage Foundation, New York City. 1909. 360 p. Out of print.

NEW YORK CITY. **Report of the Cost of Living for an Unskilled Laborer's Family in New York City.**
 By—Bureau of Standards. PUBLISHER—Committee on Salaries and Grades, Board of Estimate and Apportionment, New York City. 1916. 57 p. Out of print.

NEW YORK CITY. **The Minimum Cost of Living.** A study of families of limited income in New York City.
 By—Winifred Stuart Gibbs. PUBLISHER—Macmillan Company, New York City. 1917. 93 p. $1.25.

SURVEYS IN SPECIALIZED FIELDS

COST OF LIVING—Continued

NEW YORK CITY. **My Money Won't Reach.** The experience of 377 self-supporting families in New York City in endeavoring to make their incomes provide the essentials for healthful living.
    By—Emma A. Winslow. PUBLISHER—Charity Organization Society, New York City. 1918. 22 p. Out of print.

NEW YORK CITY. **Cost of Living in New York City.**
    By—National Industrial Conference Board. PUBLISHER—The same, New York City. 1926. 129 p. $2.00.

NORTH CAROLINA, CHARLOTTE. *See* SOUTH CAROLINA, GREENVILLE AND PELZER, in this section.

NORTH DAKOTA. **Cost of Living Survey for Women and Minor Workers in the State of North Dakota.**
    By—Minimum Wage Department, North Dakota Workmen's Compensation Bureau in cooperation with the Women's Bureau, U. S. Department of Labor. MIMEOGRAPHED—Minimum Wage Department, North Dakota Workmen's Compensation Bureau, Bismarck. 1921. 28 p. Free.

OHIO. **Women's Wages and the Cost of Living.** Report of an investigation.
    By—Ohio Council on Women and Children in Industry. PUBLISHER—The same, Toledo. 1922. 19 p. 10 cents.

OHIO, CINCINNATI. **The Cost of Living among Wage-Earners, Cincinnati.** Special Report No. 13.
    By—National Industrial Conference Board. PUBLISHER—The same, New York City. 1920. 18 p. 50 cents.

OREGON, PORTLAND. **Cost of Living Survey.** Reed College Bulletin. Vol. 4, No. 1.
    By—Jessie M. Short. PUBLISHER—Reed College, Portland. 1925. 16 p. Free.

PENNSYLVANIA. **The Cost of Living among Wage-Earners, Anthracite Region of Pennsylvania.** Special Report No. 21.
    By—National Industrial Conference Board. PUBLISHER—The same, New York City. 1922. 41 p. 50 cents.

SOUTH CAROLINA, GREENVILLE AND PELZER. **The Cost of Living among Wage-Earners, Greenville and Pelzer, South Carolina, and Charlotte, North Carolina.** Special Report No. 8.
    By—National Industrial Conference Board. PUBLISHER—The same, New York City. 1920. 25 p. 50 cents.

TENNESSEE. *See* KENTUCKY in this section.

COST OF LIVING—Continued

TEXAS. *See* KENTUCKY in this section.

UNITED STATES. **Cost of Living in American Towns.** Report of an inquiry into working class rents, housing, and retail prices, together with rates of wages in certain occupations in the principal industrial towns of the United States of America, with an introductory memorandum and a comparison of conditions in the United States and the United Kingdom.
> By—London Board of Trade. PUBLISHER—His Majesty's Stationery Office, London. 1911. 533 p. 5s. 1d.

UNITED STATES. **Family Budgets of Typical Cotton-Mill Workers.** Vol. XVI. Report on Condition of Woman and Child Wage-Earners in the United States. Senate Document No. 645.
> By—Wood F. Worcester and Daisy Worthington Worcester. PUBLISHER—Superintendent of Documents, Government Printing Office, Washington, D. C. 1911. 255 p. Out of print.

UNITED STATES. **Investigation Relative to Wages and Price of Commodities.** Senate Document No. 847. In 4 volumes.
> By—Senate Committee. PUBLISHER—Superintendent of Documents, Government Printing Office, Washington, D. C. 1911. Vol. I. 187 p. 20 cents; Vol. II. 960 p. 65 cents; Vol. III. 960 p. 65 cents; Vol. IV. 215 p. 20 cents.

UNITED STATES. **Report of Special Committee Appointed to Investigate Increased Living Costs.**
> By—Bankers Trust Company of New York. PUBLISHER—The same, New York City. 1917. 15 p. Free.

UNITED STATES. **Sociological Studies.** Composition of mining population, living costs, and wage rates. In Report of the United States Coal Commission. Reprinted from "The Coal Age."
> By—United States Coal Commission. PUBLISHER—The same, Washington, D. C. 1923. 9 p. Free.

UNITED STATES. **The Comparative Living Costs in Eight Cities.**
> By—Municipal Committee. MIMEOGRAPHED—Chamber of Commerce, Cleveland, Ohio. 1926. 21 p. Free.

UNITED STATES. **The Farmer's Standard of Living.** A socio-economic study of 2,886 white farm families of selected localities in 11 states. U. S. Department of Agriculture, Bulletin No. 1466.
> By—E. L. Kirkpatrick. PUBLISHER—Superintendent of Documents, Government Printing Office, Washington, D. C. 1926. 63 p. 10 cents.

SURVEYS IN SPECIALIZED FIELDS

COST OF LIVING—Continued

UNITED STATES. STUDIES IN THE COST OF LIVING.
  The Cost of Living in the United States, 1914–1926. 233 p. $2.50.
  The Cost of Living in the United States in 1926. Supplementing the Cost of Living in the United States, 1914–1926. 1927. 33 p. 75 cents.
   BY—National Industrial Conference Board. PUBLISHER—The same, New York City.
   In addition to the above the National Industrial Conference Board has issued yearly since 1914 reports on the cost of living in the United States. These are obtainable at 75 cents each.

In addition to reports **presenting findings** in Cost of Living Surveys, as listed above, publications dealing with **methods of conducting** such studies will be found in Part III, PURPOSE, METHOD, AND STANDARDS, page 343.

CRIME AND CRIMINALS

  See also DELINQUENCY AND CORRECTION; FEEBLEMINDED; IMMIGRATION AND AMERICANIZATION; JUVENILE DELINQUENCY; MENTAL HYGIENE; POLICE; PRISONS; PROBATION AND PAROLE; and TRUANCY AND NON-ATTENDANCE.

GEORGIA. **Notes on Negro Crime Particularly in Georgia.** A special study made under the direction of Atlanta University. Publication No. 9.
   BY—W. E. Burghardt Du Bois. PUBLISHER—University of Atlanta Press. 1904. 88 p. 40 cents.

ILLINOIS, CHICAGO. **Report of City Council Committee on Crime of the City of Chicago.**
   BY—Charles E. Merriam. PUBLISHER—Municipal Reference Library, Chicago. 1915. 196 p. 50 cents.

ILLINOIS, CHICAGO. **Delinquents and Criminals: Their Making and Unmaking** [Chicago, Ill., and Boston, Mass.]. Judge Baker Foundation Publication No. 3.
   BY—William Healy and Augusta F. Bronner. PUBLISHER—Macmillan Company, New York City. 1926. 317 p. $3.50.

MASSACHUSETTS, BOSTON. *See* ILLINOIS, CHICAGO, in this section.

MISSOURI. **The Administration of Criminal Justice in Missouri.**
   BY—Raymond Moley. PUBLISHER—Missouri Association for Criminal Justice, St. Louis. 1926. 56 p. Free.

CRIME AND CRIMINALS—Continued

MISSOURI. **The Missouri Crime Survey.** Made by the Missouri Association for Criminal Justice.
> BY—Raymond Moley, Director. PUBLISHER—Macmillan Company, New York City. 1926. 587 p. $6.00.

NEBRASKA, OMAHA. **A Survey of the Cause and Extent of Crime among Foreigners in Omaha.** University of Omaha Bulletin. Vol. VI, No. 2.
> BY—Beatrice Harvey. PUBLISHER—University of Omaha. 1924. 12 p. 15 cents.

NEW JERSEY. **Report of the Dependency and Crimes Commission of New Jersey.**
> BY—The Commission. PUBLISHER—State of New Jersey, Trenton. 1909. 23 p. Out of print.

NEW YORK, KINGS COUNTY. **A Study of Crime Conditions in the Red Hook District of Kings County.**
> BY—New York State Crime Commission. MIMEOGRAPHED—The same, New York City. 1927. 78 p. Free.

OHIO, CLEVELAND. **Criminal Justice in Cleveland.** Complete report of the Cleveland Crime Survey.
> BY—Roscoe Pound and Felix Frankfurter. PUBLISHER—Cleveland Foundation. 1921. 700 p. $3.75.

Parts of the report may be obtained as follows:

Correctional and Penal Treatment. By Burdette G. Lewis. 59 p. 50 cents.

The Criminal Courts. By Reginald Heber Smith and Herbert N. Ehrmann. 141 p. $1.00.

Criminal Justice and the American City. By Roscoe Pound. 148 p. $1.00.

Medical Science and Criminal Justice. By Herman M. Adler. 46 p. 50 cents.

Prosecution. By Alfred Bettman. 142 p. $1.00.

PENNSYLVANIA, PHILADELPHIA. **Report of the Crime Survey Committee.**
> BY—Law Association of Philadelphia. PUBLISHER—The same. 1926. 476 p. Out of print.

PENNSYLVANIA, PITTSBURGH AND ALLEGHENY COUNTY. **Crime and Its Treatment in Pittsburgh and Allegheny County.**
> BY—Commission on Social Service, Pittsburgh Council of Churches. PUBLISHER—The same. 1924. 62 p. Free.

SURVEYS IN SPECIALIZED FIELDS

CRIME AND CRIMINALS—Continued

SOUTH CAROLINA. **Crime and Its Treatment in South Carolina.** Quarterly Bulletin of the State Board of Public Welfare. Vol. 3, No. 2.
>By—G. Croft Williams. PUBLISHER—State Board of Public Welfare, Columbia. 1922. 16 p. Out of print.

UNITED STATES. **Immigration and Crime.** Reports of the Immigration Commission. Senate Document. Vol. 36, No. 750.
>By—The Commission. PUBLISHER—Superintendent of Documents, Government Printing Office, Washington, D. C. 1911. 444 p. Out of print.

UNITED STATES. **Relation between Occupation and Criminality of Women.** Vol. XV. Report on Condition of Woman and Child Wage-Earners in the United States. Senate Document No. 645.
>By—Mary Coyngton. PUBLISHER—Superintendent of Documents, Government Printing Office, Washington, D. C. 1911. 117 p. 10 cents.

UNITED STATES. **Criminal Receivers in the United States.** Social and economic problems of the "Fence"—the source of organized crime and creator of criminals—submitted to the New York State Crime Commission, the National Crime Commission, the National Trade Relations Committee of the Chamber of Commerce of the United States, and the Association of Casualty and Surety Executives.
>By—Prison Committee, Association of Grand Jurors, New York County. MIMEOGRAPHED—The same, New York City. 1927. 56 p. Free.

In addition to reports **presenting findings** in Crime and Criminals Surveys, as listed above, publications dealing with **methods of conducting** such studies will be found in Part III, PURPOSE, METHOD AND STANDARDS, page 344.

CRIPPLED, DISABLED, AND HANDICAPPED
>*See also* ACCIDENTS AND ACCIDENT PREVENTION; CARDIACS; CHILD WELFARE; DEAF; INDUSTRIAL CONDITIONS AND RELATIONS; and MENTAL HYGIENE.

CALIFORNIA, SAN FRANCISCO. **The Care of Disabled Veterans and Ex-service Men in San Francisco.** A survey.
>By—Esther De Tuberville and E. P. Van Allmen. MIMEOGRAPHED—Council of Social Agencies, San Francisco. 1924. 208 p. Free.

A BIBLIOGRAPHY OF SOCIAL SURVEYS

CRIPPLED, DISABLED, AND HANDICAPPED—Continued

CANADA, TORONTO. Report of a Survey of Physically Handicapped Children in Toronto.
>   BY—Child Welfare Council of Toronto. PUBLISHER—The same. 1924. 64 p. Free.

ILLINOIS. Report of the Survey of the Specially Handicapped Children in the State of Illinois.
>   BY—Herman M. Adler. PUBLISHER—State Department of Public Welfare, Springfield. 1925. 30 p. Free.

ILLINOIS, CHICAGO. Survey of the Care of Disabled and Ex-Service Men in Chicago.
>   BY—Evelina Belden Paulson. PUBLISHER—Community Trust, Chicago. 1923. 69 p. Free.

ILLINOIS, CHICAGO. Survey of Crippled Children in Chicago.
>   BY—Rotary Club of Chicago. PUBLISHER—Community Trust, Chicago. 1925. 87 p. Free.

INDIANA, BLOOMINGTON. A Study of Handicapped Children, Based on 150 Crippled Children Referred to the Social Service Department of Indiana University. Study No. 41.
>   BY—Helen Hare. PUBLISHER—University of Indiana, Bloomington. 1919. 64 p. 35 cents.

MASSACHUSETTS, BOSTON. Gainful Employment for Handicapped Women. A study based on 1000 case records from an employment bureau for handicapped women. Report No. 1.
>   BY—Lucile Eaves. PUBLISHER—Women's Educational and Industrial Union, Boston. 1921. 32 p. 25 cents.

NEW YORK. Report of the New York State Commission for Survey of Crippled Children.
>   BY—Henry C. Wright, Director. PUBLISHER—State of New York, Albany. 1925. 104 p. Free.

NEW YORK. Survey of Educational Facilities for Crippled Children in New York State. Bulletin No. 835.
>   BY—J. S. Orleans. PUBLISHER—University of the State of New York Press, Albany. 1925. 26 p. 5 cents.

NEW YORK CITY. The Economic Consequences of Physical Disability. A case study of civilian cripples in New York City. Publications Series I, No. 2.
>   BY—John Culbert Faries. PUBLISHER—Red Cross Institute for Crippled and Disabled Men, New York City. 1918. 11 p. Free.

SURVEYS IN SPECIALIZED FIELDS

CRIPPLED, DISABLED, AND HANDICAPPED—Continued

NEW YORK CITY. **Survey of Cripples in New York City, Made under the Auspices of a Social Committee on Survey of Cripples.**
 By—Henry C. Wright, Director. PUBLISHER—New York Committee on After-Care of Infantile Paralysis Cases, New York City. 1920. 104 p. $1.00.

NEW YORK CITY. **Securing Employment for the Handicapped.** A study of placement agencies for this group in New York City. WC 3.
 By—Mary La Dame. PUBLISHER—Welfare Council of New York City. 1927. 133 p. 50 cents.

OHIO, CLEVELAND. **Education and Occupations of Cripples, Juvenile and Adult.** A survey of all the cripples of Cleveland in 1916, made under the Direction of the Welfare Federation of Cleveland.
 By—Lucy Wright and Amy M. Hamburger. PUBLISHER—Red Cross Institute for Crippled and Disabled Men, New York City. 1918. 227 p. Free.

UNITED STATES. **The Care of Crippled Children in the United States.** A study of the distribution of institutions and work.
 By—Douglas C. McMurtrie. PUBLISHER—American Journal of Orthopedic Surgery, Boston, Massachusetts. 1912. 33 p. Out of print.

UNITED STATES. **Care and Education of Crippled Children in the United States.**
 By—Edith Reeves. PUBLISHER—Russell Sage Foundation, New York City. 1914. 252 p. $2.00.

WISCONSIN. **Rehabilitation of the Handicapped.** The Continuation Schools of Wisconsin: Vocational School Survey.
 By—Edward A. Fitzpatrick, Director. PUBLISHER—State Board of Education, Madison. 1921. 31 p. Free.

In addition to reports **presenting findings,** as listed above, a publication dealing with **methods of conducting** such studies will be found in Part III, PURPOSE, METHOD AND STANDARDS, under **Industrial Conditions and Relations.**

CZECHS

OHIO, CLEVELAND. **The Czechs of Cleveland.**
 By—Eleanor E. Ledbetter. PUBLISHER—Americanization Committee, Citizens Bureau, Cleveland. 1919. 40 p. 10 cents.

DANCE HALLS

See also VICE.

ILLINOIS, CHICAGO. **Public Dance Halls of Chicago.**
> By—Louise de Koven Bowen. PUBLISHER—Juvenile Protective Association, Chicago. 1917. 13 p. Free.

NEW YORK CITY. **Report of the Advisory Dance Hall Committee.**
> By—Maria Ward Lambin. PUBLISHER—Women's City Club and City Recreation Committee, New York City. 1924. 39 p. 25 cents.

PENNSYLVANIA, PITTSBURGH. **A Study of Dance Halls in Pittsburgh.**
> By—Collis A. Stocking. PUBLISHER—Pittsburgh Girls' Conference. 1925. 47 p. 25 cents.

UNITED STATES. **Report of the Public Dance Hall Committee.**
> By—Maria Lambin. PUBLISHER—San Francisco Center, California Civic League of Women Voters, San Francisco. 1924. 24 p. 25 cents.

DEAF

ILLINOIS, CHICAGO. **Chicago Public Schools.** A special report of the Department of Child Study and Pedagogic Investigation on children attending the public day schools for the deaf in Chicago.
> By—D. P. Macmillan, Director. PUBLISHER—Department of Education, Chicago. 1908. 88 p. Free.

DEFECTIVE (MENTAL)

> *See* CHILD WELFARE; DELINQUENCY AND CORRECTION; EDUCATION; FEEBLEMINDED; INSANE; MENTAL HYGIENE; and PSYCHIATRIC.

For publications dealing with **methods of conducting** Mental Defective Studies see Part III, PURPOSE, METHOD, AND STANDARDS, under **Mental Hygiene.**

DELINQUENCY AND CORRECTION

Reports dealing with the general question of delinquency and correction and with delinquency and correction in connection with other subjects are listed here. For reports dealing with specific phases of delinquency and correction, *see* ADOLESCENCE; CHARITIES; CHILD WELFARE; CRIME AND CRIMINALS; DETENTION; JUVENILE DELINQUENCY; LIBRARIES; POLICE; PRISONS; PSYCHIATRIC; and SEX DELINQUENCY.

SURVEYS IN SPECIALIZED FIELDS

DELINQUENCY AND CORRECTION—Continued

CALIFORNIA. STUDIES IN DELINQUENCY.
  Intelligence and Delinquency. A study of 215 cases. Bulletin No. 2. 1915. 12 p. 10 cents.
  Delinquency and Density of Population. Bulletin No. 4. 1917. 18 p. 30 cents.
    BY—J. Harold Williams. PUBLISHER—Department of Research, Whittier State School, Whittier.

COLORADO. **Report on the Care of Dependents, Delinquents, and Defectives, Including Reports on the Care and Treatment of the Insane in Colorado, a Study of the Mental Conditions of the Inmates of the Four Colorado Institutions for Minors, and the State Board of Charities and Corrections.** Report No. XVI.
  BY—Survey Committee of State Affairs of Colorado. PUBLISHER—The same, Denver. 1918. 53 p. Out of print.

CONNECTICUT, WATERBURY. **Report of a Study of the Juvenile Court and of the Adult Probation Work in the City of Waterbury.**
  BY—Francis H. Hiller. MIMEOGRAPHED—National Probation Association, New York City. 1926. 17 p. Free.

IDAHO. **A Study of Delinquency in Thirty Counties in Idaho.** In Journal of the American Institute of Criminal Law and Criminology, November.
  BY—Robert D. Leeper. PUBLISHER—Northwestern University Press, Chicago, Illinois. 1925. 48 p. $1.00 per copy.

ILLINOIS, CHICAGO. STUDIES IN DELINQUENCY.
  A Study in Adult Delinquency Based on 3000 Families. By Mary Swain. 1911. 14 p.
  On the Trail of the Juvenile Adult Offender. By A. P. Drucker. 1912. 60 p.
  What Should Be Done for Chicago's Women Offenders: Recommendations and Report. By City Council Crime Commission. 1916. 12 p.
    PUBLISHER—Juvenile Protective Association, Chicago. Out of print.

ILLINOIS, SPRINGFIELD. **The Correctional System of Springfield.** Delinquency and Correction Section of the Springfield Survey.
  BY—Zenas L. Potter. PUBLISHER—Russell Sage Foundation, New York City. 1915. 185 p. 25 cents.

DELINQUENCY AND CORRECTION—Continued

IOWA. **Dependents, Defectives, and Delinquents in Iowa.** A study of the sources of social infection.
 BY—L. H. Mounts. PUBLISHER—University of Iowa, Iowa City. 1919. 166 p. 85 cents.

KANSAS. **A Study of the Causes of Delinquency of Women Quarantined for Diseases at the State Industrial Farm for Women.** In Bulletin of the Kansas State Board of Health. Vol. XVII, No. 2.
 BY—D. D. Newby. PUBLISHER—Kansas State Department of Health, Topeka. 1921. 17 p. Free.

KANSAS, TOPEKA. **Delinquency and Correction.** Part II. Topeka Improvement Survey.
 BY—Zenas L. Potter. PUBLISHER—Russell Sage Foundation, New York City. 1914. 64 p. 15 cents.

MASSACHUSETTS. **Report of the Special Commission Relative to the Control, Custody, and Treatment of Defectives, Criminals, and Misdemeanants.**
 BY—The Commission. PUBLISHER—House of Delegates, Boston. 1919. 49 p. Free.

MISSISSIPPI. **Treatment of the Dependent, Defective, and Delinquent Classes in Mississippi.**
 BY—Nathaniel Batson Bond. PUBLISHER—Tulane University, New Orleans, Louisiana. 1923. 100 p. $1.00.

MISSOURI, ST. LOUIS. **Report of a Mental Hygiene Survey of Delinquency and Dependency Problems in St. Louis.**
 BY—V. V. Anderson, Director. PUBLISHER—Department of Public Welfare, St. Louis. 1922. 52 p. Free.

NEW YORK. **Report of a Special Committee of the State Commission of Prisons Appointed to Investigate the Matter of Mental Diseases and Delinquency.**
 BY—The Committee. PUBLISHER—State of New York, Albany. 1918. 23 p. Free.

NEW YORK. **Mental Disease and Delinquency.** A report of a special committee of the New York State Commission of Prisons. Reprint No. 50.
 BY—V. V. Anderson. PUBLISHER—National Committee for Mental Hygiene, New York City. 1919. 22 p. 10 cents.

SURVEYS IN SPECIALIZED FIELDS

DELINQUENCY AND CORRECTION—Continued

NEW YORK. **A Study of Women Delinquents in New York State.** Publications of the Bureau of Social Hygiene.
> By—Mabel Ruth Fernald and others. PUBLISHER—Century Company, New York City. 1920. 542 p. $5.00.

NEW YORK, BEDFORD HILLS. **An Experimental Study of Psychopathic Delinquent Women.** Publications of the Bureau of Social Hygiene.
> By—Edith R. Spaulding and Katharine Bement Davis. PUBLISHER—Rand McNally and Company, New York City. 1923. 368 p. $2.50.

OHIO, AKRON. **Report on the Municipal Court of Akron.**
> By—Bureau of Municipal Research. MIMEOGRAPHED—The same, Akron. 1922. 27 p. Out of print.

OHIO, CLEVELAND. **Delinquency and Spare Time.** A study of a few stories written into the court records of the city of Cleveland. Cleveland Foundation Survey.
> By—Henry W. Thurston. PUBLISHER—Survey Committee of Cleveland Foundation. 1918. 190 p. 50 cents.

OHIO, TOLEDO. **Report of a Survey of Toledo's Welfare Farm.**
> By—Charles Russell. PUBLISHER—Commission of Publicity and Efficiency, Toledo. 1920. 61 p. Free.

OREGON. **Preliminary Statistical Report of the Oregon State Survey of Mental Defect, Delinquency, and Dependency.** U. S. Public Health Service Bulletin No. 112.
> By—Chester L. Carlisle, Director. PUBLISHER—Superintendent of Documents, Government Printing Office, Washington, D. C. 1922. 77 p. 10 cents.

PENNSYLVANIA. **A Financial Survey of the State Penal and Correctional Institutions in Pennsylvania.** Reprinted from Part III of the Report to the Citizens' Committee on the Finances of the State of Pennsylvania.
> By—Louis N. Robinson. PUBLISHER—Department of State and Finance, Harrisburg. 1922. 35 p. Free.

PENNSYLVANIA, PHILADELPHIA. **Report of the Operation and Condition of the Bureau of Correction of Philadelphia.**
> By—Special Investigating Committee. PUBLISHER—Department of Public Safety, Philadelphia. 1915. 43 p. Free.

DELINQUENCY AND CORRECTION—Continued

PENNSYLVANIA, PHILADELPHIA. **Social Non-Conformity.** An analysis of 420 cases of delinquent girls and women.
>By—Frances Q. Holsopple. PUBLISHER—Philadelphia Committee, U. S. Interdepartmental Social Hygiene Board, Philadelphia. 1919. 44 p. Out of print.

PENNSYLVANIA, PHILADELPHIA. **Humanizing Justice.** A brief study of the municipal court of Philadelphia. Public Service Series No. 10.
>By—Maximilian P. E. Groszmann. PUBLISHER—Municipal Court of Philadelphia. 1922. 31 p. Free.

In addition to reports **presenting findings** in Delinquency and Correction Surveys, as listed above, publications dealing with **methods of conducting** such studies will be found in Part III, PURPOSE, METHOD, AND STANDARDS, page 344.

DEPENDENCY

>*See also* CHARITIES; CHILD WELFARE; CRIME AND CRIMINALS; DELINQUENCY AND CORRECTION; HEALTH AND SANITATION; LIBRARIES; RELIEF; and SUB-NORMAL, RETARDED, AND EXCEPTIONAL CHILDREN.

DISTRICT OF COLUMBIA. **Child Dependency in the District of Columbia.** An interpretation of data concerning dependent children under the care of public and private agencies. U. S. Department of Labor. Children's Bureau Publication No. 140.
>By—Emma O. Lundberg and Mary E. Milburn. PUBLISHER—Superintendent of Documents, Government Printing Office, Washington, D. C. 1924. 160 p. 20 cents.

MASSACHUSETTS. **Report of the Commission on the Support of Dependent Minor Children of Widowed Mothers.** House Document No. 2075.
>By—The Commission. PUBLISHER—Commonwealth of Massachusetts, Boston. 1913. 189 p. Free.

MASSACHUSETTS. **Report of a Special Inquiry Relative to the Aged and Dependent Persons in Massachusetts.**
>By—Commission on Aged and Dependent Persons. PUBLISHER—Commonwealth of Massachusetts, Boston. 1916. 107 p. Free.

NEW YORK. **Report on Standards of Placing Out, Supervision, and After-Care of Dependent Children.**
>By—Special Committee, New York State Conference of Charities and Corrections. PUBLISHER—The same, Albany. 1916. 11 p. Free.

SURVEYS IN SPECIALIZED FIELDS

DEPENDENCY—Continued

NEW YORK CITY. **Physical Examination and Employment of Dependents in City Homes (Almshouses).** Section IV. Report of the Committee on Inquiry into the Departments of Health, Charities, and Bellevue and Allied Hospitals in the City of New York.
By—Henry C. Wright, Director. PUBLISHER—City of New York. 1913. 34 p. Free.

NEW YORK, ONEIDA COUNTY. **The Causes of Dependency, Based on a Survey of Oneida County.** Eugenics and Social Welfare Bulletin No. XV.
By—Chester Lee Carlisle, Director. PUBLISHER—Division of Mental Defect and Delinquency, State Board of Charities, Albany. 1918. 465 p. Out of print.

OHIO, CLEVELAND. **The Children's Bureau of Cleveland.** A study of the care of dependent children in Cleveland. U. S. Department of Labor. Children's Bureau Publication No. 177.
By—Mary Mather Leete. PUBLISHER—Superintendent of Documents, Government Printing Office, Washington, D. C. 1927. 98 p. 15 cents.

PENNSYLVANIA. **Pennsylvania Dependents.** Report and Recommendations of the State Dependents Commission.
By—The Commission. PUBLISHER—State Department of Public Grounds and Buildings, Harrisburg. 1915. 88 p. Free.

PENNSYLVANIA. **Care of Dependent Children in Twenty-eight Counties as Administered by Poor Law Authorities.**
By—Abraham Epstein. PUBLISHER—Child Welfare Division, Public Charities Association of Pennsylvania, Philadelphia. 1924. 15 p. Free.

WISCONSIN. **The Administration of the Aid to Dependent Children's Law (Mothers' Pension Law) in Wisconsin.**
By—State Board of Control. PUBLISHER—The same, Madison. 1921. 32 p. Free.

In addition to reports **presenting findings,** as listed above, a publication dealing with **methods of conducting** such studies will be found in Part III, PURPOSE, METHOD, AND STANDARDS, under **Cost of Living.**

DEPORTATION

UNITED STATES. **Deportation Cases of 1919–1920.** A study.
By—Constantine M. Panunzio. PUBLISHER—Federal Council, Churches of Christ in America, New York City. 1921. 100 p. 50 cents.

DESERTION

ILLINOIS, CHICAGO. **Study of Family Desertion.**
By—Earle Edward Eubank. PUBLISHER—Department of Public Welfare, Chicago. 1916. 73 p. Free.

UNITED STATES. **Five Hundred and Seventy-Four Deserters and Their Families.** A descriptive study of their characteristics and circumstances.
By—Lilian Brandt. PUBLISHER—Charity Organization Society, New York City. 1905. 57 p. Out of print.

DETENTION

CANADA, TORONTO. **The Detention Home.** Interim report on the Juvenile Court of Toronto.
By—Joseph E. Howes, Director. PUBLISHER—Bureau of Municipal Research, Toronto. 1920. 14 p. Free.

ILLINOIS, COOK COUNTY. **Juvenile Detention Home.** Report of an investigation.
By—Special Committee of the Board of Commissioners. PUBLISHER—Chicago Municipal Reference Library. 1917. 16 p. Postage.

ILLINOIS, COOK COUNTY. **The Juvenile Detention Home in Relation to Juvenile Court Policy.** A study of intake in the Cook County, Chicago, Juvenile Detention Home.
By—Savilla Millis. PUBLISHER—Board of Commissioners of Cook County, Chicago. 1927. 96 p. Free.

MISSOURI, ST. LOUIS. **The Juvenile Detention Home of St. Louis.**
By—Hastings H. Hart. PUBLISHER—Missouri Welfare League, St. Louis. 1924. 8 p. Free.

UNITED STATES. **Detention Houses and Reformatories as Protective Social Agencies in the Campaign of the United States Government against Venereal Diseases.**
By—Mary Macey Dietzler. PUBLISHER—Superintendent of Documents, Government Printing Office, Washington, D. C. 1922. 227 p. 15 cents.

DISABLED

See CRIPPLED, DISABLED, AND HANDICAPPED.

SURVEYS IN SPECIALIZED FIELDS

DISASTER

NOVA SCOTIA, HALIFAX. **Catastrophe and Social Change, Based upon a Sociological Study of the Halifax Disaster.** Columbia University Studies in History, Economics, and Public Law. Vol. 94, No. 1.
 BY—S. H. Prince. PUBLISHER—Columbia University, New York City. 1920. 151 p. $2.25.

DISEASE OF THE EYE

 See BLINDNESS, SIGHT CONSERVATION, AND DISEASE OF THE EYE.

DISPENSARIES

 See CLINICS AND DISPENSARIES.

DOMESTIC WORKERS

MARYLAND, BALTIMORE. **Domestic Workers and Their Employment Relations.** A study based on the records of the Domestic Efficiency Association of Baltimore. U. S. Department of Labor. Bulletin of the Women's Bureau No. 39.
 BY—Mary V. Robinson. PUBLISHER—Superintendent of Documents, Government Printing Office, Washington, D. C. 1924. 87 p. 15 cents.

EDUCATION

Reports dealing with the general subject of education are listed here. For reports dealing with specific phases of this subject or with education in connection with other subjects see BLINDNESS, SIGHT CONSERVATION, AND DISEASE OF THE EYE; CARDIACS; CHILD LABOR; CHILD WELFARE; CONTINUATION AND PART-TIME SCHOOLS; CRIPPLED, DISABLED, AND HANDICAPPED; DEAF; FEEBLEMINDED; IMMIGRATION AND AMERICANIZATION; INDUSTRIAL CONDITIONS AND RELATIONS; INDUSTRIAL EDUCATION; KINDERGARTENS; LIBRARIES; LOANS; MENTAL HYGIENE; NEGRO EDUCATION; PENSIONS; PRE-SCHOOL; PRISONS; RECREATION; REFORMATORIES; RELIGIOUS EDUCATION; RURAL EDUCATION; SCHOOL BUILDINGS AND PLANTS; SCHOOL HEALTH AND SANITATION; SCHOOL ORGANIZATION AND ADMINISTRATION; SUB-NORMAL, RETARDED, AND EXCEPTIONAL CHILDREN; TRACHOMA; TRUANCY AND NON-ATTENDANCE; and VOCATIONAL GUIDANCE AND TRAINING.

EDUCATION—Continued

AFRICA. **Education in Africa.** A study of West, South, and Equatorial Africa by the African Educational Commission.
>By—Thomas Jesse Jones. PUBLISHER—Phelps-Stokes Fund, New York City. 1922. 223 p. Cloth $2.00.

ALABAMA. EDUCATION IN ALABAMA.
Alabama's Public School System: a Comparative Study. By State Department of Education. 1916. 32 p.
A Comparative Study of the Elementary Schools, White and Colored, of the 67 Counties of Alabama. By Thomas E. Benner. 1921. 14 p.
>PUBLISHER—State Department of Education, Montgomery. Out of print.

ALABAMA. **An Educational Study of Alabama.** U. S. Department of Interior. Bureau of Education Bulletin, 1919, No. 41.
>By—Harold W. Foght and Samuel P. Capen. PUBLISHER—Superintendent of Documents, Government Printing Office, Washington, D. C. 1919. 522 p. Out of print.

ALABAMA; COVINGTON, MACON, AND MORGAN COUNTIES. **Educational Survey of Three Counties in Alabama.** Bulletin No. 43.
>By—N. R. Baker and J. L. Shibley. PUBLISHER—Alabama Department of Education, Montgomery. 1914. 179 p. 15 cents.

ALASKA. EDUCATION IN ALASKA.
Survey of Education in Alaska. By Sheldon Jackson. 1886. 88 p. Out of print.
Reports of an Investigation of the Conditions of Educational and School Service in the District of Alaska. By Frank C. Churchill. 1906. 176 p. Out of print.
The Work of the Bureau of Education for the Natives of Alaska. Bureau of Education Bulletin, 1921, No. 35. By Bureau of Education. 1921. 12 p. 5 cents.
>PUBLISHER—Superintendent of Documents, Government Printing Office, Washington, D. C.

ALASKA. **Education in the Territories and Dependencies [Alaska, Canal Zone, Hawaii, Philippines, Porto Rico, Virgin Islands].** U. S. Department of Interior. Bureau of Education Bulletin, 1919, No. 12.
>By—Bureau of Education. PUBLISHER—Superintendent of Documents, Government Printing Office, Washington, D. C. 1919. 71 p. 10 cents.

SURVEYS IN SPECIALIZED FIELDS

EDUCATION—Continued

ARIZONA. **Educational Conditions in Arizona.** U. S. Department of Interior. Bureau of Education Bulletin, 1917, No. 44.
> By—Bureau of Education. PUBLISHER—Superintendent of Documents, Government Printing Office, Washington, D. C. 1918. 200 p. 35 cents.

ARIZONA. **A Survey of the Arizona Public School System.** A study of the elementary and secondary public schools of the state.
> By—C. Ralph Tupper, Director. PUBLISHER—State Board of Education, Phoenix. 1925. 112 p. Free.

ARIZONA, MARICOPA COUNTY. **Report of the School Survey Made in Maricopa County.**
> By—Maricopa County Teachers' Association. PUBLISHER—The same, Phoenix. 1916. 8 p. Out of print.

ARIZONA, TUCSON. **Report of a Survey of the University of Arizona.** U. S. Department of Interior. Bureau of Education Bulletin, 1922, No. 36.
> By—Park R. Kolbe, L. E. Blauch and George F. Zook. PUBLISHER—Superintendent of Documents, Government Printing Office, Washington, D. C. 1922. 89 p. 10 cents.

ARKANSAS. **Report on the Higher Educational Institutions of Arkansas.** U. S. Department of Interior. Bureau of Education Bulletin, 1922, No. 7.
> By—G. F. Zook. PUBLISHER—Superintendent of Documents, Government Printing Office, Washington, D. C. 1922. 18 p. 5 cents.

ARKANSAS. **The Public School System of Arkansas.** Part I. Digest of the General Report. U. S. Department of Interior. Bureau of Education Bulletin, 1923, No. 10.
> By—Bureau of Education. PUBLISHER—Superintendent of Documents, Government Printing Office, Washington, D. C. 1923. 79 p. 10 cents.

ARKANSAS, FAYETTEVILLE. **Educational Survey of the University of Arkansas.** Summary of conclusions and recommendations.
> By—George F. Zook, Director. PUBLISHER—University of Arkansas, Fayetteville. 1921. 43 p. Free.

ARKANSAS, FORT SMITH. **Educational Survey of Fort Smith.**
> By—College of Education, University of Arkansas. PUBLISHER—Board of Education, Fort Smith. 1920. 69 p. Free.

A BIBLIOGRAPHY OF SOCIAL SURVEYS

EDUCATION—Continued

CALIFORNIA. Report of the Special Legislative Committee on Education as Authorized by Senate Concurrent Resolution No. 21.
    By—The Committee. PUBLISHER—State Department of Education, Sacramento. 1920. 96 p. Free.

CALIFORNIA, BAKERSFIELD. **A Survey of Pupils in the Schools of Bakersfield.** Research Bulletin No. 9.
    By—J. Harold Williams. PUBLISHER—Whittier State School, Whittier. 1920. 43 p. 20 cents.

CALIFORNIA, NEVADA COUNTY. **Report of the Survey of the Schools of Nevada County.** Bulletin No. 28.
    By—Margaret S. McNaught. PUBLISHER—State Board of Education, Sacramento. 1921. 23 p. Free.

CALIFORNIA, SAN FRANCISCO. **Some Conditions in the Schools of San Francisco.**
    By—California Branch, Association of Collegiate Alumnæ. PUBLISHER—School Survey Class, San Francisco. 1914. 96 p. 20 cents.

CALIFORNIA, SAN FRANCISCO. **Public School System of San Francisco.** A report to the San Francisco Board of Education of a survey made under the direction of the United States Commissioner of Education. U. S. Department of Interior. Bureau of Education Bulletin, 1917, No. 46.
    By—P. P. Claxton, Director. PUBLISHER—Superintendent of Documents, Government Printing Office, Washington, D. C. 1917. 649 p. 60 cents.

CALIFORNIA, VALLEJO. **A Survey of the Educational Program, Organization and Administration, School Finances, and School Housing of Vallejo.**
    By—F. W. Hart and L. H. Peterson, Directors. MIMEOGRAPHED—Board of Education, Vallejo. 1926. 110 p. $1.00.

CANADA. **Education in the Maritime Provinces of Canada.** Bulletin No. 16.
    By—William S. Learned and Kenneth C. M. Sills. PUBLISHER—Carnegie Foundation for the Advancement of Teaching, New York City. 1922. 50 p. Free.

CANADA. *See also* UNITED STATES in this section.

SURVEYS IN SPECIALIZED FIELDS

EDUCATION—Continued

CANADA, SASKATCHEWAN. **Survey of Education in the Province of Saskatchewan.**
> By—Harold W. Foght. PUBLISHER—Province of Saskatchewan, REGINA. 1918. 183 p. Free.

CANAL ZONE. *See* ALASKA in this section.

COLORADO. **A General Survey of Public High School Education in Colorado.** University Bulletin. Vol. XIV, No. 10.
> By—William A. Cook. PUBLISHER—University of Colorado, Boulder. 1914. 92 p. Out of print.

COLORADO, ARCHULETA COUNTY. **A Survey of the Public Schools of Archuleta County.** University Bulletin. Vol. XX, No. 2.
> By—Frank L. Clapp, Alice Noland, and George Wheatley. PUBLISHER—University of Colorado, Boulder. 1920. 21 p. Free.

COLORADO, DENVER. **Report of the Survey of School District No. 1 in the City and County of Denver.** Part II. The Work of the Schools.
> By—Frank Bobbitt and Charles H. Judd. PUBLISHER—School Survey Committee, Denver. 1916. 180 p. Free.

COLORADO, FRUITA. **An Educational Survey of the Fruita Union High School District.**
> By—Samuel Quigley and others. PUBLISHER—Board of Education, Fruita. 1921. 111 p. 50 cents.

COLORADO, GRAND JUNCTION. **A Survey of the City Schools of Grand Junction.**
> By—Frank L. Clapp. PUBLISHER—Department of Education, Grand Junction. 1916. 64 p. Free.

COLORADO, STERLING. **A Self-Survey of the Sterling Public Schools.**
> By—Survey Committee. PUBLISHER—Colorado State Teachers College, Greeley. 1917. 82 p. Free.

CONNECTICUT. **Report of the Special Educational Commission.**
> By—The Commission. PUBLISHER—State of Connecticut, Hartford. 1909. 14 p. Free.

CONNECTICUT. EDUCATIONAL INQUIRIES.
  Chaplin. Bulletin 49. 1917. 23 p.
  East Windsor. Bulletin 45. 1917. 34 p.
  Glastonbury. Bulletin 29. 1916. 37 p.
  Kent. Bulletin 56. 1907. 33 p.
  Middlefield. Bulletin 55. 1917. 23 p.

A BIBLIOGRAPHY OF SOCIAL SURVEYS

EDUCATION—Continued
  New Hartford. Bulletin 30. 1917. 33 p.
  Newton. Bulletin 44. 1917. 43 p.
  North Stonington. Bulletin 32. 1916. 29 p.
  Seymour. Bulletin 30. 1916. 26 p.
  Trumbull. Bulletin 53. 1917. 29 p.
  Westbrook. Bulletin 33. 1917. 23 p.
      By—E. W. Ireland, N. S. Light, and G. S. Swift. PUBLISHER—State Board of Education, Hartford. Free.

CONNECTICUT. **Survey of the Writing Vocabularies of Public School Children in Connecticut.** U. S. Department of Interior. Bureau of Education Teacher's Leaflet No. 15.
      By—Williard F. Tidyman. PUBLISHER—Superintendent of Documents, Government Printing Office, Washington, D. C. 1921. 18 p. 5 cents.

CONNECTICUT, BRIDGEPORT. **Report of the Examination of the School System of Bridgeport.**
      By—J. H. VanSickle. PUBLISHER—Board of Education, Bridgeport. 1913. 129 p. Out of print.

CONNECTICUT, GREENWICH. **Report of the Special Committee and Town School Committee of Greenwich with Reference to the Needs of the Town as to Enlarged School Accommodations.**
      By—The Committee. PUBLISHER—City of Greenwich. 1911. 11 p. Out of print.

CONNECTICUT, STAMFORD. **The Mirror: As We See Ourselves, Stamford Public Schools.** A partial "Auto Survey" for the period September, 1916, to February, 1918.
      By—City Department of Education. PUBLISHER—The same, Stamford. 1918. 28 p. Free.

CONNECTICUT, STAMFORD. **Report of the Survey of the Public School System of the Town of Stamford.**
      By—Institute of Educational Research, Teachers College. PUBLISHER—Bureau of Publications, Teachers College, Columbia University, New York City. 1923. 237 p. $1.00.

CONNECTICUT, WATERBURY. **Help Your School Surveys: Waterbury Public Schools; Classroom Instruction in St. Paul.**
      By—Bureau of Municipal Research of New York City. PUBLISHER—The same. 1913. 32 p. 15 cents.

SURVEYS IN SPECIALIZED FIELDS

EDUCATION—Continued

CONNECTICUT, WEST HARTFORD. **A Survey of the Schools of West Hartford.**
> BY—Alfred D. Simpson, Director. PUBLISHER—Town School Committee of West Hartford and State Board of Education, Hartford. 1923. 151 p. Free.

DELAWARE. **Public Education in Delaware.** A report to the Public School Commission of Delaware.
> BY—General Education Board. PUBLISHER—The same, New York City. 1919. 202 p. Free.

DELAWARE, WILMINGTON. **Survey of the Schools of Wilmington.** Part II. Elementary and Secondary Courses and Special Departments. U. S. Department of Interior. Bureau of Education Bulletin, 1921, No. 2.
> BY—Frank F. Bunker, Director. PUBLISHER—Superintendent of Documents, Government Printing Office, Washington, D. C. 1921. 191 p. 25 cents.

DISTRICT OF COLUMBIA. **Preliminary Survey of the Schools of the District of Columbia.** U. S. Department of Interior. Bureau of Education Bulletin, 1920, No. 36.
> BY—P. P. Claxton. PUBLISHER—Superintendent of Documents, Government Printing Office, Washington, D. C. 1920. 15 p. 5 cents.

EUROPE. **Medical Education in Europe.** Bulletin No. 6.
> BY—Abraham Flexner and Henry C. Pritchett. PUBLISHER—Carnegie Foundation for the Advancement of Teaching, New York City. 1912. 357 p. Free.

FLORIDA. **A Study of Florida High Schools.** University of Florida Record. Vol. XVI, No. 4.
> BY—Joseph Roemer. PUBLISHER—University of Florida, Gainsville. 1921. 29 p. Free.

FLORIDA, TAMPA. **Report of the Survey of the Schools of Tampa.**
> BY—Institute of Educational Research, Teachers College. PUBLISHER—Bureau of Publications, Teachers College, Columbia University, New York City. 1926. 304 p. $1.50.

GEORGIA. EDUCATIONAL SURVEYS OF GEORGIA COUNTIES.
Bacon County. No. 38. 1922. 40 p. Out of print.
Ben Hill County. No. 24. 1918. 27 p. Out of print.

EDUCATION—Continued

Brooks County. No. 15. 1917. 25 p. Out of print.
Bulloch County. No. 10. 1915. 78 p. Out of print.
Candler County. No. 22. 1918. 29 p. Out of print.
Carroll County. No. 25. 1918. 79 p. Out of print.
Clayton and Taliaferro Counties. Nos. 2 and 3. 1915. 23 p. Out of print.
Dekalb and Union Counties. Nos. 13 and 14. 1916. 70 p. Out of print.
Dooly County. No. 37. 1922. 60 p. Free.
Grady County. No. 39. 1922. 59 p. Free.
Gwinnett County. No. 42. 1923. 80 p. Free.
Hart County. No. 16. 1917. 25 p. Out of print.
Heard County. No. 17. 1917. 28 p. Out of print.
Jackson County. No. 4. 1915. 64 p. Out of print.
Johnson County. No. 32. 1921. 59 p. Out of print.
Jones County. No. 20. 1918. 40 p. Out of print.
Laurens County. No. 30. 1921. 94 p. Out of print.
Lee County. No. 28. 1920. 25 p. Out of print.
Miller County. No. 29. 1920. 48 p. Free.
Morgan County. 1915. 77 p. Out of print.
Rabun County. No. 1. 1914. 48 p. Out of print.
Seminole County. No. 41. 1923. 21 p. Free.
Spalding County. No. 18. 1917. 31 p. Out of print.
Stephens County. No. 36. 1922. 36 p. Free.
Tatnall County. No. 11. 1916. 46 p. Out of print.
Thomas County. No. 31. 1921. 38 p. Out of print.
Tift County. No. 23. 1918. 44 p. Out of print.
Towns County. No. 19. 1917. 30 p. Out of print.
Warren County. No. 27. 1919. 39 p. Free.
Wilkes County. No. 40. 1922. 51 p. Free.

> By—M. L. Duggan and others. PUBLISHER—State Department of Education, Atlanta.

GEORGIA, ATLANTA. **Report of Survey of the Department of Health and the Department of Education.**

> By—S. G. Lindholm. PUBLISHER—Atlanta Chamber of Commerce. 1912. 44 p. Out of print.

GEORGIA, ATLANTA. **Survey of the Atlanta Public Schools.**

> By—C. S. Parish. PUBLISHER—Board of Education, Atlanta. 1914. 33 p. 2 cents postage.

SURVEYS IN SPECIALIZED FIELDS

EDUCATION—Continued

GEORGIA, ATLANTA. REPORT OF THE SURVEY OF THE PUBLIC SCHOOL SYSTEM OF ATLANTA.
Vol. I. Survey of the Public School Buildings and the School Building Program for Atlanta. By N. L. Engelhardt. 260 p.
Vol. II. The Organization and Administration of the School System, School Costs, Classification and Progress of Children, the Teaching Corps, and the Educational Program of the Schools. By N. L. Engelhardt and E. S. Evenden. 255 p.
BY—George D. Strayer, Director. PUBLISHER—Board of Education, Atlanta. 1924. $1.00 each.

GEORGIA, BRUNSWICK AND GLYNN COUNTY. Survey of the Schools of Brunswick and Glynn County. U. S. Department of Interior. Bureau of Education Bulletin, 1920, No. 27.
BY—Frank F. Bunker, Katharine M. Cook, and Alice Barrows. PUBLISHER—Superintendent of Documents, Government Printing Office, Washington, D. C. 1920. 82 p. 15 cents.

GEORGIA, DECATUR. Educational Survey of Decatur Public School System. No. 26.
BY—M. L. Duggan. PUBLISHER—State Department of Education, Atlanta. 1918. 56 p. Out of print.

HAWAII. A Survey of Education in Hawaii. U. S. Department of Interior. Bureau of Education Bulletin, 1920, No. 16.
BY—Commissioner of Education. PUBLISHER—Superintendent of Documents, Government Printing Office, Washington, D. C. 1920. 408 p. 50 cents.

HAWAII. See also ALASKA in this section.

IDAHO, BOISE. BOISE SCHOOL SURVEYS.
First Boise School Survey. By C. N. Kendall. 1910. 8 p.
Expert Survey of Public School System. By E. C. Elliott and others. 1913. 31 p.
Special Report of the Boise Public Schools. By E. C. Elliott, C. H. Judd, and George D. Strayer. 1915. 96 p.
PUBLISHER—Board of Education, Boise. Out of print.

IDAHO, BOISE. The Boise Survey. The best available concrete study of a small city school system.
BY—J. B. Sears and others. PUBLISHER—World Book Company, Yonkers, New York. 1920. 290 p. $2.40.

EDUCATION—Continued

ILLINOIS. **Illinois School Survey.** A co-operative investigation of school conditions and school efficiency.
>By—L. D. Coffman, Director. PUBLISHER—Illinois Teachers' Association, Springfield. 1917. 377 p. Out of print.

ILLINOIS. **A Statistical Survey of Illinois Colleges.**
>By—B. Warren Brown. PUBLISHER—Council of Church Board of Education, Chicago. 1917. 78 p. 30 cents.

ILLINOIS, ALTON. **Findings and Recommendations of the Survey of the Alton Public Schools.**
>By—Special Committee on School Survey. PUBLISHER—Board of Education, Alton. 1918. 87 p. Out of print.

ILLINOIS, CHICAGO. **Report of the Educational Commission of Chicago.**
>By—The Commission. PUBLISHER—The same. 1897. 249 p. Out of print.

ILLINOIS, CHICAGO. STUDIES OF CHICAGO SCHOOLS.
Report on Child Study Investigation in Chicago Public Schools. By W. S. Christopher. 1899. 48 p.
Survey of Chicago Public Schools. By Ella Flagg Young. 1914. 257 p.
Report of the Superintendent of Schools to the Committee on Survey. By the Superintendent. 1917. 16 p.
>PUBLISHER—Board of Education, Chicago. Out of print.

ILLINOIS, MARION. **A Survey of the City Schools of Marion.** University Bulletin. Vol. XXII, No. 3.
>By—Bureau of Educational Research. PUBLISHER—University of Illinois, Urbana. 1924. 60 p. 50 cents.

ILLINOIS, SPRINGFIELD. **The Public Schools of Springfield.** Educational Section of the Springfield Survey.
>By—Leonard P. Ayres. PUBLISHER—Russell Sage Foundation, New York City. 1915. 152 p. 25 cents.

ILLINOIS, WINNETKA. **A Survey of the Winnetka Public Schools.** Results of practical experiments in fitting schools to individuals. Under a subvention from the Commonwealth Fund.
>By—Carleton Washburne, Mabel Vogel, and William S. Gray. PUBLISHER—Public School Publishing Company, Bloomington. 1926. 135 p. Out of print.

SURVEYS IN SPECIALIZED FIELDS

EDUCATION—Continued

INDIANA. **The Intelligence of High School Seniors as Revealed by a State Wide Mental Survey of Indiana High Schools.**
  By—William F. Book. PUBLISHER—Macmillan Company, New York City. 1922. 371 p. $2.40.

INDIANA. **Public Education in Indiana.** A report of the Indiana Education Survey Commission.
  By—Frank P. Bachman, Director. PUBLISHER—General Education Board, New York City. 1923. 304 p. Free.

INDIANA, BLOOMINGTON. **Survey of a Public School System.** Columbia University Contributions to Education No. 82. Teachers College Series.
  By—Henry Lester Smith. PUBLISHER—Bureau of Publications, Teachers College, Columbia University, New York City. 1917. 304 p. $2.25.

INDIANA, GARY. **The Public School System of Gary.** U. S. Department of Interior. Bureau of Education Bulletin, 1914, No. 18. Whole No. 591.
  By—William Paxton Burris. PUBLISHER—Superintendent of Documents, Government Printing Office, Washington, D. C. 1914. 53 p. 15 cents.

INDIANA, GARY. GARY PUBLIC SCHOOLS.
  A General Account. By Alexander Flexner and F. P. Bachman. 1918. 265 p. 25 cents.
  Industrial Work. By Charles R. Richards. 1918. 204 p. 25 cents.
  Physical Training and Play. By Lee F. Hanmer. 1918. 35 p. 10 cents.
  Household Arts. By Eva W. White. 1918. 49 p. 10 cents.
  Science Teaching. By Otis W. Caldwell. 1919. 125 p. 10 cents.
  Measurement of Classroom Products. By Stuart A. Courtis. 1919. 532 p. 30 cents.
    PUBLISHER—General Education Board, New York City.

INDIANA, GREENE COUNTY. **Educational Survey of Greene County.**
  By—Daniel C. McIntosh. PUBLISHER—University of Indiana, Bloomington. 1916. 110 p. 50 cents.

INDIANA, SOUTH BEND. **The Public Schools of South Bend.** A survey conducted by the Department of Education of the University of Chicago. In the Biennial Report of the Superintendent of Schools.
  By—J. F. Bobbitt. PUBLISHER—Board of Education, South Bend. 1914. 92 p. Free.

EDUCATION—Continued

INDIANA, VERMILION COUNTY. **A Partial Survey of the Schools of Vermilion County.**
> BY—Roy Herbert Valentine. PUBLISHER—University of Indiana, Bloomington. 1919. 86 p. $1.00.

IOWA. **Higher Educational Institutions of Iowa.** A report to the Iowa State Board of Education of a survey made under the direction of the Commissioner of Education. U. S. Department of Interior. Bureau of Education Bulletin, 1916, No. 19.
> BY—P. P. Claxton. PUBLISHER—Superintendent of Documents, Government Printing Office, Washington, D. C. 1916. 223 p. 25 cents.

IOWA. **A Mental Educational Survey of 1550 Iowa High School Seniors.** Studies in Education. Vol. II, No. 5. First Series No. 72.
> BY—G. M. Ruch. PUBLISHER—University of Iowa, Iowa City. 1923. 29 p. 50 cents.

IOWA, CEDAR FALLS. THE INSIDE SURVEY.
Report of the Inside Survey. Bulletin Vol. XVII. Part II, No. 4. 113 p.
Supplement to the Report of the Inside Survey. Bulletin Vol. XXI. Part I, No. 2. 138 p.
> BY—Survey Committee, Iowa State Teachers College. PUBLISHER—The same, Cedar Falls. 1912. Free.

IOWA, DES MOINES. **Survey of the High Schools of Des Moines.** Extension Bulletin No. 37. First Series No. 18.
> BY—E. E. Lewis. PUBLISHER—University of Iowa, Iowa City. 1918. 64 p. Postage.

IOWA, DES MOINES. **A Survey of Musical Talent in the Public Schools.** Studies in Child Welfare. Vol. I, No. 2.
> BY—Carl E. Seashore. PUBLISHER—University of Iowa, Iowa City. 1920. 36 p. 25 cents.

IOWA, FORT DODGE. **A Partial Survey of the Public Schools of Fort Dodge.** Official Publication Vol. XVI, No. 36. Engineering Extension Bulletin No. 32.
> BY—Edward T. Snively. PUBLISHER—Iowa State College of Agriculture and Mechanic Arts. Ames. 1917. 19 p. Out of print.

IOWA, UNION. **A Survey of Some Phases of the Schools of Union.**
> BY—H. F. Martin and Leon O. Smith. PUBLISHER—Board of Education, Union. 1918. 15 p. 25 cents.

SURVEYS IN SPECIALIZED FIELDS

EDUCATION—Continued

KANSAS. **Results of Instruction in Different Types of Elementary Schools in the State of Kansas.** Report of a survey made for the State School Code Commission.
> BY—Survey Committee. PUBLISHER—State of Kansas, Topeka. 1922. 45 p. Free.

KANSAS. **Report of a Survey of the State Institutions of Higher Learning in Kansas.** U. S. Department of Interior. Bureau of Education Bulletin, 1923, No. 40.
> BY—George F. Zook, Lotus D. Coffman, and A. R. Mann. PUBLISHER—Superintendent of Documents, Government Printing Office, Washington, D. C. 1923. 159 p. 20 cents.

KANSAS, CHANUTE. **Survey Report of the Chanute School System.**
> BY—F. P. O'Brien and others. PUBLISHER—Bureau of School Service and Research, University of Kansas, Lawrence. 1924. 134 p. Free.

KANSAS, GREAT BEND. **School Survey Report for the City of Great Bend.**
> BY—F. P. O'Brien, R. A. Kent, and H. P. Smith. PUBLISHER—Bureau of School Service, University of Kansas, Lawrence. 1922. 37 p. Out of print.

KANSAS, LAWRENCE. **School Survey of Lawrence.** Report of a survey of certain features of the school system of Lawrence. University Bulletin. Vol. 23, No. 1.
> BY—F. P. O'Brien. PUBLISHER—University of Kansas, Lawrence. 1921. 100 p. Free.

KANSAS, LEAVENWORTH. **Report of a Survey of the Public Schools of Leavenworth.** University Bulletin. Vol. IV, New Series No. 2.
> BY—Walter S. Monroe, Director. PUBLISHER—Kansas State Normal School, Emporia. 1915. 202 p. Out of print.

KENTUCKY. **Public Education in Kentucky.** A report by the Kentucky Educational Commission.
> BY—Frank P. Bachman, Director. PUBLISHER—General Education Board, New York City. 1921. 213 p. Free.

KENTUCKY, LEXINGTON. **Report of the Survey Commission Appointed to Investigate the University of Kentucky.** University Bulletin. Vol. IX, No. 5.
> BY—The Commission. PUBLISHER—University of Kentucky, Lexington. 1917. 111 p. Free.

EDUCATION—Continued

KENTUCKY, PADUCAH. **Survey of the Public School System of Paducah.**
BY—Survey Staff, George Peabody College for Teachers. PUBLISHER—Board of Education, Paducah. 1919. 165 p. Free.

LOUISIANA, CADDO PARISH AND SHREVEPORT. **Survey of the Schools of Caddo Parish with Special Reference to the City of Shreveport.**
BY—Bureau of Education, U. S. Department of Interior. PUBLISHER—State Department of Education, Baton Rouge. 1922. 136 p. Free.

MAINE, AUGUSTA. **Report of the Survey Staff to the Board of Education.**
BY—Alexander Inglis, Director. PUBLISHER—Board of Education, Augusta. 1922. 242 p. $1.00.

MARYLAND. **Report of the Maryland Educational Commission.** Bulletin No. 2.
BY—The Commission. PUBLISHER—State Department of Education, Annapolis. 1910. 10 p. Out of print.

MARYLAND. **Report on the Educational Situation in Maryland by a Special Committee of the Board of State Aid and Charities.**
BY—Philip Briscoe, Thomas M. Bartlett, and H. Wirt Steele. PUBLISHER—State Board of Charities, Baltimore. 1914. 33 p. Out of print.

MARYLAND. **Public Education in Maryland.** A report to the Maryland Education Survey Commission.
BY—Abraham Flexner and Frank P. Bachman. PUBLISHER—General Education Board, New York City. 1921. 230 p. Free.

MARYLAND, BALTIMORE. **Report of the Commission Appointed to Study the System of Education in the Public Schools of Baltimore.** U. S. Department of Interior. Bureau of Education Bulletin, 1911, No. 4. Whole No. 450.
BY—Elmer Ellsworth Brown and others. PUBLISHER—Superintendent of Documents, Government Printing Office, Washington, D. C. 1911. 112 p. 30 cents.

MARYLAND, BALTIMORE. **Adjusting the School Work to the Child.** Results of a survey of three Baltimore schools. Publication No. 3.
BY—Charles B. Thompson. PUBLISHER—Mental Hygiene Society of Maryland, Baltimore. 1919. 16 p. Free.

MARYLAND, BALTIMORE. **Abstract of a Survey of Baltimore Public Schools.**
BY—George D. Strayer, Director. PUBLISHER—Board of School Commissioners, Baltimore. 1921. 53 p. Free.

SURVEYS IN SPECIALIZED FIELDS

EDUCATION—Continued

MARYLAND, BALTIMORE. **The School Curriculum.** Vol. III. The Baltimore School Survey.
> By—George D. Strayer, Director. PUBLISHER—City of Baltimore. 1921. 336 p. $5.00 with Volumes I and II.

Other volumes are listed elsewhere.

MARYLAND, LOCUST POINT [BALTIMORE]. **The Francis Scott Key School.** Report of a study of the school and local industries with reference to the enrichment of the school curriculum and the planning of new school buildings. U. S. Department of Interior. Bureau of Education Bulletin, 1920, No. 41.
> By—Charles A. Bennett. PUBLISHER—Superintendent of Documents, Government Printing Office, Washington, D. C. 1921. 31 p. 5 cents.

MASSACHUSETTS. **Report of the Special Commission on Education Appointed under the Authority of Chapter 88 of the Resolves of 1918 to Investigate the Educational System of the Commonwealth.** Senate No. 330.
> By—The Commission. PUBLISHER—State Department of Education, Boston. 1919. 197 p. Free.

MASSACHUSETTS. **Open-Air Schools.** The Commonhealth. Vol. 8, No. 1. January–February.
> By—Harriet L. Wedgwood. PUBLISHER—Massachusetts Department of Public Health, Boston. 1921. 67 p. Free.

MASSACHUSETTS. **A Comparison of the Intelligence and Training of School Children in a Massachusetts Town.** Harvard Monographs in Education. Whole No. 1, Series 1, No. 1.
> By—Edwin A. Shaw and Edward A. Lincoln. PUBLISHER—Graduate School of Education, Harvard University, Cambridge. 1922. 49 p. 60 cents.

MASSACHUSETTS. **Intelligence of Seniors in the High Schools of Massachusetts.** U. S. Department of Interior. Bureau of Education Bulletin, 1924, No. 9.
> By—Stephen S. Colvin and Andrew H. MacPhail. PUBLISHER—Superintendent of Documents, Government Printing Office, Washington, D. C. 1924. 38 p. 10 cents.

MASSACHUSETTS, BOSTON. **Report on the Boston School System by the Finance Commission of the City of Boston.**
> By—John A. Sullivan. PUBLISHER—City of Boston. 1911. 234 p. Free.

EDUCATION—Continued

MASSACHUSETTS, BROOKLINE. **Educational Survey of the Public Schools of Brookline.**
> BY—J. H. Van Sickle, George D. Strayer, and others. PUBLISHER—Department of Education, Brookline. 1917. 436 p. 75 cents.

MASSACHUSETTS, FALL RIVER. **The School Survey.** In Annual Report of the Public Schools, Fall River.
> BY—Ernest C. Moore. PUBLISHER—Board of Education, Fall River. 1917. 56 p. Out of print.

MASSACHUSETTS, HAVERHILL. **Annual Report and Summary of Survey of the Public Schools of the City of Haverhill.**
> BY—C. H. Dempsey. PUBLISHER—Department of Schools, Haverhill. 1919. 23 p. Out of print.

MASSACHUSETTS, LYNN. **Report of the Survey of the Schools of Lynn.** School Survey Series.
> BY—Institute of Educational Research, Teachers College. PUBLISHER—Bureau of Publications, Teachers College, Columbia University, New York City. 1927. 368 p. $1.50.

MASSACHUSETTS, NEW BEDFORD. **Principles, Policies, and Plans for the Improvement of the New Bedford Public Schools.**
> BY—Frank E. Spaulding. PUBLISHER—School Commissioners, New Bedford. 1922. 181 p. Out of print.

MASSACHUSETTS, SPRINGFIELD. **Survey Report of the Public School System of Springfield.** Institute of Educational Research.
> BY—George D. Strayer, Director. PUBLISHER—Bureau of Publications, Teachers College, Columbia University, New York City. 1924. 173 p. $1.25.

MASSACHUSETTS, WINCHESTER. **Survey of the Schools of Winchester.** U. S. Department of Interior. Bureau of Education Bulletin, 1920, No. 43.
> BY—Frank F. Bunker, Director. PUBLISHER—Superintendent of Documents, Government Printing Office, Washington, D. C. 1921. 193 p. 15 cents.

MICHIGAN. **Report of a School Survey of the Upper Peninsula of Michigan.**
> BY—Bureau of Research, Educational Association of the Upper Peninsula. PUBLISHER—The same, Marquette. 1913. 48 p. Out of print.

SURVEYS IN SPECIALIZED FIELDS

EDUCATION—Continued

MICHIGAN, DETROIT. STUDIES IN DETROIT PUBLIC SCHOOLS.
  A Survey of Teachers' Salaries in Detroit. Bulletin No. 1. By Arthur B. Moehlman. 1920. 47 p.
  A Preliminary Study of Standards of Growth in the Detroit Public Schools. Bulletin No. 5. By Paul C. Packer and Arthur B. Moehlman, 1921. 46 p.
  Age, Grade, and Nationality Survey. Bulletin No. 7. By Bureau of Statistics and Reference. 1922. 28 p.
    PUBLISHER—Board of Education, Detroit. Free.

MICHIGAN, GRAND RAPIDS. **School Survey of Grand Rapids.**
    BY—C. H. Judd. PUBLISHER—Board of Education, Grand Rapids. 1916. 510 p. $1.10.

MICHIGAN; KALAMAZOO, MARQUETTE, MT. PLEASANT, AND YPSILANTI.
  A Survey of the Needs of the Michigan State Normal Schools.
    BY—Arthur B. Moehlman. PUBLISHER—State Board of Education, Lansing. 1922. 250 p. Free.

MINNESOTA. **Public Education Commission's Report to the Governor.**
    BY—The Commission. PUBLISHER—State of Minnesota, St. Paul. 1914. 32 p. Free.

MINNESOTA, ARLINGTON AND SIBLEY COUNTY. **The Arlington School Survey Covering a Study of the Schools of Arlington and of Districts 14, 16, and 30 of Sibley County, Minnesota.** General Extension Division Bulletin. Vol. XXIV, No. 28.
    BY—J. B. Sears, Director. PUBLISHER—University of Minnesota, Minneapolis. 1921. 58 p. Free.

MINNESOTA, DULUTH. **Report of Educational Committee on the Duluth Public School System.**
    BY—E. A. Silberstein. PUBLISHER—Commercial Club of Duluth. 1918. 11 p. Free.

MINNESOTA, LAKE CRYSTAL. **Survey Report of the Lake Crystal Public Schools.** Educational Monograph No. 10.
    BY—Fred Engelhardt. PUBLISHER—University of Minnesota, Minneapolis. 1926. 100 p. 50 cents.

MINNESOTA, MINNEAPOLIS. REPORTS ON THE UNIVERSITY OF MINNESOTA.
  Part I. Growth of the University in the Next Quarter Century. Bulletin Vol. XXIII, No. 25. By Rodney M. West and L. V. Koos. 1920. 50 p. Out of print.

EDUCATION—Continued

Part II. **The Salary Situation and Cost of Living.** Bulletin Vol. XXIII, No. 45. By Albert J. Lobb. 1920. 56 p. Out of print.

Part III. **(a) Departments of the University. (b) Needs of the University.** Bulletin Vol. XXV, No. 5. 1922. 54 p. 50 cents.

Part IV. **The Instructional Service of the University.** Bulletin Vol. XXV, No. 6. 1922. 88 p. 75 cents.

Part V. **(a) University Income. (b) University Expenditures.** Bulletin Vol. XXV, No. 7. 1922. 62 p. 50 cents.

By—Survey Commission, University of Minnesota. PUBLISHER—University of Minnesota, Minneapolis.

MINNESOTA, ST. PAUL. **Report of a Survey of the School System of St. Paul.**

By—George D. Strayer and N. L. Engelhardt. Publisher—City Council, St. Paul. 1917. 962 p. $1.00.

MINNESOTA, ST. PAUL. See also CONNECTICUT, WATERBURY, in this section.

MISSISSIPPI. **Public Education in Mississippi.** Report of a commission appointed to make a study of the entire public education system and suggest improvements.

By—M. V. O'Shea, Director. PUBLISHER—State Department of Education, Jackson. 1926. 362 p. Free.

MISSOURI. **The Professional Preparation of Teachers for American Public Schools.** A study based upon an examination of tax-supported Normal Schools in the State of Missouri. Bulletin No. 14.

By—William S. Learned, William C. Bagley, Charles A. McMurry, George D. Strayer, Walter F. Dearborn, Isaac L. Kandel, and Homer W. Josselyn. PUBLISHER—Carnegie Foundation for the Advancement of Teaching, New York City. 1920. 475 p. Free.

MISSOURI. **Facts Concerning Public Education in Missouri.** Report of the Missouri School Survey.

By—Survey Staff. PUBLISHER—State Department of Education, Jefferson City. 1924. 139 p. Free.

MISSOURI, GENTRY COUNTY. **Survey of Gentry County Public Schools.** State Teachers College Bulletin. Vol. XVI, No. 3.

By—Burt W. Loomis, Director. PUBLISHER—State Teachers College, Maryville. 1922. 67 p. Free.

SURVEYS IN SPECIALIZED FIELDS

EDUCATION—Continued

MISSOURI, KANSAS CITY. **Kansas City, Missouri, Public Schools.** Bulletin No. 1.
> BY—Bureau of Research and Efficiency. PUBLISHER—Kansas City Public Schools. 1916. 89 p. Out of print.

MISSOURI, ST. LOUIS. **Report on Speech Defectives in the St. Louis Public Schools.** Reprinted from the Annual Report of the Board of Education. 1915–1916.
> BY—J. E. W. Wallin. PUBLISHER—Board of Education, St. Louis. 1916. 211 p. Free.

MISSOURI, ST. LOUIS. **Survey of the St. Louis Public Schools.** In 7 volumes.
> BY—Charles H. Judd and others. PUBLISHER—Board of Education, St. Louis. 1917. 961 p. Out of print.

MISSOURI, ST. LOUIS. **Survey of the St. Louis Public Schools.** In 3 parts.
> BY—Charles H. Judd and others. PUBLISHER—World Book Company, Yonkers, New York. 1918. 881 p. $6.00 per set.

MONTANA, BUTTE. **Report of a Survey of the School System of Butte.**
> BY—George D. Strayer, Director. PUBLISHER—Board of School Trustees, Butte. 1914. 163 p. 25 cents.

NEBRASKA, BUFFALO COUNTY. **A Study of Educational Inequalities. Being a Survey of Certain Aspects of Public Education in Buffalo County.**
> BY—Hans C. Olsen. PUBLISHER—Nebraska State Teachers College, Kearney. 1921. 163 p. $1.00.

NEVADA, RENO. **Report of a Survey of the University of Nevada.** U. S. Department of Interior. Bureau of Education Bulletin, 1917, No. 19.
> BY—Samuel P. Capen and Edwin B. Stevens. PUBLISHER—Superintendent of Documents, Government Printing Office, Washington, D. C. 1917. 184 p. 25 cents.

NEW JERSEY, BAYONNE. **A Study of the School Problem in Bayonne.**
> BY—Board of Education. PUBLISHER—The same, Bayonne. 1924. 73 p. Free.

NEW JERSEY, CRANFORD TOWNSHIP. **Report of the Survey of the Schools of the Township of Cranford.**
> BY—Division of Field Studies, Institute of Educational Research, Teachers College, Columbia University. PUBLISHER—Board of Education, Cranford. 1925. 70 p. Free.

EDUCATION—Continued

NEW JERSEY, EAST ORANGE. **Report of the Examination of the School System of East Orange.**
> BY—E. C. Moore. PUBLISHER—Board of Education, East Orange. 1912. 64 p. Out of print.

NEW JERSEY, FORT LEE. **Report of the Survey of the Schools of Fort Lee.** School Survey Series.
> BY—Division of Field Studies, Institute of Educational Research, Teachers College. PUBLISHER—Bureau of Publications, Teachers College, Columbia University, New York City. 1927. 136 p. 75 cents.

NEW JERSEY, HACKENSACK. **The Hackensack Schools.** Report of the survey of the public school system of Hackensack.
> BY—George D. Strayer and N. L. Engelhardt. PUBLISHER—Board of Education, Hackensack. 1921. 230 p. $1.00.

NEW JERSEY, HAMMONTON. **Report of the Survey of the Schools of the Town of Hammonton.**
> BY—Institute of Educational Research, Teachers College. PUBLISHER—Bureau of Publications, Teachers College, Columbia University, New York City. 1926. 131 p. 65 cents.

NEW JERSEY, MERCER COUNTY, LAWRENCE TOWNSHIP. **Report of the Survey of the Public School System of Lawrence Township, Mercer County.** Institute of Educational Research.
> BY—N. L. Engelhardt and E. S. Evenden. PUBLISHER—Bureau of Publications, Teachers College, Columbia University, New York City. 1922. 128 p. $1.00.

NEW JERSEY, MONTCLAIR. **Report on the Program of Studies in the Public Schools of Montclair with Some Comments on the School Plant and Its Equipment and Its Teaching.**
> BY—Paul H. Hanus. PUBLISHER—Board of Education, Montclair. 1911. 27 p. Out of print.

NEW JERSEY, MORRIS COUNTY, HANOVER TOWNSHIP. **A School Survey of Hanover Township.**
> BY—Elizabeth Hooker. PUBLISHER—Board of Education, Hanover Township, Morris Plains. 1923. 72 p. Out of print.

NEW JERSEY, NEWARK. **Nationality and Age-Grade Surveys.** Monograph No. 11.
> BY—Elmer K. Sexton. PUBLISHER—Public Schools of Newark. 1923. 45 p. 25 cents.

SURVEYS IN SPECIALIZED FIELDS

EDUCATION—Continued

NEW JERSEY, NEWARK. **The All Year Schools of Newark.**
> BY—Wilson Farrand and M. V. O'Shea. PUBLISHER—Board of Education, Newark. 1926. 96 p. Free.

NEW JERSEY, NEW BRUNSWICK. **Survey of Rutgers University.**
> BY—Arthur Jay Klein. PUBLISHER—United States Bureau of Education, Department of the Interior, Washington, D. C. 1927. 258 p. Free.

NEW JERSEY, THE ORANGES. **Report of the Study of School Systems of East Orange, Orange, South Orange, and West Orange.**
> BY—Women's Club of Orange. PUBLISHER—The same. 1922. 48 p. Free.

NEW JERSEY, PASSAIC. **The Problem of Adult Education in Passaic.** U. S. Department of Interior. Bureau of Education Bulletin, 1920, No. 4.
> BY—Alice B. Fernandez. PUBLISHER—Superintendent of Documents, Government Printing Office, Washington, D. C. 1920. 26 p. 10 cents.

NEW JERSEY, PATERSON. **The Paterson Public Schools.** A survey of school finance, school buildings, and the achievements of pupils.
> BY—George D. Strayer, Director. PUBLISHER—Board of Education, Paterson. 1918. 194 p. Out of print.

NEW MEXICO. **Report on the New Mexico State Educational Institutions to the New Mexico Special Revenue Commission.**
> BY—William C. Bagley. PUBLISHER—State Board of Education, Santa Fe. 1921. 62 p. Out of print.

NEW YORK. **Digest of the New York School Inquiry Submitted to the New York Board of Education.**
> BY—Bureau of Municipal Research. PUBLISHER—The same, New York City. 1913. 68 p. 25 cents.

NEW YORK. **Costs of Compulsory Attendance Service in the State of New York and Some Factors Affecting the Cost.**
> BY—Whittier Lorenz Hanson. PUBLISHER—Bureau of Publications, Teachers College, Columbia University, New York City. 1924. 121 p. $1.50.

NEW YORK. **A Study of Pupil Classification of the Villages of New York State.** Bulletin No. 841.
> BY—Warren W. Coxe. PUBLISHER—University of the State of New York, Albany. 1925. 59 p. 20 cents.

A BIBLIOGRAPHY OF SOCIAL SURVEYS

EDUCATION—Continued

NEW YORK, BINGHAMTON. **A Report of the Survey of the Binghamton School System.**
> BY—George M. Wiley, Director. PUBLISHER—State Department of Education, Albany. 1919. 209 p. Free.

NEW YORK, BUFFALO. **Examination of the Public School System of the City of Buffalo.**
> BY—Thomas E. Finegan, Director. PUBLISHER—State Department of Education, Albany. 1916. 208 p. Free.

NEW YORK, BUFFALO. **Adult Education in a Community.** A survey of the facilities existing in the city of Buffalo.
> BY—Buffalo Educational Council. PUBLISHER—American Association for Adult Education, New York City. 1926. 192 p. $1.00.

NEW YORK, DANSVILLE. **The Dansville High School.** A study.
> BY—J. Murray Foster. PUBLISHER—Board of Education, Dansville. 1915. 109 p. Out of print.

NEW YORK, GREAT NECK, LONG ISLAND. **Great Neck School Survey.**
> BY—George D. Strayer and M. G. Neale. PUBLISHER—Great Neck Association. 1917. 29 p. Out of print.

NEW YORK, LIVINGSTON COUNTY. **Survey of Livingston County Schools.** Bulletin No. 738.
> BY—University of the State of New York. PUBLISHER—The same, Albany. 1921. 143 p. Out of print.

NEW YORK, NASSAU COUNTY. **Report of a Survey of Public Education in Nassau County.** Bulletin No. 652.
> BY—L. S. Hawkins, George D. Strayer, and M. R. Trabue. PUBLISHER—University of the State of New York, Albany. 1918. 291 p. 25 cents.

NEW YORK CITY. **The Compulsory Attendance Service of New York City.** Bulletin No. 16.
> BY—Howard W. Nudd. PUBLISHER—Public Education Association, New York City. 1913. 20 p. 2 cents postage.

NEW YORK CITY. **Digest of the New York School Inquiry.**
> BY—Bureau of Municipal Research. PUBLISHER—The same, New York City. 1913. 85 p. Out of print.

NEW YORK CITY. **Report of the Committee on School Inquiry.** In 3 volumes.
> BY—The Committee. PUBLISHER—Committee on School Inquiry, New York City. 1913. 2573 p. Out of print.

SURVEYS IN SPECIALIZED FIELDS

EDUCATION—Continued

NEW YORK CITY. **School Efficiency.** A constructive study applied to New York City, being a summary and interpretation of the report on the educational aspects of the school inquiry.
>By—Paul H. Hanus. PUBLISHER—World Book Company, Yonkers, New York. 1913. 128 p. $1.60.

NEW YORK CITY (Brooklyn). **Report upon Divisions Four and Five, Elementary Schools.**
>By—William McAndrews. PUBLISHER—New York City Department of Education. 1915. 64 p. Out of print.

NEW YORK CITY. **Survey of the Gary and Prevocational Schools.** Reprinted from Seventeenth Annual Report of the City Superintendent of Schools. 1914–1915.
>By—Burdette R. Buckingham. PUBLISHER—Department of Education, New York City. 1916. 61 p. Out of print.

NEW YORK CITY. **Instruction in Civics in New York City High Schools.** A statistical survey. Bulletin No. 89.
>By—Anna M. Michener. PUBLISHER—Bureau of Municipal Research, New York City. 1917. 39 p. 25 cents.

NEW YORK CITY. **Private Commercial Schools: Manhattan and the Bronx.** Report of the Committee to Investigate Private Commercial Schools.
>By—Bertha Stevens. PUBLISHER—Public Education Association, New York City. 1918. 144 p. 20 cents.

NEW YORK CITY. **Self-Supporting Students in Certain New York City High Schools.** Studies in Social Work.
>By—Walter W. Pettit. PUBLISHER—New York School of Social Work, New York City. 1920. 87 p. 75 cents.

NEW YORK CITY. **Survey of Junior High Schools of New York City.**
>By—Special Survey Committee. PUBLISHER—Board of Education, New York City. 1923. 257 p. Free.

NEW YORK CITY. **Survey of the Educational Activities of the Young Men's Christian Association.**
>By—Institute of Educational Research, Teachers College. PUBLISHER—Young Men's Christian Association, New York City. 1923. 210 p. Free.

NEW YORK CITY. **Fitting the School to the Child.** An experiment in education.
>By—Elizabeth A. Irwin and Louis A. Marks. PUBLISHER—Macmillan Company, New York City. 1924. 339 p. $2.00.

A BIBLIOGRAPHY OF SOCIAL SURVEYS

EDUCATION—Continued

NEW YORK CITY. **A Study of the After-Career of Pupils of P. S. 120 Probationary.**
> BY—Bureau of Jewish Social Research. PUBLISHER—The same, New York City. 1926. 35 p. Free.

NEW YORK, NIAGARA FALLS. **The Niagara Falls School System.** Report of a survey.
> BY—State Department of Education. PUBLISHER—University of the State of New York Press, Albany. 1921. 223 p. Free.

NEW YORK, ROCHESTER. **Survey of the Needs in Commercial Education.**
> BY—Rochester Chamber of Commerce. PUBLISHER—The same. 1915. 18 p. Free.

NEW YORK, SYRACUSE. **Report of the Investigations for the Associated Charities of Syracuse.** Part I. Report on the Syracuse Public Schools. Part II. Report on the Syracuse Board of Health.
> BY—Horace Brittain and A. E. Shipley. PUBLISHER—Bureau of Municipal Research, New York City. 1912. 12 p. 10 cents.

NEW YORK, UTICA. **A Report of the Survey of the Utica School System.**
> BY—George M. Wiley. PUBLISHER—State Department of Education, Albany. 1919. 233 p. Free.

NEW YORK, WATERTOWN. **Report of the Survey of the Schools of Watertown.**
> BY—Institute of Educational Research, Teachers College, Columbia University. PUBLISHER—Board of Education, Watertown. 1926. 157 p. $1.50.

NEW YORK, WESTCHESTER COUNTY. **School Reports in Westchester County.** A study of local school conditions.
> BY—Alexander J. Inglis. PUBLISHER—Westchester County Research Bureau, White Plains. 1912. 15 p. Out of print.

NEW YORK, WESTCHESTER COUNTY. **Survey of the Need for Special Schools and Classes in Westchester County.** Bulletin No. 806.
> BY—J. Cayce Morrison, W. B. Cornell, and Warren W. Coxe. PUBLISHER—University of the State of New York, Albany. 1924. 29 p. 5 cents.

NORTH CAROLINA. **Public Education in North Carolina.** A report by the State Educational Commission.
> BY—General Education Board. PUBLISHER—The same, New York City. 1920. 137 p. Free.

SURVEYS IN SPECIALIZED FIELDS

EDUCATION—Continued

NORTH CAROLINA. **A Study of the Mill Schools of North Carolina.** Teachers College Contributions to Education No. 178.
> BY—John Harrison Cook. PUBLISHER—Bureau of Publications, Teachers College, Columbia University, New York City. 1925. 55 p. $1.25.

NORTH CAROLINA, ELIZABETH CITY. **Educational Survey of Elizabeth City.** A digest of the report of a survey made at the request of the Board of School Trustees under the direction of the United States Commissioner of Education. U. S. Department of Interior. Bureau of Education Bulletin, 1921, No. 26.
> BY—William T. Bawden. PUBLISHER—Superintendent of Documents, Government Printing Office, Washington, D. C. 1921. 43 p. 5 cents.

NORTH CAROLINA, ELIZABETH CITY. **High School Survey of Elizabeth City.**
> BY—Charles G. Maphis. PUBLISHER—University of Virginia, University. 1923. 48 p. Free.

NORTH CAROLINA, LENOIR COUNTY. **Survey of the Public Schools of Lenoir County.** Educational Publication No. 73. Division of Supervision No. 17.
> BY—L. C. Brogden, Director. PUBLISHER—State Department of Public Instruction, Raleigh. 1924. 233 p. Free.

NORTH CAROLINA, NEW HANOVER COUNTY. **Survey of the School System of New Hanover County.**
> BY—Shelton Phelps, Director. PUBLISHER—County Board of Education, Wilmington. 1920. 114 p. Free.

NORTH CAROLINA, ORANGE COUNTY. **A Study of the Public Schools in Orange County.** Extension Series No. 32.
> BY—L. A. Williams. PUBLISHER—University of North Carolina, Chapel Hill. 1919. 32 p. 25 cents.

NORTH CAROLINA, WINSTON-SALEM. **Study of the Winston-Salem Schools.**
> BY—L. A. Williams and J. H. Johnston. PUBLISHER—City of Winston-Salem. 1918. 93 p. Free.

NORTH DAKOTA. **Report of the Temporary Educational Commission.**
> BY—The Commission. PUBLISHER—The same, Grand Forks. 1912. 61 p. Out of print.

EDUCATION—Continued

NORTH DAKOTA. **State Higher Educational Institutions of North Dakota.** A report to the North Dakota State Board of Regents of a survey made under the direction of the U. S. Commissioner of Education. U. S. Department of Interior. Bureau of Education Bulletin, 1916, No. 27.
> BY—William T. Bawden, Edwin B. Craighead, and Lotus D. Coffman. PUBLISHER—Superintendent of Documents, Government Printing Office, Washington, D. C. 1917. 205 p. 30 cents.

OHIO. **Report of the Ohio State Survey Commission.** An intensive study of 659 rural village schools in 88 counties, and an extensive study of 9,000 school rooms and of 395 school systems.
> BY—H. L. Brittain, Director. PUBLISHER—Ohio State School Survey Commission, Columbus. 1914. 352 p. Postage.

OHIO, AKRON. **Report on the Schools of Akron, Made for the Educational Committee of the Akron Chamber of Commerce.**
> BY—H. L. Brittain and T. L. Hinckley. PUBLISHER—Chamber of Commerce, Akron. 1917. 234 p. Free.

OHIO, CLEVELAND. **Report of the Educational Commission Appointed by the Board of Education to Examine the Government, Supervision, and Course of Study of the Cleveland Public Schools.**
> BY—The Commission. PUBLISHER—Department of Education, Cleveland. 1906. 120 p. Out of print.

OHIO, CLEVELAND. THE CLEVELAND EDUCATION SURVEY.
  Child Accounting in the Public Schools. By Leonard P. Ayres. 68 p. 35 cents.
  Educational Extension. By Clarence A. Perry. 115 p. 35 cents.
  Household Arts and School Lunches. By Alice C. Boughton. 170 p. 35 cents.
  Measuring the Work of the Public Schools. By Charles Hubbard Judd. 291 p. 75 cents.
  Overcrowded Schools and the Platoon Plan. By Shattuck O. Hartwell. 77 p. 35 cents.
  The Teaching Staff. By Walter A. Jessup. 114 p. 35 cents.
  What the Schools Teach and Might Teach. By Franklin Bobbitt. 108 p. Out of print.
  The Cleveland School Survey (Summary Volume). By Leonard P. Ayres. 363 p. 75 cents.
> BY—Leonard P. Ayres, Director. PUBLISHER—Cleveland Foundation. 1916.

SURVEYS IN SPECIALIZED FIELDS

EDUCATION—Continued

OHIO, CLEVELAND. **Cleveland Public Schools.** The first of a series of surveys of the Department of Instruction.
    By—W. W. Theisen, Director. PUBLISHER—Cleveland Board of Education. 1922. 29 p. 50 cents.

OHIO, CLEVELAND. **Survey of Higher Education in Cleveland.**
    By—Survey Commission. PUBLISHER—Cleveland Foundation Committee. 1925. 487 p. $2.00.

OHIO, DAYTON. **Over-Age and Progress in the Public Schools of Dayton.**
    By—Arch M. Mandel, Director. PUBLISHER—Bureau of Municipal Research, Dayton. 1914. 20 p. Out of print.

OHIO, ELYRIA. **Educational Survey of Elyria, Made under the Direction of the U. S. Commissioner of Education.** U. S. Department of Interior. Bureau of Education Bulletin, 1918, No. 15.
    By—P. P. Claxton, Director. PUBLISHER—Superintendent of Documents, Government Printing Office, Washington, D. C. 1918. 300 p. 30 cents.

OHIO, FAIRFIELD COUNTY. **Survey of Educational Conditions in Fairfield County.**
    By—F. C. Landsittel. PUBLISHER—Department of Education, Columbus. 1921. 53 p. Free.

OKLAHOMA. **Public Education in Oklahoma.** A digest of a survey of public education in Oklahoma. U. S. Department of Interior. Bureau of Education Bulletin, 1923, No. 14.
    By—William T. Bawden, Director. PUBLISHER—Superintendent of Documents, Government Printing Office, Washington, D. C. 1923. 91 p. 15 cents.

OKLAHOMA; ALFALFA, GRADY, AND WAGONER COUNTIES. **School Survey Suggestions.**
    By—E. A. Duke. PUBLISHER—Department of Public Instruction, Oklahoma City. 1918. 130 p. Free.

OREGON. **County School Systems of Oregon.** The efficiency of Oregon counties in education.
    By—Fred L. Stetson and John C. Almack. PUBLISHER—State Department of Public Instruction, Salem. 1921. 26 p. Free.

OREGON, ASHLAND. **Constructive Survey of the Public School System of Ashland.** New Series Bulletin. Vol. XII, No. 11.
    By—F. C. Ayer, C. R. Frazier, and D. C. Sowers. PUBLISHER—University of Oregon, Eugene. 1915. 52 p. Free.

A BIBLIOGRAPHY OF SOCIAL SURVEYS

EDUCATION—Continued

OREGON, EUGENE. **Report of a Survey of the University of Oregon.** University Bulletin. Vol. XIII, No. 4.
 By—S. P. Capen. PUBLISHER—University of Oregon, Eugene. 1915. 28 p. Free.

OREGON, PORTLAND. **Report of the Survey of the Public School System of School District No. 1, City of Portland, Multnomah County.**
 By—Ellwood P. Cubberley, Director. PUBLISHER—City of Portland. 1913. 317 p. Out of print.

OREGON, PORTLAND. **The Portland Survey.**
 By—Ellwood P. Cubberley and others. PUBLISHER—World Book Company, Yonkers, New York. 1915. 441 p. $2.00.

OREGON, PORTLAND. **Report of Supplementary Survey of Portland Public Schools.**
 By—P. W. Horn. PUBLISHER—School Board, Portland. 1917. 64 p. Out of print.

PENNSYLVANIA, HONESDALE. **Educational Survey of Honesdale.**
 By—Daniel Wolford LaRue, Director. PUBLISHER—Honesdale School Board. 1921. 160 p. Free.

PENNSYLVANIA, PHILADELPHIA. REPORT OF THE SURVEY OF THE PUBLIC SCHOOLS OF PHILADELPHIA.
 Book II. **Administration, Finance, Elementary and High Schools.** 291 p.
 Book III. **Kindergartens, Continuation Schools, Junior High Schools, Home Economics, and Industrial Education.** 343 p.
 Book IV. **Art, Commercial Education, Foreign Languages, Health Education, School Libraries, Music, Science, and Social Studies.** 348 p.
 For Book I. *See* SCHOOL BUILDINGS AND PLANTS.
 By—State Department of Public Instruction. PUBLISHER—Public Education and Child Labor Association, Philadelphia. 1922. $5.00 for 4 Books.

PENNSYLVANIA, PHILADELPHIA. **Social Work in the First Grade of a Public School.** In the American Journal of Sociology. Vol. XXVIII, No. 4.
 By—Anna B. Pratt. PUBLISHER—University of Chicago Press. 1923. 7 p. 75 cents per copy.

SURVEYS IN SPECIALIZED FIELDS

EDUCATION—Continued

PENNSYLVANIA, PITTSBURGH. **Pittsburgh Schools.** In The Pittsburgh District Civic Frontage, The Pittsburgh Survey.
    BY—Lila Ver Planck North. PUBLISHER—Russell Sage Foundation, New York City. 1914. p. 217–306. Out of print.

PENNSYLVANIA, SCRANTON. **Survey of the Scranton Public Schools.** 1918–1920.
    BY—Board of Education. PUBLISHER—The same, Scranton. 1920. 240 p. Out of print.

PHILIPPINE ISLANDS. **A Survey of the Educational System of the Philippine Islands.**
    BY—Board of Educational Survey. PUBLISHER—Department of Public Instruction, Manila, P. I. [Available in United States through Bureau of Publications, Teachers College, Columbia University, New York City.] 1925. 677 p. $3.00.

PHILIPPINE ISLANDS. See also ALASKA in this section.

PORTO RICO. **A Study of Certain Social, Educational, and Industrial Problems in Porto Rico.**
    BY—Meyer Bloomfield. PUBLISHER—The Author, Boston, Massachusetts. 1912. 28 p. Out of print.

PORTO RICO. **A Survey of the Public Education System of Porto Rico.**
    BY—Paul Monroe, Director. PUBLISHER—Bureau of Publications, Teachers College, Columbia University, New York City 1926. 453 p. $3.50.

PORTO RICO. See also ALASKA in this section.

RHODE ISLAND, PROVIDENCE. **Report of the Survey of Certain Aspects of the Public School System of Providence.**
    BY—Division of Field Studies, Institute of Educational Research, Teachers College, Columbia University. PUBLISHER—Department of Public Schools, Providence. 1924. 222 p. Out of print.

RHODE ISLAND, SOUTH KINGSTOWN. **Survey of Public Schools of South Kingstown.** Rhode Island Education Circulars.
    BY—Survey Commission. PUBLISHER—Public Education Service, Providence. 1927. 15 p. Free.

SOUTH CAROLINA, COLUMBIA. **Public Schools of Columbia.** Report of a survey made under the direction of the U. S. Commissioner of

EDUCATION—Continued

Education. U. S. Department of Interior. Bureau of Education Bulletin, 1918, No. 28.
    By—F. F. Bunker, Director. PUBLISHER—Superintendent of Documents, Government Printing Office, Washington, D. C. 1918. 192 p. 20 cents.

SOUTH CAROLINA, OCONEE COUNTY. **Public School Survey of Oconee County.**
    By—Clemson Agricultural College, South Carolina, and Oconee County Board of Education. PUBLISHER—Clemson Agricultural College, Clemson College. 1923. 283 p. Free.

SOUTH DAKOTA. **The Educational System of South Dakota.** Report of a survey made under the direction of the United States Commissioner of Education. U. S. Department of Interior. Bureau of Education Bulletin, 1918, No. 31.
    By—P. P. Claxton. PUBLISHER—Superintendent of Documents, Government Printing Office, Washington, D. C. 1918. 304 p. 25 cents.

TENNESSEE, MEMPHIS. THE PUBLIC SCHOOL SYSTEM IN MEMPHIS. U. S. Department of Interior. Bureau of Education Bulletin, 1919, No. 50.
Part 2. Elementary and High Schools. 191 p. 20 cents.
Part 3. Civic Teaching. 60 p. 10 cents.
Part 4. Science Teaching. 23 p. 10 cents.
Part 5. Music Teaching. 74 p. 10 cents.
Part 6. Industrial Art, Home Economics, and Gardening. 48 p. 10 cents.
For Part 1, *See* SCHOOL ORGANIZATION AND ADMINISTRATION.
    By—Frank F. Bunker, Director. PUBLISHER—Superintendent of Documents, Government Printing Office, Washington, D. C. 1920.

TEXAS. TEXAS EDUCATIONAL SURVEY REPORT.
Vol. III. Secondary Education. 1924. 103 p.
Vol. IV. Educational Achievement. 1925. 233 p.
Vol. V. Courses of Study and Instruction. 1924. 524 p.
Vol. VI. Higher Education. 1925. 389 p.
Vol. VIII. General Report. 1925. 256 p.
Other volumes are listed elsewhere.
    By—George A. Works, Director. PUBLISHER—Texas Educational Survey Commission, Austin. Free.

SURVEYS IN SPECIALIZED FIELDS

EDUCATION—Continued

TEXAS, CALDWELL COUNTY. **The Schools of Caldwell County.** Teachers College. Bulletin. Vol. 13, No. 3.
>By—A. C. Burkholder. PUBLISHER—Southwest Texas State Teachers College, San Marcos. 1923. 33 p. Out of print.

TEXAS, EL PASO. **Survey of the City Schools of El Paso.** Publication, 1922, No. 1.
>By—Paul W. Horn. PUBLISHER—Board of Education, El Paso. 1922. 64 p. Free.

TEXAS, GALVESTON. **Survey of the Galveston Public Schools.** Bulletin No. 2630.
>By—Bureau of School Inquiry, Division of Extension, University of Texas. PUBLISHER—The same, Austin. 1926. 117 p. Free.

TEXAS, PORT ARTHUR. **Report of the Survey of the Schools of Port Arthur.** School Survey Series.
>By—Division of Field Studies, Institute of Educational Research, Teachers College. PUBLISHER—Bureau of Publications, Teachers College, Columbia University, New York City. 1926. 333 p. $1.50.

TEXAS, SAN ANTONIO. **The San Antonio Public School System.** A survey.
>By—J. F. Bobbitt. PUBLISHER—School Board, San Antonio. 1915. 257 p. 35 cents.

UNITED STATES. **Medical Education in the United States and Canada.** Bulletin No. 4.
>By—Abraham Flexner. PUBLISHER—Carnegie Foundation for the Advancement of Teaching, New York City. 1910. 346 p. Free.

UNITED STATES. **Comparative Study of Public School Systems in the Forty-eight States.**
>By—Division of Education, Russell Sage Foundation. PUBLISHER—The same, New York City. 1913. 32 p. Out of print.

UNITED STATES. **Report of the Committee on Teachers' Salaries and Cost of Living.**
>By—National Education Association. PUBLISHER—University of Chicago Press. 1913. 328 p. $2.00.

EDUCATION—Continued

UNITED STATES. **Jewish Students.** A survey dealing with the religious, educational, social, and fraternal activities among Jewish students at universities and colleges.
>By—Department of Synagogue and School Extension, Union of American Hebrew Congregations. PUBLISHER—The same, New York City. 1915. 28 p. Free.

UNITED STATES [APPALACHIAN MOUNTAINS]. **A Statistical Study of the Public Schools of the Southern Appalachian Mountains.** U. S. Department of Interior. Bureau of Education Bulletin, 1915, No. 11. Whole No. 636.
>By—Norman Frost. PUBLISHER—Superintendent of Documents, Government Printing Office, Washington, D. C. 1915. 71 p. 20 cents.

UNITED STATES [APPALACHIAN MOUNTAINS]. **Schools in the Bituminous Coal Regions of the Appalachian Mountains.** U. S. Department of Interior. Bureau of Education Bulletin, 1920, No. 21.
>By—W. S. Deffenbaugh. PUBLISHER—Superintendent of Documents, Government Printing Office, Washington, D. C. 1920. 31 p. 10 cents.

UNITED STATES. **Status of Certain Social Studies in High Schools.** U. S. Department of Interior. Bureau of Education Bulletin, 1923, No. 45.
>By—Harry H. Moore. PUBLISHER—Superintendent of Documents, Government Printing Office, Washington, D. C. 1923. 21 p. 5 cents.

UNITED STATES. **Dental Education in the United States and Canada.** Bulletin No. 19.
>By—William J. Gies. PUBLISHER—Carnegie Foundation for the Advancement of Teaching, New York City. 1926. 692 p. Free.

UTAH. **Survey of Education in Utah.** U. S. Department of Interior. Bureau of Education Bulletin, 1926, No. 18.
>By—John J. Tigert, Director. PUBLISHER—Superintendent of Documents, Government Printing Office, Washington, D. C. 1926. 510 p. 60 cents.

UTAH, OGDEN. **Report of the Ogden Public School Survey Commission.**
>By—W. S. Deffenbaugh. PUBLISHER—State Department of Education, Salt Lake City. 1914. 42 p. Free.

SURVEYS IN SPECIALIZED FIELDS

EDUCATION—Continued

UTAH, SALT LAKE CITY. **Report of a Survey of the School System of Salt Lake City.**
    BY—Ellwood P. Cubberley and others. PUBLISHER—Board of Education, Salt Lake City. 1915. 324 p. Out of print.

VERMONT. **Secondary Education in Vermont.** Middlebury College Bulletin. Vol. VI, No. 5.
    BY—Raymond McFarland. PUBLISHER—Middlebury College, Middlebury. 1912. 43 p. Free.

VERMONT. **Education in Vermont.** Bulletin No. 7.
    BY—Carnegie Foundation for the Advancement of Teaching. PUBLISHER—The same, New York City. 1914. 241 p. Free.

VERMONT. **Report of the Commission to Investigate the Educational System and Conditions in Vermont.**
    BY—The Commission. PUBLISHER—Department of Education, Montpelier. 1914. 391 p. Free.

VIRGINIA. **Report of the Virginia Educational Commission.** Senate Document No. 3.
    BY—The Commission. PUBLISHER—State of Virginia, Richmond. 1912. 102 p. Out of print.

VIRGINIA. VIRGINIA PUBLIC SCHOOLS.
Part I. **Reports of Education Commission on School Survey.** 1920. 400 p. $2.68.
Part II. **Educational Tests.** 1921. 235 p. $2.16.
    BY—Virginia Education Commission and Survey Staff. PUBLISHER—World Book Co., Yonkers, New York.

VIRGINIA. **School Attendance of Children Fourteen and Fifteen Years of Age in Virginia in 1925.** Publication No. 330.
    BY—Sara A. Brown. PUBLISHER—National Child Labor Committee, New York City. 1925. 8 p. 10 cents.

VIRGINIA, ALEXANDRIA. **Survey of the Schools of Alexandria.** U. S. Department of Interior. Bureau of Education Bulletin, 1923. No. 56.
    BY—W. S. Deffenbaugh, Director. PUBLISHER—Superintendent of Documents, Government Printing Office, Washington, D. C. 1924. 61 p. 10 cents.

VIRGINIA, RICHMOND. **Placement of Children in the Elementary Grades.** A study of the schools of Richmond. U. S. Department of Interior. Bureau of Education Bulletin, 1916, No. 3.
    BY—E. J. Hoke. PUBLISHER—Superintendent of Documents, Government Printing Office, Washington, D. C. 1916. 92 p. 10 cents.

EDUCATION—Continued

VIRGINIA, WINCHESTER. **Psychological and Educational Tests in the Public Schools of Winchester.** A report to the City School Board and the Handley Board of Trustees. University Record. Vol. VI, No. 6.
> BY—W. F. Dearborn and Alexander Inglis. PUBLISHER—University of Virginia, University. 1921. 54 p. Free.

VIRGIN ISLANDS. *See* ALASKA in this section.

WASHINGTON. **Survey of Educational Institutions of the State of Washington.** U. S. Department of Interior. Bureau of Education Bulletin, 1916, No. 26.
> BY—S. P. Capen, H. W. Foght, and Alexander Inglis. PUBLISHER—Superintendent of Documents, Government Printing Office, Washington, D. C. 1916. 228 p. 25 cents.

WASHINGTON, BLAINE. **A Survey of the Blaine Public Schools.** University Extension Journal. Vol. I, No. 3.
> BY—Herbert G. Lull, Director. PUBLISHER—University of Washington, Seattle. 1914. 165 p. 10 cents.

WASHINGTON, PORT TOWNSEND. **A Survey of the Port Townsend Public Schools.** Extension Series Publication No. 17.
> BY—Herbert G. Lull, Director. PUBLISHER—University of Washington, Seattle. 1915. 112 p. 10 cents.

WASHINGTON, SEATTLE. **Studies in Administrative Research: Time Allotment, the Curriculum, Upper Grade Organization, and Progress of Pupils.** Bulletin No. 1.
> BY—Fred C. Ayer. PUBLISHER—Board of Directors, Seattle. 1924. 117 p. 75 cents.

WEST VIRGINIA; BERKELEY, BRAXTON, BROOKS, GILMER, HARRISON, LOGAN, MARION, MONROE, UPSHUR, AND WETZEL COUNTIES. **School Survey of Type Counties of West Virginia.**
> BY—L. V. Cavins. PUBLISHER—State Department of Schools, Charleston. 1923. 77 p. 35 cents.

WEST VIRGINIA, GRAFTON. **Report of the Survey of the Grafton City Schools.**
> BY—J. N. Deahl and others. PUBLISHER—State Department of Free Schools, Charleston. 1913. 29 p. Free.

WEST VIRGINIA, MARSHALL COUNTY. **Educational Survey of the Schools of Clay District, Marshall County.**
> BY—Harry E. Carmichael. PUBLISHER—County Superintendent of Schools, Moundsville. 1922. 43 p. Out of print.

SURVEYS IN SPECIALIZED FIELDS

EDUCATION—Continued

WEST VIRGINIA, PHILIPPI. **Educational Survey of the Philippi School System.**
 By—L. V. Cavins. PUBLISHER—Board of Education, Philippi. 1923. 39 p. 25 cents.

WEST VIRGINIA, WHEELING. **Educational Survey of Wheeling.** U. S. Department of Interior. Bureau of Education Bulletin, 1921, No. 28.
 By—William T. Bawden, Director. PUBLISHER—Superintendent of Documents, Government Printing Office, Washington, D. C. 1921. 53 p. 10 cents.

WISCONSIN. **Preliminary Report of the Committee of Fifteen Appointed by the State Superintendent of Schools to Investigate Educational Needs and Conditions in Wisconsin.**
 By—The Committee. PUBLISHER—State Department of Education, Madison. 1912. 30 p. Out of print.

WISCONSIN. **Children Indentured by the Wisconsin State Public School.** U. S. Department of Labor. Children's Bureau Publication No. 150.
 By—Children's Bureau. PUBLISHER—Superintendent of Documents, Government Printing Office, Washington, D. C. 1925. 132 p. 20 cents.

WISCONSIN, JANESVILLE. **An Educational Survey of Janesville.**
 By—C. P. Cary. PUBLISHER—State Department of Public Instruction, Madison. 1918. 329 p. 25 cents.

WISCONSIN, MADISON. **Report of the Survey of the University of Wisconsin.**
 By—State Board of Public Affairs. PUBLISHER—The same, Madison. 1914. 957 p. Out of print.

WISCONSIN, MILWAUKEE COUNTY. **Survey of the Milwaukee County School of Agriculture and Domestic Economy.**
 By—Walter Matscheck. PUBLISHER—Taxpayers' League, Milwaukee. 1916. 73 p. Out of print.

WISCONSIN, SPARTA. **Some Recommendations for the Improvement of the School System of Sparta.** A survey by the City School Division of the U. S. Bureau of Education.
 By—W. F. Deffenbaugh. PUBLISHER—Board of Education, Sparta. 1921. 23 p. Free.

WYOMING. **Educational Survey of Wyoming.** U. S. Department of Interior. Bureau of Education Bulletin, 1916, No. 29.
 By—A. C. Monahan and Katherine M. Cook. PUBLISHER—Superintendent of Documents, Government Printing Office, Washington, D. C. 1917. 120 p. 15 cents.

EDUCATION—Continued

WYOMING, LINCOLN COUNTY. **A Survey of Five School Districts in Lincoln County.** Bulletin No. 6, Series B.
> BY—L. C. Tidball, C. R. Maxwell, and James R. Coxen. PUBLISHER—Department of Education, Cheyenne. 1922. 24 p. Free.

In addition to reports **presenting findings** in Education Surveys, as listed above, publications dealing with **methods of conducting** such studies will be found in Part III, PURPOSE, METHOD, AND STANDARDS, page 344.

EIGHT-HOUR DAY

> See also INDUSTRIAL CONDITIONS AND RELATIONS.

MASSACHUSETTS. **The Eight Hour Day for Children in Massachusetts Factories.** Publication No. 226.
> BY—Richard E. Conant. PUBLISHER—National Child Labor Committee, New York City. 1914. 5 p. 5 cents.

UNITED STATES. **Comparison of an Eight Hour Plant and a Ten Hour Plant.** Report on an investigation by Philip Sargant Florence and Associates. U. S. Public Health Service Bulletin No. 106.
> BY—Josephine Goldmark and Mary D. Hopkins. PUBLISHER—Superintendent of Documents, Government Printing Office, Washington, D. C. 1920. 213 p. 25 cents.

ELECTIONS

> See also CITY, COUNTY, AND STATE ADMINISTRATION.

ILLINOIS, CHICAGO AND COOK COUNTY. **Growing Cost of Elections in Chicago and Cook County.** 1912. 19 p. Out of print.

The High Cost of Elections in Chicago and Cook County. 1921. 24 p. Free.
> BY—Chicago Bureau of Public Efficiency. PUBLISHER—The same.

EPILEPTICS

> See also DELINQUENCY AND CORRECTION; FEEBLEMINDED; and MENTAL HYGIENE.

NEW YORK. **Nine Family Histories of Epileptics in one Rural County.** Bureau of Analysis and Investigation. Eugenics and Social Welfare. Bulletin No. VII.
> BY—Florence Givens Smith. PUBLISHER—State Board of Charities, Albany. 1916. 55 p. Free.

SURVEYS IN SPECIALIZED FIELDS

EXCEPTIONAL CHILDREN
See SUB-NORMAL, RETARDED, AND EXCEPTIONAL CHILDREN.

FAMILY WELFARE
See also CHARITIES; COST OF LIVING; DEPENDENCY; DESERTION; DISASTERS; FOOD; INDUSTRIAL CONDITIONS AND RELATIONS; MARRIAGE LAWS; PENSIONS; RELIEF; SOCIAL AGENCIES; TUBERCULOSIS; UNEMPLOYMENT; UNMARRIED MOTHERS; and VENEREAL DISEASES.

CALIFORNIA, LOS ANGELES. **Social Work with Families in Los Angeles.**
BY—Karl de Schweinitz and Ruth Hill. MIMEOGRAPHED—Community Welfare Federation, Los Angeles. 1925. 29 p. Free.

CANADA, ONTARIO. **Mothers' Allowances.** An investigation.
BY—Margaret K. Strong. PUBLISHER—Department of Labour, Toronto. 1920. 126 p. Free.

ILLINOIS. **Administration of the Aid-to-Mothers Law in Illinois.** U. S. Department of Labor. Children's Bureau Publication No. 82.
BY—Edith Abbott and Sophonisba P. Breckinridge. PUBLISHER—Superintendent of Documents, Government Printing Office, Washington, D. C. 1921. 173 p. 30 cents.

MASSACHUSETTS. **Report of the Special Commission to Investigate Maternity Benefits.** House No. 1835.
BY—The Commission. PUBLISHER—Commonwealth of Massachusetts, Boston. 1920. 92 p. Free.

MASSACHUSETTS, NEW BEDFORD. **Family Welfare Division of the Survey of New Bedford Social Agencies.**
BY—Malcolm S. Nichols. MIMEOGRAPHED—Council of Social Agencies, New Bedford. 1923. 64 p. Free.

NEW YORK CITY. **Home Service in Action.** A study of case work in the Home Service Section of the New York and Bronx County Chapters of the American Red Cross.
BY—Mary Buell Sayles. PUBLISHER—New York County Chapter, American Red Cross, New York City. 1921. 232 p. $2.00.

NEW YORK CITY. **When Fathers Drop Out.** What happened to 115 widows and their 470 children.
BY—William H. Matthews. PUBLISHER—Association for Improving the Condition of the Poor, New York City. 1924. 38 p. 20 cents.

FAMILY WELFARE—Continued

PENNSYLVANIA, PITTSBURGH. **Homestead: The Households of a Mill Town.** The Pittsburgh Survey.
>By—Margaret F. Byington. PUBLISHER—Russell Sage Foundation, New York City. 1910. 292 p. Out of print.

WASHINGTON, TACOMA. **Survey of Family Relief Work in Tacoma.**
>By—Federation of Social Agencies. MIMEOGRAPHED—The same, Tacoma. 1923. 58 p. Free.

FEEBLEMINDED

>See also MENTAL HYGIENE.

ARKANSAS. **Report of the Arkansas Commission for the Feebleminded to the General Assembly of the State of Arkansas.**
>By—The Commission. PUBLISHER—General Assembly, Little Rock. 1915. 14 p. Out of print.

ARKANSAS. **Feebleminded: Their Prevalence and Needs in the School Population of Arkansas.** Reprint No. 379, Public Health Reports, November 24, 1916.
>By—W. L. Treadway. PUBLISHER—Superintendent of Documents, Government Printing Office, Washington, D. C. 1916. 18 p. 5 cents.

CANADA, ONTARIO. **Report on the Care and Control of the Mentally Defective and Feebleminded in Ontario.**
>By—Frank Egerton Hodgins. PUBLISHER—Province of Ontario, Toronto. 1919. 236 p. $1.00.

HAWAII. **Report of the Commission to Investigate Feeblemindedness in the Territory of Hawaii.**
>By—Frank C. Atherton. PUBLISHER—Territory of Hawaii, Honolulu. 1919. 7 p. Free.

KENTUCKY. **Report of the Commission on Provision for the Feebleminded in Kentucky.**
>By—Thomas H. Haines. PUBLISHER—State Commission for the Provision of the Feebleminded, Frankfort. 1916. 23 p. Free.

MAINE. **Report of the Maine Commission for the Feebleminded and of the Survey by the National Committee for Mental Hygiene.**
>By—The Commission and Committee. PUBLISHER—Department of Public Welfare, Augusta. 1918. 95 p. Free.

SURVEYS IN SPECIALIZED FIELDS

FEEBLEMINDED—Continued

MASSACHUSETTS. **Community Supervision of the Feebleminded.** An analysis of 300 families in which there is mental defect.
> By—Amy Woods. PUBLISHER—League for Preventive Work, Boston. 1918. 14 p. Out of print.

MICHIGAN. **Report of the Commission to Investigate the Extent of Feeblemindedness, Epilepsy, and Insanity, and Other Conditions of Mental Defectiveness in Michigan.**
> By—Albert M. Barrett. PUBLISHER—Board of Corrections and Charities, Lansing. 1919. 175 p. Free.

MONTANA. **Report of the Survey of the Feebleminded in Montana.**
> By—Committee in Charge of Survey. PUBLISHER—State Board of Education, Helena. 1919. 24 p. Free.

NEW YORK. **Care of the Feebleminded in New York.** Prison Leaflet No. 49.
> By—George A. Hastings. PUBLISHER—National Committee on Prisons and Prison Labor, New York City. 1919. 9 p. Free.

NEW YORK CITY. **Study of the Feebleminded in a West Side School in New York City.** Bulletin No. 21.
> By—Elizabeth A. Irwin. PUBLISHER—Public Education Association, New York City. 1913. 15 p. Free.

OHIO. **The Feebleminded in a Rural County of Ohio.** Bureau of Juvenile Research Bulletin No. 6, Publication No. 12.
> By—Mina A. Sessions. PUBLISHER—Ohio Board of Administration, Columbus. 1918. 69 p. Free.

OHIO, CINCINNATI. **The Feebleminded or the Hub of Our Wheel of Vice, Crime, and Pauperism.**
> By—Juvenile Protective Association. PUBLISHER—The same, Cincinnati. 1915. 28 p. Free.

OHIO, CINCINNATI. **Feebleminded Ex-School Children.** A study of children who have been students in Cincinnati special schools. Studies from the Helen S. Trounstine Foundation. Vol. I, No. 7.
> By—Helen T. Wooley and Hornell Hart. PUBLISHER—Helen S. Trounstine Foundation, Cincinnati. 1921. 31 p. 50 cents.

PENNSYLVANIA. **Report of the Commission on Segregation, Care, and Treatment of Feebleminded and Epileptic Persons.**
> By—The Commission. PUBLISHER—State of Pennsylvania, Harrisburg. 1913. 70 p. Out of print.

FEEBLEMINDED—Continued

PENNSYLVANIA. **Feebleminded Citizens in Pennsylvania, Being the Report of a Survey of a Certain Locality Comprising about 700 Square Miles and Having a Population Estimated at 16,000.**
    BY—Wilhelmine E. Key. PUBLISHER—Public Charities Association of Pennsylvania, Philadelphia. 1915. 63 p. Out of print.

PENNSYLVANIA, LAURELTON. **Education of Feebleminded Women.** Teachers College Contributions to Education No. 174.
    BY—Mary Vanuxem. PUBLISHER—Bureau of Publications, Teachers College, Columbia University, New York City. 1925. 74 p. $1.20.

PENNSYLVANIA, PHILADELPHIA. **The Care of the Feebleminded in Philadelphia.** A report to the Director of Public Health of a survey.
    BY—Eleanor Hope Johnson. PUBLISHER—National Committee for Mental Hygiene, New York City. 1920. 44 p. 25 cents.

SOUTH CAROLINA. **Feeblemindedness and Its Care in South Carolina.** Quarterly Bulletin. Vol. I, No. 2.
    BY—C. Croft Williams and Louise E. Bishop. PUBLISHER—State Board of Public Welfare, Columbia. 1920. 28 p. Free.

TEXAS. **Care of the Feebleminded and Insane in Texas.** University of Texas Bulletin. Humanistic Series No. 16.
    BY—C. S. Yoakum. PUBLISHER—University of Texas, Austin. 1914. 147 p. Out of print.

WISCONSIN. **Some Aspects of Feeblemindedness in Wisconsin.** Bulletin of the Extension Division. Serial No. 940.
    BY—John L. Gillin. PUBLISHER—University of Wisconsin, Madison. 1918. 28 p. 10 cents.

FINNS

MASSACHUSETTS, LANESVILLE. **The Finns in Lanesville.** Studies in Sociology No. 13.
    BY—Helen Babson. PUBLISHER—Southern California Sociological Society, Los Angeles. 1919. 12 p. 15 cents.

FIRE

MASSACHUSETTS, BOSTON. **A Study of Fire Risks in a Business Section of Boston.** Bulletin No. 12.
    BY—Mary C. Wiggin. PUBLISHER—Consumers' League of Massachusetts, Boston. 1916. 14 p. Free.

SURVEYS IN SPECIALIZED FIELDS

FIRE—Continued

NEW YORK CITY. **Investigation of the Fire Department of New York.** A report for the Commissioners of Accounts.
>BY—Greeley S. Curtis. PUBLISHER—Merchants' Association of New York, New York City. 1908. 118 p. Out of print.

NEW YORK CITY. **Fire Hazards in Factory Buildings.** Report of a survey of fire hazards in 1168 factory buildings in New York City. Reprint from the Twelfth Annual Report of the Joint Board of Sanitary Control.
>BY—George M. Price. PUBLISHER—Joint Board of Sanitary Control, New York City. 1923. 30 p. Free.

PENNSYLVANIA, PHILADELPHIA. **Health Survey of the Police and Firemen of the City of Philadelphia.**
>BY—Frank A. Craig. PUBLISHER—Henry Phipps Institute, Philadelphia. 1923. 87 p. 50 cents.

PENNSYLVANIA, READING. **Department of Fire.** Report on a survey of the municipal departments and school district.
>BY—New York Bureau of Municipal Research. PUBLISHER—Reading Chamber of Commerce. 1913. 44 p. 10 cents.

WISCONSIN, MILWAUKEE. **Proposed Consolidation of Fire and Police Alarm Telegraph Systems.** Bulletin No. 2.
>BY—Milwaukee Bureau of Economy and Efficiency. PUBLISHER—The same. 1911. 23 p. Out of print.

In addition to reports **presenting findings,** as listed above, a publication dealing with **methods of conducting** such studies will be found in Part III, PURPOSE, METHOD, AND STANDARDS, page 347.

FOOD

>*See also* CHILD HEALTH AND HYGIENE; HEALTH IN INDUSTRY; and INDUSTRIAL CONDITIONS AND RELATIONS.

MASSACHUSETTS, BOSTON. **Food Supply in Families of Limited Means.** A study of present facts of the food problem in Boston families by six welfare agencies.
>BY—Michael M. Davis, Jr. PUBLISHER—League for Preventive Work, Boston. 1917. 24 p. 10 cents.

A BIBLIOGRAPHY OF SOCIAL SURVEYS

FOOD—Continued

MASSACHUSETTS, BOSTON. **Housing of Foodstuffs in Small Provision Stores in Boston.** Department of Food Sanitation and Distribution Bulletin. Vol. VIII, No. 4.
>BY—Dora E. Wheeler and Theodora Bailey. PUBLISHER—Women's Municipal League of Boston. 1917. 40 p. Free.

NEW YORK. **Report of the Food Problem Committee.**
>BY—The Committee. PUBLISHER—Merchants' Association of New York, New York City. 1918. 39 p. Free.

NEW YORK CITY. **Health of Food Handlers: A Cooperative Study of the Department of Health, the Metropolitan Life Insurance Company, and the American Museum of Safety.**
>BY—L. I. Harris and L. I. Dublin. PUBLISHER—Metropolitan Life Insurance Company, New York City. 1917. 24 p. Free.

GANGS

ILLINOIS, CHICAGO. **The Gang.** A study of 1,313 Gangs in Chicago.
>BY—Frederic M. Thrasher. PUBLISHER—University of Chicago Press. 1927. 571 p. $3.00.

GARBAGE, REFUSE, AND SEWAGE

>See also CITY AND REGIONAL PLANNING.

CALIFORNIA, LOS ANGELES. **Report of the Special Sewage Disposal Commission.**
>BY—George W. Fuller, George C. Whipple, and William Milholland. PUBLISHER—City of Los Angeles. 1921. 31 p. Free.

ILLINOIS, CHICAGO. **Report on a Comprehensive and Scientific Method of the Collection of Garbage, Ashes, and Miscellaneous Waste, together with Recommendations.**
>BY—Division of Public Works and Civil Service, City of Chicago. PUBLISHER—Bureau of Statistics and Municipal Reference Library, Chicago. 1913. 113 p. 50 cents.

NEW JERSEY, BRIDGETON. **A Report and Survey with Recommendations upon the Municipal Refuse Collection and Disposal of the City of Bridgeton.**
>BY—William F. Morse. PUBLISHER—City Department of Health, Bridgeton. 1920. 15 p. Free.

SURVEYS IN SPECIALIZED FIELDS

GARBAGE, REFUSE, AND SEWAGE—Continued

NEW YORK CITY. **Report on the Collection and Disposal of Solid Wastes in the City of New York.**
>By—John Kenlon. PUBLISHER—Board of Estimate and Apportionment, New York City. 1921. 15 p. Free.

NEW YORK, ROCHESTER. REPORTS ON THE GOVERNMENT OF THE CITY OF ROCHESTER.
Report on the Problem of Snow Removal in the City of Rochester. 1917. 44 p.
Report on the Problem of Refuse Collection. 1919. 138 p.
>By—Leroy E. Snyder. PUBLISHER—Rochester Bureau of Municipal Research. Free.

OREGON, PORTLAND. **The Collection and Disposal of Municipal Wastes.**
>By—City Club of Portland. PUBLISHER—The same. 1922. 12 p. Free.

UNITED STATES. **A Recent Survey of Sewage Treatment Plants.** Public Health Reports. Vol. 37, No. 25.
>By—H. H. Wagenhals. PUBLISHER—Superintendent of Documents, Government Printing Office, Washington, D. C. 1922. 14 p. 5 cents.

UNITED STATES. **Sewage Treatment in the United States.** Report on the study of fifteen representative sewage treatment plants. U. S. Public Health Service Bulletin No. 132.
>By—H. H. Wagenhals, E. J. Theriault, and H. B. Hommon. PUBLISHER—Superintendent of Documents, Government Printing Office, Washington, D. C. 1923. 260 p. 50 cents.

WISCONSIN, MILWAUKEE. BUREAU OF ECONOMY AND EFFICIENCY REPORTS.
The Refuse Incinerator. Bulletin No. 5. By M. Cerf. 1911. 75 p.
Reorganization of the System of Garbage Collections. Bulletin No. 12. By Robert E. Godell. 1912. 25 p.
>PUBLISHER—Milwaukee Bureau of Economy and Efficiency. Out of print.

GERMAN
>*See* RUSSIANS.

GIRLS
>*See* PART I, GENERAL SOCIAL SURVEYS—URBAN, and PART II, in CHILD LABOR; COST OF LIVING; DELINQUENCY AND COR-

GIRLS—Continued

RECTION; HOUSING; INDUSTRIAL CONDITIONS AND RELATIONS; INDUSTRIAL EDUCATION; JUVENILE DELINQUENCY; MARRIAGE LAWS; MENTAL HYGIENE; PROBATION AND PAROLE; PSYCHIATRIC; RECREATION; TRUANCY AND NON-ATTENDANCE; and VOCATIONAL GUIDANCE AND TRAINING.

GOVERNMENT

See CITY, COUNTY, AND STATE ADMINISTRATION.

For publications dealing with **methods of conducting** Government Surveys see Part III, PURPOSE, METHOD, AND STANDARDS, under **City, County, and State Administration.**

GREEKS

See ITALIANS.

HANDICAPPED

See CRIPPLED, DISABLED, AND HANDICAPPED.

HEALTH ADMINISTRATION

See also RURAL HEALTH AND SANITATION; and TUBERCULOSIS.

ALABAMA, BIRMINGHAM AND JEFFERSON COUNTY. **Public Health Administration, City of Birmingham and County of Jefferson, Alabama.** Public Health Reports. Vol. 31, No. 45.

By—Carroll Fox. PUBLISHER—Superintendent of Documents, Government Printing Office, Washington, D. C. 1916. 28 p. 5 cents.

ARIZONA. **Public Health Administration in Arizona.** U. S. Public Health Service Bulletin No. 122.

By—R. C. Williams. PUBLISHER—Superintendent of Documents, Government Printing Office, Washington, D. C. 1922. 49 p. 10 cents.

CALIFORNIA, ALAMEDA COUNTY. **A Survey of Medical Social Service in County Institutions, Alameda County.**

By—Marguerite L. Spiers. MIMEOGRAPHED—Alameda County Institutions' Commission, Oakland. 1927. 73 p. Free.

CANADA, TORONTO. **Administrative Study of the Toronto Department of Public Health.** Reprinted from the Public Health Journal. Issues of July, August, September, and October, 1915.

By—Toronto Bureau of Municipal Research. PUBLISHER—The same. 1915. 53 p. Free.

SURVEYS IN SPECIALIZED FIELDS

HEALTH ADMINISTRATION—Continued

COLORADO. **Public Health Administration in Colorado.** Reprint No. 383, Public Health Reports, December 29, 1916.
>By—Carroll Fox. PUBLISHER—Superintendent of Documents, Government Printing Office, Washington, D. C. 1916. 36 p. 5 cents.

FLORIDA. **Public Health Administration in Florida.** Reprint No. 230, Public Health Reports, June 2, 1916.
>By—Carroll Fox. PUBLISHER—Superintendent of Documents, Government Printing Office, Washington, D. C. 1916. 49 p. 5 cents.

ILLINOIS. **Report on Public Health Administration.**
>By—J. M. Matthews. PUBLISHER—State Efficiency and Economy Committee, Springfield. 1914. 54 p. Free.

ILLINOIS. **Public Health Administration in Illinois.** Public Health Reports. Vol. 30, No. 21.
>By—S. B. Grubbs. PUBLISHER—Superintendent of Documents, Government Printing Office, Washington, D. C. 1915. 67 p. 10 cents.

ILLINOIS, CHICAGO. **Public Health Administration in Chicago.** A study of the organization and administration of the City Health Department. Reprint No. 300, Public Health Reports, August 20, 1915.
>By—J. C. Perry. PUBLISHER—Superintendent of Documents. Government Printing Office, Washington, D. C. 1915. 139 p, 15 cents.

ILLINOIS, QUINCY. **Public Health Administration in Quincy.** Reprint No. 427, Public Health Reports, October 5, 1917.
>By—Carroll Fox. PUBLISHER—Superintendent of Documents, Government Printing Office, Washington, D. C. 1917. 16 p. 5 cents.

INDIANA, SOUTH BEND. **Public Health Administration in South Bend.** Public Health Reports. Vol. 32, No. 21.
>By—Carroll Fox. PUBLISHER—Superintendent of Documents, Government Printing Office, Washington, D. C. 1917. 30 p. 5 cents.

MAINE. PUBLIC HEALTH ADMINISTRATION IN MAINE.
>**Augusta.** Bulletin Vol. II, No. 12. By Alton S. Pope. 1919. 19 p.
>**Bangor and Bath.** Bulletin Vol. II, No. 7. By H. D. Worth and Chester S. Kingsley. 1919. 16 p.

HEALTH ADMINISTRATION—Continued

Lewiston and Auburn. Bulletin Vol. I, No. 10. By Aaron P. Pratt. 1918. 20 p.

Waterville and Biddeford. Bulletin Vol. III, No. 5. By Alton S. Pope and C. F. Kendall. 1920. 21 p.

Westbrook. Bulletin Vol. II, No. 8. By Aaron P. Pratt. 1919. 8 p.
PUBLISHER—State Department of Health, Augusta. Free.

MARYLAND. **Public Health Administration in Maryland.** A study of the State Department of Health and other agencies having sanitary functions. Reprint No. 166, Public Health Reports, January 30, 1914.
By—Carroll Fox. PUBLISHER—Superintendent of Documents, Government Printing Office, Washington, D. C. 1914. 80 p. 10 cents.

MARYLAND, BALTIMORE. **Public Health Administration in Baltimore.** A study of the organization and administration of the City Department of Health. Reprint No. 201, Public Health Reports, June 12, 1914.
By—Carroll Fox. PUBLISHER—Superintendent of Documents, Government Printing Office, Washington, D. C. 1914. 80 p. 10 cents.

MASSACHUSETTS, SPRINGFIELD. **The Organization and Administration of the Health Department of Springfield.**
By—C. E. McCombs. PUBLISHER—Bureau of Municipal Research, Springfield. 1914. 48 p. Out of print.

MINNESOTA. **Public Health Administration in Minnesota.** Reprint No. 223, Public Health Reports, October 2, 1914.
By—Carroll Fox. PUBLISHER—Superintendent of Documents, Government Printing Office, Washington, D. C. 1914. 82 p. 10 cents.

MINNESOTA, MINNEAPOLIS. **An Ideal Health Department.**
By—Hermann M. Biggs and C. E. A. Winslow. PUBLISHER—Minneapolis Civic and Commerce Association. 1912. 36 p. Out of print.

MINNESOTA, ST. PAUL. **Public Health Administration in St. Paul.** Public Health Reports. Vol. 32, No. 2.
By—G. B. Young. PUBLISHER—Superintendent of Documents, Government Printing Office, Washington, D. C. 1917. 31 p. 5 cents.

SURVEYS IN SPECIALIZED FIELDS

HEALTH ADMINISTRATION—Continued

NEBRASKA. **Public Health Administration in Nebraska.** Reprint No. 348, Public Health Reports, July 7, 1916.
 BY—Carroll Fox. PUBLISHER—Superintendent of Documents, Government Printing Office, Washington, D. C. 1916. 26 p. 5 cents.

NEVADA. **Public Health Administration in Nevada.** Reprint No. 317, Public Health Reports, December 31, 1915.
 BY—Carroll Fox. PUBLISHER—Superintendent of Documents, Government Printing Office, Washington, D. C. 1916. 33 p. 5 cents.

NEW MEXICO. **Public Health Administration in New Mexico.** Public Health Reports. Vol. 33, No. 46.
 BY—J. W. Kerr. PUBLISHER—Superintendent of Documents, Government Printing Office, Washington, D. C. 1918. 20 p. 5 cents.

NORTH DAKOTA. **Public Health Administration in North Dakota.** Reprint No. 315, Public Health Reports, December 17, 1915.
 BY—Carroll Fox. PUBLISHER—Superintendent of Documents, Government Printing Office, Washington, D. C. 1916. 30 p. 5 cents.

NORTH DAKOTA. **Report of a Survey of Public Health Administration in North Dakota.** Reprint No. 802, Public Health Reports, December 8, 1922.
 BY—Robert Olesen. PUBLISHER—Superintendent of Documents, Government Printing Office, Washington, D. C. 1923. 20 p. 5 cents.

OHIO, DAYTON. **Organization and Administration of the Department of Health of the City of Dayton.**
 BY—Bureau of Municipal Research. PUBLISHER—Department of Health, Dayton. 1913. 97 p. Out of print.

OHIO, PIQUA. **Public Health Administration in Piqua.** Public Health Reports. Vol. 32, No. 25.
 BY—Carroll Fox. PUBLISHER—Superintendent of Documents, Government Printing Office, Washington, D. C. 1917. 13 p. 5 cents.

OHIO, SPRINGFIELD. **Public Health Administration in Springfield.** Reprint No. 417, Public Health Reports, August 10, 1917.
 BY—Carroll Fox. PUBLISHER—Superintendent of Documents, Government Printing Office, Washington, D. C. 1917. 25 p. 5 cents.

HEALTH ADMINISTRATION—Continued

OHIO, TOLEDO. **Public Health Administration in Toledo.** Reprint No. 284, Public Health Reports, June 25, 1915.
> BY—Carroll Fox. PUBLISHER—Superintendent of Documents, Government Printing Office, Washington, D. C. 1915. 64 p. 10 cents.

OHIO, TOLEDO. **Public Health Administration in Toledo.** In Toledo City Journal, August 14–October 9, inclusive.
> BY—Commission of Publicity and Efficiency. PUBLISHER—The same, Toledo. 1926. 122 p. Free.

OHIO, YOUNGSTOWN. **Public Health Administration in Youngstown.** Public Health Reports. Vol. 31, No. 39.
> BY—Carroll Fox. PUBLISHER—Superintendent of Documents, Government Printing Office, Washington, D. C. 1916. 33 p. 5 cents.

PENNSYLVANIA, READING. **Report on a Survey of the Municipal Departments and School District No. 1.** Department of Health.
> BY—New York Bureau of Municipal Research. PUBLISHER—Chamber of Commerce, Reading. 1913. 37 p. 10 cents.

TENNESSEE, KNOXVILLE. **Preliminary Report on the Public Health Services, Official and Voluntary of the City of Knoxville.**
> BY—American Public Health Association Committee on Administrative Practice. PUBLISHER—City of Knoxville. 1926. 31 p. Free.

TENNESSEE, MEMPHIS. **A Review of Public Health Administration in Memphis, Based on a Survey of Health Activities and Sanitary Conditions in May, 1920.** U. S. Public Health Service Bulletin No. 113.
> BY—Paul Preble. PUBLISHER—Superintendent of Documents, Government Printing Office, Washington, D. C. 1921. 116 p. 10 cents.

UNITED STATES. **The Present Condition of Public Health Organization in the United States.** Report of the Central Committee on Public Health Organization based on a voluntary survey of organizations interested in public health.
> BY—Selskar M. Gunn. PUBLISHER—American Medical Association, Chicago, Illinois. 1913. 48 p. Out of print.

UNITED STATES. **Survey of the Activities of Municipal Health Departments in the United States.** An investigation to obtain an approxi-

SURVEYS IN SPECIALIZED FIELDS

HEALTH ADMINISTRATION—Continued

mate idea of the status of Health Department work in the United States.

By—Franz Schneider, Jr. PUBLISHER—Russell Sage Foundation, New York City. 1916. 22 p. Out of print.

UNITED STATES. REPORTS ON MUNICIPAL HEALTH DEPARTMENT PRACTICES.

First Report. U. S. Public Health Service Bulletin No. 136. 1923. 468 p. 50 cents.

Municipal Health Department Practice for the Year 1923, Based upon Surveys of the 100 Largest Cities in the United States. U. S. Public Health Service Bulletin No. 164. 1926. 782 p. $1.25.

By—Committee on Municipal Health Department Practice, American Public Health Association and the U. S. Public Health Service. PUBLISHER—Superintendent of Documents, Government Printing Office, Washington, D. C.

WASHINGTON. **Public Health Administration in the State of Washington.** Reprint No. 255, Public Health Reports, February 5, 1915.

By—Carroll Fox. PUBLISHER—Superintendent of Documents, Government Printing Office, Washington, D. C. 1915. 56 p. 10 cents.

WEST VIRGINIA. **Public Health Administration in West Virginia.** A study of the health laws and public health administration of the state of West Virginia. Reprint No. 252, Public Health Reports, January 22, 1915.

By—Taliaferro Clark. PUBLISHER—Superintendent of Documents, Government Printing Office, Washington, D. C. 1915. 50 p. 10 cents.

WISCONSIN, MILWAUKEE. **The Health Department: Education and Publications.** Bulletin No. 15.

By—Milwaukee Bureau of Economy and Efficiency. PUBLISHER —The same. 1912. 35 p. Out of print.

HEALTH AND SANITATION

Reports dealing with the general subject of health and sanitation are listed here. For reports dealing with specific phases of this subject or with health and sanitation in connection with other subjects *see* ADOLESCENCE; CANCER; CHARITIES; CHILD HEALTH AND HYGIENE; CHINESE; CLINICS AND DISPENSARIES; FIRE; FOOD; GARBAGE, REFUSE, AND SEWAGE; HEALTH ADMINISTRATION; HEALTH IN INDUSTRY; HEALTH INSURANCE; HOSPITALS

A BIBLIOGRAPHY OF SOCIAL SURVEYS

HEALTH AND SANITATION—Continued
AND SANATORIA; HOUSING; INDIANS; INFANT MORTALITY; MATERNAL DEATHS; MIDWIFE; MILK; NEGROES; NURSERIES AND NURSING; POSTURE; PRE-NATAL CARE; RURAL HEALTH AND SANITATION; SCHOOL HEALTH AND SANITATION; SLUMS; TRACHOMA; TUBERCULOSIS; and VENEREAL DISEASE.

ALASKA. **Sanitary Conditions in Alaska.** A report upon the diseases found among the Indians of Southeastern Alaska. Reprint No. 194, Public Health Reports, May 22, 1914.
BY—Emil Krulish. PUBLISHER—Superintendent of Documents, Government Printing Office, Washington, D. C. 1914. 6 p. 5 cents.

ARIZONA, TUCSON. **Survey of Tucson, Pima County.**
BY—Arizona Anti-Tuberculosis Association. MIMEOGRAPHED—Arizona State Board of Health, Phoenix. 1920. 6 p. Free.

CALIFORNIA, SAN FRANCISCO. **Report of the Commission Appointed by the Secretary of the Treasury for the Investigation of Plague in San Francisco.** U. S. Public Health Service Bulletin No. 8.
BY—U. S. Public Health Service. PUBLISHER—Superintendent of Documents, Government Printing Office, Washington, D. C. 1901. 23 p. Out of print.

CANADA, MONTREAL. **Report on the Montreal Typhoid Fever Situation.** Public Health Reports. Vol. 42, No. 29.
BY—Public Health Service. PUBLISHER—Superintendent of Documents, Government Printing Office, Washington, D. C. 1927. 5 cents.

CANADA, NEW BRUNSWICK. **Report on a Sanitary Survey of the Province of New Brunswick.**
BY—John Hall. PUBLISHER—Authority of the Government of Fredericton. 1917. 86 p. Free.

CHINA. **The Health of Missionary Families in China.** A statistical study.
BY—William G. Lennox. PUBLISHER—University of Denver, Colorado. 1921. 121 p. Free.

CHINA. *See also* JAPAN in this section.

COLORADO, DENVER. **A Survey of Some Communicable Diseases in Denver.** Pamphlet 13.
BY—Health Committee, City Club. PUBLISHER—City Club of Denver. 1927. 19 p. Free.

SURVEYS IN SPECIALIZED FIELDS

HEALTH AND SANITATION—Continued

COLORADO, STERLING. *See* OREGON, ALBANY, in this section.

CONNECTICUT, GREENWICH. **A Public Health Survey of Greenwich.**
BY—Department of Public Health, Yale School of Medicine. PUBLISHER—The same, New Haven. 1925. 32 p. Free.

CONNECTICUT, MIDDLETOWN. **Health Survey of Middletown.**
BY—Davis Greenberg and Ira D. Joel. PUBLISHER—Yale School of Medicine, New Haven. 1917. 74 p. Free.

CONNECTICUT, NEW HAVEN. **The Health of New Haven.** Documents of the Civic Federation of New Haven No. 13.
BY—Irving Fisher. PUBLISHER—Civic Federation, New Haven. 1913. 8 p. Free.

CONNECTICUT, NEW HAVEN. **Health Survey of New Haven.** Documents of the Civic Federation of New Haven No. 17.
BY—C. E. A. Winslow, James C. Greenway, and D. Greenberg. PUBLISHER—Yale University Press, New Haven. 1917. 114 p. 50 cents.

CONNECTICUT, NEW HAVEN. **Report on the New Haven Health Center Demonstration.** July 1920–June 1923.
BY—Philip S. Platt. PUBLISHER—State Department of Health, Visiting Nurse Association, New Haven Medical Association, New Haven Chapter, American Red Cross, New Haven. 1923. 108 p. Free.

GEORGIA, ATLANTA. **Report of Survey of the Department of Health and the Department of Education.**
BY—S. G. Lindholm. PUBLISHER—Atlanta Chamber of Commerce. 1912. 44 p. Out of print.

GEORGIA, ATLANTA. **A Survey of the Public Health Situation of Atlanta.**
BY—Franz Schneider, Jr. PUBLISHER—Chamber of Commerce, Atlanta. 1913. 22 p. Out of print.

GEORGIA, MILLEDGEVILLE. **Report of the Findings of the Survey of Milledgeville.**
BY—Chloe M. Jackson. MIMEOGRAPHED—W. G. Raoul Foundation, Atlanta. 1917. 5 p. Free.

GEORGIA, ROME. **Report of the Findings of the Survey of Rome.**
BY—Chloe M. Jackson. MIMEOGRAPHED—W. G. Raoul Foundation, Atlanta. 1916. 4 p. Free.

A BIBLIOGRAPHY OF SOCIAL SURVEYS

HEALTH AND SANITATION—Continued

HAWAII. **Studies in Leprosy.** U. S. Public Health Service Bulletin No. 130.
  By—H. E. Hasseltine. PUBLISHER—Superintendent of Documents, Government Printing Office, Washington, D. C. 1922. 24 p. 5 cents.

HAWAII. **The Effect of Vaccinia on Leprosy.** Reprint No. 808, Public Health Reports, January 25, 1923.
  By—H. E. Hasseltine. PUBLISHER—Superintendent of Documents, Government Printing Office, Washington, D. C. 1923. 12 p. 5 cents.

ILLINOIS. **Report on an Appraisal of Health Service for the Year 1925 in Fifteen Illinois Cities.** Illinois Health Bulletin, May-June.
  By—State Department of Health. PUBLISHER—The same, Springfield. 1926. 108 p. Free.

ILLINOIS, CHICAGO. **The Noise Problem in Chicago.** Reprinted from the City Club Bulletin. Vol. VI, No. 11.
  By—William O. Nance. PUBLISHER—City Council Committee on Health, Chicago. 1913. 11 p. Free.

ILLINOIS, CHICAGO. **Public Comfort Stations.** Bulletin of the Department of Public Welfare. Vol. 1, No. 3.
  By—Earle E. Eubank, Director. PUBLISHER—Department of Public Welfare, Chicago. 1916. 43 p. Free.

ILLINOIS, CHICAGO. **Survey of Comfort Stations on Elevated Railroads.**
  By—Benjamin and Eloise Blinstrub. PUBLISHER—Juvenile Protective Association, Chicago. 1918. 4 p. Free.

ILLINOIS, CHICAGO. **Use and Cost of Ice in Families with Children.**
  By—Elsie P. Wolcott. PUBLISHER—Department of Public Welfare, Chicago. 1925. 20 p. Free.

ILLINOIS, FREEPORT. **Sanitary and Health Survey of the City of Freeport.** Illinois Health News. Vol. 4, No. 5. New Series.
  By—Paul L. Skoog, Director. PUBLISHER—State Department of Public Health, Springfield. 1918. 31 p. Free.

ILLINOIS, QUINCY. **Sanitary Survey of Quincy.** In Fourth Annual Report of the Department of Public Health.
  By—B. K. Richardson. PUBLISHER—State of Illinois, Springfield. 1921. 25 p. Free.

SURVEYS IN SPECIALIZED FIELDS

HEALTH AND SANITATION—Continued

ILLINOIS, ROCKFORD. **Sanitary Survey of the City of Rockford, Winnebago County.**
> By—Paul L. Skoog. PUBLISHER—Illinois Department of Public Health, Springfield. 1920. 40 p. Free.

ILLINOIS, SPRINGFIELD. **Sanitary and Health Survey.** Reprint from Publications of the Academy of Political Science. Vol. II, No. 4.
> By—George Thomas Palmer. PUBLISHER—Academy of Political Science, New York City. 1912. 50 p. Out of print as a pamphlet.

ILLINOIS, SPRINGFIELD. **Public Health in Springfield.** Public Health Section of The Springfield Survey.
> By—Franz Schneider, Jr. PUBLISHER—Russell Sage Foundation, New York City. 1915. 159 p. Out of print.

INDIANA, EAST CHICAGO. **Public Health in East Chicago.** A study of life wastage from preventable disease and a plea for an adequate department of health.
> By—A. W. Hedrich. PUBLISHER—Board of Health, East Chicago. 1916. 42 p. Free.

INDIANA, LAFAYETTE. **Public Health Survey of Lafayette.**
> By—Murray P. Horwood. PUBLISHER—Tippecanoe County Tuberculosis Association, Lafayette. 1921. 252 p. $1.00.

JAPAN. **A Comparative Study of the Health of Missionary Families in Japan and China, and a Selected Group in America.**
> By—William G. Lennox. PUBLISHER—University of Denver, Colorado. 1920. 44 p. Free.

KANSAS, TOPEKA. **Public Health Survey of Topeka.** Part I. Topeka Improvement Survey.
> By—Franz Schneider, Jr. PUBLISHER—Russell Sage Foundation, New York City. 1914. 98 p. Out of print.

KENTUCKY. **Sanitary Conditions and Needs of Kentucky.** In Kentucky Medical Journal. Vol. 7, No. 13.
> By—Caroline Bartlett Crane. PUBLISHER—Kentucky Medical Association, Bowling Green. 1909. 44 p. 10 cents.

LOUISIANA, NEW ORLEANS. **Report of the Sanitary Commission of New Orleans on the Epidemic of Yellow Fever in 1853.**
> By—City Council of New Orleans. PUBLISHER—The same. 1854. 542 p. Out of print.

HEALTH AND SANITATION—Continued

LOUISIANA, NEW ORLEANS. **Report of the Health and Sanitary Survey of the City of New Orleans.**
BY—Board of Health of New Orleans and Metropolitan Life Insurance Company. PUBLISHER—City Council, New Orleans. 1919. 163 p. Free.

MARYLAND. **Influenza in Maryland.** Preliminary statistics of certain localities. Reprint No. 510, Public Health Reports, March 14, 1919.
BY—W. H. Frost and Edgar Sydenstricker. PUBLISHER—Superintendent of Documents, Government Printing Office, Washington, D. C. 1919. 15 p. 5 cents.

MASSACHUSETTS. **Outbreak of Tonsillitis or Septic Sore Throat in Eastern Massachusetts and Its Relation to an Infected Milk Supply.** Reprint from Journal of Infectious Diseases. Vol. 10. No. 1.
BY—C. E. A. Winslow. PUBLISHER—Journal of Infectious Diseases, Chicago, Illinois. 1912. 39 p. Out of print.

MASSACHUSETTS. **Lessons from a Study of One Thousand Diphtheria Deaths.** Reprinted from the Boston Medical and Surgical Journal. Vol. CLXXX, No. 3.
BY—Bernard W. Carey. PUBLISHER—Commonwealth of Massachusetts, Boston. 1920. 8 p. Free.

MASSACHUSETTS. **Survey of Endemic Thyroid Enlargement in Massachusetts.** Public Health Reports. Vol. 42, No. 12.
BY—Robert Olesen and Neil E. Taylor. PUBLISHER—Superintendent of Documents, Government Printing Office, Washington, D. C. 1927. 13 p. 5 cents.

MASSACHUSETTS, BOSTON. **A Sickness Survey of Boston.** Fourth Community Sickness Survey.
BY—Lee K. Frankel and Louis I. Dublin. PUBLISHER—Metropolitan Life Insurance Company, New York City. 1916. 23 p Free.

MASSACHUSETTS, NEW BEDFORD. **Public Health in New Bedford.**
BY—C. E. A. Winslow. PUBLISHER—Council of Social Agencies, New Bedford. 1923. 28 p. Free.

MASSACHUSETTS, QUINCY AND TAUNTON. **A Synoptic Report on a Comparative Sanitary Survey of Two Massachusetts Cities.** Reprint from American Journal of Public Health. Vol. VII, No. 8.
BY—Murray P. Horowitz. PUBLISHER—Sanitary Research Laboratory, Massachusetts Institute of Technology, Cambridge. 1916. 14 p. 10 cents.

SURVEYS IN SPECIALIZED FIELDS

HEALTH AND SANITATION—Continued

MICHIGAN, HIGHLAND PARK. **Health of Highland Park.** A study.
By—Minnie Goodnow. PUBLISHER—Thomas Thompson Foundation, Boston, Massachusetts. 1917. 32 p. Free.

MICHIGAN, SAGINAW. **A Sanitary Survey of Saginaw.**
By—Caroline Bartlett Crane. PUBLISHER—Saginaw Federation of Clubs. 1911. 42 p. Postage.

MINNESOTA. **Report on a Campaign to Awaken Public Interest in Sanitary and Sociologic Problems in the State of Minnesota.**
By—Caroline Bartlett Crane. PUBLISHER—State Board of Health, St. Paul. 1911. 239 p. 50 cents.

MINNESOTA. **Railroad Water Supplies in Minnesota.** Reprint No. 191, Public Health Reports, May 15, 1914.
By—R. H. Mullin, Director. PUBLISHER—Superintendent of Documents, Government Printing Office, Washington, D. C. 1914. 25 p. 10 cents.

MINNESOTA, MINNEAPOLIS. **Drinking Fountains.** Investigation of fountains at the University of Minnesota. Reprint No. 397, Public Health Reports, May 11, 1917.
By—H. A. Whittaker. PUBLISHER—Superintendent of Documents, Government Printing Office, Washington, D. C. 1917. 9 p. 5 cents.

MINNESOTA, ST. PAUL. **Efficiency and Next Needs of the St. Paul Health Department.** Report submitted by the New York Bureau of Municipal Research and Training School for Public Service.
By—Carl E. McCombs. PUBLISHER—St. Paul Anti-Tuberculosis Committee. 1913. 48 p. Out of print.

MINNESOTA, ST. PAUL. **Health Conditions and Health Service in St. Paul.**
By—Esther M. Flint and Carol Aronovici. PUBLISHER—Amherst H. Wilder Charity, St. Paul. 1919. 103 p. Free.

MISSOURI. **A Study of the Malaria Problem of Southeast Missouri.** Public Health Reports. Vol. 38, No. 6.
By—K. F. Maxcy. PUBLISHER—Superintendent of Documents, Government Printing Office, Washington, D. C. 1923. 17 p. 5 cents.

HEALTH AND SANITATION—Continued

MISSOURI, KANSAS CITY. **A Health Census of Kansas City.** Seventh Community Sickness Survey.
> BY—Lee K. Frankel and Louis I. Dublin. PUBLISHER—Metropolitan Life Insurance Company, New York City. 1917. 11 p. Free.

MISSOURI, ST. JOSEPH. **Report of a Sanitary Survey of St. Joseph.** Reprint No. 185, Public Health Reports, April 24, 1914.
> BY—J. H. White. PUBLISHER—Superintendent of Documents, Government Printing Office, Washington, D. C. 1914. 12 p. 5 cents.

NEW JERSEY, GLEN RIDGE. **Sanitary Survey of the Borough of Glen Ridge.**
> BY—M. P. Horowitz. PUBLISHER—Health Department, Glen Ridge. 1916. 43 p. Out of print.

NEW JERSEY, HOBOKEN. **A Sanitary Survey of Hoboken.**
> BY—W. H. Deadrick. PUBLISHER—Robert L. Stevens Fund for Municipal Research, Hoboken. 1913. 32 p. 10 cents.

NEW YORK. **Report of Special Public Health Commission.**
> BY—The Commission. PUBLISHER—State Department of Health, Albany. 1913. 36 p. Free.

NEW YORK. **Report of the New York State Commission on Ventilation.**
> BY—George T. Palmer, Director. PUBLISHER—E. P. Dutton and Company, New York City. 1923. 620 p. $15.00.

NEW YORK, AMSTERDAM. **Report of Health Inventory of the City of Amsterdam.**
> BY—C. E. Terry and Franz Schneider, Jr. PUBLISHER—Department of Health, Amsterdam. 1918. 11 p. Out of print.

NEW YORK, ITHACA. **Survey of the Public Health Situation in Ithaca.**
> BY—Franz Schneider, Jr. PUBLISHER—Russell Sage Foundation, New York City. 1915. 34 p. Out of print.

NEW YORK, JEFFERSON COUNTY. **Summary of an Investigation of the Source of Typhoid Fever Cases in Jefferson County.** In State Department of Health Annual Report, Vol. III.
> BY—F. M. Meader. PUBLISHER—State Department of Health, Albany. 1915. 35 p. Out of print.

NEW YORK CITY. **Report on the Croton Watershed: A Sanitary Survey.**
> BY—New York City Department of Health. PUBLISHER—The same. 1891. 176 p. Out of print.

SURVEYS IN SPECIALIZED FIELDS

HEALTH AND SANITATION—Continued

NEW YORK CITY. **Comfort Stations in New York City.** A social, sanitary, and economic survey. Bureau of Public Health and Hygiene. Department of Social Welfare. Publication No. 80.

BY—Donald B. Armstrong. PUBLISHER—Association for Improving the Condition of the Poor, New York City. 1913. 39 p. Out of print.

NEW YORK CITY. **Flies and Diarrheal Disease (Second Year's Investigation).**

BY—Philip S. Platt. PUBLISHER—Association for Improving the Condition of the Poor, New York City. 1915. 46 p. Free.

NEW YORK CITY. **Health Census of Chelsea Neighborhood, 14th to 42d Streets, Fifth Avenue to Hudson River.**

BY—Metropolitan Life Insurance Company and Chelsea Neighborhood Association. PUBLISHER—Metropolitan Life Insurance Company, New York City. 1917. 16 p. 5 cents.

NEW YORK CITY. **Laundries and the Public Health.** A sanitary study including bacteriologic tests. Public Health Reports. Vol. 32, No. 6.

BY—M. C. Schroeder and S. G. Southerland. Publisher—Superintendent of Documents, Government Printing Office, Washington, D. C. 1917. 22 p. 5 cents.

NEW YORK CITY. **The Cost of Clean Clothes in Terms of Health.** A study of laundries and laundry workers in New York City.

BY—Louis I. Harris and Nelle Swartz. PUBLISHER—Consumers' League and Department of Health, New York City. 1918. 96 p. Free.

NEW YORK CITY. **A Survey of the Activities during Five Years of Work of the Public Health Committee of the New York Academy of Medicine. 1911-1916.**

BY—The Committee. PUBLISHER—New York Academy of Medicine, New York City. 1918. 106 p. Free.

NEW YORK CITY. **The Health of a Neighborhood.** A social study of the Mulberry District. Publication No. 130.

BY—John C. Gebhart. PUBLISHER—Association for Improving the Condition of the Poor, New York City. 1924. 23 p. 25 cents.

NEW YORK CITY. **Better Doctoring: Less Dependency.** A study of the relation between non-medical agencies with special reference to clinics and family services.

BY—Louise Stevens Bryant. PUBLISHER—Committee on Dispensary Development, United Hospital Fund, New York City. 1927. 90 p. Free.

HEALTH AND SANITATION—Continued

NEW YORK, ROCHESTER. **A Sanitary Survey of Rochester, Made in Cooperation with the Women's Educational and Industrial Union.**
> By—Caroline Bartlett Crane. PUBLISHER—City of Rochester. 1911. 119 p. 10 cents.

NEW YORK, ROCHESTER. **Community Sickness Survey, Rochester.** Reprint No. 326, Public Health Reports, February 25, 1916.
> By—Lee K. Frankel and Louis I. Dublin. PUBLISHER—Superintendent of Documents, Government Printing Office, Washington, D. C. 1916. 16 p. 5 cents.

NEW YORK, SYRACUSE. **Report of the Investigations for the Associated Charities of Syracuse, New York.** Part I. Report on the Syracuse Public Schools. Part II. Report on the Syracuse Board of Health.
> By—Horace L. Brittain and A. E. Shipley. PUBLISHER—Bureau of Municipal Research, New York City. 1912. 12 p. 10 cents.

NORTH CAROLINA. **Malaria in North Carolina.** Reprint No. 156, Public Health Reports, December 19, 1913.
> By—Henry R. Carter. PUBLISHER—Superintendent of Documents, Government Printing Office, Washington, D. C. 1914. 21 p. 10 cents.

NORTH CAROLINA. **A Sickness Survey of North Carolina.** Public Health Reports. Vol. 31, No. 41.
> By—Lee K. Frankel. PUBLISHER—Superintendent of Documents, Government Printing Office, Washington, D. C. 1916. 25 p. 5 cents.

NORTH CAROLINA, BLEWETTS FALLS. **Survey of Blewetts Falls Impounded Waters. Their effect upon the prevalence of malaria.** Public Health Reports. Vol. 30, No. 1.
> By—H. R. Carter. PUBLISHER—Superintendent of Documents, Government Printing Office, Washington, D. C. 1915. 18 p. 5 cents.

NORTH CAROLINA, RALEIGH. **Health Survey of Raleigh.**
> By—C. E. Terry. PUBLISHER—Wake County Council of National Defense, Raleigh. 1918. 30 p. Free.

NORTH DAKOTA, FARGO. **A Survey of Public Health Work in Fargo.** The Commonwealth Fund Child Health Program Bulletin No. 5.
> By—W. F. Walker. PUBLISHER—Child Health Demonstration Committee, New York City. 1927. 32 p. Free.

SURVEYS IN SPECIALIZED FIELDS

HEALTH AND SANITATION—Continued

OHIO, CINCINNATI AND HAMILTON COUNTY. **A Survey of Community Dental Facilities.**
> BY—Anna M. Drake. PUBLISHER—Public Health Federation, Cincinnati. 1927. 51 p. Free.

OHIO, CLEVELAND. CLEVELAND HOSPITAL AND HEALTH SURVEY.
Part 1. Introduction, General Environment, and Sanitation. 90 p.
Part 2. Public Health Agencies and Private Health Agencies. 115 p.
Part 8. Education and Practice in Medicine, Dentistry, and Pharmacy. 46 p.
Other parts of this survey are listed elsewhere.

A Popular Summary of the Cleveland Hospital and Health Survey. 21 p.

Cleveland Hospital and Health Survey Two Years After. 1922. 70 p.
> BY—Haven Emerson, Director. PUBLISHER—Cleveland Hospital Council. 1920. 50 cents and postage each.

OHIO, CLEVELAND. **Typhoid Fever in Cleveland for the Years 1918, 1919, 1920.** Reprint No. 659, Public Health Reports, May 20, 1921.
> BY—Roger G. Perkins. PUBLISHER—Superintendent of Documents, Government Printing Office, Washington, D. C. 1921. 30 p. 5 cents.

OHIO, DELAWARE. **Report on the Public Water Supply of Delaware Made by the Engineering Division of the State Department of Health.** Public Health Reports. Vol. 37, No. 32.
> BY—F. H. Waring. PUBLISHER—Superintendent of Documents, Government Printing Office, Washington, D. C. 1922. 12 p. 5 cents.

OHIO, SPRINGFIELD. **Report of the Appraisal of Public Health Activities of the City of Springfield.**
> BY—W. F. Walker. PUBLISHER—Chamber of Commerce, Springfield. 1926. 16 p. Free.

OKLAHOMA, MUSKOGEE. **The Oklahoma Public Health Surveys: Muskogee.**
> BY—M. P. Horwood and Jules Schevitz. PUBLISHER—Oklahoma Tuberculosis Association, Oklahoma City. 1920. 145 p. $1.00.

OKLAHOMA, OKLAHOMA CITY. **The Oklahoma Public Health Surveys: Oklahoma City.**
> BY—M. P. Horowitz and Jules Schevitz. PUBLISHER—Oklahoma Tuberculosis Association, Oklahoma City. 1919. 157 p. $1.00.

HEALTH AND SANITATION—Continued

OREGON. **A Health Survey of the State of Oregon.**
    By—John C. Almack. MIMEOGRAPHED—University of Oregon, Eugene. 1920. 29 p. Free.

OREGON. **Report on Survey of Endemic Goiter in Oregon.** Public Health Reports. Vol. 42, No. 46.
    By—Robert Olesen. PUBLISHER—Superintendent of Documents, Government Printing Office, Washington, D. C. 1927. 19 p. 5 cents.

OREGON, ALBANY. **Outbreaks of Botulism at Albany, Oregon, and Sterling, Colorado, February, 1924.** Public Health Reports. Vol. 39, No. 14.
    By—Frederick D. Stricker and J. C. Geiger. PUBLISHER—Superintendent of Documents, Government Printing Office, Washington, D. C. 1924. 7 p. 5 cents.

OREGON, PORTLAND. **Public Health Methods and Their Application in Portland.**
    By—City Club of Portland. PUBLISHER—The same. 1922. 40 p. Out of print.

PENNSYLVANIA. **Sickness Survey of Principal Cities in Pennsylvania and West Virginia.**
    By—L. K. Frankel and L. I. Dublin. PUBLISHER—Metropolitan Life Insurance Company, New York City. 1917. 78 p. Free.

PENNSYLVANIA, ERIE. **General Sanitary Survey of Erie.**
    By—Caroline Bartlett Crane. PUBLISHER—Chamber of Commerce, Erie. 1910. 22 p. 10 cents and postage.

PENNSYLVANIA, PHILADELPHIA. **Report of the Pneumonia Commission of the City of Philadelphia.**
    By—The Commission. PUBLISHER—Department of Public Health, Philadelphia. 1922. 43 p. Free.

PENNSYLVANIA, PITTSBURGH. **Report on a Survey of the Department of Public Health.**
    By—New York Bureau of Municipal Research. PUBLISHER—City Council, Pittsburgh. 1913. 62 p. Out of print.

PENNSYLVANIA, PITTSBURGH. **Thirty-Five Years of Typhoid.** In The Pittsburgh District Civic Frontage, The Pittsburgh Survey.
    By—Frank E. Wing. PUBLISHER—Russell Sage Foundation, New York City. 1914. p. 63–87. Out of print.

SURVEYS IN SPECIALIZED FIELDS

HEALTH AND SANITATION—Continued

PENNSYLVANIA, PITTSBURGH. **Sickness Survey of Pittsburgh.**
> BY—L. K. Frankel and L. I. Dublin. PUBLISHER—Metropolitan Life Insurance Company, New York City. 1917. 22 p. Free.

PENNSYLVANIA, UNIONTOWN. **A Sanitary Survey of Uniontown.**
> BY—Caroline Bartlett Crane. PUBLISHER—Women's Civic League, Uniontown. 1914. 51 p. Out of print.

PERU, IQUITOS. **The Sanitation of Iquitos.** Reprint No. 233, Public Health Reports, November 13, 1914.
> BY—G. M. Converse. PUBLISHER—Superintendent of Documents, Government Printing Office, Washington, D. C. 1914. 12 p. 5 cents.

PHILIPPINE ISLANDS. **Sanitation of the Philippine Islands. Work of the Sanitary Commissions.** Reprint No. 371, Public Health Reports, December 27, 1916.
> BY—J. D. Long. PUBLISHER—Superintendent of Documents, Government Printing Office, Washington, D. C. 1916. 11 p. 5 cents.

RHODE ISLAND, PAWTUCKET. **Report on the Public Health Activities of the City of Pawtucket with Recommendations for Their Improvement.**
> BY—S. M. Gunn. PUBLISHER—Pawtucket Business Men's Association. 1913. 18 p. Free.

SOUTH CAROLINA, SPARTANBURG COUNTY. REPORTS OF THE THOMPSON-MCFADDAN PELLAGRA COMMISSION.
Pellagra. First Report. 1913. 148 p.
Pellagra. Second Progress Report. 1915. 169 p.
Pellagra. Third Progress Report. 1918. 454 p.
> BY—Joseph F. Siler, Director. PUBLISHER—New York Post-Graduate Medical School and Hospital, New York City. Free.

TENNESSEE. **Report of a State-Wide Smallpox Survey in Tennessee.** In Public Health Reports, Vol. 41, No. 30.
> BY—W. J. Breeding and A. E. Lane. PUBLISHER—Superintendent of Documents, Government Printing Office, Washington, D. C. 1926. 5 p. 5 cents per copy.

TENNESSEE, NASHVILLE. **General Sanitary Survey of Nashville.**
> BY—Caroline Bartlett Crane. PUBLISHER—The same, Kalamazoo, Michigan. 1910. 24 p. Free.

HEALTH AND SANITATION—Continued

TEXAS, AUSTIN. **A Social Survey of Austin: Sanitary and Health Conditions.** Bulletin of the University of Texas. Humanistic Series No. 15.
> By—William B. Hamilton. PUBLISHER—University of Texas, Austin. 1913. 88 p. Out of print.

TEXAS, GALVESTON. **Report of a Sanitary Survey of Galveston.**
> By—Commercial Association of Galveston. PUBLISHER—The same. 1913. 30 p. Out of print.

UNITED STATES. **Report of an Investigation of Diphtheria Carriers.** U. S. Public Health Service Bulletin No. 101.
> By—Joseph Goldberger and others. PUBLISHER—Superintendent of Documents, Government Printing Office, Washington, D. C. 1915. 13 p. Out of print.

UNITED STATES. **Report on State Public Health Work, Based on a Survey of State Boards of Health, Made under the Direction of the Council of Health and Public Instruction.**
> By—Charles V. Chapin. PUBLISHER—American Medical Association, Chicago. 1915. 211 p. Out of print.

UNITED STATES [Great Lakes District]. **Drinking Water on Interstate Carriers.** A study of conditions on steam vessels engaged in interstate commerce in the sanitary district of the Great Lakes. Reprint No. 368, Public Health Reports, October 13, 1916.
> By—J. O. Cobb, C. L. Williams, and H. P. Letton. PUBLISHER—Superintendent of Documents, Government Printing Office, Washington, D. C. 1916. 24 p. 10 cents.

UNITED STATES. **Influenza Studies on Certain General Statistical Aspects of the 1918 Epidemic in American Cities.** Public Health Reports. Vol. 34, No. 32.
> By—Raymond Pearl. PUBLISHER—Superintendent of Documents, Government Printing Office, Washington, D. C. 1919. 40 p. 5 cents.

UNITED STATES. **Some Recent Morbidity Data.** A summary of seven community surveys.
> By—Margaret Loomis Stecker. PUBLISHER—Metropolitan Life Insurance Company, New York City. 1919. 28 p. Free.

UNITED STATES. **A Comparative Study of State Regulations for the Control of Influenza.** Public Health Reports. Vol. 35, No. 37.
> By—L. M. Feezer. PUBLISHER—Superintendent of Documents, Government Printing Office, Washington, D. C. 1920. 6 p. 5 cents.

SURVEYS IN SPECIALIZED FIELDS

HEALTH AND SANITATION—Continued

UNITED STATES [Southwest]. **Malta Fever in Southwest United States with Special Reference to the Recent Outbreak in Phoenix, Arizona.** Public Health Reports. Vol. 37, No. 47.
> By—U. S. Public Health Service. PUBLISHER—Superintendent of Documents, Government Printing Office, Washington, D. C. 1922. 5 p. 5 cents.

UNITED STATES. **Railroad Malaria Surveys: the Missouri Pacific Railroad.** U. S. Public Health Service Bulletin No. 135.
> By—A. W. Fuchs. PUBLISHER—Superintendent of Documents, Government Printing Office, Washington, D. C. 1923. 36 p. 10 cents.

UNITED STATES. **The Distribution of Physicians in the United States.**
> By—Lewis Mayers and Leonard V. Harrison. PUBLISHER—General Education Board, New York City. 1924. 197 p. Free.

UNITED STATES. **A Health Survey of Eighty-six Cities.**
> By—Research Division, American Child Health Association. PUBLISHER—American Child Health Association, New York City. 1925. 614 p. $3.00.

UNITED STATES. **A Typhoid Fever Epidemic Caused by Oyster-Borne Infection.** Supplement No. 50 to the Public Health Reports.
> By—L. L. Lumsden, H. E. Hasseltine, J. P. Leake, and M. V. Veldee. PUBLISHER—Superintendent of Documents, Government Printing Office, Washington, D. C. 1925. 103 p. 20 cents.

UNITED STATES—*See also* JAPAN in this section.

WEST VIRGINIA. **Sickness Survey of West Virginia Cities.**
> By—L. K. Frankel and L. I. Dublin. PUBLISHER—Metropolitan Life Insurance Company, New York City. 1917. 11 p. Free.

WEST VIRGINIA.
> *See also* PENNSYLVANIA in this section.

WEST VIRGINIA, CHARLESTON. **A Sanitary Survey of Charleston.**
> By—Mayo Tolman. PUBLISHER—State Department of Health, Charleston. 1918. 168 p. Free.

WISCONSIN, MILWAUKEE. STUDIES OF THE HEALTH DEPARTMENT.
Plumbing and House Drain Inspection. Bulletin No. 10. By Fayette H. Elwell. 1911. 33 p.
The Health Department: Communicable Diseases. Bulletin No. 18. By Selskar M. Gunn. 1912. 37 p.
> PUBLISHER—Milwaukee Bureau of Economy and Efficiency. Out of print.

HEALTH AND SANITATION—Continued

WISCONSIN, SHEBOYGAN. **Investigation of Typhoid Fever Epidemic at Sheboygan.** Reprint from Report of the Lake Michigan Water Commission.

BY—J. T. Bowles. PUBLISHER—Wisconsin State Hygienic Laboratory, Madison. 1908. 6 p. Free.

In addition to reports **presenting findings** in Health and Sanitation Surveys, as listed above, publications **dealing with methods** of conducting such studies will be found in Part III, PURPOSE, METHOD, AND STANDARDS, page 347.

HEALTH IN INDUSTRY

See also HEALTH INSURANCE; INDUSTRIAL CONDITIONS AND RELATIONS; and TUBERCULOSIS.

CANADA, TORONTO. **Survey of General Conditions of Industrial Hygiene in Toronto.**

BY—Associate Committee on Industrial Fatigue, Research Council. PUBLISHER—Sub-Committee, Privy Council for Scientific and Industrial Research, Ottawa. 1921. 21 p. Free.

CONNECTICUT. **A Study of the Dust Hazard in the Wet and Dry Grinding Shops of an Ax Factory.** Reprint No. 616, Public Health Reports, October 8, 1920.

BY—C. E. A. Winslow. PUBLISHER—Superintendent of Documents, Government Printing Office, Washington, D. C. 1920. 11 p. 5 cents.

ILLINOIS. **Hours and Health of Women Workers.** Report of the Illinois Industrial Survey.

BY—James B. Herrick. PUBLISHER—State of Illinois, Springfield. 1918. 120 p. Free.

INDIANA. **Sanitary Survey of Indiana Industries Employing Women Labor.** Supplement No. 17 to Public Health Reports, July 17, 1914.

BY—M. J. White. PUBLISHER—Superintendent of Documents, Government Printing Office, Washington, D. C. 1914. 44 p. 5 cents.

MASSACHUSETTS. **Report upon the Sanitary Conditions of Factories, Workshops, and Other Establishments Where People Are Employed.**

BY—State Board of Health. PUBLISHER—The same, Boston. 1907. 144 p. Free.

SURVEYS IN SPECIALIZED FIELDS

HEALTH IN INDUSTRY—Continued

MASSACHUSETTS. **Hygiene of the Boot and Shoe Industry in Massachusetts.**
> By—William C. Hanson. PUBLISHER—State Board of Health, Boston. 1912. 38 p. Free.

MASSACHUSETTS, BOSTON. **The Food of Working Women in Boston.** An investigation by the Department of Research of the Women's Educational and Industrial Union.
> By—Lucile Eaves, Director. PUBLISHER—State Department of Health, Boston. 1917. 213 p. 80 cents.

MICHIGAN, FLINT AND PONTIAC. **Sickness Survey among 21,000 Automobile Workers.** Public Health Reports. Vol. 39, No. 16.
> By—Dean K. Brundage. PUBLISHER—Superintendent of Documents, Government Printing Office, Washington, D. C. 1924. 12 p. 5 cents.

MISSOURI, JOPLIN. **Pulmonary Diseases among Miners in the Joplin District and Its Relation to Rock Dust in the Mines.** A preliminary report. U. S. Bureau of Mines Technical Paper No. 105.
> By—A. J. Lanza and Edwin Higgins. PUBLISHER—Superintendent of Documents, Government Printing Office, Washington, D. C. 1915. 47 p. 5 cents.

NEW YORK. INVESTIGATIONS IN NEW YORK INDUSTRIES.
Health Hazards of the Cloth Sponging Industry. Special Bulletin No. 89. 1918. 24 p.
Health Hazards of the Chemical Industry. Special Bulletin No. 93. 1919. 69 p.
Sickness Among New York Factory Workers in 1919. Special Bulletin No. 108. 1921. 29 p.
A Study of Hygienic Conditions in Steam Laundries and Their Effect upon the Health of Workers. Special Bulletin No. 130. 1924. 57 p.
> By—Division of Industrial Hygiene, State Department of Labor. PUBLISHER—The same, Albany. Free.

NEW YORK. **Chronic Benzol Poisoning among Women Industrial Workers.** Special Bulletin No. 150.
> By—Adelaide Ross Smith. PUBLISHER—Bureau of Women in Industry, State Department of Labor, Albany. 1927. 64 p. Free.

HEALTH IN INDUSTRY—Continued

NEW YORK CITY. REPRINTS OF PARTS OF A REPORT OF THE NEW YORK STATE FACTORY INVESTIGATING COMMISSION.

Occupational Diseases. A preliminary report on lead poisoning in the City of New York with an appendix on arsenical poisoning. By Edward Ewing Pratt. 5 p.

Notes on an Industrial Survey of a Selected Area in New York City with Respect to Sanitary Conditions in the Factories. By Pauline Goldmark. 67 p.

PUBLISHER—State Department of Labor, Albany. 1912. Out of print.

NEW YORK CITY. STUDIES IN VOCATIONAL DISEASES.

I. Health of Garment Workers. II. Hygienic Conditions of Illumination in Workshops of the Women's Garment Industry. U. S. Public Health Bulletin, No. 71. By J. W. Schereschewsky and D. H. Tuck. 1915. 224 p. 40 cents.

Effect of Gas-Heated Appliances upon the Air of Workshops. U. S. Public Health Bulletin, No. 81. By Charles Weisman. 1917. 84 p. 15 cents.

PUBLISHER—Superintendent of Documents, Government Printing Office, Washington, D. C.

NEW YORK CITY. Health of Garment Workers. The relation of economic status to health. Public Health Reports. Vol. 31, No. 21.

BY—B. D. Brown and Edgar Sydenstricker. PUBLISHER—Superintendent of Documents, Government Printing Office, Washington, D. C. 1916. 8 p. 5 cents.

NEW YORK CITY. Occupation and Mortality as Indicated by the Mortality Returns in the City of New York for 1914. Public Health Reports. Vol. 32, No. 23.

BY—S. W. Wynne and W. H. Guilfoy. PUBLISHER—Superintendent of Documents, Government Printing Office, Washington, D. C. 1917. 17 p. 5 cents.

NEW YORK CITY. Clinical Study of the Frequency of Lead, Turpentine, and Benzine Poisoning in Four Hundred Painters. Reprint Series No. 65.

BY—Louis I. Harris. PUBLISHER—Department of Health, New York City. 1918. 32 p. Free.

SURVEYS IN SPECIALIZED FIELDS

HEALTH IN INDUSTRY—Continued

NEW YORK, NIAGARA FALLS. **Health Hazards in the Industries of Niagara Falls.** Public Health Reports. Vol. 35, No. 1.
>By—Paul M. Holmes. PUBLISHER—Superintendent of Documents, Government Printing Office, Washington, D. C. 1920. 20 p. 5 cents.

OHIO. **A Survey of Industrial Health Hazards and Occupational Diseases in Ohio.**
>By—E. R. Hayhurst. PUBLISHER—State Department of Health, Columbus. 1915. 438 p. Out of print.

OHIO, CINCINNATI. **A Study of Restaurant Kitchens.** Bulletin No. 4 of the Consumer's League of Cincinnati.
>By—Elizabeth Shelow, Director. PUBLISHER—Consumer's League of Cincinnati. 1916. 10 p. Out of print.

OHIO, CLEVELAND. **Industrial Medical Series: Woman in Industry and Children in Industry.** Part VII. Cleveland Hospital and Health Survey.
>By—Haven Emerson, Director. PUBLISHER—Cleveland Hospital Council. 1920. 114 p. 50 cents and postage.

PENNSYLVANIA. **Diseases Prevalent among Steel Workers in a Pennsylvania City.** Public Health Reports. Vol. 36, No. 52.
>By—Dean K. Brundage. PUBLISHER—Superintendent of Documents, Government Printing Office, Washington, D. C. 1920. 10 p. 5 cents.

RHODE ISLAND. **Study of a Typical Mill Village from the Standpoint of Health.**
>By—Anti-Tuberculosis Association of Rhode Island. PUBLISHER—State Department of Health, Providence. 1911. 16 p. Free.

SOUTH CAROLINA. **Disabling Sickness among the Population of Seven Cotton-Mill Villages of South Carolina in Relation to Family Income.** Reprint No. 492, Public Health Reports, November 22, 1918.
>By—Edgar Sydenstricker, G. A. Wheeler, and Joseph Goldberger. PUBLISHER—Superintendent of Documents, Government Printing Office, Washington, D. C. 1919. 16 p. 5 cents.

SOUTH CAROLINA. **A Study of the Relation of Family Income and Other Economic Factors to Pellagra Incidence in Seven Cotton-Mill Villages of South Carolina in 1916.** Public Health Reports. Vol. 35, No. 46.
>By—Joseph Goldberger. PUBLISHER—Superintendent of Documents, Government Printing Office, Washington, D. C. 1920. 41 p. 10 cents.

A BIBLIOGRAPHY OF SOCIAL SURVEYS

HEALTH IN INDUSTRY—Continued

SOUTH CAROLINA. **Disabling Sickness in Cotton-Mill Communities of South Carolina in 1917.** Public Health Reports. Vol. 39, No. 24.
 BY—Dorothy Wiehl and Edgar Sydenstricker. PUBLISHER—Superintendent of Documents, Government Printing Office, Washington, D. C. 1924. 40 p. 5 cents.

UNITED STATES. **Hookworm Disease among Cotton-Mill Operatives.** Vol. XVII. Report on Condition of Woman and Child Wage-Earners in the United States. Senate Document No. 645.
 BY—Charles Wardell Stiles. PUBLISHER—Superintendent of Documents, Government Printing Office, Washington, D. C. 1912. 42 p. 5 cents.

UNITED STATES. HOURS OF WORK AS RELATED TO OUTPUT AND HEALTH OF WORKERS.
Cotton Manufacturing. Research Report No. 4. 1918. 64 p.
Boot and Shoe Industry. Research Report No. 7. 1918. 76 p.
Wool Manufacturing. Research Report No. 12. 1918. 69 p.
Silk Manufacturing. Research Report No. 16. 1919. 54 p.
Metal Manufacturing Industries. Research Report No. 18. 1919. 62 p.
 BY—National Industrial Conference Board. PUBLISHER—The same, New York City. $1.00 each.

UNITED STATES. **Studies of the Medical and Surgical Care of Industrial Workers.** U. S. Public Health Service Bulletin No. 99.
 BY—C. D. Selby. PUBLISHER—Superintendent of Documents, Government Printing Office, Washington, D. C. 1919. 115 p. 30 cents.

UNITED STATES. **Lead Poisoning in the Pottery Trades.** U. S. Public Health Service Bulletin No. 116.
 BY—Bernard J. Newmen, William J. McConnell, Octavius M. Spencer, and Frank M. Phillips. PUBLISHER—Superintendent of Documents, Government Printing Office, Washington, D. C. 1921. 223 p. 35 cents.

UNITED STATES. **Health Conditions among Chemical Workers with Respect to Earnings.** Public Health Reports. Vol. 38, No. 40.
 BY—Frank M. Phillips. PUBLISHER—Superintendent of Documents, Government Printing Office, Washington, D. C. 1923. 3 p. 5 cents.

SURVEYS IN SPECIALIZED FIELDS

HEALTH IN INDUSTRY—Continued

UNITED STATES. **A Health Study of Ten Thousand Male Industrial Workers.** Statistical analysis of surveys in ten industries. Public Health Bulletin No. 162.
> By—Rollo H. Britten and L. R. Thompson. PUBLISHER—Superintendent of Documents, Government Printing Office, Washington, D. C. 1926. 170 p. 30 cents.

In addition to reports presenting findings in Health in Industry Surveys, as listed above, a publication dealing with methods of conducting such studies will be found in Part III, PURPOSE, METHOD, AND STANDARDS, page 349.

HEALTH INSURANCE

See also PENSIONS.

ILLINOIS. **Report of the Health Insurance Commission of the State of Illinois.**
> By—The Commission. PUBLISHER—State of Illinois, Springfield. 1919. 645 p. Free.

UNITED STATES. **Health Insurance: Its Relation to the Public Health.** U. S. Public Health Service Bulletin No. 76. Second Edition.
> By—B. S. Warren and Edgar Sydenstricker. PUBLISHER—Superintendent of Documents, Government Printing Office, Washington, D. C. 1916. 79 p. 10 cents.

HOMELESS

See also RELIEF; and SOCIAL AGENCIES.

CALIFORNIA, SAN FRANCISCO. **A Study of the Homeless Men Problem in San Francisco.**
> By—W. S. Goodrich. MIMEOGRAPHED—Joint Committee on Single Men and Unemployment, Council of Social and Health Agencies, San Francisco. 1924. 97 p. Free.

ILLINOIS, CHICAGO. **One Thousand Homeless Men.** A study of original records.
> By—Alice W. Solenberger. PUBLISHER—Russell Sage Foundation, New York City. 1914. 374 p. $1.50.

ILLINOIS, CHICAGO. **The Hobo: The Sociology of the Homeless Man.** A study prepared for the Chicago Council of Social Agencies.
> By—Nels Anderson. PUBLISHER—University of Chicago Press. 1923. 302 p. $2.50.

HOMELESS—Continued

ILLINOIS, CHICAGO. **500 Lodgers of the City.** In Annual Report of the Department of Public Welfare.
> BY—Elizabeth A. Hughes. PUBLISHER—Department of Public Welfare, Chicago. 1926. 35 p. Free.

HOSPITALS AND SANATORIA

> *See also* CHARITIES; CHINESE; CLINICS AND DISPENSARIES; HEALTH AND SANITATION; INSANE; and TUBERCULOSIS.

CALIFORNIA, SAN FRANCISCO. **A Survey of Hospital and Health Agencies of San Francisco.**
> BY—Haven Emerson and Anna C. Phillips. PUBLISHER—Council of Social and Health Agencies, San Francisco. 1923. 154 p. $1.00

KENTUCKY, LOUISVILLE. **Hospital and Health Agencies of Louisville.** A survey.
> BY—Haven Emerson and Anna C. Phillips. PUBLISHER—Health and Hospital Survey Committee, Louisville Community Chest. 1924. 174 p. 75 cents.

NEW HAMPSHIRE. **Report of the Commission on State Sanatorium for Consumptives.**
> BY—The Commission. PUBLISHER—State of New Hampshire, Concord. 1902. 74 p. Out of print.

NEW YORK, BUFFALO. **Report to the Citizens Committee on an Investigation of the Department of Hospitals and Dispensaries.**
> BY—Haven Emerson. PUBLISHER—Department of Hospitals and Dispensaries, Buffalo. 1922. 36 p. Free.

NEW YORK CITY. **Ambulance Service in Greater New York.** Report on present conditions with recommendations for reorganization. Publication No. 99.
> BY—Phil P. Jacobs. PUBLISHER—State Charities Aid Association, New York City. 1907. 36 p. Out of print.

NEW YORK CITY. **Report of the Commission on Hospitals Appointed by the Mayor of the City of New York.**
> BY—The Commission. PUBLISHER—Department of Health, New York City. 1909. 761 p. Out of print.

NEW YORK CITY. **Subsequent History of Patients Discharged from Tuberculosis Sanatoria.** Monograph Series No. 8.
> BY—Council of Jewish Women. PUBLISHER—Department of Health, New York City. 1913. 47 p. Out of print.

SURVEYS IN SPECIALIZED FIELDS

HOSPITALS AND SANATORIA—Continued

NEW YORK CITY. **The Chronic Disabled Heart Patient.** A study of the extent and cost for these patients in the hospitals, dispensaries, and convalescent homes in New York City.
    BY—Haven Emerson, Director. PUBLISHER—Association for the Prevention and Relief of Heart Disease, New York City. 1923. 6 p. 10 cents.

NEW YORK CITY. **The Hospital Situation in Greater New York.** Report of a survey of hospitals in New York City by the Public Health Committee of the New York Academy of Medicine.
    BY—E. H. Lewinski-Corwin. PUBLISHER—G. P. Putnam's Sons, New York City. 1924. 356 p. $5.00.

OHIO, CINCINNATI. **Hospitals of Cincinnati.** A survey.
    BY—Mary L. Hicks. PUBLISHER—Helen S. Trounstine Foundation, Cincinnati. 1925. 212 p. $1.00.

OHIO, CLEVELAND. **Hospitals and Dispensaries.** Part X. Cleveland Hospital and Health Survey.
    BY—Michael M. Davis, Jr. PUBLISHER—Cleveland Hospital Council. 1920. 173 p. 50 cents.

PENNSYLVANIA. **State-Aided Hospitals in Pennsylvania.** A survey of hospital finances, resources, extent of service, and the nursing situation. Bulletin No. 25.
    BY—Emil Frankel. PUBLISHER—Department of Welfare, Commonwealth of Pennsylvania, Harrisburg. 1925. 102 p. Free.

UNITED STATES. **Report of the Committee Making a Survey of Hospital Social Service.** Bulletin No. 23.
    BY—Michael M. Davis, Jr. PUBLISHER—American Hospital Association, Chicago, Illinois. 1920. 21 p. 50 cents.

In addition to reports **presenting findings** in Hospitals and Sanatoria Surveys, as listed above, publications dealing with **methods of conducting** such studies will be found in Part III, PURPOSE, METHOD, AND STANDARDS, page 349.

HOUSING
    See also PART I, GENERAL SOCIAL SURVEYS—URBAN, and PART II in COST OF LIVING; INDUSTRIAL CONDITIONS AND RELATIONS; ITALIANS, MEXICANS; and TUBERCULOSIS.
    For SCHOOL HOUSING *see* SCHOOL BUILDING AND PLANTS.

HOUSING—Continued

CALIFORNIA. REPORTS ON HOUSING CONDITIONS.
Report of the Survey on Housing. In 1st Annual Report of the Commission of Immigration and Housing. 1915. 25 p. Out of print.
Report of the Housing and Industrial Survey of Oakland, Alameda, and Berkeley District. Mimeographed. 1918. 5 p. Free.
> BY—Commission of Immigration and Housing. PUBLISHER—The same, San Francisco.

CALIFORNIA, LOS ANGELES. REPORTS ON HOUSING CONDITIONS IN LOS ANGELES.
Report of the Housing Commission. 1908. 31 p. Out of print.
Report of the Housing Commission. 1909. 29 p. Out of print.
Report of the Housing Commission. 1910. 28 p. Free.
> BY—Housing Commission of Los Angeles. PUBLISHER—The same.

CALIFORNIA, SAN FRANCISCO. REPORTS ON HOUSING.
Report of the San Francisco Housing Association. 1911. 60 p.
Second Report of the San Francisco Housing Association. 1913. 32 p.
> BY—San Francisco Housing Association. PUBLISHER—The same. Free.

CALIFORNIA, SAN FRANCISCO. A Study of Housing Conditions for the Non-Family Girl in San Francisco.
> BY—Girls' Housing Council of San Francisco. MIMEOGRAPHED—The same. 1927. 44 p. Free.

CANADA, ONTARIO. Report of the Ontario Housing Committee, Including Standards for Inexpensive Houses Adopted for Ontario and Typical Plans.
> BY—Ontario Housing Committee. PUBLISHER—Legislative Assembly of Ontario, Toronto. 1919. 187 p. Free.

CANADA, WINNIPEG. HOUSING SURVEYS IN WINNIPEG.
Report on Housing Survey of Certain Selected Areas in Winnipeg.
> BY—Ernest W. J. Hague. 1919. 86 p.
Second Housing Survey. BY—A. J. Douglas. 1921. PUBLISHER—Department of Health, Winnipeg. Free.

CONNECTICUT, BRIDGEPORT. A Brief Survey of Housing Conditions in Bridgeport.
> BY—Udetta D. Brown. PUBLISHER—Bridgeport Housing Association. 1914. 64 p. Postage.

SURVEYS IN SPECIALIZED FIELDS

HOUSING—Continued

CONNECTICUT, NEW BRITAIN. **Housing Conditions in New Britain.** An investigation made for the Health Department.
> BY—Carol Aronovici. PUBLISHER—Health Department, New Britain. 1912. 43 p. Free.

CONNECTICUT, NEW HAVEN. **Summary of the New Haven Tenement House Investigation of 1902.**
> BY—H. W. Farnam. PUBLISHER—Lowell House, New Haven. 1902. 23 p. Out of print.

CONNECTICUT, NEW HAVEN. **Housing Conditions in New Haven.** Document No. 12.
> BY—Carol Aronovici. PUBLISHER—Civic Federation of New Haven. 1913. 48 p. Free.

CONNECTICUT, WATERBURY. **Report of Committee to Investigate Charges of Excessive Rentals in Waterbury.**
> BY—Herbert Knox Smith and others. MIMEOGRAPHED—State of Connecticut, Hartford. 1918. 12 p. Free.

DELAWARE, WILMINGTON. **War-Time Housing and Community Development.**
> BY—John Nolen. PUBLISHER—Chamber of Commerce, Wilmington. 1918. 24 p. Out of print.

DISTRICT OF COLUMBIA, WASHINGTON. **Reports of the President's Home Commission Appointed by President Theodore Roosevelt.**
> BY—The Commission. PUBLISHER—The same, Washington, D. C. 1908. 281 p. Out of print.

DISTRICT OF COLUMBIA, WASHINGTON. **Inhabited Alleys of Washington.** Prepared for the Committee on Housing.
> BY—Grace Vawter Bicknell. PUBLISHER—National Civic Federation, Washington, D. C. 1912. 35 p. Free.

ILLINOIS, CHICAGO. **Tenement Conditions in Chicago.** Report by the Investigating Committee of the City Homes Association.
> BY—Robert Hunter. PUBLISHER—City Homes Association, Chicago. 1900. 208 p. Out of print.

ILLINOIS, CHICAGO. CHICAGO HOUSING CONDITIONS. Reprints from the American Journal of Sociology.
Housing of Non-Family Groups of Working Men. Vol. XVI, No. 1. 1910. 39 p. 50 cents.
Families in Furnished Rooms. Vol. XVI, No. 3. 1910. 20 p. 50 cents.

A BIBLIOGRAPHY OF SOCIAL SURVEYS

HOUSING—Continued

The Twenty-Ninth Ward Back of the Yards. Vol. XVI, No. 4. 1911. 109 p. 50 cents.

The West Side Revisited. Vol. XVIII, No. 1. 1911. 34 p. Out of print.

South Chicago at the Gates of the Steel Mills. Vol. XVII, No. 2. 1911. 32 p. 50 cents.

The Problem of the Negro. Vol. XVIII, No. 2. By Alazada P. Comstock. 1912. 19 p. Out of print.

By—Sophonisba P. Breckinridge and Edith Abbott. PUBLISHER —University of Chicago Press.

ILLINOIS, CHICAGO. **Tenement Housing Conditions in the 20th Ward of Chicago.**

By—Chicago Women's Club. PUBLISHER—The same. 1912. 16 p. Free.

ILLINOIS, CHICAGO. **Housing Survey.** In City of Chicago Municipal Tuberculosis Sanitarium Annual Report.

By—R. E. Todd. PUBLISHER—Municipal Tuberculosis Sanitarium, Chicago. 1918. 112 p. Free.

ILLINOIS, CHICAGO. **Housing of Non-Family Women in Chicago.** A survey.

By—Ann Elizabeth Trotter. PUBLISHER—Chicago Community Trust. 1922. 39 p. 50 cents.

ILLINOIS, CHICAGO. **Living Conditions for Small Wage Earners in Chicago.**

By—Elizabeth A. Hughes. PUBLISHER—Department of Public Welfare, Chicago. 1925. 62 p. Free.

ILLINOIS, PEORIA. **Report of Peoria and Vicinity Housing Survey with Map Supplement.**

By—Housing Committee of Peoria. MIMEOGRAPHED—Peoria Association of Commerce. 1918. 35 p. Free.

ILLINOIS, SPRINGFIELD. **Housing in Springfield.** Housing Section of the Springfield Survey.

By—John Ihlder. PUBLISHER—Russell Sage Foundation, New York City. 1915. 24 p. Out of print.

INDIANA, INDIANAPOLIS. **Investigation of Housing and Living Conditions in Three Districts of Indianapolis.** University Bulletin, Vol. 8, No. 8.

By—L. M. C. Adams. PUBLISHER—University of Indiana, Bloomington. 1910. 31 p. 50 cents.

SURVEYS IN SPECIALIZED FIELDS

HOUSING—Continued

IOWA, DES MOINES. **Report of the Housing Commission of Des Moines.**
 By—The Commission. PUBLISHER—The same. 1917. 64 p. Out of print.

KENTUCKY, LOUISVILLE. **Report of the Tenement House Commission of Louisville.**
 By—Janet E. Kemp. PUBLISHER—The Commission. 1909. 78 p. Free.

LOUISIANA. **Report of State Housing Commission of Louisiana.**
 By—The Commission. PUBLISHER—State of Louisiana, Baton Rouge. 1921. 12 p. Free.

MARYLAND, BALTIMORE. **Housing Conditions in Baltimore.**
 By—Janet E. Kemp. PUBLISHER—Federated Charities, Baltimore. 1907. 96 p. Out of print.

MARYLAND, BALTIMORE. **Special Survey of the Housing Situation in Baltimore.**
 By—A. S. Goldsborough. PUBLISHER—Merchants and Manufacturers Association, Baltimore. 1920. 15 p. Out of print.

MARYLAND, BALTIMORE. **A Survey of Housing Conditions in Baltimore.**
 By—Special Survey Committee. PUBLISHER—Real Estate Board of Baltimore. 1921. 14 p. Free.

MASSACHUSETTS, ATTLEBORO. **Housing Analysis of Attleboro.**
 By—George H. Schwan. MIMEOGRAPHED—Chamber of Commerce, Attleboro. 1921. 21 p. Free.

MASSACHUSETTS, BOSTON. **Report upon a Sanitary Inspection of Certain Tenement Housing Districts in Boston.**
 By—Dwight Potter. PUBLISHER—Associated Charities, Boston. 1889. 76 p. Out of print.

MASSACHUSETTS, BOSTON. **Report of the Commission to Investigate Tenement House Conditions.**
 By—S. M. Child. PUBLISHER—City of Boston. 1904. 66 p. Out of print.

MASSACHUSETTS, BOSTON. **The Lodging House Problem in Boston.** Harvard Economic Studies.
 By—Albert Benedict Wolfe. PUBLISHER—Houghton Mifflin Company, New York City. 1906. 200 p. $1.50.

HOUSING—Continued

MASSACHUSETTS, BOSTON. **Report of the Commission Appointed to Investigate Lodging House Conditions in the City of Boston.**
>BY—The Commission. PUBLISHER—State of Massachusetts, Boston. 1909. 27 p. Out of print.

MASSACHUSETTS, BOSTON. **Boston's Housing Problem.**
>BY—John S. Hodson, Louis C. Southard, and C. Howard Walker. PUBLISHER—Economic Club of Boston. 1911. 16 p. Out of print.

MASSACHUSETTS, BOSTON. **Housing Conditions of Today in Boston.** In Bulletin of the Women's Municipal League of Boston. Vol. VII, No. 3.
>BY—Department of Housing. PUBLISHER—Women's Municipal League, Boston. 1916. 70 p. Free.

MASSACHUSETTS, CAMBRIDGE. **Housing Conditions in Cambridge.**
>BY—Cambridge Housing Association. PUBLISHER—The same. 1913. 31 p. Free.

MASSACHUSETTS, FALL RIVER. **Housing Conditions in Fall River.** An investigation made by the Bureau of Social Research of New England.
>BY—Carol Aronovici. PUBLISHER—Associated Charities Housing Committee, Fall River. 1912. 29 p. 15 cents.

MASSACHUSETTS, LAWRENCE. **The Lawrence Survey.** Housing conditions and public health.
>BY—Robert E. Todd and Frank B. Sanborn. Francis H. McLean, Consultant. PUBLISHER—Trustees of the White Fund, Lawrence. 1912. 263 p. 65 cents.

MASSACHUSETTS, SPRINGFIELD. **Report of Housing Conditions in Springfield.**
>BY—Carol Aronovici. PUBLISHER—Union Relief Association, Springfield. 1913. 39 p. Postage.

MICHIGAN. **Report of the Michigan Housing Commission.**
>BY—The Commission. PUBLISHER—State Board of Health, Lansing. 1916. 69 p. Out of print.

MICHIGAN, GRAND RAPIDS. **Housing Conditions and Tendencies in Grand Rapids.**
>BY—U. D. Brown. PUBLISHER—Charity Organization Society, Grand Rapids. 1913. 42 p. Free.

SURVEYS IN SPECIALIZED FIELDS

HOUSING—Continued

MINNESOTA. **Investigation of the Housing and Rental Situation in Minnesota.** Bulletin No. 12.
 BY—J. H. Hay. PUBLISHER—State Department of Agriculture, St. Paul. 1920. 19 p. Free.

MINNESOTA, MINNEAPOLIS. **Housing Problems in Minneapolis.** A preliminary investigation.
 BY—Douglas A. Fiske. PUBLISHER—Minnesota Civic and Commerce Association, Minneapolis. 1914. 111 p. Out of print.

MINNESOTA, ST. PAUL. **Housing Conditions in the City of St. Paul.**
 BY—Carol Aronovici. PUBLISHER—Housing Commission, St. Paul. 1917. 120 p. 50 cents.

MISSOURI, KANSAS CITY. **Report on Housing Conditions in Kansas City.**
 BY—Fred R. Johnson, C. C. Stillman, and J. O. Stutsman. PUBLISHER—Board of Public Welfare, Kansas City. 1912. 93 p. Free.

MISSOURI, KANSAS CITY. **Housing Conditions among Negroes in Kansas City.**
 BY—Myrtle F. Cook, Director. PUBLISHER—Missouri Industrial Commission, Kansas City. 1921. 15 p. Free.

MISSOURI, ST. LOUIS. **Housing Conditions in St. Louis.**
 BY—Charlotte Rumbold. PUBLISHER—Civic League of St. Louis. 1908. 85 p. Out of print.

MISSOURI, ST. LOUIS. **The Housing Problem in St. Louis.**
 BY—City Plan Commission. PUBLISHER—The same, St. Louis. 1920. 50 p. Free.

NEW JERSEY. **Report of the New Jersey Tenement House Commission.**
 BY—The Commission. PUBLISHER—State of New Jersey, Trenton. 1904. 45 p. Out of print.

NEW JERSEY, JERSEY CITY. **Housing Conditions in Jersey City.**
 BY—Mary B. Sayles. PUBLISHER—American Academy of Political and Social Science, Philadelphia, Pennsylvania. 1903. 72 p. Out of print.

NEW JERSEY, NEWARK. **Housing Report to the Newark City Plan Commission.**
 BY—E. P. Goodrich and George B. Ford. PUBLISHER—City Plan Commission, Newark. 1913. 75 p. Out of print.

HOUSING—Continued

NEW JERSEY, THE ORANGES. **A Report on Housing Conditions in the Oranges.**
>By—Edith R. Hall. PUBLISHER—Women's Club, East Orange. 1915. 45 p. Out of print.

NEW JERSEY, PASSAIC. **Survey of Housing Conditions in Passaic.**
>By—Udetta D. Brown. PUBLISHER—Board of Trade, Passaic. 1915. 48 p. Out of print.

NEW JERSEY, PLAINFIELD. **Housing Conditions in Plainfield and North Plainfield.**
>By—Udetta D. Brown. PUBLISHER—Charity Organization Society, Plainfield. 1914. 36 p. Free.

NEW YORK. **Report of the Commission in the Matter of the Investigation of Housing of the People in Cities of the Second Class in the State of New York.**
>By—The Commission. PUBLISHER—State of New York, Albany. 1915. 29 p. Out of print.

NEW YORK. **Study of Housing Conditions.**
>By—Madge Headley. PUBLISHER—State Department of Health, Albany. 1916. 33 p. Out of print.

NEW YORK. **Report of the Housing Committee of the Reconstruction Commission of the State of New York.**
>By—The Committee. PUBLISHER—State of New York, Albany. 1920. 94 p. Free.

NEW YORK. REPORTS OF THE JOINT LEGISLATIVE COMMITTEE ON HOUSING.
Intermediate Report of the Joint Legislative Committee on Housing. Legislative Document (1922) No. 60. 257 p.
Final Report of the Joint Legislative Committee on Housing. Legislative Document (1923) No. 48. 153 p.
>By—The Committee. PUBLISHER—State of New York, Albany. Free.

NEW YORK. REPORTS ON HOUSING IN NEW YORK STATE.
The Present Status of the Housing Emergency. Legislative Document (1924) No. 43. 102 p.
Tax Exemption of New Housing. Legislative Document (1924) No. 78. 26 p.
Report of the Commission of Housing and Regional Planning to

SURVEYS IN SPECIALIZED FIELDS

HOUSING—Continued

Governor Alfred E. Smith and to the Legislature of the State of New York. Legislative Document (1926) No. 40. 110 p.
> By—Commission of Housing and Regional Planning. PUBLISHER—State of New York, Albany. Free.

NEW YORK. **Some Economic Aspects of the Recent Emergency Housing Legislation in New York.** Memorandum report on a fact-finding inquiry.
> By—Samuel McCune Lindsay. PUBLISHER—Law Committee of the Real Estate Board, New York City. 1924. 137 p. Free.

NEW YORK, NEWBURGH. **Housing Investigation, Newburgh.**
> By—Amy Woods. PUBLISHER—Newburgh Associated Charities. 1913. 9 p. Free.

NEW YORK CITY. **Tenement House Administration: Steps Taken to Locate and to Solve Problems of Enforcing the Tenement House Law.**
> By—Bureau of Municipal Research of New York City. PUBLISHER—The same. 1909. 175 p. 50 cents.

NEW YORK CITY. **Report of the Heights of Buildings Commission to the Committee on the Height, Size, and Arrangement of Buildings.**
> By—The Commission. PUBLISHER—Board of Estimate and Apportionment, New York City. 1913. 295 p. Out of print.

NEW YORK CITY. **Housing Conditions among Negroes in Harlem, New York City.** Bulletin of the National League on Urban Conditions Among Negroes. Vol. 4, No. 2.
> By—Housing Bureau, National League on Urban Conditions Among Negroes. PUBLISHER—The League, New York City. 1915. 29 p. Free.

NEW YORK CITY. **Study of Living Conditions of Self-Supporting Women in New York City.**
> By—Esther Packard. PUBLISHER—Metropolitan Board, Young Women's Christian Association, New York City. 1915. 96 p. Out of print.

NEW YORK CITY [BROOKLYN]. HOUSING REPORTS.
The Progress of Housing Reform and a Study of Land Overcrowding in Brooklyn. By Herbert B. Swan. 1916. 47 p.
Housing Standards in Brooklyn. An intensive study of the housing records of 3,227 workingmen's families. By J. C. Gebhart. 1918. 60 p.
> PUBLISHER—Tenement House Committee, Bureau of Charities, Brooklyn. Free.

HOUSING—Continued

NEW YORK CITY. **The Housing Situation in the City of New York.** In Monthly Bulletin of the Department of Health of New York City. Vol. XI, No. 2.
> BY—J. H. Lonergan. PUBLISHER—Department of Health, New York City. 1921. 13 p. Free.

NEW YORK CITY. **Housing Conditions of Employed Women in the Borough of Manhattan.**
> BY—Bureau of Social Hygiene. PUBLISHER—The same, New York City. 1922. 163 p. Free.

NEW YORK CITY. **Should Not the State End New York City's Rookeries?** The Survey of Housing Conditions in New York City. Reprinted articles from The Evening World.
> BY—Special Staff Investigators. PUBLISHER—The Evening World, New York City. 1924. 16 p. 5 cents.

NEW YORK, POUGHKEEPSIE. **A Report of a Housing Survey in the City of Poughkeepsie.**
> BY—Helen D. Thompson. PUBLISHER—Women's City Club, Poughkeepsie. 1919. 46 p. Free.

NEW YORK, YONKERS. **Housing of the Working People in Yonkers.** American Economic Association Studies. Vol. III, No. 5.
> BY—Ernest Ludlow Bogart. PUBLISHER—American Economic Association, Baltimore, Maryland. 1898. 75 p. Out of print.

OHIO, CINCINNATI. **A Study of Living Conditions in Rooming Houses.** Bulletin No. 2.
> BY—Consumers' League of Cincinnati. PUBLISHER—The same. 1916. 7 p. Out of print.

OHIO, CINCINNATI. **A Tenement House Survey in Cincinnati.**
> BY—Cincinnati Better Housing League. PUBLISHER—The same. 1921. 20 p. Free.

OHIO, CLEVELAND. **Housing Conditions in Cleveland.**
> BY—Housing Problem Committee. PUBLISHER—Chamber of Commerce, Cleveland. 1904. 61 p. Out of print.

OHIO, CLEVELAND. **Investigation of Housing Conditions of Cleveland's Workmen—the Best, the Average, and the Worst.**
> BY—Mildred Chadsey. PUBLISHER—Department of Public Welfare, Cleveland. 1914. 34 p. Out of print.

SURVEYS IN SPECIALIZED FIELDS

HOUSING—Continued

OHIO, CLEVELAND. **An Investigation of Housing Conditions of War Workers in Cleveland.**
> BY—Committee on Housing and Sanitation and the U. S. Home Registration Service. PUBLISHER—Cleveland Chamber of Commerce. 1918. 46 p. Out of print.

PENNSYLVANIA. **Housing Conditions in Main Line Towns** [Pennsylvania Railroad].
> BY—Marion Bosworth. PUBLISHER—Philadelphia Housing Commission. 1914. 46 p. Free.

PENNSYLVANIA, PHILADELPHIA. **Housing Conditions in Philadelphia.**
> BY—Emily W. Dinwiddie. PUBLISHER—Octavia Hill Association, Philadelphia. 1904. 42 p. Out of print.

PENNSYLVANIA, PHILADELPHIA. **Housing of the City Negro.**
> BY—B. J. Newman. PUBLISHER—Whittier Center, Philadelphia. 1914. 8 p. Free.

PENNSYLVANIA, PHILADELPHIA. STUDIES IN HOUSING.
Housing in Philadelphia. 1922. 46 p.
Housing in Philadelphia. 1924. 51 p.
> BY—Philadelphia Housing Commission. PUBLISHER—The same. Free.

The Philadelphia Housing Association, as a regular part of its work, makes periodic studies of local housing conditions and preserves the reports in its own office. Its annual reports present summaries of and excerpts from this material.

PENNSYLVANIA, PITTSBURGH. **Report of the Committee on Housing Conditions of Workmen's Dwellings.**
> BY—The Committee. PUBLISHER—Chamber of Commerce, Pittsburgh. 1911. 11 p. Out of print.

PENNSYLVANIA, PITTSBURGH. HOUSING STUDIES OF THE PITTSBURGH SURVEY. In the Pittsburgh District Civic Frontage.
The Housing of Pittsburgh's Workers. By Emily Wayland Dinwiddie. p. 87–124.
Three Studies in Housing and Responsibility. By Florence Larrabee Lattimore and F. Elizabeth Crowell. p. 124–139.
> PUBLISHER—Russell Sage Foundation, New York City. 1914. Out of print.

A BIBLIOGRAPHY OF SOCIAL SURVEYS

HOUSING—Continued

PORTO RICO. **Report on the Housing Conditions of Laborers in Porto Rico.**
    BY—J. C. Bills, Jr. PUBLISHER—Bureau of Labor, San Juan. 1914. 114 p. Free.

RHODE ISLAND; CENTRAL FALLS, NEWPORT, PAWTUCKET, PROVIDENCE, AND WOONSOCKET. **Tenement House Conditions in Five Rhode Island Cities.** Part I of the Annual Report for 1910.
    BY—Carol Aronovici. PUBLISHER—Bureau of Industrial Statistics of Rhode Island, Providence. 1911. 38 p. Out of print.

RHODE ISLAND, PROVIDENCE. **The Houses of Providence.** A study of present conditions, with notes on the surrounding communities and some mill villages.
    BY—John Ihlder, Madge Headley, and Udetta D. Brown. PUBLISHER—Committee on Housing Survey, Chamber of Commerce, Providence. 1916. 105 p. 15 cents.

TEXAS. **Housing Problem in Texas.** A study of physical conditions under which the other half lives. Reprinted articles from the Galveston-Dallas News, November 19–December 17, 1911.
    BY—George Waverly Briggs. PUBLISHER—Galveston-Dallas News, Galveston. 1911. 96 p. Postage.

TEXAS, DALLAS. **Survey of Negro Housing in Dallas.**
    BY—Dallas Committee on Inter-Racial Cooperation. MIMEOGRAPHED—The same. 1925. 13 p. Free.

TEXAS, EL PASO. **Preliminary Report of the Health Survey of El Paso: Housing Health Survey.**
    BY—Jessie P. Rich and B. L. Arms. PUBLISHER—Chamber of Commerce, El Paso. 1915. 8 p. Free.

UNITED STATES. **Housing for Women in War Work.** Report of the Housing Committee of the War Work Council, Young Women's Christian Association.
    BY—The Committee. PUBLISHER—National Board, Young Women's Christian Association, New York City. 1918. 20 p. Free.

UNITED STATES. **Sanitation of Rural Workmen's Areas with Special Reference to Housing.** Public Health Reports. Vol. 33, No. 36.
    BY—Committee on Welfare Work, Council of National Defense. PUBLISHER—Superintendent of Documents, Government Printing Office, Washington, D. C. 1918. 32 p. 5 cents.

SURVEYS IN SPECIALIZED FIELDS

HOUSING—Continued

UNITED STATES. **The Building Situation.** An investigation by the Chamber of Commerce of the United States.
By—John Ihlder. PUBLISHER—Civic Development Department, Chamber of Commerce of the United States, Washington, D. C. 1921. 18 p. Free.

UNITED STATES. **Housing of Women Students at College.** An investigation conducted by the Housing Committee of the American Association of University Women. Reprinted from the Journal of the American Association of University Women. Vol. XV, No. 4.
By—The Committee. PUBLISHER—American Association of University Women, Washington, D. C. 1922. 11 p. 25 cents.

UNITED STATES. **A Study of the Housing of Employed Women and Girls.** Service Series No. 3.
By—National Council of Catholic Women. PUBLISHER—The same, Washington, D. C. 1925. 52 p. 50 cents.

VERMONT, BURLINGTON. **Survey of the City of Burlington: Its Charities and Housing Conditions.**
By—F. H. McLean and U. D. Brown. PUBLISHER—Committee on Social Survey, Burlington. 1915. 85 p. Out of print.

VIRGINIA, RICHMOND. **Report on Housing and Living Conditions in the Neglected Sections of Richmond.**
By—G. A. Weber. PUBLISHER—Society for the Betterment of Housing and Living Conditions, Richmond. 1913. 79 p. Out of print.

WISCONSIN, MILWAUKEE. **Housing Conditions in Milwaukee.**
By—George C. Ruhland. PUBLISHER—Milwaukee Department of Health. 1916. 15 p. Out of print.

In addition to reports **presenting findings** in Housing Surveys, as listed above, publications dealing with **methods of conducting** such studies will be found in Part III, PURPOSE, METHOD, AND STANDARDS, page 350.

ILLEGITIMACY

See also SOCIAL AGENCIES; and UNMARRIED MOTHERS.

CANADA, ONTARIO. **Study of Illegitimacy in Ontario.**
By—N. Emily Mohr. PUBLISHER—Social Service Council of Ontario, Toronto. 1921. 32 p. 25 cents.

ILLEGITIMACY—Continued

CONNECTICUT. **Study of Children Born out of Wedlock in Connecticut.**
BY—Connecticut Child Welfare Association. PUBLISHER—The same, New Haven. 1927. 48 p. Free.

FRANCE. *See* UNITED STATES in this section.

GERMANY. *See* UNITED STATES in this section.

ILLINOIS, CHICAGO. **The Care of Illegitimate Children in Chicago.**
BY—Howard Moore. PUBLISHER—Juvenile Protective Association, Chicago. 1912. 37 p. Out of print.

ILLINOIS, CHICAGO. **A Study of Bastardy Cases Taken from the Court of Domestic Relations.**
BY—Louise DeKoven Bowen. PUBLISHER—Juvenile Protective Association, Chicago. 1914. 24 p. Out of print.

MARYLAND, BALTIMORE. **The Welfare of Infants of Illegitimate Birth in Baltimore. Part I. Mortality among Infants Born Out of Wedlock in 1915 and 1921. Part II. Effect of the Law on the Policies and Work of Social Agencies.** U. S. Department of Labor. Children's Bureau Publication No. 144.
BY—Rena Rosenberg and A. Madorah Donahue. PUBLISHER—Superintendent of Documents, Government Printing Office, Washington, D. C. 1925. 24 p. 5 cents.

MASSACHUSETTS. **Illegitimacy as a Child Welfare Problem. Part II.** A study of original records in the city of Boston and the state of Massachusetts. U. S. Department of Labor. Children's Bureau Publication No. 75. Dependent, Defective and Delinquent Classes Series No. 10.
BY—Emma O. Lundberg and Katharine F. Lenroot. PUBLISHER—Superintendent of Documents, Government Printing Office, Washington, D. C. 1921. 408 p. 50 cents.

MISSOURI, ST. LOUIS. **Illegitimate Births in St. Louis.** Report of Social Investigation No. 4.
BY—G. B. Mangold and L. R. Essex. PUBLISHER—School of Social Economy, St. Louis. 1914. 27 p. 25 cents.

NEW YORK CITY. **Negro Illegitimacy in New York City.** Columbia University Studies in History, Economics, and Public Law No. 277.
BY—Ruth Reed. PUBLISHER—Columbia University Press, New York City. 1926. 136 p. $2.25.

SURVEYS IN SPECIALIZED FIELDS

ILLEGITIMACY—Continued

OHIO, CINCINNATI. **Illegitimacy in Cincinnati.** Studies from the Helen S. Trounstine Foundation. Vol. I, No. 6.
> BY—Helen S. Trounstine. PUBLISHER—Helen S. Trounstine Foundation, Cincinnati. 1919. 14 p. 50 cents.

OHIO, FRANKLIN COUNTY. **Illegitimacy as Shown by a Study of the Birth Certificates from Franklin County in 1924.** Ohio Welfare Bulletin. Vol. III, No. 3.
> BY—Julia Griggs. PUBLISHER—Department of Public Welfare, Columbus. 1927. 18 p. Free.

SWITZERLAND. *See* UNITED STATES in this section.

UNITED STATES. **Illegitimacy Laws of the United States and Certain Foreign Countries** [France, Germany, Switzerland]. U. S. Department of Labor. Children's Bureau Publication No. 42. Legal Series No. 2.
> BY—Ernest Freud. PUBLISHER—Superintendent of Documents, Government Printing Office, Washington, D. C. 1919. 260 p. 35 cents.

UNITED STATES. **Illegitimacy as a Child Welfare Problem. Part I. A Brief Treatment of the Prevalence and Significance of Birth out of Wedlock, the Child's Status, and the State's Responsibility for Care and Protection.** U. S. Department of Labor. Children's Bureau Publication No. 66. Dependent, Defective, and Delinquent Classes Series No. 9.
> BY—Emma O. Lundberg and Katharine F. Lenroot. PUBLISHER—Superintendent of Documents, Government Printing Office, Washington, D. C. 1920. 105 p. 15 cents.

UNITED STATES. **Children Born out of Wedlock.** A sociological study of illegitimacy with particular reference to the United States. University Studies. Vol. III, No. 3. Social Science Series.
> BY—George B. Mangold. PUBLISHER—University of Missouri, Columbia. 1921. 209 p. $1.50.

UNITED STATES. **Illegitimacy as a Child Welfare Problem. Part III. Methods of Care in Selected Urban and Rural Communities.** U. S. Department of Labor. Children's Bureau Publication No. 128. Dependent, Defective, and Delinquent Classes Series No. 11.
> BY—Emma O. Lundberg and Katharine F. Lenroot. PUBLISHER—Superintendent of Documents, Government Printing Office, Washington, D. C. 1924. 260 p. 30 cents.

A BIBLIOGRAPHY OF SOCIAL SURVEYS

IMMIGRATION AND AMERICANIZATION

Reports dealing with the general subject of immigration and Americanization are listed here. For reports dealing with specific phases of this subject or with immigration and Americanization in connection with other subjects *see* PART I, GENERAL SOCIAL SURVEYS—URBAN and PART II, in CHILD HEALTH AND HYGIENE; CHINESE; CRIME AND CRIMINALS; CZECHS; DEPORTATION; FINNS; ITALIANS; JAPANESE; JUGO-SLAVS; JUVENILE DELINQUENCY; LITHUANIANS; MAGYARS; MENTAL HYGIENE; MEXICANS; POLES; RACE RELATIONS; RELIGION; RUSSIANS; SLAVS; SLOVAKS; and TUBERCULOSIS.

Studies covering **a number of cities** in the United States will be found under reports, **Immigrants in Cities** and **Children of Immigrants in Schools,** page 179.

CALIFORNIA. REPORTS ON IMMIGRATION IN CALIFORNIA.

Americanization of Foreign-Born Women. 1917. 24 p. Out of print.

Report of Fresno's Immigration Problem with Particular Reference to Educational Facilities and Requirements. By Ethel Richardson. 1918. 28 p. Free.

Report on Large Landholdings in Southern California. 1919. 43 p. Free.

By—Commission of Immigration and Housing. PUBLISHER—The same, San Francisco.

ELLIS ISLAND. **Report of the Commission for Investigation of the Immigration Station at Ellis Island.**

By—The Commission. PUBLISHER—Superintendent of Documents, Government Printing Office, Washington, D. C. 1904. 38 p. Out of print.

ELLIS ISLAND. MENTALITY OF IMMIGRANTS.

Mental Examination of Immigrants. Administration and line inspection at Ellis Island. Reprint No. 398, Public Health Reports, May 18, 1917. 16 p. 5 cents.

Mentality of the Arriving Immigrant. U. S. Public Health Service Bulletin No. 90. 132 p. 15 cents.

By—E. H. Mullan. PUBLISHER—Superintendent of Documents, Government Printing Office, Washington, D. C. 1917.

ELLIS ISLAND. **A Psychological Study of Immigrant Children at Ellis Island.** Mental Measurement Monographs. Serial No. 3.

By—Bertha M. Boody. PUBLISHER—Williams and Wilkins Company, Baltimore, Maryland. 1926. 163 p. $4.00.

FOREIGN COUNTRIES. See United States in this Section.

SURVEYS IN SPECIALIZED FIELDS

IMMIGRATION AND AMERICANIZATION—Continued

ILLINOIS. REPORTS ON IMMIGRANTS.
 The Educational Needs of Immigrants in Illinois. Bulletin of the Immigrants Commission No. 1. 1920. 37 p.
 The Immigrant and Coal Mining Communities of Illinois. Bulletin of the Immigrants Commission No. 2. 1920. 43 p.
  By—Grace Abbott. PUBLISHER—State Department of Registration and Education, Springfield. Out of print.

ILLINOIS, CHICAGO. Americanization in Chicago. Report of a survey.
  By—Frank D. Loomis. PUBLISHER—Chicago Community Trust. 1920. 40 p. Postage.

INDIANA. The Foreign Problem in Northwest Indiana.
  By—H. William Pilot. PUBLISHER—American Baptist Home Mission Society, New York City. 1917. 15 p. Out of print.

MASSACHUSETTS. Report of the Commission on the Problem of Immigration in Massachusetts. House Document No. 2300.
  By—Commission on Immigration. PUBLISHER—State Legislative Document Division, Boston. 1914. 295 p. Free.

MASSACHUSETTS. REPORTS ON IMMIGRANT EDUCATION.
 Adult Immigrant Education in Massachusetts. Bulletin of the Department of Education. Vol. VI, No. 4. 1921. 19 p.
 The Massachusetts Problem of Immigrant Education in 1921 and 1922. Bulletin of the Department of Education. Vol. VII, No. 6. 1922. 23 p.
  By—James A. Moyer. PUBLISHER—State Department of Education, Boston. Free.

MINNESOTA, MINNEAPOLIS AND ST. PAUL. Nationality and School Progress. A study in Americanization. School and Home Education Monograph No. 4.
  By—Riverda Harding Jordan. PUBLISHER—Public School Publishing Company, Bloomington, Illinois. 1921. 105 p. $1.25.

MISSOURI, ST. LOUIS. The Immigrant in St. Louis. A survey. Studies in Social Economics. Vol. I, No. 2.
  By—Ruth Crawford. PUBLISHER—St. Louis School of Social Economy. 1916. 108 p. 50 cents.

NEW YORK. Report of the Joint Legislative Committee on the Exploitation of Immigrants. Legislative Document (1924) No. 76.
  By—The Committee. PUBLISHER—State of New York, Albany. 1924. 166 p. Free.

IMMIGRATION AND AMERICANIZATION—Continued

OHIO, CLEVELAND. **The School and the Immigrant.** Cleveland Education Survey.
> BY—Herbert Adolphus Miller. PUBLISHER—Cleveland Foundation. 1916. 100 p. 35 cents.

OHIO, CLEVELAND. **Americanization in Cleveland.**
> BY—Americanization Committee, Citizens Bureau. PUBLISHER—The same, Cleveland. 1918. 26 p. Free.

PENNSYLVANIA, PITTSBURGH. **Immigrant Wage-Earners.** In Wage-Earning Pittsburgh, The Pittsburgh Survey.
> BY—Peter Roberts. PUBLISHER—Russell Sage Foundation, New York City. 1914. p. 33–61. Out of print.

UNITED STATES. REPORTS OF THE IMMIGRATION COMMISSION.
> **Abstracts of Reports of the Immigration Commission with Conclusions and Recommendations and Views of the Minority.** In 2 vols. Vol. I. 902 p. $1.25. Vol. 2. 900 p. $1.25.
> **Statistical Review of Immigration, 1819–1910. Distribution of Immigrants, 1850–1900.** Vol. 3. 587 p. Out of print.
> **Emigration Conditions in Europe.** Vol. 4. 424 p. 30 cents.
> **Dictionary of Races of Peoples.** Vol. 5. 150 p. 20 cents.
> **Immigrants in Industries.** Vols. 6–25 inclusive:
>> Part 1. Bituminous Coal Mining. Vol. I. 708 p. 55 cents. Vol. II. 599 p. 45 cents.
>> Part 2. Iron and Steel Manufacturing. Vol. I. 805 p. 65 cents. Vol. II. 749 p. 55 cents.
>> Part 3. Cotton Goods Manufacturing in the North Atlantic States. Part 4. Woolen and Worsted Goods Manufacturing. 950 p. 70 cents.
>> Part 5. Silk Goods Manufacturing and Dyeing. Part 6. Clothing Manufacturing. Part 7. Collar, Cuff, and Shirt Manufacturing. 790 p. 55 cents.
>> Part 8. Leather Manufacturing. Part 9. Boot and Shoe Manufacturing. Part 10. Glove Manufacturing. 903 p. 60 cents.
>> Part 11. Slaughtering and Meat Packing. 695 p. 60 cents.
>> Part 12. Glass Manufacturing. Part 13. Agricultural Implement and Vehicle Manufacturing. 812 p. 55 cents.
>> Part 14. Cigar and Tobacco Manufacturing. Part 15. Furniture Manufacturing. Part 16. Sugar Refining. 727 p. 55 cents.
>> Part 17. Copper Mining and Smelting. Part 18. Iron Ore Mining. Part 19. Anthracite Coal Mining. Part 20. Oil Refining. 929 p. 70 cents.

SURVEYS IN SPECIALIZED FIELDS

IMMIGRATION AND AMERICANIZATION—Continued

- Part 21. Diversified Industries. 500 p. 35 cents.
- Part 22. General Tables of Diversified Industries. 431 p. 40 cents.
- Part 23. Summary Reports of Immigrants in Manufacturing and Mining. Vol. I. 439 p. 35 cents. Vol. II. 1589 p. $1.10.
- Part 24. Recent Immigrants in Agriculture. Vol. I. 435 p. 35 cents. Vol. II. 580 p. 40 cents.
- Part 25. Japanese and Other Immigrant Races in the Pacific Coast and Rocky Mountain States. Vol. I. 403 p. Out of print. Vol. II. 1045 p. Out of print. Vol. III. 732 p. Out of print.

Immigrants in Cities. A study of the population of selected districts in New York, Chicago, Philadelphia, Boston, Cleveland, Buffalo and Milwaukee. Vol. 26. 816 p. Out of print. Vol. 27. 589 p. 40 cents.

Occupations of the First and Second Generations of Immigrants in the United States. Fecundity of Immigrant Women. Vol. 28. 826 p. 55 cents.

Children of Immigrants in Schools. Vols. 29–33 inclusive. Vol. I. 177 p. 55 cents. Vol. II. Baltimore, Bay City, Boston, Buffalo, Cedar Rapids, Chelsea, Chicago, Cincinnati, and Cleveland. 909 p. 60 cents. Vol. III. Detroit, Duluth, Fall River, Haverhill, Johnstown, Kansas City, Los Angeles, Lowell, Lynn, Manchester, and Meriden. 953 p. 60 cents. Vol. IV. Milwaukee, Minneapolis, Newark, New Bedford, New Britain, New Orleans, New York, and Philadelphia. 899 p. 60 cents. Vol. V. Pittsburgh, Providence, St. Louis, San Francisco, Scranton, Shenandoah, South Omaha, Worcester, Yonkers. 866 p. 60 cents.

Immigrants as Charity Seekers. Vols. 34–35. Vol. I. 404 p. 30 cents. Vol. II. 1433 p. $1.00.

Immigration and Crime. Vol. 36. 444 p. Out of print.

Steerage Conditions. Importation and Harboring of Women for Immoral Purposes. Immigrant Home and Aid Societies. Immigrant Banks. Vol. 37. 350 p. 25 cents.

Changes in Bodily Form of Descendants of Immigrants. Vol. 38. 571 p. Out of print.

Federal Immigration Legislation. Digest of Immigration Decisions. Steerage Legislation, 1819–1908. State Immigration and Alien Laws. Vol. 39. 955 p. Out of print.

IMMIGRATION AND AMERICANIZATION—Continued

The Immigration Situation in Other Countries: Canada, Australia, New Zealand, Argentina, Brazil. Vol. 40. 229 p. 35 cents.

Statements and Recommendations Submitted by Societies and Organizations Interested in the Subject of Immigration. Vol. 41. 431 p. Out of print.

> By—Immigration Commission Created by Special Act of Congress. PUBLISHER—Superintendent of Documents, Government Printing Office, Washington, D. C., 1911.

UNITED STATES. **The Foreign Student in America.** A study by the Commission on Survey of Foreign Students in the United States of America, under the auspices of the Friendly Relations Committees of the Young Men's Christian Association and the Young Women's Christian Association.

> By—Reginald Wheeler, Henry H. King, and Alexander B. Davidson. PUBLISHER—Association Press, New York City. 1925. 329 p. $1.75.

In addition to reports **presenting findings** in Immigration and Americanization Surveys, as listed above, a publication dealing with **methods of conducting** such studies will be found in Part III, PURPOSE, METHOD, AND STANDARDS, page 350.

INDIANS

See also HEALTH AND SANITATION.

NEBRASKA. **Tuberculosis among the Nebraska Winnebago.** A social study on an Indian Reservation.

> By—Margaret W. Loening. PUBLISHER—Nebraska State Historical Society, Lincoln. 1921. 48 p. Free.

NEW YORK. **The Indians of New York State.** A study of present day social, industrial, and religious conditions and needs.

> By—Arthur C. Parker and G. E. E. Lindquist. PUBLISHER—Home Mission Council, New York City. 1922. 19 p. 10 cents.

NEW YORK, ONONDAGA INDIAN RESERVATION. **Study of Sanitary Conditions on the Onondaga Indian Reservation.** In Health News, New Series. Vol. 14, No. 4.

> By—F. W. Sears. PUBLISHER—State Department of Health, Albany. 1919. 6 p. Free.

OREGON, KLAMATH COUNTY. **Klamath Indian Survey.** In Health First. Vol. V, No. 3.

> By—L. Grace Holmes. PUBLISHER—Oregon Tuberculosis Association, Portland. 1922. 10 p. Free.

SURVEYS IN SPECIALIZED FIELDS

INDIANS—Continued

UNITED STATES. **Tuberculosis among Certain Indian Tribes of the United States.** Smithsonian Institution. Bureau of American Ethnology Bulletin 42.
By—Ales Hrdlicka. PUBLISHER—Superintendent of Documents, Government Printing Office, Washington, D. C. 1909. 48 p. 50 cents.

UNITED STATES. **The Red Man in the United States.** An intimate study of the social, economic, and religious life of the American Indian.
By—G. E. E. Lindquist. PUBLISHER—George H. Doran Company, New York City. 1923. 461 p. $3.50.

UNITED STATES. **Tuberculosis among North American Indians.** Printed for the use of the Committee on Indian Affairs.
By—Committee of the National Tuberculosis Association. PUBLISHER—Superintendent of Documents, Government Printing Office, Washington, D. C. 1923. 101 p. Free.

INDUSTRIAL CONDITIONS AND RELATIONS

Reports dealing only with the general subject of industrial conditions and relations are listed here. For reports dealing with specific phases of this subject or with industrial questions in connection with other subjects *see* ACCIDENTS AND ACCIDENT PREVENTION; ADOLESCENCE; BLINDNESS, SIGHT CONSERVATION, AND DISEASE OF THE EYE; CHILD LABOR; CHINESE; COST OF LIVING; CRIPPLED, DISABLED, AND HANDICAPPED; EIGHT-HOUR DAY; FIRE; HEALTH IN INDUSTRY; HOUSING; IMMIGRATION AND AMERICANIZATION; INDUSTRIAL EDUCATION; INFANT MORTALITY; ITALIANS; JAPANESE; NEGRO EDUCATION; NEGROES, PENSIONS; POSTURE; PRISONS; RELIGION; RURAL; RURAL EDUCATION; TUBERCULOSIS; UNEMPLOYMENT; and VOCATIONAL GUIDANCE AND TRAINING.

ALABAMA. **Women in Alabama Industries.** A study of hours, wages, and working conditions. U. S. Department of Labor. Bulletin of the Women's Bureau No. 34.
By—Kathleen B. Jennison. PUBLISHER—Superintendent of Documents, Government Printing Office, Washington, D. C. 1924. 86 p. 15 cents.

INDUSTRIAL CONDITIONS AND RELATIONS—Continued

ARKANSAS. **Women in Arkansas Industries.** A study of hours, wages, and working conditions. U. S. Department of Labor. Bulletin of the Women's Bureau No. 26.
> By—Caroline Manning and Ethel L. Best. PUBLISHER—Superintendent of Documents, Government Printing Office, Washington, D. C. 1923. 86 p. 10 cents.

CALIFORNIA, LOS ANGELES. **Social Aspects of the Fishing Industry at Los Angeles Harbor.** Studies in Sociology No. 18.
> By—Edwin F. Bamford. PUBLISHER—Southern California Sociological Society, Los Angeles. 1921. 15 p. 20 cents.

CALIFORNIA; OAKLAND, ALAMEDA, AND BERKELEY. **Report of the Housing and Industrial Survey of the Oakland, Alameda, and Berkeley District.**
> By—Housing Bureau, California Commission of Immigration and Housing. MIMEOGRAPHED—The Commission, San Francisco. 1918. 5 p. Free.

CALIFORNIA, SAN FRANCISCO. **A Survey of the Garment Trades in San Francisco.** Bureau of Research in Education No. 3.
> By—Emily G. Palmer. PUBLISHER—University of California, Berkeley. 1921. 87 p. 40 cents.

CANADA. **Industrial Occupations of Women.** Department of Economics and Political Science, McGill University. Series VI, No. 5.
> By—Enid M. Price. PUBLISHER—Canadian Reconstruction Association, Montreal. 1919. 86 p. 50 cents.

CANADA. **Shop Collective Bargaining.** A study of wage determination in the men's garment industry [Canada and the United States].
> By—Francis Joseph Haas. PUBLISHER—Catholic University of America, Washington, D. C. 1922. 174 p. Free.

CANADA, WINNIPEG. **Work of Women and Girls in Department Stores of Winnipeg.**
> By—Civic Committee, University Women's Club, Winnipeg. PUBLISHER—The same. 1914. 21 p. Out of print.

COLORADO. **Child Labor and the Work of Mothers in the Beet Fields of Colorado and Michigan.** U. S. Department of Labor. Children's Bureau Publication No. 115.
> By—Ellen Nathalie Matthews, Director. PUBLISHER—Superintendent of Documents, Government Printing Office, Washington, D. C. 1923. 122 p. 20 cents.

SURVEYS IN SPECIALIZED FIELDS

INDUSTRIAL CONDITIONS AND RELATIONS—Continued

COLORADO, DENVER. **Denver and Farm Labor Families.** Publication No. 328.
>By—Sara A. Brown. PUBLISHER—National Child Labor Committee, New York City. 1925. 4 p. Free.

CONNECTICUT. REPORTS ON WOMEN IN INDUSTRY.
The Conditions of Labor of Women Factory Workers in Six Connecticut Industries. Pamphlet No. 6. By Mary S. Sims. 1912. 8 p.
The Department Store Girl and Her Friend in "The Five and Ten." Pamphlet No. 9. By Charlotte M. Holloway. 1914. 8 p.
>PUBLISHER—Consumers' League of Connecticut, Hartford. Free.

CONNECTICUT. REPORTS ON CONDITIONS OF WAGE-EARNING WOMEN AND GIRLS.
Report of the Special Commission to Investigate the Conditions of Wage-Earning Women and Minors in the State. 1913. 297 p.
Report of the Bureau of Labor on the Conditions of Wage-Earning Women and Girls. 1914. 139 p.
Report of the Bureau of Labor on the Conditions of Wage-Earning Women and Girls. 1916. 143 p.
Report of the Bureau of Labor on the Conditions of Wage-Earning Women and Girls. 1918. 144 p.
Report of the Department of Labor on the Conditions of Wage-Earners in the State. 1922. 176 p.
>By—Charlotte M. Holloway. PUBLISHER—State Bureau of Labor, Hartford. Free.

CONNECTICUT, BRIDGEPORT. **Munition Makers.** Contains a section on munition workers in England and France.
>By—Amy Hewes and Henriette R. Walter. PUBLISHER—Russell Sage Foundation, New York City. 1917. 158 p. 75 cents.

CONNECTICUT, BRIDGEPORT. **Home Work in Bridgeport.** U. S. Department of Labor. Bulletin of the Women's Bureau No. 9.
>By—Mary N. Winslow. PUBLISHER—Superintendent of Documents, Government Printing Office, Washington, D. C. 1920. 35 p. 5 cents.

CONNECTICUT, NEW HAVEN. **An Industrial Survey of a New Haven District.**
>By—Henry P. Fairchild. PUBLISHER—Civic Federation of New Haven. 1913. 14 p. Out of print.

A BIBLIOGRAPHY OF SOCIAL SURVEYS

INDUSTRIAL CONDITIONS AND RELATIONS—Continued

DELAWARE. **Women in Delaware Industries.** A study of hours, wages, and working conditions. U. S. Department of Labor. Bulletin of the Women's Bureau No. 58.

> By—Caroline Manning and others. PUBLISHER—Superintendent of Documents, Government Printing Office, Washington, D. C. 1927. 156 p. 25 cents.

DELAWARE. **Women's Employment in Vegetable Canneries in Delaware.** U. S. Department of Labor. Bulletin of the Women's Bureau No. 62.

> By—Loretta Sullivan and Ethel Erickson. PUBLISHER—Superintendent of Documents, Government Printing Office, Washington, D. C. 1927. 47 p. 10 cents.

DISTRICT OF COLUMBIA. **Hours, Earnings, and Duration of Employment of Wage-Earning Women in Selected Industries in the District of Columbia.** Bulletin of the U. S. Bureau of Labor Statistics. Whole No. 116. Women in Industry Series No. 1.

> By—Marie L. Obenauer. PUBLISHER—Superintendent of Documents, Government Printing Office, Washington, D. C. 1913. 68 p. 10 cents.

DISTRICT OF COLUMBIA, WASHINGTON. **An Industrial Survey of Washington, D. C.**

> By—Industrial Committee, Young Women's Christian Association, District of Columbia. PUBLISHER—The same, Washington. 1925. 11 p. Free.

FLORIDA, JACKSONVILLE. **Family Status of Breadwinning Women in Four Selected Cities.** [Jacksonville, Fla.; Butte, Mont.; Passaic, N. J.; Wilkes-Barre and Hanover Township, Pa.] U. S. Department of Labor. Bulletin of the Women's Bureau No. 41.

> By—Mary Anderson, Director. PUBLISHER—Superintendent of Documents, Government Printing Office, Washington, D. C. 1925. 144 p. 20 cents.

GEORGIA. **Women in Georgia Industries.** A study of hours, wages, and working conditions. U. S. Department of Labor. Bulletin of the Women's Bureau No. 22.

> By—Ethel L. Best, Director. PUBLISHER—Superintendent of Documents, Government Printing Office, Washington, D. C 1922. 89 p. 10 cents.

SURVEYS IN SPECIALIZED FIELDS

INDUSTRIAL CONDITIONS AND RELATIONS—Continued

GEORGIA, ATLANTA. **Preliminary Report of a Survey of Wages, Hours, and Conditions of Work of the Women in Industry in Atlanta, Georgia.** U. S. Department of Labor.
> By—Women's Bureau. PUBLISHER—Superintendent of Documents, Government Printing Office, Washington, D. C. 1920. 31 p. Out of print.

GREAT BRITAIN. **Economic Effects of the War upon Women and Children in Great Britain.**
> By—Irene Osgood Andrews and Margarett A. Hobbs. PUBLISHER—Carnegie Endowment for International Peace, New York City. 1918. 190 p. $1.00.

HAWAII, HONOLULU. **The Industrial Conditions of Women and Girls in Honolulu.** A social study.
> By—Frances Blascoer. PUBLISHER—Kaiulani Home for Young Women and Girls, Honolulu. 1912. 98 p. Free.

ILLINOIS. **Women in Illinois Industries.** A study of hours and working conditions. U. S. Department of Labor. Bulletin of the Women's Bureau No. 51.
> By—Ruth I. Voris. PUBLISHER—Superintendent of Documents, Government Printing Office, Washington, D. C. 1926. 108 p. 20 cents.

ILLINOIS, CHICAGO. **Working Hours of Wage-Earning Women in Selected Industries in Chicago.** Bulletin of the U. S. Bureau of Labor No. 91.
> By—Marie L. Obenauer. PUBLISHER—Superintendent of Documents, Government Printing Office, Washington, D. C. 1910. 48 p. Out of print.

ILLINOIS, CHICAGO. EMPLOYMENT OF GIRLS IN CHICAGO.
The Department Store Girl. Report based upon interviews with 200 girls. 1911. 13 p.
The Girl Employed in Hotels and Restaurants. Report of investigation of 50 hotels and 72 restaurants. 1912. 17 p.
> By—Louise de Koven Bowen. PUBLISHER—Juvenile Protective Association, Chicago. Out of print.

ILLINOIS, CHICAGO. INVESTIGATIONS MADE IN THE STOCKYARD DISTRICT
Wages and Family Budget in the Chicago Stockyard District with

A BIBLIOGRAPHY OF SOCIAL SURVEYS

INDUSTRIAL CONDITIONS AND RELATIONS—Continued

Wage Statistics from Other Industries Employing Skilled Labor. By—J. C. Kennedy. 1914. 80 p. PUBLISHER—Board of University of Chicago Settlement. 25 cents each.

ILLINOIS, CHICAGO. **The Saturday Half Holiday.** An investigation.
By—Juvenile Protective Association. PUBLISHER—The same, Chicago. 1916. 9 p. Free.

ILLINOIS, CHICAGO. **Women Street Car Conductors and Ticket Agents** [Chicago, Ill.; Boston, Mass.; Detroit, Mich.; Kansas City, Mo.]. U. S. Department of Labor. Bulletin of the Women's Bureau No. 11.
By—Mary N. Winslow. PUBLISHER—Superintendent of Documents, Government Printing Office, Washington, D. C. 1920. 90 p. 15 cents.

ILLINOIS, CHICAGO. **Women in the Candy Industry in Chicago and St. Louis.** A study of hours, wages and working conditions in 1920–1921. U. S. Department of Labor. Bulletin of the Women's Bureau No. 25.
By—Caroline Manning. PUBLISHER—Superintendent of Documents, Government Printing Office, Washington, D. C. 1923. 72 p. 10 cents.

ILLINOIS, SPRINGFIELD. **Industrial Conditions in Springfield.** Industrial Section of the Springfield Survey.
By—Louise C. Odencrantz and Zenas L. Potter. PUBLISHER—Russell Sage Foundation, New York City. 1916. 173 p. Out of print.

INDIANA. **Hours, Earnings, and Conditions of Labor of Women in Indiana Mercantile Establishments and Garment Factories.** Bulletin of the U. S. Bureau of Labor Statistics. Whole No. 160. Women in Industry Series No. 4.
By—Marie L. Obenauer and Frances W. Valentine. PUBLISHER—Superintendent of Documents, Government Printing Office, Washington, D. C. 1914. 198 p. 20 cents.

INDIANA. **Labor Laws for Women in Industry in Indiana.** Report of a survey. U. S. Department of Labor. Bulletin of the Women in Industry Service No. 2.
By—May Allinson, Director. PUBLISHER—Superintendent of Documents, Government Printing Office, Washington, D. C. 1919. 29 p. 10 cents.

SURVEYS IN SPECIALIZED FIELDS

INDUSTRIAL CONDITIONS AND RELATIONS—Continued

IOWA. **Iowa Women in Industry.** Report of the investigation in the state of Iowa of hours and working conditions of women in industry. U. S. Department of Labor. Bulletin of the Women's Bureau No. 19.
> BY—Women's Bureau. PUBLISHER—Superintendent of Documents, Government Printing Office, Washington, D. C. 1922. 78 p. 10 cents.

KANSAS. **Women's Wages in Kansas.** U. S. Department of Labor. Bulletin of the Women's Bureau No. 17.
> BY—Women's Bureau and Kansas Industrial Welfare Commission. PUBLISHER—Superintendent of Documents, Government Printing Office, Washington, D. C. 1921. 104 p. 10 cents.

KANSAS, TOPEKA. **Industrial Conditions. Part IV. Topeka Improvement Survey.**
> BY—Zenas L. Potter. PUBLISHER—Russell Sage Foundation. New York City. 1914. 56 p. 15 cents.

KENTUCKY. **Report of the Commission to Investigate the Conditions of Working Women in Kentucky.**
> BY—S. M. Hartzman. PUBLISHER—State of Kentucky, Frankfort. 1911. 55 p. Out of print.

KENTUCKY. **Women in Kentucky Industries.** A study of hours, wages, and working conditions. U. S. Department of Labor. Bulletin of the Women's Bureau No. 29.
> BY—Caroline Manning, Director. PUBLISHER—Superintendent of Documents, Government Printing Office, Washington, D. C. 1923. 114 p. 15 cents.

LOUISIANA. **Report of the State Commission to Study the Conditions of Working Women and Children in Louisiana.**
> BY—S. M. Hartzman. PUBLISHER—Louisiana Industrial Commission, State Department of Labor, Baton Rouge. 1914. 24 p. Out of print.

LOUISIANA. **Conditions of Women's Labor in Louisiana.** New Orleans and Louisiana Industrial Survey.
> BY—Janet R. Huntington. PUBLISHER—State Department of Labor, New Orleans. 1919. 139 p. 5 cents.

MARYLAND. **Women in Maryland Industries.** A study of hours and working conditions. U. S. Department of Labor. Bulletin of the Women's Bureau No. 24.
> BY—Mary V. Robinson. PUBLISHER—Superintendent of Documents, Government Printing Office, Washington, D. C. 1922. 96 p. 10 cents.

INDUSTRIAL CONDITIONS AND RELATIONS—Continued

MASSACHUSETTS. REPORT OF THE RESEARCH DEPARTMENT OF THE WOMEN'S EDUCATIONAL AND INDUSTRIAL UNION.
The Living Wage of Women Workers. A study of incomes and expenditures of 450 women in the city of Boston. By Louise Marion Bosworth. 1911. 90 p. $1.00 and postage.
The Public School and Women in Office Service. By May Allinson. 1914. 187 p. 80 cents and postage.
Industrial Home Work in Massachusetts. By Amy Hewes. 1915. 191 p. 80 cents and postage.
    PUBLISHER—Women's Educational and Industrial Union, Boston.

MASSACHUSETTS. **The Department Store.** Its holidays and vacations. Bulletin No. 6.
    BY—Consumers' League of Massachusetts. PUBLISHER—The same, Boston. 1914. 4 p. Free.

MASSACHUSETTS. **Report of the Special Committee Appointed by the House of Representatives of 1913 to Investigate the Conditions under Which Women and Children Labor in the Various Industries and Occupations.** House Document No. 2126.
    BY—The Committee. PUBLISHER—Legislative Document Division, State House, Boston. 1914. 194 p. Free.

MASSACHUSETTS. STUDIES OF WOMEN IN INDUSTRY. U. S. BUREAU OF LABOR STATISTICS BULLETINS.
The Boot and Shoe Industry in Massachusetts as a Vocation for Women. Women in Industry Series No. 7. Whole No. 180. 1915. 109 p. 15 cents.
Dressmaking as a Trade for Women in Massachusetts. Women in Industry Series No. 9. Whole No. 193. 1916. 180 p. 20 cents.
Industrial Experience of Trade-School Girls in Massachusetts. Women in Industry Series No. 10. Whole No. 215. 1917. 275 p. 25 cents.
    BY—May Allinson, Director. PUBLISHER—Superintendent of Documents, Government Printing Office, Washington, D. C.

MASSACHUSETTS. **Report of the State Board of Labor and Industry Relative to the Investigation of Prevailing Conditions in Hotels and Restaurants in Massachusetts.** House Bulletin No. 1538.
    BY—State Board of Labor and Industries. PUBLISHER—Commonwealth of Massachusetts, Boston. 1917. 17 p. Free.

SURVEYS IN SPECIALIZED FIELDS

INDUSTRIAL CONDITIONS AND RELATIONS—Continued

MASSACHUSETTS. **Wages and Hours of Labor in the Metal Trades in Massachusetts.** Department of Labor and Industries Bulletin No. 132.
> BY—Roswell F. Phelps, Director. PUBLISHER—State Department of Labor and Industries, Boston. 1920. 72 p. Free.

MASSACHUSETTS. **Some Effects of Legislation Limiting Hours of Work for Women** [Massachusetts and New Jersey]. U. S. Department of Labor. Bulletin of the Women's Bureau No. 15.
> BY—Mary N. Winslow. PUBLISHER—Superintendent of Documents, Government Printing Office, Washington, D. C. 1921. 26 p. 5 cents.

MASSACHUSETTS, BOSTON. See ILLINOIS, CHICAGO, in this section.

MASSACHUSETTS, LAWRENCE. **Report on the Industrial Situation Revealed by the Lawrence Strike.**
> BY—Committee Appointed by the Massachusetts Federation of Churches. PUBLISHER—Federal Council, Churches of Christ in America, New York City. 1920. 8 p. 10 cents.

MICHIGAN. See COLORADO in this section.

MICHIGAN, DETROIT. See ILLINOIS, CHICAGO, in this section.

MINNESOTA. **Women in Industry in Minnesota in 1918.** Bulletin of Minnesota Department of Labor and Industries. Bureau of Women and Children.
> BY—Carol Aronovici. PUBLISHER—Minnesota Commission of Public Safety, St. Paul. 1920. 35 p. Free.

MINNESOTA, MINNEAPOLIS. **A Study of Women in Clerical and Secretarial Work.**
> BY—M. C. Elmer. PUBLISHER—Woman's Occupational Bureau Minneapolis. 1925. 42 p. 25 cents.

MISSISSIPPI. **Women in Mississippi Industries.** A study of hours, wages, and working conditions. U. S. Department of Labor. Bulletin of the Women's Bureau No. 55.
> BY—Ruth I. Voris and Elizabeth A. Hyde. PUBLISHER—Superintendent of Documents, Government Printing Office, Washington, D. C. 1926. 89 p. 15 cents.

MISSOURI. **Report of the Senate Wage Commission for Women and Children in the State of Missouri.**
> BY—The Commission. PUBLISHER—State Department of Labor, Jefferson City. 1915. 108 p. Free.

INDUSTRIAL CONDITIONS AND RELATIONS—Continued

MISSOURI. **Women in Missouri Industries.** A study of hours and wages. U. S. Department of Labor. Bulletin of the Women's Bureau No. 35.
>BY—Ruth I. Voris and Elizabeth A. Hyde. PUBLISHER—Superintendent of Documents, Government Printing Office, Washington, D. C. 1924. 127 p. 15 cents.

MISSOURI, KANSAS CITY. See ILLINOIS, CHICAGO, in this section.

MISSOURI, ST. LOUIS. **Industrial Conditions among Negroes in St. Louis.** Studies in Social Economics. Vol. I, No. 1.
>BY—William August Crossland. PUBLISHER—School of Social Economy, Washington University, St. Louis. 1914. 123 p. 75 cents.

MISSOURI, ST. LOUIS. See also ILLINOIS, CHICAGO, in this section.

MONTANA, BUTTE. See FLORIDA, JACKSONVILLE, in this section.

NEW JERSEY. **Three Years under the New Jersey Workmen's Compensation Law.** Report of an investigation.
>BY—Social Insurance Committee, American Association for Labor Legislation. PUBLISHER—American Association for Labor Legislation, New York City. 1915. 71 p. Free.

NEW JERSEY. **Executive and Technical Women in Industry: Survey of Factories** [New Jersey and New York].
>BY—Janet R. Huntington. PUBLISHER—National Board, Young Women's Christian Association, New York City. 1920. 19 p. Free.

NEW JERSEY. **Desirable Improvements in the New Jersey Workmen's Compensation System.** Report of the Bureau of State Research. Vol. VIII, No. 10, Consecutive No. 19.
>BY—Paul Studensky. PUBLISHER—Bureau of State Research, Newark. 1921. 28 p. 25 cents.

NEW JERSEY. **Women in New Jersey Industries.** A study of wages and hours of labor. U. S. Department of Labor. Bulletin of the Women's Bureau No. 37.
>BY—Ruth I. Voris. PUBLISHER—Superintendent of Documents, Government Printing Office, Washington, D. C. 1924. 99 p. 15 cents.

NEW JERSEY. See also MASSACHUSETTS and PENNSYLVANIA in this section.

SURVEYS IN SPECIALIZED FIELDS

INDUSTRIAL CONDITIONS AND RELATIONS—Continued

NEW JERSEY, HUDSON COUNTY. **Sweated Work in Hudson County.**
Reprinted from Charities and the Commons, December 21, 1907.
> BY—Elizabeth B. Butler. PUBLISHER—Consumers' League of New Jersey, Newark. 1907. 8 p. Out of print.

NEW JERSEY, PASSAIC. **Night-Working Mothers in Textile Mills.**
> BY—Agnes de Lima. PUBLISHER—National Consumers' League and the Consumers' League of New Jersey, Newark. 1920. 19 p. Out of print.

NEW JERSEY, PASSAIC. **The Family Status of Breadwinning Women.**
U. S. Department of Labor. Bulletin of the Women's Bureau No. 23.
> BY—Mary Anderson, Director. PUBLISHER—Superintendent of Documents, Government Printing Office, Washington, D. C. 1922. 43 p. 10 cents.

NEW JERSEY, PASSAIC. *See also* FLORIDA, JACKSONVILLE, in this section.

NEW YORK. **Report to the Legislature of the State of New York by the Commission Appointed to Inquire into the Question of Employers' Liability and Other Matters.**
> BY—The Commission. PUBLISHER—State of New York, Albany. 1910. 270 p. Free.

NEW YORK. REPORTS OF THE FACTORY INVESTIGATING COMMISSION OF THE STATE OF NEW YORK.
Preliminary Report of the Factory Investigating Commission. In 3 volumes. By George M. Price, Director. 1912. 1986 p.
Second Report of the Factory Investigating Commission. In 4 volumes. By George M. Price, Director. 1913. 2437 p.
Third Report of the Factory Investigating Commission. By Howard B. Woolston, Director. 1914. 676 p.
Fourth Report of the Factory Investigating Commission. In 5 volumes. By Howard B. Woolston and Albert H. N. Baron, Directors. 1915. 2922 p.
> BY—The Commission. PUBLISHER—State Department of Labor, Albany. Free.

NEW YORK. **Brief Summary of Investigations and Inquiries Made between the Years of 1905 and 1915 into Typical Industries in the State of New York.**
> BY—D. J. Schweitzer. PUBLISHER—Council of Jewish Women, New York City. 1916. 42 p. Out of print.

INDUSTRIAL CONDITIONS AND RELATIONS—Continued

NEW YORK. INVESTIGATIONS IN INDUSTRIES IN NEW YORK STATE.
  The Telephone Industry. Special Bulletin No. 100. By Bureau of Women in Industry. 1920. 64 p.
  The Outer-Wear Knit Goods Industry. Special Bulletin No. 117. By Charlotte E. Carr. 1923. 19 p.
  Hours and Earnings of Women in Five Industries: Confectionery, Tobacco, Shirts and Collars, Paper Box, and Mercantile. Special Bulletin No. 121. By Charlotte E. Carr. 1923. 76 p.
  Vacation Policies in Manufacturing Industries. Special Bulletin No. 138. By Marie Elder. 1925. 11 p.
  Hours and Earnings of Women Employed in Power Laundries in New York State. By Edna Shepard, Director. 1927. 72 p.
    PUBLISHER—Bureau of Women in Industry, State Department of Labor, Albany. Free.

NEW YORK. REPORTS ON WOMEN'S WAGES.
  Women's Wages Today. 1920. 12 p.
  Behind the Scenes in a Hotel. 1922. 47 p.
    BY—Consumers' League of New York. PUBLISHER—The same, New York City. Free.

NEW YORK. Our Boys: A Study of 245,000 Sixteen, Seventeen, and Eighteen Year Old Employed Boys of the State of New York.
    BY—Howard G. Burdge. PUBLISHER—Bureau of Vocational Training, State of New York, Albany. 1921. 345 p. Free.

NEW YORK. See also NEW JERSEY in this section.

NEW YORK, BUFFALO. Nationality, Color, and Economic Opportunity in the City of Buffalo.
    BY—Niles Carpenter. PUBLISHER—Committee on Publications, Roswell Park Publication Fund, University of Buffalo. 1927. 194 p. 50 cents.

NEW YORK CITY. The Clothing Industry in New York. University of Missouri Studies. Social Science Series.
    BY—Jesse E. Pope. PUBLISHER—University of Missouri, Columbia. 1905. 340 p. $1.25.

NEW YORK CITY. INDUSTRIAL STUDIES.
  Women in the Bookbinding Trade. 1913. 270 p. $1.50.
  Working Girls in Evening Schools: A Statistical Study. 1914. 252 p. Out of print.
  A Seasonal Industry: A Study of the Millinery Trade. 1917. 276 p. $1.50.

SURVEYS IN SPECIALIZED FIELDS

INDUSTRIAL CONDITIONS AND RELATIONS—Continued
Artificial Flower Makers. 1918. 261 p. $1.50.
By—Mary van Kleeck. PUBLISHER—Russell Sage Foundation, New York City.

NEW YORK CITY. The Longshoremen.
By—Charles B. Barnes. PUBLISHER—Russell Sage Foundation, New York City. 1915. 287 p. $2.00.

NEW YORK CITY. Increased Employment of Women in Industry. A report on the problems of substituting female workers for male to meet the present labor scarcity.
By—Alfred L. Smith, Director. PUBLISHER—Merchants Association of New York, New York City. 1917. 23 p. Free.

NEW YORK CITY. Opportunities for Women in the Municipal Civil Service of the City of New York.
By—Fannie M. Witherspoon and Anna Martin Crocker. PUBLISHER—Intercollegiate Bureau of Occupations, New York City, 1918. 94 p. Free.

NEW YORK CITY. Women Street Railway Employees. In U. S. Bureau of Labor Statistics Monthly Review. Vol. VI, No. 5.
By—Benjamin M. Squires. PUBLISHER—Superintendent of Documents, Government Printing Office, Washington, D. C. 1918. 27 p. 15 cents per copy.

NEW YORK CITY. New Day for the Colored Woman Worker. A study of colored women in industry in the City of New York.
By—Jessie Clark and Gertrude E. McDougal. PUBLISHER—National Board, Young Women's Christian Association, New York City. 1919. 39 p. Free.

NEW YORK CITY. Less Than a Living Wage.
By—Consumers' League of New York. PUBLISHER—The same, New York City. 1921. 9 p. Free.

NEW YORK, NEW YORK CITY AND ROCHESTER. Homework in the Men's Clothing Industry in New York and Rochester. Special Bulletin No. 147.
By—Edna Shepard, Director. PUBLISHER—Bureau of Women in Industry, State Department of Labor, Albany. 1926. 67 p. Free.

INDUSTRIAL CONDITIONS AND RELATIONS—Continued

NEW YORK, NIAGARA FALLS. **Proposed Employment of Women during the War in the Industries of Niagara Falls.** U. S. Department of Labor. Bulletin of the Women in Industry Service No. 1.
> BY—Bureau of Labor Statistics. PUBLISHER—Superintendent of Documents, Government Printing Office, Washington, D. C. 1918. 16 p. 5 cents.

OHIO. **Preliminary Survey of Labor Camps in Ohio.**
> BY—George F. Miles. PUBLISHER—Industrial Commission of Ohio, Columbus. 1917. 22 p. Free.

OHIO. **Women in Ohio Industries.** A study of hours and wages. U. S. Department of Labor. Bulletin of the Women's Bureau No. 44.
> BY—Women's Bureau. PUBLISHER—Superintendent of Documents, Government Printing Office, Washington, D. C. 1925. 137 p. 20 cents.

OHIO, CINCINNATI. INDUSTRIAL SURVEY OF CINCINNATI.
Garment Making Industries. By Cleo Murtland and F. P. Goodwin. 113 p.
Printing Trades. By Charles R. Hebble, Director. 141 p.
> PUBLISHER—Chamber of Commerce, Cincinnati. 1915. Out of print.

OHIO, CINCINNATI. STUDIES IN INDUSTRY.
A Study of Restaurant Kitchens. Bulletin No. 4. By Elizabeth Shelow, Director. 1916. 10 p. Out of print.
Women Workers in Factories. A study of working conditions in 275 industrial establishments in Cincinnati and adjoining towns. By Annette Mann. 1918. 45 p. Free.
> PUBLISHER—Consumers' League of Cincinnati.

OHIO, CINCINNATI. **Wage-Earning Girls in Cincinnati.** The wages, employment, housing, food, recreation, and education of a sample group.
> BY—Frances Ivins Rich and Ellery Francis Reed. MIMEOGRAPHED—Helen S. Trounstine Foundation and Young Women's Christian Association, New York City. 1927. 76 p. $1.00.

OHIO, CLEVELAND. **Study of Women's Work in Cleveland.**
> BY—B. M. Stevens. PUBLISHER—Consumers' League of Cleveland. 1908. 27 p. Out of print.

OHIO, CLEVELAND. **Employee Representation in Industry.** Some plans in operation in Cleveland.
> BY—Committee on Labor Relations. PUBLISHER—Chamber of Commerce, Cleveland. 1923. 107 p. $1.00.

SURVEYS IN SPECIALIZED FIELDS

INDUSTRIAL CONDITIONS AND RELATIONS—Continued

OKLAHOMA. **Women in Oklahoma Industries.** A study of hours, wages, and working conditions. U. S. Department of Labor. Bulletin of the Women's Bureau No. 48.
> BY—Mildred M. Hawkins and Ruth I. Voris. PUBLISHER—Superintendent of Documents, Government Printing Office, Washington, D. C. 1926. 118 p. 20 cents.

OREGON. **Wages, Hours, and Conditions of Work and Cost and Standard of Living of Women Wage Earners in Oregon, with Special Reference to Portland.**
> BY—E. V. O'Hara. PUBLISHER—Social Survey Committee, Consumers' League of Oregon, Portland. 1913. 84 p. Out of print.

OREGON, PORTLAND. **Report of the Industrial Welfare Commission of the State of Oregon on the Power Laundries in Portland.**
> BY—Caroline J. Gleason. PUBLISHER—Industrial Welfare Commission, Portland. 1914. 52 p. Out of print.

PENNSYLVANIA. **Wage-Earning Women in War Time: The Textile Industry with Special Reference in Pennsylvania and New Jersey to Woolen and Worsted Yarn, and in Rhode Island to the Work of Women at Night.** Reprinted from the Journal of Industrial Hygiene, October, 1919.
> BY—Florence Kelley. PUBLISHER—National Consumers' League, New York City. 1919. 24 p. Free.

PENNSYLVANIA. **Industrial Home Work in Pennsylvania.** Prepared through the Cooperation of the Department of Labor and Industry of the Commonwealth of Pennsylvania, the Consumers' League of Eastern Pennsylvania, and the Carola Woerishoffer Graduate Department of Social Economy and Social Research of Bryn Mawr College.
> BY—Agnes Mary Hadden Byrnes. PUBLISHER—Department of Labor and Industry, Harrisburg. 1921. 189 p. Free.

PENNSYLVANIA, PHILADELPHIA. **Conditions of Women in Mercantile Establishments in Philadelphia.** Bulletin No. 1, Vol. 2.
> BY—Consumers' League of Eastern Pennsylvania. PUBLISHER—State Department of Labor and Industry, Harrisburg. 1915. 79 p. Out of print.

PENNSYLVANIA, PHILADELPHIA. **Wages of Candy Makers in Philadelphia in 1919.** U. S. Department of Labor. Bulletin of the Women in Industry Service No. 4.
> BY—Ethel L. Best and Mildred L. Jones. PUBLISHER—Superintendent of Documents, Government Printing Office, Washington, D. C. 1919. 46 p. 5 cents.

A BIBLIOGRAPHY OF SOCIAL SURVEYS

INDUSTRIAL CONDITIONS AND RELATIONS—Continued

PENNSYLVANIA, PHILADELPHIA. **Colored Women as Industrial Workers in Philadelphia.**
> BY—Consumers' League of Eastern Pennsylvania. PUBLISHER—The same, Philadelphia. 1920. 43 p. Free.

PENNSYLVANIA, PHILADELPHIA. **Attendance in Four Textile Mills in Philadelphia.** A study by the Industrial Research Department. Wharton School of Finance and Commerce. Publication No. 1660. Reprinted from Vol. CIV, Annals of the American Academy of Political and Social Science.
> BY—Anne Bezanson and others. PUBLISHER—University of Pennsylvania, Philadelphia. 1922. 34 p. 50 cents.

PENNSYLVANIA, PHILADELPHIA. **Mothers in Industry.** Wage-earning by mothers in Philadelphia.
> BY—Gwendolyn Salisbury Hughes and Carola Woerishoffer. PUBLISHER—New Republic, New York City. 1925. 265 p. $1.00.

PENNSYLVANIA, PHILADELPHIA. **The Young Employed Girl.**
> BY—Hazel Grant Ormsbee. PUBLISHER—Woman's Press, New York City. 1927. 124 p. $1.00.

PENNSYLVANIA, PITTSBURGH. THE PITTSBURGH SURVEY. Findings in six volumes.
Women and the Trades. By Elizabeth B. Butler. 1909. 440 p. Out of print.
The Steel Workers. By John A. Fitch. 1911. 380 p. Out of print.
Wage-Earning Pittsburgh. By Paul U. Kellogg and others. 1914. 582 p. $2.50.
Other volumes listed elsewhere.
> BY—Paul U. Kellogg, Editor. PUBLISHER—Russell Sage Foundation, New York City.

PENNSYLVANIA, PITTSBURGH. **Industry.** In Wage Earning Pittsburgh, The Pittsburgh Survey.
> BY—Paul U. Kellogg, Director. PUBLISHER—Russell Sage Foundation, New York City. 1914. p. 113–307. Out of print.

PENNSYLVANIA, WILKES-BARRE AND HANOVER TOWNSHIP. *See* FLORIDA, JACKSONVILLE, in this section.

SURVEYS IN SPECIALIZED FIELDS

INDUSTRIAL CONDITIONS AND RELATIONS—Continued

RHODE ISLAND. **Women in Rhode Island Industries.** A study of hours, wages and working conditions. U. S. Department of Labor. Bulletin of the Women's Bureau No. 21.
    By—Ethel L. Best and Mary V. Robinson. PUBLISHER—Superintendent of Documents, Government Printing Office, Washington, D. C. 1922. 73 p. 10 cents.

RHODE ISLAND. *See also* PENNSYLVANIA in this section.

RHODE ISLAND, LONSDALE. **Wages and Family Income in the Village of Lonsdale.** Reprint from the Annual Report of the Rhode Island Bureau of Industrial Statistics. Part 2.
    By—Carol Aronovici. PUBLISHER—Rhode Island Bureau of Industrial Statistics, Providence. 1911. 67 p. Out of print.

SOUTH CAROLINA. **Women in South Carolina Industries.** A study of hours, wages, and working conditions. U. S. Department of Labor. Bulletin of the Women's Bureau No. 32.
    By—Mary V. Robinson. PUBLISHER—Superintendent of Documents, Government Printing Office, Washington, D. C. 1923. 127 p. 15 cents.

TENNESSEE. **Women in Tennessee Industries.** A study of hours, wages, and working conditions. U. S. Department of Labor. Bulletin of the Women's Bureau No. 56.
    By—Ethel L. Best and Ruth I. Voris. PUBLISHER—Superintendent of Documents, Government Printing Office, Washington, D. C. 1926. 121 p. 20 cents.

UNITED STATES. REPORT ON CONDITION OF WOMAN AND CHILD WAGE-EARNERS IN THE UNITED STATES.
    Vol. I. **Cotton and Textile Industry.** 1910. 1035 p. Out of print.
    Vol. II. **Men's Ready-Made Clothing.** 1911. 871 p. 65 cents.
    Vol. III. **The Glass Industry.** 1911. 959 p. 75 cents.
    Vol. IV. **The Silk Industry.** 1911. 585 p. Out of print.
    Vol. V. **Wage-Earning Women in Stores and Factories.** 1910. 377 p. Out of print.
    Vol. IX. **History of Women in Industry in the United States.** By Helen L. Sumner. 1911. 263 p. Out of print.
    Vol. X. **History of Women in Trade Unions.** By John B. Andrews and W. E. F. Bliss. 1911. 229 p. Out of print.
    Vol. XI. **Employment of Women in the Metal Trades.** By Lucian W. Chaney. 1911. 101 p. 10 cents.

INDUSTRIAL CONDITIONS AND RELATIONS—Continued

Vol. XII. Employment of Women in Laundries. 1911. 118 p. Out of print.

Vol. XVIII. Employment of Women and Children in Selected Industries. 1913. 521 p. 35 cents.

Vol. XIX. Labor Laws and Factory Conditions. 1912. 1107 p. 80 cents.

Other volumes are listed elsewhere.

By—Charles P. Neill, Director. PUBLISHER—Superintendent of Documents, Government Printing Office, Washington, D. C.

UNITED STATES. REPORT ON CONDITIONS OF EMPLOYMENT IN THE IRON AND STEEL INDUSTRY IN THE UNITED STATES.

Vol. I. Wages and Hours of Labor. 1911. 522 p. 50 cents.

Vol. II. Wages and Hours of Labor. 1912. 1040 p. 70 cents.

Vol. III. Working Conditions and the Relations of Employers and Employees. 1913. 584 p. 45 cents.

By—Charles P. Neill, Director. PUBLISHER—Superintendent of Documents, Government Printing Office, Washington, D. C.

UNITED STATES. **Saleswomen in Mercantile Stores.**

By—Elizabeth B. Butler. PUBLISHER—Russell Sage Foundation, New York City. 1913. 217 p. $1.00.

UNITED STATES. **Summary of the Report on Condition of Woman and Child Wage-Earners in the United States.** Bulletin of the U. S. Bureau of Labor Statistics. Whole No. 175, Women in Industry Series No. 5.

By—Bureau of Labor Statistics. PUBLISHER—Superintendent of Documents, Government Printing Office, Washington, D. C. 1915. 445 p. 45 cents.

UNITED STATES. **Wage Worth of School Training.** An analytical study of six hundred women workers in textile factories. Teachers College Contributions to Education No. 70.

By—Anna Charlotte Hedges. PUBLISHER—Bureau of Publications, Teachers College, Columbia University, New York City. 1915. 174 p. $2.00.

UNITED STATES. **Effect of Workmen's Compensation Laws in Diminishing the Necessity of Industrial Employment of Women and Children.** U. S. Bureau of Labor Statistics Bulletin. Whole No. 217. Workmen's Insurance and Compensation Series No. 11.

By—Mary K. Conyngton. PUBLISHER—Superintendent of Documents, Government Printing Office, Washington, D. C. 1918. 170 p. 15 cents.

SURVEYS IN SPECIALIZED FIELDS

INDUSTRIAL CONDITIONS AND RELATIONS—Continued

UNITED STATES [NORTHWEST]. **Report on the Logging Camps of the Pacific Northwest with Recommendations.**
By—Worth M. Tippy. PUBLISHER—Joint Committee on War Production Communities and Commission on Church and Social Service, New York City. 1919. 29 p. 10 cents.

UNITED STATES. **Women's Wages.** A study of the wages of industrial women and measures suggested to increase them. Studies in History, Economics, and Public Law. Vol. LXXXIX, No. 1. Whole No. 202. Columbia University.
By—Emilie Josephine Hutchinson. PUBLISHER—Longmans, Green and Company, New York City. 1919. 179 p. Out of print.

UNITED STATES. **The Hours of Work Problem in Five Major Industries.** Research Report No. 27.
By—National Industrial Conference Board. PUBLISHER—The same, New York City. 1920. 91 p. $1.00.

UNITED STATES. **The New Position of Women in American Industry.** U. S. Department of Labor. Bulletin of the Women's Bureau No. 12.
By—Women's Bureau. PUBLISHER—Superintendent of Documents, Government Printing Office, Washington, D. C. 1920. 157 p. 25 cents.

UNITED STATES. **Women in Government Service.** U. S. Department of Labor. Bulletin of the Women's Bureau No. 8.
By—Bertha M. Nienburg. PUBLISHER—Superintendent of Documents, Government Printing Office, Washington, D. C. 1920. 37 p. 10 cents.

UNITED STATES. **Women Professional Workers.** A study made for the Women's Educational and Industrial Union.
By—Elizabeth K. Adams. PUBLISHER—Macmillan Company, New York City. 1921. 467 p. $2.50.

UNITED STATES [GULF COAST]. **Child Labor and the Work of Mothers in Oyster and Shrimp Canning Communities on the Gulf Coast.** U. S. Department of Labor. Children's Bureau Publication No. 98.
By—Viola I. Paradise. PUBLISHER—Superintendent of Documents, Government Printing Office, Washington, D. C. 1922. 114 p. 15 cents.

INDUSTRIAL CONDITIONS AND RELATIONS—Continued

UNITED STATES. **Industrial Unemployment.** A statistical study of its extent and causes. U. S. Department of Labor. Bureau of Labor Statistics Bulletin No. 310. Employment and Unemployment Series.
 BY—Ernest S. Bradford. PUBLISHER—Superintendent of Documents, Government Printing Office, Washington, D. C. 1922. 52 p. 10 cents.

UNITED STATES. **A Survey of Natural Illumination in an Industrial Plant.** Public Health Reports. Vol. 37, No. 15.
 BY—C.-E. A. Winslow and Leonard Greenburg. PUBLISHER—Superintendent of Documents, Government Printing Office, Washington, D. C. 1922. 12 p. 5 cents.

UNITED STATES. **Employment Hours and Earnings in Prosperity and Depression in the United States.** Results of an inquiry conducted by the National Bureau of Economic Research, with the help of the Bureau of Markets and Crop Estimates, and the Bureau of the Census for the President's Conference on Unemployment.
 BY—Willford Isbell King. PUBLISHER—National Bureau of Economic Research, New York City. 1923. 147 p. $3.10.

UNITED STATES. **The Share of Wage-Earning Women in Family Support.** U. S. Department of Labor. Bulletin of the Women's Bureau No. 30.
 BY—Mary N. Winslow. PUBLISHER—Superintendent of Documents, Government Printing Office, Washington, D. C. 1923. 163 p. 20 cents.

UNITED STATES. **Home Environment and Employment Opportunities of Women in Coal Mine Workers' Families.** U. S. Department of Labor. Bulletin of the Women's Bureau No. 45.
 BY—Women's Bureau. PUBLISHER—Superintendent of Documents, Government Printing Office, Washington, D. C. 1925. 61 p. 10 cents.

UNITED STATES. *See also* CANADA in this section.

VERMONT, BRATTLEBORO. **A Legacy to Wage-Earning Women.** A survey of gainfully employed women of Brattleboro and of relief which they have received from the Thomas Thompson Trust.
 BY—Lucile Eaves and associates. PUBLISHER—Women's Educational and Industrial Union. Boston, Massachusetts. 1925. 135 p. $1.25.

SURVEYS IN SPECIALIZED FIELDS

INDUSTRIAL CONDITIONS AND RELATIONS—Continued

VIRGINIA. **Hours and Conditions of Work for Women in Industry in Virginia.** U. S. Department of Labor. Bulletin of the Women's Bureau No. 10. Second Edition.
> BY—Mary N. Winslow. PUBLISHER—Superintendent of Documents, Government Printing Office, Washington, D. C. 1920. 32 p. 5 cents.

VIRGINIA, NORFOLK. **Child Labor and the Work of Mothers on Norfolk Truck Farms.** U. S. Department of Labor. Children's Bureau Publication No. 130.
> BY—Ellen Nathalie Matthews and Ethel M. Springer. PUBLISHER—Superintendent of Documents, Government Printing Office, Washington, D. C. 1924. 27 p. 5 cents.

VIRGINIA, PETERSBURG. **Petersburg, Economic and Municipal.**
> BY—Leroy Hodges. PUBLISHER—Chamber of Commerce, Petersburg. 1917. 166 p. $1.00.

WASHINGTON. **Report of the Industrial Welfare Commission of the State of Washington on the Wages, Conditions of Work, and Cost and Standards of Living of Women Wage-Earners in Washington.**
> BY—Caroline J. Gleason. PUBLISHER—State of Washington, Olympia. 1914. 111 p. Out of print.

WASHINGTON. **Women in the Fruit-growing and Canning Industries in the State of Washington.** A study of hours, wages, and conditions. U. S. Department of Labor. Bulletin of the Women's Bureau No. 47.
> BY—Caroline Manning, Mary V. Robinson, Blanche Halbert, and Loretta Sullivan. PUBLISHER—Superintendent of Documents, Government Printing Office, Washington, D. C. 1926. 223 p. 40 cents.

WISCONSIN. **Conditions in the Garment-Making Trades.**
> BY—Bureau of Labor and Industrial Statistics. PUBLISHER—The same, Madison. 1902. 314 p. Out of print.

WISCONSIN. **Working Hours of Women in the Pea Canneries of Wisconsin.** Bulletin of the U. S. Bureau of Labor Statistics. Whole No. 119. Women in Industry Series No. 2.
> BY—Marie L. Obenauer. PUBLISHER—Superintendent of Documents, Government Printing Office, Washington, D. C. 1913. 54 p. 5 cents.

WISCONSIN. **Investigation of Labor Camps in Wisconsin.**
> BY—Industrial Commission of Wisconsin. PUBLISHER—State of Wisconsin, Madison. 1914. 48 p. Free.

INDUSTRIAL CONDITIONS AND RELATIONS—Continued

WISCONSIN, MILWAUKEE. SURVEYS OF WAGES IN MILWAUKEE.
Garnishment of Wages. Bulletin No. 3. 27 p.
Women's Wages in Milwaukee. Bulletin No. 4. 18 p.
> BY—Milwaukee Bureau of Economy and Efficiency. PUBLISHER—The same, 1911. Out of print.

WISCONSIN, MILWAUKEE. **Employment of Women in Power Laundries in Milwaukee.** A study of working conditions and of the physical demands of the various laundry occupations. Bulletin of the U. S. Bureau of Labor Statistics. Whole No. 122. Women in Industry Series No. 3.
> BY—Marie L. Obenauer. PUBLISHER—Superintendent of Documents, Government Printing Office, Washington, D. C. 1913. 92 p. 10 cents.

In addition to reports **presenting findings** in Industrial Conditions and Relations Surveys, as listed above, publications dealing with **methods of conducting** such studies will be found in Part III, PURPOSE, METHODS, AND STANDARDS, page 351.

INDUSTRIAL EDUCATION

> *See also* CHILD WELFARE; CONTINUATION AND PART-TIME SCHOOLS; EDUCATION; RURAL EDUCATION; and VOCATIONAL GUIDANCE AND TRAINING.

DELAWARE, WILMINGTON. **Industrial Education in Wilmington.** Report of a survey made under the direction of the Commissioner of Education. U. S. Department of Interior. Bureau of Education Bulletin, 1918, No. 25.
> BY—Fred C. Whitcomb. PUBLISHER—Superintendent of Documents, Government Printing Office, Washington, D. C. 1918. 102 p. 15 cents.

GEORGIA, COLUMBUS. **Industrial Education in Columbus.** U. S. Department of Interior. Bureau of Education Bulletin No. 25. Whole No. 535.
> BY—Roland B. Daniel. PUBLISHER—Superintendent of Documents, Government Printing Office, Washington, D. C. 1913. 30 p. 5 cents.

MASSACHUSETTS, WORCESTER. **A Trade School for Girls.** A preliminary investigation in a typical manufacturing city. U. S. Department of

SURVEYS IN SPECIALIZED FIELDS

INDUSTRIAL EDUCATION—Continued

Interior. Bureau of Education Bulletin, 1913, No. 17. Whole No. 525.
> By—Susan M. Kingsbury and May Allinson. PUBLISHER—Superintendent of Documents, Government Printing Office, Washington, D. C. 1913. 59 p. 10 cents.

MICHIGAN. **Report of the Michigan Commission on Industrial and Agricultural Education.**
> By—The Commission. PUBLISHER—The same, Lansing. 1910. 95 p. Out of print.

NEW YORK CITY. **Industrial Education Survey of the City of New York.** Complete report of the Committee authorized by the Board of Estimate and Apportionment.
> By—Lewis A. Wilson, Director. PUBLISHER—Board of Estimate and Apportionment, New York City. 1918. 473 p. Free.

OHIO, CLEVELAND. **Industrial Education in the Cleveland Public Schools.**
> By—Cleveland Chamber of Commerce. PUBLISHER—The same. 1914. 7 p. Free.

OHIO, CLEVELAND. **Wage Earning and Education.** The Cleveland Education Survey.
> By—R. R. Lutz. PUBLISHER—Cleveland Foundation. 1916. 208 p. 75 cents.

> The following parts are obtainable at 35 cents each:

Boys and Girls in Commercial Work. By Bertha M. Stevens. 181 p.
Dressmaking and Millinery. By Edna Bryner. 133 p.
Railroad and Street Transportation. By Ralph D. Fleming. 76 p.
The Building Trades. By Frank L. Shaw. 107 p.
The Metal Trades. By R. R. Lutz. 130 p.
The Printing Trades. By Frank L. Shaw. 95 p.
Department Store Occupations. By Iris Prouty O'Leary. 127 p.
The Garment Trades. By Edna Bryner. 153 p.

SOUTH CAROLINA, CHARLESTON. INDUSTRIAL EDUCATION SURVEY.
Part I. Charleston Public Schools. 24 p.
Part II. Survey of Industries. 58 p.
Part III. Survey of Business Occupations. 58 p.
Part IV. Survey of Housekeeping. 48 p.
> By—Carleton B. Gibson, Director. PUBLISHER—Board of City School Commissioners, Charleston. 1920. Free.

INDUSTRIAL HYGIENE

See HEALTH IN INDUSTRY.

INFANT MORTALITY

See also ILLEGITIMACY; and MATERNAL DEATHS.

CONNECTICUT, WATERBURY. **Infant Mortality.** Results of a field study in Waterbury, based on births in one year. U. S. Department of Labor. Children's Bureau Publication No. 29. Infant Mortality Series No. 7.

 By—Estelle B. Hunter. PUBLISHER—Superintendent of Documents, Government Printing Office, Washington, D. C. 1918. 157 p. 20 cents.

INDIANA, GARY. **Infant Mortality.** Results of a field study in Gary, based on births in one year. U. S. Department of Labor. Children's Bureau Publication No. 112.

 By—Elizabeth Hughes and others. PUBLISHER—Superintendent of Documents, Government Printing Office, Washington, D. C. 1923. 122 p. 20 cents.

MARYLAND, BALTIMORE. **Infant Mortality.** Results of a field study in Baltimore, based on births in one year. U. S. Department of Labor. Children's Bureau Publication No. 119.

 By—Anne Rochester. PUBLISHER—Superintendent of Documents, Government Printing Office, Washington, D. C. 1923. 400 p. 40 cents.

MASSACHUSETTS. **A Brief Statistical Study of Infant Mortality in a Town of Massachusetts.** In The Commonhealth. Vol. 9, No. 6.

 By—Angeline D. Hamblen. PUBLISHER—State Department of Public Health, Boston. 1922. 8 p. Free.

MASSACHUSETTS, BOSTON. **Infant Mortality: Its Relation to Social and Industrial Conditions.**

 By—Henry H. Hibbs, Jr. PUBLISHER—Russell Sage Foundation, New York City. 1916. 127 p. Out of print.

MASSACHUSETTS, BROCKTON. **Infant Mortality.** Results of a field study in Brockton, based on births in one year. U. S. Department of Labor. Children's Bureau Publication No. 37. Infant Mortality Series No. 8.

 By—Mary V. Dempsey. PUBLISHER—Superintendent of Documents, Government Printing Office, Washington, D. C. 1919. 82 p. 10 cents.

SURVEYS IN SPECIALIZED FIELDS

INFANT MORTALITY—Continued

MASSACHUSETTS, FALL RIVER. **Infant Mortality in Fall River.** Report of a survey of the mortality among 832 infants born in June, July, and August, 1913.

    BY—Fall River District Nursing Association. PUBLISHER—Civic Department, Woman's Club, Fall River. 1915. 16 p. Free.

MASSACHUSETTS, NEW BEDFORD. **Infant Mortality.** Results of a field study in New Bedford, based on births in one year. U. S. Department of Labor. Children's Bureau Publication No. 68. Infant Mortality Series No. 10.

    BY—Jessamine S. Whitney. PUBLISHER—Superintendent of Documents, Government Printing Office, Washington, D. C. 1920. 114 p. 25 cents.

MICHIGAN, SAGINAW. **Infant Mortality.** Results of a field study in Saginaw, based on births in one year. U. S. Department of Labor. Children's Bureau Publication No. 52. Infant Mortality Series No. 9.

    BY—Nila F. Allen. PUBLISHER—Superintendent of Documents, Government Printing Office, Washington, D. C. 1919. 91 p. 25 cents.

NEW HAMPSHIRE, MANCHESTER. **Infant Mortality.** Results of a field study in Manchester, based on births in one year. U. S. Department of Labor. Children's Bureau Publication No. 20. Infant Mortality Series No. 6.

    BY—Beatrice Sheets Duncan and Emma Duke. PUBLISHER—Superintendent of Documents, Government Printing Office, Washington, D. C. 1917. 138 p. 25 cents.

NEW JERSEY, ESSEX COUNTY. **Infant Mortality.** Report of the Public Welfare Committee of Essex County.

    BY—Julius Levy. PUBLISHER—The Committee, Newark. 1912. 32 p. Out of print.

NEW JERSEY, MONTCLAIR. **A Study of Infant Mortality in a Suburban Community.** U. S. Department of Labor. Children's Bureau Publication No. 11. Infant Mortality Series No. 4.

    BY—Margretta A. Williamson. PUBLISHER—Superintendent of Documents, Government Printing Office, Washington, D. C. 1915. 36 p. 5 cents.

NEW YORK CITY. **Infant Mortality in New York City.** A study of the results accomplished by infant life-saving agencies. 1885–1920.

    BY—Ernst Christopher Meyer. PUBLISHER—Rockefeller Foundation International Health Board, New York City. 1921. 135 p. Free.

INFANT MORTALITY—Continued

NEW YORK, OGDENSBURG. **A Survey of Infant Mortality and Stillbirths in the City of Ogdensburg.** In Annual Report of the State Department of Health. Vol. III.
    BY—B. R. Wakeman. PUBLISHER—State Department of Health, Albany. 1915. 30 p. Out of print.

NEW ZEALAND. **A New Zealand Study in Infant Mortality.** In Journal of American Statistical Association, September.
    BY—Edward P. Neals. PUBLISHER—American Statistical Association, New York City. 1925. 14 p. $1.50 per copy.

OHIO, AKRON. **Infant Mortality.** Results of a field study of Akron, based on births in one year. U. S. Department of Labor. Children's Bureau Publication No. 72. Infant Mortality Series No. 11.
    BY—Theresa S. Haley. PUBLISHER—Superintendent of Documents, Government Printing Office, Washington, D. C. 1920. 118 p. 20 cents.

OHIO, CINCINNATI. **A Study of Infant Mortality in Cincinnati for the Year 1925.**
    BY—Anna M. Drake. PUBLISHER—Child Hygiene Council, Cincinnati Public Health Federation. 1927. 24 p. Free.

PENNSYLVANIA, JOHNSTOWN. **Infant Mortality.** Results of a study in Johnstown, based on births in one calendar year. U. S. Department of Labor. Children's Bureau Publication No. 9. Infant Mortality Series No. 3.
    BY—Emma Duke. PUBLISHER—Superintendent of Documents, Government Printing Office, Washington, D. C. 1915. 93 p. 20 cents.

PENNSYLVANIA, PITTSBURGH. **Infant Mortality in Pittsburgh.** An analysis of records for 1920 with six charts. U. S. Department of Labor. Children's Bureau Publication No. 86. Infant Mortality Series No. 12.
    BY—Glenn Steele. PUBLISHER—Superintendent of Documents, Government Printing Office, Washington, D. C. 1921. 24 p. 5 cents.

RHODE ISLAND, WOONSOCKET. **Stillbirths and Neonatal Deaths in Woonsocket in 1915.**
    BY—Sarah I. Morse. PUBLISHER—Child Welfare Division, State Board of Health, Providence. 1926. 25 p. Free.

SURVEYS IN SPECIALIZED FIELDS

INFANT MORTALITY—Continued

UNITED STATES. **Infant Mortality and Its Relation to the Employment of Mothers.** Vol. XIII. Report on Condition of Woman and Child Wage-Earners in the United States. Senate Document No. 645.
    BY—Charles P. Neill, Director. PUBLISHER—Superintendent of Documents, Government Printing Office, Washington, D. C. 1912. 174 p. 15 cents.

UNITED STATES. **Infant Mortality and Milk Stations.** Special report dealing with the problem of reducing infant mortality; work carried on in ten largest cities of the United States with details of demonstration by public and private agencies in New York City during 1911 to determine the value of milk station work as a practical means of reducing infant mortality.
    BY—Philip Van Ingen and Paul Emmons Taylor. PUBLISHER—New York Milk Committee, New York City. 1912. 175 p. $1.00.

UNITED STATES. **Causal Factors in Infant Mortality.** A statistical study based on investigations in eight cities. U. S. Department of Labor. Children's Bureau Publication No. 142.
    BY—Robert Morse Woodbury. PUBLISHER—Superintendent of Documents, Government Printing Office, Washington, D. C. 1925. 245 p. 30 cents.

INFANTILE PARALYSIS

IOWA. **Epidemiologic Studies of Acute Poliomyelitis.** I. Poliomyelitis in Iowa, 1910. II. Poliomyelitis in Cincinnati, Ohio, 1911. III. Poliomyelitis in Buffalo and Batavia, New York, 1912. Hygienic Laboratory Bulletin No. 90. U. S. Public Health Service.
    BY—Wade H. Frost. PUBLISHER—Superintendent of Documents, Government Printing Office, Washington, D. C. 1913. 71 p. Out of print.

MASSACHUSETTS. **Infantile Paralysis with Special Reference to Its Occurrence in Massachusetts.**
    BY—R. W. Lovett and M. W. Richardson. PUBLISHER—American Medical Association, Chicago, Illinois. 1911. 38 p. Free.

MASSACHUSETTS. INFANTILE PARALYSIS IN MASSACHUSETTS.
Infantile Paralysis in Massachusetts, 1907–1912, with Reports of Special Investigations. By State Department of Health. 1914. 151 p. Out of print.

A BIBLIOGRAPHY OF SOCIAL SURVEYS

INFANTILE PARALYSIS—Continued

The 1916 Infantile Paralysis Epidemic in Massachusetts. By Stanley H. Osborn and Lyman Asa Jones. 1919. 52 p. Free.
PUBLISHER—State Department of Public Health, Boston.

MONTANA. **A Study of Epidemic Poliomyelitis in Montana.** Public Health Reports. Vol. 38, No. 4.
BY—John J. Sippy. PUBLISHER—Superintendent of Documents, Government Printing Office, Washington, D. C. 1923. 5 p. 5 cents.

NEW YORK. **After-Care of Poliomyelitis in New York State.**
BY—Robert W. Lovett. PUBLISHER—State Department of Health, Albany. 1918. 31 p. Free.

NEW YORK, BUFFALO. **Study of the Acute Anterior Poliomyelitis Epidemic Which Occurred in the City of Buffalo during the Year 1912.**
BY—W. S. Goodale. PUBLISHER—Buffalo Department of Health. 1913. 62 p. Free.

NEW YORK, BUFFALO AND BATAVIA. *See also* IOWA in this section.

NEW YORK CITY. **A Monograph on the Epidemic of Poliomyelitis (Infantile Paralysis) in New York City in 1916, Based on the Official Reports of the Bureaus of the Department of Health.**
BY—City Department of Health. PUBLISHER—The same, New York City. 1917. 312 p. Free.

NEW YORK CITY AND NORTHEASTERN UNITED STATES. **Epidemiological Studies of Poliomyelitis in New York City and the Northeastern United States During the Year 1916.** U. S. Public Health Service Bulletin No. 91.
BY—C. H. Lavinder, A. W. Freemen, and W. H. Frost. PUBLISHER—Superintendent of Documents, Government Printing Office, Washington, D. C. 1918. 309 p. 25 cents.

OHIO, CINCINNATI. *See* IOWA in this section.

UNITED STATES. **State Work against Infantile Paralysis: Steps Taken by 43 Departments of Health.**
BY—Institute for Public Service. PUBLISHER—The same, New York City. 1917. 63 p. 50 cents.

WEST VIRGINIA, ELKINS. **Winter Outbreak of Poliomyelitis.** Reprint No. 437, Public Health Reports, November 30, 1917.
BY—J. P. Leake, Joseph Bolton, and H. F. Smith. PUBLISHER—Superintendent of Documents, Government Printing Office, Washington, D. C. 1918. 22 p. 5 cents.

SURVEYS IN SPECIALIZED FIELDS

INSANE

See also DELINQUENCY AND CORRECTION; FEEBLEMINDED; and MENTAL HYGIENE.

MISSOURI. **The Care and Treatment of the Insane in Missouri.** The report of a survey of all the institutions in Missouri caring for the insane.
 By—Committee for Mental Hygiene Survey. PUBLISHER—State Board of Charities and Correction, Jefferson City. 1920. 172 p. Free.

NEW YORK. **Report of the Investigation of the State Commission on Lunacy and the State Hospitals for the Insane.**
 By—The Commission. PUBLISHER—General Assembly of New York, Albany. 1895. 24 p. Out of print.

NEW YORK. **Social Aspects of the Treatment of the Insane, Based on a Study of New York Experience.** Columbia University Studies in History, Economics, and Public Law. Vol. XCVII, No. 2.
 By—Jacob A. Goldberg. PUBLISHER—Columbia University Press, New York City. 1921. 247 p. $3.00.

PENNSYLVANIA. **Treatment and Care of the Insane in Pennsylvania.** Being a report of a survey of all the institutions in Pennsylvania caring for the insane.
 By—C. Floyd Haviland. PUBLISHER—Public Charities Association of Pennsylvania, Philadelphia. 1915. 94 p. Out of print.

INSURANCE

See HEALTH INSURANCE; PENSIONS; and SOCIAL INSURANCE.

ITALIANS

See also PRISONS.

AMERICA. **Religious Work among Italians in America.** A survey for the Home Mission Council.
 By—Antonio Mangano. PUBLISHER—Home Mission Council, New York City. 1917. 51 p. Out of print.

ILLINOIS, CHICAGO. **Two Italian Districts.** Reprints from the American Journal of Sociology. Vol. XVIII, No. 4.
 By—Grace Peloubet Norton. PUBLISHER—University of Chicago Press. 1913. 33 p. 50 cents.

ITALIANS—Continued

ILLINOIS, CHICAGO. **Greeks and Italians in the Neighborhood of Hull House.** Reprint from the American Journal of Sociology. Vol. XXI, No. 3.
> By—Natalie Walker. PUBLISHER—University of Chicago Press. 1915. 31 p. 50 cents.

ILLINOIS, CHICAGO. **Housing Survey in the Italian District of the 17th Ward.** In First Annual Report of the Department of Public Welfare.
> By—Department of Public Welfare. PUBLISHER—The same, Chicago. 1915. 21 p. Free.

ILLINOIS, CHICAGO. **The Italians in Chicago.** A study made by the Bureau of Surveys of the Department of Public Welfare. Bulletin Vol. II, No. 3.
> By—Louise Osborne Rowe and Frank Orman Beck. PUBLISHER—Department of Public Welfare, Chicago. 1919. 32 p. Free.

NEW YORK, MOUNT VERNON. **Study of the Activities of the Neighborhood House and the Italians in Mount Vernon.**
> By—Jeannette Bullis. MIMEOGRAPHED—Neighborhood Association, Mount Vernon. 1922. 16 p. Free.

NEW YORK CITY. **Italian Women in Industry.** A study of conditions in New York City.
> By—Louise C. Odencrantz. PUBLISHER—Russell Sage Foundation, New York City. 1919. 345 p. $1.50.

NEW YORK CITY. **Growth and Development of Italian Children in New York City.** Publication No. 132.
> By—John C. Gebhart. PUBLISHER—Association for Improving the Condition of the Poor, New York City. 1924. 36 p. 25 cents.

NEW YORK, POUGHKEEPSIE. **The Italian Situation in Poughkeepsie.**
> By—Henry S. Huntington, Jr. MIMEOGRAPHED—The same. Rochester. 1918. 16 p. Out of print.

OHIO, CLEVELAND. **The Italians of Cleveland.**
> By—Charles W. Coulter. PUBLISHER—Americanization Committee, Citizens Bureau, Cleveland. 1919. 43 p. 10 cents.

UNITED STATES. *See* AMERICA in this section.

WISCONSIN, MILWAUKEE. **The Italians in Milwaukee.** A general survey prepared under the direction of the Associated Charities.
> By—G. La Piana. PUBLISHER—Family Welfare Association, Milwaukee. 1915. 85 p. 40 cents.

SURVEYS IN SPECIALIZED FIELDS

JAILS
    See ALMSHOUSES; MENTAL HYGIENE; PRISONS; and WORKHOUSES.

JAPANESE
    See also IMMIGRATION AND AMERICANIZATION; and RACE RELATIONS.

CALIFORNIA. **Preliminary Report on the Mental Capacity of Japanese Children in California.**
    By—M. L. Darsie. PUBLISHER—Japanese Association of America, San Francisco. 1922. 7 p. Free.

CALIFORNIA, LOS ANGELES COUNTY. **The Japanese in Rural Los Angeles County.** Bulletin No. 16.
    By—Ralph F. Burnight. PUBLISHER—Southern California Sociological Society, Los Angeles. 1920. 16 p. 20 cents.

JAPAN, OSAKA. **Cost of Living among Laborers in Osaka.** Report of Labor Research. Series X.
    By—Municipal Bureau of Labor Research of Osaka. PUBLISHER—The same. 1921. 123 p. Free.

JAPAN, TOKYO. **The Administration and Politics of Tokyo.** A survey and opinions.
    By—Charles A. Beard. PUBLISHER—Macmillan Company, New York City. 1923. 187 p. $2.50.

UNITED STATES. **Japanese and Other Immigrant Races in the Pacific Coast and Rocky Mountain States.** Vol. 24. Report of the Immigration Commission.
    By—The Commission. PUBLISHER—Superintendent of Documents, Government Printing Office, Washington, D. C. 1911. 1045 p. Out of print.

In addition to reports **presenting findings,** as listed above, a publication dealing with **methods of conducting** such studies will be found in Part III, PURPOSE, METHOD, AND STANDARDS, under **Race Relations.**

JUGO-SLAVS

OHIO, CLEVELAND. **The Jugo-Slavs in Cleveland, with a Brief Sketch of Their Historical Background.**
    By—Eleanor E. Ledbetter. PUBLISHER—Americanization Committee, Citizens Bureau, Cleveland. 1918. 30 p. 25 cents.

A BIBLIOGRAPHY OF SOCIAL SURVEYS

JUVENILE COURT
See JUVENILE DELINQUENCY.

JUVENILE DELINQUENCY
See also ADOLESCENCE; CHILD LABOR; CHILD WELFARE; DELINQUENCY AND CORRECTION; DETENTION; PROBATION AND PAROLE; and VICE.

CALIFORNIA. **Study of 150 Delinquent Boys in 1915.** Research Laboratory of the Buckel Foundation, Bulletin No. 1.
   BY—J. Harold Williams. PUBLISHER—Stanford University, Stanford. 1915. 15 p. Out of print.

CALIFORNIA, LOS ANGELES. **Causes of Delinquency among Fifty Negro Boys.** Studies in Sociology No. 14.
   BY—Homer K. Watson. PUBLISHER—Southern California Sociological Society, Los Angeles. 1919. 12 p. 15 cents.

CALIFORNIA, LOS ANGELES COUNTY. **Report of Committee on Survey of Probation Department and Juvenile Hall.**
   BY—F. E. Doty. MIMEOGRAPHED—Bureau of Efficiency, Los Angeles. 1914. 55 p. Out of print.

CONNECTICUT. **Children before the Courts of Connecticut.** U. S. Department of Labor. Children's Bureau Publication No. 43. Dependent, Defective, and Delinquent Classes Series No. 6.
   BY—William B. Bailey. PUBLISHER—Superintendent of Documents, Government Printing Office, Washington, D. C. 1918. 98 p. 10 cents.

CONNECTICUT. **The Legal Handling of Juvenile Offenders in Connecticut.** Report of the Commission on Child Welfare to the Governor.
   BY—The Commission. PUBLISHER—State of Connecticut, Hartford. 1921. 32 p. Free.

CONNECTICUT, NEW HAVEN. **A Study of the Problem of Girl Delinquency in New Haven.** Report No. 15.
   BY—Mabel A. Wiley. PUBLISHER—Civic Federation of New Haven. 1915. 39 p. Out of print.

ILLINOIS, CHICAGO. **The Delinquent Child and the Home.** A study of children in the Chicago Juvenile Court.
   BY—Sophonisba P. Breckinridge and Edith Abbott. PUBLISHER—Russell Sage Foundation, New York City. 1917. 355 p. $2.00.

SURVEYS IN SPECIALIZED FIELDS

JUVENILE DELINQUENCY—Continued

ILLINOIS, CHICAGO. **Junk Dealing and Juvenile Delinquency.** An investigation.
    BY—Harry H. Grigg and George E. Haynes. PUBLISHER—Juvenile Protective Association, Chicago. 1918. 60 p. 25 cents.

ILLINOIS, CHICAGO. **A Study of Boys Appearing in the Municipal Court of Chicago with Emphasis upon Recidivism.** Bulletin Vol. II, No. 4.
    BY—Frank Orman Beck and Mabel Gregg. PUBLISHER—Department of Public Welfare, Chicago. 1919. 39 p. Free.

ILLINOIS, CHICAGO. **The Chicago Juvenile Court.** U. S. Department of Labor. Children's Bureau Publication No. 104.
    BY—Helen Rankin Jeter. PUBLISHER—Superintendent of Documents, Government Printing Office, Washington, D. C. 1922. 111 p. 15 cents.

ILLINOIS, COOK COUNTY. **The Juvenile Court of Cook County.**
    BY—W. E. Hotchkiss. PUBLISHER—Citizens' Investigating Committee of Cook County, Chicago. 1912. 294 p. Free.

ILLINOIS, ST. CHARLES. **St. Charles Study.** A survey made by the Bureau of Social Surveys. Bulletin Vol. II, No. 1.
    BY—E. E. Eubank. PUBLISHER—Department of Public Welfare, Chicago. 1917. 19 p. Free.

INDIANA. **Juvenile Delinquency in Indiana.**
    BY—Board of State Charities. PUBLISHER—The same, Indianapolis. 1918. 20 p. Free.

INDIANA, GARY. **Juvenile Delinquency and Adult Crime.** Certain association of juvenile delinquency and adult crime in Gary, with special reference to the immigrant population. Study No. 49.
    BY—Edna Hatfield Edmondson. PUBLISHER—University of Indiana, Bloomington. 1921. 114 p. $1.00.

LOUISIANA, NEW ORLEANS. **An Experimental Study of Delinquent and Destitute Boys in New Orleans and Notes Concerning Preventive and Ameliorative Measures in the United States.**
    BY—D. S. Hill. PUBLISHER—Division of Educational Research of Public Schools, New Orleans. 1914. 130 p. 35 cents and postage.

MASSACHUSETTS, WORCESTER. **Juvenile Delinquency in Worcester.** Bulletin of the Worcester Conference for Child Welfare. Vol. I, No. 3.
    BY—Thomas C. Carrigan. PUBLISHER—Worcester Conference for Child Welfare. 1912. 16 p. Out of print.

JUVENILE DELINQUENCY—Continued

MINNESOTA. **Delinquents.** Study of 600 delinquent boys.
> By—Marie E. Burmeister. PUBLISHER—State Training School, Red Wing. 1919. 24 p. Free.

MINNESOTA, MINNEAPOLIS. STUDIES OF COMMUNITY CONDITIONS. An extension survey of environmental causes of juvenile delinquency and a summary of the programs of the constructive agencies and institutions working in the community.

North District. Publication 68, Series I. By Grace E. Pratt. 1925. 52 p.

East District. Publication 68, Series II. By Erma Robertson, Fern Chase, and Mrs. Robbins Gilman. 1926. 45 p.

South District. Publication 68, Series III. By Fern Chase. 1926. 71 p.

> PUBLISHER—Women's Cooperative Alliance, Minneapolis. 25 cents each.

MINNESOTA, ST. PAUL. **The Juvenile Delinquent in St. Paul.** A summary of a study.
> By—M. C. Elmer. PUBLISHER—Community Chest, St. Paul. 1926. 48 p. Free.

NEBRASKA, OMAHA. **Summary of the Study of the Juvenile Delinquent in Omaha.** Bulletin of the University of Omaha. Vol. I, No. 5.
> By—T. Earl Sullinger. PUBLISHER—University of Omaha. 1925. 17 p. 25 cents.

NEW YORK. **Juvenile Delinquency in Rural New York.** U. S. Department of Labor. Children's Bureau Publication No. 32.
> By—Kate Holladay Claghorn. PUBLISHER—Superintendent of Documents, Government Printing Office, Washington, D. C. 1918. 199 p. 25 cents.

NEW YORK CITY. **A Study of Delinquent and Neglected Negro Children before the New York City Children's Court.**
> By—Joint Committee on Negro Child Study in New York City, in cooperation with the Department of Research, National Urban League, and the Women's City Club. PUBLISHER—The same. 1927. 48 p. 25 cents.

NEW YORK, ROCHESTER. **Condensed Report of a Survey of Juvenile Delinquency in Rochester.**
> By—Henry W. Thurston. PUBLISHER—Child Welfare League of America, New York City. 1923. 44 p. 50 cents.

SURVEYS IN SPECIALIZED FIELDS

JUVENILE DELINQUENCY—Continued

OHIO, HAMILTON COUNTY. **Juvenile Court of Hamilton County.**
>BY—R. E. Miles. PUBLISHER—Bureau of Municipal Research, Cincinnati. 1912. 24 p. Postage.

PENNSYLVANIA, ERIE. **A Study of Girls Cared for by the Florence Crittenton Home of Erie.**
>BY—Gladys Freeman. MIMEOGRAPHED—Florence Crittenton Home, Erie. 1921. 11 p. Free.

SOUTH CAROLINA. **A Study of Fifty Delinquent Girls of South Carolina.** In State Board of Charities and Corrections Quarterly Bulletin, Vol. V, No. 1.
>BY—Louise E. Bishop. PUBLISHER—State Board of Charities and Corrections, Columbus. 1919. 6 p. Free.

UNITED STATES. **Juvenile Delinquency and Its Relation to Employment.** Vol. VIII. Report on Condition of Woman and Child Wage-Earners in the United States. Senate Document No. 645.
>BY—Charles P. Neill, Director. PUBLISHER—Superintendent of Documents, Government Printing Office, Washington, D. C. 1911. 177 p. Out of print.

UNITED STATES. **The Federal Court and the Delinquent Child.** A study of the methods of dealing with children who have violated Federal laws. U. S. Department of Labor. Children's Bureau Publication No. 103.
>BY—Ruth Bloodgood. PUBLISHER—Superintendent of Documents, Government Printing Office, Washington, D. C. 1922. 69 p. 10 cents.

KINDERGARTENS

See also EDUCATION.

MINNESOTA, MINNEAPOLIS. **Kindergartens in the Public Schools of Minneapolis.** Educational Bulletin No. 4.
>BY—Board of Education. PUBLISHER—The same, Minneapolis. 1924. 28 p. Free.

LABOR

>*See* CHILD LABOR; INDUSTRIAL CONDITIONS AND RELATIONS; JAPANESE; and RURAL.

A BIBLIOGRAPHY OF SOCIAL SURVEYS

LIBRARIES

See also EDUCATION.

CALIFORNIA, LOS ANGELES. **Social Survey Report on Library Facilities in Los Angeles.** Reprinted from the Municipal League Bulletin.
    BY—Social Welfare Committee of Municipal League. PUBLISHER—Los Angeles Public Library. 1915. 11 p. Free.

OHIO, CLEVELAND. **The Public Library and the Public Schools.** The Cleveland Education Survey.
    BY—Leonard P. Ayres and Adele McKinnie. PUBLISHER—Cleveland Foundation. 1916. 93 p. 35 cents.

PENNSYLVANIA, PITTSBURGH. **The Public Library.** In The Pittsburgh District Civic Frontage, The Pittsburgh Survey.
    BY—Frances Jenkins Olcott. PUBLISHER—Russell Sage Foundation, New York City. 1914. p. 325–337. Out of print.

PENNSYLVANIA, READING. **Public Library.** Report on a survey of the Municipal Department and School District.
    BY—New York Bureau of Municipal Research. PUBLISHER—Reading Chamber of Commerce. 1913. 9 p. 10 cents.

RHODE ISLAND, PROVIDENCE. **A Sociological Survey of the Providence Public Library.**
    BY—May Hall James. PUBLISHER—Connecticut College for Women, New London. 1926. 105 p. $1.60.

UNITED STATES. **The Libraries of the American State and National Institutions for Defectives, Dependents, and Delinquents.** Studies in Social Sciences No. 13.
    BY—Florence Rising Curtis. PUBLISHER—University of Minnesota, Minneapolis. 1918. 56 p. 50 cents.

UNITED STATES. **Our College and University Libraries.** A survey and a program. Reprinted from School and Society. Vol. XII, No. 299.
    BY—William Warner Bishop. PUBLISHER—Science Press, New York City. 1920. 10 p. 25 cents.

UNITED STATES. **Library Extension.** A study of public library conditions and needs.
    BY—Committee on Library Extension, American Library Association. PUBLISHER—American Library Association, Chicago, Illinois. 1926. 163 p. $1.75.

SURVEYS IN SPECIALIZED FIELDS

LIBRARIES—Continued

UNITED STATES. A SURVEY OF LIBRARIES IN THE UNITED STATES.
  Vol. 1. **Administrative Work of Public Libraries and of College and University Libraries.** 1926. 316 p.
  Vol. 2. **Service to Readers in Public Libraries and in College and University Libraries.** 1926. 370 p.
  Vol. 3. **Public Library Service to Children; Extension Work and Community Service of Public Libraries; and School Library Organization and Service.** 1927. 326 p.
    By—American Library Association. PUBLISHER—The same, Chicago, Illinois. $2.00 each.

WASHINGTON. **Survey of State Supported Library Activities in the State of Washington.**
    By—State Library Advisory Board. PUBLISHER—Washington State Library Commission, Olympia. 1917. 134 p. Free.

In addition to reports **presenting findings,** as listed above, a publication dealing with **methods of conducting** such studies will be found in Part III, PURPOSE, METHOD, and STANDARDS, under **General Social Surveys—Urban.**

LITHUANIANS

ILLINOIS, CHICAGO. **The Lithuanians in the 4th Ward.** Reprint from the American Journal of Sociology. Vol. XX, No. 3.
    By—Elizabeth Hughes. PUBLISHER—University of Chicago Press. 1914. 23 p. 50 cents.

OHIO, CLEVELAND. **The Lithuanians of Cleveland.**
    By—Charles W. Coulter. PUBLISHER—Americanization Committee, Citizens Bureau, Cleveland. 1920. 24 p. 10 cents.

LOANS

ILLINOIS, CHICAGO. **The Loan Shark in Chicago.** Public Welfare Bulletin. Vol. I, No. 4.
    By—E. E. Eubank. PUBLISHER—Department of Public Welfare, Chicago. 1916. 28 p. Free.

MASSACHUSETTS. **Report on the Administration of State Revenues and Loans.**
    By—Special Commission Appointed by the Governor. PUBLISHER—Commonwealth of Massachusetts, Boston. 1916. 102 p. Out of print.

LOANS—Continued

PENNSYLVANIA, PITTSBURGH. **The Loan Shark Business in Pittsburgh.** A report containing the results of an investigation of the business of lending money upon household goods and upon salaries, together with recommendations for the formation of a "Remedial Loan Company" in Pittsburgh.

 By—Special Committee, Chamber of Commerce. PUBLISHER—The same, Pittsburgh. 1909. 14 p. Free.

UNITED STATES. **Student Loan Funds.** A study of student loan funds and their administration throughout the United States.

 By—Harmon Foundation. PUBLISHER—The same, New York City. 1924. 40 p. Free.

MAGYARS

OHIO, CLEVELAND. **The Magyars of Cleveland with a Brief Sketch of Their Historical and Political Background.**

 By—Huldah F. Cook. PUBLISHER—Americanization Committee, Citizens Bureau, Cleveland. 1919. 31 p. 10 cents.

MARKETS

MINNESOTA, MINNEAPOLIS. **An Exhaustive Study and Report on Public and Municipal Markets.**

 By—Mayor's Commission on Municipal Markets. PUBLISHER—City Council, Minneapolis. 1918. 60 p. Free.

PENNSYLVANIA, READING. **Department of Markets.** Report of a Survey of the Municipal Departments and School District.

 By—New York Bureau of Municipal Research. PUBLISHER—Reading Chamber of Commerce. 1913. 10 p. 10 cents.

MARRIAGE LAWS

OHIO. **School-girl Brides.** A study of the Ohio marriage laws relating to minors.

 By—Sabina Marshall, Director. PUBLISHER—Women's Protective Association, Cleveland. 1926. 54 p. 10 cents.

UNITED STATES. **American Marriage Laws and Their Social Aspects.** A digest.

 By—Fred S. Hall and Elisabeth W. Brooks. PUBLISHER—Russell Sage Foundation, New York City. 1919. 132 p. 50 cents.

SURVEYS IN SPECIALIZED FIELDS

MATERNAL DEATHS

FOREIGN COUNTRIES. *See* UNITED STATES in this section.

MONTANA. **Study of Infant and Maternal Death Rates in a Western State.** Public Health Reports. Vol. 37, No. 15.
> BY—John J. Sippy. PUBLISHER—Superintendent of Documents, Government Printing Office, Washington, D. C. 1922. 16 p. 5 cents.

UNITED STATES. **Maternal Mortality from All Conditions Connected with Childbirth in the United States and Certain Other Countries.** U. S. Department of Labor. Children's Bureau Publication No. 19. Miscellaneous Series No. 6.
> BY—Grace L. Meigs. PUBLISHER—Superintendent of Documents, Government Printing Office, Washington, D. C. 1917. 66 p. 10 cents.

MATERNITY HOMES
> *See* SOCIAL AGENCIES.

MENTAL HYGIENE
> *See also* BLINDNESS, SIGHT CONSERVATION, AND DISEASE OF THE EYE; DELINQUENCY AND CORRECTION; FEEBLEMINDED; IMMIGRATION AND AMERICANIZATION; INSANE; JAPANESE; LIBRARIES; PSYCHIATRIC; RURAL EDUCATION; SUB-NORMAL, RETARDED, AND EXCEPTIONAL CHILDREN; and TRUANCY AND NON-ATTENDANCE.

ARIZONA. **Report of the Arizona Mental Hygiene Survey with Recommendations.** Conducted by the National Committee for Mental Hygiene.
> BY—Thomas H. Haines, Director. PUBLISHER—Department of Public Welfare, Phoenix. 1922. 124 p. Free.

CALIFORNIA. **Surveys in Mental Deviation in Prisons, Public Schools, and Orphanages in California.** Brief description of local conditions and need for custodial care and training dependent, defective, and delinquent classes.
> BY—L. M. Terman, J. H. Williams, and G. M. Fernald. PUBLISHER—California State Board of Charities and Corrections, Sacramento. 1918. 87 p. Free.

CALIFORNIA, MODOC COUNTY. **Modoc County Mental Survey.** In Department of Education, Bureau of Research Studies 4, 5, 6, 7.
> BY—Frederick J. Adams. PUBLISHER—University of California, Berkeley. 1922. 5 p. 25 cents per copy.

MENTAL HYGIENE—Continued

DELAWARE, NEW CASTLE COUNTY. **Mental Status of Rural School Children.** Report of preliminary survey made in New Castle County, Delaware, with a description of the tests employed. Reprint No. 377, Public Health Reports, November 17, 1916.
>BY—E. H. Mullan. PUBLISHER—Superintendent of Documents. Government Printing Office, Washington, D. C. 1916. 14 p. 5 cents.

DELAWARE, NEW CASTLE COUNTY. **Social Study of Mental Defectives in New Castle County.** U. S. Department of Labor. Children's Bureau Publication No. 24.
>BY—Emma O. Lundberg. PUBLISHER—Superintendent of Documents, Government Printing Office, Washington, D. C. 1917. 38 p. 5 cents.

DELAWARE, SUSSEX COUNTY. **Mental Defect in a Rural County.** A study made through the collaboration of the U. S. Public Health Service and the Children's Bureau. U. S. Department of Labor. Children's Bureau Publication No. 48.
>BY—Walter L. Treadway and Emma O. Lundberg. PUBLISHER—Superintendent of Documents, Government Printing Office, Washington, D. C. 1919. 96 p. 10 cents.

DISTRICT OF COLUMBIA. **Mental Defectives in the District of Columbia.** A brief description of local conditions and the need for custodial care and training. U. S. Department of Labor. Children's Bureau Publication No. 13. Dependent, Defective and Delinquent Classes, Series No. 2.
>BY—Emma O. Lundberg and others. PUBLISHER—Superintendent of Documents, Government Printing Office, Washington, D. C. 1915. 39 p. 5 cents.

GEORGIA. **Mental Defect in a Southern State.** Report of the Georgia Commission on Feeblemindedness and the Survey of the National Committee for Mental Hygiene. Reprint No. 61.
>BY—V. V. Anderson. PUBLISHER—National Committee for Mental Hygiene, New York City. 1919. 38 p. 10 cents.

ILLINOIS, CHICAGO. **A Study of Mentally Defective Children in Chicago.** An investigation.
>BY—John Edward Ranson and Alexander Johnson. PUBLISHER—Juvenile Protective Association, Chicago. 1915. 72 p. Out of print.

SURVEYS IN SPECIALIZED FIELDS

MENTAL HYGIENE—Continued

ILLINOIS, COOK COUNTY. **Cook County and the Mentally Handicapped.** A study of the provisions for dealing with mental problems in Cook County. Report of survey, 1916–1917.
> BY—Herman M. Adler. PUBLISHER—National Committee for Mental Hygiene, New York City. 1918. 224 p. 25 cents.

ILLINOIS, SPRINGFIELD. **Care of Mental Defectives, the Insane, and Alcoholics in Springfield.** Mental Hygiene Section of the Springfield Survey.
> BY—Walter L. Treadway. PUBLISHER—Russell Sage Foundation, New York City. 1914. 46 p. 15 cents.

INDIANA. MENTAL DEFECTIVES IN INDIANA.
Mental Defectives in Indiana. By Amos W. Butler. 1916. 33 p.
Mental Defectives in Indiana. A survey of eight counties. 1919. 56 p.
Mental Defectives in Indiana. A survey of ten counties. 1920. 60 p.
> BY—Indiana Committee on Mental Defectives. PUBLISHER—State of Indiana, Indianapolis. Free.

INDIANA. **The Social Significance of Mental Disease and Defects.** A study based on 345 mental and nervous cases referred to the Social Science Department of Indiana University. Study No. 43.
> BY—Helen Hunt Andrews. PUBLISHER—University of Indiana, Bloomington. 1919. 59 p. 35 cents.

INDIANA. **A Social Study of Mental Defectives in County H.** Indiana University Studies No. 59.
> BY—Hazel Irene Hansford. PUBLISHER—Indiana University, Bloomington. 1923. 148 p. $1.00.

KENTUCKY. **Report of the Mental Hygiene Survey of Kentucky with Recommendations.**
> BY—National Committee for Mental Hygiene. PUBLISHER—General Assembly, Commonwealth of Kentucky, Frankfort. 1923. 178 p. Free.

MARYLAND. **Report of the Maryland Mental Hygiene Survey.**
> BY—Thomas H. Haines, Director. PUBLISHER—Maryland Mental Hygiene Commission, Annapolis. 1921. 96 p. Free.

MARYLAND, BALTIMORE. **Some Adaptive Difficulties Found in School Children.** Reprint No. 80 from Mental Hygiene. Vol. IV, No. 2.
> BY—Esther Loring Richards. PUBLISHER—National Committee for Mental Hygiene, New York City. 1920. 33 p. 25 cents.

A BIBLIOGRAPHY OF SOCIAL SURVEYS

MENTAL HYGIENE—Continued

MASSACHUSETTS. **Report of the Commission to Investigate the Question of the Increase of Criminals, Mental Defectives, Epileptics and Degenerates.**
> By—The Commission. PUBLISHER—State Department of Public Welfare, Boston. 1911. 50 p. Free.

MASSACHUSETTS. **The Hill Folk.** Report of a rural community of hereditary defectives.
> By—Florence H. Danielson and Charles B. Davenport. PUBLISHER—Eugenics Record Office, Cold Spring Harbor, New York. 1912. 56 p. 75 cents.

MASSACHUSETTS. **The Mental Defective and the Public Schools of Massachusetts.** A study of special classes for mental defectives. Publication No. 2.
> By—Amy Woods. PUBLISHER—League for Preventive Work, Boston. 1917. 16 p. Out of print.

MASSACHUSETTS. **After-Care Study of the Patients Discharged from Waverly for a Period of Twenty-Five Years.** Publication No. 39.
> By—Walter E. Fernald. PUBLISHER—Massachusetts Society for Mental Hygiene, Boston. 1919. 8 p. 10 cents.

MASSACHUSETTS. **The Child and the Home.** An extract from a survey of mental health conditions in a metropolitan district. Reprint from Mental Hygiene. Vol. VIII, No. 4. Publication No. 43.
> By—Marianna Taylor. PUBLISHER—Massachusetts Society for Mental Hygiene, Boston. 1922. 39 p. 15 cents.

MASSACHUSETTS, BOSTON. **Factors in the Mental Health of Boys of Foreign Parentage.** A study of 240 boys of foreign parentage known to a child welfare agency. Public Health Reports. Vol. 39, No. 17.
> By—Mary C. Jarrett. PUBLISHER—Superintendent of Documents, Government Printing Office, Washington, D. C. 1924. 21 p. 5 cents.

MASSACHUSETTS, BOSTON. **Factors in the Mental Health of Girls of Foreign Parentage.** A study of 210 girls of foreign parentage who received advice and assistance from a social agency, 1919–1922. Public Health Reports. Vol. 39, No. 10.
> By—Mary C. Jarrett. PUBLISHER—Superintendent of Documents, Government Printing Office, Washington, D. C. 1924. 23 p. 5 cents.

SURVEYS IN SPECIALIZED FIELDS

MENTAL HYGIENE—Continued

MASSACHUSETTS, CHARLESTOWN. **Survey of 100 Cases at the Massachusetts State Prison at Charlestown.** Bulletin 16.
>BY—A. W. Stearns. PUBLISHER—Massachusetts State Board of Insanity, Boston. 1915. 6 p. Out of print.

MINNESOTA, FARIBAULT. **Occupational Efficiency of the Mentally Defective.** A survey of the inmates of the Minnesota School for Feeble-Minded and Colony for Epileptics. Educational Monograph No. 7.
>BY—G. G. Hanna. PUBLISHER—University of Minnesota, Minneapolis. 1924. 43 p. 50 cents.

MISSISSIPPI. **Mississippi Mental Deficiency Survey.**
>BY—Thomas H. Haines. PUBLISHER—Mississippi School and Colony, Ellisville. 1924. 45 p. Free.

MISSOURI. **Report of the Missouri Mental Deficiency Survey with Recommendations.**
>BY—National Committee for Mental Hygiene and Missouri Commission on Mental Deficiency. PUBLISHER—State Board of Charities and Corrections, Jefferson City. 1922. 48 p. Free.

NEW JERSEY. **Report of the New Jersey Commission on the Care of Mental Defectives.**
>BY—The Commission. PUBLISHER—State of New Jersey, Trenton. 1914. 27 p. Out of print.

NEW YORK. **Report of the State Commission to Investigate Provisions for the Mentally Deficient.** Senate Document No. 42.
>BY—The Commission. PUBLISHER—State of New York, Albany. 1915. 320 p. Free.

NEW YORK. **Case Studies in Mental Defect.** Eugenic and Social Welfare Bulletin No. XIV.
>BY—Marion Collins. PUBLISHER—State Board of Charities, Albany. 1918. 177 p. Free.

NEW YORK. **Mental Defectives in a Community.** In Ungraded. Vol. IX, No. 6.
>BY—Katherine G. Ecob. PUBLISHER—Ungraded Teachers Association, New York City. 1924. 8 p. 25 cents.

NEW YORK. **Report of the Mental Hygiene Survey of New York County Jails and Penitentiaries.**
>BY—National Committee for Mental Hygiene. PUBLISHER—The same, New York City. 1925. 148 p. 25 cents.

MENTAL HYGIENE—Continued

NEW YORK, BUFFALO. **A Brief Report on Mental Defectives in Buffalo and the Vicinity, Made to the Vassar Club by the Committee from Its Members.**
> BY—The Committee. PUBLISHER—Vassar Club, Buffalo. 1917. 13 p. Free.

NEW YORK, NASSAU COUNTY. **Survey of Mental Disorders in Nassau County.**
> BY—A. J. Rosanoff. PUBLISHER—National Committee for Mental Hygiene, New York City. 1916. 125 p. 25 cents.

NEW YORK, NEW YORK COUNTY. **Report of a Mental Hygiene Survey of New York County Jails and Penitentiaries.**
> BY—National Committee for Mental Hygiene. PUBLISHER—The same, New York City. 1925. 148 p. 25 cents.

NEW YORK, ROME. **Fifty-Two Border-Line Cases in the Rome State Custodial Asylum.** Bureau of Analysis and Investigation. Eugenics and Social Welfare Bulletin No. VI.
> BY—Committee on Idiots and Feeble-Minded. PUBLISHER—State Board of Charities, Albany. 1915. 32 p. Free.

NEW YORK, STATEN ISLAND. **Report of a Mental Health Survey of Staten Island.**
> BY—National Committee for Mental Hygiene. PUBLISHER—The same, New York City. 1925. 140 p. 25 cents.

NORTH DAKOTA. **Report of the North Dakota Mental Hygiene Survey with Recommendations.**
> BY—Thomas H. Haines, Director. PUBLISHER—National Committee for Mental Hygiene, New York City. 1923. 152 p. 25 cents.

OHIO, CINCINNATI. **Report of the Mental Hygiene Survey of Cincinnati.**
> BY—National Committee for Mental Hygiene. PUBLISHER—Mental Hygiene Council, Public Health Federation, Cincinnati. 1922. 131 p. $1.00.

OHIO, CLEVELAND. **Mental Diseases and Mental Deficiency.** Part VI. Cleveland Hospital and Health Survey.
> BY—Thomas W. Salmon and Jesse M. W. Scott. PUBLISHER—Cleveland Hospital Council. 1920. 68 p. 50 cents and postage.

OHIO, HAMILTON COUNTY. **What Shall We Do about Our Mental Hygiene Problem?** A brief summary of the report of a year's survey of the mental hygiene problem in Hamilton County.
> BY—Mental Hygiene Council, Public Health Federation. PUBLISHER—The same, Cincinnati. 1922. 15 p. Free.

SURVEYS IN SPECIALIZED FIELDS

MENTAL HYGIENE—Continued

RHODE ISLAND. **Report of the Rhode Island Mental Hygiene Survey.** Conducted under the Auspices of the National Committee for Mental Hygiene.
> By—Samuel W. Hamilton, Director. PUBLISHER—State Welfare Board, Providence. 1923. 99 p. Free.

SOUTH CAROLINA. **A Report of the South Carolina Mental Hygiene Survey with Recommendations.**
> By—V. V. Anderson. PUBLISHER—State of South Carolina, Columbia. 1922. 73 p. Free.

TEXAS. **Report of the Texas Mental Hygiene Survey.**
> By—Survey Staff. PUBLISHER—National Committee for Mental Hygiene, New York City. 1924. 86 p. 25 cents.

TEXAS. **Report of the Texas Eleemosynary Commission.** Part I. Preliminary Report of the Commission with Recommendations of Legislation. Parts II and III. Report of the Mental Hygiene Survey of Texas Made by the National Committee for Mental Hygiene, under the Auspices of the Commission and with the Financial Co-operation of the Buchanan Foundation.
> By—The Commission. PUBLISHER—State of Texas, Austin. 1925. 87 p. Free.

UNITED STATES. **Mental Hygiene with Special Reference to Migration of People.** Public Health Bulletin No. 148.
> By—Walter L. Treadway. PUBLISHER—Superintendent of Documents, Government Printing Office, Washington, D. C. 1925. 190 p. 25 cents.

UTAH. **Mental Survey of Utah Schools and Adaptation of the Army Beta Tests.** Bulletin of the University of Utah. Vol. 12, No. 6.
> By—George S. Snoddy and George E. Hyde. PUBLISHER—Department of Psychology, University of Utah, Salt Lake City. 1921. 28 p. Free.

VIRGINIA. **Mental Defectives in Virginia.** A special report to the General Assembly on weak-mindedness in the state of Virginia together with a plan for training, segregating, and preventing the procreation of the feeble-minded.
> By—Virginia State Board of Charities and Corrections. PUBLISHER—State of Virginia, Richmond. 1915. 128 p. Out of print.

MENTAL HYGIENE—Continued

WISCONSIN. **Report of the Wisconsin Mental Deficiency Survey.**
>By—National Committee for Mental Hygiene. PUBLISHER—State Board of Public Affairs, Madison. 1921. 59 p. Free.

In addition to reports **presenting findings** in Mental Hygiene Surveys, as listed above, publications dealing with **methods of conducting** such studies will be found in Part III, PURPOSE, METHOD, AND STANDARDS, page 351.

MEXICANS

CALIFORNIA, LOS ANGELES. **The Mexican Housing Problem in Los Angeles.** Studies in Sociology No. 17.
>By—Elizabeth Fuller. PUBLISHER—Southern California Sociological Society, Los Angeles. 1920. 11 p. 15 cents.

COLORADO. **Spanish and Mexican in Colorado.** A survey of the Spanish Americans and Mexicans in the State of Colorado.
>By—Robert N. McLean and Charles A. Thomson. PUBLISHER—Board of National Missions, Presbyterian Church in the U.S.A., New York City. 1924. 61 p. 25 cents.

MEXICO. **Cancer in Mexico.**
>By—Frederick L. Hoffman. PUBLISHER—Prudential Insurance Company of America, New York City. 1927. 70 p. Free.

MIDWIFE

ENGLAND. **The Midwife in England.** A study of the working of the English Midwives Act in 1902. Bulletin No. 13.
>By—Carolyn Conant Van Blarcom and J. Clifton Edgar. PUBLISHER—Committee on Prevention of Blindness, New York City. 1913. 139 p. Free.

ILLINOIS, CHICAGO. **The Midwife in Chicago.** Reprinted from the American Journal of Sociology. Vol. XX, No. 5. Publications of the Immigrant Protective League. Series 1, No. 4.
>By—Grace Abbott. PUBLISHER—Immigrant Protective League, Chicago. 1915. 15 p. Out of print.

SURVEYS IN SPECIALIZED FIELDS

MIGRATION
See CHILD WELFARE; CHINESE; IMMIGRATION AND AMERICANIZATION; MENTAL HYGIENE; NEGROES; RURAL; and TUBERCULOSIS.

MILITARY CAMPS
UNITED STATES. **A Report on the Work of Women in Military Camps in the United States.**
By—Raymond B. Fosdick. PUBLISHER—War Department Commission on Training Camp Activities, Washington, D. C. 1918. 29 p. Free.

UNITED STATES. **Survey of the Moral and Religious Forces in the Military Camps and Naval Stations in the United States.**
By—General War-Time Commission of Churches. PUBLISHER—Federal Council, Churches of Christ in America, New York City. 1918. 120 p. Free.

MILK
See also HEALTH AND SANITATION; and INFANT MORTALITY.

KANSAS. MILK SURVEYS.
A Survey of the Milk Situation in Kansas. By Leon A. Congdon. In Bulletin of the Kansas State Board of Health. Vol. XI, No. 4. 1915. 10 p.
The Milk Survey of Twenty Kansas Cities. Bulletin of the Kansas State Board of Health. Vol. XVIII, No. 11. 1922. 45 p.
By—State Board of Health. PUBLISHER—The same, Topeka. Free.

MISSOURI, ST. LOUIS. **Milk Problem in St. Louis.**
By—G. B. Mangold, E. Moore, and M. D. Weiss. PUBLISHER—School of Social Economy, St. Louis. 1911. 36 p. 10 cents.

NEW YORK CITY. **Study of the New York City Milk Problem.**
By—I. G. Jennings. PUBLISHER—National Civic Federation, New York City. 1919. 58 p. $1.00.

NEW YORK, TROY. **Report of Investigation of Distribution of Milk at Troy.** Department of Farms and Markets Bulletin. Vol. II, No. 13.
By—Eugene H. Porter. PUBLISHER—State Department of Farms and Markets, Troy. 1919. 4 p. Free.

MILK—Continued

PENNSYLVANIA, PHILADELPHIA. **Consumer Demand for Milk in Philadelphia.** A study of the effect of income, race, nationality, and publicity upon milk consumption.
>By—J. Clyde Marquis and P. R. Taylor. MIMEOGRAPHED—U. S. Department of Agriculture, Washington, D. C. 1924. 51 p. Free.

UNITED STATES. REPORTS ON MILK STANDARDS.
First Report. Reprint No. 78, Public Health Reports, May 10, 1912, 23 p.
Second Report. Reprint No. 141, Public Health Reports, August 22, 1913. 27 p.
Third Report. Reprint No. 386, Public Health Reports, February 16. 1917. 28 p.
>By—Milk Commission Appointed by the New York Milk Committee. PUBLISHER—Superintendent of Documents, Government Printing Office, Washington, D. C. 5 cents each.

WISCONSIN, MILWAUKEE. **The Health Department: Milk Supply.** Bulletin No. 13.
>By—Milwaukee Milk Committee. PUBLISHER—Milwaukee Bureau of Economy and Efficiency. 1912. 45 p. Out of print.

MINIMUM WAGE

See also INDUSTRIAL CONDITIONS AND RELATIONS.

MASSACHUSETTS. **Report of the Special Commission on Unemployment, Unemployment Compensation, and the Minimum Wage.** House No. 1325.
>By—The Commission. PUBLISHER—Commonwealth of Massachusetts, Boston. 1923. 78 p. Free.

MASSACHUSETTS. REPORTS OF THE MINIMUM WAGE COMMISSION OF THE COMMONWEALTH OF MASSACHUSETTS.
Wages of Women in the Paper-Box Factories. Bulletin No. 8. 1915. 38 p.
Wages of Women in Women's Clothing Factories. Bulletin No. 9. 1915. 37 p.
Wages of Women in Hosiery and Knit Goods Factories. Bulletin No. 10. 1916. 37 p.
Wages of Women in Men's Clothing and Raincoat Factories. Bulletin No. 13. 1916. 60 p.

SURVEYS IN SPECIALIZED FIELDS

MINIMUM WAGE—Continued

Wages of Women in Muslin Underwear, Petticoat, Apron, Kimono, Women's Neckwear, and Children's Clothing Factories. Bulletin No. 14. 1917. 58 p.

Wages of Women Employed as Office and Other Building Cleaners in Massachusetts. Bulletin No. 16. 1918. 36 p.

Wages of Women in Hotels and Restaurants in Massachusetts. Bulletin No. 17. 1918. 68 p.

Supplementary Report on the Wages in Candy Factories in Massachusetts. Bulletin No. 18. 1919. 42 p.

Wages of Women Employed in Canning and Preserving Establishments in Massachusetts. Bulletin No. 19. 1919. 51 p.

Report on the Wages of Women in the Millinery Industry. Bulletin No. 20. 1919. 69 p.

Second Report on the Wages of Women in Corset Factories. Bulletin No. 21. 1920. 49 p.

Second Report on the Wages of Women Employed in Paper-Box Factories. Bulletin No. 22. 1920. 53 p.

Report on the Wages of Women Employed in the Manufacture of Food Preparations and Minor Lines of Confectionery. Bulletin No. 23. 1920. 41 p.

Wages of Women in the Laundries. Reprint Bulletin No. 5. 1920. 41 p.

BY—The Commission. PUBLISHER—State Department of Labor and Industries, Boston. Free.

MICHIGAN. **Report of the Michigan State Commission of Inquiry into Wages and the Conditions of Labor for Women and the Advisability of Establishing a Minimum Wage.**

BY—The Commission. PUBLISHER—State of Michigan, Lansing. 1915. 496 p. Out of print.

OREGON. **Effect of Minimum Wage Determinations in Oregon.** Bulletin of the U. S. Bureau of Labor Statistics. Whole No. 176. Women in Industry Series No. 6.

BY—Marie L. Obenauer and Bertha von der Nienburg. PUBLISHER—Superintendent of Documents, Government Printing Office, Washington, D. C. 1915. 108 p. Out of print.

WISCONSIN. **Minimum Wage Investigation Report.**

BY—Janet Van Hise. PUBLISHER—Wisconsin Consumer's League, Madison. 1918. 37 p. Free.

A BIBLIOGRAPHY OF SOCIAL SURVEYS

MORTALITY

See HEALTH AND SANITATION; ILLEGITIMACY; INFANT MORTALITY; MATERNAL DEATHS; and TUBERCULOSIS.

MOTION PICTURES

ILLINOIS, CHICAGO. **Five and Ten Cent Theatres.**
 By—Louise de Koven Bowen. PUBLISHER—Juvenile Protective Association, Chicago. 1911. 11 p. Out of print.

MINNESOTA, MINNEAPOLIS. **Better Movie Movement.** Plan and report of a survey of the Minneapolis motion picture houses. Publication No. 38.
 By—Research and Investigation Department, Women's Cooperative Alliance, Minneapolis. PUBLISHER—The same. 1921. 31 p. Free.

NEW YORK CITY. **Report on the Condition of Moving Picture Shows in New York City.**
 By—Raymond B. Fosdick. PUBLISHER—Commissioner of Accounts, New York City. 1911. 19 p. Free.

OHIO, TOLEDO. **Motion Pictures in a Typical City.**
 By—John J. Phelan. PUBLISHER—Little Book Publishing Company, Toledo. 1919. 292 p. $2.00.

OREGON, PORTLAND. **Vaudeville and Motion Picture Shows.** A study of theatres in Portland. Reed College Record No. 16.
 By—William Trufant Foster. PUBLISHER—Reed College, Portland. 1914. 63 p. Free.

MUSIC

See also EDUCATION.

UNITED STATES. **Municipal Aid to Music in America.** An exposition and analysis of the findings in a survey.
 By—Kenneth S. Clark. PUBLISHER—National Bureau for the Advancement of Music, New York City. 1925. 297 p. $2.00.

UNITED STATES. **Music, Youth, and Opportunity.** A survey of settlement and community music schools. Settlement Monographs V.
 By—Janet D. Schenck. PUBLISHER—National Federation of Settlements, Boston, Massachusetts. 1926. 118 p. $1.00.

NEGRO EDUCATION

See also EDUCATION; RURAL EDUCATION; and TRUANCY AND NON-ATTENDANCE.

SURVEYS IN SPECIALIZED FIELDS

NEGRO EDUCATION—Continued

DELAWARE. **Negro School Attendance in Delaware.** A report to the State Board of Education of Delaware by the Service Citizens of Delaware.
> BY—Richard Watson Cooper and Hermann Cooper. PUBLISHER—University of Delaware Press, Newark. 1923. 398 p. $5.00.

GEORGIA, CLARKE COUNTY. **School Conditions in Clarke County with Special Reference to Negroes.** Phelps-Stokes Studies No. 3. Serial No. 266. Vol. XVI.
> BY—M. K. Johnson. PUBLISHER—University of Georgia, Athens. 1916. 50 p. 25 cents.

MISSISSIPPI. **Forty Years of the Public Schools in Mississippi with Special Reference to the Education of the Negro.** Teachers College Contributions to Education No. 94.
> BY—Stuart Grayson Noble. PUBLISHER—Bureau of Publications, Teachers College, Columbia University, New York City. 1918. 142 p. $1.60.

MISSOURI. **Report of the Missouri Negro Educational and Industrial Commission.**
> BY—Robert S. Cobb. PUBLISHER—State Board of Charities and Corrections, Jefferson City. 1920. 25 p. Free.

NEW YORK CITY. **Colored School Children in New York.**
> BY—Frances Blascoer. PUBLISHER—Public Education Association, New York City. 1915. 176 p. Out of print.

PENNSYLVANIA, PHILADELPHIA. **Negro Children in the Public Schools of Philadelphia.** Reprinted from the Annals of the American Academy of Political and Social Sciences, September 1913.
> BY—Howard W. Odum. PUBLISHER—The Annals of the American Academy of Political and Social Science, Philadelphia. 1913. 23 p. 15 cents.

UNITED STATES. **The Negro Common School.** A social study made under the direction of Atlanta University. Publication No. 6.
> BY—W. E. Burghardt DuBois. PUBLISHER—Atlanta University Press. 1901. 120 p. Out of print.

UNITED STATES. NEGRO EDUCATION. A study of the private and higher schools for colored people in the United States. Prepared in cooperation with the Phelps-Stokes Fund. U. S. Bureau of Education Bulletin. 1916. Nos. 38 and 39.

NEGRO EDUCATION—Continued

Vol. I. History of Negro Education in the United States, Educational Funds, Industrial and Church Schools, and Statistics. 423 p. $1.00.

Vol. II. Economic and Social Status of Negroes, and Educational Facilities in the Various States. 724 p. $1.25.

By—Thomas Jesse Jones. PUBLISHER—Superintendent of Documents, Government Printing Office, Washington, D. C. 1917.

UNITED STATES. REPORTS ON SCHOOLS FOR NEGROES.

Report on Negro Universities and Colleges. Occasional Papers No. 21. By W. T. Williams. 1922. 28 p.

A Study of County Training Schools for Negroes in the South. Occasional Papers No. 23. By Leo Mortimer Favrot. 1925. 85 p.

PUBLISHER—John F. Slater Fund, Charlottesville, Virginia. Free.

UNITED STATES. A Study of Home Economics Education in Teacher Training Institutions for Negroes. Federal Board for Vocational Education Bulletin No. 79. Home Economic Series No. 7.

By—Anne E. Richardson. PUBLISHER—Superintendent of Documents, Government Printing Office, Washington, D. C. 1923. 124 p. 15 cents.

UNITED STATES. Education of Negro Ministers Based on a Survey of Theological Schools for Negroes in the United States. Institute of Social and Religious Research.

By—R. L. Kelly and W. A. Daniel. PUBLISHER—George H. Doran Company, New York City. 1925. 187 p. $1.50.

VIRGINIA. The Education and Economic Development of the Negro in Virginia. Phelps-Stokes Fellowship Studies No. 6.

By—W. H. Brown. PUBLISHER—University of Virginia, Charlottesville. 1923. 150 p. 75 cents.

NEGROES

Reports dealing with the general subject of Negroes are listed here. For reports dealing with specific subjects relating to Negroes *see* CHARITIES; COST OF LIVING; CRIME AND CRIMINALS; HOUSING; ILLEGITIMACY; INDUSTRIAL CONDITIONS AND RELATIONS; JUVENILE DELINQUENCY; NEGRO EDUCATION; RECREATION; TRUANCY AND NON-ATTENDANCE; and TUBERCULOSIS.

GEORGIA. PHELPS-STOKES FELLOWSHIP STUDIES.

The Negroes of Athens. Bulletin Vol. XIV, No. 4. By T. J. Woofter, Jr. 1913. 62 p.

SURVEYS IN SPECIALIZED FIELDS

NEGROES—Continued

The Negroes of Clarke County during the Great War. Bulletin Vol. XIX, No. 8. By Francis Taylor Long. 1919. 56 p.

The Negro Women of Gainesville. Bulletin Vol. XXII, No. 1. By Ruth Reed. 1921. 61 p.
   PUBLISHER—University of Georgia, Athens. 25 cents each.

GEORGIA. **Economic Cooperation among the Negroes of Georgia.** Report of a social survey made by Atlanta University with the Proceedings of the 23d Annual Conference for the Study of the Negro Problem. Publication No. 19.
   BY—Thomas I. Brown. PUBLISHER—Atlanta University. 1917. 57 p. 50 cents.

GEORGIA, ATHENS. **Sanitary Conditions among the Negroes of Athens.** Phelps-Stokes Fellowship Studies No. 4. Bulletin Vol. XVIII, No. 7.
   BY—R. P. Brooks. PUBLISHER—University of Georgia, Athens. 1905. 25 p. 25 cents.

GEORGIA, CLARKE COUNTY. **Rural Survey of Clarke County with Special Reference to the Negroes.** Phelps-Stokes Fellowship Studies No. 2. Bulletin Vol. XV.
   BY—W. B. Hill and R. P. Brooks. PUBLISHER—University of Georgia, Athens. 1915. 63 p. 25 cents.

ILLINOIS, CHICAGO. **The Colored People of Chicago.** An investigation.
   BY—A. P. Drucker and others. PUBLISHER—Juvenile Protective Association, Chicago. 1913. 30 p. Out of print.

ILLINOIS, CHICAGO. **A Preliminary Study of Interracial Conditions in Chicago.** Made under the Survey Division of the Interchurch World Movement of North America.
   BY—Howard R. Gold, Byron K. Armstrong, and George E. Haynes. PUBLISHER—Home Mission Council, New York City. 1920. 15 p. Out of print.

ILLINOIS, CHICAGO. **The Negro in Chicago.** A study of race relations and a race riot.
   BY—Chicago Commission on Race Relations. PUBLISHER—University of Chicago Press. 1922. 672 p. $4.20.

KANSAS, WICHITA. **Survey of Negro Life and Race Relations.** Report of the Committee on Findings.
   BY—The Committee. MIMEOGRAPHED—Commission on Race Relations, Wichita Council of Churches. 1924. 15 p. Free.

NEGROES—Continued

LOUISIANA, CINCLARE AND PATTERSON. **The Negroes of Cinclare Central Factory and Calumet Plantation.** In Bulletin of the U. S. Bureau of Labor No. 38.
>BY—J. Bradford Laws. PUBLISHER—Superintendent of Documents, Government Printing Office, Washington, D. C. 1902. 25 p. 10 cents.

MARYLAND, SANDY SPRING. **The Negroes of Sandy Spring, Maryland.** A social study. In Bulletin of the U. S. Bureau of Labor No. 32.
>BY—William Taylor Thom. PUBLISHER—Superintendent of Documents, Government Printing Office, Washington, D. C. 1901. 60 p. Out of print.

MICHIGAN, DETROIT. **Negro New-Comers in Detroit.**
>BY—George E. Haynes. PUBLISHER—Home Mission Council, New York City. 1918. 42 p. 25 cents.

MICHIGAN, DETROIT. **The Negro in Detroit.**
>BY—Special Survey Staff under direction of Detroit Bureau of Governmental Research. MIMEOGRAPHED—Mayor's Interracial Committee, Detroit. 1926. 394 p. Out of print.

MICHIGAN, DETROIT. **Report on the Mayor's Committee on Race Relations, Embodying Findings and Recommendations Based upon a Survey of Race Conditions in the City.** Reprinted from Public Business, March 10, 1927.
>BY—The Committee. PUBLISHER—Detroit Bureau of Governmental Research. 1927. 16 p. Free.

MISSOURI, COLUMBIA. **The Negroes of Columbia.** A concrete study of the race problem.
>BY—William Wilson Elwang. PUBLISHER—Department of Sociology, University of Missouri, Columbia. 1904. 69 p. 50 cents.

MISSOURI, KANSAS CITY. **Our Negro Population.** A sociological study of Negroes of Kansas City.
>BY—Asa E. Marlin. PUBLISHER—Franklin Hudson Publishing Company, Kansas City. 1913. 189 p. $1.50.

NEW JERSEY. *See* PENNSYLVANIA in this section.

NEW YORK CITY. **The Negro at Work in New York City.** A study of economic progress. Columbia University Studies in History, Economics, and Public Law. Vol. 49, No. 3.
>BY—George Edmund Haynes. PUBLISHER—Longmans, Green and Company, New York City. 1912. 156 p. Out of print.

SURVEYS IN SPECIALIZED FIELDS

NEGROES—Continued

NEW YORK CITY. **A Study of Negro Employees of Apartment Houses in New York City.** Bulletin of National League on Urban Conditions among Negroes. Vol. VI, No. 5.
    BY—Forrester B. Washington. PUBLISHER—National Urban League, New York City. 1916. 36 p. Free.

NEW YORK CITY. **Health Work of Mothers and Children in a Colored Community, Including a Study of Venereal Disease as a Prenatal Problem.** Publication 131.
    BY—John C. Gebhart. PUBLISHER—Association for Improving the Condition of the Poor, New York City. 1924. 15 p. 25 cents.

OHIO, CINCINNATI. **The Cincinnati Negro Survey and Program.** Reprint from Proceedings of the National Conference of Social Work. Pamphlet 229.
    BY—James H. Robinson. PUBLISHER—National Conference of Social Work, Chicago. 1919. 7 p. 10 cents.

OHIO, XENIA. **Negroes of Xenia.** A social study. U. S. Bureau of Labor Bulletin No. 48.
    BY—Richard R. Wright. PUBLISHER—Superintendent of Documents, Government Printing Office, Washington, D. C. 1903. 38 p. Out of print.

PENNSYLVANIA. **A Study of Living Conditions among Colored People in Towns in the Outer Part of Philadelphia and in Other Suburbs, Both in Pennsylvania and New Jersey.**
    BY—Harriet E. Norris. PUBLISHER—Armstrong Association of Philadelphia. 1915. 57 p. Free.

PENNSYLVANIA. **Negro Survey of Pennsylvania.**
    BY—Forrester B. Washington, Director. PUBLISHER—Department of Welfare, Commonwealth of Pennsylvania, Harrisburg. 1927. 97 p. Free.

PENNSYLVANIA, PHILADELPHIA. **The Philadelphia Negro.** A social study. Publications of the University of Pennsylvania. Series in Political Economy and Public Law No. 14.
    BY—W. E. Burghardt DuBois. PUBLISHER—Ginn and Company, New York City. 1899. 520 p. Out of print.

PENNSYLVANIA, PHILADELPHIA. **The Standard of Living among One Hundred Negro Migrant Families in Philadelphia.** Reprinted from

NEGROES—Continued

the Annals of the American Academy of Political and Social Science, Vol. XCVIII.
>By—Sadie Tanner Mossell. PUBLISHER—University of Pennsylvania, Philadelphia. 1921. 50 p. Free.

PENNSYLVANIA, PITTSBURGH. **One Hundred Negro Steel Workers.** In Wage-Earning Pittsburgh, The Pittsburgh Survey.
>By—R. R. Wright, Jr. PUBLISHER—Russell Sage Foundation, New York City. 1914. p. 97–113. Out of print.

PENNSYLVANIA, PITTSBURGH. **The Negro Migrant in Pittsburgh.** A study in social economics.
>By—Abram Epstein. PUBLISHER—University of Pittsburgh. 1918. 75 p. 50 cents.

PENNSYLVANIA, PITTSBURGH. **The New Negro Population.** Report on the recent influx of Negroes in Pittsburgh.
>By—Charles Reed Zahniser. PUBLISHER—Commission on Social Service, Pittsburgh Council, Churches of Christ. 1918. 10 p. Out of print.

SOUTH CAROLINA. **The Negro in South Carolina during the Reconstruction.**
>By—Alrutheus Ambush Taylor. PUBLISHER—Association for the Study of Negro Life and History, Washington D. C. 1924. 341 p. $2.15.

UNITED STATES. **Condition of the Negro in Various Cities.** Bulletin of the U. S. Bureau of Labor No. 10.
>By—Joseph E. Smith, R. R. Wright, and Butler B. Wilson. PUBLISHER—Superintendent of Documents, Government Printing Office, Washington, D. C. 1897. 112 p. Out of print.

UNITED STATES. **The Negro Artisan.** A social study. Publication No. 7.
>By—W. E. Burghardt DuBois. PUBLISHER—Atlanta University Press. 1902. 192 p. 50 cents.

UNITED STATES. **Negro Migration in 1916–1917.** U. S. Department of Labor. Division of Negro Economics Bulletin.
>By—J. H. Dillard, Director. PUBLISHER—Superintendent of Documents, Government Printing Office, Washington, D. C. 1919. 158 p. 20 cents.

NEGROES—Continued

UNITED STATES. **The Negro at Work during the World War and during Reconstruction.** U. S. Department of Labor. Division of Negro Economics Bulletin.
> BY—Division of Negro Economics. PUBLISHER—Superintendent of Documents, Government Printing Office, Washington, D. C. 1921. 144 p. 25 cents.

UNITED STATES. **Negro Women in Industry.** Investigation made during the World War. U. S. Department of Labor. Bulletin of the Women's Bureau No. 20.
> BY—Emma L. Shields. PUBLISHER—Superintendent of Documents, Government Printing Office, Washington, D. C. 1922. 65 p. 10 cents.

VIRGINIA, FARMVILLE. **Negroes of Farmville.** A social study. U. S. Bureau of Labor Bulletin No. 14.
> BY—W. E. Burghardt DuBois. PUBLISHER—Superintendent of Documents, Government Printing Office, Washington, D. C. 1898. 37 p. Out of print.

VIRGINIA, LITWALTON. **Negroes of Litwalton.** A social study of the "Oyster Negro." U. S. Bureau of Labor Bulletin No. 37.
> BY—William Taylor Thom. PUBLISHER—Superintendent of Documents, Government Printing Office, Washington, D. C. 1901. 55 p. Out of print.

VIRGINIA, LYNCHBURG. **The Negroes of Lynchburg.** Phelps-Stokes Fellowship Studies. No. 5.
> BY—Benjamin Guy Childs. PUBLISHER—University of Virginia, Charlottesville. 1923. 57 p. 75 cents.

VIRGINIA, TIDEWATER. **Three Negro Communities in Tidewater.** Bulletin Vol. XIX, No. 4.
> BY—Allen B. Doggett. PUBLISHER—Hampton Normal and Agricultural Institute. 1923. 46 p. Free.

NEIGHBORHOOD HOUSES AND SETTLEMENTS

See also ITALIANS; and MUSIC.

UNITED STATES. **Thirty Neighborhood Houses.** A survey of thirty Presbyterian neighborhood houses.
> BY—Christine T. Wilson. PUBLISHER—Board of National Missions, Presbyterian Church in the United States of America, New York City. 1926. 119 p. Out of print.

NURSERIES AND NURSING

See also CHARITIES; and HOSPITALS AND SANATORIA.

CONNECTICUT. **Survey of Public Health Nursing in Connecticut.**
BY—H. F. Boyd. PUBLISHER—State Department of Health, Hartford. 1918. 28 p. Out of print.

ILLINOIS, CHICAGO. **A Study of Day Nurseries.**
BY—Helen McKee Brenton. PUBLISHER—Chicago Association of Day Nurseries. 1918. 65 p. Free.

NEW YORK CITY. **Day Nurseries in New York City.** Summary of the principal findings of the study.
BY—E. H. Lewinski-Corwin. PUBLISHER—New York Academy of Medicine, New York City. 1924. 9 p. Free.

NEW YORK CITY. **A Comparative Study of Generalized and Specialized Nursing and Health Services.**
BY—East Harlem Nursing and Health Demonstration. PUBLISHER—The same, New York City. 1926. 40 p. 35 cents.

NEW YORK, WESTCHESTER COUNTY. **Study of Public Health Nursing in Westchester County.** In Public Health Nurse. Vol. XI, No. 8.
BY—Zoe LaForge. PUBLISHER—National Organization for Public Health Nursing, New York City. 1919. 23 p. 20 cents per copy.

OHIO, CLEVELAND. **Nursing.** Part IX. Cleveland Hospital and Health Survey.
BY—Josephine Goldmark. PUBLISHER—Cleveland Hospital Council. 1920. 102 p. 50 cents.

PENNSYLVANIA. **Day Nurseries in Pennsylvania.** A study made for the Bureau of Children. Department of Welfare Bulletin 17.
BY—Helen Glenn Tyson. PUBLISHER—Commonwealth of Pennsylvania, Harrisburg. 1924. 44 p. Free.

PENNSYLVANIA, PHILADELPHIA. **A Study of the Day Nurseries of Philadelphia.**
BY—Child Federation. PUBLISHER—Philadelphia Association of Day Nurseries. 1916. 115 p. Out of print.

PENNSYLVANIA, PHILADELPHIA. **Day Nursery in Its Community Relation.** A study of the day nurseries of Philadelphia.
BY—Helen Glenn Tyson. PUBLISHER—Philadelphia Association of Day Nurseries. 1919. 42 p. 25 cents.

NURSERIES AND NURSING—Continued

UNITED STATES. **Survey of Nursing Education.** Report of the Committee for the Study of Nursing Education.
    BY—Josephine Goldmark. PUBLISHER—Macmillan Company, New York City. 1923. 585 p. $2.00.

UNITED STATES. **Report of the Committee to Study Visiting Nursing, Instituted by the National Organization for Public Health Nursing at the Request of the Metropolitan Life Insurance Company.**
    BY—The Committee. PUBLISHER—National Organization for Public Health Nursing, New York City. 1924. 196 p. Free.

UNITED STATES. **The Pupil Nurse in the Out-Patient Department.** A study of the nurse and nursing services in the Out-patient Department.
    BY—National League of Nursing Education. PUBLISHER—United Hospital Fund, New York City. 1925. 30 p. Free.

In addition to reports **presenting findings,** as listed above, publications dealing with **methods of conducting** such studies will be found in Part III, PURPOSE, METHOD, AND STANDARDS, under **Tuberculosis.**

OLD AGE
    See DEPENDENCY; PENSIONS; and SOCIAL AGENCIES.

PARISH
    See RELIGION.

For publications dealing with **methods of conducting** Parish Surveys see Part III, PURPOSE, METHOD, AND STANDARDS, under **Religion.**

PARKS
    See CITY AND REGIONAL PLANNING; and RECREATION.

PART-TIME SCHOOLS
    See CONTINUATION AND PART-TIME SCHOOLS; INDUSTRIAL EDUCATION; and VOCATIONAL GUIDANCE AND TRAINING.

PAUPER
    See also FEEBLEMINDED.

MASSACHUSETTS, SPRINGFIELD. **Organization and Administration of the Pauper Department.**
    BY—C. E. McCombs. PUBLISHER—Bureau of Municipal Research, Springfield. 1914. 32 p. Out of print.

PENAL INSTITUTIONS
See CHARITIES; and PRISONS.

PENITENTIARY
See PRISONS.

PENSIONS
See also DEPENDENCY.

CALIFORNIA, SAN FRANCISCO. **Public Pensions to Widows with Children.** A study of their administration in several American cities [San Francisco, Calif.; Chicago, Ill.; Kansas City, Mo.; Milwaukee, Wis.]
> BY—C. C. Carstens. PUBLISHER—Russell Sage Foundation, New York City. 1913. 36 p. 10 cents.

ILLINOIS, CHICAGO. **Care of the Aged in Chicago.** I. Industrial Pensions in the Care of the Aged. II. Trade Union Provisions for the Aged.
> BY—Elizabeth A. Hughes and Elsie Wolcott Hayden. PUBLISHER—Department of Public Welfare, Chicago. 1927. 132 p. Free.

ILLINOIS, CHICAGO. *See also* CALIFORNIA, SAN FRANCISCO, in this section.

INDIANA. **Report of the Committee Appointed to Investigate the Question of Old-Age Pensions.**
> BY—The Committee. PUBLISHER—State of Indiana, Indianapolis. 1925. 12 p. Free.

MASSACHUSETTS. **Old-Age Support of Women Teachers.** Provision for old age made for women teachers in the public schools of Massachusetts.
> BY—Department of Research, Women's Educational and Industrial Union. PUBLISHER—The same, Boston. 1921. 122 p. $1.25.

MASSACHUSETTS. **Report on Old-Age Pensions by the Commission on Pensions.** Senate No. 5.
> BY—The Commission. PUBLISHER—Commonwealth of Massachusetts, Boston. 1925. 280 p. Free.

SURVEYS IN SPECIALIZED FIELDS

PENSIONS—Continued

MISSOURI, KANSAS CITY. *See* CALIFORNIA, SAN FRANCISCO, in this section.

NEW YORK CITY. **Report on the Pension Funds of the City of New York.** Operation of the nine existing pension funds.
By—Henry Bruere. PUBLISHER—Commission on Pensions, New York City. 1916. 171 p. Out of print.

NEW YORK CITY. **Industrial Pensions.** Report of the Special Committee on Industrial Pensions and Report of a Survey of Industrial Pensions Systems.
By—Industrial Bureau, Merchants Association of New York. PUBLISHER—Merchants Association of New York, New York City. 1920. 49 p. Free.

OHIO. **Health Insurance and Old-Age Pensions.** Report, recommendations, and dissenting opinions.
By—Ohio Health and Old-Age Insurance Commission. PUBLISHER—State Department of Industry, Columbus. 1919. 448 p. Free.

PENNSYLVANIA. REPORTS ON OLD-AGE PENSIONS.
Report of the Pennsylvania Commission on Old-Age Pensions. 1919. 293 p. Out of print.
Report of the Pennsylvania Commission on Old-Age Assistance. 1925. 112 p. Free.
The Problem of Old-Age Pensions in Industry. 1926. 126 p. Free.
By—Abraham Epstein. PUBLISHER—Old-Age Pension Commission, Harrisburg.

TEXAS, DALLAS COUNTY. **Widows' Pensions.** A study of 53 fatherless families in Dallas County who are aided by the County Commissioners' Court, including the Texas Widows' Pension Law and its method of administration.
By—Gaynell Hawkins. PUBLISHER—Civic Federation of Dallas. 1922. 16 p. 15 cents.

WISCONSIN, MILWAUKEE. **Report of the Commission on Pension Laws of Milwaukee.**
By—The Commission. PUBLISHER—City of Milwaukee. 1920. 103 p. Free.

WISCONSIN, MILWAUKEE. *See also* CALIFORNIA, SAN FRANCISCO, in this section.

A BIBLIOGRAPHY OF SOCIAL SURVEYS

PLAYGROUNDS

See RECREATION; and SCHOOL BUILDINGS AND PLANTS.

For publications dealing with **methods of conducting** Playground Surveys see Part III, PURPOSE, METHOD, AND STANDARDS, under **Recreation**.

POLES

NEW YORK, BUFFALO. **Americanizing Eighty Thousand Poles.** In The Survey. Vol. XXIV, June 4.
> By—John Daniels. PUBLISHER—The Survey, New York City. 1910. 12 p. Out of print.

OHIO, CLEVELAND. **The Poles of Cleveland.**
> By—Charles W. Coulter. PUBLISHER—Americanization Committee, Citizens Bureau, Cleveland. 1919. 31 p. 10 cents.

POLICE

See also FIRE.

INDIANA, INDIANAPOLIS. **A Survey of the Indianapolis Police Department.**
> By—Leonard V. Harrison. PUBLISHER—Common Council of Indianapolis. 1924. 43 p. Free.

MARYLAND, BALTIMORE. **Business Methods of the Baltimore Police Department.** Parts I and II.
> By—Carl Hill. PUBLISHER—Bureau of State and Municipal Research, Baltimore. 1917. 32 p. Free.

NEW YORK, ROCHESTER. **Report of a Survey of the Police Bureau.**
> By—L. V. Harrison. PUBLISHER—Rochester Bureau of Municipal Research. 1921. 22 p. Free.

OHIO, CLEVELAND. **Police Administration: Criminal Justice in Cleveland.**
> By—Raymond B. Fosdick. PUBLISHER—Cleveland Foundation. 1921. 81 p. $1.00.

PENNSYLVANIA, HARRISBURG. **Report on a Survey of the Police Department of Harrisburg.**
> By—New York Bureau of Municipal Research. PUBLISHER—Chamber of Commerce, Harrisburg. 1917. 121 p. $1.00.

PENNSYLVANIA, READING. **Report on a Survey of the Municipal Departments and School District: Department of Police.**
> By—New York Bureau of Municipal Research. PUBLISHER—Reading Chamber of Commerce. 1913. 65 p. 10 cents.

SURVEYS IN SPECIALIZED FIELDS

POLICE—Continued

UNITED STATES. **American Police Systems.** Publication of the Bureau of Social Hygiene.
> BY—Raymond B. Fosdick. PUBLISHER—Century Company, New York City. 1920. 408 p. $2.20.

In addition to reports presenting findings, as listed above, a publication dealing with **methods of conducting** such studies will be found in Part III, PURPOSE, METHOD, AND STANDARDS, under **City, County, and State Administration.**

POLIOMYELITIS
> *See* INFANTILE PARALYSIS.

POOL ROOM

OHIO, COLUMBUS. **Pool Room Survey of Columbus.**
> BY—E. W. Burgess. PUBLISHER—Central Philanthropic Council, Columbus. 1916. 20 p. 10 cents.

OHIO, TOLEDO. **Pool, Billiards, and Bowling Alleys as a Phase of Commercialized Amusements in Toledo.**
> BY—John J. Phelan. PUBLISHER—Little Book Publishing Company, Toledo. 1919. 195 p. $1.50.

POPULATION
> *See also* Part I, GENERAL SOCIAL SURVEYS—URBAN, and Part II, in CITY AND REGIONAL PLANNING; DELINQUENCY AND CORRECTION; NEGROES; and RURAL EDUCATION.

ILLINOIS, CHICAGO. **Trends of Population in the Region of Chicago.**
> BY—Helen Rankin Jeter. PUBLISHER—University of Chicago Press. 1927. 64 p. $2.50.

NEW YORK CITY. **Study of the Population of Manhattanville.** Columbia University Studies in History, Economics, and Public Law. Vol. 35, No. 2.
> BY—H. B. Woolston. PUBLISHER—Longmans, Green and Company, New York City. 1909. 158 p. $1.25.

NEW YORK CITY. **Report of the New York Commission on Congestion of Population.**
> BY—The Commission. PUBLISHER—City Council, New York City. 1911. 272 p. Out of print.

POPULATION—Continued

NEW YORK CITY. **Statistical Sources for Demographic Studies of Greater New York.**
> By—Walter Laidlaw. PUBLISHER—1920 Census Committee, New York City. 1920. 844 p. $25.00.

WASHINGTON, SEATTLE. **A Study of Mobility of Population in Seattle.** Publications in the Social Sciences. Vol. 3, No. 1.
> By—Andrew W. Lind. PUBLISHER—University of Washington Press, Seattle. 1925. 63 p. Free.

In addition to reports **presenting findings,** as listed above, a publication dealing with methods of conducting such studies will be found in Part III, PURPOSE, METHOD, AND STANDARDS, under **Race Relations.**

POSTURE

NEW YORK. **Industrial Posture and Seating.** Special Bulletin No. 104.
> By—Edith Hilles and Wilhelmina Conger. PUBLISHER—Bureau of Women in Industry, State Department of Labor, Albany. 1921. 53 p. Free.

NEW YORK CITY. **Defective Seating and Faulty Posture.** Reprint from the Twelfth Annual Report of the Joint Board of Sanitary Control.
> By—Theresa Wolfson. PUBLISHER—Joint Board of Sanitary Control, New York City. 1923. 15 p. Free.

PRE-NATAL CARE
> See also NEGROES.

ILLINOIS, CHICAGO. **Pre-natal Care in Chicago.** A survey.
> By—Mrs. Kenneth F. Rich. PUBLISHER—Chicago Community Trust. 1922. 102 p. 50 cents.

MISSOURI, ST. LOUIS. **Pre-natal Care: The Pre-natal Care of a Group of St. Louis Women.** An investigation.
> By—St. Louis School of Social Economy. PUBLISHER—The same. 1913. 14 p. 10 cents.

PRE-SCHOOL

INDIANA, GARY. **Children of Pre-School Age in Gary.** Part I. General Conditions Affecting Children. Part II. Diet of the Children. U. S. Department of Labor. Children's Bureau Publication No. 122.
> By—Elizabeth Hughes and Lydia Roberts. PUBLISHER—Superintendent of Documents, Government Printing Office, Washington, D. C. 1922. 175 p. 20 cents.

SURVEYS IN SPECIALIZED FIELDS

PRE-SCHOOL—Continued

INDIANA, GARY. **Physical Status of Pre-School Children, Gary.** U. S. Department of Labor. Children's Bureau Publication No. 111.
> BY—Anna E. Rude. PUBLISHER—Superintendent of Documents, Government Printing Office, Washington, D. C. 1922. 84 p. 15 cents.

PRISONS

> *See also* ALMSHOUSES; CHARITIES; DELINQUENCY AND CORRECTION; MENTAL HYGIENE; PROBATION AND PAROLE; and WORKHOUSES.

CALIFORNIA. **A Study of County Jails in California.**
> BY—Stuart A. Queen. PUBLISHER—State Board of Charities and Corrections, San Francisco. 1918. 115 p. Free.

COLORADO. **The Colorado Report on the State Penal Institutions.** Bulletin No. 8.
> BY—National Society of Penal Information. PUBLISHER—The same, New York City. 1924. 39 p. 10 cents.

CONNECTICUT. **Report of the Commission on Convict Labor of the State of Connecticut.**
> BY—The Commission. PUBLISHER—State of Connecticut, Hartford. 1915. 90 p. Free.

CONNECTICUT, NEW HAVEN. **The New Haven County Jail.** An investigation of existing conditions. Document No. 16.
> BY—Hastings H. Hart and O. F. Lewis. PUBLISHER—Civic Federation of New Haven. 1918. 68 p. 25 cents.

DISTRICT OF COLUMBIA. **The Penal System of the District of Columbia.**
> BY—National Committee on Prisons and Prison Labor. PUBLISHER—Penal Commission, District of Columbia, Washington. 1920. 30 p. Free.

ENGLAND. **English Prisons Today, Being the Report of the Prison System Enquiry Committee.**
> BY—Stephen Hobhouse and A. F. Brockway. PUBLISHER—Longmans, Green and Company, New York City. 1922. 728 p. $8.50.

FLORIDA. **Survey of Florida County Jails.**
> BY—B. C. Riley. PUBLISHER—Russell Sage Foundation, New York City. 1922. 8 p. 10 cents.

PRISONS—Continued

IDAHO. **Report of the Commission on Prison Labor to the Legislature.**
> By—The Commission. PUBLISHER—Department of State, Boise. 1913. 14 p. Out of print.

ILLINOIS. **The One Hundred and One County Jails of Illinois and Why They Ought to Be Abolished, with Extracts of a Jail Survey Made by the State Charities Commission.**
> By—Edith Abbott. PUBLISHER—Juvenile Protective Association, Chicago. 1916. 23 p. Free.

ILLINOIS, CHICAGO. **Report on the Investigation of Prison Labor and Management of the House of Correction in Chicago.**
> By—Efficiency Division, Civil Service Commission. PUBLISHER—The same, Chicago. 1914. 66 p. Out of print.

ILLINOIS, COOK COUNTY. **Reports Comprising the Survey of the Cook County Jail, Made by the Chicago Community Trust.**
> By—George W. Kirchwey, Director. PUBLISHER—Board of Commissioners of Cook County, Chicago. 1922. 230 p. 10 cents and postage.

LOUISIANA. **Report upon the Penal and Other State Institutions of Louisiana.**
> By—Frederick H. Wines. PUBLISHER—Prison Reform Association of Louisiana, Baton Rouge. 1906. 46 p. Out of print.

MARYLAND. **Report of the Maryland Penitentiary Commission.**
> By—The Commission. PUBLISHER—State of Maryland, Annapolis. 1913. 341 p. Out of print.

MASSACHUSETTS. **Report on Investigation Regarding Establishing Schools in County Jails and Houses of Correction.** House Document No. 1255.
> By—Board of Education and Director of Bureau of Prisons. PUBLISHER—State Legislative Document Division, Boston. 1918. 45 p. Free.

MICHIGAN. **Prison Conditions in Michigan.** A report embodying the findings and recommendations of the Prison Conditions Committee of the Detroit Board of Commerce.
> By—The Committee. PUBLISHER—Detroit Board of Commerce. 1922. 19 p. Free.

MISSOURI. **Condition of the County Jails in Missouri.** A study.
> By—C. A. Ellwood. PUBLISHER—University of Missouri, Columbia. 1904. 20 p. Out of print.

SURVEYS IN SPECIALIZED FIELDS

PRISONS—Continued

MISSOURI. **Report of the Senate Committee on Penitentiary Reform in the State of Missouri.**
> BY—The Committee. PUBLISHER—The same, Jefferson City. 1915. 28 p. Free.

MISSOURI, ST. LOUIS. **The St. Louis Municipal Jail.**
> BY—Hastings H. Hart. PUBLISHER—Missouri Welfare League, St. Louis. 1924. 19 p. Free.

NEW JERSEY. **Report of the Commission on Prison Labor of the State of New Jersey.**
> BY—The Commission. PUBLISHER—State of New Jersey, Trenton. 1879. 33 p. Out of print.

NEW JERSEY. **Report of the Prison Inquiry Commission.** Vols. I and II.
> BY—Harry E. Barnes. PUBLISHER—State of New Jersey, Trenton. 1917. 822 p. Free.

NEW YORK. **Report of the Commission Appointed to Investigate the Affairs of the State Prisons of This State and the State Reformatory at Elmira.**
> BY—The Commission. PUBLISHER—State of New York, Albany. 1876. 810 p. Out of print.

NEW YORK. **Report of the Prison Labor Reform Commission.**
> BY—The Commission. PUBLISHER—State of New York, Albany. 1887. 33 p. Out of print.

NEW YORK. **Report of the Special Committee of the Assembly on Convict Labor in Penal Institutions.**
> BY—The Committee. PUBLISHER—State of New York, Albany. 1899. 56 p. Out of print.

NEW YORK. **Prison Methods in New York State.** A contribution to the study of the theory and practice of correctional institutions in New York State. Columbia University Studies in History, Economics, and Public Law. Vol. 40, No. 1, Whole No. 205.
> BY—Philip Klein. PUBLISHER—Longmans, Green and Company, New York City. 1920. 420 p. $3.50.

NEW YORK. **Report of the Prison Survey Committee of the State of New York.**
> BY—The Committee. PUBLISHER—State of New York, Albany. 1920. 412 p. Free.

A BIBLIOGRAPHY OF SOCIAL SURVEYS

PRISONS—Continued

NEW YORK. **A Plan for the Custody and Training of Prisoners Serving Sentences in County Jails in New York State.**
> BY—Joint Committee of 12 Organizations. PUBLISHER—State of New York, Albany. 1925. 206 p. Free.

NEW YORK, ALBANY COUNTY. **A Survey of Albany County Jail and Penitentiary from Social, Physical, and Psychiatric Viewpoints.** In Journal of Criminal Law and Criminology, May, 1924.
> BY—Clinton P. McCard. PUBLISHER—Northwestern University Press, Evanston, Illinois. 1924. 25 p. $1.00 per copy.

NEW YORK CITY. **A Study of the Conditions Which Have Accumulated under Many Administrations and Now Exist in the Prisons on Welfare Island, New York City, with a Plan for the Erection and Economical Financing of a New Penitentiary Elsewhere.**
> BY—Special Committee, Regular Grand Jury, August Term. PUBLISHER—Prison Association of New York City. 1924. 46 p. Free.

NEW YORK CITY. **Two Reports on the Reorganization and Reconstruction of the New York City Prison System.**
> BY—Hastings H. Hart. PUBLISHER—Prison Association of New York, New York City. 1925. 53 p. Free.

NORTH DAKOTA. **Poor Relief and Jails in North Dakota.** Reprinted from the Quarterly Journal of the University of North Dakota. Vol. III.
> BY—John Morris Gillette. PUBLISHER—University of North Dakota, Grand Forks. 1913. 137 p. 25 cents.

OHIO. **The Penal Problem in Ohio.** Report of the Joint Legislative Committee on Prisons and Reformatories Appointed by the 86th General Assembly of Ohio.
> BY—The Committee. PUBLISHER—State of Ohio, Columbus. 1926. 62 p. Free.

OREGON. **Report of the Commission to Investigate the Oregon State Penitentiary.**
> BY—L. J. Wentworth, E. E. Brodie, and F. W. Mulkey. PUBLISHER—Oregon State Board of Control, Salem. 1917. 76 p. Out of print.

PENNSYLVANIA. REPORTS ON PENAL SYSTEMS IN PENNSYLVANIA.
Employment and Compensation of Prisoners in Pennsylvania. 1915. 112 p. Out of print.

SURVEYS IN SPECIALIZED FIELDS

PRISONS—Continued

Report of the Pennsylvania Commission to Investigate Penal Systems. 1919. 79 p. Free.
> BY—Penal Commissions of Pennsylvania. PUBLISHER—General Assembly, Harrisburg.

PENNSYLVANIA. **A Financial Survey of the State Penal and Correctional Institutions in Pennsylvania.** Reprinted from Part III, Report to the Citizens' Committee on the Finances of the State of Pennsylvania.
> BY—Louis N. Robinson. PUBLISHER—Department of State and Finance, Harrisburg. 1922. 35 p. Free.

PENNSYLVANIA. **A Psychological and Educational Survey of 1916 Prisoners in the Western Penitentiary of Pennsylvania and a Report on the Italian Convict.**
> BY—William T. Root and Giovanni Giardini. PUBLISHER—Board of Trustees of Western Penitentiary, Pittsburgh. 1926. 246 p. Free.

TENNESSEE. **County Jails in Tennessee.** University Record Extension Series. Department of Community Service. Vol. III, No. 3.
> BY—Rollin V. Wilson. PUBLISHER—University of Tennessee Press, Knoxville. 1926. 47 p. Out of print.

TEXAS. **A Summary of the Texas Prison Survey.** Vol. I.
> BY—Texas Committee on Prisons and Prison Labor. PUBLISHER—The same, Austin. 1924. 88 p. Free.

TEXAS, HOUSTON. **Charge of Joseph C. Hutcheson to the Grand Jury of March, 1925, and Report of the Grand Jury on the Harris County Jail.**
> BY—R. L. Blaffer, Foreman. PUBLISHER—United States Court, Houston. 1925. 41 p. Free.

UNITED STATES. **Penal Servitude.** An investigation.
> BY—E. Stagg Whitin. PUBLISHER—National Committee on Prison Labor, New York City. 1912. 162 p. Out of print.

UNITED STATES. **Report of the Convict Labor Commission.** Public Document Special.
> BY—John J. Cloonan, Edward A. Fuller, and Willard B. Hodge. PUBLISHER—State of Connecticut, Hartford. 1915. 90 p. Free.

UNITED STATES. **A Study of Wage Payment to Prisoners as a Penal Method.** Reprinted from the Journal of Criminal Law and Criminology. Vol. X, No. 4 and Vol. XI, Nos. 1 and 2. February, May and August.
> BY—Lorenzo Dow Weyland. PUBLISHER—University of Chicago Library. 1920. 106 p. 50 cents.

PRISONS—Continued

UNITED STATES. **Wall Shadows.** A study in American prisons.
> By—Frank Tannenbaum. PUBLISHER—G. P. Putnam's Sons, New York City. 1922. 168 p. $2.00.

UNITED STATES. HANDBOOKS OF AMERICAN PRISONS.
Handbook of American Prisons Covering the Prisons of the New England and Middle Atlantic States. 1925. 311 p.
Handbook of American Prisons. 1926. 623 p.
> By—National Society for Penal Information. PUBLISHER— G. P. Putnam's Sons, New York City. $2.50 each.

UNITED STATES. **United States Prisoners in County Jails.** Report of the Committee of the American Prison Association on Lockups, Municipal and County Jails, together with suggestions for grand jury surveys of conditions under which federal prisoners are kept in county jails.
> By—Hastings H. Hart. PUBLISHER—Russell Sage Foundation, New York City. 1926. 64 p. 40 cents.

In addition to reports **presenting findings** in Prisons Surveys, as listed above, publications dealing with **methods of conducting** such studies will be found in Part III, PURPOSE, METHOD, AND STANDARDS, page 352.

PROBATION AND PAROLE

> *See also* DELINQUENCY AND CORRECTION; and JUVENILE DELINQUENCY.

MARYLAND, BALTIMORE. **Probation and Penal Treatment in Baltimore.**
> By—James M. Hepbron. PUBLISHER—Criminal Justice Commission, Baltimore. 1927. 15 p. Free.

MASSACHUSETTS. **The Delinquent Girl.** A study of the girl on parole in Massachusetts.
> By—Edith N. Burleigh and Frances R. Harris. PUBLISHER— New York School of Social Work, New York City. 1923. 118 p. 60 cents.

MISSOURI, ST. LOUIS. **Report on Probation in St. Louis.** In The Community Courier. Vol. 3, No. 9.
> By—Charles L. Chute. PUBLISHER—Community Council of St. Louis. 1924. 7 p. Free.

NEW YORK. **Report of the Probation Commission of the State of New York.**
> By—The Commission. PUBLISHER—Assembly of New York State, Albany. 1906. 300 p. Out of print.

SURVEYS IN SPECIALIZED FIELDS

PROBATION AND PAROLE—Continued

NEW YORK. **Methods of Supervising Persons on Probation.**
>BY—New York State Probation Commission. PUBLISHER—State of New York, Albany. 1922. 74 p. Free.

NEW YORK. **Report to the Commission of the Sub-Commission on Adjustment of Sentences.**
>BY—The Sub-Commission. PUBLISHER—Crime Commission of New York State, Albany. 1927. 30 p. Free.

WISCONSIN. **Probation in Wisconsin.** Report of a survey by the National Probation Association assisted by the American Social Hygiene Association, the University of Wisconsin, and the State Board of Control of Wisconsin.
>BY—Francis H. Hiller. PUBLISHER—National Probation Association, New York City. 1926. 106 p. Free.

PROHIBITION

NEW YORK CITY. **The Bowery.** A survey of the district in 1923 compared with pre-prohibition days.
>BY—World League Against Alcoholism. PUBLISHER—The same, New York City. 1923. 16 p. Free.

UNITED STATES. **The Prohibition Situation.** Research Bulletin No. 5.
>BY—Department of Research and Education, Federal Council, Churches of Christ in America. PUBLISHER—The same, New York City. 1925. 83 p. 25 cents.

UNITED STATES. **Does Prohibition Work?** A study of the operation of the Eighteenth Amendment, made by the National Federation of Settlements, assisted by social workers in different parts of the United States.
>BY—Martha Bensley Bruere, Director. PUBLISHER—Harper and Brothers, New York City. 1927. 329 p. $1.50.

PROSTITUTION

>*See also* PSYCHIATRIC; SOCIAL EVIL; and VICE.

NEW YORK CITY. **Commercialized Prostitution in New York City with a Supplementary Chapter by Katharine Bement Davis.** A study of prostitutes committed from New York City to the State Reformatory for Women at Bedford Hills. Bureau of Social Hygiene.
>BY—George J. Kneeland. PUBLISHER—Century Company, New York City. 1913. 334 p. $2.50.

PROSTITUTION—Continued

NEW YORK CITY. COMMERCIALIZED PROSTITUTION IN NEW YORK CITY.
A Comparison between 1912 and 1915. 1915. 15 p.
A Comparison between 1912, 1915, and 1916. 1916. 16 p.
A Comparison between 1912, 1915, 1916 and 1917. 1917. 18 p.
> BY—Bureau of Social Hygiene. PUBLISHER—The same, New York City. Out of print.

UNITED STATES. **Prostitution in the United States.**
> BY—Howard B. Woolston. PUBLISHER—The Century Company, New York City. 1921. 360 p. $2.50.

PSYCHIATRIC

> *See also* CONVALESCENCE; and PRISONS.

KANSAS. **Psychiatric Studies of Delinquents.** Part III. Social and Environmental Factors in the Moral Delinquency of Girls Committed to the Kansas State Industrial Farm. Public Health Reports. Vol. 35, No. 26.
> BY—Alice M. Hill. PUBLISHER—Superintendent of Documents, Government Printing Office, Washington, D. C. 1920. 36 p. 5 cents.

KANSAS, LANSING. **Psychiatric Studies of Delinquents.** Part I. A Psychiatric Study of Delinquent Women in Lansing. Public Health Reports. Vol. 35, No. 21.
> BY—Walter L. Treadway. PUBLISHER—Superintendent of Documents, Government Printing Office, Washington, D. C. 1920. 95 p. 5 cents.

KENTUCKY, LOUISVILLE. **Psychiatric Studies of Delinquents.** Part II. A Study of Physical and Mental Conditions of 100 Delinquent White Women in Louisville. Public Health Reports. Vol. 35, No. 22.
> BY—L. O. Weldon. PUBLISHER—Superintendent of Documents, Government Printing Office, Washington, D. C. 1920. 18 p. 5 cents.

UNITED STATES. **Psychiatric Studies of Delinquents.** Part IV. Some Constitutional Facts in Prostitution. Public Health Reports. Vol. 35, No. 27.
> BY—Walter L. Treadway. PUBLISHER—Superintendent of Documents, Government Printing Office, Washington, D. C. 1920. 5 p. 5 cents.

SURVEYS IN SPECIALIZED FIELDS

RACE RELATIONS

See also IMMIGRATION AND AMERICANIZATION; and NEGROES.

CANADA AND UNITED STATES. **Tentative Findings of the Survey of Race Relations.** A Canadian-American study of the Oriental on the Pacific Coast.

By—Survey of Race Relations and Institute of Social and Religious Research. PUBLISHER—Stanford University, Stanford, California. 1925. 24 p. Free.

In addition to reports **presenting findings** in Race Relations Surveys, as listed above, publications dealing with **methods of conducting** such studies will be found in Part III, PURPOSE, METHOD, AND STANDARDS, page 352.

RECREATION

Reports dealing with the general subject of recreation are listed here. For reports dealing with specific phases of this subject see DANCE HALLS; INDUSTRIAL CONDITIONS AND RELATIONS; MOTION PICTURES; POOL ROOM; and VICE.

CALIFORNIA. **Report of the State Recreational Inquiry Committee.**

By—The Committee. PUBLISHER—State of California, Sacramento. 1914. 60 p. Free.

CALIFORNIA, SAN FRANCISCO. **Public Recreation.** Transactions of the Commonwealth Club of California. Vol. 8, No. 5.

By—Francis T. North. PUBLISHER—Commonwealth Club of California, San Francisco. 1913. 129 p. 25 cents.

CALIFORNIA, SAN FRANCISCO. **Character Building Resources: A Recreation Study.**

By—Josephine D. Randall, E. P. Von Allmen, and Esther DeTuberville. PUBLISHER—Council of Social and Health Agencies, San Francisco. 1926. 217 p. Free.

DISTRICT OF COLUMBIA. **Facilities for Children's Play in the District of Columbia.** U. S. Department of Labor. Children's Bureau Publication No. 22. Miscellaneous Series No. 8.

By—Children's Bureau and Playground Department, District of Columbia. PUBLISHER—Superintendent of Documents, Government Printing Office, Washington, D. C. 1917. 72 p. 30 cents.

DISTRICT OF COLUMBIA. **Playground Facilities in the District of Columbia.**

By—Eva W. White and others. MIMEOGRAPHED—Children's Bureau, U. S. Department of Labor, Washington, D. C. 1921. 59 p. Free.

A BIBLIOGRAPHY OF SOCIAL SURVEYS

RECREATION—Continued

DISTRICT OF COLUMBIA, WASHINGTON. **Recreation and Amusement among Negroes in Washington.**
> BY—William H. Jones. PUBLISHER—Howard University Press, Washington. 1927. 216 p. $2.00.

ILLINOIS, ELGIN. **Playgrounds and Organized Public Recreation for Elgin.**
> BY—Francis R. North. PUBLISHER—Playground and Recreation Association of America, New York City. 1915. 6 p. Out of print.

ILLINOIS, GALESBURG. **Report of the Recreation Conditions and Problems of Galesburg with Recommendations and Suggestions.**
> BY—James Edward Rogers. PUBLISHER—Playground and Recreation Association of America, New York City. 1916. 28 p. Out of print.

ILLINOIS, PEORIA. **Report of the Recreation Conditions and Problems of Peoria with Recommendations and Suggested System.** In Child Welfare Bulletin. Vol. 4, No. 11.
> BY—James E. Rogers. PUBLISHER—Child Welfare League of Peoria. 1916. 32 p. 10 cents per copy.

ILLINOIS, SPRINGFIELD. **Recreation in Springfield.** Recreation Section of the Springfield Survey.
> BY—Lee F. Hanmer and Clarence Arthur Perry. PUBLISHER—Russell Sage Foundation, New York City. 1915. 133 p. Out of print.

INDIANA. **Vocational Recreation in Indiana.** Indiana University Extension Division Bulletin. Vol. III, No. 5.
> BY—Lebert H. Weir. Publisher—Indiana University, Bloomington. 1918. 126 p. Out of print.

INDIANA, GARY. **Gary Public Schools. Physical Training and Play.**
> BY—Lee F. Hanmer. PUBLISHER—General Education Board, New York City. 1918. 35 p. 10 cents.

INDIANA, INDIANAPOLIS. **Indianapolis Recreation Survey.**
> BY—Francis R. North. PUBLISHER—Chamber of Commerce, Indianapolis. 1914. 60 p. Out of print.

INDIANA, SOUTH BEND. **Playground and Public Recreation Facilities for South Bend.** A study of conditions and recommendations for an adequate recreation system.
> BY—Francis R. North. PUBLISHER—Playground and Recreation Committee, South Bend. 1914. 9 p. Out of print.

SURVEYS IN SPECIALIZED FIELDS

RECREATION—Continued

KENTUCKY, LOUISVILLE. **Survey of Private Recreation Facilities in Louisville.**
> BY—Recreation Division of the Community Chest. MIMEOGRAPHED—Community Chest, Louisville. 1925. 22 p. Free.

MAINE, PORTLAND. **Portland Recreation Survey.** Prepared under the Direction of the Playground and Recreation Association of America.
> BY—Francis R. North. PUBLISHER—Board of Trade, Portland. 1913. 82 p. 5 cents.

MASSACHUSETTS, IPSWICH. **Play and Recreation in a Town of 6,000.** A recreation survey of Ipswich.
> BY—Howard R. Knight. PUBLISHER—Russell Sage Foundation, New York City. 1915. 99 p. Out of print.

MASSACHUSETTS, WALTHAM. **A Recreation Survey of the City of Waltham.**
> BY—Francis R. North. PUBLISHER—City Council of Waltham. 1913. 96 p. Out of print.

MICHIGAN, DETROIT. **Detroit Recreation Survey.**
> BY—Rowland Haynes and Mrs. Haynes. PUBLISHER—Board of Commerce, Detroit. 1913. 71 p. Free.

MISSOURI, KANSAS CITY. **Recreation Survey of Kansas City.** In Second Annual Report of the Recreation Department of the Kansas City Board of Public Welfare.
> BY—Rowland T. Haynes. PUBLISHER—Board of Public Welfare, Kansas City. 1912. 100 p. Out of print.

MISSOURI, KANSAS CITY. **Rotary Club Survey of the Recreational Conditions of Kansas City Boyhood.**
> BY—Boys' Work Committee, Rotary Club. PUBLISHER—The same, Kansas City. 1921. 10 p. Free.

MISSOURI, ST. LOUIS. **Recreation in St. Louis.**
> BY—City Plan Commission. PUBLISHER—The same, St. Louis. 1917. 48 p. Out of print.

NEBRASKA, OMAHA. **One City's Program for Leisure Time.** Reprinted from the Journal of Social Forces, September, 1924.
> BY—T. Earl Sullenger. PUBLISHER—University of Omaha. 1924. 4 p. 10 cents.

NEBRASKA, OMAHA. **Social Ministry in an American City.** A recreational survey of the churches of Omaha.
> BY—T. Earl Sullenger. PUBLISHER—University of Omaha. 1924. 14 p. 15 cents.

RECREATION—Continued

NEW JERSEY, NEWARK. **Girls' Recreation Survey of Newark.**
> BY—Recreation Committee, Civic Department of Contemporary Club. PUBLISHER—Contemporary Club, Newark. 1923. 34 p. Free.

NEW JERSEY, PATERSON. **Playgrounds and Organized Public Recreation for Paterson.**
> BY—F. R. North. PUBLISHER—Playground Commission, Paterson. 1914. 9 p. Out of print.

NEW YORK, BUFFALO. **Study of the Social and Recreational Resources of the Jewish Community of Buffalo.**
> BY—Jewish Welfare Board. MIMEOGRAPHED—The same, New York City. 1923. 51 p. Free.

NEW YORK, BUFFALO. **Recreation Survey of Buffalo.**
> BY—L. H. Weir, Director. PUBLISHER—City Planning Committee, Department of Parks and Public Buildings; and Buffalo City Planning Association. 1925. 369 p. 25 cents.

NEW YORK CITY. **Statement Relating to Recreation in Greater New York.**
> BY—Parks and Playgrounds Association. PUBLISHER—The same, New York City. 1910. 25 p. Free.

NEW YORK CITY. **The Exploitation of Pleasure.** A study of commercial recreation in New York City.
> BY—Michael M. Davis, JR. PUBLISHER—Russell Sage Foundation, New York City. 1911. 61 p. Out of print.

NEW YORK CITY. **Report by the Committee on Recreation, City of New York.**
> BY—The Committee. PUBLISHER—The same, New York City. 1916. 23 p. Out of print.

NEW YORK CITY. **Planning for Play.** Some of the methods and results of the Recreation Survey of Greater New York for the Regional Plan of New York and Its Environs. In The Survey, July 15.
> BY—Lee F. Hanmer. PUBLISHER—The Survey, New York City. 1925. 3 p. 25 cents per copy.

NORTH CAROLINA, CHARLOTTE. **Recreation in Charlotte.**
> BY—Ivan G. Wright. PUBLISHER—Parks and Playground Association, Charlotte. 1915. 39 p. Out of print.

SURVEYS IN SPECIALIZED FIELDS

RECREATION—Continued

OHIO, CINCINNATI. **Recreation Survey of Cincinnati.**
    By—Juvenile Protective Association. PUBLISHER—The same, Cincinnati. 1913. 48 p. Free.

OHIO, CLEVELAND. **Report of the Committee on Public Recreation of the Cleveland Chamber of Commerce.**
    By—The Committee. PUBLISHER—Cleveland Chamber of Commerce. 1912. 22 p. Out of print.

OHIO, CLEVELAND. THE CLEVELAND RECREATION SURVEY.
    Education through Recreation. By George E. Johnson. 1916. 94 p. 35 cents.
    School Work and Spare Time. By F. G. Bonser. 1918. 176 p. 50 cents.
    Wholesome Citizens and Spare Time. By John L. Gillin. 1918. 182 p. 50 cents.
    The Sphere of Private Agencies. By L. E. Bowman and others. 1918. 178 p. 50 cents.
    Commercial Recreation. By Charlotte Rumbold and Raymond Moley. 1920. 155 p. 50 cents.
    Public Provision for Recreation. By Rowland Haynes and Stanley P. Davies. 1920. 198 p. 50 cents.
    A Community Recreation Program. By Rowland Haynes and C. K. Matson. 1920. 116 p. 50 cents.
        By—Rowland Haynes, Director. PUBLISHER—Cleveland Foundation.

OHIO, TOLEDO. **Play Facilities in Toledo.**
    By—E. B. DeGroot. PUBLISHER—Toledo Playground Association. 1914. 8 p. Out of print.

PENNSYLVANIA, PITTSBURGH. **The Playgrounds of Pittsburgh.** In The Pittsburgh District Civic Frontage, The Pittsburgh Survey.
    By—Beulah Kennard. PUBLISHER—Russell Sage Foundation, New York City. 1914. p. 306–325. Out of print.

PENNSYLVANIA, PITTSBURGH. **Pittsburgh Playgrounds.** Study and recommendations.
    By—Citizen's Committee on City Planning. PUBLISHER—The same, Pittsburgh. 1920. 40 p. Free.

PENNSYLVANIA, SCRANTON. **Recreation Survey of Scranton.**
    By—Lavera Berlew. PUBLISHER—Playground Association, Scranton. 1913. 21 p. Out of print.

RECREATION—Continued

RHODE ISLAND, PROVIDENCE. **Recreation Survey of the City of Providence.**
>By—Francis R. North. PUBLISHER—Playground Association, Providence. 1912. 65 p. Postage.

UNITED STATES. **How People Play in Forty American Cities.** Based on facts gathered in recreation surveys.
>By—Playground and Recreation Association of America. MIMEOGRAPHED—The same, New York City. 1916. 56 p. 40 cents.

UNITED STATES. **State Parks and Recreational Uses of State Forests in the United States.** Report of a survey.
>By—Raymond H. Torrey. PUBLISHER—National Conference on State Parks, Washington, D. C. 1926. 259 p. Available to members.

WISCONSIN, MADISON. **The Four Lake City Recreational Survey.**
>By—C. W. Hetherington. PUBLISHER—Board of Commerce, Madison. 1915. 103 p. 50 cents.

WISCONSIN, MILWAUKEE. **Recreation Survey.** Bulletin No. 17.
>By—Rowland Haynes. PUBLISHER—Bureau of Economy and Efficiency. 1912. 32 p. Out of print.

WISCONSIN, MILWAUKEE. **Recreation Survey.** In The Playground, May.
>By—Rowland Haynes. PUBLISHER—Playground and Recreation Association of America, New York City. 1912. 33 p. 25 cents per copy.

WISCONSIN, MILWAUKEE. **Amusements and Recreation in Milwaukee.**
>By—Committee on Public Amusements and Morals, Public Parks and Playgrounds; and Public Education and Buildings. PUBLISHER—City Club, Milwaukee. 1914. 56 p. Free.

In addition to reports **presenting findings** in Recreation Surveys, as listed above, publications dealing with **methods of conducting** such studies will be found in Part III, PURPOSE, METHOD, AND STANDARDS, page 352.

REFORMATORIES

>*See also* CHARITIES; DETENTION; PRISONS; and PROSTITUTION.

MISSOURI, BOONEVILLE. **The Missouri Reformatory.** Report and recommendations. Bi-Monthly Bulletin Vol. 24, No. 8.
>By—A. F. Kuhlman. PUBLISHER—State Board of Charities and Corrections, Jefferson City. 1922. 12 p. Free.

SURVEYS IN SPECIALIZED FIELDS

REFORMATORIES—Continued

UNITED STATES. **The American State Reformatory with Special Reference to its Educational Aspects.** University of California Publication. Vol. 5, No. 3.
> By—Frank Fielding Nalder. PUBLISHER—University of California Press, Berkeley. 1920. 178 p. $1.80.

REGIONAL PLANNING
> See CITY AND REGIONAL PLANNING.

RELIEF
> See also BLINDNESS, SIGHT CONSERVATION, AND DISEASE OF THE EYE; CHILD WELFARE; FAMILY WELFARE; PRISONS; SOCIAL AGENCIES; TUBERCULOSIS; and UNEMPLOYMENT.

CALIFORNIA. **County Outdoor Relief in California.** Revised edition.
> By—E. P. VonAllmen and Esther DeTuberville. PUBLISHER—State Board of Charities and Corrections, Sacramento. 1918. 33 p. Free.

CONNECTICUT, WATERBURY. **Report of the Special Commission on Public Poor Relief.**
> By—The Commission. PUBLISHER—Municipal Council, Waterbury. 1894. 19 p. Out of print.

INDIANA, MARION COUNTY. **Report to the Board of Commissioners of Marion County on the County Institutions and Poor Relief.**
> By—Henry C. Wright. PUBLISHER—Board of Commissioners of Marion County, Indianapolis. 1920. 23 p. Free.

MISSOURI. **Outdoor Relief in Missouri.** A study of its administration by county officers.
> By—George A. Warfield. PUBLISHER—Russell Sage Foundation, New York City. 1915. 142 p. Out of print.

NEW YORK. **Report of the New York State Commission on Relief for Widowed Mothers.**
> By—The Commission. PUBLISHER—State of New York, Albany. 1914. 584 p. Free.

NEW YORK, DUTCHESS COUNTY. **Public Outdoor Relief.** An inquiry into the administration of public outdoor relief in Dutchess County for the three year period, October, 1910, to September, 1913.
> By—State Charities Aid Association. PUBLISHER—The same, New York City. 1913. 29 p. Free.

RELIEF—Continued

OHIO, CINCINNATI. **The House of Refuge.** Submitted to the Mayor and the Board of Social Service.
>By—Bureau of Municipal Research. PUBLISHER—The same, Cincinnati. 1912. 23 p. Free.

OREGON, PORTLAND. **The Public Welfare Bureau of Portland.** A study of its administration and methods for disbursing county relief funds.
>By—City Club of Portland. PUBLISHER—The same. 1922. 8 p. Free.

PENNSYLVANIA. **Poor Relief in Pennsylvania.** A state-wide survey. Bulletin 21.
>By—Emil Frankel. PUBLISHER—State Department of Welfare, Harrisburg. 1925. 149 p. Free.

PENNSYLVANIA, PHILADELPHIA. **The Philadelphia Relief Study.** A study of the family relief needs and resources of Philadelphia.
>By—William H. Pear, Director. PUBLISHER—Committee on the Philadelphia Relief Study, Philadelphia. 1926. 30 p. 25 cents.

WISCONSIN. **Organized Poor Relief in Wisconsin.** Bulletin of the Extension Division.
>By—Katherine L. VanWyck. PUBLISHER—University of Wisconsin, Madison. 1915. 12 p. 5 cents.

RELIGION

>*See also* PART I, GENERAL SOCIAL SURVEYS—URBAN and RURAL, and PART II, in EDUCATION; INDIANS; ITALIANS; MILITARY CAMPS; NEGRO EDUCATION; RECREATION; RELIGIOUS EDUCATION; RURAL; and SOCIAL AGENCIES.

CALIFORNIA, ORANGE COUNTY AND STANISLAUS COUNTY. **Irrigation and Religion.** A study of two prosperous California counties. Committee on Social and Religious Surveys.
>By—Edmund deS. Brunner and Mary V. Brunner. PUBLISHER—George H. Doran Company, New York City. 1922. 127 p. 75 cents.

CALIFORNIA, SAN FRANCISCO. **The Church in Greater San Francisco.** A study in church efficiency.
>By—Robert S. Donaldson. PUBLISHER—Board of Home Missions, Presbyterian Church in the U. S. A., New York City. 1921. 24 p. 5 cents.

SURVEYS IN SPECIALIZED FIELDS

RELIGION—Continued

COLORADO. **The Church and Industrial Warfare.** A report on the labor troubles in Colorado and Michigan.
>By—Henry F. Atkinson. PUBLISHER—Federal Council, Churches of Christ in America, New York City. 1920. 8 p. 10 cents.

FOREIGN COUNTRIES. *See* UNITED STATES AND FOREIGN COUNTRIES in this section.

ILLINOIS, CHICAGO. **A Modern Church to Meet a Modern Situation.** The story of a survey of the Fourth Presbyterian Church community.
>By—Charles Stelzle. PUBLISHER—Board of Home Missions, Presbyterian Church in the U. S. A., New York City. 1912. 16 p. Out of print.

INDIANA, JENNINGS COUNTY. **Church and Community Survey in Jennings County.**
>By—Martha Robinson. PUBLISHER—Committee on Social and Religious Surveys, New York City. 1920. 18 p. Free.

INDIANA, JENNINGS COUNTY. *See also* IOWA, CLAY COUNTY, in this section.

IOWA, CLAY COUNTY. **Rural Church Life in the Middle West as Illustrated by Clay County, Iowa, and Jennings County, Indiana, with Comparative Data from Studies of 35 Middle Western Counties.** Committee on Social and Religious Surveys.
>By—Benson Y. Landis. PUBLISHER—George H. Doran Company, New York City. 1922. 90 p. Out of print.

KANSAS [NORTHEASTERN]. **Factors Which Have to Do with the Decline of the Country Church.** A study based on surveys made in three rural counties and three rural communities [Northeastern Kan.; Western Me.; Salt River Presbytery, Mo.; Sullivan Co., Mo.; Westchester Co., N. Y.; Gibson Co., Tenn.]. Reprinted from the American Journal of Sociology. Vol. XXII, No. 2.
>By—Anton T. Boisen. PUBLISHER—Social Service Department, Congregational Churches, Boston, Massachusetts. 1916. 15 p. Free.

KANSAS, SEDGWICK COUNTY. **A Church and Community Survey of Sedgwick County.** Committee on Social and Religious Surveys.
>By—Benson Y. Landis. PUBLISHER—George H. Doran Company, New York City. 1922. 83 p. 90 cents.

MAINE [WESTERN]. *See* KANSAS [NORTHEASTERN] in this section.

RELIGION—Continued

MARYLAND, GRACEHAM. **Survey of Graceham, Frederick County.**
 By—H. E. Stocker and Edmund deS. Brunner. PUBLISHER—Moravian Country Church Commission, Easton, Pennsylvania. 1915. 9 p. Postage.

MARYLAND, HARFORD COUNTY. **The Country Church in Industrial Zones** [Harford Co., Md., and Columbia Co., Pa.]. Committee on Social and Religious Surveys.
 By—H. N. Morse. PUBLISHER—George H. Doran Company, New York City. 1922. 120 p. 75 cents.

MASSACHUSETTS, BOSTON. **Community Survey of Morgan Memorial Parish, Boston.** In Treasurer's Annual Report for 1916.
 By—Helen Lacount and Pauline Helms. PUBLISHER—Morgan Memorial Church, Boston. 1916. 32 p. 25 cents.

MASSACHUSETTS, SPRINGFIELD. **The Springfield Church Survey.** Institute of Social and Religious Research.
 By—H. Paul Douglass. PUBLISHER—George H. Doran Company, New York City. 1926. 445 p. $4.00.

MICHIGAN. *See* COLORADO in this section.

MICHIGAN, DETROIT. **A Study of Detroit for Baptists.**
 By—Detroit Baptist Union. PUBLISHER—The same. 1918. 26 p. 10 cents.

MINNESOTA, REDWOOD COUNTY. **Canvass of Religious Life and Work in Redwood County.**
 By—L. F. Badger. PUBLISHER—Board of Home Missions, Presbyterian Church in the U. S. A., New York City. 1912. 22 p. Out of print.

MISSOURI, ST. LOUIS. **The St. Louis Church Survey.** A religious investigation with a social background. Institute of Social and Religious Research.
 By—H. Paul Douglass. PUBLISHER—George H. Doran Company, New York City. 1924. 327 p. $4.00.

MISSOURI, SULLIVAN COUNTY AND SALT RIVER PRESBYTERY. *See* KANSAS [NORTHEASTERN] in this section.

NEW JERSEY, NEWARK. **Religious and Sociological Investigation of Newark.**
 By—Department of Immigration, Presbyterian Board of Home Missions. MIMEOGRAPHED—The same, New York City. 1910. 14 p. Out of print.

SURVEYS IN SPECIALIZED FIELDS

RELIGION—Continued

NEW JERSEY, SALEM COUNTY. **A Church and Community Survey of Salem County.** Committee on Social and Religious Surveys.
>By—Edmund deS. Brunner. PUBLISHER—George H. Doran Company, New York City. 1922. 92 p. 75 cents.

NEW YORK CITY [BROOKLYN]. **Community Study.** Parish of the Clinton Avenue Congregational Church, Brooklyn.
>By—Henry A. Atkinson and Morrison Russell Boynton. PUBLISHER—Clinton Avenue Congregational Church, Brooklyn. 1915. 60 p. Out of print.

NEW YORK CITY. **The Survey of the Young Men's Christian Association of the City of New York.**
>By—Arthur L. Swift, Jr., Director. PUBLISHER—Association Press, New York City. 1927. 632 p. $10.00.

NEW YORK, TOMPKINS COUNTY. **The Country Church: the Decline of Its Influence and the Remedy** [Tompkins Co., N. Y., and Windsor Co., Vt.].
>By—Charles Otis Gill and Gifford Pinchot. PUBLISHER—Macmillan Company, New York City. 1913. 222 p. $1.60.

NEW YORK, TOMPKINS AND WARREN COUNTIES. **The Country Church in Colonial Counties** [Tompkins and Warren Counties, N. Y., and Addison County, Vt.]. Committee on Social and Religious Surveys.
>By—Marjorie Patten. PUBLISHER—George H. Doran Company, New York City. 1922. 106 p. 75 cents.

NEW YORK, WESTCHESTER COUNTY. *See* KANSAS [NORTHEASTERN] in this section.

NORTH CAROLINA. **The Church and Landless Men.** University Extension Division. Vol. I, No. 11.
>By—L. G. Wilson. PUBLISHER—University of North Carolina, Chapel Hill. 1921. 26 p. Free.

OHIO. **Six Thousand Country Churches.**
>By—Charles Otis Gill and Gifford Pinchot. PUBLISHER—Macmillan Company, New York City. 1919. 237 p. $1.50.

OHIO. **Survey Reports of Churches and Communities with Tentative Suggestions on Each of the Counties in Ohio.**
>By—B. F. Lamb and others. PUBLISHER—Ohio Federation of Churches, Columbus. 1920–1922. 15 p. each. Free.

RELIGION—Continued

OHIO, CLEVELAND. RELIGIOUS SURVEYS IN CLEVELAND.
Survey of the Protestant Churches of Cleveland. 1916. 14 p.
Religious Survey of Greater Cleveland. 1920. 32 p.
The Churches and the Foreign Situation in Greater Cleveland. 1921. 12 p.
>By—Comity Committee, Federated Churches. PUBLISHER—The same, Cleveland. Free.

PENNSYLVANIA; BEDFORD, BLAIR, CENTER, CLEARFIELD, HUNTINGDON AND JUNIATA COUNTIES. **Survey of Huntingdon Presbytery.**
>By—G. B. St. John. PUBLISHER—Board of Home Missions, Presbyterian Church in the U. S. A., New York City. 1910. 50 p. Postage.

PENNSYLVANIA, COLUMBIA COUNTY. *See* MARYLAND, HANFORD COUNTY, in this section.

PENNSYLVANIA; COLUMBIA, LUZERNE, MONTOUR, NORTHUMBERLAND, AND UNION COUNTIES. **Sunbury District Survey.**
>By—A. S. Williams, Director. PUBLISHER—Home Missionary Society, Central Methodist Episcopal Church, Newberry. 1918. 24 p. Postage.

PENNSYLVANIA, COOPERSBURG. **Co-operation in Coopersburg.**
>By—Edmund deS. Brunner. PUBLISHER—Missionary Education Movement, United States and Canada, New York City. 1916. 95 p. 50 cents.

PENNSYLVANIA, PHILADELPHIA. **Social Survey of the Parish of Christ Church.**
>By—Francis M. Wetherill. PUBLISHER—Christ Church, Philadelphia. 1915. 42 p. Free.

PENNSYLVANIA, PITTSBURGH. **The Strip: a Socio-Religious Survey of a Typical Problem Section of Pittsburgh.**
>By—R. E. Boyd, Director. PUBLISHER—Christian Social Service Union, Pittsburgh. 1915. 55 p. 25 cents.

PENNSYLVANIA, PITTSBURGH. **The Up-Town: a Socio-Religious Survey of a Section of Pittsburgh.**
>By—Elizabeth Summerson, Director. PUBLISHER—Pittsburgh Council, Churches of Christ. 1917. 34 p. Out of print.

PENNSYLVANIA, RANKIN. **An Interchurch Survey, Rankin.**
>By—Interchurch World Movement and Pittsburgh Council of Churches. PUBLISHER—The same. 1920. 47 p. Out of print.

SURVEYS IN SPECIALIZED FIELDS

RELIGION—Continued

PENNSYLVANIA, SUSQUEHANNA COUNTY. **Susquehanna County Survey.** Interchurch World Movement of North America.
    By—F. E. Cholerton. PUBLISHER—Interchurch Press, New York City. 1920. 52 p. 50 cents.

TENNESSEE, GIBSON COUNTY. *See* KANSAS [NORTHEASTERN] in this section.

UNITED STATES. **The Social Welfare Work of Unitarian Churches.** A report of an investigation by the Department of Social and Public Service of the American Unitarian Association. Bulletin No. 1.
    By—Elmer S. Forbes. PUBLISHER—American Unitarian Association, Boston, Massachusetts. 1910. 38 p. Free.

UNITED STATES [NEW ENGLAND]. **The Survey.** In New England Methodism.
    By—H. J. Bergstahler. PUBLISHER—Methodist Book Concern, New York City. 1915. 79 p. 50 cents per copy.

UNITED STATES. **The Centenary Survey of the Board of Home Missions and Church Extension of the Methodist Episcopal Church.**
    By—Joint Centenary Committee, Methodist Church. PUBLISHER—The same, New York City. 1918. 83 p. 50 cents.

UNITED STATES. **General Survey of the Needs and Activities of the Episcopal Church.**
    By—Isabel Y. Douglas and Nannette B. Lincoln. PUBLISHER—Nation-Wide Campaign of the Episcopal Church, New York City. 1919. 176 p. Out of print.

UNITED STATES. **Religion among American Men as Revealed by a Study of Conditions in the Army.**
    By—Committee on War and Religious Outlook. PUBLISHER—Association Press, New York City. 1920. 155 p. Out of print.

UNITED STATES. **From Survey to Service.**
    By—Harlan Paul Douglass. PUBLISHER—Missionary Education Movement, New York City. 1921. 182 p. 75 cents.

UNITED STATES. **The Church on the Changing Frontier.** A study of the homesteader and his church. Committee on Social and Religious Surveys.
    By—Helen O. Belknap. PUBLISHER—George H. Doran Company, New York City. 1922. 143 p. 75 cents.

RELIGION—Continued

UNITED STATES [SOUTH]. **Church Life in the Rural South.** A study of the opportunity of Protestantism, based upon data from 70 counties. Committee on Social and Religious Surveys.
    BY—Edmund deS. Brunner. PUBLISHER—George H. Doran Company, New York City. 1923. 117 p. Out of print.

UNITED STATES. **The Town and Country Church in the United States.** Second Edition. Institute of Social and Religious Research.
    BY—H. N. Morse and Edmund deS. Brunner. PUBLISHER—George H. Doran Company, New York City. 1925. 179 p. $1.50.

UNITED STATES. **The Church in the Changing City.** Case studies illustrating adaptation. Institute of Social and Religious Research.
    BY—H. Paul Douglass. PUBLISHER—George H. Doran Company, New York City. 1927. 453 p. $4.00.

UNITED STATES [MIDDLE WEST]. *See* IOWA, CLAY COUNTY, in this section.

UNITED STATES AND FOREIGN COUNTRIES. **Survey of the Field and Work of the Northern Baptist Convention** [Africa, Central America, China, Cuba, Europe, India, Japan, Mexico, Philippine Islands, Porto Rico, South America, United States].
    BY—Special Committee on Survey. PUBLISHER—General Board of Promotion, Northern Baptist Convention, New York City. 1919. 151 p. Free.

VERMONT, ADDISON COUNTY. *See* NEW YORK, TOMPKINS AND WARREN COUNTIES, in this section.

VERMONT, WINDSOR COUNTY. *See* NEW YORK, TOMPKINS COUNTY, in this section.

WASHINGTON, PEND OREILLE COUNTY. **A Church and Community Survey of Pend Oreille County.** Committee on Social and Religious Surveys.
    BY—Edmund deS. Brunner. PUBLISHER—George H. Doran Company, New York City. 1922. 51 p. 60 cents.

WISCONSIN, SHEBOYGAN COUNTY AND PRICE COUNTY. **The New and the Old Immigrant on the Land.** A study of Americanization and the rural church. Committee on Social and Religious Surveys.
    BY—C. Luther Fry. PUBLISHER—George H. Doran Company, New York City. 1922. 119 p. 75 cents.

In addition to reports **presenting findings** in Religion Surveys, as listed above, publications dealing with **methods of conducting** such studies will be found in Part III, PURPOSE, METHOD, AND STANDARDS, page 353.

SURVEYS IN SPECIALIZED FIELDS

RELIGIOUS EDUCATION

See also CHINESE; and NEGRO EDUCATION.

AMERICA. **Theological Education in America.** An evaluation of the education of Protestant ministers in the United States and Canada, based upon a critical study of 161 theological seminaries. Institute of Social and Religious Research.
BY—Robert L. Kelly. PUBLISHER—George H. Doran Company, NEW York City. 1924. 456 p. $5.00.

INDIANA. **The Religious Education of Protestants in an American Commonwealth.** Vol. I. Indiana Survey of Religious Education. Institute of Social and Religious Research.
BY—Walter S. Athearn. PUBLISHER—George H. Doran Company, New York City. 1923. 580 p. $5.00.

NEW YORK CITY. SURVEYS OF RELIGIOUS EDUCATION.
Jewish Religious Education in the Bronx. In Annual Report of the New York Committee and a Survey of the Bronx. 1916. 41 p.
Survey of Jewish Religious School Conditions in Harlem. 1921. 19 p.
BY—Union of American Hebrew Congregations. PUBLISHER—The same, Cincinnati, Ohio. Free.

UNITED STATES. **A Survey of Week-Day Religious Education.** In Religious Education. Vol. XVII, No. 2.
BY—Erwin L. Shaver. PUBLISHER—Religious Education, Chicago, Illinois. 1922. 59 p. $1.00 per copy.

In addition to reports **presenting findings** in Religious Education Surveys, as listed above, publications dealing with **methods of conducting** such studies will be found in Part III, PURPOSE, METHOD, AND STANDARDS, page 354.

RURAL

Reports dealing with general conditions in rural communities are listed in Part I, GENERAL SOCIAL SURVEYS—URBAN and RURAL. Reports dealing with specific phases of this subject are listed here and under CHILD HEALTH AND HYGIENE; CHILD LABOR; CHILD WELFARE; COST OF LIVING; EPILEPTICS; FEEBLE-MINDED; HOUSING; ILLEGITIMACY; IMMIGRATION AND AMERICANIZATION; INDUSTRIAL CONDITIONS AND RELATIONS; JAPANESE; JUVENILE DELINQUENCY; MENTAL HYGIENE; NEGROES; RELIGION; RURAL

A BIBLIOGRAPHY OF SOCIAL SURVEYS

RURAL—Continued

EDUCATION; RURAL HEALTH AND SANITATION; SOCIAL AGENCIES; TRACHOMA; TRUANCY AND NON-ATTENDANCE; and UNEMPLOYMENT.

CALIFORNIA. **A Study of Farm Labor in California.** Agricultural Experiment Station Circular No. 193.

By—R. L. Adams and T. R. Kelly. PUBLISHER—University of California, Berkeley. 1918. 75 p. Free.

LOUISIANA. **Standards of Labor on the Hill Farms of Louisiana.** U. S. Department of Agriculture Bulletin No. 961.

By—M. Bruce Oates. PUBLISHER—Superintendent of Documents, Government Printing Office, Washington, D. C. 1921. 27 p. 10 cents.

MICHIGAN, ST. JOSEPH COUNTY. **A Survey of Farm Homes.** Reprinted from the Journal of Home Economics. Vol. XIII, No. 8.

By—Ilena M. Bailey and Melissa Farrell Snyder. PUBLISHER— Bureau of Home Economics, Washington, D. C. 1921. 10 p. Free.

MINNESOTA. **Family Living on Successful Minnesota Farms.** Bulletin 240.

By—John D. Black and Carle C. Zimmerman. PUBLISHER— Agricultural Experiment Station, University of Minnesota, St. Paul. 1927. 25 p. Free.

NEBRASKA. STUDIES OF NEBRASKA FARMS.

Reading Matter in Nebraska Farm Homes. Bulletin 180. 1922. 27 p. Out of print.

Nebraska Farm Tenancy: Some Community Phases. Bulletin 196. 1923. 50 p. Free.

The Nebraska Farm Family: Some Land Tenure Phases. Bulletin 185. 1923. 31 p. Free.

Nebraska Farm Homes: a Comparison of Some Living Conditions of Owners, Part-Owners, and Tenants. Bulletin 191. 1923. 48 p. Free.

By—J. O. Rankin. PUBLISHER—Agricultural Experiment Station, Lincoln.

NEW JERSEY. **Truck-Farm Labor in New Jersey, 1922.** U. S. Department of Agriculture Bulletin No. 1285.

By—Josiah C. Folsom. PUBLISHER—Superintendent of Documents, Government Printing Office, Washington, D. C. 1925. 37 p. 10 cents.

SURVEYS IN SPECIALIZED FIELDS

RURAL—Continued

NEW YORK, BELLEVILLE. **The National Influence of a Single Farm Community.** A story of the flow into national life of migration from the farms. U. S. Department of Agriculture Bulletin No. 984.
> BY—Emily F. Hoag. PUBLISHER—Superintendent of Documents, Government Printing Office, Washington, D. C. 1921. 55 p. 20 cents.

NEW YORK, TOMPKINS COUNTY. **Agricultural Survey.**
> BY—G. F. Warren and K. C. Livermore. PUBLISHER—College of Agriculture, Cornell University, Ithaca. 1911. 568 p. Out of print.

NORTH CAROLINA, WAKE COUNTY. **Rural Organization.** A study of primary groups in Wake County. Bulletin 245.
> BY—Carle C. Zimmerman and Carl C. Taylor. PUBLISHER—North Carolina Agricultural Experiment Station, Raleigh. 1922. 42 p. Free.

NORTH DAKOTA, ALICE. **Rural Survey of Alice, Cass County.** Pamphlet No. 16.
> BY—Charles J. Bornman. PUBLISHER—Moravian Country Church Commission, Easton, Pennsylvania. 1917. 11 p. 5 cents.

OHIO. RURAL SURVEYS.
Rural Survey of Sharon Parish. 1915. 7 p. Out of print.
Survey of Fry's Valley. Pamphlet No. 13. 1916. 8 p. Postage.
> BY—Edmund deS. Brunner. PUBLISHER—Moravian Country Church Commission, Easton, Pennsylvania.

TEXAS. **Studies in Agricultural Economics by the Texas Applied Economics Club.**
> BY—Lewis H. Haney, Investigator. PUBLISHER—University of Texas, Austin. 1913. 132 p. Out of print.

UNITED STATES. **What the Farm Contributes Directly to the Farmer's Living.** Farmers' Bulletin 635.
> BY—W. C. Funk. PUBLISHER—U. S. Department of Agriculture, Washington, D. C. 1914. 21 p. Out of print.

UNITED STATES. **The Farm Woman's Problems.** A survey of farm home conditions. U. S. Department of Agriculture Circular 148.
> BY—Florence E. Ward. PUBLISHER—Superintendent of Documents, Government Printing Office, Washington, D. C. 1920. 24 p. 5 cents.

RURAL—Continued

UNITED STATES. REPORT OF THE JOINT COMMISSION OF AGRICULTURAL INQUIRY.
  The Agricultural Crisis and Its Causes. Part I. 1921. 240 p. 15 cents.
  Credit. Part II. 1922. 159 p. 10 cents.
  Transportation. Part III. 1922. 686 p. 75 cents.
  Marketing and Distribution. Part IV. 1922. 266 p. 30 cents.
   By—Sydney Anderson, Director. PUBLISHER—Superintendent of Documents, Government Printing Office, Washington, D. C.

VERMONT. **Status of Rural Vermont.**
   By—George F. Wells. PUBLISHER—Vermont State Agricultural Commission, Montpelier. 1903. 53 p. Out of print.

WEST VIRGINIA, FRENCH CREEK. **French Creek as a Rural Community.** Agricultural Experiment Station Bulletin 176.
   By—A. J. Dadisman. PUBLISHER—West Virginia University, Morgantown. 1921. 23 p. Free.

WISCONSIN. **Farm Tenancy.** An analysis of the occupancy of 500 farms. Research Bulletin 44.
   By—C. J. Galpin and Emily F. Hoag. PUBLISHER—Agricultural Experiment Station, University of Wisconsin, Madison. 1919. 18 p. Free.

WISCONSIN, WALWORTH COUNTY. **The Social Anatomy of an Agricultural Community.** Research Bulletin 34.
   By—C. J. Galpin. PUBLISHER—Agricultural Experiment Station, University of Wisconsin, Madison. 1915. 34 p. Out of print.

In addition to reports **presenting findings,** as listed above, publications dealing with **methods of conducting** such studies will be found in Part III, PURPOSE, METHOD, AND STANDARDS, under **General Social Surveys,** both **Urban** and **Rural; Religion; Rural; Rural Education;** and **Rural Health and Sanitation.**

RURAL EDUCATION

   See also Part I, GENERAL SOCIAL SURVEYS—RURAL, and Part II, in EDUCATION; MENTAL HYGIENE; SCHOOL BUILDINGS AND PLANTS; TRUANCY AND NON-ATTENDANCE; and VOCATIONAL GUIDANCE AND TRAINING.

SURVEYS IN SPECIALIZED FIELDS

RURAL EDUCATION—Continued

ALABAMA. **Rural School Attendance in Alabama.** In Child Labor Bulletin. Vol. 7, No. 2.
> By—Eva Joffe. PUBLISHER—National Child Labor Committee, New York City. 1918. 25 p. 50 cents per copy.

CALIFORNIA, SAN MATEO COUNTY. **Reorganizing a County System of Rural Schools.** Report of a study of the schools of San Mateo County. U. S. Department of Interior. Bureau of Education Bulletin, 1916, No. 16.
> By—J. Harold Williams. PUBLISHER—Superintendent of Documents, Government Printing Office, Washington, D. C. 1916. 49 p. Out of print.

CANADA. **Rural Schools in Canada.** Their organization, administration, and supervision. Teachers College Contributions to Education No. 61.
> By—James Collins Miller. PUBLISHER—Bureau of Publications, Teachers College, Columbia University, New York City. 1913. 236 p. $1.50.

CANADA, ONTARIO. **The School System of Ontario with Special Reference to Rural Schools.** U. S. Department of Interior. Bureau of Education Bulletin, 1915, No. 32. Whole No. 659.
> By—Harold W. Foght. PUBLISHER—Superintendent of Documents, Government Printing Office, Washington, D. C. 1915. 58 p. 15 cents.

COLORADO. **The Rural and Village Schools of Colorado: an Eight Year Survey of Each School District.**
> By—C. G. Sargent. PUBLISHER—Colorado Agricultural College, Fort Collins. 1914. 99 p. Free.

COLORADO, WELD COUNTY. **The Farm and the School.** A résumé of a survey of the public schools of Weld County. State Teachers College Bulletin. Series XVIII, No. 6.
> By—Herbert M. Baker and Edgar Dunnington Randolph. PUBLISHER—State Teachers College, Greeley. 1918. 63 p. Free.

DELAWARE. **Possible Consolidation of Rural Schools in Delaware, Based on a Survey of the Public Schools of Delaware.** Vol. 1, No. 4.
> By—George D. Strayer, N. L. Engelhardt, and F. W. Hart. PUBLISHER—Service Citizens of Delaware, Wilmington. 1919. 60 p. Free.

RURAL EDUCATION—Continued

DELAWARE. **The One-Teacher School in Delaware.** A study in attendance.
>By—Richard Watson Cooper and Hermann Cooper. PUBLISHER—University of Delaware Press, Newark. 1925. 434 p. Free.

FLORIDA. **A Study of the Conditions of the Rural Schools in Peninsula Florida.** University Record. Vol. XVII, No. 4.
>By—Gertrude McArthur. PUBLISHER—University of Florida, Gainesville. 1922. 81 p. Free.

ILLINOIS. **A Farm and Home Survey.** Board for Vocational Education Bulletin No. 24.
>By—A. W. Nolan. PUBLISHER—Department of Public Instruction, Springfield. 1922. 16 p. Free.

INDIANA. **Report of the Indiana Rural Education Survey Committee.**
>By—The Committee. PUBLISHER—State Department of Public Instruction, Indianapolis. 1926. 130 p. Free.

INDIANA, BARTHOLOMEW COUNTY. **Rural Schools.** Sanitary survey of schools in Bartholomew County. Reprint No. 177, Public Health Reports, February 6, 1914.
>By—J. A. Nydegger. PUBLISHER—Superintendent of Documents, Government Printing Office, Washington, D. C. 1914. 16 p. 5 cents.

INDIANA, PORTER COUNTY. **Rural School Sanitation Including Physical and Mental Status of School Children in Porter County.** U. S. Public Health Service Bulletin No. 77.
>By—Taliaferro Clark, George L. Collins, and W. L. Treadway. PUBLISHER—Superintendent of Documents, Government Printing Office, Washington, D. C. 1916. 126 p. 15 cents.

KENTUCKY. **Farmwork and Schools in Kentucky.** Pamphlet 274.
>By—Edward N. Clopper. PUBLISHER—National Child Labor Committee, New York City. 1917. 30 p. 10 cents.

MARYLAND, MONTGOMERY COUNTY. **Educational Survey of a Suburban and Rural County.** U. S. Department of Interior. Bureau of Education Bulletin, 1913, No. 32. Whole No. 543.
>By—H. N. Morse, E. Fred Eastman, and A. C. Monahan. PUBLISHER—Superintendent of Documents, Government Printing Office, Washington, D. C. 1913. 68 p. Out of print.

SURVEYS IN SPECIALIZED FIELDS

RURAL EDUCATION—Continued

MASSACHUSETTS. **Report of the Commission on the Investigation of Agricultural Education.**
> By—The Commission. PUBLISHER—Commonwealth of Massachusetts, Boston. 1918. 61 p. Free.

MICHIGAN. **Report of the Michigan State Commission on Industrial and Agricultural Education.**
> By—The Commission. PUBLISHER—The same, Lansing. 1910. 95 p. Out of print.

MICHIGAN, KALAMAZOO COUNTY. **A County Study in Rural Education.**
> By—Ernest Burnham. PUBLISHER—Western State Normal School, Kalamazoo. 1926. 89 p. Free.

MICHIGAN, OAKLAND COUNTY. **A Rural School Survey of Oakland County.**
> By—Department of Rural Education, Michigan State Normal School. PUBLISHER—The same, Ypsilanti. 1924. 64 p. Free.

MINNESOTA. **Rural School System of Minnesota.** A study in school efficiency. U. S. Department of Interior. Bureau of Education Bulletin, 1915, No. 20. Whole No. 647.
> By—H. W. Foght. PUBLISHER—Superintendent of Documents, Government Printing Office, Washington, D. C. 1915. 56 p. 20 cents.

MINNESOTA, RAMSEY COUNTY. **A Survey of the Environmental Sanitation of the Rural Schools of Ramsey County.**
> By—H. A. Whittaker, Director. PUBLISHER—State Board of Health, St. Louis. 1916. 14 p. Free.

MISSOURI. **Survey of the Rural Schools Including the One-Room School.** In Sixty-Ninth Report of the Public Schools of the State of Missouri for the year ending June 30, 1918.
> By—Uel W. Lamkin. PUBLISHER—State Department of Education, Jefferson City. 1919. 114 p. Out of print.

MISSOURI. **Rural School Health Survey.**
> By—Elizabeth Moore. PUBLISHER—Missouri Tuberculosis Association, St. Louis. 1922. 46 p. Free.

MISSOURI, SALINE COUNTY. **A Study of the Rural Schools of Saline County.** Bulletin Vol. 16, No. 22. Education Series 11.
> By—Joseph Doliver Elliff and Abner Jones. PUBLISHER—University of Missouri, Columbia. 1915. 32 p. Free.

RURAL EDUCATION—Continued

NEW YORK. RURAL SCHOOL SURVEY OF NEW YORK STATE.
  Vol. I. Preliminary Report. 1922. 272 p. 75 cents.
  Vol. II. Administration and Supervision. By Charles H. Judd. 1923. 629 p. $1.00.
  Vol. III. Financial Support. By Harlan Updegraff. 1922. 272 p. 75 cents.
  Vol. IV. The Teaching Personnel. By William C. Bagley, Orville G. Brim, and Mabel Carney. 1923. 279 p. 75 cents.
  Vol. V. Buildings and Grounds. By Julian E. Butterworth. 1922. 131 p. 75 cents.
  Vol. VI. Educational Achievement. By M. E. Haggerty. 1922. 223 p. 75 cents.
  Vol. VII. The Rural High School. By Emery N. Ferriss. 1922. 187 p. 75 cents.
  Vol. VIII. Vocational Education. By Theodore H. Eaton. 1922. 293 p. 75 cents.
  Summary of the Rural School Survey of New York State. 1922. 272 p. 75 cents.
    BY—G. A. Works, Director. PUBLISHER—Joint Committee on Rural Schools, Ithaca.

NORTH DAKOTA. **Report of the Rural School Commission.**
  BY—The Commission. PUBLISHER—The same, Grand Forks. 1912. 30 p. Out of print.

OHIO. **A Study of Rural School Conditions in Ohio.**
  BY—Vernon M. Riegel. PUBLISHER—State Superintendent of Public Instruction, Columbus. 1920. 175 p. Free.

PENNSYLVANIA. **Report on Rural Schools.**
  BY—State Educational Association. PUBLISHER—The Same, Harrisburg. 1914. 103 p. Free.

PENNSYLVANIA. **Status of the Rural Teacher in Pennsylvania.** U. S. Department of Interior. Bureau of Education Bulletin, 1922, No. 86.
  BY—Leroy Albert King. PUBLISHER—Superintendent of Documents, Government Printing Office, Washington, D. C. 1922. 86 p. 10 cents.

PENNSYLVANIA, LACKAWANNA COUNTY. **Survey of the One-Teacher Elementary Schools of Lackawanna County.**
  BY—Thomas Francis. MIMEOGRAPHED—Lackawanna County Schools, Scranton. 1926. 24 p. Free.

SURVEYS IN SPECIALIZED FIELDS

RURAL EDUCATION—Continued

TEXAS. RURAL SCHOOLS IN TEXAS. Bulletins of the Bureau of Extension.
  A Study of the Rural Schools of Texas. By E. V. White and E. E. Davis. 1914. 167 p. Out of print.
  The Rural Schools of Karnes County. By T. H. Shelby. 1922. 68 p. 10 cents.
  A Study of Rural Schools in Runnels County. By J. L. Tennant and E. E. Davis. 1924. 95 p. 10 cents.
  The Rural Schools of Travis County. By E. E. Davis. 1916. 53 p. Out of print.
  The Rural Schools of Wichita County. By T. H. Shelby. 1922. 60 p. 10 cents.
  The Rural Schools of Williamson County. By E. E. Davis. 1922. 55 p. 10 cents.
    PUBLISHER—University of Texas Press, Austin.

UNITED STATES [SOUTH]. **Study of 15 Consolidated Rural Schools.** Their organization, cost, efficiency, and affiliated interests.
    BY—G. W. Knorr. PUBLISHER—Southern Education Board, Washington, D. C. 1911. 55 p. Out of print.

UNITED STATES. **The Status of Rural Education in the United States.** U. S. Department of Interior. Bureau of Education Bulletin, 1913, No. 8. Whole No. 515.
    BY—A. C. Monahan. PUBLISHER—Superintendent of Documents, Government Printing Office, Washington, D. C. 1913. 72 p. Out of print.

UNITED STATES. **Factors Controlling Attendance in Rural Schools.** Teachers College Contributions to Education No. 108.
    BY—George H. Reaves. PUBLISHER—Bureau of Publications, Teachers College, Columbia University, New York City. 1920. 69 p. $1.50.

UNITED STATES. **Farm Labor vs. School Attendance.** Publication No. 300.
    BY—Gertrude Folks. PUBLISHER—National Child Labor Committee, New York City. 1920. 19 p. 10 cents.

UNITED STATES. **Supervision of Rural Schools.** U. S. Department of Interior. Bureau of Education Bulletin, 1922, No. 10.
    BY—Katherine M. Cook. PUBLISHER—Superintendent of Documents, Government Printing Office, Washington, D. C. 1922. 111 p. 15 cents.

A BIBLIOGRAPHY OF SOCIAL SURVEYS

RURAL EDUCATION—Continued

UNITED STATES. **Analytic Survey of State Courses of Study for Rural Elementary Schools.** U. S. Department of Interior. Bureau of Education Bulletin, 1922, No. 42.
>By—Charles M. Reinoehl. PUBLISHER—Superintendent of Documents, Government Printing Office, Washington, D. C. 1923. 114 p. 20 cents.

UNITED STATES. **High School Education of the Farm Population in Selected States.** U. S. Department of Interior. Bureau of Education Bulletin, 1925, No. 6.
>By—E. E. Windes. PUBLISHER—Superintendent of Documents, Government Printing Office, Washington, D. C. 1925. 24 p. 5 cents.

VERMONT, WINDSOR COUNTY. **Do You Know the Facts?** Some conditions and needs among the rural schools of Windsor County.
>By—F. T. Kidder. PUBLISHER—Windsor County Young Men's Christian Association, White River Junction. 1913. 12 p. 5 cents.

WEST VIRGINIA, MARSHALL COUNTY. **Educational Survey of the Clay District Schools, Marshall County.**
>By—H. E. Carmichael and C. M. Koon. PUBLISHER—Superintendent of Schools, Moundsville. 1922. 43 p. Free.

WISCONSIN. **Preliminary Report on Conditions and Needs of Rural Schools in Wisconsin.** Results of field study reported to the Wisconsin State Board of Public Affairs by the Training School for Public Service.
>By—W. H. Allen, Director. PUBLISHER—State Board of Public Affairs, Madison. 1912. 92 p. Out of print.

In addition to reports **presenting findings** in Rural Education Surveys, as listed above, publications dealing with **methods of conducting** such studies will be found in Part III, PURPOSE, METHOD, AND STANDARDS, page 355.

RURAL HEALTH AND SANITATION

>*See also* PART I, GENERAL SOCIAL SURVEYS—RURAL and PART II, in CHILD HEALTH AND HYGIENE; HOUSING; INDIANS; RURAL EDUCATION; TRACOMA; and TUBERCULOSIS.

GEORGIA. **Maternity and Infant Care in a Mountain County in Georgia.** U. S. Department of Labor. Children's Bureau Publication No. 120.
>By—Glenn Steele. PUBLISHER—Superintendent of Documents, Government Printing Office, Washington, D. C. 1923. 58 p. 15 cents.

SURVEYS IN SPECIALIZED FIELDS

RURAL HEALTH AND SANITATION—Continued

ILLINOIS, WHITE COUNTY. **Health Survey of White County, Made under the Auspices of the Illinois State Board of Health and the Illinois State Association for the Prevention of Tuberculosis.**
> BY—I. A. Foster and Harriet Fulmer. PUBLISHER—State Board of Health, Springfield. 1915. 23 p. Free.

INDIANA; BARTHOLOMEW, BOONE, DAVIESS, MARSHALL, AND MONTGOMERY COUNTIES. **A Rural Sanitary Survey of Five Counties in Indiana.** In Indiana Bulletin of Charities and Corrections, June, 1914.
> BY—John N. Hurty. PUBLISHER—Department of Charities and Corrections, Indianapolis. 1914. 6 p. Free.

KANSAS. **Maternity and Infant Care in a Rural County in Kansas.** U. S. Department of Labor. Children's Bureau Publication No. 26. Rural Child Welfare Series No. 1.
> BY—Elizabeth Moore. PUBLISHER—Superintendent of Documents, Government Printing Office, Washington, D. C. 1917. 50 p. 10 cents.

KANSAS, SUMNER COUNTY. **Sumner County Sanitary and Social Survey.** Bulletin Vol. XI, No. 5.
> BY—S. J. Grumbine. PUBLISHER—Kansas State Board of Health, Topeka. 1915. 160 p. Out of print.

MAINE. **Public Health Administration in Rural Districts.** Bulletin, Vol. I, Nos. 7 and 8.
> BY—Leverett D. Bristol. PUBLISHER—State Department of Health, Augusta. 1918. 10 p. Free.

MISSISSIPPI. **Maternity and Child Care in Selected Rural Areas of Mississippi.** U. S. Department of Labor. Children's Bureau Publication No. 88. Rural Child Welfare Series No. 5.
> BY—Helen M. Dart. PUBLISHER—Superintendent of Documents, Government Printing Office, Washington, D. C. 1921. 60 p. 10 cents.

MONTANA. **Maternity Care and Welfare of Young Children in a Homesteading County in Montana.** U. S. Department of Labor. Children's Bureau Publication No. 34. Rural Welfare Series No. 3.
> BY—Viola I. Paradise. PUBLISHER—Superintendent of Documents, Government Printing Office, Washington, D. C. 1919. 98 p. 20 cents.

RURAL HEALTH AND SANITATION—Continued

NEW YORK. RURAL HEALTH IN NEW YORK STATE.
  Rural Death Rate of the State of New York. By Frederick L. Hoffman. 1913. 49 p. Out of print.
  Preliminary Inquiry into the Health Needs of Rural People of the State of New York. By C. J. Durkee. 1916. 60 p. Free.
    PUBLISHER—State Department of Health, Albany.

NEW YORK, ALBANY COUNTY. **Rural Health Survey, Albany County.**
    By—Josephine Durkee. PUBLISHER—Division of Public Health Nursing, State Department of Health, Albany. 1915. 14 p. Free.

NEW YORK, DUTCHESS COUNTY. **Sickness in Dutchess County.** Its extent, care and prevention.
    By—Committee on Hospitals, State Charities Aid Association. PUBLISHER—The same, New York City. 1915. 102 p. Out of print.

NEW YORK, ERIE COUNTY. **Child Health in Erie County.** The report of a brief cooperative inquiry into conditions relating to child health and the agencies for dealing with them in the rural sections and villages in Erie County.
    By—National Child Health Council. PUBLISHER—American Child Hygiene Association, Washington, D. C. 1922. 90 p. 20 cents.

NORTH CAROLINA, YANCEY COUNTY. **Pellagra in the Mountains of Yancey County.** Reprint No. 619, Public Health Reports, October 22, 1920.
    By—G. A. Wheeler. PUBLISHER—Superintendent of Documents, Government Printing Office, Washington, D. C. 1920. 8 p. 5 cents.

OHIO, KELLEY'S ISLAND. **An Epidemiological Study of the 1920 Epidemic of Influenza in an Isolated Rural Community.** Reprint No. 678, Public Health Reports, July 22, 1921.
    By—Charles Armstrong and Rose Hopkins. PUBLISHER—Superintendent of Documents, Government Printing Office, Washington, D. C. 1921. 32 p. 5 cents.

UNITED STATES [ROCKY MOUNTAINS]. **Rocky Mountain Spotted Fever.** A report of its investigation and of work in tick eradication for its control during 1913. Reprint No. 169, Public Health Reports, February 20, 1913.
    By—L. D. Fricks. PUBLISHER—Superintendent of Documents, Government Printing Office, Washington, D. C. 1914. 12 p. 5 cents.

SURVEYS IN SPECIALIZED FIELDS

RURAL HEALTH AND SANITATION—Continued

UNITED STATES [15 COUNTIES]. **Rural Sanitation.** A report of special studies made in 15 counties in 1914, 1915, 1916. U. S. Public Health Service Bulletin No. 94.
    BY—L. L. Lumsden. PUBLISHER—Superintendent of Documents, Government Printing Office, Washington, D. C. 1918. 336 p. 50 cents.

WISCONSIN. **Maternity and Infant Care in Two Rural Counties in Wisconsin.** U. S. Department of Labor. Children's Bureau Publication No. 46. Child Welfare Series No. 4.
    BY—Florence S. Sherbon and Elizabeth Moore. PUBLISHER—Superintendent of Documents, Government Printing Office, Washington, D. C. 1919. 92 p. 10 cents.

In addition to reports **presenting findings** in Rural Health and Sanitation Surveys, as listed above, a publication dealing with **methods of conducting** such studies will be found in Part III, PURPOSE, METHOD, AND STANDARDS, page 355.

RUSSIANS

CALIFORNIA, LOS ANGELES. **The Russians in Los Angeles.** Bulletin No. 11.
    BY—Lillian Sokoloff. PUBLISHER—Southern California Sociological Society, Los Angeles. 1918. 16 p. 15 cents.

UNITED STATES. **Social Study of the Russian-German.** Studies of the University of Nebraska. Vol. XVI, No. 3.
    BY—Hattie Plum Williams. PUBLISHER—University of Nebraska, Lincoln. 1916. 99 p. 75 cents.

SANATORIA

    See HOSPITALS AND SANATORIA.

SANITATION

    See HEALTH AND SANITATION; RURAL HEALTH AND SANITATION; and SCHOOL HEALTH AND SANITATION.

For publications dealing with methods of conducting Sanitation Surveys see Part III, PURPOSE, METHOD, AND STANDARDS, under **Health and Sanitation; Rural Health and Sanitation;** and **School Health and Sanitation.**

A BIBLIOGRAPHY OF SOCIAL SURVEYS

SCHOOL BUILDINGS AND PLANTS

See also EDUCATION; RURAL EDUCATION; and SCHOOL ORGANIZATION AND ADMINISTRATION.

CALIFORNIA, EUREKA. **A School Building Survey and School Housing Program.**
By—Frank W. Hart and L. H. Peterson, Directors. PUBLISHER—Board of Education, Eureka. 1924. 59 p. Free.

CALIFORNIA, NAPA. **A School Building Survey and School Housing Program for Napa.** Bureau of Research Studies in Education No. 2.
By—Frank W. Hart. PUBLISHER—University of California, Berkeley. 1921. 64 p. 50 cents.

CALIFORNIA, SAN RAFAEL. **A School Building Survey and School Housing Program for San Rafael.** Bureau of Research Studies in Education No. 8.
By—Frank W. Hart and L. H. Peterson. PUBLISHER—University of California, Berkeley. 1922. 70 p. 50 cents.

CALIFORNIA, SANTA MONICA. **School Housing Survey of the Santa Monica City Schools.** University of Southern California Studies. Second Series No. 4.
By—Osman R. Hull and Willard S. Ford. PUBLISHER—University of Southern California, Los Angeles. 1927. 66 p. 50 cents.

CANADA, TORONTO. REPORTS ON SCHOOL BUILDINGS.
Interim Reports of the Toronto School Survey. 1. The Physical Plant of the Toronto Public Schools. 2. The Building Department of the Toronto Board of Education. 1920. 87 p. Free.
A Twelve Hour Working Day for School Buildings 300 Days in the Year. 1921. 8 p. 10 cents.
By—Bureau of Municipal Research, Toronto. PUBLISHER—The same.

COLORADO, DENVER. **Report of the School Survey of School District No. 1 in the City and County of Denver.** Part V. The Building Situation and Medical Inspection.
By—Lewis M. Terman. PUBLISHER—School Survey Committee, Denver. 1916. 75 p. Free.

CONNECTICUT, MERIDEN. **A School Building Program for Meriden.** U. S. Department of Interior. Bureau of Education Bulletin, 1920, No. 22.
By—Alice Barrows Fernandez. PUBLISHER—Superintendent of Documents, Government Printing Office, Washington, D. C. 1920. 26 p. 5 cents.

SURVEYS IN SPECIALIZED FIELDS

SCHOOL BUILDINGS AND PLANTS—Continued

DELAWARE. REPORTS ON SCHOOL BUILDINGS.
   Report and Recommendations on Certain School Buildings of Delaware. By Service Citizens of Delaware. 80 p.
   General Reports on School Buildings and Grounds of Delaware. By George D. Strayer, N. L. Englehardt, and F. W. Hart. 222 p.
      PUBLISHER—Service Citizens of Delaware, Wilmington. 1919. Free.

DISTRICT OF COLUMBIA. **Special Report on Schoolhouse Accommodations Submitted to the Board of Education of the District of Columbia.**
   By—Superintendent of Schools. PUBLISHER—Board of Education, Washington. 1920. 71 p. Free.

GEORGIA, ATHENS. **A School Building Program for Athens.** U. S. Department of Interior. Bureau of Education Bulletin, 1921, No. 25.
   By—Alice B. Fernandez. PUBLISHER—Superintendent of Documents, Government Printing Office, Washington, D. C. 1921. 70 p. 10 cents.

IOWA, MUSCATINE. **Survey of the School Buildings of Muscatine.** Extension Bulletin No. 41. First Series No. 22.
   By—E. J. Ashbaugh. PUBLISHER—University of Iowa, Iowa City. 1918. 39 p. Out of print.

KANSAS, DODGE CITY. **School Survey and Building Program.**
   By—F. P. O'Brien, Director. PUBLISHER—Bureau of School Service, University of Kansas, Lawrence. 1923. 100 p. Free.

KANSAS, OTTAWA. **Survey Report on School Building Program for the City of Ottawa.**
   By—F. P. O'Brien, Director. PUBLISHER—Bureau of School Service, University of Kansas, Lawrence. 1923. 63 p. Free.

KENTUCKY, LEXINGTON. **Financial and Building Needs of the Schools of Lexington, Kentucky.** U. S. Department of Interior. Bureau of Education Bulletin, 1919, No. 68.
   By—Frank F. Bunker, Director. PUBLISHER—Superintendent of Documents, Government Printing Office, Washington, D. C. 1919. 50 p. 10 cents.

MAINE, BANGOR. **Bangor, Maine, School Building Survey.** A program of the school building needs for the City of Bangor.
   By—N. L. Engelhardt. PUBLISHER—School Board of Bangor. 1922. 20 p. Free.

SCHOOL BUILDINGS AND PLANTS—Continued

MARYLAND, BALTIMORE. **The School Plant and the School Building Program.** Vol. I. The Baltimore School Survey.
> By—George D. Strayer, Director. PUBLISHER—City of Baltimore. 1921. 373 p. $5.00 with Volumes II and III.

MASSACHUSETTS, GLOUCESTER. **A School Building Program for Gloucester.** U. S. Department of Interior. Bureau of Education Bulletin, 1920. No. 23.
> By—Bureau of Education. PUBLISHER—Superintendent of Documents, Government Printing Office, Washington, D. C. 1920. 16 p. 5 cents.

MICHIGAN, HAMTRAMCK. **Housing the Children: a Community Project.** Hamtramck Public Schools Research Series No. 1.
> By—Self-Survey Committee. PUBLISHER—Board of Education, Hamtramck. 1926. 123 p. Free.

MINNESOTA, WINONA. **A School Building Program of the City of Winona.**
> By—M. G. Neale and S. B. Severson. PUBLISHER—University of Minnesota, Minneapolis. 1922. 66 p. 50 cents.

MISSOURI, ST. JOSEPH. **Report of the Survey of the Public School Buildings and a Proposed School Building Program for St. Joseph.**
> By—George D. Strayer and N. L. Engelhardt. PUBLISHER—Board of Directors of the St. Joseph School District. 1923. 103 p. $1.00.

NEW JERSEY. **School Building Survey.**
> By—Commissioner of Education. PUBLISHER—State Department of Public Instruction, Trenton. 1922. 128 p. Free.

NEW JERSEY, NUTLEY. **Report of a Study of the Need for Further School Accommodations in the Town of Nutley.**
> By—George D. Strayer and N. L. Engelhardt. PUBLISHER—Board of Education, Nutley. 1925. 15 p. Free.

NEW YORK. **Buildings and Grounds.** Vol. V. Rural School Survey of New York State.
> By—Julian E. Butterworth. PUBLISHER—Joint Committee on Rural Schools, Ithaca. 1922. 131 p. 75 cents.

NEW YORK CITY. **Report Submitted to the Committee on School Inquiry on the Condition of Efficiency of Public School Buildings of the City of New York.**
> By—C. G. Armstrong. PUBLISHER—City Department of Education, New York City. 1912. 68 p. Out of print.

SURVEYS IN SPECIALIZED FIELDS

SCHOOL BUILDINGS AND PLANTS—Continued

NEW YORK CITY. **A Study of 40 School Buildings in New York City.**
BY—Joint Committee on Education. MIMEOGRAPHED—National Civic Federation, New York City. 1922. 28 p. Free.

NEW YORK, ROCHESTER. **Summary of School Building Survey.**
BY—Arthur L. Weeks. MIMEOGRAPHED—Rochester Bureau of Municipal Research. 1923. 24 p. Free.

NEW YORK, WHITE PLAINS. **A School Building Program for White Plains.**
BY—George D. Strayer, N. L. Engelhardt, and Paul C. Packer. PUBLISHER—Board of Education, White Plains. 1923. 32 p. Free.

NORTH CAROLINA, WASHINGTON. **A School Building Program.** U. S. Department of Interior. Bureau of Education Bulletin, 1923, No. 2.
BY—Alice Barrows. PUBLISHER—Superintendent of Documents. Government Printing Office, Washington, D. C. 1923. 20 p. 5 cents.

OHIO, CLEVELAND. **School Buildings and Equipment.** The Cleveland Education Survey.
BY—Leonard P. and May Ayres. PUBLISHER—Cleveland Foundation. 1916. 117 p. 35 cents.

OHIO, CLEVELAND HEIGHTS. **Survey of Public School Building Requirements in Cleveland Heights.**
BY—Board of Education. PUBLISHER—The same, Cleveland. 1920. 39 p. Out of print.

OHIO, DAYTON. **Building New Schools for Dayton's Children.** Reports on Dayton's School Administration No. 1.
BY—Walter Matscheck. PUBLISHER—Department of Education, Dayton. 1917. 19 p. Out of print.

OHIO, NILES. **The School Housing Problem of Niles.** Report of a survey made on request of the Board of Education.
BY—George R. Twiss. PUBLISHER—McKinley High School, Niles. 1922. 38 p. Free.

OHIO, YOUNGSTOWN. **A Survey and Building Program for the Youngstown City Schools.**
BY—N. H. Chaney. PUBLISHER—Board of Education, Youngstown. 1921. 35 p. Free.

PENNSYLVANIA, HARRISBURG. **A Study of the Public Schools of Harrisburg and Recommendations for a Building Program.**
BY—Frank E. Spaulding. PUBLISHER—Board of Education, Harrisburg. 1922. 30 p. Free.

A BIBLIOGRAPHY OF SOCIAL SURVEYS

SCHOOL BUILDINGS AND PLANTS—Continued

PENNSYLVANIA, PHILADELPHIA. **Report of the Survey of the Public Schools of Philadelphia.** Book I. School Plant and Building Program.
> By—State Department of Public Instruction. PUBLISHER—Public Education and Child Labor Association, Philadelphia. 1922. 369 p. $5.00 for 4 Books.

Books II, III, and IV are listed in the Education section.

PENNSYLVANIA, READING. **Report on the School Plant Survey and the School Building Program for the City of Reading.**
> By—Bureau of School Buildings. PUBLISHER—Board of School Directors, Reading. 1923. 222 p. $2.00.

SOUTH CAROLINA, YORK COUNTY. **School Survey of York County.** A study of school plants, costs, and programs. Bulletin, Vol. XIV. No. 1.
> By—John F. Thomason. PUBLISHER—Winthrop College, Rock Hill. 1920. 87 p. Free.

TENNESSEE, KNOXVILLE. **A Survey of the School Building Needs of Knoxville.**
> By—Board of Education. PUBLISHER—The same, Knoxville. 1924. 78 p. Free.

VIRGINIA, NORFOLK COUNTY AND SOUTH NORFOLK CITY. **School Housing Survey.**
> By—Charles M. Robinson. PUBLISHER—Board of Education, Norfolk. 1921. 24 p. Free.

VIRGINIA, PORTSMOUTH. **Report and Survey of School Housing Conditions.**
> By—Charles M. Robinson. PUBLISHER—Portsmouth Public Schools. 1921. 18 p. Free.

WISCONSIN, APPLETON. **A School Building Survey of Appleton.**
> By—C. J. Anderson, Director. PUBLISHER—State Department of Public Instruction, Madison. 1922. 81 p. Free.

WISCONSIN, MILWAUKEE. **A Constructive Survey of Milwaukee School Buildings and Sites with a Ten Year Building Program.**
> By—F. M. Harbach and Hornell Hart. PUBLISHER—Board of Directors, Milwaukee. 1916. 42 p. Free.

In addition to reports **presenting findings** in School Buildings and Plants, as listed above, a publication dealing with **methods of conducting** such studies will be found in Part III, PURPOSE, METHOD, AND STANDARDS, page 356.

SURVEYS IN SPECIALIZED FIELDS

SCHOOL HEALTH AND SANITATION

See also RURAL EDUCATION; SCHOOL BUILDINGS AND PLANTS; and TRACHOMA.

CALIFORNIA, RIVERSIDE. **Survey of the Contagious Disease Situation in the Elementary Schools of the City of Riverside during the School Year, 1917–1918.** In California State Board of Health Bulletin. Vol. 14, Nos. 3 and 4.
BY—Edward A. Ingham. PUBLISHER—California State Board of Health, Sacramento. 1918. 5 p. Free.

CANADA, TORONTO. **The Prevalence of Malnutrition in the Public School Children of Toronto.** Reprinted from the Canadian Medical Association Journal, February, 1921.
BY—Alan Brown and G. Albert Davis. PUBLISHER—Canadian Medical Association Journal, Montreal. 1921. 3 p. Free.

FLORIDA, MANATEE COUNTY. **School Hygiene.** Survey of schools in Manatee County. Supplement No. 25 to the Public Health Reports, July 30, 1915.
BY—J. A. Nydegger. PUBLISHER—Superintendent of Documents, Government Printing Office, Washington, D. C. 1915. 35 p. 5 cents.

ILLINOIS, OAK PARK. **An Investigation of the Health of School Children.** A two year study of the physical status of the children of the elementary schools of Oak Park.
BY—Maude A. Brown, Director. PUBLISHER—Elizabeth McCormick Memorial Fund, Chicago. 1926. 144 p. 25 cents.

IOWA. **Hygienic Conditions in Iowa Schools.** A report on conditions in schools in 181 cities and towns in Iowa. Extension Division Bulletin No. 11.
BY—Irving King. PUBLISHER—University of Iowa, Iowa City. 1915. 33 p. Free.

MARYLAND. **Heights and Weights of School Children.** A study of heights and weights of 14,335 native white school children in Maryland, North and South Carolina, and Virginia. Reprint No. 750, Public Health Reports, May 19, 1922.
BY—Taliaferro Clark. PUBLISHER—Superintendent of Documents, Government Printing Office, Washington, D. C. 1922. 36 p. 10 cents.

SCHOOL HEALTH AND SANITATION—Continued

MARYLAND, BALTIMORE. **Correcting Physical Defects in School Children.** A study of the results of the correction of certain physical defects in the growth and development of 146 school children in Baltimore. Public Health Reports. Vol. 37, No. 16.

    BY—Taliaferro Clark. PUBLISHER—Superintendent of Documents, Government Printing Office, Washington, D. C. 1922. 16 p. 5 cents.

MARYLAND, HAGERSTOWN. **Morbidity among School Children in Hagerstown.** Public Health Reports. Vol. 39, No. 38.

    BY—Selwyn D. Collins. PUBLISHER—Superintendent of Documents, Government Printing Office, Washington, D. C. 1924. 31 p. 5 cents.

MASSACHUSETTS, BOSTON. **Tuberculosis among School Children.** Report of the Commission appointed by the School Committee of the City of Boston to investigate the problem of tuberculosis among school children.

    BY—The Commission. PUBLISHER—Board of Education, Boston. 1909. 11 p. Out of print.

MASSACHUSETTS, NEWTON. **A School Health Study of Newton.** Monograph No. 5. School Health Bureau Welfare Division.

    BY—Jean V. Latimer. PUBLISHER—Metropolitan Life Insurance Company, New York City. 1927. 87 p. Free.

MICHIGAN, GRAND RAPIDS. **A Survey of Thyroid Enlargement among the School Children of Grand Rapids.** In Michigan Department of Health Monthly Bulletin. Vol. XI, No. 8.

    BY—Torrence Reed. PUBLISHER—State Department of Health, Lansing. 1923. 33 p. Free.

MINNESOTA, MINNEAPOLIS. **School Health Supervision in Minneapolis.** Reprint No. 683, Public Health Reports, August 12, 1921.

    BY—Taliaferro Clark. PUBLISHER—Superintendent of Documents, Government Printing Office, Washington, D. C. 1921. 36 p. 5 cents.

MISSOURI. **The Relation of Physical Defects to Sickness.** A study of absence from school on account of sickness among 3,876 children in four localities in Missouri.

    BY—Selwyn D. Collins. PUBLISHER—Superintendent of Documents, Government Printing Office, Washington, D. C. 1922. 10 p. 5 cents.

SURVEYS IN SPECIALIZED FIELDS

SCHOOL HEALTH AND SANITATION—Continued

NORTH CAROLINA. **School Hygiene.** A report of a sanitary survey of schools and of medical inspection of school children in certain sections of North and South Carolina. Reprint No. 211, Public Health Reports, July 31, 1914.

    BY—A. D. Foster. PUBLISHER—Superintendent of Documents, Government Printing Office, Washington, D. C. 1914. 12 p. 5 cents.

NORTH CAROLINA. *See also* MARYLAND in this section.

OHIO, CINCINNATI. **Thyroid Survey of 47,493 Elementary School Children in Cincinnati.** Public Health Reports. Vol. 39, No. 30.

    BY—Robert Oleson. PUBLISHER—Superintendent of Documents, Government Printing Office, Washington, D. C. 1924. 25 p. 5 cents.

OHIO, CLEVELAND. **Health Work in the Public Schools.** The Cleveland Education Survey.

    BY—Leonard P. and May Ayres. PUBLISHER—Cleveland Foundation. 1916. 59 p. 35 cents.

OHIO, Cleveland. **Stamp it out of the Schools.** A study of the menace of diphtheria with suggestions for its prevention.

    BY—Medical Division of the Board of Education. PUBLISHER—Chamber of Commerce, Cleveland. 1922. 13 p. Free.

OHIO, WOOD COUNTY. **Report of the Wood County Survey with Special Reference to the Sanitary Conditions of the Schools.** In Ohio Public Health Journal. Vol. VII, No. 1–3.

    BY—W. E. Obetz. PUBLISHER—Ohio State Board of Health, Columbus. 1916. 18 p. Free.

PENNSYLVANIA. **The Medical Inspection of 469,000 School Children in Pennsylvania.** Pennsylvania Health Bulletin No. 71.

    BY—Samuel G. Dixon, Director. PUBLISHER—State Department of Health, Harrisburg. 1915. 12 p. Out of print.

SOUTH CAROLINA. *See* MARYLAND and NORTH CAROLINA in this section.

UNITED STATES. **The Status of Hygiene Programs in Institutions of Higher Education in the United States.** A report for the Presidents' Committee of Fifty on College Hygiene. University Series. Medical Sciences. Vol. II, No. 1.

    BY—Thomas A. Storey. PUBLISHER—Stanford University Press, Stanford, California. 1927. 125 p. $1.00.

A BIBLIOGRAPHY OF SOCIAL SURVEYS

SCHOOL HEALTH AND SANITATION—Continued

VIRGINIA. See MARYLAND in this section.

VIRGINIA, ORANGE COUNTY. **Sanitary Survey of the Schools of Orange County.** Report of an investigation by the Virginia State Board of Health, the Department of Education of the University of Virginia, and the Virginia State Department of Education. U. S. Department of Interior. Bureau of Education Bulletin, 1914, No. 17.
 By—Roy K. Flannagan. PUBLISHER—Superintendent of Documents, Government Printing Office, Washington, D. C. 1914. 28 p. 10 cents.

WISCONSIN, MILWAUKEE. **Medical Inspection in the Schools of Milwaukee.**
 By—City Club of Milwaukee. PUBLISHER—The same. 1919. 16 p. Free.

In addition to reports **presenting findings** in School Health and Sanitation Surveys, as listed above, publications dealing with **methods of conducting** such studies will be found in Part III, PURPOSE, METHOD, AND STANDARDS, page 356.

SCHOOL ORGANIZATION AND ADMINISTRATION

 See also EDUCATION; RURAL EDUCATION; and TAXATION.

ALABAMA. See ARKANSAS in this section.

ALASKA. See ILLINOIS in this section.

ARKANSAS. **The Public School System of Arkansas.** Part II. Public School Finance. U. S. Department of Interior. Bureau of Education Bulletin, 1923, No. 11.
 By—Fletcher Harper Swift. PUBLISHER—Superintendent of Documents, Government Printing Office, Washington, D. C. 1923. 107 p. 15 cents.

ARKANSAS. **Studies in Public School Finance.** The South: Arkansas, Oklahoma, Alabama, and Tennessee. Research Publication. Education Series No. 4.
 By—Fletcher Harper Swift and John Harold Goldthorpe. PUBLISHER—University of Minnesota, Minneapolis. 1925. 224 p. $2.50.

CALIFORNIA. **Studies in Public School Finance.** The West: California and Colorado. Research Publication. Education Series No. 1.
 By—Fletcher Harper Swift. PUBLISHER—University of Minnesota, Minneapolis. 1922. 221 p. $3.00.

SURVEYS IN SPECIALIZED FIELDS

SCHOOL ORGANIZATION AND ADMINISTRATION—Continued

CALIFORNIA. **The Cost of Education in California.** Publications of the Educational Finance Inquiry Commission. Vol. VII.
 By—Jesse B. Sears and Ellwood P. Cubberley. PUBLISHER— Macmillan Company, New York City. 1924. 353 p. $1.25.

CALIFORNIA, LOS ANGELES. **Report of the Advisory Committee of the Board of Education on Certain Aspects of the Organization and Administration of the Public School System.**
 By—Albert Shields and W. A. Jessup. PUBLISHER—Board of Education, Los Angeles. 1916. 177 p. Free.

CALIFORNIA, OAKLAND. **Summary of a Survey of the School Department of Oakland: Its Organization, Business Management, Revenues and Expenditures with Recommendations.** Report No. 19.
 By—Tax Association of Alameda County. PUBLISHER—The same, Oakland. 1915. 20 p. 10 cents.

COLORADO. STUDIES OF COLORADO SCHOOLS.
A Study of Colorado School Revenues. 1916. 31 p.
Consolidated Schools of the Mountains, Valleys, and Plains of Colorado. 1921. 60 p.
 By—C. G. Sargent. PUBLISHER—Colorado Agricultural College, Fort Collins. Free.

COLORADO. **Report of an Inquiry into the Administration and Support of the Colorado School System.** U. S. Department of Interior. Bureau of Education Bulletin. 1917. No. 5.
 By—A. C. Monahan and Katherine M. Cook. PUBLISHER— Superintendent of Documents, Government Printing Office, Washington, D. C. 1917. 93 p. 10 cents.

COLORADO. **The Financing of Public Higher Education in Colorado.** University Bulletin. Vol. XXIV, No. 9.
 By—Don C. Sowers. PUBLISHER—University of Colorado, Boulder. 1924. 199 p. Free.

COLORADO. *See also* CALIFORNIA in this section.

COLORADO, DENVER. REPORT OF THE SCHOOL SURVEY OF SCHOOL DISTRICT NO. 1 IN THE CITY AND COUNTY OF DENVER.
Part I. General Organization and Management. By Franklin Bobbitt. 116 p.
Part IV. The Business Management. By J. T. Byrne. 107 p.

SCHOOL ORGANIZATION AND ADMINISTRATION—Continued

Part VI. **Summary of Recommendations Relating to General Organization and Administration.** 13 p.
>By—School Survey Committee. PUBLISHER—The same, Denver. 1916. Free.

CONNECTICUT. **A Survey of the Organization and Administration of High Schools in the State of Connecticut.** High School Bulletin No. 1, Series 1921–1922.
>By—Jesse B. Davis. PUBLISHER—State Board of Education, Hartford. 1921. 37 p. Free.

DELAWARE, WILMINGTON. **Survey of the Schools of Wilmington.** Part I. School Organization, Supervision, Finance, and a School Building Program. U. S. Department of Interior. Bureau of Education Bulletin, 1921, No. 2.
>By—Frank F. Bunker, Director. PUBLISHER—Superintendent of Documents, Government Printing Office, Washington, D. C. 1921. 132 p. 25 cents.

ILLINOIS. **Report on Educational Administration Prepared for the Efficiency and Economy Committee Created under the Authority of the 48th General Assembly.**
>By—J. M. Mathews. PUBLISHER—Efficiency and Economy Committee, Springfield. 1914. 83 p. Out of print.

ILLINOIS. PUBLICATIONS OF THE EDUCATIONAL FINANCE INQUIRY COMMISSION.

Vol. IX. **The Financing of Public Schools in the State of Illinois.** By Henry C. Morrison. 162 p.

Vol. X. **The Political Unit of Public School Finance in Illinois.** By Floyd W. Reeves. 166 p.

Vol. XI. **The Public School Debt in Illinois.** By George W. Willett. 97 p.

Vol. XII. **A Study of School Costs in Illinois Cities.** By Nelson B. Henry. 82 p.

Other volumes of this study are listed elsewhere.
>PUBLISHER—Macmillan Company, New York City. 1924. $1.00 each.

ILLINOIS. **Studies in Public School Finance.** The Middle West: Illinois, Minnesota, and South Dakota with a Supplement on Alaska. Research Publication. Education Series No. 3.
>By—Fletcher Harper Swift, Frances Kelley del Plaine, and Oliver Leonard Troxel. PUBLISHER—University of Minnesota, Minneapolis. 1925. 329 p. $3.50.

SURVEYS IN SPECIALIZED FIELDS

SCHOOL ORGANIZATION AND ADMINISTRATION—Continued

ILLINOIS, CHICAGO. **Recommendations for the Reorganization of the Public School System of the City of Chicago.** Report of an investigation.
 BY—Committee on Investigation. PUBLISHER—City Council of Chicago. 1917. 83 p. Out of print.

ILLINOIS, CHICAGO. **Chicago School Finances, 1915–1925.** General summary and conclusions of a report.
 BY—Chicago Bureau of Public Efficiency. PUBLISHER—The same. 1927. 36 p. Free.

INDIANA, GARY. GARY PUBLIC SCHOOLS.
 Organization and Administration. By George D. Strayer and F. P. Bachman. 129 p. 15 cents.
 Costs: School Year 1915–1916. By Frank P. Bachman and Ralph Bowman. 86 p. 25 cents.
 PUBLISHER—General Education Board, New York City. 1918.

IOWA. **The Financing of Education in Iowa.** Publications of the Educational Finance Inquiry Commission. Vol. VIII.
 BY—William F. Russell, Thomas C. Holy, Raleigh W. Stone and others. PUBLISHER—Macmillan Company, New York City. 1925. 279 p. $1.00.

MARYLAND, BALTIMORE. **The Administration of the Public Schools.** Vol. II. The Baltimore School Survey.
 BY—George D. Strayer, Director. PUBLISHER—City of Baltimore. 1921. 362 p. $5.00 with Volumes I and III.
Volumes I and III are listed in the Education section.

MASSACHUSETTS. **Studies in Public School Finance.** The East: Massachusetts, New York, and New Jersey. Research Publication. Education Series No. 2.
 BY—Fletcher Harper Swift, Richard A. Graves, and Ernest Walter Tiegs. PUBLISHER—University of Minnesota, Minneapolis. 1923. 240 p. $2.00.

MASSACHUSETTS, BOSTON. **Report of a Study of Certain Phases of the Public School System of Boston.** Document No. 87.
 BY—George D. Strayer, Director. PUBLISHER—Boston Finance Commission. 1916. 219 p. Free.

MASSACHUSETTS, BOSTON. ORGANIZATION AND ADMINISTRATION OF INTERMEDIATE SCHOOLS OF BOSTON.
 Bulletin No. XVII of the Department of Educational Investigation and Measurement. School Document No. 13. 1918. 75 p.

SCHOOL ORGANIZATION AND ADMINISTRATION—Continued

Supplementary Report on Organization and Administration of Intermediate Schools of Boston. 1919. 23 p.
    By—Frank W. Ballou. PUBLISHER—Department of Education, Boston. Out of print.

MINNESOTA. **A Study of State Aid to Public Schools in Minnesota.** Studies in the Social Sciences No. 11.
    By—Raymond Asa Kent. PUBLISHER—University of Minnesota, Minneapolis. 1918. 183 p. $1.00.

MINNESOTA. **Public School Finance in Minnesota.** Summary of a report prepared for the Minnesota Education Association Committee on school tax and sources of school support.
    By—Fletcher Harper Swift and Frances Kelley del Plaine. PUBLISHER—Minnesota Teachers' Association, St. Paul. 1922. 59 p. Free.

MINNESOTA. *See also* ILLINOIS in this section.

MINNESOTA, MINNEAPOLIS. **Report of the Survey of the Business Administration of the Public Schools, Made at the Request of the Board of Education.**
    By—F. S. Staley, Director. PUBLISHER—Minneapolis Civic and Commerce Association. 1915. 43 p. Out of print.

NEW JERSEY. **Report of the Senate Committee to Investigate the Methods and Practices, Expenses, and Disbursements of the Public Schools of New Jersey.**
    By—The Committee. PUBLISHER—State of New Jersey, Trenton. 1911. 67 p. Out of print.

NEW JERSEY. **Report of the Survey of Accounting and Business Systems of the School Districts in New Jersey.**
    By—State Commissioner of Education. PUBLISHER—State Department of Public Instruction, Trenton. 1921. 45 p. Free.

NEW JERSEY. *See also* MASSACHUSETTS in this section.

NEW JERSEY, MONTCLAIR. REPORT OF THE SCHOOL SURVEY COMMITTEE APPOINTED BY THE HOME AND SCHOOL COUNCIL.
Part I. Teachers' Salaries. 24 p.
Part II. Administration and Costs. 51 p.
    By—New York Bureau of Municipal Research. PUBLISHER—Home and School Council, Montclair. 1922. Free.

SURVEYS IN SPECIALIZED FIELDS

SCHOOL ORGANIZATION AND ADMINISTRATION—Continued

NEW YORK. **The Cost of Government and the Support of Education.**
Teachers College Contributions to Education No. 145.
> BY—Harold F. Clark. PUBLISHER—Bureau of Publications, Teachers College, Columbia University, New York City. 1924. 77 p. $1.25.

NEW YORK. PUBLICATIONS OF THE EDUCATIONAL FINANCE INQUIRY COMMISSION.
Vol. I. The Financing of Education in the State of New York. By George D. Strayer and Robert Murray Haig. 205 p.
Vol. II. Elementary School Costs in the State of New York. By R. O. Stoops. 123 p.
Vol. III. The Cost and Support of Secondary Schools in the State of New York. By Charles W. Hunt. 107 p.
> PUBLISHER—Macmillan Company, New York City. 1924. $1.00 each.

NEW YORK. *See also* MASSACHUSETTS in this section.

NEW YORK CITY. **Reports of an Investigation Concerning the Cost of Maintaining the Public School System of the City of New York.**
> BY—Department of Finance of the Department of Education. PUBLISHER—Department of Education, New York City. 1905. 82 p. Out of print.

NEW YORK CITY. **How New York City Administers Its Schools.** A constructive study.
> BY—Ernest Carroll Moore. PUBLISHER—World Book Company, Yonkers, New York. 1913. 321 p. $2.00.

NORTH CAROLINA, CURRITUCK COUNTY. **Suggestions for the Reorganization of the Schools in Currituck County.** U. S. Department of Interior. Bureau of Education Bulletin, 1921, No. 24.
> BY—Katherine M. Cook. PUBLISHER—Superintendent of Documents, Government Printing Office, Washington, D. C. 1921. 31 p. 5 cents.

OHIO, CLEVELAND. THE CLEVELAND EDUCATION SURVEY.
Financing the Public Schools. By Earle Clark. 133 p.
School Organization and Administration. 134 p.
> BY—Leonard P. Ayres, Director. PUBLISHER—Cleveland Foundation. 1916. 35 cents each.

OKLAHOMA. *See* ARKANSAS in this section.

SCHOOL ORGANIZATION AND ADMINISTRATION—Continued

OREGON. **A Study of School Finance in Oregon.** The Commonwealth Review of the University of Oregon. Vol. VII, No. 3.
    By—Homer P. Rainey. PUBLISHER—University of Oregon, Eugene. 1925. 132 p. 50 cents.

PENNSYLVANIA. **Report of the Citizens' Committee on the Finances of Pennsylvania.** Part II. A Survey of the Fiscal Policies of the State of Pennsylvania in the Field of Education.
    By—The Committee. PUBLISHER—Department of State and Finance, Harrisburg. 1922. 207 p. Out of print.

PENNSYLVANIA, HARRISBURG. **Report upon the Business and Financial Administration of the Harrisburg School District.**
    By—New York Bureau of Municipal Research. PUBLISHER—Chamber of Commerce, Harrisburg. 1917. 216 p. $1.00.

PENNSYLVANIA, NEW CASTLE. **Report of the Administration of the Schools of New Castle.** U. S. Bureau of Education. City School Leaflet No. 24.
    By—W. S. Deffenbaugh. PUBLISHER—Superintendent of Documents, Government Printing Office, Washington, D. C. 1927. 8 p. 5 cents.

PENNSYLVANIA, PITTSBURGH. **Survey of the Salaries of Teachers in the Public Schools of Pittsburgh in Relation to Cost of Living.**
    By—Marion K. McKay and Colston E. Warne. PUBLISHER—Pittsburgh Teachers' Association. 1927. 98 p. Free.

PENNSYLVANIA, READING. **Report on a Survey of the Board of Education.** Pamphlet No. 10.
    By—New York Bureau of Municipal Research. PUBLISHER—Chamber of Commerce, Reading. 1913. 28 p. 10 cents.

SOUTH DAKOTA. *See* ILLINOIS in this section.

TENNESSEE. *See* ARKANSAS in this section.

TENNESSEE, MEMPHIS. **The Public School System of Memphis.** Part I. An Industrial and Social Study of Memphis; School Organization, Supervision, and Finance; and the Building Problem. U. S. Department of Interior. Bureau of Education Bulletin, 1919, No. 50.
    By—Frank F. Bunker, Director. PUBLISHER—Superintendent of Documents, Government Printing Office, Washington, D. C. 1920. 160 p. 20 cents.

SURVEYS IN SPECIALIZED FIELDS

SCHOOL ORGANIZATION AND ADMINISTRATION—Continued

TEXAS. **Organization and Administration of Institutions of Higher Education in Texas.**
> BY—Arthur Lefevre. PUBLISHER—Organization for the Enlargement of State Institutions of Higher Education, Houston. 1914. 524 p. Out of print.

TEXAS. **County Unit of School Administration in Texas.** University Bulletin No. 2226.
> BY—T. H. Shelby and E. E. Davis. PUBLISHER—University of Texas, Austin. 1922. 63 p. 15 cents.

TEXAS. TEXAS EDUCATIONAL SURVEY REPORT.
> **Vol. I. Organization and Administration.** 446 p.
> **Vol. II. Financial Support.** 152 p.
>> BY—George A. Works, Director. PUBLISHER—Texas Educational Survey Commission, Austin. 1925. Free.

UNITED STATES. **A Study of Expenses of City School Systems.** U. S. Department of Interior. Bureau of Education Bulletin, 1912, No. 5.
> BY—Harlan Updegraff. PUBLISHER—Superintendent of Documents, Government Printing Office, Washington, D. C. 1912. 96 p. 10 cents.

UNITED STATES. **School Administration in the Smaller Cities.** U. S. Department of Interior. Bureau of Education Bulletin, 1915, No. 44.
> BY—W. S. Deffenbaugh. PUBLISHER—Superintendent of Documents, Government Printing Office, Washington, D. C. 1915. 238 p. 25 cents.

UNITED STATES. **Administration and Supervision of Village Schools.** U. S. Department of Interior. Bureau of Education Bulletin, 1919, No. 86.
> BY—W. S. Deffenbaugh and J. C. Muerman. PUBLISHER—Superintendent of Documents, Government Printing Office, Washington, D. C. 1920. 63 p. 10 cents.

UNITED STATES. **Digest of a Study of Public Education Costs.**
> BY—N. B. Henry. PUBLISHER—Committee on Education, Chicago Association of Commerce. 1923. 29 p. Free.

UNITED STATES. PUBLICATIONS OF THE EDUCATIONAL FINANCE INQUIRY COMMISSION.
> **Vol. IV. Bibliography on Educational Finance.** By Carter Alexander. 257 p.
> **Vol. V. The Fiscal Administration of City School Systems.** By J. R. McGaughy. 95 p.

A BIBLIOGRAPHY OF SOCIAL SURVEYS

SCHOOL ORGANIZATION AND ADMINISTRATION—Continued

Vol. VI. **Financial Statistics of Public Education in the United States.** 1910–1920. By Mabel Newcomer. 188 p.

Vol. XIII. **Unit Costs of Higher Education.** By Edwin B. Stevens and Edward C. Elliott. 212 p.

Other volumes of this study are listed elsewhere.

 PUBLISHER—The Macmillan Company, New York City. 1924. $1.00 each.

UTAH, SALT LAKE CITY. **School Organization and Administration.** A concrete study based on the Salt Lake City Survey.

 BY—Ellwood P. Cubberley and others. PUBLISHER—World Book Company, Yonkers, New York. 1916. 346 p. $2.68.

WISCONSIN. THE CONTINUATION SCHOOLS OF WISCONSIN: VOCATIONAL SCHOOL SURVEY.

Financing Continuation Schools. 1922. 16 p.

State and Local Administration of Continuation Schools. 1922. 27 p.

 BY—Edward A. Fitzpatrick, Director. PUBLISHER—State Board of Education, Madison. Free.

In addition to reports **presenting findings,** as listed above, publications dealing with **methods of conducting** such studies will be found in Part III, PURPOSE, METHOD, AND STANDARDS, under **Education.**

SETTLEMENTS

 See NEIGHBORHOOD HOUSES AND SETTLEMENTS.

SEX DELINQUENCY

 See also ADOLESCENCE; PROSTITUTION; SOCIAL EVIL; and UNMARRIED MOTHERS.

ILLINOIS, CHICAGO. **The Morals Court of Chicago.** A study of specialized courts dealing with sex delinquency. Reprinted from the Journal of Social Hygiene, October, 1921. Publication No. 348.

 BY—George E. Worthington and Ruth Topping. PUBLISHER—American Social Hygiene Association, New York City. 1922. 60 p. 10 cents.

ILLINOIS, CHICAGO. **Specialized Courts Dealing with Sex Delinquency.** A study of procedure in Chicago, Boston, Philadelphia, and New York.

 BY—George E. Worthington and Ruth Topping. PUBLISHER—Bureau of Social Hygiene, New York City. 1925. 460 p. $3.00.

SEX DELINQUENCY—Continued

MASSACHUSETTS, BOSTON. **The Second Sessions of the Municipal Court of the City of Boston.** A study of specialized courts dealing with sex delinquency. Reprinted from the Journal of Social Hygiene, April, 1922. Publication No. 364.
>By—George E. Worthington and Ruth Topping. PUBLISHER—American Social Hygiene Association, New York City. 1922. 55 p. 10 cents.

MASSACHUSETTS, BOSTON. See also ILLINOIS, CHICAGO, in this section.

NEW YORK CITY. **The Women's Day Court of Manhattan and the Bronx, New York City.** A study of specialized courts dealing with sex delinquency. Reprinted from the Journal of Social Hygiene, October, 1922. Publication No. 379.
>By—George E. Worthington and Ruth Topping. PUBLISHER—American Social Hygiene Association, New York City. 1922. 117 p. 10 cents.

NEW YORK CITY. See also ILLINOIS, CHICAGO, in this section.

PENNSYLVANIA. PHILADELPHIA. **Unmarried Girls with Sex Experience.** Bulletin No. 1.
>By—Bureau of Social Research, Seybert Institution. PUBLISHER—The same, Philadelphia. 1916. 48 p. 25 cents.

PENNSYLVANIA, PHILADELPHIA. **The Misdemeanants' Division of the Philadelphia Municipal Court.** A study of specialized courts dealing with sex delinquency. Reprinted from the Journal of Social Hygiene, January, 1922. Publication No. 361.
>By—George E. Worthington and Ruth Topping. PUBLISHER—American Social Hygiene Association, New York City. 1922. 150 p. 10 cents.

PENNSYLVANIA, PHILADELPHIA. See also ILLINOIS, CHICAGO, in this section.

SIGHT CONSERVATION
>See BLINDNESS, SIGHT CONSERVATION, AND DISEASE OF THE EYE.

SLAVS

NEW JERSEY, JERSEY CITY. **Investigation of Slavic Conditions in Jersey City.**
>By—Elizabeth T. White. PUBLISHER—Whittier House, Jersey City. 1907. 8 p. Free.

SLAVS—Continued

UNITED STATES. **Our Slavic Fellow Citizens.**
By—Emily Greene Balch. PUBLISHER—Charities Publication Committee, New York City. 1910. 536 p. Out of print.

SLOVAKS

ILLINOIS, CHICAGO. **Among the Slovaks of the 20th Ward.** Reprint from the American Journal of Sociology. Vol. XX, No. 2.
By—Helen L. Wilson. PUBLISHER—University of Chicago Press. 1914. 24 p. 50 cents.

OHIO, CLEVELAND. **The Slovaks of Cleveland with Some General Information on the Race.**
By—Eleanor E. Ledbetter. PUBLISHER—Americanization Committee, Citizens Bureau, Cleveland. 1919. 32 p. 25 cents.

SLUMS

CANADA, TORONTO. **Report of the Medical Health Officer Dealing with the Recent Investigation of Slum Conditions in Toronto Embodying Recommendations for the Amelioration of the Same.**
By—Department of Health. PUBLISHER—The same, Toronto, 1911. 35 p. 25 cents.

MARYLAND, BALTIMORE. **The Slums of Baltimore, Chicago, New York, and Philadelphia.** Special Report No. 7. U. S. Bureau of Labor.
By—Victor H. Olmsted. PUBLISHER—Superintendent of Documents, Government Printing Office, Washington, D. C. 1894. 620 p. 45 cents.

NEW YORK CITY. **Plague in Its Stronghold: a Study of Tuberculosis in New York City Slums.**
By—Ernest Poole. PUBLISHER—University Settlement, New York City. 1903. 29 p. Out of print.

SOCIAL AGENCIES

See also CHARITIES; CHILD WELFARE; and FAMILY WELFARE.

ALABAMA. **Social Problems of Alabama.** A study of the social institutions and agencies of the State of Alabama as related to its war activities.
By—Hastings H. Hart. PUBLISHER—Russell Sage Foundation, New York City. 1918. 78 p. 10 cents.

SURVEYS IN SPECIALIZED FIELDS

SOCIAL AGENCIES—Continued

ALABAMA. **Social Progress in Alabama.** A second study of the social institutions and agencies of the State of Alabama.
> BY—Hastings H. Hart. PUBLISHER—State of Alabama, Montgomery. 1922. 62 p. 4 cents postage.

CALIFORNIA, ALAMEDA COUNTY. **Survey of Social Agencies of Alameda County.**
> BY—Jean Howard McDuffie. PUBLISHER—Board of Public Welfare, Oakland. 1917. 56 p. Free.

CALIFORNIA, BERKELEY. **Study of Social Work in Berkeley.**
> BY—Margery Carpenter. PUBLISHER—Commission of Public Charities, Berkeley. 1926. 78 p. Free.

CANADA, MONTREAL. **Social and Financial Survey of Protestant Non-Sectarian Social Agencies of an Undenominational Character in the City of Montreal.**
> BY—Howard L. Folk, Director. PUBLISHER—Montreal Council of Social Agencies. 1919. 56 p. Out of print.

COLORADO, COLORADO SPRINGS. **Report on the Philanthropic Work and Social Agencies of Colorado Springs.**
> BY—Francis H. McLean. PUBLISHER—American Association of Societies for Organizing Charity, New York City. 1913. 15 p. Out of print.

CONNECTICUT, NEW HAVEN. **Report of the Survey Committee to the Executive Committee.** Part I. Child Welfare Work, Family Welfare Work, Work for Homeless and Transient Men.
> BY—Survey Committee. PUBLISHER—Council of Social Agencies, New Haven. 1924. 24 p. Free.

ILLINOIS, CHICAGO. **The Financing of Social Agencies.** A fact-finding report with special reference to raising annual operating budgets.
> BY—Chicago Council of Social Agencies. PUBLISHER—Commercial Club of Chicago. 1924. 190 p. Free.

MASSACHUSETTS, BOSTON. **Aged Clients of Boston Social Agencies.** Cooperative Social Research. Report No. III.
> BY—Group of Investigators and Social Workers. PUBLISHER—Women's Educational and Industrial Union, Boston. 1925. 152 p. $1.25.

SOCIAL AGENCIES—Continued

MICHIGAN, DETROIT. **Trouble Cases.** A study of the more difficult family problems and the work upon them of the Detroit Social Agencies.
> By—Arthur Evans Wood and Harry L. Lurie. PUBLISHER—Detroit Community Union. 1919. 89 p. 50 cents.

MINNESOTA. **A Study of Maternity Homes in Minnesota and Pennsylvania.** U. S. Department of Labor. Children's Bureau Publication No. 167.
> By—Ethel M. Watters, Director. PUBLISHER—Superintendent of Documents, Government Printing Office, Washington, D. C. 1926. 92 p. 15 cents.

MINNESOTA, MINNEAPOLIS. **Report of the Committee on the East Lake District.**
> By—M. C. Elmer. MIMEOGRAPHED—Minneapolis Council of Social Agencies. 1920. 23 p. Free.

MINNESOTA, MINNEAPOLIS. **Survey of Child Caring Institutions of Minneapolis.**
> By—Committee on Children's Institutions, Council of Social Agencies. MIMEOGRAPHED—Minneapolis Council of Social Agencies. 1922. 19 p. Free.

MINNESOTA, ST. LOUIS COUNTY. **Report on the Organization of the Public Welfare Agencies of St. Louis County.**
> By—Tax Payers' League of St. Louis County. PUBLISHER—60th State Senatorial District, Duluth. 1923. 82 p. Free.

NEW JERSEY, NEWARK. **Survey of Jewish Philanthropic Organizations of Newark.**
> By—Bureau of Jewish Social Research. PUBLISHER—The same, New York City. 1922. 100 p. Free.

NEW YORK CITY. **Positions in Social Work.** A study of the number, salaries, experience, and qualifications of professional workers in official social agencies in New York City based upon an investigation made by Florence Woolston.
> By—Edward T. Devine and Mary van Kleeck. PUBLISHER—New York School of Social Work, New York City. 1916. 55 p. Out of print.

NEW YORK CITY. **The Finances of New York's Social Work.** Reprinted from Better Times, June 1, 1925.
> By—Edith Shatto King and Augusta H. Frear. PUBLISHER—Bureau of Advice and Information, Charity Organization Society, New York City. 1925. 10 p. 25 cents.

SURVEYS IN SPECIALIZED FIELDS

SOCIAL AGENCIES—Continued

OHIO, CINCINNATI. **Community Responsibility.** A review of the Cincinnati Social Unit Experiment, with statistics of health services in the unit district.
> By—Courtnay Dinwiddie and Bennet L. Mead. PUBLISHER—New York School of Social Work, New York City. 1921. 170 p. 35 cents.

OHIO, CLEVELAND. **Cleveland's Relief Agencies.**
> By—S. C. Kingsley, Amelia Sears, and Allen T. Burns. PUBLISHER—Survey Committee, Cleveland Foundation. 1915. 91 p. Out of print.

OHIO, SUMMIT COUNTY. **Public Welfare Activities of Summit County.**
> By—Bureau of Municipal Research. MIMEOGRAPHED—The same, Akron. 1920. 27 p. Free.

PENNSYLVANIA. *See* MINNESOTA in this section.

PENNSYLVANIA, DELAWARE COUNTY. **The Family and Child Welfare Agencies of Delaware County.**
> By—Family and Children's Division, Delaware County Council of Health and Social Agencies. MIMEOGRAPHED—The same, Media. 1926. 15 p. Free.

PENNSYLVANIA, PHILADELPHIA. **The Functional Relation of Fifteen Case Working Agencies as Shown by a Study of 421 Individual Families.** Bureau for Social Research.
> By—Helen C. Wallerstein, Director. PUBLISHER—Seybert Institution, Philadelphia. 1919. 176 p. 75 cents.

SOUTH CAROLINA. **The War Program of the State of South Carolina.** A study of agencies and institutions.
> By—Hastings H. Hart. PUBLISHER—Russell Sage Foundation, New York City. 1918. 61 p. Out of print.

TENNESSEE, MEMPHIS. **The Larger Plan for Memphis.**
> By—Francis H. McLean and Edgar E. Brooks. PUBLISHER—Social Agencies Endorsement Committee, Memphis Chamber of Commerce. 1921. 19 p. Free.

UNITED STATES. **Report of a Study of the Interrelation of the Work of National Social Agencies in 14 American Communities.**
> By—Porter R. Lee, Walter W. Pettit, and Jane M. Hoey. PUBLISHER—National Information Bureau, New York City. 1921. 152 p. $1.00.

SOCIAL AGENCIES—Continued

UNITED STATES. **Social Salvage.** A study of the central organization and administration of the Salvation Army.
   By—Porter R. Lee and Walter W. Pettit. PUBLISHER—National Information Bureau, New York City. 1924. 124 p. 50 cents.

UNITED STATES. **How Shall Country Youth Be Served?** A study of the "rural" work of certain national character-building agencies. Institute of Social and Religious Research.
   By—H. Paul Douglass. PUBLISHER—George H. Doran Company, New York City. 1926. 259 p. $2.50.

VIRGINIA, RICHMOND. **Survey of Social Agencies of Richmond.**
   By—Francis H. McLean and Hilda K. Mills. PUBLISHER—Department of Public Welfare, Richmond. 1923. 159 p. Free.

In addition to reports **presenting findings,** as listed above, publications dealing with methods of conducting such studies will be found in Part III, PURPOSE, METHOD, AND STANDARDS, under **General Social Surveys—Urban.**

SOCIAL EVIL

   See also PROSTITUTION; SEX DELINQUENCY; and VICE.

HAWAII. **Report in Reference to Proposed Government Regulation of the Social Evil.**
   By—Civic Federation, Territory of Hawaii. PUBLISHER—The same, Honolulu. 1905. 20 p. Out of print.

HAWAII, HONOLULU. **Report of the Committee on the Social Evil.**
   By—Social Survey Committee. PUBLISHER—The same, Honolulu. 1914. 40 p. Free.

ILLINOIS, CHICAGO. **The Social Evil in Chicago.** A study of existing conditions with recommendations.
   By—Vice Commission of Chicago. PUBLISHER—The same. 1911. 399 p. 50 cents.

LOUISIANA, BATON ROUGE. **The Social Evil in Baton Rouge.**
   By—Baton Rouge Purity League. PUBLISHER—The same. 1914. 11 p. Out of print.

MAINE, PORTLAND. **First Report of the Citizens' Committee of Portland to Investigate the Social Evil.**
   By—The Committee. PUBLISHER—The same, Portland. 1914. 77 p. Free.

SURVEYS IN SPECIALIZED FIELDS

SOCIAL EVIL—Continued

MICHIGAN, BAY CITY. **The Social Evil in Bay City.** A report of existing conditions with recommendations.

 By—Social Purity Committee. PUBLISHER—The same, Bay City. 1914. 39 p. 25 cents.

MICHIGAN, GRAND RAPIDS. **Report on the Social Evil.**

 By—Public Welfare Commission. PUBLISHER—The same, Grand Rapids. 1913. 33 p. Free.

MISSOURI, KANSAS CITY. **Social Evil in Kansas City.** In Annual Report of Board of Public Welfare, 1910–1911.

 By—F. R. Johnson. PUBLISHER—Board of Public Welfare, Kansas City. 1911. 16 p. Out of print.

NEW JERSEY, NEWARK. **Report of the Social Evil Conditions of Newark.**

 By—American Vigilance Committee. PUBLISHER—Citizens' Committee on Social Evil, Newark. 1914. 170 p. Free.

NEW YORK CITY. **Social Evil in New York, by Committee of Fourteen for the Suppression of the Raines Law Hotels.**

 By—Committee of Fourteen. PUBLISHER—E. L. Kellogg, New York City. 1910. 268 p. Out of print.

NEW YORK CITY. **The Social Evil with Special Reference to Conditions Existing in the City of New York.**

 By—E. R. A. Seligman. PUBLISHER—G. P. Putnam's Sons, New York City. 1912. 303 p. $1.75.

NEW YORK, SYRACUSE. **The Social Evil of Syracuse.** Being a report of an investigation of the moral condition of the city.

 By—Committee of Eighteen. PUBLISHER—Morals Survey Committee, Syracuse. 1913. 127 p. 50 cents.

SOCIAL INSURANCE

 See also INDUSTRIAL CONDITIONS AND RELATIONS.

CALIFORNIA. **Report of the Social Insurance Commission of the State of California.**

 By—The Commission. PUBLISHER—The same, San Francisco. 1917. 340 p. Free.

SPANISH

See MEXICANS.

STREETS

See CITY AND REGIONAL PLANNING; and CITY, COUNTY, AND STATE ADMINISTRATION.

SUB-NORMAL, RETARDED, AND EXCEPTIONAL CHILDREN

See also CHILD WELFARE; and TRUANCY AND NON-ATTENDANCE.

CALIFORNIA, SANTA ANA. **Exceptional Children in the Schools of Santa Ana.** A survey by the Research Staff of the Whittier State School, Bulletin No. 6.
>By—J. Harold Williams. PUBLISHER—Whittier State School. Whittier. 1918. 40 p. 30 cents.

CONNECTICUT, NEW HAVEN. **Exceptional Children and Public School Policy Including a Mental Survey of the New Haven Elementary Schools.**
>By—Arnold Gesell. PUBLISHER—Yale University Press, New Haven. 1921. 66 p. Free.

DELAWARE, WILMINGTON. **A Study of Non-Promotion in the Wilmington Elementary Schools for the Term Ending June, 1921.** Bulletin of the Consumers' League of Delaware. Vol. 1, No. 2.
>By—Edith C. Rhoads, Director. PUBLISHER—Consumers' League of Delaware, Wilmington. 1923. 4 p. Free.

LOUISIANA, NEW ORLEANS. **Exceptional Children in the Public Schools of New Orleans.**
>By—Public School Alliance. PUBLISHER—The same, New Orleans. 1913. 36 p. Out of print.

LOUISIANA, NEW ORLEANS. **Notes on the Problem of Extreme Individual Differences in Children of the Public Schools.** A report to the superintendent concerning a preliminary study of the problems of exceptional children and of certain related questions.
>By—David Spence Hill. PUBLISHER—Department of Education, New Orleans. 1913. 92 p. Out of print.

SURVEYS IN SPECIALIZED FIELDS

SUB-NORMAL, RETARDED, AND EXCEPTIONAL CHILDREN—Continued

MARYLAND, BALTIMORE. **The Sub-Normal Child.** A survey of the school population in the Locust Point District of Baltimore. Reprint No. 1 from Mental Hygiene. Vol. 1, No. 1.
> BY—C. Macfie Campbell. PUBLISHER—National Committee for Mental Hygiene, New York City. 1917. 52 p. Out of print.

MINNESOTA, MINNEAPOLIS. **The Relation between Dependency and Retardation.** A study of 1,351 public school children known to the Minneapolis Associated Charities. Research Publication. Vol. VIII, No. 1. Current Problems No. 10.
> BY—Margaret Kent Beard. PUBLISHER—University of Minnesota, Minneapolis. 1919. 17 p. 25 cents.

NEW JERSEY, CAMDEN. **A Clinical Study of One Thousand Retarded Children in the Public Schools of Camden.**
> BY—Jacob Daniel Heilman. PUBLISHER—University of Pennsylvania, Philadelphia. 1910. 106 p. $1.00.

OHIO, CINCINNATI. **Retardation in Cincinnati Public Elementary Schools.** Studies from the Helen S. Trounstine Foundation. Vol. I, No. 1.
> BY—Helen S. Trounstine and Hornell Hart. PUBLISHER—Helen S. Trounstine Foundation, Cincinnati. 1918. 44 p. 50 cents.

OHIO, CINCINNATI. **Diagnosis and Treatment of Young School Failures.** U. S. Department of Interior. Bureau of Education Bulletin, 1923, No. 1.
> BY—Helen Thompson Woolley and Elizabeth Ferris. PUBLISHER—Superintendent of Documents, Government Printing Office, Washington, D. C. 1923. 113 p. 15 cents.

OHIO, CLEVELAND. **Schools and Classes for Exceptional Children.** The Cleveland Education Survey.
> BY—David Mitchell. PUBLISHER—Cleveland Foundation. 1916. 122 p. 35 cents.

PENNSYLVANIA, PHILADELPHIA. **Report of the Committee on Investigation of Backward Children.**
> BY—The Committee. PUBLISHER—Board of Education, Philadelphia. 1911. 68 p. Out of print.

UNITED STATES. **Laggards in Our Schools.** A study of retardation and elimination in city school systems.
> BY—Leonard P. Ayres. PUBLISHER—Russell Sage Foundation, New York City. 1913. 236 p. Out of print.

TAXATION

NOTE: The following list of studies in taxation is selective rather than inclusive; it presents only those found in a search in which interest centered chiefly upon the social-welfare rather than the strictly fiscal aspects of the question.

See also CITY, COUNTY, AND STATE ADMINISTRATION; and HOUSING.

CALIFORNIA. **Report of the State Tax Commission of California.**

By—C. L. Seavey. PUBLISHER—State of California, Sacramento. 1917. 280 p. Free.

COLORADO. **The Work of the Colorado Tax Commission.** A report prepared for the Survey Committee of State Affairs. No. XII.

By—Robert Murray Haig. PUBLISHER—Tax Committee, Denver. 1916. 57 p. Free.

ILLINOIS. **Taxation and Revenue System of Illinois.** Report of Special Tax Commission.

By—John A. Fairlie. PUBLISHER—State of Illinois, Springfield. 1910. 256 p. Out of print.

INDIANA. **Report of the Commission on Taxation to the Governor.**

By—The Commission. PUBLISHER—The same, Indianapolis. 1916. 408 p. Out of print.

KENTUCKY. **Taxation in Kentucky.** Studies in Economics and Sociology. Vol. I, No. 1.

By—Simeon E. Leland. PUBLISHER—University of Kentucky, Lexington. 1920. 170 p. $1.00.

MASSACHUSETTS. **Report of the Commission to Investigate the Subject of Taxation and to Codify, Revise, and Amend the Laws Relating Thereto.**

By—Guy W. Cox. PUBLISHER—Commonwealth of Massachusetts, Boston. 1908. 234 p. Out of print.

MASSACHUSETTS. **Report of the Special Commission on Taxation.** House Document No. 1700.

By—The Commission. PUBLISHER—Legislative Document Division, State House, Boston. 1916. 126 p. Free.

MASSACHUSETTS, CAMBRIDGE. **Final Report of the Special Tax Committee of Cambridge by the Special Committee on Study of Local Real Estate Assessment.**

By—The Committee. PUBLISHER—City of Cambridge. 1920. 33 p. Free.

SURVEYS IN SPECIALIZED FIELDS

TAXATION—Continued

MICHIGAN. **Report of the Michigan Committee on Inquiry into Taxation.**
BY—The Committee. PUBLISHER—Department of Legislative Reference, Lansing. 1923. 63 p. Free.

NEW HAMPSHIRE. **Report of a Special Investigation Relative to Municipal Finance and Accounts by the New Hampshire State Tax Commission.**
BY—A. O. Brown and others. PUBLISHER—State of New Hampshire, Manchester. 1917. 61 p. Free.

NEW YORK. **Report of the Joint Legislative Committee on Taxation of the State of New York.** Senate No. 26.
BY—The Committee. PUBLISHER—State of New York, Albany. 1916. 295 p. Free.

NEW YORK. REPORT OF THE SPECIAL JOINT COMMITTEE ON TAXATION AND RETRENCHMENT.
Retrenchment Section. Legislative Document (1920) No. 80. 155 p.
Taxation Section. Legislative Document (1921) No. 57. 67 p.
Critical Survey of Revenue System of the State of New York, with a Statistical Analysis of the Tax Burden on Corporations in the State of New York. Legislative Document (1922) No. 72. 383 p.
Retrenchment in County, Town, and Village Government. Legislative Document (1923) No. 55. 310 p.
Forest Taxation, with Sections Dealing with Public Utility Taxation, the Gasoline Tax, the Bank Tax, and County Salary Standardization. Legislative Document (1924) No. 91.
Summary of the Report of the Special Joint Committee on Taxation and Retrenchment. Legislative Document (1925) No. 97. 259 p.
State Expenditures, Tax Burden, and Wealth. A study of the growth of the functions and expenditures of the state government and the relation of total tax burden to the income of the people of the State. Legislative Document (1926) No. 68. 157 p.
The Gasoline Tax. Legislative Document (1926) No. 69. 22 p.
The Debt of the State of New York, Past, Present, and Future. Legislative Document (1926) No. 70. 104 p.
Tax Exemption in the State of New York. Legislative Document (1927) No. 86.
BY—The Committee. PUBLISHER—State of New York, Albany. Free.

TAXATION—Continued

NEW YORK. **Financial Support.** Vol. III. Rural School Survey of New York State.
>   By—Harlan Updegraff. PUBLISHER—Joint Committee on Rural Schools, Ithaca. 1922. 272 p. 75 cents.

NEW YORK CITY. **Final Report of the Committee on Taxation of the City of New York.**
>   By—The Committee. PUBLISHER—City of New York. 1916. 398 p. Free.

NEW YORK, ROCHESTER. **Report on the Assessment of Real Property in the City of Rochester.**
>   By—Rochester Bureau of Municipal Research. PUBLISHER—The same. 1921. 57 p. Free.

NEW YORK, TROY. **Report of Survey of the Department of Finance of Troy.**
>   By—Bureau of Municipal Research. PUBLISHER—Troy Chamber of Commerce. 1918. 143 p. Free.

OHIO. **Report on Taxation in Ohio.**
>   By—Civic League of Cleveland. PUBLISHER—The same. 1915. 17 p. Free.

OHIO. **Finances of Ohio Cities: Debt and Taxation.**
>   By—Ohio Legislative Reference Department. PUBLISHER—The same, Columbus. 1917. 81 p. Out of print.

PENNSYLVANIA. **Report of the Committee on Taxation Study to the Council of the City of Pittsburgh.**
>   By—The Committee. PUBLISHER—City Council of Pittsburgh. 1916. 105 p. Free.

PENNSYLVANIA, DELAWARE COUNTY. **A Survey of the Revenue System of Delaware County with Special Reference to the Methods of Assessment and Collection of Taxes.**
>   By—Gordon Watkins. PUBLISHER—People's Association of Delaware County, Media. 1918. 80 p. Out of print.

PENNSYLVANIA, PHILADELPHIA COUNTY. **Organization and Administrative Methods of the Board of Revision of Taxes of Philadelphia County.**
>   By—The Board. PUBLISHER—Bureau of Municipal Research, Philadelphia. 1913. 63 p. Free.

SURVEYS IN SPECIALIZED FIELDS

TAXATION—Continued

PENNSYLVANIA, PITTSBURGH. **The Disproportion of Taxation in Pittsburgh.** In the Pittsburgh District Civic Frontage. The Pittsburgh Survey.
>By—Shelby M. Harrison. PUBLISHER—Russell Sage Foundation, New York City. 1914. p. 156–217. Out of print.

VIRGINIA. **Report of the Joint Committee on Tax Revision.**
>By—The Committee. PUBLISHER—Office of State Tax Board Richmond. 1914. 298 p. Free.

WEST VIRGINIA. **The Tax Problem in West Virginia.**
>By—L. R. Gottlieb. PUBLISHER—National Industrial Conference Board, New York City. 1925. 223 p. $2.50.

WISCONSIN. **The Tax Problem in Wisconsin.**
>By—L. R. Gottlieb. PUBLISHER—National Industrial Conference Board, New York City. 1924. 163 p. $2.50.

WISCONSIN, MILWAUKEE. **Increased Taxes in Milwaukee.** Their causes and their significance.
>By—Hornell Hart. PUBLISHER—City Club, Milwaukee. 1914. 25 p. Free.

TEACHERS
>*See* EDUCATION; PENSIONS; RURAL EDUCATION; and SCHOOL ORGANIZATION AND ADMINISTRATION.

TENEMENTS
>*See* CHILD WELFARE; and HOUSING.

THEATRES
>*See* MOTION PICTURES.

TRACHOMA

GEORGIA. *See* TENNESSEE in this section.

KENTUCKY. **Trachoma.** A survey of its prevalence in the mountain section of Eastern Kentucky. Reprint No. 263, Public Health Reports, March 5, 1915.
>By—John McMullen. PUBLISHER—Superintendent of Documents, Government Printing Office, Washington, D. C. 1915. 11 p. 5 cents.

KENTUCKY, JEFFERSON COUNTY. **Trachoma.** Report of a sanitary inspection of the schools of Jefferson County with special reference to

TRACHOMA—Continued
>the prevalence of trachoma. Reprint No. 196, Public Health Reports, May 29, 1914.
>>By—J. H. Oakley, Dunlop Moore, and Lawrence Kolb. PUBLISHER—Superintendent of Documents, Government Printing Office, Washington, D. C. 1914. 7 p. 5 cents.
>
>KENTUCKY, KNOTT COUNTY. **Results of a Three Year Trachoma Campaign in Knott County in 1913 as Shown by a Survey Made in the Same Locality 10 Years Later.** Public Health Reports. Vol. 38, No. 43.
>>By—John McMullen. PUBLISHER—Superintendent of Documents, Government Printing Office, Washington, D. C. 1923. 5 p. 5 cents.
>
>MINNESOTA. REPORTS ON TRACHOMA IN MINNESOTA.
>
>**Investigation of the Prevalence of Trachoma in the State of Minnesota.** Reprint No. 134, Public Health Reports, June 27, 1913. 1913. 26 p.
>
>**The Trachoma Problem in the State of Minnesota.** Public Health Reports. Vol. 38, No. 9. 1923. 13 p.
>>By—Taliaferro Clark. PUBLISHER—Superintendent of Documents, Government Printing Office, Washington, D. C. 5 cents each.
>
>NORTH CAROLINA. **Trachoma.** A survey of its prevalence in the mountain sections of North and South Carolina. Reprint No. 207, Public Health Reports, July 10, 1914.
>>By—A. D. Foster. PUBLISHER—Superintendent of Documents, Government Printing Office, Washington, D. C. 1914. 13 p. 5 cents.
>
>PORTO RICO. **Trachoma in the Schools of Porto Rico.** Reprint No. 241, Public Health Reports, December 18, 1914.
>>By—W. W. King. PUBLISHER—Superintendent of Documents, Government Printing Office, Washington, D. C. 1914. 15 p. 5 cents.
>
>SOUTH CAROLINA. *See* NORTH CAROLINA in this section.
>
>TENNESSEE. **Trachoma.** A study of its prevalence in the mountain sections of East Tennessee and Northern Georgia. Reprint No. 220, Public Health Reports, September 18, 1914.
>>By—Charles A. Bailey. PUBLISHER—Superintendent of Documents, Government Printing Office, Washington, D. C. 1914. 19 p. 5 cents.

SURVEYS IN SPECIALIZED FIELDS

TRACHOMA—Continued

VIRGINIA AND WEST VIRGINIA. **Trachoma.** A survey of its prevalence in the mountain sections of Virginia and West Virginia. Reprint No. 198, Public Health Reports, June 5, 1914.
 BY—Taliaferro Clark. PUBLISHER—Superintendent of Documents, Government Printing Office, Washington, D. C. 1914. 31 p. 5 cents.

TRUANCY AND NON-ATTENDANCE

 See also CHILD WELFARE; and RURAL EDUCATION.

CALIFORNIA, LOS ANGELES. STUDIES IN TRUANCY.
 Causes of Truancy among Boys. Vol. II, No. 2. By Ernest J. Lickley. 12 p.
 Causes of Truancy among Girls. Vol. III, No. 3. By Inez D. Dunham. 14 p.
  PUBLISHER—Southern California Sociological Society, Los Angeles. 1917.

ILLINOIS, ALEXANDER COUNTY. **A Study of Truancy in One Rural Southern Illinois Community.** In Welfare Magazine, January.
 BY—Mary L. Whitehead. PUBLISHER—State Department of Public Welfare, Springfield. 1926. 24 p. Free.

ILLINOIS, CHICAGO. **Intensive Study of the Causes of Truancy in Eight Chicago Public Schools.**
 BY—Gertrude Howe Britton. PUBLISHER—Chicago Board of Education. 1905. 47 p. Out of print.

ILLINOIS, CHICAGO. **Truancy and Non-Attendance in the Chicago Schools.** A study of the social aspects of the compulsory education and child labor legislation of Illinois.
 BY—Edith Abbott and Sophonisba P. Breckinridge. PUBLISHER—University of Chicago Press. 1917. 472 p. $2.10.

NEW YORK CITY. **Truancy.** A study of the mental, physical, and social factors of the problem of non-attendance at school.
 BY—Elizabeth A. Irwin. PUBLISHER—Public Education Association, New York City. 1915. 66 p. Free.

NEW YORK CITY. **A Study of 201 Truants in the New York City Schools.**
 BY—Sub-Commission on Causes and Effects of Crime. PUBLISHER—Crime Commission of New York State, Albany. 1927. 20 p. Free.

TRUANCY AND NON-ATTENDANCE—Continued

OHIO, CLEVELAND. **Absenteeism among White and Negro School Children in Cleveland.** Reprint No. 908, Public Health Reports, March 21, 1924.
>By—G. E. Harmon and G. E. Whitman. PUBLISHER—Superintendent of Documents, Government Printing Office, Washington, D. C. 1924. 9 p. 5 cents.

OKLAHOMA. **Causes of Absence from Rural Schools in Oklahoma.** Pamphlet 281. Reprinted from the Child Labor Bulletin. Vol. VI, No. 2.
>By—Edward N. Clopper, Director. PUBLISHER—National Child Labor Committee, New York City. 1917. 26 p. 10 cents.

UNITED STATES. **Truant Problem and the Parental School.** U. S. Department of Interior. Bureau of Education Bulletin, 1915, No. 29.
>By—James S. Hiatt. PUBLISHER—Superintendent of Documents, Government Printing Office, Washington, D. C. 1915. 35 p. 5 cents.

TUBERCULOSIS

>*See also* CHARITIES; CLINICS AND DISPENSARIES; HEALTH IN INDUSTRY; HOSPITALS AND SANATORIA; HOUSING; INDIANS; SCHOOL HEALTH AND SANITATION; and SLUMS.

ARIZONA. **Interstate Migration of Tuberculous Persons.** Its bearing on the public health with special reference to the states of Arizona and Colorado. Reprint No. 283, Public Health Reports, June 18, 1915.
>By—A. J. Lanza. PUBLISHER—Superintendent of Documents, Government Printing Office, Washington, D. C. 1915. 21 p. 5 cents.

ARIZONA, PHOENIX. **A Report of the Indigent Migratory Consumptive in Certain Cities of the Southwest** [Phoenix, Ariz.; Los Angeles, Calif.; Colorado Springs and Denver, Colo.; El Paso and San Antonio, Texas]. Reprint No. 824, Public Health Reports, March 23, 1923.
>By—Jessamine S. Whitney. PUBLISHER—Superintendent of Documents, Government Printing Office, Washington, D. C. 1923. 30 p. 10 cents.

CALIFORNIA. **Report of the California Tuberculosis Commission.**
>By—The Commission. PUBLISHER—State of California, Sacramento. 1914. 152 p. Out of print.

SURVEYS IN SPECIALIZED FIELDS

TUBERCULOSIS—Continued

CALIFORNIA. **Interstate Migration of Tuberculous Persons.** Its bearing on public health with reference to the state of California. Reprint No. 266, Public Health Reports, March 19, 1915.
 By—P. M. Carrington. PUBLISHER—Superintendent of Documents, Government Printing Office, Washington, D. C. 1915. 16 p. 5 cents.

CALIFORNIA, LOS ANGELES. *See* ARIZONA, PHOENIX, in this section.

CANADA, SASKATCHEWAN. **Report to the Government of Saskatchewan by the Anti-Tuberculosis Commission.**
 By—The Commission. PUBLISHER—Bureau of Public Health, Regina. 1922. 94 p. Free.

COLORADO. *See* ARIZONA in this section.

COLORADO, COLORADO SPRINGS. *See* ARIZONA, PHOENIX, in this section.

COLORADO, DENVER. **A Limited Investigation of Housing Conditions for the Tuberculous in Denver.**
 By—Denver Tuberculosis Society. MIMEOGRAPHED—The same. 1920. 18 p. Free.

COLORADO, DENVER. **Results of a Survey of Tuberculosis as a Community Problem in the City of Denver, Covering the Year September 1, 1919, to September 1, 1920.**
 By—Jessamine S. Whitney. PUBLISHER—Denver Tuberculosis Society. 1920. 13 p. Free.

COLORADO, DENVER. *See* ARIZONA, PHOENIX, in this section.

CONNECTICUT. **Report of Special Commission to Investigate Tuberculosis in Connecticut.**
 By—The Commission. PUBLISHER—Board of Control, New Haven. 1908. 86 p. Out of print.

CONNECTICUT. **The Incidence of Tuberculosis among Polishers and Grinders in an Ax Factory.** Reprint No. 640, Public Health Reports, February 4, 1921.
 By—W. Herbert Drury. PUBLISHER—Superintendent of Documents, Government Printing Office, Washington, D. C. 1921. 22 p. 5 cents.

GEORGIA. **Crusade against Tuberculosis in Georgia.** A survey of the conditions in Georgia bearing upon the prevalence of tuberculosis.
 By—Jessamine S. Whitney. PUBLISHER—W. G. Raoul Foundation, Atlanta. 1914. 31 p. Free.

TUBERCULOSIS—Continued

ILLINOIS, CHICAGO. **Study of Tuberculosis in Chicago.**
  By—Alice Hamilton. PUBLISHER—City Homes' Association, Chicago. 1905. 21 p. Out of print.

ILLINOIS, CHICAGO. **Tuberculosis Problem of the City of Chicago.** Reprint from the American Journal of Public Health.
  By—J. D. Roberts. PUBLISHER—American Public Health Association, New York City. 1918. 11 p. 50 cents.

ILLINOIS, CHICAGO. **The Tuberculosis Survey.** City of Chicago Municipal Tuberculosis Sanitarium Bulletin, July.
  By—Helen W. O'Malley. PUBLISHER—Municipal Tuberculosis Sanitarium, Chicago. 1926. 24 p. Free.

ILLINOIS, MACON COUNTY. **A Tuberculosis Survey.**
  By—C. M. Jack, Director. PUBLISHER—Macon County Tuberculosis and Visiting Nurse Association, Decatur. 1920. 18 p. Free.

INDIANA. **Report of the Indiana Tuberculosis Commission.**
  By—The Commission. PUBLISHER—State of Indiana, Indianapolis. 1906. 33 p. Out of print.

INDIANA, RICHMOND. **Public Health Administration in Richmond.** A report of a survey to determine the incidence of tuberculosis. Supplement No. 26 to Public Health Reports, October 8, 1915.
  By—J. C. Perry. PUBLISHER—Superintendent of Documents, Government Printing Office, Washington, D. C. 1915. 62 p. 10 cents.

LOUISIANA. **A Program for Tuberculosis Control in the State of Louisiana Based upon Observations.**
  By—H. A. Pattison. PUBLISHER—Louisiana State Board of Health, New Orleans. 1924. 68 p. Free.

MARYLAND. REPORTS OF THE TUBERCULOSIS COMMISSION OF MARYLAND.
  Report of the Commission. 1902–1904. 1904. 108 p.
  Second Report of the Commission. 1906. 32 p.
    By—The Commission. PUBLISHER—Department of Health, Annapolis. Free.

MARYLAND, BALTIMORE. **Report of the Municipal Tuberculosis Commission of the City of Baltimore.**
  By—The Commission. PUBLISHER—City of Baltimore. 1911. 94 p. Out of print.

SURVEYS IN SPECIALIZED FIELDS

TUBERCULOSIS—Continued

MASSACHUSETTS. **Report of the Commission to Investigate Measures for the Relief of Consumptives.**
BY—The Commission. PUBLISHER—State Department of Health, Boston. 1907. 78 p. Out of print.

MASSACHUSETTS. **Tuberculosis in Massachusetts.** Prepared for the International Congress on Tuberculosis Held in Washington, D. C., September–October, 1908.
BY—Edwin A. Locke. PUBLISHER—Massachusetts State Committee on Tuberculosis, Boston. 1908. 223 p. Free.

MASSACHUSETTS. **Report of the Commission to Investigate and Report upon a System of Caring for Tubercular Patients by State and Local Authorities.**
BY—The Commission. PUBLISHER—State Department of Health, Boston. 1910. 89 p. Out of print.

MASSACHUSETTS. **Report of the Special Recess Committee Appointed to Investigate Methods Employed in Checking the Spread of Tuberculosis.** House No. 2113.
BY—The Committee. PUBLISHER—State Department of Health, Boston. 1914. 55 p. Free.

MASSACHUSETTS, BARNSTABLE COUNTY. **Barnstable County Tuberculosis Survey.** In The Commonhealth, August.
BY—B. W. Billings. PUBLISHER—Massachusetts State Department of Health, Boston. 1918. 4 p. Free.

MASSACHUSETTS, BOSTON. **Tuberculosis Study in Boston Hospital Out-Patients Departments.** In Eighteenth Annual Report, Boston Tuberculosis Association.
BY—Committee of Boston Tuberculosis Association. PUBLISHER—The same. 1921. 8 p. Free.

MASSACHUSETTS, BOSTON. **Tuberculosis Survey of Boston.**
BY—Murray P. Horwood. PUBLISHER—Boston Tuberculosis Association. 1926. 215 p. $1.00.

MASSACHUSETTS, BROCKTON. **Report of a Tuberculosis Survey of the City of Brockton.**
BY—James H. Drohan and others. PUBLISHER—Department of Health, Brockton. 1920. 19 p. Free.

TUBERCULOSIS—Continued

MASSACHUSETTS, FRAMINGHAM. **Tuberculosis Findings.** Monograph No. 5.
> By—Framingham Community Health and Tuberculosis Demonstration. PUBLISHER—The same. 1919. 35 p. 5 cents.

MICHIGAN. **Report of the Tuberculosis Survey of the State Board of Health for the Twelve Months from October 1, 1915, to October 1, 1916.**
> By—John L. Burkhart. PUBLISHER—State Board of Health, Lansing. 1917. 89 p. Out of print.

MINNESOTA. **The Spread of Tuberculosis.** Report of the spread of infection in certain tuberculous families in five counties in Minnesota. Reprint No. 249, Public Health Reports, January 8, 1915.
> By—H. G. Lampson. PUBLISHER—Superintendent of Documents, Government Printing Office, Washington, D. C. 1915. 16 p. 5 cents.

MINNESOTA, MINNEAPOLIS. **A Study of the Spread of Tuberculosis in Families.** Studies in Public Health No. 1.
> By—Herbert G. Lampson. PUBLISHER—University of Minnesota, Minneapolis. 1913. 50 p. Free.

MISSOURI. **Miners' Consumption.** A study of 433 cases of the disease among zinc miners in southwestern Missouri. U. S. Public Health Service Bulletin No. 85.
> By—A. J. Lanza. PUBLISHER—Superintendent of Documents, Government Printing Office, Washington, D. C. 1917. 39 p. Out of print.

MONTANA, BUTTE. **A Preliminary Report of an Investigation of Miners' Consumption in the Mines of Butte, Made in the Years of 1916–1919.** Department of Interior Paper 260.
> By—Daniel Harrington and A. J. Lanza. PUBLISHER—Superintendent of Documents, Government Printing Office, Washington, D. C. 1921. 19 p. 5 cents.

NEW JERSEY. **A Tuberculosis Survey of New Jersey and Report.**
> By—Jules Schevitz. PUBLISHER—New Jersey Anti-Tuberculosis League, Newark. 1917. 48 p. Free.

NEW JERSEY. **The Tuberculosis Problem in New Jersey.**
> By—H. A. Pattison. PUBLISHER—State Department of Institutions and Agencies, Trenton. 1922. 86 p. Free.

SURVEYS IN SPECIALIZED FIELDS

TUBERCULOSIS—Continued

NEW MEXICO. *See* TEXAS in this section.

NEW YORK, AMSTERDAM. **The Houses of Amsterdam with Some Notes on the Prevalence of Tuberculosis.**
BY—Udetta D. Brown. PUBLISHER—Amsterdam Committee on Tuberculosis, State Charities Aid Association. 1917. 61 p. Out of print.

NEW YORK CITY. **Tuberculosis Families in Their Homes.**
BY—Association of Tuberculosis Clinics and Committee on Prevention of Tuberculosis, Charity Organization Society, New York City. PUBLISHER—Charity Organization Society, New York City. 1916. 77 p. Free.

NEW YORK CITY. **Tuberculosis among Different Nationalities in New York.** Bulletin Vol. IV, No. 3.
BY—Godias J. Drolet. PUBLISHER—New York Tuberculosis Association, New York City. 1923. 5 p. Free.

NEW YORK CITY. **Tuberculosis a Family Problem.** The story of the Home Hospital of the A.I.C.P.
BY—John C. Gebhart. PUBLISHER—Association for Improving the Condition of the Poor, New York City. 1924. 19 p. 25 cents.

NEW YORK, SARANAC LAKE. **Tuberculosis Survey of the Residents of Saranac Lake.** In the American Review of Tuberculosis. Vol. II, No. 4.
BY—Forest B. Ames. PUBLISHER—National Tuberculosis Association, New York City. 1918. 30 p. 35 cents.

NORTH CAROLINA. **Interstate Migration of Tuberculous Persons.** Its bearing on public health with special reference to the states of North and South Carolina. Reprint No. 265, Public Health Reports, March 12, 1915.
BY—A. D. Foster. PUBLISHER—Superintendent of Documents, Government Printing Office, Washington, D. C. 1915. 29 p. 10 cents.

NORTH CAROLINA. **A Resume of a Tuberculosis Survey of a Silk Mill Village in North Carolina.** Reprint from the American Review of Tuberculosis. Vol. XIV, No. 12.
BY—L. B. McBrayer. PUBLISHER—North Carolina Sanatorium for the Treatment of Tuberculosis, Sanatorium. 1921. 6 p. Free.

TUBERCULOSIS—Continued

OHIO. **Survey of the Tuberculosis Situation in the State of Ohio.**
 By—Ohio Society for the Prevention of Tuberculosis. PUBLISHER—State Board of Health, Columbus. 1912. 49 p. Out of print.

OHIO, CINCINNATI. **Tuberculosis among Industrial Workers.** Report of an investigation made in Cincinnati, with special reference to predisposing causes. U. S. Public Health Service Bulletin No. 73.
 By—D. E. Robinson and J. G. Wilson. PUBLISHER—Superintendent of Documents, Government Printing Office, Washington, D. C. 1916. 143 p. 25 cents.

OHIO, CLEVELAND. **Tuberculosis.** Part IV. Cleveland Hospital and Health Survey.
 By—Donald B. Armstrong. PUBLISHER—Cleveland Hospital Council. 1920. 51 p. 50 cents and postage.

PENNSYLVANIA, PHILADELPHIA. **Summary of Philadelphia Tuberculosis Survey.**
 By—Philadelphia Health Council and Tuberculosis Committee. MIMEOGRAPHED—The same. 1922. 32 p. Free.

PENNSYLVANIA, PHILADELPHIA. **A Study of the Negro Tuberculosis Problem in Philadelphia.**
 By—Whittier Center, Henry Phipps Institute, and the Philadelphia Health Council. PUBLISHER—Henry Phipps Institute, Philadelphia. 1923. 29 p. Free.

PENNSYLVANIA, PHILADELPHIA. **A Tuberculosis Survey of Philadelphia.** Reprinted from January and February, 1924, issues of the American Journal of Public Health.
 By—Murray P. Horwood. PUBLISHER—American Public Health Association, New York City. 1924. 21 p. 5 cents.

PENNSYLVANIA, PITTSBURGH. **Tuberculosis and Infant Welfare.** An intensive study of eight city squares. First survey report of the Dispensary Aid Society.
 By—Alice E. Stewart and Violet S. Simmons. PUBLISHER—Tuberculosis League of Pittsburgh. 1916. 65 p. Free.

PORTO RICO. **Tuberculosis Survey of the Island of Porto Rico.** U. S. Public Health Service Bulletin No. 138.
 By—J. B. Townsend. PUBLISHER—Superintendent of Documents, Government Printing Office, Washington, D. C. 1924. 74 p. 35 cents.

SURVEYS IN SPECIALIZED FIELDS

TUBERCULOSIS—Continued

RHODE ISLAND. **The Tuberculosis Problem in Rhode Island.** A survey conducted for the Rhode Island Tuberculosis Association.
> By—C.-E. A. Winslow. PUBLISHER—Rhode Island Tuberculosis Association, Providence. 1920. 81 p. 30 cents.

SOUTH CAROLINA. **Tuberculosis in South Carolina.** A survey with recommendations.
> By—H. A. Pattison. PUBLISHER—National Tuberculosis Association, New York City. 1925. 64 p. Free.

SOUTH CAROLINA. *See also* NORTH CAROLINA in this section.

TEXAS. **Interstate Migration of Tuberculous Persons.** Its bearing on the public health with special reference to the states of Texas and New Mexico. Reprint No. 269, Public Health Reports, April 9, 16, and 23, 1915.
> By—Ernest A. Sweet. PUBLISHER—Superintendent of Documents, Government Printing Office, Washington, D. C. 1915. 92 p. 10 cents.

TEXAS, EL PASO. *See* ARIZONA, PHOENIX, in this section.

TEXAS, SAN ANTONIO. *See* ARIZONA, PHOENIX, in this section.

UNITED STATES. **Agricultural and Industrial Community for Arrested Cases of Tuberculosis and Their Families.** A study. Federal Board for Vocational Education. Bulletin 32. Reeducation Series No. 6.
> By—H. A. Pattison. PUBLISHER—Federal Board for Vocational Education, Washington, D. C. 1919. 45 p. Out of print.

UNITED STATES. **Mortality from Pulmonary Tuberculosis in Recent Years.** Public Health Reports. Vol. 37, No. 46.
> By—Rollo H. Britten. PUBLISHER—Superintendent of Documents, Government Printing Office, Washington, D. C. 1922. 17 p. 5 cents.

UNITED STATES. **Tuberculosis among Ex-Service Men with Special Reference to Its Bearing on Public Health.** U. S. Public Health Reports. Vol. 37, No. 37.
> By—Hugh S. Cummings. PUBLISHER—Superintendent of Documents, Government Printing Office, Washington, D. C. 1922. 13 p. 5 cents.

VERMONT. **Report of the Vermont Tuberculosis Commission.**
> By—The Commission. PUBLISHER—State Department of Health, Montpelier. 1904. 29 p. Out of print.

A BIBLIOGRAPHY OF SOCIAL SURVEYS

TUBERCULOSIS—Continued

VIRGINIA. **Report of the Virginia Tuberculosis Committee.**
> BY—The Committee. PUBLISHER—State Board of Health, Richmond. 1920. 72 p. Free.

WEST VIRGINIA, HARRISON COUNTY. **A Tuberculosis Survey of Harrison County.**
> BY—Lilla M. Hescock. PUBLISHER—West Virginia Tuberculosis Association. Charleston. 1925. 23 p. 5 cents.

WEST VIRGINIA, MARION COUNTY. **A Tuberculosis Survey of Marion County.**
> BY—Francina McMahon. PUBLISHER—West Virginia Tuberculosis Association, Charleston. 1922. 16 p. 15 cents.

WEST VIRGINIA, OHIO COUNTY. **Report of a Tuberculosis Survey of Ohio County.**
> BY—Jesse A. Bloch. PUBLISHER—State Board of Health, Charleston. 1922. 76 p. Free.

WISCONSIN. **Report of the Wisconsin State Tuberculosis Commission.**
> BY—The Commission. PUBLISHER—State Board of Health, Madison. 1905. 43 p. Out of print.

WISCONSIN. **Tuberculosis in Rural Districts.** I. Dunn County Survey. II. Lafayette County Survey. III. What the Rural Crusade Teaches the Farmer.
> BY—Wisconsin Anti-Tuberculosis Association. PUBLISHER—The same, Milwaukee. 1911. 6 p. Out of print.

WISCONSIN. **Tuberculosis or Consumption with Special Reference to Wisconsin Conditions.** University Extension Series. Bulletin Vol. I, No. 3.
> BY—W. D. Frost. PUBLISHER—University of Wisconsin, Madison. 1913. 70 p. 40 cents.

In addition to reports **presenting findings** in Tuberculosis Surveys, as listed above, publications dealing with **methods of conducting** such studies will be found in Part III, PURPOSE, METHOD, AND STANDARDS, page 357.

UNEMPLOYMENT
> *See also* CHILD WELFARE; FAMILY WELFARE; INDUSTRIAL CONDITIONS AND RELATIONS; and MINIMUM WAGE.

SURVEYS IN SPECIALIZED FIELDS

UNEMPLOYMENT—Continued

CALIFORNIA. **Unemployment.** Transactions of the Commonwealth Club of California. Vol. IV, No. 13.
> By—Section on Investigation of Unemployment. PUBLISHER—Commonwealth Club of California, San Francisco. 1914. 43 p. 25 cents.

CALIFORNIA. REPORTS ON UNEMPLOYMENT.
Report on Unemployment to His Excellency, Governor Hiram W. Johnson. 1914. 73 p.
Report on Relief of the Destitute Unemployed. 1914–1915. 1915. 24 p.
> By—Commission of Immigration and Housing in California. PUBLISHER—The same, San Francisco. Out of print.

CANADA, ONTARIO. **Report of the Ontario Commission on Unemployment.**
> By—The Commission. PUBLISHER—Legislative Assembly of Ontario, Toronto. 1916. 333 p. Out of print.

COLORADO. **Report of the Committee on Unemployment and Relief.**
> By—Albert A. Reed. PUBLISHER—State of Colorado, Denver. 1916. 47 p. Free.

ENGLAND, YORK. **Unemployment.** A social study of York.
> By—Seebohm Rowntree and Bruno Lasker. PUBLISHER—Macmillan Company, New York City. 1911. 311 p. $2.00.

ILLINOIS, CHICAGO. **Report of the Mayor's Commission on Unemployment.**
> By—The Commission. PUBLISHER—City Council of Chicago. 1914. 173 p. Out of print.

MASSACHUSETTS. **Report of the Massachusetts Board to Investigate the Subject of the Unemployed.** House Document No. 50.
> By—The Board. PUBLISHER—State of Massachusetts, Boston. 1895. 130 p. Out of print.

MASSACHUSETTS, BOSTON. **Unemployment among Women in Department and Other Retail Stores of Boston.** U. S. Department of Labor. Bureau of Labor Statistics Bulletin. Whole No. 182. Women in Industry Series No. 8.
> By—U. S. Commission on Industrial Relations. PUBLISHER—Superintendent of Documents, Government Printing Office, Washington, D. C. 1916. 72 p. 15 cents.

UNEMPLOYMENT—Continued

MICHIGAN, DETROIT. **Report on Unemployment in the Winter of 1914–1915 in Detroit and the Institutions and Measures of Relief.**
> BY—Walter E. Kruesi. PUBLISHER—City of Detroit. 1915. 30 p. Out of print.

MINNESOTA, ST. PAUL. **Report of the Citizens' Committee for the Relief of the Unemployed.**
> BY—The Committee. PUBLISHER—City of St. Paul. 1894. 51 p. Out of print.

MISSOURI, ST. LOUIS. **St. Louis after the War.**
> BY—Harland Bartholomew. PUBLISHER—Board of Public Welfare, St. Louis. 1918. 31 p. Free.

NEW YORK. **Unemployment and Lack of Farm Labor.** Third Report to the Legislature of the State of New York by the Commission appointed to inquire into the question of employers' liability and other matters.
> BY—William M. Leiserson. PUBLISHER—State of New York, Albany. 1911. 245 p. Free.

NEW YORK CITY. **Public Employment Exchanges.** Report of the Committee appointed by the trustees of the City Club of New York to inquire into the need of public employment exchanges in New York.
> BY—The Committee. PUBLISHER—City Club of New York City. 1914. 35 p. Out of print.

NEW YORK CITY. **Unemployment in New York City.** U. S. Department of Labor. Bureau of Labor Statistics Bulletin. Whole No. 172. Miscellaneous Series No. 10.
> BY—U. S. Department of Labor. PUBLISHER—Superintendent of Documents, Government Printing Office, Washington, D. C. 1915. 24 p. 5 cents.

NEW YORK CITY. **Report of the Mayor's Committee on Unemployment.**
> BY—The Committee. PUBLISHER—City of New York. 1916. 109 p. Out of print.

OHIO. **Ohio and Unemployment in 1920–1921.**
> BY—Council on Women and Children in Industry. PUBLISHER—The same, Toledo. 1921. 40 p. Out of print.

OREGON. **Unemployment in Oregon.** Its nature, extent, and remedies.
> BY—Frank O'Hara. PUBLISHER—State of Oregon, Salem. 1914. 39 p. Out of print.

SURVEYS IN SPECIALIZED FIELDS

UNEMPLOYMENT—Continued

OREGON, PORTLAND. **A Study of the Unemployed in Portland.** Reed College. Record No. 18.
> By—Arthur E. Wood. PUBLISHER—Reed College, Portland. 1914. 32 p. Free.

OREGON, PORTLAND. **Report on the Problem of Unemployment during the Winter 1914–1915.**
> By—W. L. Brewster. PUBLISHER—City of Portland. 1915. 18 p. Out of print.

PENNSYLVANIA, PHILADELPHIA. **Philadelphia Unemployment with Special Reference to the Textile Industries.**
> By—J. H. Willitts. PUBLISHER—City Department of Unemployment, Philadelphia. 1915. 170 p. Out of print.

UNITED STATES. **Unemployment Survey.** American Labor Legislative Review. Vol. V, No. 3. Publication 30.
> By—Margaret A. Hobbs. PUBLISHER—American Association for Labor Legislation, New York City. 1915. 631 p. $1.00.

UNITED STATES. **Unemployment in the United States.** U. S. Department of Labor. Bureau of Labor Statistics Bulletin. Whole No. 195. Employment and Unemployment Series No. 2.
> By—Bureau of Labor Statistics. PUBLISHER—Superintendent of Documents, Government Printing Office, Washington, D. C. 1916. 115 p. 15 cents.

UNITED STATES. **Fluctuations in Unemployment in Cities of the United States, 1902–1917.** Studies from the Helen S. Trounstine Foundation. Vol. I, No. 2.
> By—Hornell Hart. PUBLISHER—Helen S. Trounstine Foundation, Cincinnati, Ohio. 1918. 59 p. 25 cents.

UNITED STATES. **Business Cycles and Unemployment.** An investigation under the auspices of the National Bureau of Economic Research made for a committee of the President's Conference on Unemployment.
> By—National Bureau of Economic Research. PUBLISHER—McGraw-Hill Book Company, New York City. 1923. 405 p. $4.00.

UNITED STATES. **Cycles of Unemployment in the United States. 1903–1922.**
> By—W. A. Berridge. PUBLISHER—Houghton Mifflin Company, New York City. 1923. 88 p. $1.25.

In addition to reports presenting **findings** in Unemployment Surveys, as listed above, a publication dealing with **methods of conducting** such studies will be found in Part III, PURPOSE, METHOD, AND STANDARDS, page 357.

UNMARRIED MOTHERS

See also SOCIAL AGENCIES.

MASSACHUSETTS, BOSTON. **What Becomes of the Unmarried Mother?** A study of 82 cases.
> BY—Alberta S. B. Guibord and Ida R. Parker. PUBLISHER—Research Bureau on Social Case Work, Boston. 1922. 76 p. 50 cents.

OHIO, CLEVELAND. **The Unwed Mother and Her Child.** Report and recommendations of the Cleveland Conference on Illegitimacy and Its Committee.
> BY—The Committee. MIMEOGRAPHED—Cleveland Federation for Charity and Philanthropy. 1922. 15 p. Free.

UNITED STATES. **Unmarried Mothers.** A study of 500 cases.
> BY—Percy Gamble Kammerer. PUBLISHER—Little, Brown and Company, Boston. 1918. 342 p. $3.00.

VAGRANTS

NEW YORK CITY. **Why There Are Vagrants.** A study based upon an examination of 100 men.
> BY—F. C. Lenbach. PUBLISHER—Longmans, Green and Company, New York City. 1916. 128 p. Out of print.

VENEREAL DISEASE

See also CLINICS AND DISPENSARIES; DETENTION; and NEGROES.

CALIFORNIA. SAN FRANCISCO. REPORTS OF INVESTIGATIONS OF VENEREAL DISEASES IN CALIFORNIA.
The Red Plague. 1st Report. Vol. VI, No. 1. 1911. 83 p.
The Red Plague. 2nd Report. Vol. VIII, No. 7. 1913. 99 p.
> BY—Commonwealth Club of California. PUBLISHER—The same, San Francisco. 19 cents each.

OHIO, CLEVELAND. **Venereal Disease.** Part V. Cleveland Hospital and Health Survey.
> BY—Haven Emerson, Director. PUBLISHER—Cleveland Hospital Council. 1920. 38 p. 50 cents and postage.

UNITED STATES. **The Venereal Diseases.** A sociologic study. Bulletin No. 8.
> BY—Iowa State Board of Health. PUBLISHER—The same, Des Moines. 1918. 62 p. Free.

SURVEYS IN SPECIALIZED FIELDS

VENEREAL DISEASE—Continued

UNITED STATES. **Syphilis of the Innocent.** A study of the social effects of syphilis on the family and the community.
>BY—Harry C. Solomon and Maida Herman Solomon. PUBLISHER—United States Interdepartmental Social Hygiene Board, Washington, D. C. 1922. 239 p. Out of print.

VICE
>*See also* FEEBLEMINDED; PROSTITUTION; and SOCIAL EVIL.

ARKANSAS, LITTLE ROCK. **Report of the Little Rock Vice Commission.**
>BY—The Commission. PUBLISHER—City of Little Rock. 1913. 29 p. Out of print.

CANADA, TORONTO. **Report of the Social Survey Commission of Toronto.**
>BY—The Commission. PUBLISHER—Board of Control, Toronto. 1915. 72 p. Out of print.

COLORADO, DENVER COUNTY. **Report of the Morals Commission of the City and County of Denver Concerning Licensed Cafes and Restaurants.**
>BY—The Commission. PUBLISHER—Denver Council. 1913. 15 p. Out of print.

CONNECTICUT, BRIDGEPORT. **The Report and Recommendations of the Bridgeport Vice Commission.**
>BY—The Commission. PUBLISHER—City of Bridgeport. 1916. 94 p. Free.

CONNECTICUT, HARTFORD. **Report of the Vice Commission of Hartford.**
>BY—Ernest A. Wells. PUBLISHER—Vice Commission of Hartford. 1913. 90 p. 25 cents.

GEORGIA, ATLANTA. **Report of the Vice Commission.**
>BY—The Commission. PUBLISHER—City Council of Atlanta. 1912. 26 p. Free.

ILLINOIS. **Report of the Senate Vice Committee Created under the Authority of the Senate of the 49th General Assembly.**
>BY—The Committee. PUBLISHER—State of Illinois, Springfield. 1916. 979 p. Out of print.

ILLINOIS, CHICAGO. **The Road to Destruction Made Easy in Chicago.** An investigation [of excursion steamers, cabarets, dance halls, and other places of amusement].
>BY—Louise de Koven Bowen. PUBLISHER—Juvenile Protective Association, Chicago. 1916. 15 p. Free.

A BIBLIOGRAPHY OF SOCIAL SURVEYS

VICE—Continued

KENTUCKY, LEXINGTON. **Report of the Vice Commission of Lexington.**
 By—The Commission. PUBLISHER—City Council, Lexington. 1915. 62 p. 20 cents.

KENTUCKY, LOUISVILLE. **Report of the Vice Commission.** Survey of existing conditions with recommendations to the Mayor.
 By—The Commission. PUBLISHER—City Council of Louisville. 1915. 94 p. Postage.

KENTUCKY, PADUCAH. **Report of the Paducah Vice Commission.**
 By—George J. Kneeland. PUBLISHER—City Council of Paducah. 1916. 63 p. Free.

LOUISIANA, SHREVEPORT. **Brief and Recommendations.**
 By—Shreveport Vice Commission. PUBLISHER—The same. 1915. 18 p. Postage.

MASSACHUSETTS. **Report of the Commission for the Investigation of the White Slave Traffic.** House No. 2281.
 By—The Commission. PUBLISHER—Commonwealth of Massachusetts, Boston. 1914. 86 p. Free.

MICHIGAN, GRAND RAPIDS. **Report of the Investigation of the Vice Committee of Forty-One.**
 By—John S. McDonald. PUBLISHER—Vice Committee of Forty-One, Grand Rapids. 1913. 16 p. Out of print.

MINNESOTA, MINNEAPOLIS. **Report of the Minneapolis Vice Commission to the Mayor.**
 By—The Commission. PUBLISHER—City Council, Minneapolis. 1911. 134 p. 25 cents.

NEW YORK, ELMIRA. **A Report on Vice Conditions in Elmira, Being a Report of an Investigation of the Moral Condition of the City.**
 By—George J. Kneeland. PUBLISHER—Women's League for Good Government, Elmira. 1913. 76 p. Free.

NEW YORK, ROCKLAND COUNTY. **Report of the Survey Made in Rockland County.**
 By—Committee of Fifty. PUBLISHER—The same, Orangetown. 1915. 39 p. Free.

OHIO, CLEVELAND. **Report of the Vice Commission of the Cleveland Baptist Brotherhood.**
 By—The Commission. PUBLISHER—Cleveland Baptist Brotherhood. 1911. 15 p. 10 cents.

SURVEYS IN SPECIALIZED FIELDS

VICE—Continued

OHIO, CLEVELAND. **Vice Conditions in Cleveland.**
> By—Committee on Vice Conditions, Federated Churches of Cleveland. PUBLISHER—The same. 1916. 22 p. Free.

OREGON, PORTLAND. **Report of the Portland Vice Commission to the Mayor and City Council of the City of Portland.**
> By—The Commission. PUBLISHER—The same, Portland. 1913. 216 p. Out of print.

PENNSYLVANIA, LANCASTER. REPORTS ON VICE CONDITIONS.
Report on Vice Conditions in the City of Lancaster. 1913. 95 p. Out of print.
A Second Report on Vice Conditions in the City of Lancaster. 1915. 57 p. 10 cents.
> By—George J. Kneeland. PUBLISHER—American Vigilance Association.

PENNSYLVANIA, PHILADELPHIA. **Report of the Vice Commission of Philadelphia.**
> By—The Commission. PUBLISHER—American Social Hygiene Association, New York City. 1913. 164 p. 40 cents.

PENNSYLVANIA, PITTSBURGH. **Report and Recommendations of the Morals Efficiency Commission.**
> By—George Seibel. PUBLISHER—Morals Efficiency Commission, Pittsburgh. 1913. 43 p. Out of print.

SOUTH CAROLINA, CHARLESTON. **Special Report of the Law and Order League of Charleston.**
> By—The League. PUBLISHER—The same, Charleston. 1913. 84 p. 25 cents.

WISCONSIN. **Report and Recommendations of Wisconsin Vice Committee to Investigate the White Slave Traffic and Kindred Subjects.**
> By—The Committee. PUBLISHER—The same, Madison. 1914. 242 p. Free.

VIOLENT DEATHS

GEORGIA, ATLANTA. **A Study of Violent Deaths Registered in Atlanta, Birmingham, Memphis, and New Orleans for the Years 1921 and 1922.**
> By—J. J. Durrett and W. G. Stromquist. PUBLISHER—Department of Health, Memphis, Tennessee. 1924. 38 p. Free.

VOCATIONAL GUIDANCE AND TRAINING

See also CHILD LABOR; CONTINUATION AND PART-TIME SCHOOLS; INDUSTRIAL EDUCATION; RECREATION; and RURAL EDUCATION.

CALIFORNIA, FRESNO. **A Study of Vocational Conditions in the City of Fresno.** General Vocational Education Series No. 2. Division Bulletin No. 20.

By—Emily G. Palmer. PUBLISHER—Division of Vocational Education, University of California, Berkeley. 1926. 260 p. 50 cents.

CALIFORNIA, OAKLAND. **Vocational Guidance and Junior Placement in Twelve Cities in the United States** [Oakland, Calif.; Atlanta, Ga.; Chicago, Ill.; Boston, Mass.; Minneapolis, Minn.; New York City and Rochester, N. Y.; Cincinnati, Ohio; Philadelphia and Pittsburgh, Pa.; Providence, R. I.; Seattle, Wash.]. U. S. Department of Labor. Children's Bureau Publication No. 149. Employment Service Publication A.

By—Children's Bureau and Junior Division, U. S. Employment Service. PUBLISHER—Superintendent of Documents, Government Printing Office, Washington, D. C. 1925. 438 p. 65 cents.

CANADA. **Report of the Royal Commission on Industrial Training and Technical Education.** In 4 volumes.

By—The Commission. PUBLISHER—Order of Canadian Parliament, Ottawa. 1913. 2354 p. Free.

COLORADO, DENVER. **Report of the School Survey of School District No. 1 in the City and County of Denver.** Part III. Vocational Education.

By—C. A. Prosser and W. H. Henderson. PUBLISHER—School Survey Committee, Denver. 1916. 91 p. Free.

GEORGIA, ATLANTA. See CALIFORNIA, OAKLAND, in this section.

ILLINOIS, CHICAGO. **Vocational Training in Chicago and Other Cities.**

By—City Club of Chicago. PUBLISHER—The same. 1912. 315 p. Out of print.

ILLINOIS, CHICAGO. See also CALIFORNIA, OAKLAND, in this section.

INDIANA. **A Study of the People of Indiana and Their Occupation for Purposes of Vocational Education.** University Studies. Vol. XII, No. 17. Bulletin No. 26.

By—Robert J. Leonard. PUBLISHER—University of Indiana, Bloomington. 1915. 137 p. 50 cents.

SURVEYS IN SPECIALIZED FIELDS

VOCATIONAL GUIDANCE AND TRAINING—Continued

INDIANA, EVANSVILLE. **Report of the Evansville Survey for Vocational Education.** Indiana Survey Series No. 4. Educational Bulletin No. 19.
>By—Charles H. Winslow. PUBLISHER—Vocational Division, Indiana State Board of Education, Indianapolis. 1917. 510 p. Free.

INDIANA, HAMMOND. **Some Facts Concerning the People, Industries, and Schools of Hammond and a Suggested Program for Elementary, Industrial, Prevocational, and Vocational Education.**
>By—Robert J. Leonard. PUBLISHER—Board of Education, Hammond. 1915. 165 p. 5 cents.

INDIANA, INDIANAPOLIS. **Report of the Indianapolis Survey for Vocational Education.** Indiana Survey Series No. 6. Educational Bulletin No. 21.
>By—Charles H. Winslow. PUBLISHER—Indiana State Board of Education, Indianapolis. 1917. Vol. I. 400 p. Vol. II. 527 p. Free.

INDIANA, JEFFERSON COUNTY. **Report of the Jefferson County Survey for Vocational Education.** Indiana Survey Series No. 5. Educational Bulletin No. 20.
>By—Committee on Vocational Education. PUBLISHER—Indiana State Board of Education, Indianapolis. 1917. 86 p. Free.

INDIANA, RICHMOND. **Report of the Richmond Survey for Vocational Education.** Indiana Survey Series No. 3. Educational Bulletin No. 18.
>By—Robert J. Leonard. PUBLISHER—State Board of Education, Indianapolis. 1916. 599 p. Out of print.

IOWA. **Vocational Education and Vocational Guidance.** A survey and preliminary report.
>By—Committee from Iowa Teachers' Association. PUBLISHER—State Department of Public Instruction, Des Moines. 1914. 96 p. Out of print.

IOWA. **Work, Wages, and Schooling of 800 Iowa Boys in Relation to the Problems of Vocational Guidance.** Extension Bulletin No. 9. New Series No. 90.
>By—Ervin E. Lewis. PUBLISHER—University of Iowa, Iowa City. 1915. 34 p. Free.

VOCATIONAL GUIDANCE AND TRAINING—Continued

KENTUCKY, LOUISVILLE. **Vocational Guidance Survey.**
> By—Women's Club of Louisville. PUBLISHER—The same. 1918. 22 p. Free.

LOUISIANA, NEW ORLEANS. VOCATIONAL SURVEY FOR THE ISAAC DELGADO TRADES SCHOOL.
> Part I. Facts about the Public Schools of New Orleans in Relation to Vocation. 1914. 58 p.
> Part II. Industry and Education. A preliminary study of manufacturing establishments of New Orleans and mechanical occupations of boys and men with reference to education and a plan for the Delgado School. 1916. 409 p.
>> By—David S. Hill. PUBLISHER—Board of Education, New Orleans. Free.

MASSACHUSETTS, BOSTON. **The Public Schools and Women in Office Service.** Department of Research. Vol. VIII.
> By—May Allinson, Director. PUBLISHER—Women's Educational and Industrial Union, Boston. 1914. 187 p. 80 cents.

MASSACHUSETTS, BOSTON. **Training for Store Service.** The vocational experience and training of juvenile employees of retail department stores in Boston.
> By—Lucile Eaves. PUBLISHER—Women's Educational and Industrial Union, Boston. 1920. 143 p. 80 cents and postage.

MASSACHUSETTS, BOSTON. *See also* CALIFORNIA, OAKLAND, in this section.

MICHIGAN, DETROIT. **Occupations of Junior Workers in Detroit.** Vocational Education Department Special Studies No. 1.
> By—Alexander C. Crockett and Jennie M. Clow. PUBLISHER—School of Education, University of Michigan, Ann Arbor. 1925. 76 p. Free.

MINNESOTA, MINNEAPOLIS. **Vocational Survey of Minneapolis.**
> By—Minneapolis Teachers' Club. PUBLISHER—The same. 1913. 9 p. Out of print.

MINNESOTA, MINNEAPOLIS. **Vocational Education Survey of Minneapolis.** U. S. Department of Labor. Bureau of Labor Statistics Bulletin. Vocational Education Series No. 1. Whole No. 199.
> By—Society for the Promotion of Industrial Education. PUBLISHER—Superintendent of Documents, Government Printing Office, Washington, D. C. 1917. 592 p. 65 cents.

SURVEYS IN SPECIALIZED FIELDS

VOCATIONAL GUIDANCE AND TRAINING—Continued

MINNESOTA, MINNEAPOLIS. *See also* CALIFORNIA, OAKLAND, in this section.

NEW YORK, ELMIRA. **Report of a Vocational Survey Made under the Direction and Supervision of the Vocational Committee and the Superintendent of Schools for the Board of Education.** Elmira School Bulletin. Vol. IX, No. 2.
>BY—The Committee. PUBLISHER—Department of Public Education, Elmira. 1919. 16 p. Free.

NEW YORK CITY. **Report of the Vocational Guidance Survey.**
>BY—Alice P. Barrows. PUBLISHER—Public Education Association, New York City. 1912. 15 p. Free.

NEW YORK CITY. **Vocational Guidance and Placement Work for Juniors in New York City.** Report of a survey.
>BY—Josette Frank and Samuel S. Board. PUBLISHER—Committee on Vocational Guidance, Children's Welfare Federation, New York City. 1923. 55 p. 25 cents.

NEW YORK CITY. *See also* CALIFORNIA, OAKLAND, in this section.

NEW YORK, ROCHESTER. *See* CALIFORNIA, OAKLAND, in this section.

OHIO, CINCINNATI. *See* CALIFORNIA, OAKLAND, in this section.

PENNSYLVANIA, PHILADELPHIA. **A Survey of Opportunities for Vocational Education in and near Philadelphia.**
>BY—Jane R. Harper. PUBLISHER—Public Education and Child Labor Association of Pennsylvania, Philadelphia. 1921. 140 p. $1.00.

PENNSYLVANIA, PHILADELPHIA. *See also* CALIFORNIA, OAKLAND, in this section.

PENNSYLVANIA, PITTSBURGH. **A Study of Five Hundred Employed Pupils.**
>BY—Helen M. McClure and Margaret G. Woodside. PUBLISHER—Department of Vocational Guidance, Pittsburgh Public Schools. 1925. 16 p. Free.

PENNSYLVANIA, PITTSBURGH. *See also* CALIFORNIA, OAKLAND, in this section.

PENNSYLVANIA, WILKES-BARRE. **Vocational Guidance and Child Labor with a Review of a Survey of Girls at Work in Wilkes-Barre.**
>BY—National Child Labor Committee. PUBLISHER—The same, New York City. 1915. 15 p. 5 cents.

VOCATIONAL GUIDANCE AND TRAINING—Continued

RHODE ISLAND, PROVIDENCE. *See* CALIFORNIA, OAKLAND, in this section.

TEXAS. **Texas Educational Survey Report.** Vol. VII. Vocational Education.
> BY—George A. Works, Director. PUBLISHER—Texas Educational Survey Commission, Austin. 1924. 166 p. Free.

UNITED STATES. **Apprentice Education.** A survey of part-time education and other forms of extension training in their relation to apprenticeship in the United States. Federal Board for Vocational Education Bulletin No. 87. Industrial Series No. 25.
> BY—Jennie McMullin Turner. PUBLISHER—Superintendent of Documents, Government Printing Office, Washington, D. C. 1923. 519 p. 55 cents.

UNITED STATES. **Effectiveness of Vocational Education in Agriculture.** A study of the value of vocational instruction in agriculture in secondary schools as indicated by the occupational distribution of former students. Federal Board for Vocational Education.
> BY—Charles Everett Myers. PUBLISHER—Superintendent of Documents, Government Printing Office, Washington, D. C. 1923. 63 p. 10 cents.

VIRGINIA. **Vocational Agriculture in the Secondary Schools of Virginia.** Bulletin State Board of Education. Vol. II, No. 3.
> BY—Thomas D. Eason. PUBLISHER—State Board of Education, Richmond. 1919. 71 p. Free.

VIRGINIA, RICHMOND. **Vocational Education Survey of Richmond.** U. S. Department of Labor. Bureau of Labor Statistics Bulletin. Whole No. 162. Miscellaneous Series No. 7.
> BY—Leonard P. Ayres and Charles H. Winslow. PUBLISHER—Superintendent of Documents, Government Printing Office, Washington, D. C. 1916. 333 p. 40 cents.

WASHINGTON, SEATTLE. **Newsboy Service.** A study in educational and vocational guidance.
> BY—Anna Y. Reed. PUBLISHER—World Book Company, Yonkers, New York. 1917. 175 p. $1.20.

WASHINGTON, SEATTLE. *See also* CALIFORNIA, OAKLAND, in this section.

In addition to reports **presenting findings** in Vocational Guidance and Training Surveys, as listed above, publications dealing with **methods of conducting** such studies will be found in Part III, PURPOSE, METHOD, AND STANDARDS, page 357.

SURVEYS IN SPECIALIZED FIELDS

WAGES
See COST OF LIVING; INDUSTRIAL CONDITIONS AND RELATIONS; PENSIONS; and UNEMPLOYMENT.

WARD
See PART I, GENERAL SOCIAL SURVEY—URBAN, and PART II, in HOUSING.

WHITE SLAVE TRAFFIC
See VICE.

WIDOWS
See CHARITIES; DEPENDENCY; FAMILY WELFARE; PENSIONS; and RELIEF.

WORKHOUSES
See also ALMSHOUSES.

DELAWARE, WILMINGTON. **The Newcastle County Workhouse, Wilmington.** A study made on request of the Board of Trustees.
BY—Hastings H. Hart. PUBLISHER—National Committee on Prisons and Prison Labor, New York City. 1920. 29 p. Free.

DISTRICT OF COLUMBIA. **Report of the Commission Appointed to Investigate Jails, Workhouses, etc., in the District of Columbia.** Senate Document No. 648.
BY—The Commission. PUBLISHER—Superintendent of Documents, Government Printing Office, Washington, D. C. 1909. 49 p. 5 cents.

ZONING
See CITY AND REGIONAL PLANNING.

For publications dealing with **methods of conducting** Zoning Surveys see Part III, PURPOSE, METHOD, AND STANDARDS, under **General Social Surveys—Urban;** and **City and Regional Planning.**

A number of other reports of surveys in specialized fields, which have appeared since this listing was closed, are given on pages xli of the Introduction.

PART III

PUBLICATIONS ON PURPOSE, METHOD, AND STANDARDS IN SURVEYS

1. GENERAL SOCIAL SURVEYS—URBAN

See also RACE RELATIONS; and RELIGION below.

Social Surveys: Reasons, Methods, and Results. In Proceedings of the National Conference of Charities and Corrections.

By—John Daniels. PUBLISHER—National Conference of Charities and Corrections, Fort Wayne, Indiana. 1910. 5 p. Out of print.

Application of the Social Survey to Small Communities. In Papers and Proceedings of the Sixth Annual Meeting of the American Sociological Society.

By—John Lewis Gillin. PUBLISHER—University of Chicago Press. 1911. 12 p. $3.00 for membership and publications.

Knowing One's Own Community. Suggestions for social surveys of small cities and towns. Social Science Series Bulletin No. 20. Revised Edition.

By—Carol Aronovici. PUBLISHER—American Unitarian Association, New York City. 1911. 82 p. Free.

Sociology and Social Surveys. In American Journal of Sociology. Vol. XVI, May.

By—Thomas J. Riley. PUBLISHER—University of Chicago Press. 1911. 15 p. Out of print.

Community Study for Cities.

By—Warren H. Wilson. PUBLISHER—Missionary Education Movement of the United States and Canada, New York City. 1912. 119 p. 35 cents.

Need and Scope of a Social Survey for Montclair.

By—Allan T. Burns. PUBLISHER—Survey Committee of Montclair, New Jersey. 1912. 24 p. Out of print.

The Social Survey. Five papers reprinted from the Proceedings of the Academy of Political Science. Vol. II, No. 4.

By—Paul U. Kellogg, Shelby M. Harrison, George T. Palmer, Pauline Goldmark, and Robert E. Chaddock. PUBLISHER—Russell Sage Foundation, New York City. 1912. 62 p. Out of print.

Statistical Methods in Survey Work. Reprinted from the Proceedings of the Academy of Political Science. Vol. II, No. 4.
> By—Robert Emmet Chaddock. Publisher—Academy of Political Science, New York City. 1912. 6 p. Out of print.

Development of Social Surveys. In Report of the Proceedings of the National Conference of Charities and Corrections.
> By—Shelby M. Harrison. Publisher—National Conference of Charities and Corrections, Chicago, Illinois. 1913. 9 p. Out of print.

Report of a Brief Investigation of Social Conditions in the City [Toronto, Canada] Which Indicate the Need of an Intensive Social Survey, the Lines of Which Are Herein Suggested.
> By—Board of Temperance and Moral Reform, Methodist Church, and Board of Social Service and Evangelism, Presbyterian Church. Publisher—The same, Toronto. 1913. 29 p. Out of print.

Outline of a Social Survey for the Community. Recommended by the Commission on Social Service of the Interchurch Federation of Philadelphia.
> By—The Commission. Publisher—Interchurch Federation of Philadelphia, Pennsylvania. 1914. 12 p. Out of print.

Social Surveys of Urban Communities.
> By—Manuel C. Elmer. Publisher—University of Chicago Press. 1914. 73 p. Out of print.

The Collection of Social Survey Material.
> By—Florence Rising Curtis. Publisher—American Library Association, Chicago, Illinois. 1915. 15 p. 15 cents.

Handbook of Civic Improvement.
> By—Herman G. James. Publisher—University of Texas, Austin. 1915. 119 p. $1.00.

Purpose and Benefit of Social Surveys. In Kansas Municipalities. Vol. I, No. 10.
> By—F. W. Blackmar. Publisher—State of Kansas, Topeka. 1915. 3 p. Out of print.

Social Survey and Its Further Development. In American Statistical Association Publications. New Series No. 111, Vol. 14.
> By—J. L. Gillin. Publisher—American Statistical Association, Boston, Massachusetts. 1915. 8 p. Out of print.

The "Block System" of the Juvenile Protective Association of Chicago.
> By—Louise de Koven Bowen. Publisher—Juvenile Protective Association, Chicago, Illinois. 1916. 8 p. Free.

A BIBLIOGRAPHY OF SOCIAL SURVEYS

Community Action through Surveys. A paper describing the main features of the social survey including a discussion of survey results.
By—Shelby M. Harrison. PUBLISHER—Russell Sage Foundation, New York City. 1916. 29 p. 10 cents.

The Social Survey.
By—Carol Aronovici. PUBLISHER—Harpers Press, Philadelphia, Pennsylvania. 1916. 255 p. $1.25.

The Social Survey. University of Iowa Extension Bulletin No. 26. First Series No. 7.
By—Bessie A. McClenahan. PUBLISHER—University of Iowa, Iowa City. 1916. 25 p. Out of print.

A Scale for Grading Neighborhood Conditions. Department of Research Bulletin No. 5.
By—J. Harold Williams. PUBLISHER—Whittier State School, Whittier, California. 1917. 17 p. Out of print.

The Social Survey: Its History and Methods. University of Missouri Bulletin. Vol. 20, No. 28. Social Science Series 3.
By—Carl C. Taylor. PUBLISHER—University of Missouri, Columbia. 1919. 91 p. 15 cents.

Community Studies for Young Women's Christian Association Workers in Cities.
By—Research Bureau for the City Committee. PUBLISHER—National Board, Young Women's Christian Association, New York City. 1920. 49 p. 50 cents.

The Community Survey: A Basis for Social Action. A. The Urban and Industrial Community. B. The Rural and Agricultural Community.
By—Social Service Council of Canada. PUBLISHER—The same, Toronto, Canada. 1920. 19 p. 25 cents.

Essentials of a Survey Plan. Papers and Proceedings, Fifteenth Annual Meeting, American Sociological Society, Vol. XV.
By—Shelby H. Harrison. PUBLISHER—University of Chicago Press. 1920. 3 p. Out of print.

Field Work and Social Research. The Century Social Science Series.
By—F. Stuart Chapin. PUBLISHER—Century Company, New York City. 1920. 224 p. $1.75.

The Social Survey and the Science of Sociology. In the American Journal of Sociology. Vol. XXV, No. 6.
By—Carl C. Taylor. PUBLISHER—University of Chicago Press. 1920. 25 p. 75 cents per copy.

PURPOSE, METHOD, AND STANDARDS IN SURVEYS

Standard Methods in Research Surveys. In Proceedings of the National Conference of Social Work.
  By—C. B. Davenport. PUBLISHER—National Conference of Social Work, Cincinnati, Ohio. 1920. 4 p. $2.00 per volume.

Technique of Social Surveys. Revised edition.
  By—Manuel C. Elmer. PUBLISHER—University of Minnesota, Minneapolis. 1920. 117 p. Out of print.

Plan and Scope of the Social Welfare Study of the Archdiocese of Toronto.
  By—Neil McNeil. PUBLISHER—National Catholic Welfare Council, Toronto, Canada. 1921. 8 p. Free.

The Social Survey; Survey Methods and Data; Types of Survey Schedules; and Symbols for a Neighborhood Survey. In Organizing the Community.
  By—B. A. McClenahan. PUBLISHER—Century Company, New York City. 1922. 69 p. $1.75 per copy.

Know Your Town. Ten sets of questions.
  By—National League of Women Voters. PUBLISHER—The same, Washington, D. C. 1923. 12 p. 5 cents.

The Social Survey in Town and Country Areas. A statistical and graphic summary of survey data from 179 typical counties with an analysis of the aim and method of the social survey as applied to the study of town and country problems. Institute of Social and Religious Research.
  By—H. N. Morse. PUBLISHER—George H. Doran Company, New York City. 1924. 138 p. $2.50.

Two Major Ills of the Social Survey. In Journal of Applied Sociology. Vol. VIII, No. 4.
  By—Seba Eldridge. PUBLISHER—University of Southern California, Los Angeles. 1924. 10 p. 40 cents per copy.

What Social Workers Should Know about Their Own Communities. An outline. Fourth edition. Rewitten.
  By—Margaret F. Byington. PUBLISHER—Russell Sage Foundation, New York City. 1924. 66 p. 25 cents.

Making Social Science Studies. Third revised edition.
  By—Emory S. Bogardus. PUBLISHER—Jesse Ray Miller Press, Los Angeles, California. 1925. 106 p. $1.00.

The Social Survey. In Community Organization, Chapter XII.
  By—Jesse Frederick Steiner. PUBLISHER—Century Company, New York City. 1925. 16 p. $2.25 per copy.

How Good Is Your Town? Measurement standards for town planning and zoning, industry, education, health, public administration,

A BIBLIOGRAPHY OF SOCIAL SURVEYS

social service, recreation, the public library, town-country relations, and religion. Publication No. 36.

By—Wisconsin Conference of Social Work. MIMEOGRAPHED—The same, Madison. 1926. 155 p. $1.00.

How to Study Your Association and the Community. An outline dealing with the methods and technique for making a survey.

By—Frank Ritchie. PUBLISHER—Association Press, New York City. 1926. 62 p. $2.00.

Outline for a "Master" Community Survey.

By—Civic Development Department, Chamber of Commerce of the United States. MIMEOGRAPHED—The same, Washington, D. C. 1927. 52 p. Free.

Survey Information.

By—Illinois Chamber of Commerce. MIMEOGRAPHED—The same, Springfield. 1927. 11 p. Free.

Technique of Social Surveys. Third edition, entirely rewritten and enlarged.

By—Manuel C. Elmer. PUBLISHER—Jesse Ray Miller, Los Angeles, California. 1927. 229 p. $2.00.

Town-Country Relations. Citizens' Survey. Measurement standards for community activities. Publication No. 72.

By—Wisconsin Conference of Social Work. MIMEOGRAPHED—The same, Madison. 1927. 13 p. Free.

2. GENERAL SOCIAL SURVEYS—RURAL

See also GENERAL SOCIAL SURVEYS—URBAN above, and RELIGION below.

A Social Survey for Rural Communities. A practical scheme for the investigation of the structure, problems, and the possibilities of rural, village, and other communities from the point of view of the church and its work.

By—George Frederick Wells. PUBLISHER—The same, New York City. 1911. 23 p. 10 cents.

Survey Idea in Country Life Work.

By—L. H. Bailey. PUBLISHER—Cornell University, Ithaca, New York. 1911. 21 p. Out of print.

Community Study for Country Districts. A method of investigating a small village or section of the open country.

By—Anna B. Taft. PUBLISHER—Missionary Education Movement, United States and Canada, New York City. 1912. 137 p. 35 cents.

PURPOSE, METHOD, AND STANDARDS IN SURVEYS

A Method of Making a Social Survey of a Rural Community. An analysis of a rural community. Agricultural Experiment Station. Circular of Information No. 29. Revised Edition.
> By—C. J. Galpin. PUBLISHER—University of Wisconsin, Madison. 1912. 11 p. Out of print.

The Georgia Club at the State Normal School, Athens, Georgia, for the Study of Rural Sociology. U. S. Department of Interior. Bureau of Education Bulletin, 1913, No. 23. Whole No. 533.
> By—E. C. BRANSON. PUBLISHER—Superintendent of Documents, Government Printing Office, Washington, D. C. 1913. 41 p. Out of print.

A Mode of Rural Survey for Record and Purpose of Practical Exhibit. In The Church at the Center.
> By—Warren H. Wilson. PUBLISHER—Missionary Education Movement, United States and Canada, New York City. 1914. 8 p. 50 cents per copy.

Study of a Rural Parish. A method of survey.
> By—Ralph A. Felton. PUBLISHER—Missionary Education Movement, United States and Canada, New York City. 1916. 135 p. Out of print.

The Rural Survey and the Rural Crisis. In Proceedings of the National Conference of Social Work.
> By—Warren H. Wilson. PUBLISHER—National Conference of Social Work, Cincinnati, Ohio. 1917. 8 p. $2.00 per copy.

Validity of the Survey Method of Research. United States Department of Agriculture Bulletin No. 529.
> By—W. J. Spillman. PUBLISHER—Superintendent of Documents, Government Printing Office, Washington, D. C. 1917. 15 p. 5 cents.

Rural Life Survey.
> By—O. J. Kern. PUBLISHER—University of California, Berkeley. 1919. 15 p. Free.

3. PUBLICATIONS IN SPECIALIZED FIELDS
BOY LIFE

Boy Life Surveys. An outline dealing with plans and methods.
> By—Roy E. Dickerson. PUBLISHER—Grand Council Order of DeMolay, Kansas City, Missouri. 1926. 24 p. Free.

A BIBLIOGRAPHY OF SOCIAL SURVEYS

BOY LIFE—Continued

Report and Outline of Proposed Survey of the Unreached Boy for Brooklyn Boys' Work Council.
>By—Committee on Survey. PUBLISHER—Brooklyn Chamber of Commerce and Brooklyn Bureau of Charities, Brooklyn, New York. 1926. 11 p. Free.

CHARITIES
>See CRIME AND CRIMINALS below.

CHILD HEALTH AND HYGIENE
>See also HEALTH AND SANITATION; and SCHOOL HEALTH AND SANITATION below.

The Hygiene of Maternity and Childhood. Separate No. 1. Child Care and Child Welfare: Outlines for Study. Children's Bureau Publication No. 90.
>By—Children's Bureau and Federal Board for Vocational Education. PUBLISHER—Superintendent of Documents, Government Printing Office, Washington, D. C. 1921. 308 p. 30 cents.

Child Health Demonstration, Mansfield and Richland County, Ohio. 1922 to 1925.
>By—American Child Health Association. PUBLISHER—The same, New York City. 1926. 354 p. $1.00.

CHILD LABOR

Child Labor in Your State: A Study Outline. Pamphlet No. 267.
>By—Florence I. Taylor. PUBLISHER—National Child Labor Committee, New York City. 1916. 15 p. 5 cents.

Child Labor. Separate No. 4. Child Care and Child Welfare: Outlines for Study. Publication No. 93.
>By—Children's Bureau and Federal Board for Vocational Education. PUBLISHER—Superintendent of Documents, Government Printing Office, Washington, D. C. 1921. 65 p. 10 cents.

CHILD WELFARE
>See also BOY LIFE; CHILD HEALTH AND HYGIENE; and CHILD LABOR above: and HEALTH AND SANITATION; RECREATION; and SCHOOL HEALTH AND SANITATION below.

Minimum Standards of Child Welfare. U. S. Department of Labor. Children's Bureau Publication No. 62. Conference Series No. 2.
>By—Washington and Regional Conferences on Child Welfare. PUBLISHER—Superintendent of Documents, Government Printing Office, Washington, D. C. 1919. 14 p. 5 cents.

CHILD WELFARE—Continued

Standards of Child Welfare. A report of the Children's Bureau Conferences, May and June, 1919. U. S. Department of Labor. Children's Bureau Publication No. 60. Conference Series No. 1.
    By—William L. Chenery and Ella A. Merritt. PUBLISHER—Superintendent of Documents, Government Printing Office, Washington, D. C. 1919. 459 p. Out of print.

CHILD CARE AND CHILD WELFARE. Outlines for study.
    Separate No. 2. Child Mentality and Management. Publication No. 91. 42 p. 5 cents.
    Separate No. 5. Children in Need of Special Care. Publication No. 94. 12 p. 5 cents.
    Other parts of this study are listed elsewhere.
    By—Children's Bureau and Federal Board for Vocational Education. PUBLISHER—Superintendent of Documents, Government Printing Office, Washington, D. C., 1921.

Standards of Public Aid to Children in Their Own Homes. U. S. Department of Labor. Children's Bureau Publication No. 118.
    By—Florence Nesbitt. PUBLISHER—Superintendent of Documents, Government Printing Office, Washington, D. C. 1923. 145 p. 15 cents.

CHINESE
    See RACE RELATIONS below.

CHURCHES
    See GENERAL SOCIAL SURVEYS, both URBAN and RURAL, above: and RELIGION below.

CITY AND REGIONAL PLANNING
    See also GENERAL SOCIAL SURVEYS—URBAN above.

Carrying Out the City Plan. The practical application of American law in the execution of city plans.
    By—Flavel Shurtleff and Frederick L. Olmsted. PUBLISHER—Russell Sage Foundation, New York City. 1914. 349 p. $2.00.

Notes for a Study of City Planning in Champaign and Urbana, Illinois.
    By—Class in Civic Design at the University of Illinois. PUBLISHER—University of Illinois, Urbana. 1915. 51 p. Free.

The City Beautiful. A study of town planning and municipal art.
    By—Kate Louise Roberts. PUBLISHER—H. W. Wilson Company, New York City. 1916. 16 p. 25 cents.

CITY AND REGIONAL PLANNING—Continued

City Planning. Bulletin No. 8.

By—Frank G. Bates. PUBLISHER—Bureau of Legislative Information, Indianapolis, Indiana. 1916. 31 p. Out of print.

City Planning for Milwaukee, Wisconsin. What it means and why it must be secured.

By—Werner Hegemann. PUBLISHER—City Club, Milwaukee. 1916. 36 p. Out of print.

Town Planning. A program of civic preparedness for Vermont communities. Norwich University Studies. Political Science Series No. 2.

By—K. R. B. Flint. PUBLISHER—Norwich University, Northfield, Vermont. 1919. 70 p. Free.

Report of Advisory Committee on Zoning: Zoning Primer. U. S. Department of Commerce.

By—The Committee. PUBLISHER—Superintendent of Documents, Government Printing Office, Washington, D. C. 1922. 7 p. 5 cents.

A Standard of Community Excellence or the Kind of a Town We Would Like to Live In.

By—John Ihlder. PUBLISHER—Chamber of Commerce of the United States, Washington, D. C. 1924. 14 p. Free.

City Planning Procedure. Series III, No. 1.

By—Frederic A. Delano, Harland Bartholomew, George B. Ford. Lawson Purdy, and Harlean James. PUBLISHER—American Civic Association, Washington, D. C. 1926. 31 p. 25 cents.

Round Table on Regional Planning: Some Regional Problems and Methods of Their Study. In Report of the Third National Conference on the Science of Politics.

By—Shelby M. Harrison. PUBLISHER—American Political Science Association, University of Wisconsin, Madison. 1926. 8 p. 30 cents per copy.

Town Planning and Zoning. Citizens' Survey. Measurement standards for community activities. Publication No. 66.

By—Wisconsin Conference of Social Work. MIMEOGRAPHED—The same, Madison. 1927. 24 p. Free.

CITY, COUNTY, AND STATE ADMINISTRATION

See also GENERAL SOCIAL SURVEYS—URBAN; and CITY AND REGIONAL PLANNING above: and CRIME AND CRIMINALS below.

Plan and Methods. Bulletin No. 1.

By—B. M. Rastall. PUBLISHER—Bureau of Economy and Efficiency, Milwaukee, Wisconsin. 1911. 29 p. Out of print.

PURPOSE, METHOD, AND STANDARDS IN SURVEYS

CITY, COUNTY, AND STATE ADMINISTRATION—Continued

How to Start a Survey of Your City's Business. In the American City. Vol. VIII, No. 3.

By—William H. Allen. PUBLISHER—The Civic Press, New York City. 1913. 3 p. Out of print.

Administrative Government in Delaware. The Spirit and Purpose of a Recent Survey.

By—Charles A. Beard. PUBLISHER—The same, New York City. 1918. 8 p. Out of print.

Municipal Administration Surveys: Round Table on Municipal Administration. In reprint of Report of Third National Conference on the Science of Politics held in New York City, September 7–11, 1925.

By—Luther Gulick. PUBLISHER—American Political Science Association, University of Wisconsin, Madison. 1926. 5 p. 30 cents.

Measuring Municipal Government. Suggested standards for measuring the results of fire, health, police, and public works departments. Publication No. 4.

By—Clarence E. Ridley. PUBLISHER—Municipal Administration Service and School of Citizenship and Public Affairs, Syracuse University, Syracuse, New York. 1927. 88 p. 25 cents.

Municipal Government. Citizens' Survey. Measurement standard for community activities. Publication No. 69.

By—Wisconsin Conference of Social Work. MIMEOGRAPHED—The same, Madison. 1927. 19 p. Free.

COMMUNITY STUDIES

See GENERAL SOCIAL SURVEYS, both URBAN and RURAL; and CITY AND REGIONAL PLANNING above: and EDUCATION; HOSPITALS AND SANATORIA; RECREATION; RELIGION; and RURAL EDUCATION below.

COST OF LIVING

Standards of Living. A compilation of budgetary studies.

By—Bureau of Applied Economics. PUBLISHER—The same, Washington, D. C. 1919. 49 p. $1.00.

Workingmen's Standard of Living in Philadelphia.

By—William C. Beyer, Director. PUBLISHER—Bureau of Municipal Research, Philadelphia. 1919. 125 p. $2.25.

Chicago Standard Budget for Dependent Families. Bulletin No. 5.

By—Florence Nesbit. PUBLISHER—Chicago Council of Social Agencies. 1920. 45 p. 25 cents.

COST OF LIVING—Continued

Standards of Living and Wage-Earners' Budgets. In Social Problems and Social Policy.
>By—James Ford. PUBLISHER—Ginn and Company, New York City. 1923. 23 p. $4.00.

CRIME AND CRIMINALS

An Outline of the Cleveland Crime Survey.
>By—Raymond Moley. PUBLISHER—Cleveland Foundation, Cleveland, Ohio. 1922. 64 p. Free.

Report of a Crime and Courts Study for the Courts Committee of the Brooklyn Bureau of Charities.
>By—W. Bruce Cobb. PUBLISHER—Brooklyn, Bureau of Charities, Brooklyn, New York. 1926. 17 p. Free.

State Crime Commissions: What They Are, How They Should Be Organized, What They Should Do.
>By—Raymond Moley. PUBLISHER—National Crime Commission, New York City. 1926. 30 p. Free.

CRIPPLED, DISABLED, AND HANDICAPPED
>See INDUSTRIAL CONDITIONS AND RELATIONS below.

DEFECTIVE
>See MENTAL HYGIENE below.

DELINQUENCY AND CORRECTION

Correctional Reforms and Correctional Surveys. In The Delinquent. Vol. 5, April.
>By—Zenas L. Potter. PUBLISHER—Prison Association of New York, New York City. 1915. 4 p. 10 cents per copy.

The Study of the Delinquent as a Person. In the American Journal of Sociology. Vol. XXVIII, No. 6.
>By—E. W. Burgess. PUBLISHER—University of Chicago Press. 1923. 23 p. 75 cents.

DEPENDENCY
>See COST OF LIVING above.

EDUCATION
>See also GENERAL SOCIAL SURVEYS—URBAN above: and HEALTH AND SANITATION; INDUSTRIAL CONDITIONS AND RELATIONS; RE-

EDUCATION—Continued
    LIGIOUS EDUCATION; RURAL EDUCATION; SCHOOL BUILDINGS AND PLANTS; SCHOOL HEALTH AND SANITATION; and VOCATIONAL GUIDANCE AND TRAINING below.

Standards and Tests for Measuring the Efficiency of Schools or Systems of Schools. U. S. Department of Interior. Bureau of Education Bulletin, 1913, No. 13. Whole No. 521.
    BY—George D. Strayer. PUBLISHER—Superintendent of Documents, Government Printing Office, Washington, D. C. 1913. 23 p. Out of print.

American Citizenship in Educational Surveys. Reprint from the Report of the Commissioner of Education. Vol. I, Chapter XXV.
    BY—James Mahoney. PUBLISHER—Superintendent of Documents, Government Printing Office, Washington, D. C. 1914. 33 p. Out of print.

Plans for Organizing School Surveys and a Summary of Typical School Surveys. In 13th Year Book, Part 2.
    BY—National Society for the Study of Education. PUBLISHER—University of Chicago Press. 1914. 85 p. Out of print.

School Surveys. In Report of Commissioner, U. S. Bureau of Education. Vol. I.
    BY—Edward Franklin Buchner. PUBLISHER—Superintendent of Documents, Government Printing Office, Washington, D. C. 1914. 49 p. Out of print.

See also later reports of the Commissioner for references to and further discussion of school surveys.

Announcement of School and Community Survey and Community Welfare Week.
    BY—E. G. Gowans. PUBLISHER—Extension Division and School of Education, University of Utah, Salt Lake City. 1915. 32 p. Free.

School Surveys. In School and Society. Vol. I, No. 17.
    BY—Leonard P. Ayres. PUBLISHER—Science Press, New York City. 1915. 5 p. 10 cents per copy.

Suggestive Studies of School Conditions. An outlined study in school problems for women's clubs, parent-teacher associations, and community organizations.
    BY—Janet R. Rankin. PUBLISHER—State Department of Education, Madison, Wisconsin. 1916. 101 p. Free.

EDUCATION—Continued

Teachers' Year Book of Educational Investigations. New York City Department of Education. Division of Reference and Research. Publication No. 14.
> By—Isadore Springer. PUBLISHER—Department of Education, New York City. 1916. 53 p. Out of print.

Self-Surveys by College and Universities. [Wisconsin State Normal Schools]. Educational Survey Series.
> By—William H. Allen. PUBLISHER—World Book Company, Yonkers, New York. 1917. 394 p. $2.80.

Self-Surveys by Teacher-Training Schools [Wisconsin State Normal Schools]. Educational Survey Series.
> By—William H. Allen and Carroll G. Pearse. PUBLISHER—World Book Company, Yonkers, New York. 1917. 207 p. $2.20.

The Bureau of Education and the Educational Survey Movement. U. S. Department of Interior. Bureau of Education. Higher Education Circular No. 11.
> By—S. P. Capen. PUBLISHER—Superintendent of Documents, Government Printing Office, Washington, D. C. 1918. 6 p. Free.

Methods and Standards for Local School Surveys.
> By—Don C. Bliss and George D. Strayer. PUBLISHER—D. C. Heath and Company, New York City. 1918. 264 p. $1.60.

School Surveys. Bulletin of the University of South Carolina No. 66.
> By—S. H. Edmunds. PUBLISHER—University of South Carolina, Columbia. 1918. 29 p. Free.

Preliminary Suggestions for a Self-Survey of State Universities. Bulletin of the National Association of State Universities.
> By—Samuel P. Capen. PUBLISHER—University of Kentucky, Lexington. 1921. 9 p. Out of print.

School Surveys: Certain Guiding Principles. In Connecticut Schools. Vol. 3, No. 9.
> By—Alfred D. Simpson. PUBLISHER—Connecticut Board of Education, Hartford. 1922. 4 p. Free.

Research Bureaus in City School Systems. Bureau of Education City School Leaflet No. 5.
> By—W. S. Deffenbaugh. PUBLISHER—Superintendent of Documents, Government Printing Office, Washington, D. C. 1923. 23 p. 5 cents.

PURPOSE, METHOD, AND STANDARDS IN SURVEYS

EDUCATION—Continued

The School Survey. A textbook on the use of school surveying in the administration of public schools.
    By—Jesse B. Sears. PUBLISHER—Houghton Mifflin Company, New York. 1925. 440 p. $2.25.

Education: Citizens' Survey. Measurement standards for community activities. Publication No. 67.
    By—Wisconsin Conference of Social Work. MIMEOGRAPHED—The same, Madison. 1927. 23 p. Free.

FIRE
    See also CITY, COUNTY, AND STATE ADMINISTRATION above.

Standard Schedule for Grading Cities and Towns of the United States with Reference to Their Fire Defenses and Physical Conditions.
    By—National Board of Fire Underwriters. PUBLISHER—The same, New York City. 1917. 80 p. Free.

GOVERNMENT
    See CITY, COUNTY, AND STATE ADMINISTRATION above.

HEALTH AND SANITATION
    See also GENERAL SOCIAL SURVEYS—URBAN; and CHILD HEALTH AND HYGIENE above: and HEALTH IN INDUSTRY; RURAL HEALTH AND SANITATION; SCHOOL HEALTH AND SANITATION; and TUBERCULOSIS below.

An Outline for a Health Survey. In Organized Health Work in Schools. U. S. Department of Interior. Bureau of Education Bulletin, 1913, No. 44.
    By—Ernest Bryant Hoag. PUBLISHER—Superintendent of Documents, Government Printing Office, Washington, D. C. 1913. 5 p. 10 cents per copy.

Relation of the Social Survey to Public Health Authorities. Reprinted from the Public Health Journal, Toronto, Canada, October, 1913.
    By—Franz Schneider, Jr. PUBLISHER—Russell Sage Foundation, New York City. 1913. 4 p. Out of print.

Anopheline Surveys. Methods of conduct and relation to anti-malarial work. Reprint No. 272, Public Health Reports, April 20, 1915.
    By—R. H. van Ezdorf. PUBLISHER—Superintendent of Documents, Government Printing Office, Washington, D. C. 1915. 12 p. 5 cents.

HEALTH AND SANITATION—Continued

The Sanitary Survey: What It Is.
> By—L. H. VanBuskirk. PUBLISHER—Ohio State Board of Health, Columbus. 1915. 6 p. Out of print.

Sanitary Surveys of Institutions.
> By—C.-E. A. Winslow. PUBLISHER—American Home Economics Association, Baltimore, Maryland. 1916. 9 p. Free.

The Application of the Statistical Method to Public Health Research. Reprint from the American Journal of Public Health. Vol. 7, No. 1.
> By—Louis I. Dublin. PUBLISHER—Metropolitan Life Insurance Company, New York City. 1917. 14 p. Free.

Methods of Investigation in Social and Health Problems. Three Papers on: The Necessity for Health Standards, Some Shortcomings of Socio-sanitary Investigations, The Application of Statistical Method to Public Health Research.
> By—Donald B. Armstrong, Franz Schneider, Jr., and Louis I. Dublin. PUBLISHER—Russell Sage Foundation, New York City. 1917. 24 p. 20 cents.

Method of Survey; Bibliography of Survey; Index. Part XI. Cleveland Hospital and Health Survey.
> By—Haven Emerson, Director. PUBLISHER—Cleveland Hospital Council, Cleveland, Ohio, 1920. 89 p. 50 cents and postage.

How to Make a Sanitary Survey. In Health News, May–June.
> By—Theodore Horton. PUBLISHER—New York State Department of Health, Albany. 1921. 14 p. Free.

Hygiene of Maternity and Childhood. Separate No. 1. Child Care and Child Welfare: Outlines for Study. Publication No. 90.
> By—Children's Bureau and Federal Board for Vocational Education. PUBLISHER—Superintendent of Documents, Government Printing Office, Washington, D. C. 1921. 308 p. 30 cents.

Public Health Surveys. What They Are. How to Make Them. How to Use Them.
> By—Murray P. Horwood. PUBLISHER—John Wiley and Sons, New York City. 1921. 403 p. $4.50.

The Value of the Public Health Survey in the Public Health Campaign. Reprinted from February, 1921, issue of the American Journal of Public Health.
> By—Murray P. Horwood and Jules Schevitz. PUBLISHER—American Public Health Association, New York City. 1921. 6 p. 50 cents.

HEALTH AND SANITATION—Continued

The Nature and Purpose of a Health Survey. In New Jersey Public Health News, December, 1922, January, 1923.

    By—Haven Emerson. PUBLISHER—Department of Health, Trenton, New Jersey. 1923. 11 p. Free.

Eighty-Six Cities Studied by Objective Standards. American Journal of Public Health. Vol. XV, No. 5.

    By—American Public Health Association. PUBLISHER—The same, New York City. 1925. 7 p. 50 cents.

Appraisal Form for City Health Work.

    By—Committee on Administrative Practice. PUBLISHER—American Public Health Association, New York City. 1927. 68 p. 50 cents.

Standard Methods for the Control of Communicable Diseases. Reprinted from March, 1927, issue of American Journal of Public Health.

    By—Committee on Standard Regulations for the Control of Communicable Diseases. PUBLISHER—American Public Health Association, New York City. 1927. 24 p. 25 cents.

Committees of the American Public Health Association have made a number of reports setting up standards in reference to other public health questions which will be of value in surveys.

HEALTH IN INDUSTRY

Methods for Field Study of Industrial Fatigue. Reprint No. 458, Public Health Reports, March 15, 1918.

    By—P. Sargent Florence. PUBLISHER—Superintendent of Documents, Government Printing Office, Washington, D. C. 1918. 7 p. 5 cents.

HOSPITALS AND SANATORIA

    See also HEALTH AND SANITATION above.

A County Hospital Survey with Outline of a Survey to Prove the Need for a County Hospital. Public Health Bulletin. Vol. II, No. III.

    By—Robert J. Newton. PUBLISHER—Texas Anti-Tuberculosis Association, Austin. 1913. 4 p. Out of print.

Hospital Survey of a Community. Reprinted from Modern Hospital. State Charities Aid Association Bulletin No. 145.

    By—Joseph J. Weber. PUBLISHER—State Charities Aid Association, New York City. 1917. 6 p. Out of print.

A BIBLIOGRAPHY OF SOCIAL SURVEYS

HOSPITALS AND SANATORIA—Continued

How Should Community Hospital Surveys be Conducted? In Modern Hospital. January, 1926.
> By—Michael M. Davis, Jr., and Haven Emerson. PUBLISHER—Modern Hospital Publishing Company, New York City. 1926. 3 p. 35 cents per copy.

Why the Community Should Be Surveyed. Reprinted from Modern Hospital, March, 1927.
> By—E. H. Lewinski-Corwin. PUBLISHER—United Hospital Fund, New York City. 1927. 5 p. Free.

HOUSING

Housing Reform. A handbook for practical use in American cities. 1910. 213 p. Out of print.

A Model Housing Law. 1920. 430 p. $4.00.
> By—Lawrence Veiller. PUBLISHER—Russell Sage Foundation, New York City.

A Housing Survey. In Annals of the American Academy of Political and Social Science. Vol. LI, January.
> By—Carol Aronovici. PUBLISHER—American Academy of Political and Social Science, Philadelphia, Pennsylvania. 1914. 7 p. Out of print.

Plan for a Housing Survey.
> By—California Commission of Immigration and Housing. PUBLISHER—The same, San Francisco. 1916. 14 p. Free.

Standards Recommended for Permanent Industrial Housing Developments. U. S. Department of Labor. Bureau of Industrial Housing and Transportation.
> By—The Bureau. PUBLISHER—Superintendent of Documents, Government Printing Office, Washington, D. C. 1918. 15 p. Free.

Standards for Improved Housing Laws. In the National Municipal Review. Vol. XVI, No. 10. Total No. 136.
> By—George B. Ford. PUBLISHER—National Municipal League, New York City. 1927. 6 p. 50 cents per copy.

IMMIGRATION AND AMERICANIZATION

See also EDUCATION above.

Is Your Latch-string Out? Suggestions for studying the foreign language groups in your community.
> By—Ruth Walkinshaw. PUBLISHER—National Board, Young Women's Christian Association, New York City. 1920. 26 p. 35 cents.

PURPOSE, METHOD, AND STANDARDS IN SURVEYS

INDUSTRIAL CONDITIONS AND RELATIONS
    See also GENERAL SOCIAL SURVEYS—URBAN; COST OF LIVING; HEALTH IN INDUSTRY; and HOUSING, above.

The Relation of the Short Intensive Industrial Survey to the Problem of Soldier Re-Education. Publications of the Red Cross Institute for Crippled and Disabled Men. Series 1, No. 10.
    BY—G. A. Boate. PUBLISHER—Red Cross Institute for Crippled and Disabled Men, New York City. 1918. 11 p. Free.

The Labor Audit. A method of industrial investigation. Bulletin No. 43. Employment Management Series No. 8.
    BY—Ordway Tead. PUBLISHER—Federal Board for Vocational Education, Washington, D. C. 1920. 47 p. Free.

Standard and Scheduled Hours of Work for Women in Industry. A study based on hour data from thirteen states. U. S. Department of Labor. Bulletin of the Women's Bureau No. 43.
    BY—Ruth I. Voris. PUBLISHER—Superintendent of Documents, Government Printing Office, Washington, D. C. 1925. 68 p. 15 cents.

Industry. Citizens' Survey. Measurement standards for community activities. Publication No. 68.
    BY—Wisconsin Conference of Social Work. MIMEOGRAPHED—The same, Madison. 1927. 47 p. Free.

JAPANESE
    See RACE RELATIONS below.

LIBRARIES
    See GENERAL SOCIAL SURVEYS—URBAN above.

MENTAL HYGIENE
    See also CHILD WELFARE above.

Routine Mental Tests as the Proper Basis of Practical Measures in Social Service. A first study made from 30,000 cases cared for by 27 organizations in Boston and surrounding districts. In Bulletin of the Massachusetts Commission on Mental Diseases. Vol. I, Nos. 1 and 2.
    BY—Helen M. Wright. PUBLISHER—Department of Mental Diseases, Commonwealth of Massachusetts, Boston. 1917. 35 p. Free.

Standardized Fields of Inquiry for Clinical Studies of Borderline Defectives. Reprint No. 8 from Mental Hygiene. Vol. 1, No. 2.
    BY—Walter E. Fernald. PUBLISHER—National Committee for Mental Hygiene, New York City. 1922. 24 p. 25 cents.

NURSERIES AND NURSING
See TUBERCULOSIS below.

PARISH
See RELIGION below.

PLAYGROUNDS
See RECREATION below.

POLICE
See CITY, COUNTY, AND STATE ADMINISTRATION above.

POPULATION
See RACE RELATIONS below.

PRISONS
Suggestions for Grand Jury Survey of Conditions under Which Prisoners Are Kept in County Jails.
>By—Hastings H. Hart. PUBLISHER—Russell Sage Foundation, New York City. 1926. 15 p. Free.

Humanizing Georgia's County Jails. A handbook of standards and information. Second edition.
>By—State Department of Public Welfare. PUBLISHER—The same, Atlanta, Georgia. 1927. 78 p. Free.

RACE RELATIONS
A Race Relations Survey. Suggestions for a study of the oriental population of the Pacific Coast. In Journal of Applied Psychology. Vol. VIII, No. 4.
>By—Robert E. Park. PUBLISHER—University of Southern California, Los Angeles. 1924. 10 p. 40 cents per copy.

The New Social Research.
>By—Emory S. Bogardus. PUBLISHER—Jesse Ray Miller, Los Angeles, California. 1926. 287 p. $3.00.

RECREATION
See also GENERAL SOCIAL SURVEYS—URBAN above.

How a Community May Find Out and Plan for Its Recreation Needs. In Proceedings of the National Education Association.
>By—Rowland Haynes. PUBLISHER—National Education Association, Washington, D. C. 1912. 4 p. Out of print.

PURPOSE, METHOD, AND STANDARDS IN SURVEYS

RECREATION—Continued

Making a Recreation Survey. Reprinted from The Playground, April, 1913.
> By—Rowland Haynes. PUBLISHER—Playground and Recreation Association of America, New York City. 1913. 9 p. 5 cents.

Playground Survey. In American Journal of Sociology. Vol. XIX, No. 6.
> By—Henry S. Curtis. PUBLISHER—American Journal of Sociology, Chicago, Illinois. 1914. 21 p. 50 cents.

Play and Recreation. Separate No. 3. Child Care and Child Welfare: Outlines for Study. Publication No. 92.
> By—Children's Bureau and Federal Board for Vocational Education. PUBLISHER—Superintendent of Documents, Government Printing Office, Washington, D. C. 1921. 44 p. 5 cents.

Community Recreation: Citizens' Survey. Measurement standards for community activities. Publication No. 70.
> By—Wisconsin Conference of Social Work. MIMEOGRAPHED—The same, Madison. 1927. 30 p. Free.

Fundamentals in Community Recreation.
> By—Playground and Recreation Association of America. PUBLISHER—The same, New York City. 1927. 9 p. Free.

RELIGION

> See also GENERAL SOCIAL SURVEYS, both URBAN and RURAL, above: and RELIGIOUS EDUCATION below.

The Community Survey in Relation to Church Efficiency. A guide for workers in the city, town, and country church.
> By—Charles E. Carroll. PUBLISHER—Abingdon Press, New York City. 1915. 122 p. $1.00.

How to Make a Survey. In The Way to Win: Successful Methods in the Local Church.
> By—Fred B. Fisher. PUBLISHER—Methodist Book Concern, New York City. 1915. 28 p. $1.15 per copy.

What Every Church Should Know about Its Community.
> By—Harry F. Ward and Henry A. Atkinson. Rewritten by Shelby M. Harrison and Worth M. Tippy. PUBLISHER—Federal Council, Churches of Christ in America, New York City. 1917. 28 p. Out of print.

RELIGION—Continued

The Malden [Mass.] Survey. A report of the church plants of a typical city, showing the use of the Interchurch World Movement Score Card and Standards for rating city church plants.

By—Walter Scott Athearn, Director. PUBLISHER—Interchurch World Movement of North America [Available through Mr. Athearn, Boston University]. 1919. 213 p. $2.50.

Standards for City Church Plants. To be used with the Interchurch World Movement Score Card for Rating City Churches and Religious Education Plants.

By—N. L. Englehardt and E. S. Evenden. PUBLISHER—Interchurch Press, New York City. 1920. 75 p. Out of print.

The Value of the Social Survey for Religion. In the Journal of Religion. Vol. II, No. 4.

By—Worth M. Tippy. PUBLISHER—University of Chicago Press. 1922. 15 p. 65 cents per copy.

Diagnosing the Rural Church. A study in method. Institute of Social and Religious Research.

By—C. Luther Fry. PUBLISHER—George H. Doran Company, New York City. 1924. 234 p. $1.50.

Surveying Your Community. A handbook of method for the rural church. Institute of Social and Religious Research.

By—Edmund deS. Brunner. PUBLISHER—George H. Doran Company, New York City. 1925. 109 p. $1.00.

Ten Steps towards Your Neighborhood Community. A brief and pioneering survey of a local city church parish.

By—William P. Shriver. PUBLISHER—Federal Council, Churches of Christ in America, New York City. 1926. 16 p. 10 cents.

1000 City Churches. Phases of adaptation to urban environment. Institute of Social and Religious Research.

By—H. Paul Douglass. PUBLISHER—George H. Doran Company, New York City. 1926. 380 p. $4.00.

Standard Religion: Citizens' Survey. Measurement standards for community activities. Publication No. 73.

By—Wisconsin Conference of Social Work. MIMEOGRAPHED—The same, Madison. 1927. 13 p. Free.

RELIGIOUS EDUCATION

See also RELIGION above.

INDIANA SURVEY OF RELIGIOUS EDUCATION. Institute of Social and Religious Research.

RELIGIOUS EDUCATION—Continued

Vol. II. Measurements and Standards in Religious Education. 565 p.

Vol. III. Religious Education Survey Schedules. 271 p.

Vol. I is listed in Part II under Religious Education.

By—Walter S. Athearn. PUBLISHER—George H. Doran Company, New York City. 1924. $5.00 each.

RURAL

See also GENERAL SOCIAL SURVEYS, both URBAN and RURAL; and RELIGION above: and RURAL EDUCATION; and RURAL HEALTH AND SANITATION below.

STUDIES OF FARM LIFE.

An Economic Study of a Farm Layout. By W. I. Myers. 1920. 139 p.

The Standard of Life in a Typical Section of Diversified Farming. By E. L. Kirkpatrick. 1923. 133 p.

PUBLISHER—Agricultural Experiment Station, Cornell University, Ithaca. Free.

RURAL EDUCATION

The Rural School and the Community. A study of the methods and application of the social survey.

By—Howard T. Lewis. PUBLISHER—Gorham Press, Boston, Massachusetts. 1918. 91 p. $1.50.

Social Surveys of Rural School Districts: How Made and How Utilized. Circular 122.

By—C. J. Galpin, C. W. Davies, and Grace Wyman Stone. PUBLISHER—University of Wisconsin, Madison. 1920. 24 p. 10 cents.

Surveying Rural Schools. Bulletin of the Iowa State Teachers College, Vol. XXII, No. 3.

By—Fred D. Cram. PUBLISHER—Iowa State Teachers College, Cedar Falls. 1922. 75 p. Free.

RURAL HEALTH AND SANITATION

Appraisal Form for Rural Health Work. For experimental use in rural counties, districts, or other similar areas.

By—Committee on Administrative Practice. PUBLISHER—American Public Health Association, New York City. 1927. 72 p. 50 cents.

SANITATION

See HEALTH AND SANITATION; and RURAL HEALTH AND SANITATION above: and SCHOOL HEALTH AND SANITATION below.

SCHOOL BUILDINGS AND PLANTS

Score Card for City School Buildings. Teachers College Bulletin. Seventh Series No. 12.

By—George Drayton Strayer. PUBLISHER—Teachers College, Columbia University, New York City. 1916. 11 p. Out of print.

SCHOOL HEALTH AND SANITATION

Sanitary Survey for Schools and Diagnostic Table. Reprint from the Health Index of Children.

By—Ernest B. Hoag. PUBLISHER—Whitaker and Ray-Wiggin Company, San Francisco, California. 1910. 21 p. Out of print.

Sanitary Schoolhouses. Legal requirements in Indiana and Ohio. U. S. Department of Interior. Bureau of Education Bulletin, 1913, No. 52. Whole No. 563.

By—Bureau of Education. PUBLISHER—Superintendent of Documents, Government Printing Office, Washington, D. C. 1913. 40 p. 5 cents.

Schoolhouse Sanitation. A study of the laws and regulations governing the hygiene and sanitation of schoolhouses. U. S. Department of Interior. Bureau of Education Bulletin, 1915, No. 21. Whole No. 648.

By—William A. Cook. PUBLISHER—Superintendent of Documents, Government Printing Office, Washington, D. C. 1915. 69 p. 10 cents.

Sanitary School Surveys as a Health Protective Measure.

By—J. H. Berkowitz. PUBLISHER—New York Association for Improving the Condition of the Poor, New York City. 1916. 9 p. Out of print.

Health Trends in Secondary Education. Fifty-three schools analyze their health programs.

By—Emma Dolfinger and others. PUBLISHER—American Child Health Association, New York City. 1927. 153 p. $1.00.

SCHOOL ORGANIZATION AND ADMINISTRATION

See EDUCATION above.

SOCIAL AGENCIES

See GENERAL SOCIAL SURVEYS—URBAN above.

TUBERCULOSIS

A Survey Nurse and a Nurse's Tuberculosis Survey for a Small Community. Reprint from the Trained Nurse and Hospital Review, January and February, 1917.
    By—Philip P. Jacobs. PUBLISHER—Trained Nurse and Hospital Review, New York City. 1917. 8 p. Out of print.

A Method for Making a County Tuberculosis Survey. In Tuberculosis Survey Number of Health News. New Series. Vol. XIV, No. 3.
    By—Halsey J. Hall. PUBLISHER—State Department of Health, Albany. 1919. 5 p. Free.

The County Tuberculosis Survey. Suggestions for making, recording, analyzing, and reporting tuberculosis surveys.
    By—Frank W. LeClere, Director. PUBLISHER—Illinois Tuberculosis Association, Springfield. 1920. 6 p. Free.

Suggestions for Making a Tuberculosis Survey. In the Public Health Nurse. Vol. 13.
    By—Jessamine S. Whitney. PUBLISHER—National Association for Public Health Nursing, New York City. 1921. 7 p. 25 cents per copy.

Survey and Statistical Methods. Chapter XVI of the Tuberculosis Worker.
    By—Philip P. Jacobs. PUBLISHER—Williams and Wilkins Company, Baltimore, Maryland. 1923. 11 p. $3.00.

Tuberculosis Case-finding Surveys. Technical Series No. 3.
    By—Jessamine S. Whitney. PUBLISHER—National Tuberculosis Association, New York City. 1925. 32 p. Free.

UNEMPLOYMENT

Public Employment Offices. Their purpose, structure, and methods.
    By—Shelby M. Harrison in collaboration with Bradley Buell, Mary LaDame, Leslie E. Woodcock, and Frederick A. King. PUBLISHER—Russell Sage Foundation, New York City. 1924. 685 p. $3.50.

VOCATIONAL GUIDANCE AND TRAINING

The Educational Survey Preparatory to the Organization of Vocational Education. In Teachers College Record. Vol. XIV, No. 1.
    By—Leonard Righter. PUBLISHER—Teachers College, Columbia University, New York City. 1913. 40 p. 30 cents per copy.

Vocational Education and Guidance of Youth; an Outline for Study.
    By—Emily Robison. PUBLISHER—H. W. Wilson Company, New York City. 1917. 66 p. 35 cents.

ZONING

See GENERAL SOCIAL SURVEYS—URBAN; and CITY AND REGIONAL PLANNING above.

A number of other publications dealing with purpose, methods, and standards in surveys, which have appeared since this listing was closed, are given on page xxxiii of the Introduction.

PART IV
GEOGRAPHICAL INDEX
Surveys Classified by Localities

	Page
AFRICA	
Education in Africa, 1922	92
Survey of Field and Work [Religion], 1919 [Under United States]	266
ALABAMA	
Cry of Children. Study of child labor, 1908	29
Child Welfare in Alabama, 1918	38
Study of Alabama Laws Affecting Children, 1922	38
Alabama's Public School System, 1916	92
Comparative Study of Elementary Schools, 1921	92
Educational Study of Alabama, 1919	92
Women in Alabama Industries, 1924	181
Rural School Attendance, 1918	271
Studies in Public School Finance, 1925 [Under Arkansas]	288
Social Problems, 1918	298
Social Progress, 1922	299
Birmingham	
Birmingham, 1912	1
Newsboys in Birmingham, 1922	29
City Plan for Birmingham, 1919	48
Public Health Administration, 1916	134
Study of Violent Deaths, 1924 [Under Georgia, Atlanta]	327
Covington County	
Educational Survey of Three Counties, 1914	92
Jefferson County	
Public Health Administration, 1916	134
Macon County	
Educational Survey, 1914	92
Morgan County	
Educational Survey, 1914	92
ALASKA	
Survey of Education in Alaska, 1886	92
Reports of Investigation . . . of School Service, 1906	92
Work of Bureau of Education, 1921	92
Education in Territories and Dependencies, 1919	92
Sanitary Conditions in Alaska, 1914	140
Studies in Public School Finance, 1925 [Under Illinois]	290
AMERICA	
Religious Work among Italians, 1917	209
Theological Education in America, 1924	267

A BIBLIOGRAPHY OF SOCIAL SURVEYS

PAGE

ARGENTINA
    Immigration Situation in Other Countries, 1911 [Under United States]. 180

ARIZONA
    Social Survey of Arizona, 1921 10
    Educational Conditions in Arizona, 1918 93
    Survey of Arizona Public School System, 1925 93
    Public Health Administration, 1922 134
    Report of Mental Hygiene Survey, 1922 219
    Interstate Migration of Tuberculous Persons, 1915 312
    Maricopa County
        Report of School Survey, 1916. 93
    Phoenix
        Malta Fever in Southwest, 1922 [Under United States] . . . 153
        Report of Indigent Migratory Consumptives, 1923 312
    Tucson
        Report of Survey of University, 1922 93
        Survey of Tucson [Health], 1920 140

ARKANSAS
    Rural Survey in Arkansas, 1913 10
    Report on Higher Educational Institutions, 1922 93
    Public School System of Arkansas, 1923. 93
    Report of Commission for Feebleminded, 1915 128
    Feebleminded: Their Prevalence and Needs, 1916 . . . 128
    Women in Arkansas Industries, 1923 182
    Public School System, 1923 288
    Studies in Public School Finance, 1925 288
    Bradley County
        Survey of Conditions Affecting Children [Health], 1923 . . . 27
    Fayetteville
        Educational Survey of University of Arkansas, 1921 . . . 93
    Fort Smith
        Educational Survey, 1920 93
    Little Rock
        Community Study of Little Rock, 1921 1
        Report on Park System for Little Rock, 1913 48
        Report of Vice Commission, 1913 325
    Warren
        Survey of Conditions Affecting Children [Health], 1923 . . . 27

ASIA MINOR, Smyrna
    Survey of Some Social Conditions, 1921. 1

GEOGRAPHICAL INDEX

                                                                    PAGE
AUSTRALIA
    Immigration Situation in Other Countries, 1911 [Under United
      States] 180

BELGIUM
    Part-Time Schools, 1922 [Under United States] 72

BRAZIL
    Immigration Situation in Other Countries, 1911 [Under United
      States] 180

CALIFORNIA
    ACCIDENTS AND ACCIDENT PREVENTION
      Report to Industrial Accident Commission, 1919 16
    CHILD WELFARE
      Child Welfare Work in California, 1916 38
      Experimental Study of Abnormal Children, 1918 38
    CONTINUATION AND PART-TIME SCHOOLS
      Administration of Part-Time Schools, 1924 71
    COST OF LIVING
      Cost of Living Survey, 1923 73
    DELINQUENCY AND CORRECTION
      Intelligence and Delinquency, 1915 85
      Delinquency and Density of Population, 1917 85
    EDUCATION
      Report of Special Legislative Committee, 1920 94
    HOUSING
      Report of Survey on Housing, 1915 162
    IMMIGRATION AND AMERICANIZATION
      Americanization of Foreign-born Women, 1917 176
      Report on Large Landholdings in Southern California, 1919 . . 176
    JAPANESE
      Preliminary Report on Mental Capacity, 1922 211
    JUVENILE DELINQUENCY
      Study of 150 Delinquent Boys, 1915 212
    MENTAL HYGIENE
      Surveys in Mental Deviation in Prisons, 1918 219
    PRISONS
      Study of County Jails in California, 1918 245
    RECREATION
      Report of State Recreational Inquiry Committee, 1914 . . . 253
    RELIEF
      County Outdoor Relief, 1918 259
    RURAL
      Study of Farm Labor, 1918 268
    SCHOOL ORGANIZATION AND ADMINISTRATION
      Studies in Public School Finance, 1922 288

A BIBLIOGRAPHY OF SOCIAL SURVEYS

	PAGE
Cost of Education in California, 1924	289
SOCIAL INSURANCE	
Report of Social Insurance, 1917	303
TAXATION	
Report of State Tax Commission, 1917	306
TUBERCULOSIS	
Report of Tuberculosis Commission, 1914	312
Interstate Migration, 1915	313
UNEMPLOYMENT	
Unemployment, 1914	321
Report on Unemployment, 1914	321
Report on Relief, 1915	321

Alameda
Report of Housing, 1918 162

Alameda County
Survey of Medical Social Service, 1927 134
Report of Housing and Industrial Survey, 1918 182
Survey of Social Agencies, 1917 299

Bakersfield
Survey of Pupils in Schools, 1920 94

Berkeley
Report on City Plan, 1915 48
Report of Housing, 1918 162
Report of Housing and Industrial Survey, 1918 182
Study of Social Work, 1926 299

Eureka
School Building Survey, 1924 280

Fresno
Report of Immigration Problem, 1918 176
Study of Vocational Conditions, 1926 328

Los Angeles
GENERAL SOCIAL SURVEYS—URBAN
    Better City, 1907 1
    Community Survey, 1918 1
    Study of Housing and Social Conditions, 1918 . . . 2
BOY LIFE
    City Boy and His Problems, 1926 22
CITY AND REGIONAL PLANNING
    Report of Municipal Art Commission, 1909 48
CITY, COUNTY, AND STATE ADMINISTRATION
    Administrative Methods of City Government, 1913 . . 61
COST OF LIVING
    Relation of Wages to Cost of Living, 1921 74

GEOGRAPHICAL INDEX

	PAGE
FAMILY WELFARE	
Social Work with Families, 1925	127
GARBAGE, REFUSE, AND SEWAGE	
Report of Special Sewage Disposal, 1921	132
HOUSING	
Reports of Housing Commission, 1908–09–10	162
IMMIGRATION AND AMERICANIZATION	
Children of Immigrants in Schools, 1911 [Under United States]	179
INDUSTRIAL CONDITIONS AND RELATIONS	
Social Aspects of Fishing Industry, 1921	182
JUVENILE DELINQUENCY	
Causes of Delinquency, 1919	212
LIBRARIES	
Social Survey Report, 1915	216
MEXICANS	
Mexican Housing Problem, 1920	226
RUSSIANS	
Russians in Los Angeles, 1918	279
SCHOOL ORGANIZATION AND ADMINISTRATION	
Report of Advisory Committee, 1916	289
TRUANCY AND NON-ATTENDANCE	
Causes of Truancy among Boys, 1917	311
Causes of Truancy among Girls, 1917	311
TUBERCULOSIS	
Report of Indigent Migratory Consumptives, 1923 [Under Arizona, Phoenix]	312
Los Angeles County	
Causes of Fatal Accidents, 1916	16
Japanese in Rural Los Angeles County, 1920	211
Report of Committee, 1914	212
Marin County	
Rural Survey of Marin and Sonoma Counties, 1916	10
Modoc County	
Modoc County Mental Survey, 1922	219
Napa	
School Building Survey, 1921	280
Nevada County	
Report of Survey of Schools, 1921	94
Oakland	
San Francisco Cancer Survey, 1922–24–25–26 [Under California, San Francisco]	23
Plan of Civic Improvement, 1913	48
Report on City Plan, 1915	48
Report of Housing and Industrial Survey, 1918	182

A BIBLIOGRAPHY OF SOCIAL SURVEYS

                                                                   PAGE

  Summary of Survey of School Department, 1915 289
  Vocational Guidance and Junior Placement, 1925 328

Orange County
  Irrigation and Religion, 1922 260

Pasadena
  Progress Report of City Planning Commission, 1917 48

Riverside
  Survey of Contagious Disease Situation, 1918 285

Sacramento
  Report of Commission on Investigation [City and Regional Planning], 1916 48

San Diego
  Pathfinder Social Survey, 1914 2
  Comprehensive Plan for Improvement [City and Regional Planning], 1908 48

San Francisco
  BOY LIFE
    Study of . . . Boy Scouts, 1924 22
  CANCER
    Cancer Survey, 1922–24–25–26 23
  CHILD LABOR
    Child Labor on Stage, 1924 29
  CITY AND REGIONAL PLANNING
    Report on Improvement and Adornment, 1904 49
  CITY, COUNTY, AND STATE ADMINISTRATION
    Survey Report of Government of City and County, 1916 . . 62
  CRIPPLED, DISABLED, AND HANDICAPPED
    Care of Disabled Veterans and Ex-Service Men, 1924 . . . 81
  EDUCATION
    Some Conditions in Schools, 1914 94
    Public School System, 1917 94
  HEALTH AND SANITATION
    Report of Commission . . . for Investigation of Plague, 1901. 140
  HOMELESS
    Study of Homeless Men Problem, 1924 159
  HOSPITALS AND SANATORIA
    Survey of Hospital and Health Agencies, 1923 160
  HOUSING
    Reports of Housing Association, 1911–13 162
    Study of Housing Conditions, 1927 162
  IMMIGRATION AND AMERICANIZATION
    Children of Immigrants in Schools, 1911 [Under United States] . 179
  INDUSTRIAL CONDITIONS AND RELATIONS
    Survey of Garment Trades, 1921 182

GEOGRAPHICAL INDEX

	PAGE
PENSIONS	
Public Pensions to Widows with Children, 1913	240
RECREATION	
Public Recreation, 1913	253
Character Building Resources, 1926	253
RELIGION	
Church in Greater San Francisco, 1921	260
VENEREAL DISEASE	
Red Plague, 1st Report, 1911	324
Red Plague, 2d Report, 1913	324
San Jose	
Beautifying of San Jose, 1909	49
San Mateo County	
Reorganizing a County System [Rural Education], 1916	271
San Rafael	
School Building Survey, 1922	280
Santa Ana	
Exceptional Children in Schools, 1918	304
Santa Barbara	
Report Regarding Civic Affairs, 1909	49
Santa Monico	
School Housing Survey, 1927	280
Sonoma County	
Rural Survey of Marin and Sonoma County, 1916	10
Stanislaus County	
Irrigation and Religion, 1922	260
Tulare County	
Rural Survey, 1915	10
Vallejo	
Survey of Educational Progress, 1926	94

CANADA

Rural Survey of Swan River Valley, 1913	10
Report of Rural Survey, 1914	10
Rural Planning and Development, 1917	10
Part-Time Schools, 1922 [Under United States]	72
Medical Education in United States and Canada, 1910 [Under United States]	121
Education in Maritime Provinces of Canada, 1922	94
Dental Education in United States and Canada, 1926 [Under United States]	122
Immigration Situation in Other Countries, 1911 [Under United States]	180
Industrial Occupations for Women, 1919	182

A BIBLIOGRAPHY OF SOCIAL SURVEYS

	PAGE
Shop Collective Bargaining, 1922	182
Tentative Findings of Survey, 1925	253
Theological Education in America, 1924 [Under America]	267
Rural Schools in Canada, 1913.	271
Report of Royal Commission on Industrial Training, 1913	328

British Columbia
Report of British Columbia Child Welfare Study, 1927 . . . 38

Fort William
Preliminary and General Social Survey, 1913 2

Hamilton
Preliminary and General Social Survey, 1913 2

Hull
Report of Federal Plan Commission, 1915 49

London
Preliminary and General Social Survey, 1913 2

Montreal
City below the Hill [General], 1897 2
Child Health Studies in Montreal, 1921 27
Social Study along Health Lines, 1920 70
Report on Montreal Typhoid Fever, etc., 1927 140
Social and Financial Survey [Social Agencies], 1919 . . . 299

New Brunswick
Report on Sanitary Survey, 1917 140

Ontario
Mothers' Allowances [Family Welfare], 1920 127
Report on Care . . . of Mentally Deficient, 1919 . . 128
Report of Ontario Housing Committee, 1919 162
Study of Illegitimacy, 1921 173
School System of Ontario, 1915 271
Report of Commission on Unemployment, 1916 321

Ottawa
Report of Federal Plan Commission [City and Regional Planning], 1915 49

Port Arthur
Report of Preliminary and General Social Survey, 1913 . . . 2

Province of Quebec
Child Health Studies, 1921 27

Regina
Report of Preliminary and General Social Survey, 1913 . . . 2

Saskatchewan
Survey of Education, 1918 95
Report to Government [Tuberculosis], 1922 313

GEOGRAPHICAL INDEX

                                                                                                PAGE

Sydney
    Report of Preliminary and General Social Survey, 1913 . . . 2

Toronto
    GENERAL SOCIAL SURVEYS—URBAN
        What Is Ward Going to Do with Toronto? 1918 2
    CHARITIES
        Report of Charities Commission, 1912 24
    CITY AND REGIONAL PLANNING
        Report of Civic Improvement Committee, 1911 49
    CRIPPLED, DISABLED, AND HANDICAPPED
        Report of Survey of Physically Handicapped, 1924 . . . 82
    DETENTION
        Detention Home, 1920 90
    HEALTH ADMINISTRATION
        Administrative Study of Toronto Department, 1915 . . . 134
    HEALTH IN INDUSTRY
        Survey of General Conditions, 1921 154
    SCHOOL BUILDINGS AND PLANTS
        Interim Reports of Toronto School Survey, 1920 280
        Twelve Hour Working Day for School Buildings, 1921 . . 280
    SCHOOL HEALTH AND SANITATION
        Prevalence of Malnutrition, 1921. 285
    SLUMS
        Report . . . Dealing with Recent, 1911 298
    VICE
        Report of Social Survey Commission, 1915 325
    PURPOSE, METHOD, AND STANDARDS
        Report of Brief Investigation, 1913 335
        Plan and Scope of Social Welfare Study, 1921 337

Vancouver
    Report of Preliminary and General Social Survey, 1913 . . . 2

Winnipeg
    Report on Housing Survey, 1919 162
    Second Housing Survey, 1921 162
    Work of Women and Girls, 1914 182

CANAL ZONE
    Education in Territories and Dependencies, 1919 [Under Alaska] . 92

CENTRAL AMERICA
    Survey of Field and Work, 1919 [Under United States] . . . 266

CHINA
    Enquiry into Scientific Efficiency, 1920 47
    Christian Education in China, 1922 47
    Comparative Study of Health, 1920 [Under Japan] 143

A BIBLIOGRAPHY OF SOCIAL SURVEYS

	PAGE
Health of Missionary Families, 1921	140
Survey of Field and Work, 1919 [Under United States]	266

Peking
Social Survey, 1921	2
Peking Rugs and Peking Boys, 1925	47

Phenix Village (Kwantung)
Country Life in South China, 1925	10

Sung-Ka-Hong
Social Survey, 1924	2

Yenshan County, Chihli Province
Economic and Social Survey, 1926	10

COLORADO

CHILD LABOR
Child Labor in Sugar-Beet Fields, 1916	29
Children Working on Farms, 1925	30

CHILD WELFARE
Child Welfare Work, 1920	38

CITY, COUNTY, AND STATE ADMINISTRATION
Reports on State Affairs (8 reports), 1916	62

DELINQUENCY AND CORRECTION
Report on Care of Dependents, Delinquents, 1918	85

EDUCATION
General Survey of Public High School, 1914	95

HEALTH ADMINISTRATION
Public Health Administration, 1916	135

INDUSTRIAL CONDITIONS AND RELATIONS
Child Labor and Work of Mothers, 1923	182

MEXICANS
Spanish and Mexican in Colorado, 1924	226

PRISONS
Colorado Report on State Penal Institutions, 1924	245

RELIGION
Church and Industrial Warfare, 1920	261

RURAL EDUCATION
Rural and Village Schools, 1914	271

SCHOOL ORGANIZATION AND ADMINISTRATION
Study of Colorado School Revenues, 1916	289
Consolidated Schools, 1921	289
Report of Inquiry into Administration, 1917	289
Studies in Public School Finance, 1922 [Under California]	288
Financing of Public Higher Education, 1924	289

TAXATION
Work of Colorado Tax Commission, 1916	306

GEOGRAPHICAL INDEX

                                                                                                PAGE

TUBERCULOSIS
    Interstate Migration of Tuberculous Persons, 1915 [Under Arizona] 312
UNEMPLOYMENT
    Report of Committee on Unemployment, 1916 321

Archuleta County
    Public Schools of Archuleta County, 1920 95

Boulder
    Improvement of Boulder [City Planning], 1910 49

Boulder County
    Boulder County Studies [General], 1921 2

Colorado Springs
    Colorado Springs: A City Beautiful, 1912 49
    Report on Philanthropic Work and Social Agencies, 1913 . . . 299
    Report of Indigent Migratory Consumptives, 1923 [Under Arizona, Phoenix] 312

Denver
    CHARITIES
        Summary Report of Field Survey, 1916 24
    CITY AND REGIONAL PLANNING
        Proposed Plan for City of Denver, 1906 49
    CITY, COUNTY, AND STATE ADMINISTRATION
        Report on Survey of Certain Departments, 1914 62
    EDUCATION
        Report of School Survey, Part II, 1916 95
    HEALTH AND SANITATION
        Survey of Some Communicable Diseases, 1927 140
    INDUSTRIAL CONDITIONS AND RELATIONS
        Denver and Farm Labor Families, 1925 183
    SCHOOL BUILDINGS AND PLANTS
        Report of School Survey, 1916 280
    SCHOOL ORGANIZATION AND ADMINISTRATION
        General Organization and Management, 1916 289
        Business Management, 1916 289
        Summary of Recommendations, 1916 290
    TUBERCULOSIS
        Limited Investigation of Housing, 1920 313
        Results of Survey of Tuberculosis, 1920 313
        Report of Indigent Migratory Consumptives, 1923 [Under Arizona, Phoenix] 312
    VICE
        Report of Morals Commission, 1913 325
    VOCATIONAL GUIDANCE AND TRAINING
        Report of School Survey, 1916 328

A BIBLIOGRAPHY OF SOCIAL SURVEYS

PAGE

Denver County
  Report on Survey, 1914 62
  Report of Morals Commission, 1913 325
Fruita
  Educational Survey of Fruita, 1921 95
Grand Junction
  Survey of City Schools, 1916 95
Sterling
  Self-Survey of Sterling Public Schools, 1917 95
  Outbreaks of Botulism, 1924 [Under Oregon, Albany] . . . 150
Weld County
  Farm and School, 1918 271

CONNECTICUT
  ALMSHOUSES
    Some American Almshouses, 1927 19
  CHILD LABOR
    Administration of Child Labor Laws, 1915 30
    Child Laborers, 1916 30
    Industrial Instability of Child Workers, 1920 30
  CHILD WELFARE
    Report of Connecticut Commission, 1883 38
    Problem of County Home Child, 1921 39
  EDUCATION
    Report of Special Educational Commission, 1909 . . . 95
    Survey of Writing Vocabularies, 1921 96
  HEALTH IN INDUSTRY
    Study of Dust Hazards, 1920 154
  ILLEGITIMACY
    Study of Children Born Out of Wedlock, 1927 174
  INDUSTRIAL CONDITIONS AND RELATIONS
    Conditions of Labor of Women Factory Workers, 1913 . . 183
    Department Store Girl, 1914 183
    Report of Special Commission, 1913–14–16–18–22 . . . 183
  JUVENILE DELINQUENCY
    Children before the Courts, 1918 212
    Legal Handling of Juvenile Offenders, 1921 212
  NURSERIES AND NURSING
    Survey of Public Health Nursing, 1918 238
  PRISONS
    Report of Commission on Convict Labor, 1915 245
  SCHOOL ORGANIZATION AND ADMINISTRATION
    Survey of Organization and Administration, 1921 . . . 290
  TUBERCULOSIS
    Report of Special Commission, 1908 313
    Incidence of Tuberculosis among Polishers, 1921 . . . 313

GEOGRAPHICAL INDEX

PAGE

Bridgeport
Report on Department of Public Charities, 1912 25
Preliminary Report [City and Regional Planning], 1915 . . . 49
Better City Planning, 1916 49
Report of Study of Financial Conditions, 1921 62
Report of Examination of School System, 1913 96
Brief Survey of Housing Conditions, 1914 162
Munition Makers, 1917 183
Home Work in Bridgeport, 1920 183
Report and Recommendations [Vice], 1916 325

Bristol
Local Survey and City Planning Proposals, 1920 50

Chaplin
Educational Inquiry, 1917 95

East Windsor
Educational Inquiry, 1917 95

Glastonbury
Educational Inquiry, 1916 95

Greenwich
Report of Special Committee [Education], 1911 . . . 96
Public Health Survey, 1925 141

Hartford
Plan of City of Hartford, 1912 50
Report of Vice Commission, 1913 325

Kent
Educational Inquiry, 1907 95

Meriden
Children of Immigrants in Schools, 1911 [Under United States] . . 179
School Building Program for Meriden, 1920 280

Middlefield
Educational Inquiry, 1917 95

Middletown
Health Survey of Middletown, 1917 141

New Britain
Housing Conditions in New Britain, 1912 163
Children of Immigrants in Schools, 1911 [Under United States] . . 179

New Hartford
Educational Inquiry, 1917 96

New Haven
Report of Civic Improvement Commission, 1910 . . . 50
Health of New Haven, 1913 141

A BIBLIOGRAPHY OF SOCIAL SURVEYS

	PAGE
Health Survey, 1917	141
Report on New Haven Health Center, 1923	141
Summary of New Haven Tenement House Investigation, 1902	163
Housing Conditions in New Haven, 1913	163
Industrial Survey, 1913	183
Study of Problem of Girl Delinquency, 1915	212
New Haven County Jail, 1918	245
Report of Survey Committee [Social Agencies], 1924	299
Exceptional Children and Public School Policy, 1921	304

New London
Suggestions Concerning Closer Unity [Charities], 1913 . . . 25

Newton
Educational Inquiry, 1917 96

North Stonington
Educational Inquiry, 1916 96

Seymour
Educational Inquiry, 1916 96

Stamford
Mirror: As We See Ourselves [Education], 1918 96
Report of Survey of Public School System, 1923 96

Trumbull
Educational Inquiry, 1917 96

Waterbury
Survey of Cost of Living, 1920. 74
Report of Study of Juvenile Court, 1926 85
Help Your School Surveys, 1913 96
Report of Committee [Housing], 1918 163
Infant Mortality, 1918 204
Report of Special Commission [Relief], 1894 259

Westbrook
Educational Inquiry, 1917 96

West Hartford
Survey of Schools of West Hartford, 1923 97

CUBA
Survey of Field and Work, 1919 [Under United States] . . 266

CZECHOSLOVAKIA
Survey of Economic and Social Conditions, 1924 2

Prague
American Spirit in Heart of Europe, 1921 3

DELAWARE
People Who Go to Tomatoes, 1914 39
Chance of Delaware Child, 1920 39

GEOGRAPHICAL INDEX

	PAGE
Children Deprived of Parental Care, 1921	39
County Administration, 1919	62
Public Education, 1919	97
Women in Delaware Industries, 1927	184
Women's Employment in Vegetable Canneries, 1927	184
Negro School Attendance, 1923	231
Possible Consolidation of Rural Schools, 1919	271
One Teacher School, 1925	272
Report and Recommendations, 1919	281
General Report on School Buildings and Grounds, 1919	281
Administrative Government, 1918	343

Hare's Corner
Special Investigation, 1920 39

New Castle County
Mental Status, 1916 220
Social Study of Mental Defectives, 1917 220

Sussex County
Mental Defect, 1919 220

Wilmington
Survey of Schools, 1921 97
War-Time Housing, 1918 163
Industrial Education in Wilmington, 1918 202
Survey of Schools of Wilmington, 1921 290
Study of Non-Promotion, 1923 304
New Castle County Workhouse, 1920 333

DENMARK
Part-Time Schools, 1922 [Under United States] . . . 72

DISTRICT OF COLUMBIA
Report of Committee [Child Welfare], 1915 . . . 39
Child Welfare, 1924 39
Law and Public Welfare, 1925 40
High Cost of Living, 1919 74
Child Dependency, 1924 88
Preliminary Survey of Schools, 1920 97
Hours, Earnings, and Duration of Employment, 1913 . . 184
Mental Defectives, 1915 220
Penal System of District of Columbia, 1920 245
Facilities for Children's Play, 1917 253
Playground Facilities, 1921 253
Special Report on Schoolhouse Accommodations, 1920 . . 281
Report of Commission Appointed to Investigate [Workhouses], 1909 333

Washington
Neglected Neighbors, 1909 3

A BIBLIOGRAPHY OF SOCIAL SURVEYS

	PAGE
Child Labor at National Capital, 1912	30
Preliminary Report [City and Regional Planning], 1924	50
Reports of President's Home Commission, 1908	163
Inhabited Alleys, 1912	163
Industrial Survey, 1925	184
Recreation and Amusement among Negroes, 1927	254

ELLIS ISLAND

Report of Commission [Immigration], 1904	176
Mental Examination of Immigrants, 1917	176
Mentality of Arriving Immigrant, 1917	176
Psychological Study of Immigrant Children, 1926	176

ENGLAND

Part-Time Schools, 1922 [Under United States]	72
Munition Makers, 1917 [Under Connecticut, Bridgeport]	183
Midwife in England, 1913	226
English Prisons Today, 1922	245

York

Unemployment: A Social Study, 1911	321

EUROPE

Medical Education in Europe, 1912	97
Survey of Field and Work, 1919 [Under United States]	266

FLORIDA

Study of Florida High Schools, 1921	97
Public Health Administration, 1916	135
Survey of Florida County Jails, 1922	245
Study of Conditions of Rural Schools, 1922	272

Jacksonville

Family Status of Breadwinning Women, 1925	184

Manitee County

School Hygiene, 1915	285

Tampa

Report of Survey of Schools, 1926	97

FRANCE

Part-Time Schools, 1922 [Under United States]	72
Illegitimacy Laws, 1919 [Under United States]	175
Munition Makers, 1917 [Under Connecticut, Bridgeport]	183

GEORGIA

Cry of Children, 1908 [Under Alabama]	29
Child Labor in Georgia, 1910	30
Dependent and Delinquent Children, 1926	40
Notes on Negro Crime, 1904	79

GEOGRAPHICAL INDEX

	PAGE
Women in Georgia Industries, 1922	184
Mental Defect in a Southern State, 1919	220
Economic Cooperation among Negroes, 1917	233
Maternity and Infant Care [Rural], 1923	276
Trachoma, 1914 [Under Tennessee]	310
Crusade against Tuberculosis in Georgia, 1914	313
Humanizing Georgia's County Jails, 1927	352

Athens
Report of Survey, 1921	3
Sanitary Conditions among Negroes, 1905	233
Negroes of Athens, 1913	232
School Building Program, 1921	281
Georgia Club at State Normal School, 1913	339

Atlanta
Organization . . . of City Government, 1912	62
Report of Survey of . . . Health and Education, 1912	98
Survey of Atlanta Public Schools, 1914	98
Report of Survey of Public School System, 1924	99
Report of Survey of Department of Health, 1912	141
Survey of Public Health Situation, 1913	141
Preliminary Report of Survey of Wages, 1920	185
Report of Vice Commission, 1912	325
Vocational Guidance and Junior Placement, 1925 [Under California, Oakland]	328
Study of Violent Deaths, 1924	327

Augusta
Augusta Survey, 1924	3

Bacon County
Educational Survey, 1922	97

Ben Hill County
Educational Survey, 1918	97

Bibb County
Social and Economic Survey, 1913	11

Brooks County
Educational Survey, 1917	98

Brunswick
Survey of Schools, 1920	99

Bulloch County
Educational Survey, 1915	98

Candler County
Educational Survey, 1918	98

Carroll County
Educational Survey, 1918	98

A BIBLIOGRAPHY OF SOCIAL SURVEYS

PAGE

Clarke County
Report of Survey of Athens and Clarke County, 1921 . . . 3
School Conditions in Clarke County, 1916 231
Rural Survey of Clarke County [Negroes], 1915 233
Negroes of Clarke County, 1919 233

Clayton County
Educational Survey, 1915 98

Columbus
City Plan, 1926 50
Industrial Education, 1913 202

Decatur
Educational Survey, 1918 99

Dekalb County
Educational Survey, 1916 98

Dooly County
Educational Survey, 1922 98

Floyd County
Social and Economic Survey [Rural], 1917 11

Fulton County
Social and Economic Survey [Rural], 1913 11

Gainesville
Negro Women of Gainesville, 1921 233

Glynn County
Survey of Schools, 1920 99

Grady County
Educational Survey, 1922 98

Gwinnett County
Educational Survey, 1923 98

Hart County
Educational Survey, 1917 98

Heard County
Educational Survey, 1917 98

Jackson County
Educational Survey, 1915 98

Johnson County
Educational Survey, 1921 98

Jones County
Educational Survey, 1918 98

Laurens County
Educational Survey, 1921 98

Lee County
Educational Survey, 1920 98

GEOGRAPHICAL INDEX

	PAGE
Miller County	
Educational Survey, 1920	98
Millidgeville	
Report of Findings of Survey [Health], 1917	141
Morgan County	
Educational Survey, 1915	98
Muscogee County	
Social and Economic Survey [Rural], 1917	11
Putnam County	
Social and Economic Survey [Rural], 1912	11
Rabun County	
Educational Survey, 1914	98
Richmond County	
Augusta Survey, 1924	3
Rome	
Report of Findings of Survey [Health], 1916	141
Seminole County	
Educational Survey, 1923	98
Spalding County	
Educational Survey, 1917	98
Stephens County	
Educational Survey, 1922	98
Taliaferro County	
Educational Survey, 1915	98
Tatnall County	
Educational Survey, 1916	98
Thomas County	
Educational Survey, 1921	98
Tift County	
Educational Survey, 1918	98
Towns County	
Educational Survey, 1917	98
Union County	
Educational Survey, 1916	98
Warren County	
Educational Survey, 1919	98
Webster County	
Social and Economic Survey [Rural], 1912	11
Wilkes County	
Educational Survey, 1922	98

A BIBLIOGRAPHY OF SOCIAL SURVEYS

PAGE

GERMANY
Part-Time Schools, 1922 [Under United States] 72
Illegitimacy Laws, 1919 [Under United States] 175

GREAT BRITAIN
Economic Effects of War upon Women and Children, 1918 . . 185

HAWAII
Education in Territories and Dependencies, 1919 [Under Alaska] . 92
Survey of Education in Hawaii, 1920 99
Report of Commission to Investigate Feeblemindedness, 1919 . 128
Studies in Leprosy, 1922 142
Effect of Vacinnia on Leprosy, 1923 142
Report in Reference to Proposed Government Regulation [Social Evil], 1905 302

Honolulu
Beautifying Honolulu, 1907 50
Industrial Conditions of Women and Girls, 1912 185
Report of Committee on Social Evil, 1914 302

HOLLAND
Part-Time Schools, 1922 [Under United States] 72

IDAHO
Child Welfare Work, 1920 40
Study of Delinquency, 1925 85
Report of Commission on Prison Labor, 1915 246

Boise
First School Survey, 1910 99
Expert Survey of Public School System, 1913 99
Special Report of Boise Public Schools, 1915 99
Boise Survey [Education], 1920 99

ILLINOIS
GENERAL SOCIAL SURVEYS—RURAL
Rural Survey, 1912 11
CHARITIES
Report on Charitable and Correctional Institutions, 1914 . . 25
CHILD LABOR
Work of Children, 1926 30
CITY, COUNTY, AND STATE ADMINISTRATION
Report of Efficiency and Economy Committee, 1914 . . . 63
Report of Efficiency and Economy Committee, 1915 . . . 63
CRIPPLED, DISABLED, AND HANDICAPPED
Report of Survey of Specially Handicapped, 1925 82
EDUCATION
Illinois School Survey, 1917 100
Statistical Survey, 1917 100

378

GEOGRAPHICAL INDEX

	PAGE
FAMILY WELFARE	
Administration of Aid-to-Mothers' Law, 1921	127
HEALTH ADMINISTRATION	
Report on Public Health Administration, 1914	135
Public Health Administration, 1915	135
HEALTH AND SANITATION	
Report on Appraisal of Health Service, 1926	142
HEALTH IN INDUSTRY	
Hours and Health of Women Workers, 1918	154
HEALTH INSURANCE	
Report of Health Insurance Commission, 1919	159
IMMIGRATION AND AMERICANIZATION	
Educational Needs of Immigrants, 1920	177
Immigrant and Coal Mining Communities, 1920	177
INDUSTRIAL CONDITIONS AND RELATIONS	
Women in Illinois Industries, 1926	185
PRISONS	
One Hundred and One County Jails, 1916	246
RURAL EDUCATION	
Farm and Home Survey, 1922	272
SCHOOL ORGANIZATION AND ADMINISTRATION	
Report on Educational Administration, 1914	290
Financing of Public Schools, 1924	290
Political Unit of Public School Finance, 1924	290
Public School Debt in Illinois, 1924	290
Study of School Costs in Illinois Cities, 1924	290
Studies in Public School Finance, 1925	290
TAXATION	
Taxation and Revenue System of Illinois, 1910	306
VICE	
Report of Senate Vice Committee, 1916	325
Alexander County	
Study of Truancy, 1926	311
Alton	
Advancement of Alton [City and Regional Planning], 1914	50
Findings and Recommendations of Survey [Education], 1918	100
Aurora	
Cost of Living Survey, 1921	74
Champaign	
Notes for Study of City Planning, 1915	341
Chicago	
GENERAL SOCIAL SURVEYS—URBAN	
American Girl in Stockyard District, 1913	3
Community Survey, 1913	3

A BIBLIOGRAPHY OF SOCIAL SURVEYS

	PAGE
BOY LIFE	
Preliminary Inquiry into Boys's Work, 1921	22
CANCER	
San Francisco Cancer Survey, 1922–24–25–26 [Under California, San Francisco]	23
CHILD LABOR	
Chicago Children in Street Trades, 1917	30
CHILD WELFARE	
Opportunities in School, 1912	40
Baby Farms, 1917	40
Children of Wage-Earning Mothers, 1922	40
CITY AND REGIONAL PLANNING	
Zoning Chicago, 1922	50
CITY, COUNTY, AND STATE ADMINISTRATION	
Bureau of Streets, etc., 1911	63
Park Governments of Chicago, 1911	63
Nineteen Local Governments, 1915	63
City Manager Plan, 1917	63
Primary Days and Election Days, 1917	64
Unification of Local Governments, 1917	64
Water Works System, 1917	64
Conditions of Municipal Employment, 1925	63
COST OF LIVING	
Wages and Family Budget, 1914	74
CRIME AND CRIMINALS	
Report of City Council, 1915	79
Delinquents and Criminals, 1926	79
CRIPPLED, DISABLED, AND HANDICAPPED	
Survey of Care of Disabled Ex-Service Men, 1923	82
Survey of Crippled Children in Chicago, 1925	82
DANCE HALLS	
Public Dance Halls, 1917	84
DEAF	
Chicago Public Schools, 1908	84
DELINQUENCY AND CORRECTION	
Study of Adult Delinquency, 1911	85
On Trail of Juvenile Adult Offender, 1912	85
What Should Be Done for . . . Women Offenders, 1916	85
DESERTION	
Study of Family Desertion, 1916	90
EDUCATION	
Report of Educational Commission, 1897	100
Report of Child Study Investigation, 1899	100
Survey of Chicago Public Schools, 1914	100
Report of Superintendent of Schools, 1917	100

GEOGRAPHICAL INDEX

	PAGE
ELECTIONS	
Growing Cost of Elections, 1912	126
High Cost of Elections, 1921	126
GANGS	
The Gang, 1927	132
GARBAGE, REFUSE, AND SEWAGE	
Report on . . . Method of Collection, 1913	132
HEALTH ADMINISTRATION	
Public Health Administration, 1915	135
HEALTH AND SANITATION	
Noise Problem in Chicago, 1913	142
Public Comfort Stations, 1916	142
Survey of Comfort Stations, 1918	142
Use and Cost of Ice, 1925	142
HOMELESS	
One Thousand Homeless Men, 1914	159
The Hobo, 1923	159
500 Lodgers of City, 1926	160
HOUSING	
Tenement Conditions in Chicago, 1900	163
Housing of Non-Family Groups, 1910	163
Families in Furnished Rooms, 1910	163
South Chicago, 1911	164
Twenty-Ninth Ward, 1911	164
West Side Revisited, 1911	164
Problem of Negro, 1912	164
Tenement Housing Conditions, 1912	164
Housing Survey, 1918	164
Housing of Non-Family Women, 1922	164
Living Conditions for Small Wage-Earners, 1925	164
ILLEGITIMACY	
Care of Illegitimate Children, 1912	174
Study of Bastardy Cases, 1914	174
IMMIGRATION AND AMERICANIZATION	
Children of Immigrants in Schools, 1911 [Under United States]	179
Immigrants in Cities, 1911 [Under United States]	179
Americanization in Chicago, 1920	177
INDUSTRIAL CONDITIONS AND RELATIONS	
Working Hours of Wage-Earning Women, 1910	185
Department Store Girl, 1911	185
Girl Employed in Hotels and Restaurants, 1912	185
Wages and Family Budget in Chicago, 1914	185
Saturday Half Holiday, 1916	186
Women Street Car Conductors, 1920	186
Women in Candy Industry, 1923	186

A BIBLIOGRAPHY OF SOCIAL SURVEYS

PAGE

ITALIANS
- Two Italian Districts, 1913 209
- Greeks and Italians in Neighborhood of Hull House, 1915 . . 210
- Housing Survey in Italian District, 1915 210
- Italians in Chicago, 1919 210

JUVENILE DELINQUENCY
- Delinquent Child and Home, 1917 212
- Junk Dealing and Juvenile Delinquency, 1918 213
- Study of Boys Appearing in Municipal Court, 1919 . . 213
- Chicago Juvenile Court, 1922 213

LITHUANIANS
- Lithuanians in 4th Ward, 1914 217

LOANS
- Loan Shark in Chicago, 1916 217

MENTAL HYGIENE
- Study of Mentally Defective Children, 1915 220

MIDWIFE
- Midwife in Chicago, 1915 226

MOTION PICTURES
- Five and Ten Cent Theatres, 1911 230

NEGROES
- Colored People in Chicago, 1913 233
- Preliminary Study of Inter-Racial Conditions, 1920 . . . 233
- Negro in Chicago, 1922 233

NURSERIES AND NURSING
- Study of Day Nurseries, 1918 238

PENSIONS
- Public Pensions to Widows, 1913 [Under California, San Francisco] 240
- Care of Aged in Chicago, 1927 240

POPULATION
- Trends of Population, 1927 243

PRE-NATAL CARE
- Pre-Natal Care in Chicago, 1922 244

PRISONS
- Report on Investigation of Prison Labor, 1914 . . . 246

RELIGION
- Modern Church to Meet a Modern Situation, 1912 . . 261

SCHOOL ORGANIZATION AND ADMINISTRATION
- Recommendations for Reorganization of Public School System, 1917– 291
- Chicago School Finances, 1927 291

SEX DELINQUENCY
- Morals Court of Chicago, 1922 296
- Specialized Courts Dealing with Sex Delinquency, 1925 . . 296

GEOGRAPHICAL INDEX

	PAGE
SLOVAKS	
Among Slovaks of the 20th Ward, 1914	298
SLUMS	
Slums of Baltimore, Chicago, New York, and Philadelphia, 1894 [Under Maryland, Baltimore]	298
SOCIAL AGENCIES	
Financing of Social Agencies, 1924	299
SOCIAL EVIL	
Social Evil in Chicago, 1911	302
TRUANCY AND NON-ATTENDANCE	
Intensive Study of Causes of Truancy, 1905	311
Truancy and Non-Attendance in Chicago Schools, 1917	311
TUBERCULOSIS	
Study of Tuberculosis in Chicago, 1905	314
Tuberculosis Problem, 1918	314
Tuberculosis Survey, 1926	314
UNEMPLOYMENT	
Report of Mayor's Commission on Unemployment, 1914	321
VICE	
Road to Destruction Made Easy, 1916	325
VOCATIONAL GUIDANCE AND TRAINING	
Vocational Training in Chicago, 1912	328
Vocational Guidance and Junior Placement, 1925 [Under California, Oakland]	328
PURPOSE, METHOD, AND STANDARDS	
Block System, 1916	335
Chicago Standard Budget, 1920	343
Cook County	
Administration of Office of Recorder, 1911	63
Administration of Office of Sheriff, 1911	63
Judges and County Fee Officers, 1911	63
Methods of Preparing . . . Budget, 1911	63
Administration of Office of Clerk, 1912	63
Offices of Clerks of Circuit and Superior Court, 1912	63
Office of Sheriff, 1912	63
Office of County Treasurer, 1913	63
Juvenile Detention Home, 1917	90
Juvenile Detention Home in Relation, 1927	90
Growing Cost of Elections, 1912	126
High Cost of Elections, 1921	126
Juvenile Court of Cook County, 1912	213
Cook County and Mentally Handicapped, 1918	221
Reports Comprising Survey, 1922	246
Decatur	
Decatur Plan, 1920	50

A BIBLIOGRAPHY OF SOCIAL SURVEYS

	PAGE
East St. Louis	
City Plan for East St. Louis, 1920	50
Elgin	
Plan of Elgin, 1917	51
Playgrounds and Organized Public Recreation, 1915	254
Freeport	
Sanitary and Health Survey, 1918	142
Galesburg	
Analysis of Social Structure, 1896	3
Report of Recreation Conditions and Problems, 1916	254
Jacksonville	
Community Study [General], 1920	3
Joliet	
Joliet City Plan, 1921	51
Macon County	
Tuberculosis Survey, 1920	314
Marion	
Survey of City Schools, 1924	100
Morgan County	
Community Study, 1920	3
Oak Park	
Investigation of Health of School Children, 1926	285
Peoria	
Report of Peoria . . . Housing Survey, 1918	164
Report of Recreation Conditions, 1916	254
Quincy	
Public Health Administration, 1917	135
Sanitary Survey, 1921	142
Rockford	
Plan for Improvement, 1918	51
Sanitary Survey, 1920	143
St. Charles	
St. Charles Study [Juvenile Delinquency], 1917	213
Springfield	
Springfield Survey, 1918	4
Social Conditions, 1920	4
Charities of Springfield, 1915	25
City and County Administration, 1917	64
Correctional System, 1915	85
Public Schools, 1915	100
Sanitary and Health Survey, 1912	143
Public Health in Springfield, 1915	143

GEOGRAPHICAL INDEX

	PAGE
Housing in Springfield, 1915	164
Industrial Conditions, 1916	186
Care of Mental Defectives, 1914	221
Recreation in Springfield, 1915	254

Urbana
Notes for Study of City Planning, 1915 341

White County
Health Survey of White County, 1915 277

Winnetka
Survey of Public Schools, 1926. 100

INDIA
Survey of Field and Work [Religion], 1919 [Under United States] . 266

INDIANA
GENERAL SOCIAL SURVEYS—URBAN
Social and Economic Survey, 1916 4
GENERAL SOCIAL SURVEYS—RURAL
Rural Survey, 1911 11
CHILD LABOR
Child Labor in Indiana, 1908 31
School or Work in Indiana, 1927. 31
CHILD WELFARE
Report of Committee, 1908 40
CITY, COUNTY, AND STATE ADMINISTRATION
Report of Committee, 1925 64
Report of Investigation, 1911 [Under New York] . . . 66
EDUCATION
Intelligence of High School Seniors, 1922 101
Public Education in Indiana, 1923 101
HEALTH IN INDUSTRY
Sanitary Survey of Indiana Industries, 1914 154
IMMIGRATION AND AMERICANIZATION
Foreign Problem in Northwest Indiana, 1917 177
INDUSTRIAL CONDITIONS AND RELATIONS
Hours, Earnings, and Conditions of Labor, 1914 . . . 186
Labor Laws for Women, 1919 186
JUVENILE DELINQUENCY
Juvenile Delinquency, 1918 213
MENTAL HYGIENE
Mental Defectives (3 reports) 1916–19–20 221
Social Significance of Mental Disease, 1919 221
Social Study of Mental Defectives, 1923 221
PENSIONS
Report of Committee . . . Old Age Pensions, 1925. . . 240

A BIBLIOGRAPHY OF SOCIAL SURVEYS

PAGE

RECREATION
Vocational Recreation, 1918 254
RELIGIOUS EDUCATION
Religious Education of Protestants, 1923 267
RURAL EDUCATION
Report of Indiana Rural Education Survey Committee, 1926 . 272
TAXATION
Report of Commission on Taxation, 1916 306
TUBERCULOSIS
Report of Indiana Tuberculosis Commission, 1906 314
VOCATIONAL GUIDANCE AND TRAINING
Study . . . for Purposes of Vocational Education, 1915. . 328
PURPOSE, METHOD, AND STANDARDS
Measurement and Standards in Religious Education, 1924 . . 355
Religious Education Survey Schedules, 1924 355
Sanitary Schoolhouses, 1913 356

Bartholomew County
Rural Schools, 1914 272
Rural Sanitary Survey of Five Counties, 1914 277

Bloomington
Social Aspect of Cardiac Case, 1919 24
Study of Handicapped Children, 1919 82
Survey of Public School System, 1917 101

Boone County
Rural Sanitary Survey, 1914 277

Daviess County
Rural Sanitary Survey, 1914 277

East Chicago
Public Health in East Chicago, 1916 143

Elkhart
Planning Prospects for Elkhart, 1923 51

Evansville
Report of Evansville Survey for Vocational Education, 1917 . . 329

Fort Wayne
Report to Civic Improvement Association [City and Regional Planning], 1909 51

Gary
Public School System of Gary, 1914 101
Gary Public Schools, 1918–1919 101
Infant Mortality, 1923 204
Juvenile Delinquency and Adult Crime, 1921 213
Children of Pre-School Age, 1922 244
Physical Status of Pre-School Children, 1922 245
Gary Public Schools, 1918. 254

GEOGRAPHICAL INDEX

	PAGE
Organization and Administration, 1918	291
Costs [School Organization and Administration], 1918	291

Greene County
Educational Survey of Greene County, 1916 101

Hammond
Some Facts Concerning People, Industries [Vocational Guidance and Training], 1915 329

Indianapolis
Indianapolis Survey [Charities], 1919 25
Summary of Recommendations [City Administration], 1918 . . 64
Investigation of Housing and Living Conditions, 1910 . . . 164
Survey of Indianapolis Police Department, 1924 242
Indianapolis Recreation Survey, 1914 254
Report of Indianapolis Survey for Vocational Education, 1917 . 329

Jefferson County
Report of Survey for Vocational Education, 1917 329

Jennings County
Church and Community Survey, 1920 261
Rural Church Life, 1922 [Under Iowa, Clay County] . . . 261

Lafayette
Public Health Survey, 1921 143

Marion County
Summary of Recommendations [City Administration], 1918 . . 64
Report to Board of Commissioners [Relief], 1920 259

Marshall County
Rural Sanitary Survey, 1914 277

Montgomery County
Rural Sanitary Survey, 1914 277

Porter County
Rural School Sanitation, 1916 272

Richmond
Public Health Administration, 1915 314
Report of Richmond Survey for Vocational Education, 1916 . 329

South Bend
Public Schools of South Bend, 1914 101
Public Health Administration, 1917 135
Playground and Public Recreation Facilities, 1914 254

Sugar Creek Township
Know Your Community Better Study, 1920 4

Thorntown
Know Your Community Better Study, 1920 4

Vermilion County
Partial Survey of Schools, 1919 102

A BIBLIOGRAPHY OF SOCIAL SURVEYS

IOWA   PAGE

GENERAL SOCIAL SURVEYS—RURAL
Social Surveys of Three Rural Townships, 1917 11
CITY, COUNTY, STATE ADMINISTRATION
Report of Investigation, 1911 [Under New York] 66
CHILD WELFARE
Juvenile Delinquency, 1918 40
Analytical Study, 1921 41
Selective Migration as Factor in Child Welfare, 1921 [Under United States] 46
CONTINUATION AND PART-TIME SCHOOLS
Special Investigation of Children, 1926 72
COST OF LIVING
Household Expenditures, 1926 74
DELINQUENCY AND CORRECTION
Dependents, Defectives, and Delinquents, 1919 86
EDUCATION
Higher Educational Institutions, 1916 102
Mental Educational Survey, 1923 102
INDUSTRIAL CONDITIONS AND RELATIONS
Iowa Women in Industry, 1922 187
INFANTILE PARALYSIS
Epidemiologic Studies, 1913 207
SCHOOL HEALTH AND SANITATION
Hygienic Conditions in Iowa Schools, 1915 285
SCHOOL ORGANIZATION AND ADMINISTRATION
Financing of Education, 1925 291
VOCATIONAL GUIDANCE AND TRAINING
Vocational Education and Vocational Guidance, 1914 . . . 329
Work, Wages, and Schooling, 1915 329

Blackhawk County
Rural Social Survey, 1918 11
Rural Social Survey, 1924 11

Boone County
Economic and Sociological Study, 1926 74

Buchanan County
Rural Social Survey, 1924 11

Cedar Falls
Report of Inside Survey [Education], 1912 102
Supplement to Report of Inside Survey, 1912 102

Cedar Rapids
Report with Regard to Civic Affairs, 1908 51
Children of Immigrants in Schools, 1911 [Under United States] . . 179

Clay County
Rural Social Survey, 1920 11
Rural Church Life, 1922 261

GEOGRAPHICAL INDEX

	PAGE
Davenport	
City Planning for Davenport, 1918	51
Des Moines	
Survey of High Schools, 1918	102
Survey of Musical Talent, 1920	102
Report of Housing Commission, 1917	165
Dubuque	
Report on Improvement [City and Regional Planning], 1907	51
Fort Dodge	
Partial Survey of Public Schools, 1917	102
Mason City	
Civic Survey of Iowa Municipality, 1925	51
Muscatine	
Survey of School Buildings, 1918	281
Sac County	
Economic and Sociological Study, 1926	74
Story County	
Economic and Sociological Study, 1926	74
Union	
Survey of Some Phases of Schools, 1918	102
Waterloo	
Well-Being of Waterloo [City Planning], 1910	51
ITALY	
Part-Time Schools, 1922 [Under United States]	72
JAPAN	
Comparative Study of Health, 1920	143
Survey of Field and Work, 1919 [Under United States]	266
Osaka	
Cost of Living among Laborers, 1921	211
Tokyo	
Administration and Politics, 1923	211
KANSAS	
Cost of Living Survey, 1921	74
Study of Causes of Delinquency, 1921	86
Results of Instruction, 1922	103
Report of Survey, 1923	103
Women's Wages, 1921	187
Survey of Milk Situation, 1915	227
Milk Survey of Twenty Kansas Cities, 1922	227
Psychiatric Studies of Delinquents, 1920	252
Factors Which Have to Do with Decline, 1916	261
Maternity and Infant Care, 1917	277

A BIBLIOGRAPHY OF SOCIAL SURVEYS

PAGE

Amourdale
Report of Social Survey, 1919 4
Belleville
Belleville School Survey, 1915 4
Chanute
Survey Report of . . . School System, 1924 . . . 103
Clay Center
Social Survey of Clay Center, 1918 4
Council Grove
Social Survey of Council Grove, 1917 4
Dodge City
School Survey and Building Program, 1923 281
Great Bend
School Survey Report, 1922 103
Lansing
Psychiatric Studies of Delinquent Women, 1920 252
Lawrence
Social Survey of Lawrence, 1917 4
School Survey, 1921 103
Leavenworth
Report of Survey of Public Schools, 1915 103
Minneapolis
Social Survey of Minneapolis, 1918 4
Ottawa
Survey Report on School Building Program, 1923 . . . 281
Sedgwick County
Church and Community Survey, 1922 261
Sumner County
Sumner County Sanitary and Social Survey, 1915 . . . 277
Topeka
Topeka Improvement Survey, 1914 5
Municipal Administration in Topeka, 1914 64
Delinquency and Correction, 1914 86
Public Health Survey, 1914 143
Industrial Conditions, 1914 187
Wichita
Comprehensive City Plan, 1923 52
Survey of Negro Life, 1924 233

KENTUCKY
GENERAL SOCIAL SURVEYS—RURAL
Rural Survey in Kentucky, 1912 11

390

GEOGRAPHICAL INDEX

                                                                                  PAGE

CHILD HEALTH AND HYGIENE
    Nutrition and Care of Children, 1922 27
CHILD LABOR
    Enforcement of Child Labor Law, 1925 31
CHILD WELFARE
    Child Welfare in Kentucky, 1919 41
COST OF LIVING
    Cost of Living among Colored Farm Families, 1925 . . . 75
EDUCATION
    Public Education in Kentucky, 1921 103
FEEBLEMINDED
    Report of Commission, 1916 128
HEALTH AND SANITATION
    Sanitary Conditions and Needs, 1909 143
INDUSTRIAL CONDITIONS AND RELATIONS
    Report of Commission, 1911 187
    Women in Kentucky Industries, 1923 187
MENTAL HYGIENE
    Report of Mental Hygiene Survey, 1923 221
RURAL EDUCATION
    Farmwork and Schools in Kentucky, 1917. 272
TAXATION
    Taxation in Kentucky, 1920 306
TRACHOMA
    Trachoma: Survey of Its Prevalence, 1915 309

Jefferson County
    Trachoma, 1914 309

Knott County
    Results of Three Year Trachoma Campaign, 1923 . . . 310

Lexington
    Report on Charities, 1918 25
    Report of Survey Commission [Education], 1917 103
    Financial and Building Needs [School], 1919 281
    Report of Vice Commission, 1915 326

Louisville
    Jewish Neighborhood Survey, 1916 5
    Child Welfare Work, 1919 41
    Hospital and Health Agencies, 1924 160
    Report of Tenement House Commission, 1909 165
    Psychiatric Studies of Delinquents, 1920 252
    Survey of Private Recreational Facilities, 1925 255
    Report of Vice Commission, 1915 326
    Vocational Guidance Survey, 1918 330

A BIBLIOGRAPHY OF SOCIAL SURVEYS

PAGE

Paducah
Survey of Public School System, 1919 104
Report of Paducah Vice Commission, 1916 326

LOUISIANA
Report of State Housing Commission, 1921 165
Report of State Commission to Study . . . Working Women, 1914 187
Conditions of Women's Labor, 1919 187
Report upon Penal and Other State Institutions, 1906 . . . 246
Standards of Labor [Rural], 1921 268
Program for Tuberculosis Control, 1924 314

Baton Rouge
Social Evil in Baton Rouge, 1914 302

Caddo Parish
Survey of Schools of Caddo Parish, 1922 104

Cinclare
Negroes of Cinclare . . . and Calumet Plantation, 1902 . . 234

New Orleans
San Francisco Cancer Survey, 1922–24–25–26 [Under California, San Francisco] 23
Administrative Survey of Government, 1922. 64
Report of Sanitary Commission, 1854 143
Report of Health and Sanitary Survey, 1919 144
Children of Immigrants in Schools, 1911 [Under United States] . 179
Experimental Study of Delinquent and Destitute Boys, 1914 . . 213
Exceptional Children in Public Schools, 1913 304
Notes on Problems of . . . Exceptional Children, 1913 . 304
Study of Violent Deaths, 1924 [Under Georgia, Atlanta] . . 327
Vocational Survey, 1914–16 330

Patterson
Negroes of Cinclare, etc., 1902 234

Shreveport
Survey of Schools, 1922 104
Brief and Recommendations [Vice], 1915 326

MAINE
Cry of Children, 1908 [Under Alabama] 29
Report of Maine Commission for Feebleminded, 1918. . . . 128
Factors Which Have to Do [Religion], 1916 [Under Kansas] . . 261
Public Health Administration in Rural Districts, 1918 . . . 277

Auburn
Public Health . . . in Lewiston and Auburn, 1918 . . 136

Augusta
Augusta Survey, 1921 5

GEOGRAPHICAL INDEX

	PAGE
Report of Survey Staff [Education], 1922	104
Public Health Administration, 1919	135

Bangor
Bangor City Plan, 1911 52
Public Health Administration, 1919 135
Bangor School Building Survey, 1922 281

Bath
Public Health Administration, 1919 135

Biddeford
Public Health Administration, 1920 136

Lewiston
Public Health . . . in Lewiston and Auburn, 1918 . . . 136

Portland
Portland Recreation Survey, 1913 255
First Report of Citizens' Committee [Social Evil], 1914 . . . 302

Waterville
Public Health Administration in Waterville and Biddeford, 1920 . 136

Westbrook
Public Health Administration in Westbrook, 1919 136

MARYLAND

GENERAL SOCIAL SURVEYS—RURAL
    Rural Survey in Maryland, 1912 11
BLINDNESS, SIGHT CONSERVATION, AND DISEASE OF THE EYE
    Report of Commission, 1907 20
CHILD LABOR
    Administration of Child Labor Laws, 1919 31
    Child Labor on Maryland Truck Farms, 1923 31
CHILD WELFARE
    People Who Go to Tomatoes, 1914 [Under Delaware] . . . 39
EDUCATION
    Report of Maryland Educational Commission, 1910 . . . 104
    Report on Educational Situation, 1914 104
    Public Education in Maryland, 1921 104
HEALTH ADMINISTRATION
    Public Health Administration, 1914 136
HEALTH AND SANITATION
    Influenza in Maryland, 1919 144
INDUSTRIAL CONDITIONS AND RELATIONS
    Women in Maryland Industries, 1922. 187
MENTAL HYGIENE
    Report of Maryland Mental Hygiene Survey, 1921 . . . 221
PRISONS
    Report of Maryland Penitentiary Commission, 1913 . . . 246

A BIBLIOGRAPHY OF SOCIAL SURVEYS

	PAGE
SCHOOL HEALTH AND SANITATION	
Heights and Weights of School Children, 1922	285
TUBERCULOSIS	
Report of Tuberculosis Commission, 1904	314
Second Report of the Commission, 1906	314

Baltimore

GENERAL SOCIAL SURVEYS—URBAN	
Study of Social Statistics, 1919	5
CITY AND REGIONAL PLANNING	
Partial Report on City Plan, 1910	52
Port Development Plan, 1922	52
COST OF LIVING	
Wage-Earning Women . . . Study of Cost of Living, 1921	75
DOMESTIC WORKERS	
Domestic Workers and Their Employment, 1924	91
EDUCATION	
Report of Commission, 1911	104
Adjusting School Work to Child, 1919	104
Abstract of Survey, 1921	104
Francis Scott Key School, 1921	105
School Curriculum, 1921	105
HEALTH ADMINISTRATION	
Public Health Administration, 1914	136
HOUSING	
Housing Conditions, 1907	165
Special Survey of Housing Situation, 1920	165
Survey of Housing Conditions, 1921	165
ILLEGITIMACY	
Welfare of Infants, 1925	174
IMMIGRATION AND AMERICANIZATION	
Children of Immigrants in Schools, 1911 [Under United States]	179
INFANT MORTALITY	
Infant Mortality, 1923	204
MENTAL HYGIENE	
Some Adaptive Difficulties Found, 1920	221
POLICE	
Business Methods of Baltimore Police Department, 1917	242
PROBATION AND PAROLE	
Probation and Penal Treatment, 1927	250
SCHOOL BUILDINGS AND PLANTS	
School Plant and Building Program, 1921	282
SCHOOL HEALTH AND SANITATION	
Correcting Physical Defects, 1922	286
SCHOOL ORGANIZATION AND ADMINISTRATION	
Administration of Public Schools, 1921	291

GEOGRAPHICAL INDEX

	PAGE
SLUMS	
Slums of Baltimore, 1894	298
SUB-NORMAL, RETARDED, AND EXCEPTIONAL CHILDREN	
Sub-Normal Child, 1917	305
TUBERCULOSIS	
Report of Municipal Tuberculosis Commission, 1911	314
Graceham	
Survey of Graceham [Religion], 1915	262
Hagerstown	
Morbidity among School Children, 1924	286
Harford County	
Country Church in Industrial Zones, 1922	262
Montgomery County	
Educational Survey of Suburban and Rural County, 1913	272
Sandy Spring	
Negroes of Sandy Spring, 1901	234

MASSACHUSETTS

ACCIDENTS AND ACCIDENT PREVENTION	
One Thousand Industrial Accidents, 1922	16
Industrial Accidents to Employed Minors, 1926 [Under Wisconsin]	18
ADOLESCENCE	
Influence of Occupation on Health, 1916	18
BLINDNESS, SIGHT CONSERVATION, AND DISEASE OF THE EYE	
Report of Massachusetts Commission, 1904	20
Ophthalmia Neonatorum, 1911	20
Report of Ten-Year Survey Committee, 1917	20
Report of Special Commission, 1920	21
Final Report of Special Commission, 1925	21
CHILD LABOR	
Cry of Children, 1908 [Under Alabama]	29
Report of Effect of Child Labor Law, 1914	31
Child Labor, 1926	31
CHILD WELFARE	
Survey of Rural Children, 1921	41
Children in Need of Special Care, 1923	41
Fit and Proper, 1927	41
CITY, COUNTY, AND STATE ADMINISTRATION	
Report on Reorganization of Boards, 1914	64
Report of Committee, 1922	65
CONTINUATION AND PART-TIME SCHOOLS	
Needs and Possibilities of Part-Time Education, 1913	72
Continuation Schools of Massachusetts, 1924	72
Intelligence of Continuation-School Children, 1924	72

A BIBLIOGRAPHY OF SOCIAL SURVEYS

	PAGE
COST OF LIVING	
Report of Commission, 1910	75
Reports of Commission on Necessaries of Life, 1920–21–22–23	75
DELINQUENCY AND CORRECTION	
Report of Special Commission, 1919	86
DEPENDENCY	
Report of Commission . . . Dependent Minor Children, 1913	88
Report of Special Inquiry, 1916	88
EDUCATION	
Report of Special Commission, 1919	105
Open-Air Schools, 1921	105
Comparison of Intelligence and Training, 1922	105
Intelligence of Seniors, 1924	105
EIGHT-HOUR DAY	
Eight-Hour Day for Children in Massachusetts Factories, 1914	126
FAMILY WELFARE	
Report of Special Commission, 1920	127
FEEBLEMINDED	
Community Supervision of Feebleminded, 1918	129
HEALTH AND SANITATION	
Outbreak of Tonsillitis, 1912	144
Lessons from Study of One Thousand Diphtheria Deaths, 1920	144
Survey of Endemic Thyroid Enlargement, 1927	144
HEALTH IN INDUSTRY	
Report upon Sanitary Conditions, 1907	154
Hygiene of Boot and Shoe Industry, 1912	155
ILLEGITIMACY	
Illegitimacy as Child Welfare Problem, 1921	174
IMMIGRATION AND AMERICANIZATION	
Report of Commission, 1914	177
Adult Immigrant Education, 1921	177
Massachusetts Problem of Immigrant Education, 1922	177
INDUSTRIAL CONDITIONS AND RELATIONS	
Living Wage of Women Workers, 1911	188
Public School and Women in Office Service, 1914	188
Industrial Home Work in Massachusetts, 1915	188
Department Store, 1914	188
Report of Special Committee, 1914	188
Boot and Shoe Industry, 1915	188
Dressmaking as Trade for Women, 1916	188
Industrial Experience of Trade-School Girls, 1917	188
Report of State Board of Labor and Industry, 1917	188
Wages and Hours of Labor, 1920	189
Some Effects of Legislation Limiting Hours, 1921	189

GEOGRAPHICAL INDEX

	PAGE
INFANT MORTALITY	
Brief Statistical Study of Infant Mortality, 1922	204
INFANTILE PARALYSIS	
Infantile Paralysis, 1911	207
Infantile Paralysis, 1914	207
1916 Infantile Paralysis Epidemic, 1919	208
LOANS	
Report on Administration of State Revenues, 1916	217
MENTAL HYGIENE	
Report of Commission, 1911	222
Hill Folk, 1912	222
Mental Defective and Public Schools, 1917	222
After-Care Study, 1919	222
Child and Home, 1922	222
MINIMUM WAGE	
Reports of Minimum Wage Commission, 1915–1920	228
Report of Special Commission, 1923	228
PENSIONS	
Old-Age Support of Women Teachers, 1921	240
Report of Old-Age Pensions, 1925	240
PRISONS	
Report on Investigation Regarding . . . County Jails, 1918	246
PROBATION AND PAROLE	
Delinquent Girl, 1923	250
RURAL EDUCATION	
Report of Commission, 1918	273
SCHOOL ORGANIZATION AND ADMINISTRATION	
Studies in Public School Finance, 1923	291
TAXATION	
Report of Commission on Taxation, 1908	306
Report of Special Commission on Taxation, 1916	306
TUBERCULOSIS	
Report of Commission, 1907	315
Tuberculosis in Massachusetts, 1908	315
Report of Commission, 1910	315
Report of Special Recess Committee, 1914	315
UNEMPLOYMENT	
Report of Massachusetts Board to Investigate, 1895	321
VICE	
Report of Commission, 1914	326

Andover
Child Welfare Needs, 1922 41

Attleboro
Housing Analysis, 1921 165

A BIBLIOGRAPHY OF SOCIAL SURVEYS

PAGE

Barnstable County
Tuberculosis Survey, 1918. 315

Boston
GENERAL SOCIAL SURVEYS—URBAN
City Wilderness, 1898 5
Americans in Process, 1902 5
Trend of Jewish Population, 1921 5
CANCER
San Francisco Cancer Survey, 1922–24–25–26 [Under California, San Francisco] 23
CHILD HEALTH AND HYGIENE
Physical Defects in Children, 1920 28
CHILD LABOR
Working Children of Boston, 1922 31
CITY AND REGIONAL PLANNING
Port of Boston, 1916 52
Survey and Comprehensive Plan, 1916 52
North End, 1919 52
Metropolitan Planning and Development, 1922 52
CRIME AND CRIMINALS
Delinquents and Criminals, 1926 [Under Illinois, Chicago] . . 79
CRIPPLED, DISABLED, AND HANDICAPPED
Gainful Employment for Handicapped Women, 1921 . . . 82
EDUCATION
Report on Boston School System, 1911 105
FIRE
Study of Fire Risks, 1916 130
FOOD
Food Supply in Families of Limited Means, 1917 . . . 131
Housing of Foodstuffs, 1917 132
HEALTH AND SANITATION
Sickness Survey of Boston, 1916 144
HEALTH IN INDUSTRY
Food of Working Women, 1917 155
HOUSING
Report upon Sanitary Inspection, 1889 165
Report of Commission, 1904 165
Lodging House Problem, 1906 165
Report of Commission, 1909 166
Boston Housing Problem, 1911 166
Housing Conditions of Today, 1916 166
IMMIGRATION AND AMERICANIZATION
Children of Immigrants in Schools, 1911 [Under United States] . 179
Immigrants in Cities, 1911 [Under United States] . . . 179
INDUSTRIAL CONDITIONS AND RELATIONS
Women Street Car Conductors, 1920 [Under Illinois, Chicago] . 186

GEOGRAPHICAL INDEX

	PAGE
INFANT MORTALITY	
Infant Mortality, 1916	204
MENTAL HYGIENE	
Factors in Mental Health of Boys, 1924	222
Factors in Mental Health of Girls, 1924	222
RELIGION	
Community Survey, 1916	262
SCHOOL HEALTH AND SANITATION	
Tuberculosis among School Children, 1909	286
SCHOOL ORGANIZATION AND ADMINISTRATION	
Report of Study of Certain Phases, 1916	291
Organization . . . of Intermediate Schools, 1918	291
Supplementary Report, 1919	292
SEX DELINQUENCY	
Second Sessions of Municipal Court, 1922	297
Specialized Courts, 1925 [Under Illinois, Chicago]	296
SOCIAL AGENCIES	
Aged Clients of Boston Social Agencies, 1925	299
TUBERCULOSIS	
Tuberculosis Study, 1921	315
Tuberculosis Survey of Boston, 1926	315
UNEMPLOYMENT	
Unemployment among Women, 1916	321
UNMARRIED MOTHERS	
What Becomes of Unmarried Mother, 1922	324
VOCATIONAL GUIDANCE AND TRAINING	
Public Schools and Women, 1914	330
Training for Store Service, 1920	330
Vocational Guidance and Junior Placement, 1925 [Under California, Oakland]	328
PURPOSE, METHOD, AND STANDARDS	
Routine Mental Tests, 1917	351
Brockton	
Infant Mortality, 1919	204
Report of Tuberculosis Survey, 1920	315
Brookline	
Educational Survey, 1917	106
Cambridge	
Housing Conditions, 1913	166
Final Report of Special Tax Committee, 1920	306
Charlestown	
Survey of 100 Cases [Mental Hygiene], 1915	223
Chelsea	
Children of Immigrants in Schools, 1911 [Under United States]	179

A BIBLIOGRAPHY OF SOCIAL SURVEYS

PAGE

East Boston
Survey and Comprehensive Plan [City and Regional Planning], 1916 . 52

Fall River
Report of City Planning Board, 1922 52
Cost of Living among Wage-Earners, 1919 75
School Survey, 1917 106
Housing Conditions, 1912 166
Children of Immigrants in Schools, 1911 [Under United States] . . 179
Infant Mortality, 1915 205

Framingham
Tuberculosis Findings, 1919 316

Gardner
Recommendations for Development of Town, 1921 52

Gloucester
School Building Program, 1920 282

Haverhill
Annual Report and Summary, 1919 106
Children of Immigrants in Schools, 1911 [Under United States] . . 179

Ipswich
Play and Recreation, 1915 255

Lanesville
Finns in Lanesville, 1919 130

Lawrence
Child Welfare Needs, 1922 41
Cost of Living among Wage-Earners, 1919 75
Lawrence Survey. Housing Conditions, 1912 166
Report on Industrial Situation, 1920 189

Lowell
Record of City [General], 1912 5
Children of Immigrants in Schools, 1911 [Under United States] . . 179

Lynn
Report of Survey of Schools, 1927 106
Children of Immigrants in Schools, 1911 [Under United States] . . 179

Malden
Malden Survey [Method], 1919 354

Methuen
Child Welfare Needs, 1922 41

New Bedford
Study of Children's Agencies, 1923 41
Cost of Living, 1921 75
Principles, Policies, and Plans, 1922 106
Family Welfare Division of Survey, 1923 127

400

GEOGRAPHICAL INDEX

	PAGE
Public Health in New Bedford, 1923	144
Children of Immigrants, 1911 [Under United States]	179
Infant Mortality, 1920	205

Newton
Efficiency Survey, [City Administration] 1916	65
School Health Survey, 1927	286

North Andover
Child Welfare Needs, 1922	41

Norwood
Report of Planning Board, 1923	52

Quincy
Synoptic Report on Comparative Sanitary Survey, 1916	144

Springfield
Newsboys in Springfield, 1923	32
Unemployment and Child Welfare, 1923	42
City Plan for Springfield, 1922	52
City Plan for Springfield, 1923	53
Organization and Administration of City Government, 1913	65
Survey Report of Public School System, 1924	106
Organization and Administration of Health Department, 1914	136
Report on Housing Conditions, 1913	166
Organization and Administration of Pauper Department, 1914	239
Springfield Church Survey, 1926	262

Taunton
Synoptic Report on . . . Sanitary Survey, 1916	144

Waltham
From School to Work, 1917	32
Recreation Survey, 1913	255

Winchester
Survey of Schools, 1921	106

Worcester
City Plan for Worcester, 1924	53
Cost of Living among Wage-Earners, 1920	75
Children of Immigrants, 1911 [Under United States]	179
Trade School for Girls, 1913	202
Juvenile Delinquency in Worcester, 1912	213

MEXICO
Cancer in Mexico, 1927	226
Survey of Field and Work, 1919 [Under United States]	266

MICHIGAN
CHARITIES
Report on Penal, Reformatory, and Charitable, 1871	25

A BIBLIOGRAPHY OF SOCIAL SURVEYS

PAGE

CHILD LABOR
  People Who Go to Beets, 1919 32
  Child Labor in Sugar Beet Fields, 1923 32
  Minors in Automobiling . . . Manufacturing, 1923 . . 32
EDUCATION
  Report of a School Survey, 1913 106
FEEBLEMINDED
  Report of Commission, 1919 129
HOUSING
  Report of Michigan Housing Commission, 1916 166
INDUSTRIAL CONDITIONS AND RELATIONS
  Child Labor and Work of Mothers, 1923 [Under Colorado] . . 182
INDUSTRIAL EDUCATION
  Report of Michigan Commission, 1910 203
MINIMUM WAGE
  Report of Michigan State Commission, 1915 229
PRISONS
  Prison Conditions in Michigan, 1922 246
RELIGION
  Church and Industrial Warfare, 1920 [Under Colorado] . . . 261
RURAL EDUCATION
  Report of Michigan Commission, 1910 273
TAXATION
  Report of Michigan Committee, 1923 307
TUBERCULOSIS
  Report of Tuberculosis Survey, 1917 316

Battle Creek
  San Francisco Cancer Survey, 1922–24–25–26 [Under California, San Francisco] 23

Bay City
  Children of Immigrants in Schools, 1911 [Under United States] . . 179
  Social Evil in Bay City, 1914 303

Detroit
  CHILD LABOR
    Wage-Earning School Children, 1918 32
  CITY AND REGIONAL PLANNING
    Conditions in Detroit, 1915 53
    Detroit Suburban Planning, 1921 53
    Zoning and Its Application to Detroit, 1922 53
  COST OF LIVING
    Cost of Living among Wage-Earners, 1921 76
  EDUCATION
    Survey of Teachers' Salaries, 1920 107
    Preliminary Study of Standards of Growth, 1921 107
    Age-Grade and Nationality Survey, 1922 107

402

GEOGRAPHICAL INDEX

	PAGE
IMMIGRATION AND AMERICANIZATION	
Children of Immigrants in Schools, 1911 [Under United States]	179
INDUSTRIAL CONDITIONS AND RELATIONS	
Women Street Car Conductors, 1920 [Under Illinois, Chicago]	186
NEGROES	
Negro New-Comers in Detroit, 1918	234
Negro in Detroit, 1926	234
Report on Mayor's Committee, 1927	234
RECREATION	
Detroit Recreation Survey, 1913	255
RELIGION	
Study of Detroit for Baptists, 1918	262
SOCIAL AGENCIES	
Trouble Cases, 1919	300
UNEMPLOYMENT	
Report on Unemployment, 1915	322
VOCATIONAL GUIDANCE AND TRAINING	
Occupations of Junior Workers, 1925	330

Flint
City Plan of Flint, 1920	53
Sickness Survey among 21,000 Automobile Workers, 1924	155

Grand Rapids
Survey of Charities and Philanthropies, 1911	25
Wage-Earning School Children, 1918	32
Preliminary Report for City Plan, 1909	53
School Survey of Grand Rapids, 1916	107
Housing Conditions and Tendencies, 1913	166
Survey of Thyroid Enlargement, 1923	286
Report on Social Evil, 1913	303
Report of Investigation of Vice Committee, 1913	326

Hamtramck
Survey of Social, Educational, and Civic Conditions, 1915	6
Housing Children [Schools], 1926	282

Highland Park
Health of Highland Park, 1917	145

Kalamazoo
City Planning for Kalamazoo, 1921	53
Survey of Needs [Education], 1922	107

Kalamazoo County
County Study in Rural Education, 1926	273

Lansing
Lansing Plan, 1922	53

Marquette
Survey of Needs [Education], 1922	107

A BIBLIOGRAPHY OF SOCIAL SURVEYS

PAGE

Mt. Pleasant
Survey of Needs [Education], 1922 107

Oakland County
Rural School Survey, 1924 273

Pontiac
Sickness Survey among 21,000 Automobile Workers, 1924 . . . 155

Saginaw
Sanitary Survey of Saginaw, 1911 145
Infant Mortality, 1919 205

St. Joseph County
Survey of Farm Homes, 1921 268

Ypsilanti
Survey of Needs [Education], 1922 107

MINNESOTA
GENERAL SOCIAL SURVEYS—RURAL
Social and Economic Survey of Rural Township, 1913 . . . 12
Social and Economic Survey, 1915 12
Social and Economic Survey . . . Red River, 1915. . . 12
BLINDNESS, SIGHT CONSERVATION, AND DISEASE OF THE EYE
Report of Minnesota Commission, 1923 21
CHILD WELFARE
Public Child-Caring Work, 1927 42
COST OF LIVING
Cost of Living on Minnesota Farms, 1916 76
EDUCATION
Public Education Commission's Report, 1914 107
HEALTH ADMINISTRATION
Public Health Administration, 1914 136
HEALTH AND SANITATION
Report on Campaign . . . Sanitary and . . . Problems,
1911 145
Railroad Water Supplies, 1914 145
HOUSING
Investigation of Housing and Rental Situation, 1920 . . . 167
INDUSTRIAL CONDITIONS AND RELATIONS
Women in Industry, 1920 189
JUVENILE DELINQUENCY
Delinquents, 1919 214
RURAL
Family Living, 1927 268
RURAL EDUCATION
Rural School System, 1915 273

GEOGRAPHICAL INDEX

	PAGE
SCHOOL ORGANIZATION AND ADMINISTRATION	
Study of State Aid to Public Schools, 1918	292
Public School Finance, 1922	292
Studies in Public School Finance, 1925 [Under Illinois]	290
SOCIAL AGENCIES	
Study of Maternity Homes, 1926	300
TRACHOMA	
Investigation of Prevalence of Trachoma, 1913	310
Trachoma Problem, 1923	310
TUBERCULOSIS	
Spread of Tuberculosis, 1915	316

Arlington
Arlington School Survey, 1921 107

Duluth
Report of Educational Committee, 1918 107
Children of Immigrants in Schools, 1911 [Under United States] . 179

Faribault
Occupational Efficiency of Mentally Defective, 1924 . . . 223

Hennepin County
Mound District, 1922. 6

Lake Crystal
Survey Report of . . . Public Schools, 1926 107

Minneapolis
CHILD WELFARE
Survey of Child Caring Institutions, 1922 42
CITY AND REGIONAL PLANNING
Plan of Minneapolis, 1917 53
CITY, COUNTY, AND STATE ADMINISTRATION
Report on Survey of Business Administration, 1915 . . . 65
Survey of Bonded Debt, 1922 65
COST OF LIVING
Salary Situation and Cost of Living, 1920 76
EDUCATION
Reports on University of Minnesota, 1920–1922 . . . 107
HEALTH ADMINISTRATION
Ideal Health Department, 1912 136
HEALTH AND SANITATION
Drinking Fountains, 1917 145
HOUSING
Housing Problems, 1914 167
IMMIGRATION AND AMERICANIZATION
Children of Immigrants in Schools, 1911 [Under United States] . 179
Nationality and School Progress, 1921 177

A BIBLIOGRAPHY OF SOCIAL SURVEYS

	PAGE
INDUSTRIAL CONDITIONS AND RELATIONS	
Study of Women in Clerical and Secretarial Work, 1925	189
JUVENILE DELINQUENCY	
Study of Community Conditions . . . North District, 1925	214
Study of Community Conditions, East District, 1926	214
Study of Community Conditions, South District, 1926	214
KINDERGARTENS	
Kindergartens in Public Schools, 1924	215
MARKETS	
Exhaustive Study on . . . Municipal Markets, 1918	218
MOTION PICTURES	
Better Movie Movement, 1921	230
SCHOOL HEALTH AND SANITATION	
School Health Supervision, 1921	286
SCHOOL ORGANIZATION AND ADMINISTRATION	
Report of Survey, 1915	292
SOCIAL AGENCIES	
Report of Committee, 1920	300
Survey of Child-Caring Institutions, 1922	300
SUB-NORMAL, RETARDED, AND EXCEPTIONAL CHILDREN	
Relation between Dependency and Retardation, 1919	305
TUBERCULOSIS	
Study of Spread of Tuberculosis, 1913	316
VICE	
Report of Minneapolis Vice Commission, 1911	326
VOCATIONAL GUIDANCE AND TRAINING	
Vocational Survey, 1913	330
Vocational Education Survey, 1917	330
Vocational Guidance and Junior Placement, 1925 [Under California, Oakland]	328
Ramsey County	
Survey of Environmental Sanitation [Rural Education], 1916	273
Redwood County	
Canvass of Religious Life, 1912	262
Rochester	
San Francisco Cancer Survey, 1922–24–25–26 [Under California, San Francisco]	23
St. Louis County	
Report on Organization of Public Welfare Agencies, 1923	300
St. Paul	
CITY AND REGIONAL PLANNING	
Plan for St. Paul, 1922	53
EDUCATION	
Report of Survey of School System, 1917	108
Help Your School Surveys, 1913 [Under Connecticut, Waterbury]	96

GEOGRAPHICAL INDEX

	PAGE
HEALTH ADMINISTRATION	
Public Health Administration, 1917	136
HEALTH AND SANITATION	
Efficiency and Next Needs, 1913	145
Health Conditions and Health Service, 1919	145
HOUSING	
Housing Conditions, 1917	167
IMMIGRATION AND AMERICANIZATION	
Nationality and School Progress, 1921	177
JUVENILE DELINQUENCY	
Juvenile Delinquent, 1926	214
UNEMPLOYMENT	
Report of Citizens' Committee, 1894	322
Sibley County	
Arlington School Survey, 1921	107
South Minneapolis	
Neighborhood in South Minneapolis, 1922	6
Stillwater	
Report of Social Survey [General], 1920	6
Plan of Stillwater, 1918	54
Winona	
School Building Program, 1922	282
MISSISSIPPI	
Treatment of Dependent, Defective, 1923	86
Public Education in Mississippi, 1926	108
Women in Mississippi Industries, 1926	189
Mississippi Mental Deficiency Survey, 1924	223
Forty Years of Public Schools, 1918	231
Maternity and Child Care (Rural Health], 1921	277
MISSOURI	
GENERAL SOCIAL SURVEYS—RURAL	
Rural Survey in Missouri, 1912	12
ALMSHOUSES	
Condition of County Almshouse, 1904	19
CHILD HEALTH AND HYGIENE	
Progress Report on Field Investigations, 1920	28
CHILD LABOR	
Children Working in Missouri, 1927	32
CRIME AND CRIMINALS	
Administration of Criminal Justice in Missouri, 1926	79
Missouri Crime Survey, 1926	80
EDUCATION	
Professional Preparation of Teachers, 1920	108
Facts Concerning Public Education, 1924	108

A BIBLIOGRAPHY OF SOCIAL SURVEYS

PAGE

HEALTH AND SANITATION
  Study of Malaria Problem, 1923 145
INDUSTRIAL CONDITIONS AND RELATIONS
  Report of Senate Wage Commission, 1915 189
  Women in Missouri Industries, 1924 190
INSANE
  Care and Treatment of Insane, 1920 209
MENTAL HYGIENE
  Report of Missouri Mental Deficiency Survey, 1922 . . . 223
NEGRO EDUCATION
  Report of Missouri Negro Educational . . . Commission, 1920 231
PRISONS
  Condition of County Jails, 1904 246
  Report of Senate Committee on Penitentiary Reform, 1915 . . 247
RELIEF
  Outdoor Relief in Missouri, 1915 259
RELIGION
  Factors Which Have to Do, 1916 [Under Kansas], ... 261
RURAL EDUCATION
  Survey of Rural Schools, 1919 273
  Rural School Health Survey, 1922 273
SCHOOL HEALTH AND SANITATION
  Relation of Physical Defects, 1922 286
TUBERCULOSIS
  Miners' Consumption, 1917 316

Ashland
  Ashland Community Survey [Rural], 1920 12
Booneville
  Missouri Reformatory, 1922 258
Columbia
  What You Should Know about Your City [General], 1913 . . 6
  Negroes of Columbia, 1904 234
Gentry County
  Survey of Gentry County Public Schools, 1922 108
Joplin
  Pulmonary Disease among Miners, 1915 155
Kansas City
  ACCIDENTS AND ACCIDENT PREVENTION
    Report of Investigation of 100, 1912 16
  CITY AND REGIONAL PLANNING
    Kansas City Zone Plan, 1922 54
  EDUCATION
    Kansas City Public Schools, 1916 109

GEOGRAPHICAL INDEX

	PAGE
HEALTH AND SANITATION	
Health Census of Kansas City, 1917	146
HOUSING	
Report on Housing Conditions, 1912	167
Housing Conditions among Negroes, 1921	167
IMMIGRATION AND AMERICANIZATION	
Children of Immigrants in Schools, 1911 [Under United States]	179
INDUSTRIAL CONDITIONS AND RELATIONS	
Women Street Car Conductors, 1920 [Under Illinois, Chicago]	186
NEGROES	
Our Negro Population, 1913	234
PENSIONS	
Public Pensions to Widows, 1913 [Under California, San Francisco]	240
RECREATION	
Recreation Survey, 1912	255
Rotary Club Survey, 1921	255
SOCIAL EVIL	
Social Evil in Kansas City, 1911	303

Morgan County

Rural Survey of Morgan County, 1916	12

St. Joseph

Survey of Work of Associated Charities, 1920	25
Report of Sanitary Survey, 1914	146
Report of Survey of Public School Buildings, 1923	282

St. Louis

CHILD LABOR	
Newsboys of St. Louis, 1910	32
CHILD WELFARE	
Report of Municipal Commission, 1911	42
CITY AND REGIONAL PLANNING	
City Plan for St. Louis, 1907	54
River DesPeres Plan, 1916	54
Major Street Plan, 1917	54
Problems of St. Louis, 1917	54
Public Building Group Plan, 1919	54
Zone Plan, 1919	54
St. Louis Transit System, 1920	54
Plan of St. Louis, 1927	54
CITY, COUNTY, AND STATE ADMINISTRATION	
Organization and Administration of City Government, 1910	65
DELINQUENCY AND CORRECTION	
Report of Mental Hygiene Survey, 1922	86
DETENTION	
Juvenile Detention Home, 1924	90

A BIBLIOGRAPHY OF SOCIAL SURVEYS

	PAGE
EDUCATION	
Report on Speech Defectives, 1916	109
Survey of St. Louis Public Schools, 1917	109
Survey of St. Louis Public Schools, 1918	109
HOUSING	
Housing Conditions in St. Louis, 1908	167
Housing Problem in St. Louis, 1920	167
ILLEGITIMACY	
Illegitimate Births, 1914	174
IMMIGRATION AND AMERICANIZATION	
Children of Immigrants in Schools, 1911 [Under United States]	179
Immigrant in St. Louis, 1916	177
INDUSTRIAL CONDITIONS AND RELATIONS	
Industrial Conditions among Negroes, 1914	190
Women in Candy Industry, 1923 [Under Illinois, Chicago]	186
MILK	
Milk Problem in St. Louis, 1911	227
PRE-NATAL CARE	
Pre-Natal Care of Group of . . . Women, 1913	244
PRISONS	
St. Louis Municipal Jail, 1924	247
PROBATION AND PAROLE	
Report on Probation in St. Louis, 1924	250
RECREATION	
Recreation in St. Louis, 1917	255
RELIGION	
St. Louis Church Survey, 1924	262
UNEMPLOYMENT	
St. Louis after the War, 1918	322

Saline County
Study of Rural Schools, 1915 273

Springfield
Springfield Social Survey [General], 1911 6

Sullivan County
Factors Which Have to Do with Decline, 1916 [Under Kansas] . 261

MONTANA

Report of Survey of Feebleminded, 1919 129
Study of Epidemic Poliomyelitis, 1923 208
Study of Infant and Maternal Death Rates, 1922 . . . 219
Maternity Care and Welfare of Young Children [Rural Health],
1919 277

Butte
Report of Survey of School System, 1914 109

GEOGRAPHICAL INDEX

	PAGE
Family Status of Bread Winning Women, 1925 [Under Florida, Jacksonville]	184
Preliminary Report [Tuberculosis], 1921	316

Ravalli County

Social Study of Ravalli County [Rural], 1923	12

NEBRASKA

Report of Nebraska Children's Code Commission, 1920	42
Public Health Administraton, 1916	137
Tuberculosis among Nebraska Winnebago, 1921	180
Reading Matter in Nebraska Farm Homes, 1922	268
Nebraska Farm Family, 1923	268
Nebraska Farm Homes, 1923	268
Nebraska Farm Tenancy, 1923	268

Buffalo County

Study of Educational Inequalities, 1921	109

Omaha

City Planning Needs of Omaha, 1919	54
Survey of Cause and Extent of Crime, 1924	80
Summary of Study of Juvenile Delinquent, 1925	214
One City's Program for Leisure Time, 1924	255
Social Ministry in American City [Recreation], 1924.	255

South Omaha

Children of Immigrants in Schools, 1911 [Under United States]	179

NEVADA

Public Health Administration, 1916	137

Reno

Report of Survey of University, 1917	109

NEW HAMPSHIRE

Cry of Children, 1908 [Under Alabama]	29
Report of Children's Commission, 1915	42
Report of Commission on State Sanatorium, 1902	160
Report of Special Investigation [Taxation], 1917	307

Coos County

Child Welfare Needs, 1922	42

Dover

Civic Survey, 1918	65

Manchester

Children of Immigrants, 1911 [Under United States]	179
Infant Mortality, 1917	205

NEW JERSEY

GENERAL SOCIAL SURVEYS—RURAL

Social Aspects of Jewish Colonies, 1921	12

A BIBLIOGRAPHY OF SOCIAL SURVEYS

PAGE

ACCIDENTS AND ACCIDENT PREVENTION
  Industrial Accidents to Employed Minors, 1926 [Under Wisconsin]   18
  Industrial Accidents to Women, 1927 16
ALMSHOUSES
  Some American Almshouses, 1927 [Under Connecticut] . . . 19
CHILD LABOR
  Pennsylvania Children on New Jersey Cranberry Farms, 1923 . 33
  Work of Children on Truck . . . Farms, 1924 . . . 33
CHILD WELFARE
  Report of New Jersey Commission, 1898 42
  Child Welfare in New Jersey, 1927 43
CITY AND REGIONAL PLANNING
  Joint Report of New York and New Jersey Port, 1920 [Under New York City] 56
CITY, COUNTY, AND STATE ADMINISTRATION
  Report of Commission, 1916 65
  Analysis of Laws Affecting . . . Finances, 1920 . . . 65
CRIME AND CRIMINALS
  Report of Dependency and Crimes Commission, 1909 . . . 80
HOUSING
  Report of New Jersey Tenement House Commission, 1904 . . 167
INDUSTRIAL CONDITIONS AND RELATIONS
  Three Years under New Jersey Workmen's Law, 1915 . . . 190
  Wage-Earning Women in War Time, 1919 [Under Pennsylvania] . 195
  Executive and Technical Women in Industry, 1920 . . . 190
  Desirable Improvements in . . . Compensation System, 1921 190
  Some Effects of Legislation, 1921 [Under Massachusetts] . . 189
  Women in New Jersey Industries, 1924 190
MENTAL HYGIENE
  Report of New Jersey Commission, 1914 223
NEGROES
  Study of Living Conditions among Colored People, 1915 [Under Pennsylvania] 235
PRISONS
  Report of Commission on Prison Labor, 1879 247
  Report of Prison Inquiry Commission, 1917 247
RURAL
  Truck-Farm Labor in New Jersey, 1925 268
SCHOOL BUILDINGS AND PLANTS
  School Building Survey, 1922 282
SCHOOL ORGANIZATION AND ADMINISTRATION
  Report of . . . Committee to Investigate, 1911 . . . 292
  Report of Survey of Accounting and Business Systems, 1921 . 292
  Studies in Public School Finance, 1923 [Under Massachusetts] 291

GEOGRAPHICAL INDEX

	PAGE
TUBERCULOSIS	
Tuberculosis Survey, 1917	316
Tuberculosis Problem, 1922	316
Bayonne	
Study of School Problem, 1924	109
Bridgeton	
Report and Survey . . . upon Municipal Refuse, 1920.	132
Camden	
Clinical Study of One Thousand Retarded Children, 1910	305
Cranford Township	
Report of Survey of Schools, 1925	109
Dover	
Town Planning for Dover, 1913	54
East Orange	
San Francisco Cancer Survey, 1922–24–25–26 [Under California, San Francisco]	23
City Plan of East Orange, 1922	54
Report of Examination of School System, 1912	110
Report of Study of School Systems, 1922	111
Englewood	
Report of Committee [Charities], 1911	26
Essex County	
Infant Mortality, 1912	205
Fort Lee	
Report of Survey of Schools, 1927	110
Glen Ridge	
Glen Ridge. Preservation of natural beauty, 1909	54
Sanitary Survey, 1916	146
Hackensack	
Hackensack Schools, 1921	110
Hammonton	
Report of Survey of Schools, 1926	110
Hoboken	
Sanitary Survey of Hoboken, 1913	146
Hudson County	
Cost of Living among Wage-Earners, 1920	76
Sweated Work in Hudson County, 1907	191
Jersey City	
Study of First Ward, 1912	6
Report of Suggested Plan [City and Regional Planning], 1913	55
Housing Conditions in Jersey City, 1903	167
Investigation of Slavic Conditions, 1907	297

A BIBLIOGRAPHY OF SOCIAL SURVEYS

PAGE

Mercer County, Lawrence Township
Report of Survey of Public School System, 1922 110
Montclair
Montclair. Preservation of its natural beauty, 1908 55
Report on Program of Studies in Public Schools, 1911 . . . 110
Study of Infant Mortality, 1915 205
Teachers' Salaries, 1922 292
Administration and Costs, 1922 292
Need and Scope of Social Survey, 1912 334
Morris County, Hanover Township
School Survey of Hanover Township, 1923 110
Newark
GENERAL SOCIAL SURVEYS—URBAN
Ironbound District, 1912 6
ALMSHOUSES
Poor and Alms Department and Almshouse, 1919 . . . 19
CANCER
San Francisco Cancer Survey, 1922–24–25–26 [Under California, San Francisco] 23
CITY AND REGIONAL PLANNING
Preliminary Report to City Plan Commission, 1912 . . . 55
City Planning for Newark, 1913 55
Comprehensive Plan for Newark, 1915 55
CITY, COUNTY, AND STATE ADMINISTRATION
Introduction and Explanatory Excerpts, 1919 66
EDUCATION
Nationality and Age-Grade Surveys, 1923 110
All Year Schools of Newark, 1926 111
HOUSING
Housing Report, 1913 167
IMMIGRATION AND AMERICANIZATION
Children of Immigrants in Schools, 1911 [Under United States] . 179
RECREATION
Girls' Recreation Survey, 1923 256
RELIGION
Religious and Sociological Investigation, 1910 . . . 262
SOCIAL AGENCIES
Survey of Jewish Philanthropic Organizations, 1922 . . . 300
SOCIAL EVIL
Report on Social Evil Conditions, 1914 303
New Brunswick
Survey of Rutgers University, 1927 111
Nutley
Report of Study . . . Further School Accommodations, 1925 . 282

GEOGRAPHICAL INDEX

	PAGE
Oranges	
Report of Study of School Systems, 1922	111
Report on Housing Conditions, 1915	168
Passaic	
Problem of Adult Education, 1920	111
Survey of Housing Conditions, 1915	168
Night-Working Mothers, 1920	191
Family Status of Breadwinning Women, 1922	191
Family Status of Breadwinning Women, 1925 [Under Florida, Jacksonville]	184
Paterson	
Zoning: First Step in Planning, 1921	55
Thoroughfares and Traffic of Paterson, 1922	55
Paterson Public Schools, 1918	111
Playgrounds and . . . Recreation, 1914	256
Plainfield	
Housing Conditions in Plainfield, 1914	168
Princeton	
Some Unsolved Problems of a University Town, 1920	6
Ridgewood	
Improvement of Ridgewood, 1908	55
Salem County	
Church and Community Survey, 1922	263
South Orange	
Report of Study of School System, 1922	111
Trenton	
Some Salient Facts [Boy Life], 1922	23
West Orange	
Report of Study . . . of School System, 1922	111

NEW MEXICO

Report on New Mexico State Educational Institutions, 1921	111
Public Health Administration, 1918	137
Interstate Migration of Tuberculous Persons, 1915 [Under Texas]	319

NEW YORK

ACCIDENTS AND ACCIDENT PREVENTION

Causes and Prevention of Industrial Accidents, 1911	17
Asphyxiation in Garages, 1920	17
Analysis of One Hundred Accidents, 1924	17
Analysis of Three Hundred Accidents, 1925	17
Children's Work Accidents, 1923	17
Some Social and Economic Effects, 1924	17
Some Recent Figures, 1926	17

A BIBLIOGRAPHY OF SOCIAL SURVEYS

PAGE

ALMSHOUSES
Some American Almshouses, 1927 [Under Connecticut] . . 19
BLINDNESS, SIGHT CONSERVATION, AND DISEASE OF THE EYE
Report of Commission, 1906 21
CHARITIES
Report of State Commissioner, 1916 26
CHILD HEALTH AND HYGIENE
Child Health Survey, 1922 28
Health of Working Child, 1924 28
CHILD LABOR
Unrestricted Forms of Child Labor, 1911 33
Administration of Child Labor Laws, 1917 . . . 33
Children in Industry, 1919 33
Trend of Child Labor, 1923 33
CHILD WELFARE
How Foster Children Turn Out, 1924 43
Report on Manufacturing in Tenements, 1924 43
Public Child-Caring Work, 1927 [Under Minnesota] . . 42
CITY, COUNTY, AND STATE ADMINISTRATION
Report of Investigation . . . State Institutions, 1911 . . 66
Report of New York State Legislature Joint Committee, 1911 . 66
COST OF LIVING
Investigations into Living Costs, 1919 76
CRIPPLED, DISABLED, AND HANDICAPPED
Report of New York State Commission for Survey, 1925 . . 82
Survey of Educational Facilities for Crippled Children, 1925 . . 82
DELINQUENCY AND CORRECTION
Report of Special Committee, 1918 86
Mental Disease and Delinquency, 1919 86
Study of Women Delinquents, 1920 87
DEPENDENCY
Report on Standards of Placing Out, 1916 88
EDUCATION
Digest of New York School Inquiry, 1913 111
Costs of Compulsory Attendance Service, 1924 . . . 111
Study of Pupil Classification, 1925 111
EPILEPTICS
Nine Family Histories of Epileptics, 1916 126
FEEBLEMINDED
Care of Feebleminded, 1919 129
FOOD
Report of Food Problem Committee, 1918 132
HEALTH AND SANITATION
Report of Special Public Health Commission, 1913 . . . 146
Report of New York State Commission, 1923 146

GEOGRAPHICAL INDEX

PAGE

HEALTH IN INDUSTRY
    Health Hazards of Cloth Sponging Industry, 1918 155
    Health Hazards of Chemical Industry, 1919 155
    Sickness among New York Factory Workers, 1919 . . . 155
    Study of Hygienic Conditions in Steam Laundries, 1924 . . 155
    Chronic Benzol Poisoning, 1927 155

HOUSING
    Report of Commission, 1915 168
    Study of Housing Conditions, 1916 168
    Report of Housing Committee, 1920 168
    Intermediate Report of Joint Legislative Committee, 1922 . . 168
    Final Report of Joint Legislative Committee, 1923 168
    Present Status of Housing Emergency, 1924 168
    Tax Exemption of New Housing, 1924 168
    Report of Commission of Housing and Regional Planning, 1926 . 168
    Some Economic Aspects, 1924 169

IMMIGRATION AND AMERICANIZATION
    Report of Joint Legislative Committee, 1924 177

INDIANS
    Indians of New York State, 1922 180

INDUSTRIAL CONDITIONS AND RELATIONS
    Report to Legislature . . . of Employers' Liability, 1910 . 191
    Preliminary Report of Factory Investigating Commission, 1912 . 191
    Second Report   "   "   "   " 1913 . 191
    Third Report   "   "   "   " 1914 . 191
    Fourth Report   "   "   "   " 1915 . 191
    Brief Summary of Investigations, 1916 191
    Telephone Industry, 1920 192
    Outer-Wear Knit Goods Industry, 1923 192
    Hours and Earnings of Women, 1923 192
    Vacation Policies, 1925 192
    Women's Wages Today, 1920 192
    Behind Scenes in Hotel, 1922 192
    Executive and Technical Women in Industry, 1920 [Under New
        Jersey] 190
    Our Boys, 1921 192

INFANTILE PARALYSIS
    After-Care of Poliomyelitis, 1918 208

INSANE
    Report of Investigation of State Commission, 1895 . . . 209
    Social Aspects of Treatment of Insane, 1921 209

JUVENILE DELINQUENCY
    Juvenile Delinquency, 1918 214

MENTAL HYGIENE
    Report of State Commission, 1915 223

A BIBLIOGRAPHY OF SOCIAL SURVEYS

	PAGE
Case Studies in Mental Defect, 1918	223
Mental Defectives in Community, 1924	223
Report of Mental Hygiene Survey, 1925	223

POSTURE
Industrial Posture and Seating, 1921 244

PRISONS
Report of Commission, 1876 247
Report of Prison Labor Reform Commission, 1887 . . 247
Report of Special Committee, 1899 247
Prison Methods in New York State, 1920 247
Report of Prison Survey Committee, 1920. . . . 247
Plan for Custody and Training of Prisoners, 1925 . . . 248

PROBATION AND PAROLE
Report of Probation Commission, 1906 250
Methods of Supervising Persons on Probation, 1922 . . 251
Report to Commission, 1927. 251

RELIEF
Report of New York State Commission, 1914 . . . 259

RURAL EDUCATION
Rural School Survey of New York State, 1922 . . . 274

RURAL HEALTH AND SANITATION
Rural Death Rate, 1913 278
Preliminary Inquiry into Health Needs, 1916 . . . 278

SCHOOL BUILDINGS AND PLANTS
Buildings and Grounds, 1922 282

SCHOOL ORGANIZATION AND ADMINISTRATION
Studies in Public School Finance, 1923 [Under Massachusetts] . 291
Cost of Government and Support of Education, 1924 . . 293
Financing of Education, 1924 293
Elementary School Costs, 1924 293
Cost and Support of Secondary Schools, 1924 . . . 293

TAXATION
Report of Joint Legislative Committee, 1916 . . . 307
Report of Special Joint Committee, 1920–27 . . . 307
Financial Support, 1922. 308

UNEMPLOYMENT
Unemployment and Lack of Farm Labor, 1911 . . . 322

PURPOSE, METHOD, AND STANDARDS
Economic Study of Farm Layout, 1920 355
Standard of Life in Typical Section, 1923 355

Albany
San Francisco Cancer Survey, 1922–24–25–26 [Under California, San Francisco] 23

Albany County
Survey of Albany County Jail and Penitentiary, 1924 . . . 248
Rural Health Survey, 1915 278

GEOGRAPHICAL INDEX

                                                                                       PAGE

Amsterdam
- Report of Health Inventory, 1918 146
- Houses of Amsterdam with . . . Tuberculosis, 1917 . . 317

Batavia
- Epidemiologic Studies [Under Iowa], 1913 207

Bedford Hills
- Experimental Study of Psychopathic Delinquent Women, 1923 . 87

Belleville
- National Influence of Single Farm Community, 1921 . . . 269

Binghamton
- Better Binghamton, 1911 . . . . . . *. . . 55
- Report of Survey of Binghamton School System, 1919 . . 112

Brooklyn
- Neighborhood Survey, 1927 7
- Report upon Divisions Four and Five, 1915 113
- Progress of Housing Reform, 1916 169
- Housing Standards in Brooklyn, 1918 169
- Community Study [Religion], 1915 263
- Report and Outline of Proposed Survey, 1926 340
- Report of Crime and Courts Study, 1926 344

Buffalo
- San Francisco Cancer Survey, 1922–24–25–26 [Under California, San Francisco] 23
- Examination of Public School System, 1916 112
- Adult Education in Community, 1926 112
- Report to Citizens' Committee [Hospitals and Sanatoria], 1922 . 160
- Nationality, Color, and Economic Opportunity, 1927 . . 192
- Children of Immigrants in Schools, 1911 [Under United States] . 179
- Epidemiologic Studies [Under Iowa], 1913 207
- Study of Acute Anterior Poliomyelitis Epidemic, 1913 . . 208
- Brief Report on Mental Defectives, 1917 224
- Americanizing Eighty Thousand, 1910 242
- Study of Social and Recreational Resources, 1923 . . . 256
- Recreation Survey of Buffalo, 1925 256

Dansville
- Dansville High School, 1915 112

Dutchess County
- Public Outdoor Relief, 1913 259
- Sickness in Dutchess County, 1915 278

Elmira
- Report of Commission [Under New York], 1876 247
- Report on Vice Conditions, 1913 326
- Report of Vocational Survey, 1919 331

A BIBLIOGRAPHY OF SOCIAL SURVEYS

PAGE

Erie County
Study of Activities of . . . Board of Child Welfare, 1921 . . 43
Child Health in Erie County, 1922 278

Great Neck
Great Neck School Survey, 1917 112

Ithaca
Survey of Public Health Situation, 1915 146

Jamestown
Jamestown Eye Survey, 1926 21
First Annual Report . . . and Comprehensive Plan, 1908 . 55
Government of City of Jamestown, 1917 66

Jefferson County
Summary of Investigation of Source of Typhoid Fever, 1915 . . 146

Kings County
Study of Crime Conditions, 1927 80

Livingston County
Survey of Livingston County Schools, 1921 112

Madison County
San Francisco Cancer Survey, 1922–24–25–26 [Under California, San Francisco] 23

Mount Vernon
Community Survey, 1925 6
Study of Activities of Neighborhood House, 1922 . . . 210

Nassau County
Report of Survey of Public Education, 1918 112
Survey of Mental Disorders, 1916 224

Newburgh
Newburgh Survey, 1913 7
Housing Investigation, 1913 169

NEW YORK CITY

GENERAL SOCIAL SURVEYS—URBAN
Middle West Side, 1914 7
Boyhood and Lawlessness, 1914 7
Social Survey of Washington Street District, 1914 . . . 7

ADOLESCENCE
Adolescent Offender, 1923 18
Determinants of Sex Delinquency, 1923 19

BLINDNESS, SIGHT CONSERVATION, AND DISEASE OF THE EYE
Care and Treatment of Jewish Blind, 1918 21

BOY LIFE
Survey of New York City Boys, 1926. 23

CARDIACS
Special Report on Cardiac Classes, 1923 24

420

GEOGRAPHICAL INDEX

	PAGE
CHARITIES	
Report of Committee on Inquiry, 1913	26
Brief Summary of Final Report, 1920	26
CHILD HEALTH AND HYGIENE	
Health of Thousand Newsboys, 1926	28
Study of 106 Malnourished Children, 1927	28
CHILD LABOR	
Heights and Weights of New York City Children, 1916	33
Child Labor and Juvenile Delinquency, 1918	33
CHILD WELFARE	
Child in Foster Home, 1921	43
CITY AND REGIONAL PLANNING	
Report of Committee, 1912	55
Development and Present Status, 1914	56
Final Report of Commission, 1916	56
Establishment of Setbacks, 1917	56
Street Tree System, 1916	56
Joint Report of New York and New Jersey, 1920	56
Port of New York Authority, 1921	56
Plan of New York and Its Environs, 1923	56
Predicted Growth, 1924	56
Highway Traffic, 1925	56
Transit and Transportation, 1926	56
Land Values, 1927	56
Chemical Industry, 1924	57
Metal Industry, 1924	57
Food Manufacturing Industries, 1924	57
Wood Industries, 1924	57
Tobacco Products Industry, 1924	57
Printing Industry, 1924	57
Clothing and Textile Industries, 1925	57
Retail Shopping and Financial Districts, 1927	57
Wholesale Markets, 1925	57
CITY, COUNTY, AND STATE ADMINISTRATION	
Administrative Reorganization, 1915	66
Government of City of New York, 1915	66
Study of County Government, 1915	66
New York City's Administrative Progress, 1916	66
CLINICS AND DISPENSARIES	
Work of New York's Tuberculosis Clinics, 1910	70
Dispensary Situation in New York City, 1920	70
Tuberculosis Clinics, 1920	70
Venereal Disease Clinics, 1920	70
Community Dental Service, 1924	70
Medical Care for Million People, 1927	71

A BIBLIOGRAPHY OF SOCIAL SURVEYS

PAGE

CONVALESCENCE
Convalescent Treatment of Heart Disease, 1921 73
Provision for Care of Convalescents, 1923 73
Study of Country Convalescent, 1923. 73
Convalescence for Neuropsychiatric Patients, 1926 73

COST OF LIVING
Wage-Earners' Budgets, 1907 76
Standard of Living among Workingmen's Families, 1909 . . 76
Report of Cost of Living, 1916 76
Minimum Cost of Living, 1917 76
My Money Won't Reach, 1918 77
Cost of Living in New York City, 1926 77

CRIPPLED, DISABLED, AND HANDICAPPED
Economic Consequences of Physical Disability, 1918 . . . 82
Survey of Cripples, 1920 83
Securing Employment for Handicapped, 1927 83

DANCE HALLS
Report of Advisory Dance Hall Committee, 1924 84

DEPENDENCY
Physical Examination and Employment, 1913 89

EDUCATION
Compulsory Attendance Service, 1913 112
Digest of New York School Inquiry, 1913 112
Report of Committee on School Inquiry, 1913 112
School Efficiency, 1913 113
Survey of Gary and Prevocational Schools, 1916 113
Instruction in Civics, 1917 113
Private Commercial Schools, 1918 113
Self-Supporting Students, 1920 113
Survey of Junior High Schools, 1923 113
Survey of Educational Activities, 1923 113
Fitting School to Child, 1924 113
Study of After-Career, 1926 114

FAMILY WELFARE
Home Service in Action, 1921 127
When Fathers Drop Out, 1924 127

FEEBLEMINDED
Study of Feebleminded, 1913 129

FIRE
Investigation of Fire Department, 1908 131
Fire Hazards in Factory Buildings, 1923 131

FOOD
Health of Food Handlers, 1917 132

GARBAGE, REFUSE, AND SEWAGE
Report on Collection and Disposal of Solid Wastes, 1921 . . 133

GEOGRAPHICAL INDEX

PAGE

HEALTH AND SANITATION
Report on Croton Watershed, 1891 146
Comfort Stations in New York City, 1913 147
Flies and Diarrheal Diseases, 1915 147
Health Census, 1917 147
Laundries and Public Health, 1917 147
Cost of Clean Clothes, 1918 147
Survey of Activities, 1918 147
Health of Neighborhood, 1924 147
Better Doctoring, 1927 147

HEALTH IN INDUSTRY
Occupational Disease, 1912 156
Notes on Industrial Survey, 1912 156
Health of Garment Workers, 1915 156
Effect of Gas . . . upon Air of Workshops, 1917 . . 156
Health of Garment Workers, 1916 156
Occupation and Mortality, 1917 156
Clinical Study of Frequency of Lead, 1918 156

HOSPITALS AND SANATORIA
Ambulance Service, 1907 160
Report of Commission on Hospitals, 1909 160
Subsequent History of Patients, 1913 160
Chronic Disabled Heart Patient, 1923 161
Hospital Situation in Greater New York, 1924 . . . 161

HOUSING
Tenement House Administration, 1909 169
Report of Heights of Buildings Commission, 1913 . . 169
Housing Conditions among Negroes, 1915 169
Study of Living Conditions, 1915 169
Housing Situation, 1921 170
Housing Conditions of Employed Women, 1922 . . . 170
Should Not State End New York City's Rookeries, 1924 . 170

ILLEGITIMACY
Negro Illegitimacy, 1926 174

IMMIGRATION AND AMERICANIZATION
Children of Immigrants in Schools, 1911 [Under United States] . 179
Immigrants in Cities, 1911 [Under United States] . . . 179

INDUSTRIAL CONDITIONS AND RELATIONS
Clothing Industry of New York, 1905 192
Women in Bookbinding Trade, 1913 192
Working Girls in Evening Schools, 1914 192
Seasonal Industry, 1917 192
Artificial Flower Makers, 1918 193
Longshoremen, 1915 193
Increased Employment of Women in Industry, 1917 . . 193

A BIBLIOGRAPHY OF SOCIAL SURVEYS

	PAGE
Opportunities for Women, 1918	193
Women Street Railway Employees, 1918	193
New Day for Colored Women Workers, 1919	193
Less than a Living Wage, 1921	193
Home Work in Men's Clothing Industry, 1926	193

INDUSTRIAL EDUCATION
    Industrial Education Survey, 1918 203
INFANT MORTALITY
    Infant Mortality in New York City, 1921 205
INFANTILE PARALYSIS
    Monograph on Epidemic of Poliomyelitis, 1917 . . . 208
    Epidemiological Studies of Poliomyelitis, 1918 . . . 208
ITALIANS
    Italian Women in Industry, 1919 210
    Growth and Development of Italian Children, 1924 . . 210
JUVENILE DELINQUENCY
    Study of Delinquent and Neglected Negro Children, 1927 . 214
MILK
    Study of New York City Milk Problem, 1919 227
MOTION PICTURES
    Report on Condition of Moving Picture Shows, 1911 . . 230
NEGRO EDUCATION
    Colored School Children, 1915 231
NEGROES
    Negro at Work in New York City, 1912 234
    Study of Negro Employees, 1916 235
    Health Work of Mothers and Children, 1924 235
NURSERIES AND NURSING
    Day Nurseries, 1924 238
    Comparative Study, 1926 238
PENSIONS
    Report on Pension Funds, 1916 241
    Industrial Pensions, 1920 241
POPULATION
    Study of Population, 1909 243
    Report of New York State Commission, 1911 243
    Statistical Sources, 1920 244
POSTURE
    Defective Seating and Faulty Posture, 1923 244
PRISONS
    Study of Conditions, 1924 248
    Two Reports on Reorganization, 1925 248
PROHIBITION
    Bowery, 1923 251

GEOGRAPHICAL INDEX

	PAGE
PROSTITUTION	
Commercialized Prostitution, 1913	251
Comparison between 1912 and 1915, 1915	252
" " " " 1915 and 1916, 1916	252
" " " " 1915, 1916, and 1917, 1917	252
RECREATION	
Statement Relating to Recreation, 1910	256
Exploitation of Pleasure, 1911	256
Report by Committee on Recreation, 1916	256
Planning for Play, 1925	256
RELIGION	
Survey of Young Men's Christian Association, 1927	263
RELIGIOUS EDUCATION	
Jewish Religious Education in Bronx, 1916	267
Survey of Jewish Religious School Conditions, 1921	267
SCHOOL BUILDINGS AND PLANTS	
Report Submitted to Committee, 1912	282
Study of 40 School Buildings, 1922	283
SCHOOL ORGANIZATION AND ADMINISTRATION	
Reports of Investigation, 1905	293
How New York City Administers Its Schools, 1913	293
SEX DELINQUENCY	
Women's Day Court of Manhattan, 1922	297
Specialized Courts Dealing with Sex Delinquency, 1925 [Under Illinois, Chicago]	296
SLUMS	
Slums of Baltimore, etc., 1894 [Under Maryland, Baltimore]	298
Plague in Its Stronghold, 1903	298
SOCIAL AGENCIES	
Positions in Social Work, 1916	300
Finances of New York's Social Work, 1925	300
SOCIAL EVIL	
Social Evil, 1910	303
Social Evil, 1912	303
TAXATION	
Final Report of Committee, 1916	308
TRUANCY AND NON-ATTENDANCE	
Truancy, 1915	311
Study of 201 Truants, 1927	311
TUBERCULOSIS	
Tuberculosis Families in Their Homes, 1916	317
Tuberculosis among Different Nationalities, 1923	317
Tuberculosis Family Problem, 1924	317
UNEMPLOYMENT	
Public Employment Exchanges, 1914	322

A BIBLIOGRAPHY OF SOCIAL SURVEYS

	PAGE
Unemployment in New York City, 1915	322
Report of Mayor's Committee, 1916	322

VAGRANTS
    Why There Are Vagrants, 1916 324
VOCATIONAL GUIDANCE AND TRAINING
    Report of Vocational Guidance Survey, 1912 331
    Vocational Guidance and Placement Work, 1923 . . . 331
    Vocational Guidance and Junior Placement, 1925 [Under
      California, Oakland] 328
PURPOSE, METHOD, AND STANDARDS
    Teachers' Year Book of . . . Investigations, 1916 . . 346

New York County
Report of Mental Hygiene Survey, 1925 224

Niagara Falls
Niagara Falls School System, 1921 114
Health Hazards in Industries, 1920 157
Proposed Employment of Women, 1918 194

Ogdensburg
Report of Improvement Commission [City and Regional Planning],
  1907 57
Survey of Infant Mortality, 1915 206

Oneida County
Causes of Dependency, 1918 89

Onondaga
Study of Sanitary Conditions, 1919. 180

Poughkeepsie
Report of Housing Survey, 1919 170
Italian Situation in Poughkeepsie, 1918 210

Rochester
GENERAL SOCIAL SURVEYS—URBAN
    Fourth Ward Survey: Know Your City, 1911 7
CHARITIES
    Abstract of Report on Department of Charities, 1918 . . 26
CITY AND REGIONAL PLANNING
    City Plan for Rochester, 1911 57
CITY, COUNTY, AND STATE ADMINISTRATION
    Critical Appraisal and Constructive Suggestions, 1915 . . 67
    Report on Problem of Street Cleaning, 1918 67
    Report on Administration of Bureau of Buildings, 1921 . . 67
EDUCATION
    Survey of Needs in Commercial Education, 1915 . . . 114
GARBAGE, REFUSE, AND SEWAGE
    Report on Problem of Snow Removal, 1917 133
    Report on Problem of Refuse Collection, 1919 133

GEOGRAPHICAL INDEX

	PAGE
HEALTH AND SANITATION	
Sanitary Survey, 1911	148
Community Sickness Survey, 1916	148
INDUSTRIAL CONDITIONS AND RELATIONS	
Homework in Men's Clothing Industry, 1926	193
JUVENILE DELINQUENCY	
Condensed Report of Survey, 1923	214
POLICE	
Report of Survey of Police Bureau, 1921	242
SCHOOL BUILDINGS AND PLANTS	
Summary of School Building Survey, 1923	283
TAXATION	
Report on Assessment of Real Property, 1921	308
VOCATIONAL GUIDANCE AND TRAINING	
Vocational Guidance and Junior Placement, 1925 [Under California, Oakland]	328

Rockland County

Report of Survey Made in Rockland County [Vice], 1915 . . . 326

Rome

Fifty-Two Border-Line Cases [Mental Hygiene], 1915 . . . 224

Sag Harbor

Sag Harbor Survey [General], 1911 7

Saranac Lake

Tuberculosis Survey, 1918 317

Staten Island

Report of Mental Health Survey, 1925 224

Syracuse

Report of Investigations, 1912 26
Child Welfare in Syracuse, 1919 43
City Planning for Syracuse, 1919 57
Report of Investigations [Education], 1912 114
Report of Investigation [Health], 1912 148
Social Evil, 1913 303

Tompkins County

Country Church, 1913 263
Country Church in Colonial Counties, 1922 263
Agricultural Survey, 1911 269

Troy

Report of Investigation of . . . Milk, 1919 . . . 227
Report of Survey of Department of Finance, 1918 . . . 308

Utica

Report of Committee on Improving . . . Utica, 1908 . . 57
Plan for Development of . . . Streets, 1922 58
Report of Survey of Utica School System, 1919 114

A BIBLIOGRAPHY OF SOCIAL SURVEYS

PAGE

Warren County
Country Church in Colonial Counties, 1922 263
Watertown
Report of Survey of Schools, 1926 114
Westchester County
School Reports, 1912 114
Survey of Need for Special Schools, 1924 114
Study of Public Health Nursing, 1919 238
Factors Which Have to Do with Decline, 1916 [Under Kansas] . 261
White Plains
Administration of Child Labor . . . Laws, 1920 34
School Building Program, 1923 283
Yonkers
Housing of Working People, 1898 170
Children of Immigrants in Schools, 1911 [Under United States] . 179

NEW ZEALAND

New Zealand Study in Infant Mortality, 1925 206
Immigration Situation in Other Countries, 1911 [Under United States] 180

NORTH CAROLINA

CHILD LABOR
Child Labor in the Carolinas, 1910 34
CHILD WELFARE
Child Welfare in North Carolina, 1918 43
Rural Children in Selected Counties, 1918 44
Public Child-Caring Work, 1927 [Under Minnesota] . . . 42
EDUCATION
Public Education in North Carolina, 1920 114
Study of Mill Schools, 1925 115
HEALTH AND SANITATION
Malaria in North Carolina, 1914 148
Sickness Survey, 1916 148
RELIGION
Church and Landless Men, 1921 263
SCHOOL HEALTH AND SANITATION
School Hygiene, 1914 287
Heights and Weights of School Children, 1922 [Under Maryland] . 285
Trachoma, 1914 310
Interstate Migration of Tuberculous Persons, 1915 . . . 317
Resumé of Tuberculosis Survey, 1921 317
Blewetts Falls
Survey of Blewetts Falls [Health], 1915 148

GEOGRAPHICAL INDEX

PAGE

Charlotte
    Agricultural Mecklenburg and Industrial Charlotte, 1926 . . 7
    Cost of Living among Wage-Earners, 1920 [Under South Carolina,
        Greenville and Pelzer] 77
    Recreation in Charlotte, 1915 256

Currituck County
    Suggestions for Reorganization of Schools, 1921 293

Elizabeth City
    Educational Survey, 1921 115
    High School Survey, 1923 115

Forsyth County
    Economic and Social Study, 1924 12

Gaston County
    Economic and Social Study, 1920 12

Halifax County
    Economic and Social Study, 1920 12

Lenoir County
    Survey of Public Schools, 1924. 115

Mecklenburg County
    Agricultural Mecklenburg, 1926 7

New Hanover County
    Survey of School System, 1920 115

Orange County
    Study of Public Schools, 1919 115

Pitt County
    Economic and Social Study, 1920 12

Raleigh
    City Plan for Raleigh, 1913 58
    Health Survey of Raleigh, 1918 148

Rockingham County
    Economic and Social Study, 1918 12

Rutherford County
    Economic and Social Study, 1918 13

Sampson County
    Economic and Social Study, 1917 13

Wake County
    Economic and Social Study, 1918 13
    Rural Organization, 1922 269

Washington
    School Building Program, 1923 283

Winston-Salem
    Study of Winston-Salem Schools, 1918 115

Yancey County
   Pellagra in Mountains of Yancey County, 1920 278

NORTH DAKOTA
   Child Labor in North Dakota, 1923 34
   Report of Children's Code Commission, 1922 44
   Dependent and Delinquent Children, 1926 44
   Cost of Living Survey, 1921 77
   Report of Temporary Educational Commission, 1912 . . 115
   State Higher Educational Institutions, 1917 116
   Public Health Administration, 1916 137
   Report of Survey of Public Heath Administration, 1923 . . 137
   Report of North Dakota Mental Hygiene Survey, 1923 . . 224
   Poor Relief and Jails, 1913 248
   Report of Rural School Commission, 1912 274

Alice
   Rural Survey of Alice, 1917 269

Fargo
   Social Survey of Fargo, 1915 7
   Survey of Public Health Work, 1927 148

NORWAY
   Part-Time Schools, 1922 [Under United States] 72

NOVA SCOTIA
Halifax
   Catastrophe and Social Change, 1920 91

OHIO
   GENERAL SOCIAL SURVEYS—RURAL
     Southeastern Ohio, 1913 13
     Southwestern Ohio, 1913 13
     Northwestern Ohio, 1914 13
   ACCIDENTS AND ACCIDENT PREVENTION
     Accidents to Working Children, 1927 17
     Industrial Accidents to Women, 1927 [Under New Jersey] . . 16
   BLINDNESS, SIGHT CONSERVATION, AND DISEASE OF THE EYE
     Mental Survey of . . . Blind, 1916 21
   CITY, COUNTY, AND STATE ADMINISTRATION
     Report of Committee for Investigation, 1915 67
     Report of Joint Committee, 1921 67
     Report on State Institutions, 1921 67
   COST OF LIVING
     Women's Wages and Cost of Living, 1922 77
   EDUCATION
     Report of Ohio State Survey Commission, 1914 . . . 116

GEOGRAPHICAL INDEX

	PAGE
FEEBLEMINDED	
Feebleminded in Rural County, 1918	129
HEALTH IN INDUSTRY	
Survey of Industrial Health Hazards, 1915	157
INDUSTRIAL CONDITIONS AND RELATIONS	
Preliminary Survey of Labor Camps, 1917	194
Women in Ohio Industries, 1925	194
MARRIAGE LAWS	
School Girl Brides, 1926	218
PENSIONS	
Health Insurance, 1919	241
PRISONS	
Penal Problem in Ohio, 1926	248
RELIGION	
Six Thousand Country Churches, 1919	263
Survey Reports of Churches, 1920–22	263
RURAL	
Rural Survey of Sharon Parish, 1915	269
Survey of Fry's Valley, 1916	269
RURAL EDUCATION	
Study of Rural School Conditions, 1920	274
TAXATION	
Report on Taxation, 1915	308
Finances of Ohio Cities, 1917	308
TUBERCULOSIS	
Survey of Tuberculosis Situation, 1912	318
UNEMPLOYMENT	
Ohio and Unemployment, 1921	322
PURPOSE, METHOD, AND STANDARDS	
Sanitary Schoolhouses, 1913	356

Akron

City Plan for Akron, 1919	58
Tentative Zoning Plan for Akron, 1921	58
Report on Municipal Court, 1922	87
Report on Schools of Akron, 1917	116
Infant Mortality, 1920	206

Cincinnati

ALMSHOUSES	
Hamilton County Home, 1927	19
CHILD LABOR	
Experimental Study of Children at Work, 1926	34
Study of Industrial Injuries to Working Children, 1927	34
CITY AND REGIONAL PLANNING	
Official Plan of City of Cincinnati, 1925	58

A BIBLIOGRAPHY OF SOCIAL SURVEYS

	PAGE
CITY, COUNTY, AND STATE ADMINISTRATION	
Government of Cincinnati and Hamilton County, 1924	67
COST OF LIVING	
Cost of Living among Wage-Earners, 1920	77
FEEBLEMINDED	
Feebleminded or Hub of Our Wheel of Vice, 1915	129
Feebleminded Ex-School Children, 1921	129
HEALTH AND SANITATION	
Survey of Community Dental Facilities, 1927	149
HEALTH IN INDUSTRY	
Study of Restaurant Kitchens, 1916	157
HOSPITALS AND SANATORIA	
Hospitals of Cincinnati, 1925	161
HOUSING	
Study of Living Conditions, 1916	170
Tenement House Survey, 1921	170
ILLEGITIMACY	
Illegitimacy in Cincinnati, 1919	175
IMMIGRATION AND AMERICANIZATION	
Children of Immigrants in Schools, 1911 [Under United States]	179
INDUSTRIAL CONDITIONS AND RELATIONS	
Garment Making Industries, 1915	194
Printing Trades, 1915	194
Study of Restaurant Kitchens, 1916	194
Women Workers in Factories, 1918	194
Wage-Earning Girls in Cincinnati, 1927	194
INFANT MORTALITY	
Study of Infant Mortality, 1927	206
INFANTILE PARALYSIS	
Epidemiologic Studies, 1913 [Under Iowa]	207
MENTAL HYGIENE	
Report of Mental Hygiene Survey, 1922	224
NEGROES	
Cincinnati Negro Survey and Program, 1919	235
RECREATION	
Recreation Survey of Cincinnati, 1913	257
RELIEF	
House of Refuge, 1912	260
SCHOOL HEALTH AND SANITATION	
Thyroid Survey of 47,493 Elementary School Children, 1924	287
SOCIAL AGENCIES	
Community Responsibility, 1921	301
SUB-NORMAL, RETARDED, AND EXCEPTIONAL CHILDREN	
Retardation in Cincinnati Public Elementary Schools, 1918	305
Diagnosis and Treatment of Young School Failures, 1923	305

GEOGRAPHICAL INDEX

                                                                                   PAGE

TUBERCULOSIS
    Tuberculosis among Industrial Workers, 1916 318
VOCATIONAL GUIDANCE AND TRAINING
    Vocational Guidance and Junior Placement, 1925 [Under California, Oakland] 328

Clermont County
Rural Life Survey, 1914 13

Cleveland
GENERAL SOCIAL SURVEYS—URBAN
    Review of Surveys of Cleveland Foundation, 1923 7
BLINDNESS, SIGHT CONSERVATION, AND DISEASE OF THE EYE
    Blind in Cleveland, 1918 21
CHILD HEALTH AND HYGIENE
    Program for Child Health, 1920 28
CITY AND REGIONAL PLANNING
    Report of Committee on Grouping Plan, 1899 58
    Billboards, 1921 58
    Cleveland Thorofare Plan, 1921 58
    Cleveland Zone Plan, 1922 58
    Plan for Greater Cleveland, 1923 58
CONTINUATION AND PART-TIME SCHOOLS
    Continuation Schools, 1913 72
CRIME AND CRIMINALS
    Criminal Justice in Cleveland, 1921 80
    Correctional and Penal Treatment, 1922 80
    Criminal Courts, 1922 80
    Criminal Justice and American City, 1922 80
    Medical Science and Criminal Justice, 1922 80
    Prosecution, 1922 80
CRIPPLED, HANDICAPPED, AND DISABLED
    Education and Occupations of Cripples, 1918 83
CZECHS
    Czechs of Cleveland, 1919 83
DELINQUENCY AND CORRECTION
    Delinquency and Spare Time, 1918 87
DEPENDENCY
    Children's Bureau of Cleveland, 1927 89
EDUCATION
    Report of Educational Commission, 1906 116
    Child Accounting in Public Schools, 1916 116
    Educational Extension, 1916 116
    Household Arts and School Lunches, 1916 116
    Measuring Work of Public Schools, 1916 116
    Overcrowded Schools and Platoon Plan, 1916 116
    Teaching Staff, 1916 116

A BIBLIOGRAPHY OF SOCIAL SURVEYS

	PAGE
What Schools Teach, 1916	116
Cleveland School Survey, 916	116
Cleveland Public Schools, 1922	117
Survey of Higher Education, 1925	117

HEALTH AND SANITATION

Education and Practice in Medicine, 1920	149
Introduction, General Environment, and Sanitation, 1920	149
Popular Summary of Cleveland Hospital Survey, 1920	149
Public Health Agencies, 1920	149
Typhoid Fever in Cleveland, 1921	149
Cleveland Hospital and Health Survey, 1922	149

HEALTH IN INDUSTRY

Industrial Medical Series, 1920	157

HOSPITALS AND SANATORIA

Hospitals and Dispensaries, 1920	161

HOUSING

Housing Conditions in Cleveland, 1904	170
Investigation of Housing Conditions, 1914	170
Investigation of Housing Conditions of War Workers, 1918	171

IMMIGRATION AND AMERICANIZATION

Children of Immigrants in Schools, 1911 [Under United States]	179
Immigrants in Cities, 1911 [Under United States]	179
School and Immigrant, 1916	178
Americanization in Cleveland, 1918	178

INDUSTRIAL CONDITIONS AND RELATIONS

Study of Women's Work in Cleveland, 1908	194
Employee Representation in Industry, 1923	194

INDUSTRIAL EDUCATION

Industrial Education in . . . Public Schools, 1914	203
Boys and Girls in Commercial Work, 1916	203
Dressmaking and Millinery, 1916	203
Railroad and Street Transportation, 1916	203
Building Trades, 1916	203
Metal Trades, 1916	203
Printing Trades, 1916	203
Department Store Occupations, 1916	203
Garment Trades, 1916	203
Wage-Earning and Education, 1916	203

ITALIANS

Italians of Cleveland, 1919	210

JUGO-SLAVS

Jugo-Slavs in Cleveland, 1918	211

LIBRARIES

Public Library and Public School, 1916	216

GEOGRAPHICAL INDEX

	PAGE
LITHUANIANS	
Lithuanians of Cleveland, 1920	217
MAGYARS	
Magyars of Cleveland, 1919	218
MENTAL HYGIENE	
Mental Disease and Mental Deficiency, 1920	224
NURSERIES AND NURSING	
Nursing, 1920	238
POLES	
Poles of Cleveland, 1919	242
POLICE	
Police Administration, 1921	242
RECREATION	
Report of Committee on Public Recreation, 1912	257
Education through Recreation, 1916	257
School Work and Spare Time, 1918	257
Wholesome Citizens and Spare Time, 1918	257
Sphere of Private Agencies, 1918	257
Commercial Recreation, 1920	257
Public Provision for Recreation, 1920	257
Community Recreation Program, 1920	257
RELIGION	
Survey of Protestant Churches, 1916	264
Religious Survey, 1920	264
Churches and Foreign Situation, 1921	264
SCHOOL BUILDINGS AND PLANTS	
School Buildings and Equipment, 1916	283
Survey of Public School Building Requirements, 1920	283
SCHOOL HEALTH AND SANITATION	
Health Work in Public Schools, 1916	287
Stamp It Out of Schools, 1922	287
SCHOOL ORGANIZATION AND ADMINISTRATION	
Financing Public Schools, 1915	293
School Organization and Administration, 1916	293
SLOVAKS	
Slovaks of Cleveland, 1919	298
SOCIAL AGENCIES	
Cleveland's Relief Agencies, 1915	301
SUB-NORMAL, RETARDED, AND EXCEPTIONAL CHILDREN	
Schools and Classes for Exceptional Children, 1916	305
TRUANCY AND NON-ATTENDANCE	
Absenteeism among White and Negro School Children, 1924	312

A BIBLIOGRAPHY OF SOCIAL SURVEYS

PAGE

TUBERCULOSIS
  Tuberculosis, 1920 318
UNMARRIED MOTHERS
  Unwed Mother and Her Child, 1922 324
VENEREAL DISEASE
  Venereal Disease, 1920 324
VICE
  Report of Vice Commission, 1911 326
  Vice Conditions in Cleveland, 1916 327
PURPOSE, METHOD, AND STANDARDS
  Outline of Cleveland Crime Survey, 1922 344
  Method of Survey, 1920 348

Columbus
  Neighborhood, 1922 8
  Columbus Zone Plan, 1923 58
  Report on Survey of City Government, 1916 67
  Pool Room Survey, 1916 243

Cuyahoga County
  Jury System of Cuyahoga County, 1916 67

Dayton
  Over-Age and Progress [Education], 1914 117
  Organization and Administration of Department of Health, 1913 . 137
  Building New Schools, 1917 283

Delaware
  Report on Public Water Supply, 1922 149

Elyria
  Educational Survey, 1918 117

Fairfield County
  Survey of Educational Conditions, 1921. 117

Franklin County
  Illegitimacy as Shown by Study, 1927 175

Greene County
  Rural Life Survey, 1914 13

Hamilton
  City Plan of Hamilton, 1921 58

Hamilton County
  Blindness in Hamilton County, 1918 22
  Government of Cincinnati and Hamilton County, 1924 [Under Ohio,
    Cincinnati and Hamilton County] 67
  Survey of Communities' Dental Facilities, 1927 . . . 149
  Juvenile Court of Hamilton County, 1912 215
  What Shall We Do about Our Mental Hygiene Problem? 1922 . 224

GEOGRAPHICAL INDEX

	PAGE
Kelly's Island	
Epidemiological Study, 1921	278
Mansfield	
Child Health Demonstration, 1926	340
Niles	
School Housing Problem, 1922	283
Piqua	
Public Health Administration, 1917	137
Richland County	
Child Health Demonstration, 1926	340
Springfield	
Public Health Administration, 1917	137
Report of Appraisal of Public Health Activities, 1926	149
Summit County	
Public Welfare Activities, 1920	301
Toledo	
Toledo Children Who Leave School for Work, 1918	34
Toledo School Children in Street Trades, 1922	34
Industrial Survey, 1924	58
Major Street Plan, 1924	58
Port Study, 1924	59
Progress Report, 1924	59
Railroad Transportation, 1924	59
Transit Problem, 1924	59
Report of Survey of Toledo's Welfare Farm, 1920	87
Public Health Administration, 1915	138
Public Health Administration, 1926	138
Motion Pictures in Typical City, 1919	230
Pool, Billiards, and Bowling Alleys, 1919	243
Play Facilities in Toledo, 1914	257
Wood County	
Report of Wood County Survey [School Health and Sanitation], 1916	287
Xenia	
Negroes of Xenia, 1903	235
Youngstown	
Public Health Administration, 1916	138
Survey and Building Program, 1921	283
OKLAHOMA	
Child Welfare in Oklahoma, 1917	44
Public Education in Oklahoma, 1923	117
Women in Oklahoma Industries, 1926	195
Studies in Public School Finance, 1925 [Under Arkansas]	288
Causes of Absences from Rural Schools, 1917	312

A BIBLIOGRAPHY OF SOCIAL SURVEYS

PAGE

Alfalfa County
School Survey Suggestions, 1918 117
Grady County
School Survey Suggestions, 1918 117
Muskogee
Oklahoma Public Health Surveys, 1920 149
Oklahoma City
Report on Plan for Outer Parkway, 1910 59
Oklahoma Public Health Surveys, 1919 149
Wagoner County
School Survey Suggestions, 1918 117

OREGON
Child Labor in Fruit and Hop Growing Districts, 1926 . . . 34
Child Welfare Work in Oregon, 1918 44
Preliminary Statistical Report [Delinquency and Correction], 1922 . 87
County School Systems of Oregon, 1921 117
Health Survey of State of Oregon, 1920 150
Report on Survey of Endemic Goiter, 1927 150
Wages, Hours and Conditions of Work, 1913 195
Effect of Minimum Wage Determinations, 1915 229
Report of Commission to Investigate . . Penitentiary, 1917 . 248
Study of School Finance in Oregon, 1925 294
Unemployment in Oregon, 1914 322
Albany
Outbreaks of botulism, 1924 150
Ashland
Constructive Survey of Public School System, 1915 . . . 117
Eugene
Report of Survey of University of Oregon, 1915 118
Klamath County
Klamath Indian Survey, 1922 180
Lane County
Community Life in Lane County, 1920 8
Rural Survey of Lane County, 1916 13
Portland
CITY AND REGIONAL PLANNING
Zoning and City Planning, 1919 59
Proposed Building Zones, 1919 59
Major Traffic Street Plan, 1921 59
Survey of Port of Portland, 1921 59
CITY, COUNTY, AND STATE ADMINISTRATION
Organization and Business Methods of City Government, 1913 . 67

438

GEOGRAPHICAL INDEX

	PAGE
COST OF LIVING	
Cost of Living Survey, 1925	77
EDUCATION	
Report of Survey of Public School System, 1913	118
Portland Survey, 1915	118
Report of Supplementary Survey, 1917	118
GARBAGE, REFUSE, AND SEWAGE	
Collection and Disposal of Municipal Wastes, 1922	133
HEALTH AND SANITATION	
Public Health Methods, 1922	150
INDUSTRIAL CONDITIONS AND RELATIONS	
Wages, Hours, and Conditions of Work, 1913	195
Report of Industrial Welfare Commission, 1914	195
MOTION PICTURES	
Vaudeville and Motion Picture Shows, 1914	230
RELIEF	
Public Welfare Bureau, 1922	260
UNEMPLOYMENT	
Study of Unemployed in Portland, 1914	323
Report on Problem of Unemployment, 1915	323
VICE	
Report of Portland Vice Commission, 1913	327

PENNSYLVANIA

GENERAL SOCIAL SURVEYS—RURAL	
Rural Survey, 1914	13
ACCIDENTS, AND ACCIDENT PREVENTION	
Accidents to Working Children, 1927	17
ALMSHOUSES	
Some American Almshouses, 1927 [Under Connecticut]	19
BLINDNESS, SIGHT CONSERVATION, AND DISEASE OF THE EYE	
Report of Commission to Study Conditions, 1925	22
CHARITIES	
Report of Citizens' Committee, 1922	26
CHILD LABOR	
Child Labor and Welfare of Children, 1922	35
Pennsylvania Children, 1923 [Under New Jersey]	33
CHILD WELFARE	
Child Welfare Work, 1915	44
Report on Subsidized Institutions, 1915	44
Summary of Child Welfare Work, 1915	45
Report to General Assembly, 1925	45
Child Welfare Conditions and Resources, 1927	45
CITY, COUNTY, AND STATE ADMINISTRATION	
State Budget Systems, 1922	68
Survey of Fiscal Policies, 1922	68

A BIBLIOGRAPHY OF SOCIAL SURVEYS

	PAGE
CLINICS AND DISPENSARIES	
Survey of Fiscal Policies, 1922	71
COST OF LIVING	
Cost of Living, 1922	77
DELINQUENCY AND CORRECTION	
Financial Survey of State Penal . . . Institutions, 1922	87
DEPENDENCY	
Pennsylvania Dependents, 1915	89
Care of Dependent Children, 1924	89
FEEBLEMINDED	
Report of Commission on Segregation, 1913	129
Feebleminded Citizens, 1915	130
HEALTH AND SANITATION	
Sickness Survey, 1917	150
HEALTH IN INDUSTRY	
Diseases Prevalent among Steel Workers, 1920	157
HOSPITALS AND SANATORIA	
State-Aided Hospitals in Pennsylvania, 1925	161
HOUSING	
Housing Conditions in Main Line Towns, 1914	171
INDUSTRIAL CONDITIONS AND RELATIONS	
Wage-Earning Women in War Time, 1919	195
Industrial Home Work, 1921	195
INSANE	
Treatment and Care of Insane, 1915	209
NEGROES	
Study of Living Conditions among Colored People, 1915	235
Negro Survey of Pennsylvania, 1927	235
NURSERIES AND NURSING	
Day Nurseries in Pennsylvania, 1924	238
PENSIONS	
Report of . . . on Old-Age Pensions, 1919	241
Report of . . . on Old-Age Assistance, 1925	241
Problem of Old-Age Pensions in Industry, 1926	241
PRISONS	
Employment and Compensation of Prisoners, 1915	248
Report of Pennsylvania Commission, 1919	249
Financial Survey of State Penal . . . Institutions, 1922	249
Psychological and Educational Survey, 1926	249
RELIEF	
Poor Relief in Pennsylvania, 1925	260
RURAL EDUCATION	
Report on Rural Schools, 1914	274
Status of Rural Teacher, 1922	274

GEOGRAPHICAL INDEX

PAGE

SCHOOL HEALTH AND SANITATION
   Medical Inspection of . . . School Children, 1915 . . 287
SCHOOL ORGANIZATION AND ADMINISTRATION
   Report of Citizens' Committee, 1922 294
SOCIAL AGENCIES
   Study of Maternity Homes, 1926 [Under Minnesota] . . . 300
TAXATION
   Report of Committee on Taxation, 1916 308

Allegheny County
   Crime and Its Treatment, 1924 80

Bedford County
   Survey of Huntingdon Presbytery, 1910 264

Blair County
   Survey of Huntingdon Presbytery, 1910 264

Bucks County
   Social Survey of Bucks County, 1915 13

Center County
   Survey of Huntingdon Presbytery, 1910 264

Clearfield County
   Survey of Huntingdon Presbytery, 1910 264

Columbia County
   Sunbury District Survey, 1918 264
   Country Church in Industrial Zones, 1922 [Under Maryland, Harford County] 262

Coopersburg
   Coopersburg Survey, 1915. 8
   Cooperation in Coopersburg, 1916 264

Delaware County
   Family and Child Welfare Agencies, 1926 301
   Survey of Revenue System, 1918 308

Erie
   Greater Erie [City and Regional Planning], 1913 59
   General Sanitary Survey, 1910 150
   Study of Girls Cared for by Florence Crittenton Home, 1921 . . 215

Hanover Township
   Family Status of Breadwinning Women, 1925 [Under Florida, Jacksonville] 184

Harrisburg
   Report on Survey of Police Department, 1917 242
   Study of Public Schools of Harrisburg, 1922 283
   Report upon Business and Financial Administration [Schools], 1917 . 294

Honesdale
   Educational Survey of Honesdale, 1921 118

A BIBLIOGRAPHY OF SOCIAL SURVEYS

	PAGE
Huntingdon County	
Survey of Huntingdon Presbytery, 1910	264
Johnstown	
Children of Immigrants in Schools, 1911 [Under United States]	179
Infant Mortality, 1915	206
Juniata County	
Survey of Huntingdon Presbytery, 1910	264
Lackawanna County	
Survey of One-Teacher Elementary Schools, 1926	274
Lancaster	
Report on Vice Conditions, 1913	327
Second Report on Vice Conditions, 1915	327
Laurelton	
Education of Feebleminded Women, 1925	130
Lehigh County	
Coopersburg Survey, 1915 [Under Pennsylvania, Coopersburg]	8
Luzerne County	
Sunbury District Survey, 1918	264
Montour County	
Sunbury District Survey, 1918	264
New Castle	
Report of Administration of Schools, 1927	294
Northumberland County	
Sunbury District Survey, 1918	264
Philadelphia	
GENERAL SOCIAL SURVEYS—URBAN	
Study of Housing and Social Conditions, 1915	8
Preliminary Study, 1921	8
CHILD LABOR	
Report of Study of Out-of-School Work, 1923	35
CITY AND REGIONAL PLANNING	
Regional Plan for Philadelphia, 1924	59
CITY, COUNTY, AND STATE ADMINISTRATION	
Water Supply Problem, 1922	68
CRIME AND CRIMINALS	
Report of Crime Survey Committee, 1926	80
DELINQUENCY AND CORRECTION	
Report of Operation of . . . Correction, 1915	87
Social Non-Conformity, 1919	88
Humanizing Justice, 1922	88
EDUCATION	
Report of Survey of Public Schools, 1922	118
Social Work in First Grade, 1923	118

GEOGRAPHICAL INDEX

	PAGE
FEEBLEMINDED	
Care of Feebleminded, 1920	130
FIRE	
Health Survey of . . . and Firemen, 1923	131
HEALTH AND SANITATION	
Report of Pneumonia Commission, 1922	150
HOUSING	
Housing Conditions in Philadelphia, 1904	171
Housing of City Negro, 1914	171
Housing in Philadelphia, 1922	171
Housing in Philadelphia, 1924	171
IMMIGRATION AND AMERICANIZATION	
Immigrants in Cities, 1911 [Under United States]	179
Children of Immigrants in Schools, 1911 [Under United States]	179
INDUSTRIAL CONDITIONS AND RELATIONS	
Conditions of Women in Mercantile Establishments, 1915	195
Wages of Candy Makers in Philadelphia, 1919	195
Colored Women as Industrial Workers, 1920	196
Attendance in Four Textile Mills, 1922	196
Mothers in Industry, 1925	196
Young Employed Girl, 1927	196
MILK	
Consumers' Demand for Milk, 1924	228
NEGRO EDUCATION	
Negro Children in Public Schools, 1913	231
NEGROES	
Philadelphia Negro, 1899	235
Standard of Living, 1921	235
NURSERIES AND NURSING	
Study of Day Nurseries, 1916	238
Day Nursery in Its Community Relation, 1919	238
RELIEF	
Philadelphia Relief Study, 1926	260
RELIGION	
Social Survey of Parish of Christ Church, 1915	264
SCHOOL BUILDINGS AND PLANTS	
Report of Survey of Public Schools, 1922	284
SEX DELINQUENCY	
Unmarried Girls with Sex Experience, 1916	297
Misdemeanants' Division of Philadelphia Municipal Court, 1922	297
Specialized Courts Dealing with Sex Delinquency, 1925 [Under Illinois, Chicago]	296
SLUMS	
Slums of Baltimore, Chicago, New York, and Philadelphia, 1894 [Under Maryland, Baltimore]	298

A BIBLIOGRAPHY OF SOCIAL SURVEYS

PAGE

SOCIAL AGENCIES
   Functional Relation of Fifteen Case-Working Agencies, 1919 . 301
SUB-NORMAL, RETARDED, AND EXCEPTIONAL CHILDREN
   Report of Committee on Investigation of Backward Children, 1911 . 305
TUBERCULOSIS
   Summary of Philadelphia Tuberculosis Survey, 1922 . 318
   Study of Negro Tuberculosis Problem, 1923 . 318
   Tuberculosis Survey of Philadelphia, 1924 . 318
UNEMPLOYMENT
   Philadelphia Unemployment, 1915 . 323
VICE
   Report of Vice Commission, 1913 . 327
VOCATIONAL GUIDANCE AND TRAINING
   Survey of Opportunities for Vocational Education, 1921 . 331
   Vocational Guidance and Junior Placement, 1925 [Under California, Oakland] . 328
PURPOSE, METHOD, AND STANDARDS
   Workingmen's Standard of Living, 1919 . 343

Philadelphia County
   Organization and Administrative Methods, 1913 . 308

Pittsburgh
GENERAL SOCIAL SURVEYS—URBAN
   Pittsburgh Survey, 1909 . 8
   Pittsburgh District, 1914 . 8
   Social Survey of 22d and 23d Wards, 1915 . 8
   Pittsburgh Survey, 1909–1916 . 9
   Report of Economic Survey, 1921 . 8
ACCIDENTS AND ACCIDENT PREVENTION
   Work Accidents and Law, 1910 . 18
CHILD WELFARE
   Pittsburgh as Foster Mother, 1914 . 45
CITY AND REGIONAL PLANNING
   Main Thoroughfares and Downtown District, 1910 . 59
   Civic Improvement, 1914 . 59
   Major Street Plan, 1921 . 60
   Transit, 1923 . 60
   Parks, 1923 . 60
   Railroads of Pittsburgh District, 1923 . 60
   Waterways, 1923 . 60
CRIME AND CRIMINALS
   Crime and Its Treatment, 1924 . 80
DANCE HALLS
   Study of Dance Halls, 1925 . 84

GEOGRAPHICAL INDEX

	PAGE
EDUCATION	
Pittsburgh Schools, 1914	119
FAMILY WELFARE	
Homestead, 1910	128
HEALTH AND SANITATION	
Report on Survey of . . . Health, 1913	150
Thirty-Five Years of Typhoid, 1914	150
Sickness Survey, 1917	151
HOUSING	
Report of Committee on Housing, 1911	171
Housing of Pittsburgh's Workers, 1914	171
Three Studies, 1914	171
IMMIGRATION AND AMERICANIZATION	
Children of Immigrants in Schools, 1911 [Under United States]	179
Immigrant Wage-Earners, 1914	178
INDUSTRIAL CONDITIONS AND RELATIONS	
Women and Trades, 1909	196
Steel Workers, 1911	196
Wage-Earning Pittsburgh, 1914	196
Industry, 1914	196
INFANT MORTALITY	
Infant Mortality in Pittsburgh, 1921	206
LIBRARIES	
Public Library, 1914	216
LOANS	
Loan Shark Business, 1909	218
NEGROES	
One Hundred . . . Steel Workers, 1914	236
Negro Migrant in Pittsburgh, 1918	236
New Negro Population, 1918	236
RECREATION	
Playgrounds of Pittsburgh, 1914	257
Pittsburgh Playgrounds, 1920	257
RELIGION	
"The Strip," 1915	264
The Uptown, 1917	264
SCHOOL ORGANIZATION AND ADMINISTRATION	
Survey of Salaries of Teachers, 1927	294
TAXATION	
Disproportion of Taxation, 1914	309
TUBERCULOSIS	
Tuberculosis and Infant Welfare, 1916	318
VICE	
Report and Recommendations, 1913	327

      PAGE
VOCATIONAL GUIDANCE AND TRAINING
 Study of Five Hundred Employed Pupils, 1925 331
 Vocational Guidance and Junior Placement, 1925 [Under California, Oakland] 328

Rankin
 Interchurch Survey, 1920 264

Reading
 Replanning Reading, 1910 60
 Department of Parks, 1913 68
 Department of Water, 1913 68
 Department of Fire, 1913 131
 Report on Survey of Municipal Departments, 1913 . . . 138
 Public Library, 1913 216
 Department of Markets, 1913 218
 Report on Survey, 1913 242
 Report on School Plant Survey, 1923 284
 Report on Survey of Board of Education, 1913 294

Scranton
 Scranton in Quick Review, 1913 9
 Survey of Scranton Public Schools, 1920 119
 Children of Immigrants in Schools, 1911 [Under United States] . 179
 Recreation Survey of Scranton, 1913 257

Shenandoah
 Children of Immigrants in Schools, 1911 [Under United States] . 179

Susquehanna County
 Susquehanna County Survey [Religion], 1920 265

Union County
 Sunbury District Survey [Religion], 1918 264

Uniontown
 Sanitary Survey, 1914 151

Wilkes-Barre
 Survey of Wage-Earning Girls, 1915 35
 Family Status of Breadwinning Women, 1925 [Under Florida, Jacksonville] 184
 Vocational Guidance and Child Labor, 1915 331

PERU
Iquitos
 Sanitation of Iquitos, 1914 151

PHILIPPINE ISLANDS
 Education in Territories and Dependencies, 1919 [Under Alaska] . 92
 Survey of Educational System, 1925 119

GEOGRAPHICAL INDEX

	PAGE
Sanitation of Philippine Islands, 1916	151
Survey of Field and Work, 1919 [Under United States]	266

PORTO RICO
Child Welfare in Insular Possessions, 1923	45
Study of Certain . . . Problems, 1912	119
Education in Territories and Dependencies, 1919 [Under Alaska]	92
Survey of Public Education System, 1926	119
Report on Housing Conditions of Laborers, 1914	172
Survey of Field and Work, 1919 [Under United States]	266
Trachoma in Schools of Porto Rico, 1914	310
Tuberculosis Survey, 1924	318

RHODE ISLAND
Is Rhode Island a Thoughtful Father? 1920	45
Study of Typical Mill Village, 1911	157
Wage-Earning Women in War-Time, 1919 [Under Pennsylvania]	195
Women in Rhode Island Industries, 1922	197
Report of Rhode Island Mental Hygiene Survey, 1923	225
Tuberculosis Problem in Rhode Island, 1920	319

Central Falls
Industrial Home Work of Children, 1922	35
Tenement House Conditions, 1911	172

Lonsdale
Wages and Family Income, 1911	197

Newport
Newport Survey of Social Problems, 1911	9
Tenement House Conditions, 1911	172

Pawtucket
Industrial Home Work, 1922	35
Report on Public Health, 1913	151
Tenement House Conditions, 1911	172

Providence
Modern City, 1909	9
Community Fund, 1925	26
Industrial Home Work, 1922	35
Providence Zone Plan, 1923	60
Municipal Street Cleaning, 1911	68
Report of Survey, 1924	119
Tenement House Conditions, 1911	172
Houses of Providence, 1916	172
Children of Immigrants in Schools, 1911 [Under United States]	179
Sociological Survey of . . . Library, 1926	216
Recreation Survey, 1912	258

A BIBLIOGRAPHY OF SOCIAL SURVEYS

PAGE

Vocational Guidance and Junior Placement, 1925 [Under California, Oakland] 328

South Kingstown
Survey of Public Schools, 1927. 119

Woonsocket
Tenement House Conditions, 1911 172
Stillbirths and Neonatal Deaths, 1926 206

SCOTLAND
Part-Time Schools, 1922 [Under United States] 72

SOUTH AMERICA
Survey of Field and Work, 1919 [Under United States] . . . 266

SOUTH CAROLINA

ALMSHOUSES
   Handbook of . . . Almshouse Management, 1918 . . . 20
CHILD LABOR
   Child Labor in Carolinas, 1910 [Under North Carolina] . . . 34
CRIME AND CRIMINALS
   Crime and Its Treatment, 1922 81
FEEBLEMINDED
   Feeblemindedness and Its Care, 1920 130
HEALTH IN INDUSTRY
   Disabling Sickness, 1919 157
   Study of Relation of Family Income, 1920 157
   Disabling Sickness, 1924 158
INDUSTRIAL CONDITIONS AND RELATIONS
   Women in South Carolina Industries, 1923 197
JUVENILE DELINQUENCY
   Study of Fifty Delinquent Girls, 1919 215
MENTAL HYGIENE
   Report of South Carolina Mental Hygiene, 1922 225
NEGROES
   Negro in South Carolina, 1924 236
SCHOOL HEALTH AND SANITATION
   School Hygiene, 1914 [Under North Carolina] 287
   Heights and Weights of School Children, 1922 [Under Maryland] 285
SOCIAL AGENCIES
   War Program of State of South Carolina, 1918. 301
TRACHOMA
   Trachoma, 1914 [Under North Carolina] 310
TUBERCULOSIS
   Interstate Migration of Tuberculous Persons, 1915 [Under North Carolina] 317
   Tuberculosis in South Carolina, 1925 319

GEOGRAPHICAL INDEX

	PAGE
Anderson County	
Economic and Social Study, 1923	13
Charleston	
Report on Survey of Government, 1924	68
Industrial Education Survey, 1920	203
Special Report of Law and Order League [Vice], 1913	327
Chesterfield County	
Economic and Social Study, 1922	13
Columbia	
Public Schools of Columbia, 1918	119
Dillon County	
Economic and Social Study, 1922	13
Fairfield County	
Economic and Social Study, 1924	13
Florence County	
Economic and Social Study, 1921	13
Greenville	
Beautifying and Improving Greenville, 1907	60
Cost of Living among Wage-Earners, 1920	77
Greenville County	
Economic and Social Study, 1921	13
Kershaw County	
Economic and Social Study, 1923	14
Lancaster County	
Economic and Social Study, 1923	14
Lexington County	
Economic and Social Study, 1923	14
Marion County	
Economic and Social Study, 1923	14
Oconee County	
Public School Survey, 1923	120
Orangeburg County	
Economic and Social Study, 1923	14
Pelzer	
Cost of Living among Wage-Earners, 1920	77
Richland County	
Economic and Social Study, 1924	14
Spartanburg County	
Pellagra, First Report, 1913	151
Pellagra, Second Report, 1915	151
Pellagra, Third Report, 1918	151

Sumter County
Economic and Social Study, 1922 14
Union County
Economic and Social Study, 1923 14
York County
Study of School Plants, 1920 284

SOUTH DAKOTA
Dependent and Delinquent Children, 1926 [Under North Dakota] . 44
Report on Administrative Organization, 1922 68
Educational System of South Dakota, 1918 120
Studies in Public School Finance, 1925 [Under Illinois] . . . 290

SWEDEN
Part-Time Schools, 1922 [Under United States] 72

SWITZERLAND
Part-Time Schools, 1922 [Under United States] 72
Illegitimacy Laws, 1919 [Under United States] 175

TENNESSEE
Rural Survey in Tennessee, 1912 14
Child Welfare in Tennessee, 1920 45
Cost of Living among Colored Farm Families, 1925 [Under Kentucky] 75
Report of State-Wide Small-Pox Survey, 1926 151
Women in Tennessee Industries, 1926 197
County Jails in Tennessee, 1926 249
Studies in Public School Finance, 1925 [Under Arkansas] . . 288
Trachoma, 1914 310

Bledsoe County
Educational, Economic, and Community Survey, 1927 . . . 14
Chattanooga
Report on Charitable Organizations, 1913 27
Crockett County
Survey of Crockett County, 1924 14
Gibson County
Factors Which Have to Do with Decline, 1916 [Under Kansas] . 261
Hamilton County
Report of Study of Hamilton County . . . Almshouse, 1917 . 20
Jackson
Social Survey of City of Jackson, 1920 9
Knoxville
Preliminary Report on Public Health, 1926 138
Survey of School Building Needs, 1924 284

GEOGRAPHICAL INDEX

	PAGE
Madison County	
Social Survey of . . . and Madison County, 1920	9
Memphis	
Comprehensive City Plan, 1924	60
Public School System, 1920	120
Review of Public Health Administration, 1921	138
Public School System, 1920	294
Larger Plan for Memphis [Social Agencies], 1921	301
Study of Violent Deaths, 1924 [Under Georgia, Atlanta]	327
Nashville	
General Sanitary Survey, 1910	151
Union County	
Survey of Union County, 1924	14

TEXAS

CHILD WELFARE
- Child Caring Institutions, 1916 46
- Welfare of Children, 1924 46

CITY, COUNTY, AND STATE ADMINISTRATION
- County Government in Texas, 1917 68

COST OF LIVING
- Cost of Living among Colored Farm Families, 1925 [Under Kentucky] 75

EDUCATION
- Texas Educational Survey, 1924–1925 120

FEEBLEMINDED
- Care of Feebleminded and Insane, 1914 130

HOUSING
- Housing Problem in Texas, 1911 172

MENTAL HYGIENE
- Report of Texas Mental Hygiene Survey, 1924 . . . 225
- Report of Texas Eleemosynary Commission, 1925 . . . 225

PRISONS
- Summary of Texas Prison Survey, 1924 249

RURAL
- Studies in Agricultural Economics, 1913 269

RURAL EDUCATION
- Study of Rural Schools of Texas, 1914 275

SCHOOL ORGANIZATION AND ADMINISTRATION
- Organization and Administration of Institutions, 1914 . . 295
- County Unit of School Administration, 1922 295
- Texas Educational Survey Report, 1925 295

TUBERCULOSIS
- Interstate Migration of Tuberculous Persons, 1915 . . . 319

VOCATIONAL GUIDANCE AND TRAINING
- Texas Educational Survey Report, 1924 332

A BIBLIOGRAPHY OF SOCIAL SURVEYS

PAGE

Amarillo
Boy Life Survey, 1922 23
Austin
Social Survey of Austin [Child Health], 1917 28
Social Survey of Austin, 1913 152
Brazos County
Child Labor among Cotton Growers, 1925 35
Burleson County
Child Labor among Cotton Growers, 1925 35
Caldwell County
Schools of Caldwell County, 1923 121
Dallas
Newsboys of Dallas, 1921 35
City Plan for Dallas, 1911 60
Survey of Negro Housing in Dallas, 1925 172
Dallas County
Widow's Pensions, 1922 241
El Paso
City Plan of El Paso, 1925 60
Survey of City Schools, 1922 121
Preliminary Report of Health Survey, 1915 172
Report of Indigent Migratory Consumptives, 1923 [Under Arizona, Phoenix] 312
Galveston
Survey of Galveston Public Schools, 1926 121
Report of Sanitary Survey, 1913 152
Hill County
Child Labor among Cotton Growers, 1925 35
Houston
Houston: Tentative Plans [City Planning], 1913 60
Charge of Joseph C. Hutcheson [Prisons], 1925 249
Karnes County
Rural Schools of Karnes County, 1922 275
Nacogdoches County
Child Labor among Cotton Growers, 1925 35
Paris
General City Plan for Paris, 1915 60
Port Arthur
Report of Survey of Schools, 1926 121
Runnels County
Study of Rural Schools, 1924 275

GEOGRAPHICAL INDEX

	PAGE
San Antonio	
Wheel of Fortune [Boy Life], 1921	23
San Antonio Public School System, 1915	121
Report of Indigent Migratory Consumptives, 1923 [Under Arizona, Phoenix]	312
Taylor County	
Child Labor among Cotton Growers, 1925	35
Travis County	
Social and Economic Survey, 1916	14
Rural Schools of Travis County, 1916	275
Washington County	
Child Labor among Cotton Growers, 1925	35
Wichita County	
Rural Schools of Wichita County, 1922	275
Williamson County	
Rural Schools of Williamson County, 1922	275

TURKEY—Constantinople
Constantinople Today, 1922 9

UNITED STATES
GENERAL SOCIAL SURVEYS—RURAL
Rural Primary Groups, 1921 14
ACCIDENTS AND ACCIDENT PREVENTION
Accidents and Accident Prevention, 1913 18
Accidents and Accident Prevention, 1917 18
Causes and Prevention of Accidents, 1922 18
BLINDNESS, SIGHT CONSERVATION, AND DISEASE OF THE EYE
Eye Hazards in Industrial Occupations, 1917 22
Eyesight Conservation Survey, 1925 22
BURIAL
Reasons for Present-day Funeral Costs, 1927 23
CANCER
Free Tumor Diagnosis, 1916 24
CHARITIES
Study of Nine Hundred and Eighty-Five Widows, 1913 . . 27
CHILD HEALTH AND HYGIENE
Survey of Evidence, 1917 29
Infectious Diseases, 1918 29
CHILD LABOR
Child Labor and Night Messenger Service, 1910 . . . 36
Child Labor in Canneries, 1910 36
Child Labor in Street Trades, 1910 36
Conditions under Which, 1910 36
Glass Industry and Child Labor, 1911 36

A BIBLIOGRAPHY OF SOCIAL SURVEYS

	PAGE
Work of School Children, 1917	36
Administration of First Federal, 1921	36
Child Labor in . . . Areas, 1926	36

CHILD MARRIAGES
- Child Marriages, 1925 37

CHILD WELFARE
- Selective Migration as Factor, 1921 46
- Work of Child-Placing Agencies, 1927 46

CHINESE
- Chinese Migration, 1923 47

CITY, COUNTY, AND STATE ADMINISTRATION
- Administration of "Full Crew" Laws, 1917 69

CLINICS AND DISPENSARIES
- Present Status, 1920 71

CONTINUATION AND PART-TIME SCHOOLS
- Part-Time Schools, 1922 72

COST OF LIVING
- Cost of Living, 1911 78
- Family Budget, 1911 78
- Investigation Relative to Wages, 1911 78
- Report of Special Committee, 1917 78
- Sociological Studies, 1923 78
- Comparative Living Costs, 1926 78
- Farmer's Standard of Living, 1926 78
- Cost of Living in United States, 1926 79
- Cost of Living in United States, 1927 79

CRIME AND CRIMINALS
- Immigration and Crime, 1911 81
- Relation between Occupation and Criminality, 1911 . . . 81
- Criminal Receivers, 1927 81

CRIPPLED, DISABLED, AND HANDICAPPED
- Care of Crippled Children, 1912 83
- Care and Education of Crippled Children, 1914 . . . 83

DANCE HALLS
- Report of Public Dance Hall Committee, 1924 . . . 84

DEPORTATION
- Deportation Cases, 1921 89

DESERTION
- Five Hundred and Seventy-Four Deserters, 1905 . . . 90

DETENTION
- Detention Houses and Reformatories, 1922 90

EDUCATION
- Medical Education in United States and Canada, 1910 . . 121
- Comparative Study of Public School Systems, 1913 . . 121
- Report of Committee on Teachers' Salaries, 1913 . . . 121

GEOGRAPHICAL INDEX

	PAGE
Jewish Students, 1915	122
Statistical Study of Public Schools, 1915	122
Schools in Bituminous Coal Regions, 1920.	122
Status of Certain Social Studies in High School, 1923	122
Dental Education in United States and Canada, 1926	122

EIGHT-HOUR DAY
Comparison of Eight-Hour Plant and Ten-Hour Plant, 1920	126

GARBAGE, REFUSE, AND SEWAGE
Recent Survey of Sewage Treatment Plants, 1922	133
Sewage Treatment in United States, 1923	133

HEALTH ADMINISTRATION
Present Condition of Public Health Organization, 1913	138
Survey of Activities of Municipal Health Departments, 1916	138
Report of Committee on Municipal Health Department, 1923	139
Municipal Health Department Practice, 1926	139

HEALTH AND SANITATION
Report of Investigation of Diphtheria Carriers, 1915	152
Report on State Public Health Work, 1915	152
Drinking Water on Interstate Carriers, 1916	152
Influenza Studies on . . . Statistical Aspects, 1919.	152
Some Recent Morbidity Data, 1919	152
Comparative Study of State Regulations, 1920.	152
Comparative Study of Health, 1920 [Under Japan]	143
Malta Fever in Southwest United States, 1922	153
Railroad Malaria Surveys, 1923	153
Distribution of Physicians, 1924	153
Health Survey of Eighty-Six Cities, 1925	153
Typhoid Fever Epidemic, 1925	153

HEALTH IN INDUSTRY
Hookworm Disease among Cotton-Mill Operatives, 1912	158
Hours of Work . . . Cotton Manufacturing, 1918	158
Hours of Work . . . Boot and Shoe Industry, 1918	158
Hours of Work . . . Wool Manufacturing, 1918	158
Hours of Work . . . Silk Manufacturing, 1919	158
Hours of Work . . . Metal Manufacturing, 1919	158
Studies of Medical and Surgical Care, 1919	158
Lead Poisoning in Pottery Trades, 1921	158
Health Conditions among Chemical Workers, 1923	158
Health Study of 10,000 Male Industrial Workers, 1926	159

HEALTH INSURANCE
Health Insurance, 1916	159

HOSPITALS AND SANATORIA
Report of Committee, 1920	161

HOUSING
Housing for Women in War Work, 1918	172

A BIBLIOGRAPHY OF SOCIAL SURVEYS

                                                                                          PAGE

Sanitation of Rural Workmen's Areas, 1918 172
Building Situation, 1921 173
Housing of Women Students at College, 1922 173
Study of Housing of Employed Women and Girls, 1925 . . 173
ILLEGITIMACY
  Illegitimacy Laws of United States, 1919 175
  Illegitimacy as a Child Welfare Problem, 1920 . . . 175
  Children Born Out of Wedlock, 1921 175
  Illegitimacy as a Child Welfare Problem, 1924 . . . 175
IMMIGRATION AND AMERICANIZATION
  Reports of Immigration Commission, 1911 178
  Foreign Student in America, 1925 180
INDIANS
  Tuberculosis among Certain Indian Tribes, 1909 . . . 181
  Red Man in United States, 1923 181
  Tuberculosis among North American Indians, 1923 . . 181
INDUSTRIAL CONDITIONS AND RELATIONS
  Cotton and Textile Industry, 1910 197
  Men's Ready-Made Clothing, 1911 197
  Glass Industry, 1911 197
  Silk Industry, 1911 197
  Wage-Earning Women in Stores and Factories, 1910 . . 197
  History of Women in Industry, 1911 197
  History of Women in Trade Unions, 1911 197
  Employment of Women in Metal Trades, 1911 . . . 197
  Employment of Women in Laundries, 1911 198
  Employment of Women and Children in Selected Industries, 1913 . 198
  Labor Laws and Factory Conditions, 1912 198
  Summary of Report . . . Woman and Child Wage-Earners, 1915 198
  Wages and Hours of Labor, 1911. 198
  Wages and Hours of Labor, 1912. 198
  Working Conditions and Relations, 1913 198
  Saleswomen in Mercantile Stores, 1913 198
  Wage-Worth of School Training, 1915 198
  Effect of Workmen's Compensation Laws, 1918 . . . 198
  Report on Logging Camps, 1919 199
  Women's Wages, 1919 199
  Hours of Work Problem, 1920 199
  New Position of Women, 1920 199
  Women Professional Workers, 1921 199
  Women in Government Service, 1920 199
  Child Labor and Work of Mothers, 1922 199
  Industrial Unemployment, 1922 200
  Shop Collective Bargaining, 1922 [Under Canada] . . . 182

GEOGRAPHICAL INDEX

	PAGE
Survey of Natural Illumination, 1922	200
Employment, Hours, and Earnings in Prosperity, 1923	200
Share of Wage-Earning Women in Family Support, 1923	200
Home Environment and Employment Opportunities, 1925	200

INFANT MORTALITY
- Infant Mortality and Its Relation to Employment, 1912 . . . 207
- Infant Mortality and Milk Stations, 1912 207
- Causal Factors in Infant Mortality, 1925 207

INFANTILE PARALYSIS
- State Work against Infantile Paralysis, 1917 208
- Epidemiological Studies of Poliomyelitis, 1918 [Under New York City] 208

ITALIANS
- Religious Work Among Italians, 1917 [Under America] . . . 209

JAPANESE
- Japanese and Other Immigrant Races, 1911 211

JUVENILE DELINQUENCY
- Juvenile Delinquency and Its Relation, 1911 215
- Federal Court and Delinquent Child, 1922 215

LIBRARIES
- Libraries of American State, 1918 216
- Our College and University Libraries, 1920 216
- Library Extension, 1926 216
- Survey of Libraries in United States, 1926 217

LOANS
- Student Loan Funds, 1924 218

MARRIAGE LAWS
- American Marriage Laws, 1919 218

MATERNAL DEATHS
- Maternal Mortality from All Conditions, 1917 219

MENTAL HYGIENE
- Mental Hygiene, 1925 225

MILITARY CAMPS
- Report on Work of Women in Military Camps, 1918 . . . 227
- Survey of Moral and Religious Forces, 1918 227

MILK
- First Report on Milk Standards, 1912 228
- Second Report, 1913 228
- Third Report, 1917 228

MUSIC
- Municipal Aid to Music, 1925 230
- Music, Youth, and Opportunity, 1926 230

NEGRO EDUCATION
- Negro Common School, 1901 231
- History of Negro Education, 1917 232

A BIBLIOGRAPHY OF SOCIAL SURVEYS

PAGE

   Economic and Social Status of Negroes, 1917 232
   Report on Negro Universities and Colleges, 1922 . . . 232
   Study of County Training Schools for Negroes, 1925 . . . 232
   Study of Home Economics Education, 1923 232
   Education of Negro Ministers, 1925 232

NEGROES
   Condition of Negro in Various Cities, 1897 236
   Negro Artisan, 1902 236
   Negro Migration, 1919 236
   Negro at Work during World War, 1921 237
   Negro Women in Industry, 1922 237

NEIGHBORHOOD HOUSES AND SETTLEMENTS
   Thirty Neighborhood Houses, 1926 237

NURSERIES AND NURSING
   Survey of Nursing Education, 1923 239
   Report of Committee to Study, 1924 239
   Pupil Nurse, 1925 239

POLICE
   American Police Systems, 1920 243

PRISONS
   Penal Servitude, 1912 249
   Report of Convict Labor Commission, 1915 249
   Study of Wage-Payment to Prisoners, 1920 249
   Wall Shadows, 1922 250
   Handbook of American Prisons, 1925 250
   Handbook of American Prisons, 1926 250
   United States Prisoners in County Jails, 1926 250

PROHIBITION
   Prohibition Situation, 1925 251
   Does Prohibition Work? 1927 251

PROSTITUTION
   Prostitution in United States, 1921 252

PSYCHIATRIC
   Psychiatric Studies of Delinquents, 1920 252

RACE RELATIONS
   Tentative Findings of Survey of Race Relations, 1925 [Under
     Canada] 253

RECREATION
   How People Play in Forty American Cities, 1916 . . . 258
   State Parks and Recreational Uses of State Forests, 1926 . . 258

REFORMATORIES
   American State Reformatory, 1920 259

RELIGION
   Social Welfare Work of Unitarian Churches, 1910 . . . 265
   Survey, 1915 265

GEOGRAPHICAL INDEX

	PAGE
Centenary Survey, 1918	265
General Survey of Needs and Activities, 1919	265
Religion among American Men, 1920	265
From Survey to Service, 1921	265
Church on Changing Frontier, 1922	265
Church Life in Rural South, 1923	266
Town and Country Church, 1925	266
Church in Changing City, 1927	266
Survey of Field and Work, 1919	266
Rural Church Life, 1922 [Under Iowa, Clay County]	261

RELIGIOUS EDUCATION

Survey of Week-Day Religious Education, 1922	267
Theological Education, 1924 [Under America]	267

RURAL

What the Farm Contributes Directly to Farmer's Living, 1914	269
Farm Woman's Problems, 1920	269
Agricultural Crisis and Its Causes, 1921	270
Credit, 1922	270
Transportation, 1922	270
Marketing and Distribution, 1922	270

RURAL EDUCATION

Study of 15 Consolidated Rural Schools, 1911	275
Status of Rural Education, 1913	275
Factors Controlling Attendance in Rural Schools, 1920	275
Farm Labor vs. School Attendance, 1920	275
Supervision of Rural Schools, 1922	275
Analytic Survey of State Courses of Study, 1923	276
High School Education of Farm Population, 1925	276

RURAL HEALTH AND SANITATION

Rocky Mountain Spotted Fever, 1914	278
Rural Sanitation, 1918	279

RUSSIANS

Social Study of Russian-German, 1916	279

SCHOOL HEALTH AND SANITATION

Status of Hygiene Programs, 1927	287

SCHOOL ORGANIZATION AND ADMINISTRATION

Study of Expenses of City School Systems, 1912	295
School Administration in Smaller Cities, 1915	295
Administration and Supervision of Village Schools, 1920	295
Digest of Study of Public Education Costs, 1923	295
Fiscal Administration of City School Systems, 1924	295
Financial Statistics of Public Education, 1924	296
Unit Costs of Higher Education, 1924	297

SLAVS

Our Slavic Fellow Citizens, 1910	298

A BIBLIOGRAPHY OF SOCIAL SURVEYS

PAGE

Social Agencies
  Report of Study of Interrelation of Work . . . Social Agencies, 1921 301
  Social Salvage, 1924 302
  How Shall Country Youth Be Served, 1926 302
Sub-Normal, Retarded, and Exceptional Children
  Laggards in Our Schools, 1913 305
Truancy and Non-Attendance
  Truant Problem and Parental School, 1915 312
Tuberculosis
  Agricultural and Industrial Community, 1919 . . . 319
  Mortality from Pulmonary Tuberculosis, 1922 . . . 319
  Tuberculosis among Ex-Service Men, 1922 319
Unemployment
  Unemployment Survey, 1915 323
  Unemployment in United States, 1916 323
  Fluctuations in Unemployment, 1918 323
  Business Cycle and Unemployment, 1923 323
  Cycles of Unemployment in United States, 1923 . . . 323
Unmarried Mothers
  Unmarried Mothers, 1918 324
Venereal Disease
  Venereal Diseases, 1918 324
  Syphilis of Innocent, 1922 325
Vocational Guidance and Training
  Apprentice Education, 1923 332
  Effectiveness of Vocational Education, 1923 332

UTAH
  Survey of Education in Utah, 1926 122
  Mental Survey of Utah Schools, 1921 225
  Escalante
    Social Survey, 1925 15
  Ogden
    Report of Ogden Public School Survey Commission, 1914 . . . 122
  Salt Lake City
    Report of Survey of School System, 1915 123
    School Organization and Administration, 1916 296

VERMONT
  Secondary Education in Vermont, 1912 123
  Education in Vermont, 1914 123
  Report of Commission [Education], 1914 123
  Status of Rural Vermont, 1903 270
  Report of Vermont Tuberculosis Commission, 1904 . . . 319
  Town Planning, 1919 342

GEOGRAPHICAL INDEX

	PAGE
Addison County	
Country Church in Colonial Counties, 1922 [Under New York, Tompkins and Warren Counties]	263
Brattleboro	
Legacy to Wage-Earning Women, 1925	200
Burlington	
Survey of City of Burlington [Charities and Housing], 1915	27
Manchester	
Children of Immigrants in Schools, 1911 [Under United States]	179
Windsor County	
Country Church, 1913 [Under New York, Tompkins County]	263
Do You Know the Facts? 1913	276

VIRGINIA

Southwest Virginia County Almshouse Survey, 1926	20
Child Labor in Virginia, 1912	37
Report of Virginia Educational Commission, 1912	123
Reports of Education Commission, 1920	123
Educational Tests, 1921	123
School Attendance, 1925	123
Hours and Conditions of Work, 1920	201
Mental Defectives in Virginia, 1915	225
Education and Economic Development of Negro, 1923	232
Heights and Weights of School Children, 1922 [Under Maryland]	285
Report of Joint Committee on Tax Revision, 1914	309
Trachoma, 1914	311
Report of Tuberculosis Committee, 1920	320
Vocational Agriculture in Secondary Schools, 1919	332
Albemarle County	
Economic and Social Survey, 1922	15
Alexandria	
Survey of Schools, 1924	123
Clarke County	
Economic and Social Survey, 1925	15
Fairfax County	
Economic and Social Survey, 1924	15
Farmville	
Negroes of Farmville, 1898	237
King and Queen County	
Economic and Social Survey, 1925	15
Litwalton	
Negroes of Litwalton, 1901	237
Lynchburg	
Negroes of Lynchburg, 1923	237

A BIBLIOGRAPHY OF SOCIAL SURVEYS

PAGE

Norfolk
Survey of City Government, 1915 69
Child Labor and Work of Mothers, 1924 201
School Housing Survey, 1921 284

Norfolk County
School Housing Survey, 1921 284

Orange County
Sanitary Survey of Schools, 1914 288

Petersburg
Economic and Municipal [Industrial Conditions and Relations], 1917   201

Portsmouth
Report and Survey of School Housing Conditions, 1921 . . . 284

Princess Anne County
Economic and Social, 1924 15

Richmond
Report on Survey of City Government, 1917 69
Placement of Children in Elementary Grades, 1916 123
Report on Housing and Living Conditions, 1913 173
Survey of Social Agencies, 1923 302
Vocational Education Survey of Richmond, 1916 332

Roanoke
Remodeling Roanoke, 1907 61

Rockingham County
Economic and Social Survey, 1924 15

South Norfolk
School Housing Survey, 1921 284

Tidewater
Three Negro Communities, 1923 237

Winchester
Psychological and Educational Tests, 1921 124

VIRGIN ISLANDS
Education in Territories and Dependencies, 1919 [Under Alaska]   . 92

WASHINGTON
Child Labor in Fruit and Hop Growing Districts, 1926 [Under Oregon]   34
Conditions in State Institutions, 1912 69
Survey of Educational Institutions, 1916 124
Public Health Administration, 1915 139
Report of Industrial Welfare Commission, 1914 201
Women in Fruit-Growing and Canning Industries, 1926 . . . 201
Survey of State Supported Library Activities, 1917 217

Blaine
Survey of Blaine Public Schools, 1914 124

GEOGRAPHICAL INDEX

	PAGE
Pend Oreille County	
Church and Community Survey, 1922	266
Port Townsend	
Survey of Port Townsend Public Schools, 1915	124
Seattle	
Plan of Seattle, 1911	61
Studies in Administrative Research [Education], 1924.	124
Study of Mobility of Population, 1925	244
Newsboy Service, 1917	332
Vocational Guidance and Junior Placement, 1925 [Under California, Oakland]	328
Tacoma	
Child Life in Tacoma, 1926	46
Survey of Family Relief Work in Tacoma, 1923	128

WEST VIRGINIA

Rural Child Welfare, 1922	46
Public Health Administration, 1915	139
Sickness Survey of Principal Cities, 1917 [Under Pennsylvania]	150
Sickness Survey, 1917	153
Tax Problems in West Virginia, 1925	309
Trachoma, 1914	311
Berkeley County	
School Survey of Type Counties, 1923	124
Braxton County	
School Survey of Type Counties, 1923	124
Brooke County	
School Survey of Type Counties, 1923	124
Charleston	
Sanitary Survey, 1918	153
Elkins	
Winter Outbreak of Poliomyelitis, 1918	208
French Creek	
French Creek as a Rural Community, 1921	270
Gilmer County	
School Survey of Type Counties, 1923	124
Grafton	
Report of Survey of Grafton City Schools, 1913	124
Harrison County	
School Survey of Type Counties, 1923	124
Tuberculosis Survey, 1925.	320
Logan County	
School Survey of Type Counties, 1923	124

Marion County
  School Survey of Type Counties, 1923 124
  Tuberculosis Survey, 1922. 320
Marshall County
  Educational Survey, 1922 124
Monroe County
  School Survey of Type Counties, 1923 124
Ohio County
  Report of Tuberculosis Survey, 1922 320
Philippi
  Educational Survey, 1923 125
Raleigh County
  Welfare of Children in . . . Communities, 1923 . . . 46
Upshur County
  School Survey of Type Counties, 1923 124
Wetzel County
  School Survey of Type Counties, 1923 124
Wheeling
  Abstracts of Reports upon . . . a City Plan, 1920 . . . 61
  Educational Survey of Wheeling, 1921 125

WISCONSIN
  ACCIDENTS AND ACCIDENT PREVENTION
    Industrial Accidents, 1926. 18
    Industrial Accidents to Women, 1927 [Under New Jersey] . . 16
  CHILD LABOR
    Administration of Child Labor Laws, 1921 37
  CONTINUATION AND PART-TIME SCHOOLS
    Continuation Schools of Wisconsin, 1921–1922 72
  CRIPPLED, DISABLED, AND HANDICAPPED
    Rehabilitation of Handicapped, 1921 83
  DEPENDENCY
    Administration of Aid to Dependent Children's Law, 1921 . . 89
  EDUCATION
    Preliminary Report of Committee, 1912. 125
    Children Indentured by Wisconsin State Public School, 1925 . 125
  FEEBLEMINDED
    Some Aspects of Feeblemindedness, 1918 130
  INDUSTRIAL CONDITIONS AND RELATIONS
    Conditions in Garment-Making Trades, 1902 201
    Working Hours of Women, 1913 201
    Investigation of Labor Camps, 1914 201
  MENTAL HYGIENE
    Report of Wisconsin Mental Deficiency Survey, 1921 . . . 226

GEOGRAPHICAL INDEX

	PAGE
MINIMUM WAGE	
Minimum Wage Investigation Report, 1918	229
PROBATION AND PAROLE	
Probation in Wisconsin, 1926	251
RELIEF	
Organized Poor Relief in Wisconsin, 1915	260
RURAL	
Farm Tenancy, 1919	270
RURAL EDUCATION	
Preliminary Report on . . . Rural Schools, 1912	276
RURAL HEALTH AND SANITATION	
Maternity and Infant Care, 1919	279
SCHOOL ORGANIZATION AND ADMINISTRATION	
Financing Continuation Schools, 1922	296
State and Local Administration, 1922	296
TAXATION	
Tax Problem in Wisconsin, 1924	309
TUBERCULOSIS	
Report of Wisconsin State Tuberculosis Commission, 1905	320
Tuberculosis in Rural Districts, 1911	320
Tuberculosis or Consumption, 1913	320
VICE	
Report and Recommendations of . . Vice Committee, 1914	327

Appleton
School Building Survey of Appleton, 1922 284

Ashland
Citizens' Survey of Ashland, 1927 9

Dunn County
Tuberculosis in Rural Districts, 1911 320

Janesville
Educational Survey of Janesville, 1918 125

Lafayette County
Tuberculosis in Rural Districts, 1911 320

Madison
Madison: Model City, 1911 61
Report of Survey of University, 1914 125
Four Lake City Recreational Survey, 1915 258

Milwaukee
CHILD LABOR
   Newsboys of Milwaukee, 1911 37
CITY AND REGIONAL PLANNING
   Preliminary Reports of . . . Commission, 1911 . . . 61
CITY, COUNTY, AND STATE ADMINISTRATION
   Citizens' Free Employment Bureau, 1911 69

465

A BIBLIOGRAPHY OF SOCIAL SURVEYS

	PAGE
Free Legal Aid, 1911	69
Review of Bureau's Work, 1911	69
Water Works Efficiency: Present Capacity, 1911	69
Water Works Efficiency: Water Wastes, 1912	69
Water Works Efficiency: Operating Efficiency, 1912	69
Eighteen Months' Work, 1912	69
Report on Preliminary Survey, 1913	69
Report to Public, 1915	69

FIRE
Proposed Consolidation of Fire, 1911 131

GARBAGE, REFUSE, AND SEWAGE
Refuse Incinerator, 1911 133
Reorganization of System of Garbage Collection, 1912 . . 133

HEALTH ADMINISTRATION
Health Department, 1912 139

HEALTH AND SANITATION
Plumbing and House Drain Inspection, 1911 153
Health Department: Communicable Diseases, 1912 . . . 153

HOUSING
Housing Conditions in Milwaukee, 1916 173

IMMIGRATION AND AMERICANIZATION
Children of Immigrants in Schools, 1911 [Under United States] . 179
Immigrants in Cities, 1911 [Under United States] . . . 179

INDUSTRIAL CONDITIONS AND RELATIONS
Garnishment of Wages, 1911 202
Women's Wages in Milwaukee, 1911 202
Employment of Women in Power Laundries, 1913 . . . 202

ITALIANS
Italians in Milwaukee, 1915 210

MILK
Health Department: Milk Supply, 1912 228

PENSIONS
Public Pensions to Widows, 1913 [Under California, San Francisco] 240
Report of Commission on Pension Laws, 1920 241

RECREATION
Recreation Survey, 1912 258
Amusements and Recreation in Milwaukee, 1914 . . . 258

SCHOOL BUILDINGS AND PLANTS
Constructive Survey of Milwaukee School Buildings, 1916 . . 284

SCHOOL HEALTH AND SANITATION
Medical Inspection in Schools, 1919 288

TAXATION
Increased Taxes in Milwaukee, 1914 309

GEOGRAPHICAL INDEX

	PAGE
PURPOSE, METHOD, AND STANDARDS	
City Planning for Milwaukee, 1916	342
Milwaukee County	
Milwaukee County Government, 1916	70
Survey of . . . School of Agriculture, 1916	125
Price County	
New and Old Immigrant on Land [Religion], 1922	266
Racine	
Unemployment and Child Welfare, 1923 [Under Massachusetts, Springfield]	42
Sheboygan	
Investigation of Typhoid Fever Epidemic, 1908	154
Sheboygan County	
New and Old Immigrant on Land [Religion], 1922	266
Sparta	
Some Recommendations for Improvement [Education], 1921	125
Walworth County	
Social Anatomy of Agricultural Community, 1915	270
WYOMING	
Educational Survey, 1917	125
Lincoln County	
Survey of Five School Districts, 1922	126